Merle Johnson's

AMERICAN FIRST EDITIONS

Other volumes by Jacob Blanck

PETER PARLEY TO PENROD
(*Out of Print*)

HARRY CASTLEMON: BOYS' OWN AUTHOR
APPRECIATION AND BIBLIOGRAPHY

A SELECTIVE BIBLIOGRAPHY OF 19TH CENTURY
AMERICAN JUVENILE BOOKS
(*In Preparation*)

MERLE JOHNSON'S

American First Editions

FOURTH EDITION

REVISED AND ENLARGED BY

Jacob Blanck

NEW YORK: R. R. BOWKER CO.

Second Printing

Photo-Lithoprint Reproduction
EDWARDS BROTHERS, INC.
Lithoprinters
ANN ARBOR, MICHIGAN
1947

CONTRIBUTORS

TO AMERICAN FIRST EDITIONS

Manley Aaron, Francis H. Allen, William O. Andersen, Whitman Bennett, John H. Birss, M. M. Breslow, Karl Brown, I. R. Brussel, Andrew Burris, H. A. Cheney, Herman Cohen, Paul S. Clarkson, Louis Henry Cohn, Louis A. Discher, Philip C. Duschnes, Frances Edwards, Burton Emmett, Maurice Firuski, Bradford Fullerton, Rodman Gilder, Laurence Gomme, Charles R. Green, O. L. Griffith, E. J. Guilder, Irving Haas, Irving Halpern, Evelyn Harter, R. H. Hathaway, Fred Huntsberger, Albert Jackson, W. W. Lange, E. Walter Latendorf, Harold S. Latham, Alfred P. Lee, J. B. McGee, A. C. Mears, Frederic G. Melcher, Aaron Mendoza, Meade Minnegerode, David Moss, Vrest Orton, L. W. Payne, Jr., Alfred C. Potter, Lawrence Clark Powell, Henry C. Quinby, Dr. Charles Rohlfs, George E. Schilling, Don C. Seitz, Paul S. Seybolt, Frank Shay, Mildred C. Smith, Marian Gailor Squire, Aubrey H. Starke, Frank Stone, Arthur Swann, Frank R. Thoms, Charles E. Tuttle, R. W. G. Vail, E. Jacoby Van De Water, Frank C. Willson, Carroll A. Wilson, Carl Zigrosser.

PREFACE to the FOURTH EDITION

"Those who have had the good fortune to discover a new machine, or to
make any material improvements on such as have already been discovered,
must lay their account to encounter innumerable difficulties; they must arm
themselves with patience to abide disappointments; to correct a thousand
imperfections (which the trying hand of experience alone can point out)
to endure the smarting shafts of wit, and, what is perhaps more intolerable
than all the rest put together (on the least failure of any experiments) to
bear up against the heavy abuse and bitter scoffs of ill-natured ignorance.
These never fail to represent the undertaker as an impostor, and his
motives the most knavish: Happy for him if he escape with so gentle
an appelative as that of madman."

> JAMES RUMSEY in his *"A Short Treatise on the Application
> of Steam, Whereby is Clearly Shewn, from Actual Ex-
> periments, That Steam May be Applied to Propel Boats or
> Vessels ..."* Philadelphia, 1788.

THIS is the fourth edition of "Merle Johnson's American First
Editions." The first edition was issued in 1929 and the three
succeeding editions (1932, 1936 and the present edition) contain corrections and additions, each bringing the book closer to what Louise
Imogen Guiney called that "unscaled pinnacle of the bibliophile's bliss,"
completion. Sooner or later all must know that completion is not to be
attained; bibliographers discover that fact earlier than most.

Since first publication, "American First Editions" has seen changes
in book-collecting. A significant period in American book-collecting
habits was that that saw the rise and the current decline of collecting
by list. It is more than barely possible that there will be an even more
marked return to the older (and wiser) method of collecting everything by a given author, rather than the collecting of a selected group
of books which, for one reason or another, have eclipsed far too many
books that are worth the attention of the bibliophile. Another change,
somewhat less marked but nevertheless apparent, is the decrease in
the production of de luxe, large paper "rarities." Certain publishers
continue to issue them but in decreasing numbers. Another important

trend is toward the closer study of those books by Americans which were first published in England. The most serious work in this field was I. R. Brussel's "Anglo-American First Editions, West to East" (*London & New York*, 1936), which established priority for certain American works issued in England before publication in the United States.

But perhaps the most important of all the influences that have come to book-collecting is the fact that the past few years have seen a tremendous increase in the publication of ephemeral material. This has become an era of pamphleteers, with swiftly moving events requiring printed comment produced, literally, between overnight changes in frontiers. The bibliographer of tomorrow is fortunate in that the collector of today is actively gathering and preserving these ephemeral productions. Consider, and the cases are quite similar, the difficulties of securing a complete set of Thomas Paine's pamphlets or those issued by Marat during the French Revolution. The collector of the late eighteenth century could have done the collector of this century a service if he had been so inclined. But then, the collector of that age was concerned with events more important than bibliomania.

Another feature of collecting, far more pronounced today than formerly, is the more frequent occurrence of so-called advance copies. In some instances the advance copies are issued in quantities so large that they well might qualify as first issues. The collector must redefine "advance copy" and decide whether it is what it proclaims itself, or whether it is in fact the first issue. In either case, a certain amount of judgment must be used, for if one insists on having the advance copy rather than the regularly issued first issue, then why not the page-proofs (which preceded the advance copies), and if the page-proofs, then why not the galley-sheets ... and so on *ad absurdum*.

No bibliography, it must be repeated, is the work of one person. The best bibliography is the result of many contributors working toward a common end and, in that respect, bibliography is the exception to the adage regarding broth. Therefore, it is a pleasure to record the fact that the present revision of "American First Editions" is the result of hundreds of letters of comment and addition from dealers, librarians and collectors. Specifically, the editor is grateful for the assistance of Miss Alice Hackett of *The Publishers' Weekly;* Mr. John S. Van E. Kohn and his associate Dr. R. F. Roberts; Mr. David A. Randall; Mr. Edward Lazare, editor of "American Book Prices Current"; Miss Virginia Warren; Mr. Gabriel Engel; Mr. Frank C. Willson; Mr. Frank Stone who contributed, among other lists, that of Kenneth Roberts; Maj. John T. Winterich who has not permitted a war to consume all his working hours; Mr. Philip C. Duschnes; Mr. Carroll A. Wilson whose continuing interest in American first editions is reflected in many of the present lists; Capt. Louis Henry Cohn who contributed heavily to the lists of the more modern authors; Miss Jane Wise who permitted me to use her unpublished bibliography of Elinor Wylie; Col. Nathan N. Wallack whose collection was made available for the purposes of study; Mr. Colton Storm; Mr. Walter Pforzheimer, Jr.; Mrs. Dorothy Russo; and surely, to Mr. Frank J. Hogan who gave the editor free access to his notable collection of books. In the final checking the full use of the collections at the Library of Congress was invaluable.

JACOB BLANCK

Washington, D. C.
July 28, 1941

PREFACE to the THIRD EDITION

'If this were only cleared away,'
    They said, 'it would be grand!'

'If seven maids with seven mops
    Swept it for half a year,
Do you suppose,' the Walrus said,
    'That they could get it clear?'
'I doubt it,' said the Carpenter,
    And shed a bitter tear.

AND so with bibliography. One may sweep the sands of this vast subject and retire with a sense of triumph, tempered by the realization that only in simple mathematics is perfection possible, to discover later that errors have been committed. Unfortunately, the errors are usually discovered after the last *t* is crossed, the last *i* dotted and the book delivered in its final form. Nevertheless, it is essential that a body of American Bibliography be developed and if the present volume is a contribution to that growth then surely it is worthy the position occupied by the preceding two editions.

In the preface to the second edition of this work, the late Merle Johnson stated that "a certain number of stumps remained to be uprooted, stones to be removed. Perfection is not claimed, guarantees not admitted for these revised lists, but most of the earlier imperfections have been cleared away." The present revision is offered in the same spirit, with no apology for the errors but with an honest admission of the shortcomings, pointing out that many of the old stumps and stones have been cleared away, certain doubts removed, and certain once questionable points of issue definitely determined. This volume is not intended as a substitute for the extant bibliographies of American authors, but as a source of information concerning those authors whose enthusiasts have not yet offered a complete bibliographical record. The collector is at all times urged to consult the standard bibliographies, if such there are.

PREFACE

In the case of certain books it is known that more than one state exists. If it has been possible to determine the first state, a brief description of such first state is given; if the first state remains in doubt, such doubt is expressed. In the determination of states and issues the much discussed (and much misunderstood) "broken type theory" has been employed. No one knew better than the theory's own chief advocate, Merle Johnson, how much ridicule had been heaped on the head of that revealing system of bibliography. In his "High Spots of American Literature" (*New York,* 1929) he wrote: "Behind the raised palms it is being whispered that I am a crank as to 'broken type.' Bless you, my old dears, that is only modern scientific methods getting into the determination of first editions. A good practical printer can tell more about first editions than all your experts."

But for his death he would have issued a brochure on the subject. Briefly the theory is this: that as type or plates are used certain evidences of wear occur. In the case of a book suspected of existing in two or more states, it is obvious that those copies showing the least wear or lacking damaged type (always assuming until otherwise proved that the damage occurred during printing and not before) preceded copies with the defects under observation. The presence of the defects does not indicate a later issue—but it is an *indication* of *when* the sheet was printed. Thus, by following the progression of the wear or damage, it is possible to determine the earliest printed copies which almost invariably are those containing the typographical errors, usually points positive of the first state.

Bindings are understood to be in cloth unless otherwise indicated. Every effort has been made to describe the variant or special bindings in which a book has been noted. The first bindings of the early American authors may never be determined. The productions of Cooper, as an example, exist in both boards and leather and it is for the collector to decide which is the more desirable.

The importance of publisher's advertisements, unless they are an integral part of the book, is not over-emphasized. It is known that books were issued with inserted advertisements variously dated, a fact that may be explained by binder's whim or expedience.

The checklists are presented in standard form as to capitalization and punctuation. Dates which appear on the title page in Roman numerals are here expressed in Arabic. Brackets [ ] about a date or any other part of the listing indicate that the material contained within the brackets does not appear on the title page but is derived from other sources. In stating place of publication only the principal place is given, although the title page may list the home office of the publisher together with a dozen branches from Portland, Maine, to San Francisco. If such imprints are of bibliographical significance attention is called to the fact, otherwise the standard method is used.

In noting special editions the use of the word *Also* indicates: "in addition to the regularly published edition."

In no case is there an attempt to list all the minor productions of an author. Authors such as Whittier, Longfellow, Morley and Howells have scattered contributions to countless books other than their own. Each list has a representative selection of such material following the main body of the checklist; for a fuller listing the collector is referred to the formal bibliographies. Magazine appearances are not considered.

In the compilation of these lists I have been aided by so many that it becomes embarrassingly difficult to express my gratitude. Looking back over the period in which this book was produced I recall the kind co-operation of the many booksellers, publishers and collectors who gave freely of their time and knowledge. Not the least of these are Miss Alice Hackett of the *Publishers' Weekly;* Mr. John S. Van E. Kohn; Mr. David A. Randall; Mr. Herman Cohen; Mr. Edward Lazare; Miss Marian Squire; Mr. Bernard G. Otto; Miss Virginia Warren; Mr. Frank C. Willson and Mr. Paul S. Seybolt, both of whom spent many a Boston night with me poring over countless questionable entries; Mr. Carroll A. Wilson, who allowed me the privilege of drawing on his vast storehouse of information; Capt. Louis Henry Cohn, whose extensive knowledge of modern authors was of immeasurable value; to G. A.

PREFACE

Baker and Company, under whose hospitable roof much of this book was done. But above all am I grateful to one of the greatest influences in American Bibliography—good friend and mentor, Merle Johnson.

JACOB BLANCK

New York
1936

List of Authors

The present edition of "American First Editions" does not reprint the checklists of the following authors: Andy Adams, Ray Stannard Baker (David Grayson), George Bancroft, Thomas Beer, Alice Brown, Robert W. Chambers, Hart Crane, Adelaide Crapsey, Mazo de la Roche, Edgar Fawcett, Arthur Davison Ficke, Zona Gale, Ben Hecht, William James, Percy MacKaye, Mary Noailles Murfree (Charles Egbert Craddock), David Graham Phillips, Ezra Pound, Morgan Robertson, Upton Sinclair, Harriet Prescott Spofford, Carl Van Vechten and Stark Young. Lists of the preceding may be found in the 1936 edition of the present work. Exclusions are based on the degree (or lack) of collector interest as displayed in "Trade Prices Current," an annual compilation of American first editions offered by the country's leading rare book dealers.

The following authors have been added to the present edition: James Boyd, Charles Waddell Chesnutt, Walter Edmonds, James T. Farrell, Charles Fenno Hoffman, Don Marquis, Allan Pinkerton, Katherine Anne Porter, Kenneth Roberts, John Steinbeck, T. S. Stribling.

Adams, Henry 3
Ade, George 6
Aiken, Conrad 9
Alcott, Louisa May 12
Aldrich, Thomas Bailey 16
Allen, Hervey 20
Allen, James Lane 23
Anderson, Sherwood 25
Atherton, Gertrude 28
Audubon, John James 31

Austin, Jane G. 33
Austin, Mary 35
Bacheller, Irving 37
Bangs, John Kendrick 39
Beebe, William 43
Bellamy, Edward 45
Benét, Stephen Vincent 46
Benét, William Rose 50
Bierce, Ambrose 53
Bird, Robert Montgomery 56

Boyd, James 57
Brackenridge, Hugh Henry 58
Bradford, Gamaliel 60
Bradford, Roark 63
Bromfield, Louis 64
Brown, Charles Brockden 66
Bryant, William Cullen 67
Buck, Pearl 71
Bunner, H. C. 73
Burgess, Gelett 76
Burroughs, John 79
Bynner, Witter 82
Byrne, Donn 84
Cabell, James Branch 87
Cable, George W. 92
Caldwell, Erskine 94
Carman, Bliss 96
Cather, Willa 103
Chesnutt, Charles Waddell 106
Chivers, Thomas Holley 107
Churchill, Winston 108
Clemens, Samuel L. 110
Cobb, Irvin S. 116
Cooke, John Esten 121
Cooper, James Fenimore 123
Crane, Stephen 128
Cummings, E. E. 131
Curtis, George William 133
Dana, Richard Henry 135
Davis, Richard Harding 137

Deland, Margaret 141
Dickinson, Emily 144
Dodge, Mary Mapes 146
Dos Passos, John 147
Drake, Joseph Rodman 150
Dreiser, Theodore 151
Dunbar, Paul Laurence 156
Dunne, Finley Peter 158
Edmonds, Walter D. 159
Eggleston, Edward 161
Emerson, Ralph Waldo 163
Farrell, James T. 168
Faulkner, William 170
Ferber, Edna 173
Field, Eugene 176
Fisher, Vardis 180
Ford, Paul Leicester 182
Forester, Frank (*pseud*.) 238
Fox, John 185
Frederic, Harold 187
Freeman, Mary E. Wilkins 189
Freneau, Philip 192
Frost, Robert 194
Fuller, Henry Blake 198
Garland, Hamlin 200
Glasgow, Ellen 204
Green, Anna Katharine 206
Guiney, Louise Imogen 208
Halleck, Fitz-Greene 210
Harris, Joel Chandler 212

Harte, Bret 216
Hawthorne, Nathaniel 222
Hay, John 227
Hearn, Lafcadio 229
Hemingway, Ernest 235
Henry, O. (*pseud.*) 420
Herbert, Henry Willian 238
Herford, Oliver 243
Hergesheimer, Joseph 247
Heyward, Du Bose 250
Hoffman, Charles Fenno 252
Holmes, Oliver Wendell 253
Hough, Emerson 263
Hovey, Richard 266
Howells, William Dean 268
Huneker, James Gibbons 274
Irving, Washington 276
Jackson, Helen Hunt 280
James, Henry 282
James, Will 287
Janvier, Thomas A. 289
Jeffers, Robinson 291
Jewett, Sarah Orne 294
Johnston, Mary 296
Kennedy, John Pendleton 298
Kent, Rockwell 300
Kilmer, Joyce 304
Lanier, Sidney 306
Lardner, Ring 309
Lewis, Sinclair 311

Lindsay, Vachel 315
London, Jack 318
Longfellow, Henry Wadsworth 323
Lowell, Amy 330
Lowell, James Russell 332
McCutcheon, George Barr 337
McFee, William 340
MacLeish, Archibald 344
Markham, Edwin 347
Marquis, Don 349
Marvel, Ik (*pseud.*) 369
Masters, Edgar Lee 352
Melville, Herman 355
Mencken, H. L. 358
Millay, Edna St. Vincent 362
Miller, Joaquin 365
Mitchell, Donald G. 369
Mitchell, S. Weir 372
Moody, William Vaughn 376
Morley, Christopher 377
Muir, John 386
Nathan, George Jean 388
Nathan, Robert 391
Neihardt, John G. 394
Newton, A. Edward 396
Norris, Frank 399
O. Henry (*pseud.*) 420
O'Neill, Eugene 401
Page, Thomas Nelson 404

Parker, Dorothy 408

Parkman, Francis 409

Paulding, James Kirke 411

Pinkerton, Allan 414

Poe, Edgar Allan 416

Porter, Katherine Anne 419

Porter, William Sydney 420

Pyle, Howard 423

Remington, Frederic 426

Repplier, Agnes 428

Riley, James Whitcomb 430

Roberts, Elizabeth Madox 434

Roberts, Kenneth 435

Robinson, Edwin Arlington 438

Robinson, Rowland E. 443

Roosevelt, Theodore 444

Rowson, Susan 449

Saltus, Edgar 451

Sandburg, Carl 455

Santayana, George 458

Seton-Thompson, Ernest 461

Simms, William Gilmore 464

Smith, F. Hopkinson 469

Steinbeck, John 472

Sterling, George 474

Stockton, Frank R. 477

Stowe, Harriet Beecher 481

Stribling, T. S. 485

Tabb, John Bannister 487

Tarkington, Booth 489

Teasdale, Sara 496

Thompson, Daniel Pierce 498

Thompson, Maurice 499

Thompson-Seton, Ernest 461

Thoreau, Henry David 501

Trowbridge, John T. 505

Twain, Mark (*pseud.*) 110

Van Loon, Hendrik Willem 509

Wallace, Lew 512

Wescott, Glenway 514

Westcott, Edward Noyes 516

Wharton, Edith 517

Whistler, James A. McNeill 521

White, Stewart Edward 523

White, William Allen 526

Whitman, Walt 528

Whittier, John Greenleaf 533

Wilder, Thornton 541

Wilson, Harry Leon 543

Wilson, Woodrow 545

Wister, Owen 547

Wolfe, Thomas 549

Wylie, Elinor 551

AMERICAN FIRST EDITIONS

Henry (Brooks) Adams

1838–1918

CIVIL-SERVICE REFORM. *Boston, 1869.*

CHAPTERS OF ERIE AND OTHER ESSAYS. *Boston;* 1871.
With Charles Francis Adams. Cloth or wrappers. The following are by Henry
Adams: "The New York Gold Conspiracy," "Captain John Smith," "The Bank
of England Restriction," "British Finance in 1816," "The Legal Tender Act."
The last was written in collaboration with F. A. Walker.

THE LIFE OF ALBERT GALLATIN. *Philadelphia,* 1879.

DEMOCRACY: AN AMERICAN NOVEL. *New York,* 1880.
Anonymous. No. 112 in "Leisure Hour Series." End papers printed with publisher's advertisements do not list the present title; publisher's address given as
29 West 23 Street. A copy has been noted with the number as *111;* internal
evidence indicates a later printing. For a full collation and bibliographical discussion of this title see *The Publishers' Weekly,* July 15, 1939, "One Hundred Good
Novels," by David A. Randall and John T. Winterich.

JOHN RANDOLPH. *Boston,* 1882.

ESTHER: A NOVEL. *New York,* 1884.
Frances Snow Compton, *pseudonym.* No. 3 in "American Novel Series." A facsimile edition, with an introduction by Robert E. Spiller, was issued *New York,*
1938.

HISTORY OF THE UNITED STATES OF AMERICA [1801-1817]. *New York,*
1889-1891.
9 vols. Vols. 1-2, "... During the First Administration of Thomas Jefferson,"
1889; Vols. 3-4, "... During the Second Administration ... ," 1890; Vols. 5-6,
"... First Administration of James Madison," 1890; Vols. 7-8-9, "... Second
Administration," 1891. Volumes 5-6 were previously privately printed, 6 copies
only, *Cambridge,* 1888.

HISTORICAL ESSAYS. *New York,* 1891.

MONT SAINT MICHEL AND CHARTRES. *Washington,* 1904.
Anonymous. Privately printed. Revised and enlarged, *Washingon,* 1912; published edition, *Boston,* 1913.

THE EDUCATION OF HENRY ADAMS. *Washington,* 1907.
Privately printed. 100 copies only. Leather label on spine. With revisions and additions, *Boston,* 1918, edited by Henry Cabot Lodge.

A LETTER TO AMERICAN TEACHERS OF HISTORY. *Washington,* 1910.

ADAMS

THE LIFE OF GEORGE CABOT LODGE. *Boston*, 1911.

THE DEGRADATION OF THE DEMOCRATIC DOGMA. *New York*, 1919.

LETTERS TO A NIECE AND PRAYER TO THE VIRGIN OF CHARTRES. *Boston*, 1920.
Contains also: "A Niece's Memories," by Mabel La Farge.

A CYCLE OF ADAMS LETTERS, 1861-1865. *Boston*, 1920.
Worthington Chauncey Ford, editor. 2 vols.

LETTERS ... (1858-1891). *Boston*, 1930.
Worthington Chauncey Ford, editor.

LETTERS ... (1892-1918). *Boston*, 1938.
Worthington Chauncey Ford, editor. Also 200 numbered copies.

A Radical Indictment! The Administration ... Its Corruptions And Shortcomings ... ₁*Washington*, 1872₁.
Anonymous.

Syllabus. History II. Political History of Europe From the 10th to the 15th Century. *Cambridge*, 1874.
Wrappers.

Essays in Anglo-Saxon Law. *Boston*, 1876.
Contains Adams' "The Anglo-Saxon Courts of Law."

Documents Relating to New-England Federalism, 1800-1815. *Boston*, 1877.
Edited by Adams.

The Writings of Albert Gallatin. *Philadelphia*, 1879.
3 vols. Edited.

Pocahontas and Captain Smith. ₁*Bangor, Me.*, 1881₁.
Wrappers.

Memoirs of Marau Taaroa, Last Queen of Tahiti. ₁*n.p.*, 1893₁.
Privately printed. Edited by Adams. Reissued, *Paris*, 1901, as "Memoirs of Arii Taimai."

American Historical Association Report for 1894. *Washington*, 1895.
Contains Adams' "The Tendency of History," published separately, *Washington*, 1896.

Recognition of Cuban Independence. ₁*Washington*, 1896₁.

Jefferson and His Inauguration. ₁*Boston*, 1902₁.
Old South Leaflets, No. 104. Reprinted from "History of the United States."

Clarence King Memoirs. *New York*, 1904.
Boards. Contribution.

Letters of John Hay and Extracts From His Diary. *Washington*, 1908.
3 vols. Privately printed. Selected by Adams.

Proceedings of the Massachusetts Historical Society for 1910.
Contains Adams' "Washington in 1861."

4

A Catalogue of the Books of John Quincy Adams ... *Boston*, 1938.
300 copies only. Contains some Henry Adams material.

BIOGRAPHICAL AND BIBLIOGRAPHICAL

A Case of Hereditary Bias: Henry Adams as a Historian, by "Housatonic." [*New York*, 1891].

Charles Francis Adams, 1835-1916, An Autobiography. *Boston*, 1916. Contains biographical material.

Commemorative Tribute to Henry Adams, by Paul Elmer More. [*New York*] 1922.

Bibliography of the Writings of Henry Adams, by James Truslow Adams. *New York*, 1930.

Henry Adams, by James Truslow Adams. *New York*, 1933.

5

George Ade

1866–

ARTIE. *Chicago*, 1896.

PINK MARSH. *Chicago*, 1897.

DOC' HORNE. *Chicago*, 1899.

FABLES IN SLANG. *Chicago*, 1900.

MORE FABLES. *Chicago*, 1900.

FORTY MODERN FABLES. *New York*, 1901.
   R. H. Russell imprint. Boards, cloth back.

THE GIRL PROPOSITION. *New York*, 1902.
   R. H. Russell imprint.

PEOPLE YOU KNOW. *New York*, 1903.
   R. H. Russell imprint. First edition so stated on copyright page.

CIRCUS DAY. *Akron*, 1903.
   An unauthorized reprint from an as yet unlocated collection of short stories to
   which Ade contributed.

HANDSOME CYRIL. [*Phoenix*, 1903.]
   No. 1 in "The Strenuous Lad's Library." 592 copies on laid paper, 60 on handmade paper, 20 on Japan vellum, 2 on vellum.

CLARENCE ALLEN. [*Phoenix*, 1903.]
   No. 2 in "The Strenuous Lad's Library." 374 copies only.

ROLLO JOHNSON. [*Phoenix*, 1904.]
   No. 3 in "The Strenuous Lad's Library." 374 copies only. Colored wrappers. The
   colophon states that the book was printed during the latter part of 1903 and the
   first part of 1904; published 1904. This, and the two preceding burlesques, was
   reprinted in "Bang! Bang!" All three list Ade as the author of "Eddie Parks, The
   Newsboy." Thus far no such title has been located.

IN BABEL. *New York*, 1903.
   Also 374 de luxe copies. *Published, September, 1903* on copyright page.

BREAKING INTO SOCIETY. *New York*, 1904.
   Published March, 1904 on copyright page.

TRUE BILLS. *New York*, 1904.
   Published October, 1904 on copyright page.

IN PASTURES NEW. *New York*, 1906.
Also 374 de luxe copies. *Published, October, 1906* on copyright page.

THE SLIM PRINCESS. *Indianapolis* [1907].
April on copyright page.

I KNEW HIM WHEN ———. *Chicago*, 1910.
1,000 copies only for members of the Indiana Society of Chicago.

HOOSIER HAND BOOK. [*Chicago*, 1911].
1,000 copies only for members of the Indiana Society. Flexible boards.

VERSES AND JINGLES. *Indianapolis* [1911].
1,000 copies only for members of the Indiana Society.

KNOCKING THE NEIGHBORS. *Garden City*, 1912.

ADE'S FABLES. *Garden City*, 1914.

HAND-MADE FABLES. *Garden City*, 1920.

SINGLE BLESSEDNESS AND OTHER OBSERVATIONS. *Garden City*, 1922.
First edition so stated on the copyright page.

STAY WITH ME FLAGONS. *New York* [1922].
Privately printed for members of the Lotos Club.

BANG! BANG! *New York* [1928].
Boards, cloth back, paper labels.

THE OLD-TIME SALOON. *New York*, 1931.

REVIVED REMARKS ON MARK TWAIN. *Chicago*, 1936.
500 numbered copies only, signed.

ONE AFTERNOON WITH MARK TWAIN. [*Chicago*] 1939.
350 numbered copies only. Stiff wrappers.

PLAYS

The Sultan of Sulu. *New York*, 1903.
Published May, 1903 on the copyright page. Printed wrappers.
Marse Covington. *Washington*, 1918.
Printed wrappers.
Nettie. *New York*, 1923.
Printed wrappers.
Speaking to Father. *New York*, 1923.
The Mayor and the Manicure. *New York*, 1923.
Printed wrappers.
Just Out of College. *New York*, 1924.
Father and the Boys. *New York*, 1924.

ADE

The College Widow. *New York,* 1924.
The County Chairman. *New York,* 1924.

Ade is the author of numerous other plays including "The Old Town," "Mrs. Peckham's Carouse," "The Fair Co-Ed," "The Bad Samaritan," "The Sho-Gun," and "Peggy From Paris."

BOOKS WITH CONTRIBUTIONS, ETC., ETC.

The Humbler Poets. *New York,* 1903.
  Contains a poem by Ade.
Short Story Classics. *New York* [1905].
  William Patten, Editor. Vol. 5 contains Ade's "To Make a Hoosier Holiday."
The Humbler Poets: Second Series. *Chicago,* 1911.
  Contains a poem by Ade.
The Morris Book Shop. *Chicago,* 1912.
  Contribution.
An Invitation to You and Your Folks From Jim and Some More of the Home Folks. *Indianapolis* [1916].
  Pamphlet. Compiled by Ade for the Indiana Historical Commission.
Services in Memory of James Whitcomb Riley ... October 29, 1916 ... at Chicago. *Chicago,* 1916.
  Contains a four-page eulogy by Ade.
Some Torch Bearers in Indiana. *Indianapolis* [1917].
  Edited by Charity Dye. Contribution by Ade.
Dinner to George Ade Given by the Lotos Club, New York, December 18, 1920. *New York,* 1920.
  Contains a speech by Ade. Privately printed.
My Maiden Effort. *Garden City,* 1921.
  Contains a contribution by Ade.
The Stag Cook Book. *New York* [1922].
  C. Mac Sheridan, editor. Contains a recipe by Ade.
Webster's Poker Book, by H. T. Webster. *New York,* 1925.
  Introduction by Ade.
The Paths of Long Ago, by Wilbur D. Nesbit. *Chicago* [1926].
  Preface by Ade.
Literary Treasures of 1926. [*Chicago,* 1927].
  5,000 copies only. Contains Ade's "When I Sowed my Wild Oat."
Samples. *New York* [1927].
  Lillie Ryttenberg and Beatrice Lang, editors. Contains "Tall-Stoy" by Ade.
Thirty Fables. *New York,* 1933.
  Illustrations by Peggy Bacon. Reprinted selections.
The Call of the Wild. [*n.p., n.d.*]
  Printed wrappers. Issued by the Chesapeake Steamship Company as an advertisement.

8

Conrad (Potter) Aiken

1889–

EARTH TRIUMPHANT AND OTHER TALES IN VERSE. *New York,* 1914.

TURNS AND MOVIES AND OTHER TALES IN VERSE. *Boston,* 1916.
Printed wrappers over boards.

THE JIG OF FORSLIN: A SYMPHONY. *Boston,* 1916.

NOCTURNE OF REMEMBERED SPRING AND OTHER POEMS. *Boston,* 1917.

THE CHARNEL ROSE, SENLIN: A BIOGRAPHY, AND OTHER POEMS. *Boston,*
1918.
Issued in both light and dark blue cloths; Mr. Aiken states that the dark blue was
first. "Senlin" was separately issued, *London,* 1925, revised "but the revision was
abandoned in favour of the earlier" for the "Selected Poems," 1929.

SCEPTICISMS. *New York,* 1919.
Noted in two types of binding, with no known priority, as follows: red cloth,
black stamping, top edges stained red, borzoi on back cover. Or, green cloth, red
stamping, top edges unstained, no borzoi on back cover.

THE HOUSE OF DUST: A SYMPHONY. *Boston,* 1920.

PUNCH: THE IMMORTAL LIAR. *New York,* 1921.

PRIAPUS AND THE POOL. *Cambridge,* 1922.
425 copies only of which 50 were printed on handmade paper and signed.
Boards. New edition with added poems, *New York,* 1925.

THE PILGRIMAGE OF FESTUS. *New York,* 1923.
Boards, paper label.

BRING! BRING! *New York,* 1925.

BLUE VOYAGE. *New York,* 1927.
Also 125 copies numbered and signed.

COSTUMES BY EROS. *New York,* 1928.

PRELUDE. [*New York*] 1929.
475 copies only in the Random House "Poetry Quartos."

SELECTED POEMS. *New York,* 1929.
Also 210 large paper copies, numbered and signed by the author.

JOHN DETH, A METAPHYSICAL LEGEND, AND OTHER POEMS. *New York,* 1930.
First edition has code letter *A* on copyright page.

GEHENNA. *New York,* 1930.
875 copies only in the Random House "Prose Quartos." Stiff wrappers.

THE COMING FORTH BY DAY OF OSIRIS JONES. *New York,* 1931.
First edition has code letter *A* on copyright page. Mr. Aiken states that "the first printing had to be recalled (where possible) and a substitute page 37 tipped in, owing to the fact that the words *The music,* top of page, had mistakenly been printed as a section-title. A few uncorrected copies are in existence."

PRELUDES FOR MEMNON. *New York,* 1931.

GREAT CIRCLE. *New York,* 1933.
First edition has code letter *A* on copyright page.

AMONG THE LOST PEOPLE. *New York,* 1934.
First printing has code letter *A* on copyright page.

LANDSCAPE WEST OF EDEN. *New York,* 1935.

KING COFFIN. *New York,* 1935.
First edition has publisher's code letter *A* on copyright page.

TIME IN THE ROCK. *New York,* 1936.
First edition has code letter *A* on copyright page.

A HEART FOR THE GODS OF MEXICO. *London,* 1939.

AND IN THE HUMAN HEAT. *New York* [1940].
First edition so indicated on copyright page.

CONVERSATION, OR, PILGRIMS' PROGRESS. *New York* [1940].
First edition so indicated on copyright page.

Two Wessex Tales, by Thomas Hardy. *Boston* [1919].
Simulated leather wrappers. Foreword by Aiken.
The Borzoi, 1920. *New York,* 1920.
Contribution.
Modern American Poets. *London* [1922].
Edited.
Best Short Stories of 1922. *Boston* [1923].
Edward J. O'Brien, editor. Contains Aiken's "The Dark City." Also published in "Stories From the Dial," *New York,* 1924.
Best Poems of 1923. *Boston,* 1924.
Contains "The House," by Aiken.

Selected Poems of Emily Dickinson. *London* [1924].
    Edited by Aiken.
Modern American Poets. *New York* [1927].
    Edited.
Conrad Aiken. *New York* [1927].
    In "The Pamphlet Poets" series edited by Louis Untermeyer
American Poetry, 1671-1928. *New York* [1929].
    Edited.
The Melody of Chaos, by Houston Peterson. *New York,* 1931.
    Contains critical material.
Creeps by Night. *New York* [1931].
    Dashiell Hammett, editor. Contains a short story by Aiken.
O. Henry Memorial Award Prize Stories. *Garden City,* 1933.
    Harry Hansen, editor. Contains Aiken's "Impulse."
Designed for Reading. *New York,* 1934.
    Contribution.

Many of Aiken's poems were first collected in the "A Miscellany of American Poetry" annuals, 1920, 1922, 1925 and 1927. The last two carry first edition notices on the copyright page.

Louisa May Alcott

1832–1888

FLOWER FABLES. *Boston*, 1855.

HOSPITAL SKETCHES. *Boston*, 1863.
Cloth copies have leaf of advertisements announcing Wendell Phillips' speeches as ready for September 1st; board copies have review of Phillips' book on back cover. Obviously the copies with first form are earlier. Later issued with *New York and Boston* imprint, in wrappers. Reissued with revisions, enlarged, as "Hospital Sketches and Camp and Fireside Stories," *Boston*, 1869.

ON PICKET DUTY AND OTHER TALES. *Boston* [1864].

THE ROSE FAMILY. *Boston*, 1864.
Cloth or printed wrappers.

MOODS. *Boston*, 1865.
Noted with copyright notice on a pasted in slip but status of such copies is undetermined. A copy has been noted, undated on title page, copyright 1864, but since Alcott is listed as the author of books published as late as 1869 such copies are obviously later. The first state of binding does not have author's name on spine. Revised and reissued, *Boston*, 1882.

THE MYSTERIOUS KEY AND WHAT IT OPENED. *Boston* [1867].
Wrappers. No. 50 in the "Ten Cent Novelettes" series. Suppressed by the author but another edition was published by Lupton, *New York, ca.*, 1891.

MORNING-GLORIES, AND OTHER STORIES. *Boston*, 1868.
An edition, *New York, 1867*, has been noted containing about half the material contained in the Boston edition. Since the Boston edition was received for copyright in December 1867, it is possible that the New York edition was later.

KITTY'S CLASS DAY. *Boston*, 1868.
Wrappers. Copyright notice pasted in. Later issue, copyrighted about a week later, has the copyright notice printed in.

AUNT KIPP. *Boston*, 1868.
Wrappers.

NELLY'S HOSPITAL. [*Washington, D. C.* 1868(?).]
6 pp. pamphlet. Issued by the U. S. Sanitary Commission "for the encouragement of alert clubs, schools, and all other organizations of little children working for soldiers."

PSYCHE'S ART. *Boston* [1868].
Wrappers dated 1868. This, together with "Kitty's Class Day" and "Aunt Kipp,"

reissued as "Three Proverb Stories," *Boston* [n.d.], but carrying an 1868 copyright notice; issued in 1871 and not in 1868 as the copyright date suggests.

LITTLE WOMEN, or, MEG, JO, BETH, AND AMY. *Boston*, 1868.
Has no announcement for "Little Women, Part Two" at foot of last page of text; does not state *Part One* on spine. The final signature is of six leaves as follows: text, pp. 337-341, blank [p. 342], advertisements paged 3, 2, 11, 12, 8, 11. On the third page of advertisements "Little Women," without review, is priced at $1.25.

LITTLE WOMEN, or, MEG, JO, BETH, AND AMY: PART SECOND. *Boston*, 1869.
First state has no notice regarding "Little Women: Part One" at p. iv. The advertisements at the back for Jean Ingelow's books end with "A Sister's Bye-Hours"; in later states the title "Mopsa's Darling" is added.

AN OLD-FASHIONED GIRL. *Boston*, 1870.
Exists in three known states as follows: *1st:* no advertisements on the copyright page and with the word *at* repeated, p. 159, line 17. *2nd:* advertisements on copyright page, word *at* repeated as in first state; *3rd:* advertisements on copyright page, error on p. 159 corrected. Noted with paper label on spine. Dramatized by John D. Ravold, *New York*, 1935.

LITTLE MEN: LIFE AT PLUMFIELD WITH JO'S BOYS. *Boston*, 1871.
4 pp. of advertisements at front list "Pink and White Tyranny" as *nearly ready.* "Miss Alcott has taken advantage of the law by which American citizens may secure copyright for their books, both in America and throughout the British dominions, by residing on British soil when the book is simultaneously published in both countries."—*American Literary Gazette and Publishers' Circular*, June 15, 1871.

AUNT JO'S SCRAP-BAG.
Series title for the following:
My Boys, *Boston*, 1872.
    Preceded by the London edition of 1871.
Shawl-Straps, *Boston*, 1872.
Cupid and Chow-Chow, *Boston*, 1874.
My Girls, *Boston*, 1878.
Jimmy's Cruise in the Pinafore, *Boston*, 1879.
An Old-Fashioned Thanksgiving, *Boston*, 1882.

WORK. *Boston*, 1873.

EIGHT COUSINS; or, THE AUNT-HILL. *Boston*, 1875.

SILVER PITCHERS: AND INDEPENDENCE, A CENTENNIAL LOVE STORY. *Boston*, 1876.

ROSE IN BLOOM: A SEQUEL TO "EIGHT COUSINS." *Boston*, 1876.

ALCOTT

A MODERN MEPHISTOPHELES. *Boston*, 1877.
Anon. In the "No Name Series." Reprinted with preface by the author, *Boston*, 1889.

UNDER THE LILACS. *Boston*, 1878.

MEADOW BLOSSOMS. *New York* [1879].
Boards.

SPARKLES FOR BRIGHT EYES. *New York* [1879].
Boards.

WATER CRESSES. *New York* [1879].
Boards.

JACK AND JILL: A VILLAGE STORY. *Boston*, 1880.

PROVERB STORIES. *Boston*, 1882.

SPINNING-WHEEL STORIES. *Boston*, 1884.

JO'S BOYS AND HOW THEY TURNED OUT: A SEQUEL TO "LITTLE MEN." *Boston*, 1886.
The book exists in two states. Type-wear indicates that "thick" copies, measuring slightly over 1″ across the top of sheets (exclusive of cover), are earlier than those copies measuring slightly under 1″.

A GARLAND FOR GIRLS. *Boston*, 1888.
Apparently this book does not exist with title page dated 1887. The copyright deposit copy is dated 1888, copyrighted 1887.

A MODERN MEPHISTOPHELES AND A WHISPER IN THE DARK. *Boston*, 1889.
First edition for the second title. First title published anonymously in "The No Name Series," *Boston*, 1877.

LOUISA MAY ALCOTT: HER LIFE, LETTERS AND JOURNALS. *Boston*, 1889.
Ednah D. Cheney, editor. Copies have been noted untrimmed.

Echoes of Harper's Ferry, by James Redpath. *Boston*, 1860.
Contains a tribute to Thoreau by Alcott.
Concord Sketches ... Twelve Photographs ... By May Alcott. *Boston*, 1869.
Edited anonymously by Louisa May Alcott; contains a short preface.
The Sunny Side ... by Charles W. Wendté and H. S. Perkins. *New York* [1875].
Contribution.
The Horn of Plenty of Home Poems and Home Pictures. *Boston*, 1876.
Compiled by Sophie May [Rebecca Sophia Clark]. Contribution by Alcott.
A Masque of Poets. *Boston;* 1878.
Contains "Transfiguration" by Alcott. Ordinary edition black cloth, red stamping, 2,000 copies, published November, 1878; "Red Line" edition, 500 copies

only, bound in various colors of cloth, published December 1878. There is a possibility that the "Red Line" edition preceded the trade edition in time of printing. Trade edition occasionally has a slip addressed to editors tipped in at the title page.

Lulu's Library. *Boston*, 1886-87-89.

3 vols. Reprints of previously collected writings together with some material here first collected. Volume 1 has been noted in two states: with the figure *1* on spine in gilt and with no mention of the present title in terminal advertisements. Or, with the *1* on the spine in color and this title described in the advertisements. The first described is probably the first state.

Comic Tragedies: Written by "Jo" and "Meg" and Acted by the "Little Women." *Boston*, 1893.

Thoreau's Flute. *Detroit*, 1899.

The Little Men Play. *Boston*, 1900.

Adapted by Elizabeth Lincoln Gould.

The Little Women Play. *Boston*, 1900.

Adapted by Elizabeth Lincoln Gould.

Effie's Christmas Dream. *Boston*, 1912.

Three act play adapted by Laure Clair Foucher from Alcott's "A Christmas Dream and How It Came True."

Little Women Letters from the House of Alcott. *Boston*, 1914.

Selected by Jessie Bonstelle and Marian de Forest.

Alcott Memoirs. *Boston* [1915].

"Posthumously compiled from papers, journals and memoranda of the late Dr. Frederick L. H. Willis ..."

Three Unpublished Poems, by Louisa M. Alcott. [*Boston*, 1919].

Wrappers.

The following are reprints: "May Flowers," "A Hole in the Wall," "The Candy Country," "Poppies and Wheat," "A Christmas Dream," "Little Button Rose," "The Doll's Journey," "Pansies and Water-Lilies," "Mountain Laurel and Maidenhair," "Morning Glories and Queen Aster," "A Modern Cinderella," "Marjorie's Three Gifts," "Becky's Christmas Dream."

BIOGRAPHICAL AND BIBLIOGRAPHICAL

Louisa May Alcott: The Children's Friend, by Ednah D. Cheney. *Boston* [1888].

Louisa May Alcott, by Belle Moses. *New York*, 1909.

Louisa May Alcott: A Bibliography, by Lucile Gulliver. *Boston*, 1932.

Thomas Bailey Aldrich

1836–1907

THE BELLS: A COLLECTION OF CHIMES. *Boston & New York,* 1855.
By *T. B. A.* Also issued with joint imprint *Boston & New York & Cincinnati.*

DAISY'S NECKLACE: AND WHAT CAME OF IT. *New York,* 1857.
Note of erratum following text. There were 2,000 copies in the first printing of which about half were remaindered, bound together with the work of another author. The remainder was issued with binder's title: "The Stain of Birth, and, Daisy's Necklace."

THE COURSE OF TRUE LOVE NEVER DID RUN SMOOTH. *New York,* 1858.
Copies have been noted in gift or presentation bindings.

THE BALLAD OF BABIE BELL AND OTHER POEMS. *New York,* 1859.
First state has Broadway address of publisher; second state has Grand Street address. It has been stated that a separate edition of the title poem was issued in 1856; the compiler has never seen this although two early references indicate its existence. A separate printing of the title poem was issued: *Boston,* 1878.

PAMPINEA AND OTHER POEMS. *New York,* 1861.
Various colors of cloth binding. All first editions noted have *Poems of the Year* stamped on the spine.

OUT OF HIS HEAD: A ROMANCE. *New York,* 1862.
Noted on thick and thin paper with no established priority. "Père Antoine's Date Palm," *Cambridge,* 1866, 20 copies only, privately printed, is reprinted from this volume.

POEMS. *New York,* 1863.

THE POEMS OF THOMAS BAILEY ALDRICH. *Boston,* 1865.
First state omits *been* end of third verse, first stanza, p. 102.

PANSIE'S WISH: A CHRISTMAS FANTASY. *Boston,* 1867.

THE STORY OF A BAD BOY. *Boston,* 1870.
First state, p. 14, line 20 reads *scattered* for *scatters;* p. 197, line 10 reads *abroad* for *aboard.* Also, a large paper state, said to be but six copies, of which half were destroyed by fire. A large paper copy was sold at the E. C. Stedman Sale (1911) inscribed by Aldrich: "... one of an edition of 12 copies ..." Reissued with new preface, *Boston,* 1895.

MARJORIE DAW, AND OTHER PEOPLE. *Boston,* 1873.
Reissued with added material, Aldine Edition, *Boston,* 1885.

PRUDENCE PALFREY: A NOVEL. *Boston*, 1874.

FLOWER AND THORN: LATER POEMS. *Boston*, 1877.

THE QUEEN OF SHEBA. *Boston*, 1877.

A MIDNIGHT FANTASY AND THE LITTLE VIOLINIST. *Boston*, 1877.
Second title separately issued, *Boston*, 1880.

THE STILLWATER TRAGEDY. *Boston*, 1880.

THE POEMS OF THOMAS BAILEY ALDRICH. *Boston*, 1882.
Parchment or cloth bindings. Also six copies on Japan vellum.

FROM PONKAPOG TO PESTH. *Boston*, 1883.

MERCEDES AND LATER LYRICS. *Boston*, 1884.
Also copies with paper label on spine.

POEMS: HOUSEHOLD EDITION. *Boston*, 1885.

THE SECOND SON: A NOVEL. *Boston*, 1888.
With M. O. W. OLIPHANT.

WYNDHAM TOWERS. *Boston*, 1890.
It is stated that the Edinburgh edition preceded this.

THE SISTERS' TRAGEDY, WITH OTHER POEMS, LYRICAL AND DRAMATIC. *Boston*, 1891.
Also 50 copies with paper label.

AN OLD TOWN BY THE SEA. *Boston*, 1893.
Also 100 copies with paper label.

TWO BITES AT A CHERRY, WITH OTHER TALES. *Boston*, 1894.
Also 50 copies with paper label. It is stated that the Edinburgh edition preceded this.

MERCEDES: A DRAMA IN TWO ACTS. *Boston*, 1894.

UNGUARDED GATES AND OTHER POEMS. *Boston*, 1895.
Also 50 copies with paper label.

JUDITH AND HOLOFERNES. *Boston*, 1896.
Also 50 copies with paper label. This is a revision of the original poem as it appeared in "Cloth of Gold," 1874.

POETICAL WORKS. *Boston*, 1897.
2 vols.

A SEA TURN AND OTHER MATTERS. *Boston*, 1902.
Also 200 uncut copies with paper label. *Published September, 1902* on copyright page.

PONKAPOG PAPERS. *Boston*, 1903.
Also 200 uncut copies with paper label, stating *First Edition*.

JUDITH OF BETHULÎA: A TRAGEDY. *Boston*, 1904.
"... in part a dramatization of ... *Judith and Holofernes*."

Songs of the Soldiers. *New York*, 1864.
Frank Moore, editor. Contributions.

Père Antoine's Date Palm. *Cambridge*, 1866.
20 copies only, privately printed. Reprinted from "Out of His Head," 1862.

The Atlantic Almanac for 1868. *Boston* [1867].
Contains "Autumn Days," by Aldrich.

Leaves From The Quarry of the Mind. Pearls Gathered From the Shores of Life ...
Boston, 1868.
James H. Head, editor. Contains "Lycidas" by Aldrich.

The Pellet. *Boston*, 1872.
Contributions. Wrappers.

Jubilee Days: An Illustrated Record of the Humorous Features of the World's Peace
Jubilee. *Boston*, 1872.
16 daily numbers in wrappers, or boards with leather back. Edited anonymously
by Aldrich together with William Dean Howells.

Cameos. *Boston*, 1874.
With EDMUND CLARENCE STEDMAN. Selections from the work of Walter Savage
Landor. Edited and with introduction.

Cloth of Gold. *Boston*, 1874.
A reprint of "all the poems which the author cares to retain of the edition published ... in 1865."

Miss Mehetabel's Son and Père Antoine's Date Palm. *Boston*, 1877.
Reprinted from "Marjorie Daw," 1873.

A Rivermouth Romance. *Boston*, 1877.
Reprinted from "Marjorie Daw," 1873.

A Masque of Poets. *Boston*, 1878.
Contains an epilogue, a prologue and "A Preacher" by Aldrich. See under
Alcott for further discussion of this item.

The Story of a Cat. *Boston*, 1879.
Translated from the French of de la Bédollièrre. Printed boards.

Autograph Birthday Book. *Boston* [1881].
Amanda B. Harris, editor. Contribution.

XXXVI Lyrics and XII Sonnets. *Boston*, 1881.
Selections from previously published works. Page 88, verse 9, reads: "... *elud's
ɟmy art, ...*"

Friar Jerome's Beautiful Book and Other Poems. *Boston*, 1881.
Selections from previously published works. Various later reissues with a limited
(250 copies) large paper edition in 1896.

St. Nicholas Songs. *New York* [1888].
Contains, set to music, Aldrich's "Bronze-Brown Eyes," and "Marjorie's
Almanac."

The Hermitage and Later Poems, by E. R. Sill. *Boston*, 1889.
  Edited and with a memorial of the author by Aldrich.
Monody on the Death of Wendell Phillips. [*Boston?*] 1891.
Later Lyrics. *Boston*, 1896.
  Selected from previously published works.
The Works of Thomas Bailey Aldrich. *Boston*, 1896.
  8 vols. Also 250 large paper sets. Vol. 9 added 1907.
Wishmakers' Town, by William Young. *Boston*, 1898.
  Introduction by Aldrich.
Poems of Robert Herrick. *New York*, 1900.
  Introduction by Aldrich.
A Book of Songs and Sonnets. *Boston*, 1906.
  430 copies only. Selected reprints. Boards.
The Set of Turquoise. [*n.p., n.d.*].
  8 pp. Said to be but four copies issued before copyright. Later published with
  the *Werner* imprint. Appears also in "The Ballad of Babie Bell, etc.," 1859.
The Shadow of the Flowers. *Boston* [1912].
  Reprinted material.

BIOGRAPHICAL

The Life of Thomas Bailey Aldrich, by Ferris Greenslet. *Boston*, 1908.
  500 copies only. Contains a bibliography.
Crowding Memories, by Mrs. Thomas Bailey Aldrich. *Boston*, 1920.

(William) Hervey Allen

1889–

BALLADS OF THE BORDER. THE WEAKLING AND OTHER PICTURES OF THE MOBILIZATION. [*El Paso, Texas*] 1916.
Wrappers. Several printings with no distinction. It is probable that the earliest copies misspell the author's name in the copyright notice, thus: *Hervy*.

WAMPUM AND OLD GOLD. *New Haven,* 1921.
Printed wrappers over boards. 500 copies only.

THE BRIDE OF HUITZIL: AN AZTEC LEGEND. *New York,* 1922.
350 signed copies only. A few experimental copies were issued in green boards. Regular edition in gold and orange boards.

CAROLINA CHANSONS. *New York,* 1922.
With DU BOSE HEYWARD. Boards, cloth back, paper label on front cover.

EARTH MOODS AND OTHER POEMS. *New York,* 1925.
First edition so stated on copyright page. Earliest printing has code letters *C-Z* on copyright page.

TOWARD THE FLAME. *New York* [1926].
Publisher's monogram on copyright page.

POE'S BROTHER. *New York,* 1926.
With THOMAS OLLIVE MABBOTT. 1,000 copies only.

ISRAFEL: THE LIFE AND TIMES OF EDGAR ALLAN POE. *New York,* 1926.
2 vols. Also untrimmed copies in three quarter leather binding. First state has wine glass on table in Longfellow portrait, p. 529.

SARAH SIMON: CHARACTER ATLANTEAN. *Garden City,* 1929.
311 copies only, numbered and signed. Boards, cloth back.

SONGS FOR ANNETTE. *New York,* 1929.
100 copies only.

NEW LEGENDS. *New York,* 1929.
Also 175 large paper copies, signed. Trade edition states *First Regular Edition* on copyright page.

ANTHONY ADVERSE. *New York,* 1933.
Also 105 de luxe copies, 3 volumes, signed. Trade edition is in one volume and has publisher's monogram on copyright page. Earliest copies have numerous typographical errors; for purposes of identification the following are given:

p. 352, line 6, *Xaxier* for *Xavier*.

p. 1086, line 18, *ship* for *shop*.

p.397, line 22, the word *found* is repeated.

Several subsequently published de luxe or illustrated editions. Reissued with a new introduction by The Limited Editions Club, *New York*, 1937, 1,500 copies only.

Some time before publication of the first edition the publishers issued a 16 pp. pamphlet, "The Syllabus of a Novel to be Called 'Anthony Adverse' by Hervey Allen," 1,000 copies only.

THE SOURCES OF ANTHONY ADVERSE. [*New York*, 1934].

Wrappers.

ACTION AT AQUILA. *New York* [1938].

First edition so indicated on the copyright page; also, first printing has publisher's monogram on copyright page. Some copies issued in advance of publication, these being 4to page proofs in wrappers.

IT WAS LIKE THIS. *New York* [1940].

Publisher's monogram on the copyright page. 750 copies of the introduction were issued in wrappers in advance of publication.

When Shady Avenue Was Shady Lane. [*n.p.*] 1919.

Broadside.

The Christmas Herald: An Intelligencer of Good Wishes, Vol. 1, No. 1. *Charleston*, 1921.

The Year Book of the Poetry Society of South Carolina. *Charleston*, 1921.

Issues of 1922, 1923, 1924 also contain contributions.

Three Experimental Imprints. *Peterborough*, 1922.

25 copies only; privately printed.

The Bookman Anthology of Verse, 1922. [*New York*] 1922.

Contains Allen's "The Dead Men." First state is bound in boards and has publisher's device on the copyright page.

A Bulletin of the Poetry Society of South Carolina. 1922-3.

Contribution.

The Peterborough Anthology. *New York*, 1923.

Boards, cloth back, paper labels. Contains Allen's "Funeral at High Tide," "Walls," and "Black Roses."

A Book of the Year Nineteen-Twenty-Two: The Poetry Society of Texas. *Dallas* [1923].

Contains a letter by Allen.

The Blindman: A Ballad of Nogent L'Artaud. *New Haven*, 1923.

Boards. Reprinted from "Wampum and Old Gold."

Christmas Epithalamium. *New York*, 1925.

Boards. 325 copies only. Previously printed, privately, 20 copies only [1923].

DuBose Heyward: A Critical and Biographical Sketch. *New York* [1926].

Wrappers.

HERVEY ALLEN

The Works of Edgar Allan Poe. *New York* [1927].
  Introduction.
The Notable Library of Major W. Van R. Whitall. *New York*, 1927.
  Contains "An Appreciation" by Allen.
The Lyric South. *New York*, 1928.
  Addison Hibbard, editor. Contains several poems by Allen.
The Gold Bug, by Edgar Allan Poe. *New York*, 1928.
  Trade edition, 1929. Foreword by Allen.
The Book of Poe. *Garden City*, 1929.
  Addison Hibbard, editor. Introduction by Allen.
Preface to [a New] Edition of Toward the Flame. [*New York*, 1933].
  4 pp. leaflet.
So Red the Nose. *New York* [1935].
  Contribution.
Bermudiana. *New York* [1936].
  Preface.
The Limited Editions Club ... Eighth Series. *New York* [1936].
  Contains "An Opinion" by Hervey Allen.
Editor at Work, by Julie Edesheim. *New York* [1939].
  Introduction.

James Lane Allen

1849–1925

FLUTE AND VIOLIN. *New York,* 1891.

The probable first state measures 1 $\frac{7}{8}$" across top of covers. Reissued with a new introduction by the author, *New York,* 1899.

THE BLUE-GRASS REGION OF KENTUCKY. *New York,* 1892.

JOHN GRAY: A KENTUCKY TALE OF THE OLDEN TIME. *Philadelphia,* 1893.

Previously published in *Lippincott's Magazine,* June, 1892, copies of which were bound in boards, cloth back. See note under "The Choir Invisible," 1897.

A KENTUCKY CARDINAL. *New York,* 1895.

First state does not have advertisement at back for "Aftermath" or "A Kentucky Cardinal." Revised edition, *New York,* 1900, of which there were 100 large paper copies, signed. This 1900 edition also contained a reprinting of "Aftermath."

AFTERMATH. *New York,* 1896.

Part second of "A Kentucky Cardinal." First state does not have advertisement for "Aftermath." Revised and reissued with "A Kentucky Cardinal," new preface *New York,* 1900, of which there were also 100 large paper copies, signed. Uncut copies in green silk binding with red cardinal stamped on front cover are not necessarily first.

SUMMER IN ARCADY. *New York,* 1896.

THE CHOIR INVISIBLE. *New York,* 1897.

Based on "John Gray," 1893. Revised edition, *New York,* 1898.

CHIMNEY CORNER GRADUATES. *Springfield, Mass.,* [1900].

THE REIGN OF LAW: A TALE OF THE KENTUCKY HEMP FIELDS. *New York,* 1900.

The first state does not have the word *facing* before the numerals on p. vii; also, illustrations are in photogravure. Issued in England as "The Increasing Purpose."

THE METTLE OF THE PASTURE. *New York,* 1903.

THE BRIDE OF THE MISTLETOE. *New York,* 1909.

THE DOCTOR'S CHRISTMAS EVE. *New York,* 1910.

Published November, 1910 on copyright page.

THE HEROINE IN BRONZE. *New York,* 1912.

Top edges gilt. *Published October, 1912* on copyright page.

J. L. ALLEN

THE LAST CHRISTMAS TREE. *Portland, Me.,* 1914.
Boards. 950 copies only.

THE SWORD OF YOUTH. *New York,* 1915.
Published, February, 1915 on copyright page. The publishers issued about two dozen copies uncut.

A CATHEDRAL SINGER. *New York,* 1916.
Published, March, 1916 on copyright page.

THE KENTUCKY WARBLER. *Garden City,* 1918.

THE EMBLEMS OF FIDELITY: A COMEDY IN LETTERS. *Garden City,* 1919.

THE ALABASTER BOX. *New York,* 1923.

THE LANDMARK. *New York,* 1925.

From Dixie. *Richmond,* 1893.
Contains Allen's "The Wanderer."
Two Gentlemen of Kentucky. *New York,* 1899.
Reprinted from "Flute and Violin."

BIOGRAPHICAL

James Lane Allen: A Sketch of His Life and Work. *New York* [n.d.]
16 pp. pamphlet.
James Lane Allen and His Books. *New York* [1897].
16 pp. pamphlet.
Mr. James Lane Allen's Novel: The Reign of Law. A Controversy and Some Opinions Regarding It. *New York,* 1900.
James Lane Allen and the Genteel Tradition, by Grant C. Knight. *Chapel Hill,* 1935.
James Lane Allen, by John Wilson Townsend. *Louisville,* 1927.
100 copies only.

Sherwood Anderson

1876–1941

WINDY MC PHERSON'S SON. *New York*, 1916.
Revised and with new concluding chapter, *New York*, 1922.

MARCHING MEN. *New York*, 1917.

MID-AMERICAN CHANTS. *New York*, 1918.

WINESBURG, OHIO. *New York*, 1919.
Top stained yellow, same shade as cloth binding. Some copies, possibly of the first printing, with either unstained or orange tops. Paper label on spine. The earliest copies have perfect type at p. 251, line 3, the word *the*.

POOR WHITE. *New York*, 1920.
Top stained blue. Reissued by the Modern Library, *New York* [1926] with a new introduction.

THE TRIUMPH OF THE EGG. *New York*, 1921.
Top stained yellow. Dramatized by Raymond O'Neill, *Chicago*, 1932.

MANY MARRIAGES. *New York*, 1923.
Top stained orange.

HORSES AND MEN. *New York*, 1923.
Top stained orange.

A STORY TELLER'S STORY. *New York*, 1924.
Top stained yellow.

DARK LAUGHTER. *New York*, 1925.
Also 350 numbered and signed copies; and 20 lettered and signed copies.

THE MODERN WRITER. *San Francisco* [1925].
Boards. 1,000 copies only; 950 on B. R. Book Paper numbered 51-1,000, and 50 on Japan vellum numbered 1-50.

SHERWOOD ANDERSON'S NOTEBOOK. *New York*, 1926.
Also 225 large paper copies, numbered and signed.

TAR: A MIDWEST CHILDHOOD. *New York*, 1926.
Also 350 large paper copies, numbered and signed.

A NEW TESTAMENT. *New York*, 1927.
Also 265 large paper copies, numbered and signed.

ALICE AND THE LOST NOVEL. *London*, 1929.
500 signed copies only.

HELLO TOWNS! *New York,* 1929.
Page 35, line 30, *fingers* is misspelled.

NEARER THE GRASS ROOTS. *San Francisco,* 1929.
500 signed copies only.

THE AMERICAN COUNTY FAIR. *New York,* 1930.
875 copies only, in the "Random House Prose Quartos." Wrappers, paper label.

PERHAPS WOMEN. *New York* [1931].

BEYOND DESIRE. *New York* [1932].
Also limited signed edition.

DEATH IN THE WOODS. *New York* [1933].

NO SWANK. *Philadelphia,* 1934.
1,000 unnumbered copies only of which 50 were signed by the author.

PUZZLED AMERICA. *New York,* 1935.
First printing has code letter *A* on copyright page.

KIT BRANDON: A PORTRAIT. *New York,* 1936.
The first printing has the code letter *A* on the copyright page.

HOME TOWN. *New York* [1940].

Free and Other Stories, by Theodore Dreiser. *New York* [1918].
Introduction by Anderson. First edition has *B-L* monogram on title page.
These United States. *New York* [1923].
Contains Anderson's "Ohio."
The Best Short Stories of 1922. *Boston* [1923].
Edward J. O'Brien, editor. Contains Anderson's "I'm a Fool."
Hands and other Stories. *Girard, Kansas* [1919, i.e., 1925].
Printed wrappers. Reprinted from "Winesburg, Ohio."
Cinema, by Eugene Jolas. *New York,* 1926.
Introduction.
The Works of Stephen Crane. *New York* [1925-26].
12 vols. Vol. XI contains an introduction by Anderson.
Short Stories from Vanity Fair. *New York* [1928].
Contains four stories by Anderson.
The Colophon, No. 1 [*New York,* 1930].
Contains Anderson's "On Being Published."
Big Town, by Philip McKee. *New York* [1931].
Foreword by Anderson.
Harlan Miners Speak. *New York* [1932].
Contribution by Anderson.
Leaves of Grass, by Walt Whitman. *New York* [1933].
Introduction.

Peace on Earth, by George Sklar and Albert Maltz. *New York, 1934.*
  Foreword.
The American Spectator Year Book. *New York, 1934.*
  Co-editor and contributor.
America and Alfred Stieglitz. *Garden City, 1934.*
  Waldo Frank and others, editors. Contains Anderson's "City Plowman."
The Colophon, New Series, No. 1. *New York, 1935.*
  Contains "Burt Emmett," by Anderson.
Contemporary One-Act Plays from Nine Countries. *Boston, 1936.*
  Percival Wilde, editor. Contains "Mother," by Anderson.
Plays: Winesburg and Others. *New York, 1937.*
  The first printing has code letter *A* on copyright page.
Breaking into Print. *New York, 1937.*
  Elmer Adler, editor. Contribution.
Cowboy Dances, by Lloyd Shaw. *Caldwell, Idaho, 1939.*
  Foreword.
A Writer's Conception of Realism. *Olivet, Michigan, 1939.*
  Wrappers.
The Free Company Presents ... *New York* [1941].
  Contains "Above Suspicion" by Anderson. Later issued in pamphlet form.
The Intent of the Artist. *Princeton, 1941.*
  Augusto Centeno, editor. Contribution.

BIOGRAPHICAL AND CRITICAL

Sherwood Anderson, by C. B. Chase. *New York, 1927.*
The Phenomenon of Sherwood Anderson, by N. B. Fagin. *Balitmore, 1927.*

Gertrude (Franklin) Atherton

1857–

WHAT DREAMS MAY COME. *Chicago* [etc.] [1888].
Frank Lin, *pseud.* Cloth or wrappers. *London,* 1889, with author's name.

HERMIA SUYDAM. *New York* [1889].
Cloth or wrappers.

LOS CERRITOS. *New York,* 1890.

A QUESTION OF TIME. *New York* [1891].

THE DOOMSWOMAN. *New York,* 1892.
Originally in *Lippincott's Magazine,* September, 1892, copies of which were issued with title page, bound in boards, cloth back.

BEFORE THE GRINGO CAME. *New York* [1894].
Reprints the preceding title. Contains also "Rezánov," separately published, *New York,* 1906. The whole, revised and enlarged, *New York,* 1902, as "The Splendid Idle Forties."

A WHIRL ASUNDER. *New York* [1895].
Copies measuring 6″ high are probably first state.

PATIENCE SPARHAWK AND HER TIMES. *New York,* 1897.

HIS FORTUNATE GRACE. *New York,* 1897.

AMERICAN WIVES AND ENGLISH HUSBANDS. *New York,* 1898.
Reissued, 1919, as "Transplanted."

THE CALIFORNIANS. *New York,* 1898.
Revised and enlarged, *New York,* 1935.

THE VALIANT RUNAWAYS. *New York,* 1898.

A DAUGHTER OF THE VINE. *New York,* 1899.

SENATOR NORTH. *New York,* 1900.

THE ARISTOCRATS. *New York,* 1901.

THE SPLENDID IDLE FORTIES. *New York,* 1902.
See: "Before the Gringo Came" [1894].

THE CONQUEROR. *New York,* 1902.
First state: p. 546, numeral in upper left corner; second state: numeral at bottom of page. Second printing, so marked, contains revisions. Regular edition is

bound in maroon cloth, gilt and white decorations. Copies have been noted with no decorative stamping; a letter from the author suggests that such copies were bound for her personal use, but a reprint has been noted in the plain binding.

RULERS OF KINGS. *New York*, 1904.
First state is bound in brown cloth, lettered in gold, ornament on front cover. Second state is lettered in red. Copies have been noted in printed boards; status unknown.

THE BELL IN THE FOG. *New York*, 1905.
Published February, 1905 on the copyright page.

THE TRAVELLING THIRDS. *New York*, 1905.
Published October, 1905 on the copyright page.

REZÁNOV. *New York*, 1906.
See: "Before the Gringo Came" [1894].

ANCESTORS. *New York*, 1907.
Published September, 1907 on the copyright page.

THE GORGEOUS ISLE. *New York*, 1908.
Pictorial end papers. *Published, October, 1908* on the copyright page.

TOWER OF IVORY. *New York*, 1910.

JULIA FRANCE AND HER TIMES. *New York*, 1912.

PERCH OF THE DEVIL. *New York* [1914].
August, 1914 on the copyright page.

CALIFORNIA. *New York*, 1914.
K-O on copyright page.

MRS. BALFAME. *New York* [1916].

LIFE IN THE WAR ZONE. [*New York*] 1916.

THE LIVING PRESENT. *New York* [1917].

THE WHITE MORNING. *New York* [1918].

THE AVALANCHE. *New York* [1919].

THE SISTERS-IN-LAW. *New York* [1921].

SLEEPING FIRES. *New York* [1922].

BLACK OXEN. *New York* [1923].
Also 250 copies numbered and signed by the author.

THE CRYSTAL CUP. *New York*, 1925.

THE IMMORTAL MARRIAGE. *New York*, 1927.

THE JEALOUS GODS. *New York*, 1928.

DIDO, QUEEN OF HEARTS. *New York*, 1929.

THE SOPHISTICATES. *New York* [1931].

ADVENTURES OF A NOVELIST. *New York* [1932].

THE FOGHORN. *Boston*, 1934.

GOLDEN PEACOCK. *Boston*, 1936.

CAN WOMEN BE GENTLEMEN? *Boston*, 1938.

THE HOUSE OF LEE. *New York*, 1940.
    First printing has the symbol (1) below last line of text.

Mrs. Pendleton's Four-in-Hand. *New York*, 1903.
    Reprinted from "A Question of Time" [1891].
A Few of Hamilton's Letters. *New York*, 1903.
    Edited.
The Spinners' Book of Fiction. *San Francisco* [1907].
    Bound in rough buckram. Contains "Concha Argüello, Sister Dominica," by
    Mrs. Atherton.
Mirror Images, by Dorothe Bendon. [*New York*] 1931.
    Foreword by Mrs. Atherton.
The Woman Accused. *New York*, 1933.
    Contribution by Mrs. Atherton.
What Is a Book? *Boston*, 1935.
    Dale Warren, editor. Contains Mrs. Atherton's "Wanted: Imagination."
Less Than Kin, by Charles Caldwell Dobie. *New York*, 1935.
    Foreword by Mrs. Atherton.
Rezánov and Doña Concha. *New York* [1937].
    Reprint. See: "Before the Gringo Came" [1894]; "Doña Concha" reprinted from
    "The Spinners' Book of Fiction" [1907].
Love Stories of Old California, by Mrs. Fremont Older. *New York* [1940].
    Foreword.

John James Audubon
1780–1851

THE BIRDS OF AMERICA FROM ORIGINAL DRAWINGS. *London, 1827-1838.*
435 plates. 87 parts or four double elephant folios. Vol. 1: 1827-30; Vol. 2: 1831-34; Vol. 3: 1834-35; Vol. 4: 1835-38 (dates given are those of the plates). The plates exist in varying states. "Audubon's Birds of America, A Check List of First Issues of the Plates ..." by E. F. Hannaburgh, *Buchanan, New York,* 1941, is the first serious attempt to identify the first states. Partially reissued, *New York,* 1858-60, 14 numbers of ten plates each plus a supplement of ten additional plates. Issued, states Sabin of the original edition, "without any text, to avoid the necessity of furnishing gratis copies to the public libraries in England ..." *See item following.*

ORNITHOLOGICAL BIOGRAPHY; or, AN ACCOUNT OF THE HABITS OF THE BIRDS OF THE UNITED STATES OF AMERICA. *Edinburgh, 1831-1839.*
5 vols. Vol. 5 misdated 1849. Text for the preceding.

A SYNOPSIS OF THE BIRDS OF AMERICA. *Edinburgh and London, 1839.*

THE BIRDS OF AMERICA FROM DRAWINGS MADE IN THE UNITED STATES AND THEIR TERRITORIES. *New York, 1840-1844.*
8vo reissue with textual changes of the first two items here listed. 500 plates. 100 paper covered parts or 7 vols. Several later reissues, the reissue of 1856 being the first to have colored backgrounds for the plates. The reissues are in either 7 or 8 vols. Popular reissue, *New York,* 1937, edited by William Vogt, of which there were also 2,500 de luxe copies.

THE VIVIPAROUS QUADRUPEDS OF NORTH AMERICA. *New York, 1845-1848.*
In collaboration with John Bachman. 150 plates. 30 paper covered parts or 3 vols. Vol. 1: 1845; Vol. 2: 1846; Vol. 3: 1848. Each volume is composed of ten of the paper parts. Issued without text. Text issued, *New York,* 3 vols., 1846, 1851, 1853 respectively. Occasionally the three volumes are found bound in two. A supplement, 93 pp., 6 plates, issued 1854.

THE QUADRUPEDS OF NORTH AMERICA. *New York, 1849-1854.*
Reissue of the preceding. 31 parts or 3 vols. dated 1849, 1851, 1854 respectively. Includes all but one of the plates in the supplement described under preceding item.

DELINEATIONS OF AMERICAN SCENERY AND CHARACTER. *New York, 1926.*
With an introduction and brief bibliography by Francis Hobart Herrick. 500 copies printed for the English trade with London imprint. Also, 42 copies, all edges untrimmed, numbered and signed by Frank Walters, containing an inserted leaf with certificate of issue and a frontispiece portrait of Audubon printed from the original (1835) engraved plate by F. Cruickshank.

JOURNAL OF JOHN JAMES AUDUBON. *Boston*, 1929.
 2 vols. Boards. Howard Corning, editor. Printed for the Club of Odd Volumes. Vol. 1: 1820-1821, 301 copies; Vol. 2: 1840-1843, 225 copies. Reissued with trade imprint.

LETTERS OF JOHN JAMES AUDUBON. *Boston*, 1930.
 2 vols. 225 copies printed for the Club of Odd Volumes. Howard Corning, editor. Boards.

A Story of Meadville. *Boston*, 1846.
 Anonymous. Pamphlet. Probably the first of Audubon's journals to be published.

BIOGRAPHICAL

Audubon: The Naturalist in the New World, by Mrs. Horace St. John. *London*, 1856.
 The first published biography of Audubon.
Life of John James Audubon, by Mrs. L. B. [Mrs. John James] Audubon. *New York*, 1869.
Life and Adventures of John James Audubon. *London*, 1869.
 Robert Buchanan, editor. From Mrs. Audubon's notes.
Audubon and His Journals, by Maria R. Audubon. *New York*, 1897.
 2 vols.
John James Audubon, by John Burroughs. *Boston*, 1902.
 Also 350 large paper copies.
Audubon the Naturalist: A History of His Life and Time, by Francis Hobart Herrick. *New York*, 1917.
 2 vols. The first edition has the figure (1) at the foot of last page of text in each volume. A definitive life containing a complete bibliography.
Audubon's Bibliography, by Francis Herrick. [*Cambridge*, 1919].
 Reprinted "from 'The Auk' Vol. XXXVI, No. 3, July, 1919." Wrappers.
Audacious Audubon, by Edward Muschamp. *New York* [1929].
Singing in the Wilderness: A Salute to John James Audubon, by Donald Culross Peattie. *New York*, 1935.
Audubon, by Constance Rourke. *New York* [1936].
I Who Should Command All, by Alice Jaynes Tyler. *New Haven* [1937].
 First edition so indicated on the copyright page. Also contains first edition material by Audubon.
Audubon's America. *Boston*, 1940.
 Edited by Donald Culross Peattie.

Jane G[oodwin] Austin
1831–1894

FAIRY DREAM. *Boston* [1859].

DORA DARLING: THE DAUGHTER OF THE REGIMENT. *Boston*, 1865.
Anonymous.

THE NOVICE. *Boston* [1865].
Printed wrappers.

THE TAILOR BOY. *Boston*, 1865.
Anonymous.

OUTPOST. *Boston*, 1867.

CIPHER. *New York*, 1869.

THE SHADOW OF MOLOCH MOUNTAIN. *New York*, 1870.

MOONFOLK. *New York*, 1874.

MRS. BEAUCHAMP BROWN. *Boston*, 1880.
Anonymous. In: "The No Name Series," second series.

A NAMELESS NOBLEMAN. *Boston*, 1881.
Anonymous. In Osgood's "Round Robin Series." Later editions published by
Houghton-Mifflin.

THE DESMOND HUNDRED. *Boston*, 1882.
Anonymous. In Osgood's "Round Robin Series."

NANTUCKET SCRAPS. *Boston*, 1883.

THE STORY OF A STORM. *New York*, 1886.

DOLORES. *New York*, 1889.

STANDISH OF STANDISH. *Boston*, 1889.
Noted in both smooth grey-green cloth and rough tan buckram; the former is
probably first. Dramatized by Annie Russell Marble, *Boston*, 1919.

DOCTOR LE BARON AND HIS DAUGHTERS. *Boston*, 1890.

BETTY ALDEN. *Boston*, 1891.
Sequel to "Standish of Standish."

DAVID ALDEN'S DAUGHTER AND OTHER STORIES OF COLONIAL TIMES. *Boston*, 1892.

J. G. AUSTIN

THE TWELVE GREAT DIAMONDS. *New York* [1892].
No. 4 in "Idle Hour Series." Printed wrappers.

IT NEVER DID RUN SMOOTH. *New York* [1892].
No. 20 in "Idle Hour Series." Printed wrappers.

QUEEN TEMPEST. *New York* [1892].
No. 271 in "Ivers' American Series." Printed wrappers.

THE CEDAR SWAMP MYSTERY. [*New York*] 1901.

Short Stories for Spare Moments. Second Series. *Philadelphia,* 1869.
Printed wrappers. Contains "Nor Living, Nor Dead" by Austin.
Rougegorge and Other Short Stories. *Philadelphia,* 1870.
Printed wrappers. Contains "Harneyhow's Hummock" by Austin.
Vignettes: Real and Ideal. *Boston* [1890].
Frederic Edward McKay, editor. Contains Austin's "Safe in Purgatory."
Twenty Complete Novelettes by Popular Authors. *New York* [1894].
Contains Austin's "The Sailor's Secret."
The Mysterious Voyage of the Daphne and Other Stories. *Boston,* 1895.
Contains Austin's "The Powder Monkey."

Mary (Hunter) Austin
1868–1934

THE LAND OF LITTLE RAIN. *Boston*, 1903.

THE BASKET WOMAN. *Boston*, 1904.
Published October 1904 on copyright page. School edition, *Boston* [1910].

ISIDRO. *Boston*, 1905.
Published April 1905 on copyright page.

THE FLOCK. *Boston*, 1906.

SANTA LUCIA. *New York*, 1908.
Published April, 1908 on copyright page.

LOST BORDERS. *New York*, 1909.

OUTLAND. *London*, 1910.
Gordon Stairs, *pseud*. With author's name on title page, *New York* [1919].

THE ARROW MAKER: A DRAMA IN THREE ACTS. *New York*, 1911.
Revised and reissued, *Boston*, 1915.

A WOMAN OF GENIUS. *Garden City*, 1912.

CHRIST IN ITALY. *New York*, 1912.

THE GREEN BOUGH. *Garden City*, 1913.
Boards.

THE LOVELY LADY. *Garden City*, 1913.

LOVE AND THE SOUL MAKER. *New York*, 1914.
First printing has the symbol (1) below last line of text.

CALIFORNIA: THE LAND OF THE SUN. *New York*, 1914.
Reissued, *Boston*, 1927, as "The Land of the Sun."

THE MAN JESUS. *New York* [1915].
Revised and enlarged edition, *New York* [1925] with title "A Small Town Man."

THE FORD. *Boston*, 1917.
Published April 1917 on copyright page.

THE TRAIL BOOK. *Boston*, 1918.
Published October 1918 on copyright page.

M. H. AUSTIN

THE YOUNG WOMAN CITIZEN. *New York,* 1918.

NO. 26 JAYNE STREET. *Boston,* 1920.

THE AMERICAN RHYTHM. *New York* [1923].
Revised and enlarged edition, *Boston,* 1930.

THE LAND OF JOURNEY'S ENDING. *New York* [1924].

EVERYMAN'S GENIUS. *Indianapolis* [1925].

THE CHILDREN SING IN THE FAR WEST. *Boston,* 1928.

STARRY ADVENTURE. *Boston,* 1931.

EXPERIENCES FACING DEATH. *Indianapolis* [1931].
First edition so stated on copyright page.

EARTH HORIZON. *Boston,* 1932.
Also Literary Guild edition.

ONE-SMOKE STORIES. *Boston,* 1934.

CAN PRAYER BE ANSWERED. *New York,* 1934.
First edition has publisher's monogram on copyright page.

The California Earthquake. *San Francisco,* 1907.
David Starr Jordan, editor. Contains "The Temblor" by Austin.
The Spinners' Book of Fiction. *San Francisco* [1907].
Rough buckram. Contains Austin's "The Ford of Crèvecoeur."
What the Mexican Conference Really Means. *New York* [1915?].
The Sturdy Oak. *New York,* 1917.
A novel by several authors; one chapter and theme supplied by Mary Austin.
The Path on the Rainbow. *New York,* 1918.
George W. Cronyn, editor. Introduction by Mary Austin.
Recent Gains in American Civilization. *New York* [1928].
Kirby Page, editor. Contains "American Liberty Moves On."
Taos Pueblo, Photographed by Ansel Easton Adams, and Described by Mary Austin. *San Francisco,* 1930.
108 copies only, numbered and signed by author and illustrator.
Indian Poetry. [*New York,* 1931].
Enjoy Your Museum. *Pasadena,* 1934.
Contains "Indian Pottery of the Rio Grande," by Mary Austin.
When I Am Dead. [*Santa Fé,* 1935].
Privately printed.
Road to Mammon. *New York,* 1938.
Mary Austin: Woman of Genius, by Helen MacKnight Doyle. *New York* [1939].
First edition so indicated on copyright page.

Irving (Addison) Bacheller

1859–

THE MASTER OF SILENCE. *New York*, 1892.

THE STILL HOUSE OF O'DARROW. *London*, 1894.

THE STORY OF A PASSION. [*East Aurora*, 1899].
Reissued 1917.

EBEN HOLDEN. *Boston* [1900].
First state reads at p. 400, line 13, *go to fur* etc. Later: *go tew fur* etc. First state
of binding has pine-cones on spine with rounded top; later, flat top. Trimmed
and untrimmed copies noted. At a dinner to Bacheller, *Boston*, 1901, 250 copies
were issued containing several pages of additional material.

D'RI AND I. *Boston* [1901].

DARREL OF THE BLESSED ISLES. *Boston* [1903].
Published April, 1903 on copyright page.

VERGILIUS. *New York*, 1904.
Published August, 1904 on copyright page.

SILAS STRONG. *New York*, 1906.
Published March, 1906 on copyright page.

EBEN HOLDEN'S LAST DAY A-FISHING. *New York*, 1907.
Published September, 1907 on copyright page.

THE HAND-MADE GENTLEMAN. *New York*, 1909.
Published April, 1909 on copyright page.

THE MASTER. *New York*, 1909.
Published, October, 1909 on copyright page.

IN VARIOUS MOODS. *New York*, 1910.

KEEPING UP WITH LIZZIE. *New York*, 1911.

"CHARGE IT"; or, KEEPING UP WITH HARRY. *New York*, 1912.
Code letters *H-M* on copyright page.

THE TURNING OF GRIGGSBY. *New York*, 1913.
Published May, 1913 on copyright page.

THE MARRYERS. *New York*, 1914.
Code letters *D-O* on copyright page.

THE LIGHT IN THE CLEARING. *Indianapolis* [1917].

KEEPING UP WITH WILLIAM. [I]ndianapolis [1918].
First state lacks initial *I* in *Indianapolis* on title page.

A MAN FOR THE AGES. *Indianapolis* [1919].
Also large paper edition, boards, cloth back. The first state of the trade edition has *Braunworth & Co* slug on the copyright page.

THE PRODIGAL VILLAGE. *Indianapolis* [1920].
Printed boards.

IN THE DAYS OF POOR RICHARD. *Indianapolis* [1922].

THE SCUDDERS. *New York*, 1923.
Published April, 1923 on copyright page.

FATHER ABRAHAM. *Indianapolis* [1925].

OPINIONS OF A CHEERFUL YANKEE. *Indianapolis* [1926].

DAWN. *New York*, 1927.

THE HOUSE OF THE THREE GANDERS. *Indianapolis* [1928].
First edition so indicated on copyright page.

COMING UP THE ROAD. *Indianapolis* [1928].

A CANDLE IN THE WILDERNESS. *Indianapolis* [1930].
First edition so indicated on copyright page.

THE MASTER OF CHAOS. *Indianapolis* [1932].
First edition so stated on copyright page.

UNCLE PEEL. *New York*, 1933.
Appeared serially as "The Mad Years."

THE HARVESTING. *New York*, 1934.

THE OXEN OF THE SUN. *New York*, 1935.

A BOY FOR THE AGES. *New York* [1937].

FROM STORES OF MEMORY. *New York* [1938].
First printing has the publisher's monogram on the copyright page.

Best Things from American Literature. *New York*, 1899.
Edited by Bacheller.
Masterpieces of American Eloquence. *New York*, 1900.
Contains "Rural Life in the East," by Bacheller.

BIBLIOGRAPHICAL

A Bibliography of the Writings of Irving Bacheller, by A. J. Hanna. *Winter Park* [1939].
Printed wrappers.

John Kendrick Bangs
1862–1922

THE LORGNETTE. *New York* [1886].
Anon. *By J. K. B.*

ROGER CAMERDEN. *New York,* 1887.
Anon. Cloth or wrappers.

NEW WAGGINGS OF OLD TALES. *Boston,* 1888.
Anon. *By Two Wags.* With FRANK DEMPSTER SHERMAN. Prose by Bangs.

KATHARINE: A TRAVESTY. [*New York*] 1888.
Printed wrappers. A presentation copy has been noted in what seems to be pub-lisher's leather binding.

MEPHISTOPHELES: A PROFANATION. *New York,* 1889.
Printed wrappers.

TIDDLEDYWINK TALES. *New York,* 1891.

THE TIDDLEDYWINK'S POETRY BOOK. *New York,* 1892.

IN CAMP WITH A TIN SOLDIER. *New York,* 1892.

COFFEE AND REPARTEE. *New York,* 1893.
In "Harper's Black and White Series." Reissued, *New York,* 1900, of which there was also an "Author's Autograph Edition" distinguished by an inserted slip, numbered and signed by the author, limited to 500 copies.

HALF-HOURS WITH JIMMIEBOY. *New York,* 1893.

TOPPLETON'S CLIENT. *New York,* 1893.
Preceded by London edition.

THREE WEEKS IN POLITICS. *New York,* 1894.
In "Harper's Black and White Series."

THE WATER GHOST AND OTHERS. *New York,* 1894.

MR. BONAPARTE OF CORSICA. *New York,* 1895.

THE IDIOT. *New York,* 1895.
Reissued, *New York,* 1900, of which there was also an "Author's Autograph Edition" distinguished by an inserted slip, numbered and signed by the author, limited to 500 copies.

A HOUSE-BOAT ON THE STYX. *New York,* 1896.
Reissued, *New York,* 1899, "Biographical Edition."

BANGS

THE MANTEL-PIECE MINSTRELS. *New York*, 1896.
Pictorial boards.

A CHAFING DISH PARTY. *New York* [1896].

THE BICYCLERS AND THREE OTHER FARCES. *New York*, 1896.
The title story reprinted separately [1896].

A REBELLIOUS HEROINE. *New York*, 1896.

PASTE JEWELS. *New York*, 1897.

THE PURSUIT OF THE HOUSE-BOAT. *New York*, 1897.

THE YOUNG FOLK'S MINSTRELS. *New York*, 1897.

A PROPHECY AND A PLEA. *New York*, 1897.
Privately printed. Wrappers. 250 numbered copies only.

GHOSTS I HAVE MET AND SOME OTHERS. *New York*, 1898.

THE ENCHANTED TYPEWRITER. *New York*, 1899.
Also "Author's Autograph Edition," 500 copies, with inserted slip, numbered and signed by the author.

THE DREAMERS: A CLUB. *New York*, 1899.

COBWEBS FROM A LIBRARY CORNER. *New York*, 1899.

PEEPS AT PEOPLE. *New York*, 1899.

THE BOOMING OF ACRE HILL. *New York*, 1900.

THE IDIOT AT HOME. *New York*, 1900.

MR. MUNCHAUSEN. *Boston*, 1901.
First state has *Small Maynard* copyright; 2nd state has added rubber stamped copyright notice of *Noyes, Platt;* 3rd state has *Small Maynard* copyright over which is press printed *Noyes Platt* copyright; 4th state has *Noyes Platt* copyright with no mention of *Small Maynard*. A copy has been noted in plain grey wrappers with no copyright notice save one written out in ink for *Noyes Platt*.

OVER THE PLUM-PUDDING. *New York*, 1901.
Two states of frontispiece noted. Boards, cloth back. *October, 1901* on copyright page.

OLYMPIAN NIGHTS. *New York*, 1902.
Published June, 1902 on copyright page.

UNCLE SAM, TRUSTEE. *New York*, 1902.

BIKEY THE SKICYCLE. *New York*, 1902.

MOLLIE AND THE UNWISEMAN. *Philadelphia* [1902].
  Published November, 1902 on copyright page.

EMBLEMLAND. *New York,* 1902.
  With CHARLES RAYMOND MACAULEY.

THE INVENTIONS OF THE IDIOT. *New York,* 1904.
  Published April, 1904 on copyright page.

MONSIEUR D'EN BROCHETTE. *New York,* 1905.
  With BERT LESTON TAYLOR and ARTHUR HAMILTON FOLWELL.

MRS. RAFFLES. *New York,* 1905.
  Published October, 1905 on copyright page.

A PROPOSAL UNDER DIFFICULTIES. *New York,* 1905.

THE WORSTED MAN: A MUSICAL PLAY FOR AMATEURS. *New York,* 1905.

ANDIRON TALES. *Philadelphia* [1906].

R. HOLMES & CO. *New York,* 1906.
  Published June, 1906 on copyright page.

ALICE IN BLUNDERLAND. *New York,* 1907.

POTTED FICTION. *New York,* 1908.
  Pictorial wrappers. *Published, July, 1908* on copyright page.

THE GENIAL IDIOT. *New York,* 1908.
  Published October, 1908 on copyright page.

THE AUTOBIOGRAPHY OF METHUSELAH. *New York,* 1909.

THE REAL THING. *New York,* 1909.

SONGS OF CHEER. *Boston,* 1910.

MOLLIE AND THE UNWISEMAN ABROAD. *Philadelphia,* 1910.

JACK AND THE CHECKBOOK. *New York,* 1911.

A LITTLE BOOK OF CHRISTMAS. *Boston,* 1912.
  Published, September, 1912 on copyright page.

ECHOES OF CHEER. *Boston,* 1912.

A LINE O' CHEER FOR EACH DAY O' THE YEAR. *Boston,* 1913.

THE FOOTHILLS OF PARNASSUS. *New York,* 1914.

A QUEST FOR SONG. *Boston,* 1915.
  500 copies only, numbered and signed by the author.

BANGS

FROM PILLAR TO POST. *New York*, 1916.

HALF HOURS WITH THE IDIOT. *Boston*, 1917.
  Published, May, 1917 on copyright page.

The following is representative of the secondary Bangs items.

Peter Newell's Pictures and Rhymes. *New York*, 1899.
  Contains a biographical sketch of Newell by Bangs.
To The Rough Riders. [*n.p.*, 1899].
  Printed gray wrappers. Privately printed.
A House Party. *Boston*, 1901.
  Contains "Dawson's Dilemma" by Bangs.
The Whole Family. *New York*, 1908.
  Contains a chapter by Bangs.
Harper's Book of Little Plays. *New York*, 1910.
  Contains Bangs' "The Tables Turned."
"Eight Brand New Bits" of Christmas Cheer. *New York* [1911].
Loss or Gain. *New York* [1918].
  Pamphlet.
The Cheery Way. *New York* [1920].
An Address to the Graduates of the Yonkers High School. ... [*n.p., n.d.*].
  Wrappers.

"As You Were" ... *New York*, 1919.
  Edited by John Kendrick Bangs [*jr.*]; not by the subject of this list. There have
  been numerous separate reissues of Bangs' stories.

BIOGRAPHICAL

John Kendrick Bangs, Humorist of the Nineties, by Francis Hyde Bangs. *New York*, 1941.

(Charles) William Beebe

1877–

TWO BIRD-LOVERS IN MEXICO. *Boston*, 1905.
C. *William Beebe* on title page. Green or yellow-orange cloth. First state of binding has *Charles M. Beebe* on front cover. Second state: original stamped name buffed out and C. *William Beebe* stamped over. Third state lacks gold sky background. Fourth state lacks pictorial design and is merely lettered.

THE BIRD. *New York*, 1906.

THE LOG OF THE SUN. *New York*, 1906.
Gilt edges. Reissued with a new introduction, *New York* [1938].

OUR SEARCH FOR A WILDERNESS. *New York*, 1910.
With MARY BLAIR. *Published April, 1910* on the copyright page.

TROPICAL WILD LIFE IN BRITISH GUIANA. *New York*, 1917.
With G. INNESS HARTLEY and PAUL HOWES. Vol. I only issued.

A MONOGRAPH OF THE PHEASANTS. *London*, 1918-1922.
4 vols. Essentially the same material as "Pheasants: Their Lives and Homes," *Garden City*, 1926, 2 vols.; of which there were also 250 large paper sets, signed.

JUNGLE PEACE. *New York*, 1918.
First state does not contain the introduction by Theodore Roosevelt.

EDGE OF THE JUNGLE. *New York*, 1921.
It was originally intended to issue this book with a frontispiece entitled *Kartabo*. The illustration was omitted "because of extremely poor printing" although a few copies (said to be but four) were issued.

GALAPAGOS: WORLD'S END. *New York*, 1924.
Also 100 large paper copies, numbered and signed.

JUNGLE DAYS. *New York*, 1925.

THE ARCTURUS ADVENTURE. *New York*, 1926.
Also 50 large paper copies, numbered and signed.

PHEASANT JUNGLES. *New York*, 1927.

BENEATH TROPIC SEAS: A RECORD OF DIVING AMONG THE CORAL REEFS OF HAITI. *New York*, 1928.

NONSUCH: LAND OF WATER. *New York*, 1932.

FIELD BOOK OF THE SHORE FISHES OF BERMUDA. *New York*, 1933.
With JOHN TEE-VAN.

BEEBE

HALF MILE DOWN. *New York* [1934].

ZACA VENTURE. *New York* [1938].
   First edition so indicated on copyright page.

Harper Essays. *New York,* 1927.
   Contains "Pagan Personalities," by Beebe. Edited by Henry Seidel Canby. First edition so indicated on the copyright page.
Exploring with Beebe. *New York,* 1932.
   Selections from previously published writings arranged for children.
Fishes: Their Journeys and Migrations, by Louis Roule. *New York,* 1933.
   Introduction by Beebe.
Green Mansions, by W. H. Hudson. *New York,* 1935.
   Limited Editions Club edition. Introduction by Beebe.
Termite City, by Alfred E. Emerson and Eleanor Fish. *Chicago* [1937].
   Foreword by Beebe.
The Life Story of the Fish, by Brian Curtis. *New York,* 1938.
   Introduction by Beebe.

Dr. Beebe is also the author of numerous papers in "Zoologica," published by The New York Zoological Society.

Edward Bellamy
1850–1898

SIX TO ONE: A NANTUCKET IDYL. *New York*, 1878.
Printed wrappers or cloth.

DR. HEIDENHOFF'S PROCESS. *New York*, 1880.
Printed wrappers.

MISS LUDINGTON'S SISTER. *Boston*, 1884.

LOOKING BACKWARD, 2000-1887. *Boston*, 1888.
First state has printer's imprint on copyright page. Copies in wrappers carry an advertisement for a later publication and are consequently subsequent to copies in cloth. A contemporary newspaper notice states that paper covered copies were issued in the Fall of 1888; cloth bound copies the preceding Spring. *The Publishers' Weekly*, January 28, 1888, reports receipt of copies in cloth; copies in printed paper wrappers were not listed as received by that periodical until the issue of June 23, 1888.

EQUALITY. *New York*, 1897.
Sequel to "Looking Backward."

THE BLINDMAN'S WORLD AND OTHER STORIES. *Boston*, 1898.

THE DUKE OF STOCKBRIDGE. *New York*, 1900.

Stories by American Authors. *New York*, 1884.
  Contains "Lost" by Bellamy.
Plutocracy or Nationalism. *Philadelphia*, 1889.
Principles and Purposes of Nationalism. *Philadelphia*, 1889.
The State Management of the Liquor Traffic. [*n.p., n.d.*].
How to Employ the Unemployed in Mutual Maintenance. [*Boston*, 1893].
The Program of the Nationalists. *Philadelphia* [1894].
Socialism, The Fabian Essays. *Boston* [1894].
  George Bernard Shaw, editor. Introduction by Bellamy.
The Parable of the Water Tank. [*Chicago*, 19—?].
  Reprinted from "Equality."
Edward Bellamy Today, by M. Bellamy. *Chicago*, 1936.
Edward Bellamy Speaks Again! *Kansas City*, 1937.
  First edition so indicated on the copyright page.
Talks on Nationalism. *Chicago* [1938].
  First edition so indicated on the copyright page.

Stephen Vincent Benét
1898–

FIVE MEN AND POMPEY. *Boston*, 1915.
Wrappers over boards. Also a few copies on handmade paper. First state of trade edition, purple wrapper. Second state, brown wrapper.

THE DRUG-SHOP; OR, ENDYMION IN EDMONSTOUN. [*New Haven*] 1917.
Privately printed. Printed wrappers. 100 copies only.

YOUNG ADVENTURE. *New Haven*, 1918.
First published, September, 1918 on copyright page. Boards.

HEAVENS AND EARTH. *New York*, 1920.
Boards.

THE BEGINNING OF WISDOM. *New York*, 1921.

YOUNG PEOPLE'S PRIDE. *New York*, 1922.
First Printing, August 1922 on copyright page.

BALLAD OF WILLIAM SYCAMORE, 1790-1880. *New York-New Haven-Princeton* [1923].
500 copies only. Boards.

JEAN HUGUENOT. *New York*, 1923.
First Printing July, 1923 on copyright page. All examined copies have the leaf comprising pp. 201-202 tipped in on a stub.

KING DAVID. *New York*, 1923.
350 copies only. Printed boards, paper label on front cover.

TIGER JOY. *New York* [1925].
Publisher's insignia on copyright page. Boards, cloth back, paper labels.

SPANISH BAYONET. *New York* [1926].
Publisher's insignia on copyright page.

JOHN BROWN'S BODY. [*Garden City*, 1928].
Also 201 large paper copies, signed. First trade edition so stated on copyright page.

THE BAREFOOT SAINT. *Garden City*, 1929.
367 numbered copies only.

THE LITTER OF THE ROSE LEAVES. *New York*, 1930.
875 copies only in "The Random House Prose Quartos." Wrappers, paper label.

BALLADS AND POEMS: 1915-1930. *Garden City,* 1931.
Also 201 large paper copies, signed. First trade edition so stated on copyright page.

A BOOK OF AMERICANS. *New York,* 1933.
With ROSEMARY BENÉT. Also 125 signed copies. First state has publisher's monogram on copyright page. The publishers issued some specimen pages in pamphlet form in advance of publication.

JAMES SHORE'S DAUGHTER. *Garden City,* 1934.
First edition so stated on copyright page. Also 307 large paper copies, signed.

BURNING CITY. *New York* [1936].
Also 275 signed copies published June 4; trade edition published June 15. The first printing has the publisher's monogram on the copyright page.

THIRTEEN O'CLOCK. *New York* [1937].
The first printing has the publisher's monogram on the copyright page. Also 150 signed copies.

THE DEVIL AND DANIEL WEBSTER. *Weston, Vt.* [1937].
700 numbered copies, signed by the author and illustrator. Trade edition issued *New York* [1937]. Reissued as a play in one act [*New York,* 1939] in printed wrappers, the dramatization being by the author. Also adapted by the author as an opera in one act, *New York* [1939]. The story had previous appearance in "Post Stories of 1936."

THE HEADLESS HORSEMAN, AN OPERETTA IN ONE ACT. *Boston* [1937].
Printed wrappers.

JOHNNY PYE AND THE FOOL KILLER. *Weston, Vt.* [1938].
750 numbered copies, signed by the author and illustrator. Trade edition issued *New York* [1938].

TALES BEFORE MIDNIGHT. *New York* [1939].
The first printing has the publisher's monogram on the copyright page.

THE BALLAD OF THE DUKE'S MERCY. *New York,* 1939.
250 numbered and signed copies only.

The Poets of the Future. *Boston* [1918].
H. T. Schnittkind, editor. Contribution.
The Yale Book of Student Verse 1910-1919. *New Haven,* 1919.
Co-editor. Contains 14 poems by Benét. Boards.
Tamburlaine the Great, by Christopher Marlowe. *New Haven,* 1919.
Acting version by Benét and E. M. Woolley.
The History of the Class of Nineteen Nineteen. *New Haven,* 1919.
Contribution.

S. V. BENÉT

The Stag Cook Book. *New York* [1922].
    C. Mac Sheridan, editor. Contains recipe for "Zitelli's Macaroni Stew," by Benét.
O. Henry Memorial Award Prize Stories of 1924. *Garden City*, 1925.
    Contains Benét's "Uriah's Sons."
Yale College Class of 1919. Decennial Record. [*New Haven*] 1929.
    Boards. Contribution.
The [*New York*] *World's* Best Short Stories of 1929. *New York*, 1929.
    Contains "The Story About the Ant-Eater," by Benét.
Odes aux Voiles du Nord, by L. L. Le Marois. *Paris* [1928].
    Translated. 300 numbered copies only. Wrappers.
O. Henry Memorial Award Prize Stories of 1929. *Garden City*, 1930.
    Contains "The King of Cats," by Benét.
The Story of the United Press. [*New York*, 1933].
    Pamphlet.
The Collected Prose of Elinor Wylie. *New York*, 1933.
    Contains a preface by Benét.
The Dark Hills Under, by Shirley Barker. *New Haven*, 1933.
    Foreword by Benét.
Fifty Poets. *New York* [1933].
    William Rose Benét, editor. Paragraph by Stephen Vincent Benét.
A Portrait and a Poem. *Paris*, 1934.
    50 numbered copies only. The poem by Benét.
Designed for Reading. *New York*, 1934.
    Christopher Morley, William Rose Benét and others, editors. Contribution by Stephen Vincent Benét.
The Smart Set Anthology. *New York* [1934].
    Burton Rascoe and Groff Conklin, editors. Contains "Summer Thunder," by Benét. First state of binding has *Roscoe* for *Rascoe* on spine.
O. Henry Memorial Award Prize Stories of 1935. *Garden City*, 1935.
    Harry Hansen, editor. Contains "The Professor's Punch," by Benét.
Theory of Flight, by Muriel Rukeyser. *New Haven*, 1935.
    Foreword by Benét.
The Yale Literary Magazine. *New Haven*, 1936.
    Centennial number. Boards or wrappers. Contribution by Benét.
Post Stories of 1935. *Boston*, 1936.
    Contains "The Curfew Tolls," by Benét. Editions of 1936, 1937, 1940 also contain contributions.
The Magic of Poetry and The Poet's Art. *Chicago* [1936].
    Wrappers. Reprinted from the nineteenth edition of "Compton's Pictured Encyclopedia."
The Deer Come Down, by Edward Weismiller. *New Haven*, 1936.
    Edited by Benét.
Portraits and Self-Portaits, by Georges Schreiber. *Boston*, 1936.
    Contribution.
Blood of the Martyrs, by Percival Wilde. *New York* [etc.] 1937.
    Printed wrappers. Based on a story by Benét.

The Gardener Mind, by Margaret Haley. *New Haven*, 1937.
  Foreword.
Breaking Into Print. *New York*, 1937.
  Edited by Elmer Adler. Contribution.
Sherlockiana. *Ysleta*, 1938.
  4 pp. pamphlet.
The Barly Fields, by Robert Nathan. *New York*, 1938.
  Introduction by Benét.
Letter to a Comrade, by Joy Davidman. *New Haven*, 1938.
  Edited.
Gauley Mountain, by Louise McNeill. *New York* [1939].
  First edition so indicated on copyright page. Foreword.
The Connecticut River and Other Poems, by R. Denney. *New Haven*, 1939.
  Foreword.
An Announcement of The Tree of Liberty. A Novel by Elizabeth Page. [*New York*, 1939].
  Printed wrappers. Contains a letter, the latter also occurring as a facsimile broadside.
Reunion Ode. [*New Haven*, 1939].
  4 pp. leaflet.
Ake and His World by Bertil Malmberg. *New York* [1940].
  First printing has the publisher's monogram on the copyright page. Introduction by Benét. The latter, together with a few other leaves, issued in advance of publication as an advertising feature.
Return Again, Traveler, by Norman Rosten. *New Haven*, 1940.
  Edited.
Zero Hour. *New York* [1940].
  Contribution. First printing has publisher's monogram on copyright page.
Nightmare at Noon. *New York* [1940].
  First printing has the publisher's monogram on the copyright page. Printed wrappers on boards.
National Institute of Arts and Letters Public Ceremonial. [*New York*] 1941.
  4 pp.
A Summons to the Free. *New York* [1941].
  Printed wrappers.
The Free Company Presents ... *New York* [1941].
  Contains "Freedom's a Hard-Bought Thing."
The Rivers of America Series. *New York*, 1940-194-.
  Co-editor of this series.

William Rose Benét

1886–

MERCHANTS FROM CATHAY AND OTHER POEMS. *New York*, 1913.
Title poem privately printed, *New Haven*, 1920.

THE FALCONER OF GOD AND OTHER POEMS. *New Haven*, 1914.

THE GREAT WHITE WALL. *New Haven*, 1916.

THE BURGLAR OF THE ZODIAC AND OTHER POEMS. *New Haven*, 1918.
Boards.

PERPETUAL LIGHT: A MEMORIAL. *New Haven*, 1919.

MOONS OF GRANDEUR. *New York* [1920].

THE FIRST PERSON SINGULAR. *New York* [1922].
First printing has GHD insignia on copyright page.

THE FLYING KING OF KURIO. *New York* [1926].
First printing has GHD insignia on copyright page.

WILD GOSLINGS. *New York* [1927].
First printing has GHD insignia on copyright page.

MAN POSSESSED. *New York* [1927].
First printing has GHD insignia on copyright page.

SAGACITY. *New York*, 1929.
475 copies only in "The Random House Poetry Quartos."

RIP TIDE. *New York*, 1932.
"A Novel in Verse." 1,200 copies; first edition so stated at [p. 81].

STARRY HARNESS. *New York* [1933].

GOLDEN FLEECE. *New York* [1935].
First edition so stated on copyright page.

HARLEM AND OTHER POEMS. *London*, 1935.

WITH WINGS AS EAGLES. *New York* [1940].

THE DUST WHICH IS GOD.
Announced for 1941 publication.

ADOLPHUS: or, THE ADOPTED DOLPHIN AND THE PIRATE'S DAUGHTER.
Announced for 1941 publication.

Yale Verse. *New Haven,* 1909.
  Robert Moses, editor. Contains 2 poems by Benét.
The East I Know, by Paul Claudel. *New Haven,* 1914.
  Translated by Benét and Teresa Frances Thompson.
The Yale Book of Student Verse, 1910-1919. *New Haven,* 1919.
  Boards. Contribution.
Saturday Papers: Essays on Literature from the Literary Review. *New York,* 1921.
  With Amy Loveman and Henry Seidel Canby.
Dry Points: Studies in Black and White, by Henry Martyn Hoyt. *New York,* 1921.
  Contains a biographical sketch by Benét.
Poems for Youth. *New York* [1925].
  Compiled.
A Miscellany of American Poetry, 1925. *New York* [1925].
  Contributions by William Rose Benét. First edition so stated.
A Miscellany of American Poetry, 1927. *New York* [1927].
  Contributions by William Rose Benét. First edition so stated.
Twentieth Century Poetry. [*Boston*] 1929.
  Edited, with Henry Seidel Canby and John Drinkwater.
Adventures in English Literature. *New York,* 1931.
  Joint editor. Various later revised editions.
Collected Poems of Elinor Wylie. *New York,* 1932.
  Edited and with a foreword by Benét.
Fifty Poets: An Auto-Anthology. *New York* [1933].
  Edited.
Reviewing Ten Years. [*New York,* 1933].
  Compiled.
The Prose and Poetry of Elinor Wylie. *Norton, Mass.,* 1934.
The Pocket University. *Garden City,* 1934.
  13 vols. Vol. 13 edited with Henry Seidel Canby and Christopher Morley.
The Smart Set Anthology. *New York* [1934].
  Burton Rascoe and Groff Conklin, editors. Contains Benét's "The Sensible Convict." The first state of the binding has *Roscoe* for *Rascoe.*
Guide to Daily Reading. *Garden City,* 1934.
  Edited.
Designed for Reading. *New York,* 1934.
  Edited by Benét and others.
The Masquerade. *Boston,* 1934.
  Contains Benét's "Swing Song."
A Baker's Dozen of Emblems ... Verses by William Rose Benét. *Brooklyn,* 1935.
  About 125 copies specially bound in stiff wrappers; ordinary edition in wrappers.
Great Poems of the English Language. *New York,* 1936.
  Edited by Wallace Alvin Briggs and Benét.
From Robert and Elizabeth Browning: A Further Selection of the Barrett-Browning Family Correspondence. *London & New York,* 1936.
  Edited by Benét.
Portraits and Self-Portraits, By Georges Schreiber. *Boston,* 1936.
  Contribution.

W. R. BENÉT

Columbia Poetry. *New York,* 1936.
  Introduction by Benét.
Paradise Lost and Paradise Regain'd, by John Milton. *San Francisco [for] The Limited Editions Club, New York,* 1936.
  Contribution. 1,500 copies only.
Mother Goose. *New York* [1936].
  Heritage Club edition. Edited.
Collected Poems by Ford Madox Ford. *New York,* 1936.
  Introduction by Benét.
From a Paris Scrapbook, by Richard LeGallienne. *New York* [1938].
  Introduction.
The Oxford Anthology of American Literature. *New York,* 1938.
  First edition so indicated on copyright page. Edited.
Poems for Modern Youth. *Boston* [1938].
  Edited, with others.

Ambrose (Gwinnett) Bierce
1842–1914(?)

THE FIEND'S DELIGHT. *London* [1872].
Dod Grile, *pseudonym*. American edition, *New York*, 1873, with no publisher's advertisements at the back.

NUGGETS AND DUST. *London* [1872].
Dod Grile, *pseudonym*. Printed wrappers.

COBWEBS. *London* [1873].
Dod Grile, *pseudonym*. Imprint of *Fun* office. Reissued, *London*, 1874, same text, as "Cobwebs from an Empty Skull."

THE DANCE OF DEATH. [*San Francisco*, 1877].
William Herman, *pseudonym*. First state has no press notices at the back of book. Second edition, with added material, carries imprint of *Henry Keller & Co., 543 Clay Street, 1877*. "The Dance of Life: An Answer," by Mrs. Dr. J. Milton Bowers, *San Francisco*, 1877, is often collected as a companion piece.

TALES OF SOLDIERS AND CIVILIANS. *San Francisco*, 1891.
A copy has been noted with *Compliments of* press-printed on the preliminary end paper, below which appears Bierce's autograph. Reissued, *New York*, 1898, with three added stories, as "In the Midst of Life."

THE MONK AND THE HANGMAN'S DAUGHTER. *Chicago*, 1892.
Wrappers and gray cloth. A translation with G. A. Danziger [pseudonym for Adolphe De Castro]. Reissued with new preface, 1907.

BLACK BEETLES IN AMBER. *San Francisco and New York*, 1892.
Must have imprint of *Western Authors Publishing Company*. Cloth and wrappers.

CAN SUCH THINGS BE? *New York* [1893].
Cloth and wrappers. Reissued, *Washington*, 1903, with a brief new preface.

IN THE MIDST OF LIFE. *New York*, 1898.
See: "Tales of Soldiers and Civilians," 1891.

FANTASTIC FABLES. *New York*, 1899.
Light brown cloth, pictorial stamping. A probable remainder binding is plain blue cloth with red lettering.

SHAPES OF CLAY. *San Francisco*, 1903.
First state of first issue has lines 5 and 6 transposed, p. 71, reading: *We've nothing better here than bliss.* | *Walk in. But I must tell you this:* |

THE CYNIC'S WORD BOOK. *New York, 1906.*

Probable first state does not contain frontispiece; the copyright deposit copy does not have one. *Published October, 1906* on copyright page. Reissued as "The Devil's Dictionary."

THE SHADOW ON THE DIAL. *San Francisco, 1909.*

WRITE IT RIGHT. *New York, 1909.*

Wrappers or cloth. Leaves of the first issue are 5½" tall.

COLLECTED WORKS. *New York and Washington, 1909-1912.*

12 vols. Contains material here first collected.

BATTLE SKETCHES. *London, 1930.*

Boards. 350 copies in vellum for members of the First Editions Club.

Tom Hood's Comic Annual, 1873-1876. *London* [1873-1876].

4 vols. Contributions by Bierce.

The Lantern. *London,* May 18, 1874 and July 15, 1874.

An occasional paper of which there were but these two issues. Entirely written by Bierce in the interest of the former empress of France, Eugénie.

Petrarch and Other Essays, by Timothy H. Rearden. *San Francisco, 1893.*

Contains "A Man of Letters," by Bierce. Also 10 copies on large paper (untrimmed copies?) of which but five were bound by the publisher.

How Blind Is He? [*n.p., n.d.* 1896?].

Privately printed facsimile manuscript.

Tales from Town Topics. *New York, 1896.*

Contains "That Damned Thing," by Bierce.

To Ambrose Bierce, by George Sterling. *Washington, 1910.*

4 pp. leaflet.

The Woman Who Lost Him, by J. C. McCrackin. *Pasadena, 1913.*

Introduction by Bierce. Boards.

A Gracious Visitation, by E. F. Dawson. *San Francisco, 1921.*

Contains an appreciation by Bierce.

Twenty-One Letters of Ambrose Bierce. *Cleveland, 1922.*

Samuel Loveman, editor. Also 50 copies on Japan vellum.

The Letters of Ambrose Bierce. *San Francisco, 1922.*

Bertha Clarke Pope, editor. 415 copies only.

Containing Four Ambrose Bierce Letters. [*New York, 1923*].

Title printed on envelope. Privately printed. 200 copies only.

Ten Tales. *London, 1925.*

Reprint material.

The Testimony of the Suns, 1875. *San Francisco, 1927.*

Contribution by Bierce. 300 copies only.

Invocation. *San Francisco, 1928.*

Privately printed. Introduction by George Sterling and with notes by Oscar Lewis. Boards. 300 copies only.

A Letter and a Likeness, 1875. [n.p., 1930].
  10 copies only privately printed.
Battlefields and Ghosts. [Palo Alto] 1931.
  Privately printed.
Selections From Prattle. [San Francisco] 1936.
  Wrappers. 500 copies only.
Does the Coyote Howl? [n.p., n.d.]
  Broadside.

BIOGRAPHICAL

Ambrose Bierce, by Vincent Starrett. *Chicago*, 1920.
  250 numbered copies only.
Ambrose Bierce As He Really Was, by Adolphe de Castro, 1926.
  In: *The American Parade*, a bound periodical, October, 1926.
The Life of Ambrose Bierce, by Walter Neale. *New York*, 1929.
Bitter Bierce, by C. Hartley Grattan. *Garden City*, 1929.
A Bibliography of the Writings of Ambrose Bierce, by Vincent Starrett. *Philadelphia*, 1929.
  350 numbered copies only.
A Portrait of Ambrose Bierce, by Adolphe de Castro. *New York*, 1929.
Ambrose Bierce, by Carey McWilliams. *New York*, 1929.
Bierce and the Poe Hoax, by Carroll D. Hall. *San Francisco*, 1934.
  250 numbered copies only.
Footloose in Arcadia: A Personal Record, by Joseph Noel. *New York* [1940].

Among the numerous separate reprints of Bierce's stories are "A Son of the Gods and A Horseman in the Sky," "A Watcher by the Dead," "The Man and the Snake," and "My Favorite Murder."

Robert Montgomery Bird

1806–1854

CALAVAR; OR, THE KNIGHT OF THE CONQUEST. *Philadelphia, 1834.*
  2 vols. Anonymous. Cloth, paper labels. Reissued with a new introduction.
  Philadelphia, 1847.

THE INFIDEL; OR, THE FALL OF MEXICO. *Philadelphia, 1835.*
  2 vols. Cloth, paper labels.

THE HAWKS OF HAWK-HOLLOW. *Philadelphia, 1835.*
  2 vols. Cloth, paper labels.

SHEPPARD LEE. *New York, 1836.*
  2 vols. Anonymous: *By Himself.*

NICK OF THE WOODS. *Philadelphia, 1837.*
  2 vols. Cloth, paper labels. Revised edition, *New York, 1853.*

PETER PILGRIM; OR, A RAMBLER'S RECOLLECTIONS. *Philadelphia, 1838.*
  2 vols. Anonymous. Cloth, paper labels.

THE ADVENTURES OF ROBIN DAY. *Philadelphia, 1839.*
  2 vols.

THE CITY LOOKING GLASS: A PHILADELPHIA COMEDY. *New York, 1933.*
  Arthur Hobson Quinn, editor. 465 unnumbered copies only.

THE COWLED LOVER AND OTHER PLAYS. *Princeton, 1941.*
  Edward H. O'Neill, editor.

The Difficulties of Medical Science. *Philadelphia, 1841.*
  Pamphlet.
Valedictory Address ... Pennsylvania Medical College. Session of 1841-1842. *Philadelphia, 1842.*
  Pamphlet.
Valedictory Address ... Pennsylvania Medical College. Session of 1842-1843. *Philadelphia, 1843.*
  Pamphlet.
Representative American Plays. *New York, 1917.*
  Arthur Hobson Quinn, editor. Contains a five act tragedy by Bird, "A Broker of Bogota."
The Life and Dramatic Works of Robert Montgomery Bird, by Clement Edgar Foust. *New York, 1919.*

James Boyd

1888–

DRUMS. *New York-London,* 1925.

Advance copies, publisher's file copy and deposit copies at The Library of Congress have the imprint: *New York-London.* Copies have been noted, possibly of a later printing, which have *New York* only as place of publication.

Of the first edition 255 sets of sheets were sold to The H. R. Huntting Company, to be bound in buckram; these were distributed sometime after publication of the regular Scribner edition.

Several typographical errors have been noted but since they persist in the second printing they are of no bibliographical value.

Reissued in a revised edition of 525 de luxe copies signed by the author and the illustrator, N. C. Wyeth, *New York* [1928].

MARCHING ON. *New York,* 1927.

Advance copies, a presentation copy, publisher's file copy, copyright deposit copies, carry no statement of printing on the copyright page. The publishers state that reprints are marked: *First Printing, May, 1927.*

LONG HUNT. *New York,* 1930.

First printing marked with code letter *A* on the copyright page. Also 260 large paper copies, numbered, signed by the author.

ROLL RIVER. *New York,* 1935.

First printing marked with code letter *A* on the copyright page. P. 364, third line from the bottom, *senitmental* for *sentimental.*

BITTER CREEK. *New York,* 1939.

First printing marked with code letter *A* on the copyright page.

As We Are, Stories of Here and Now. *New York* [1923].
    Walter B. Pitkin, editor. Contains "Shif'less" by Boyd.
Hunting Sketches, by Anthony Trollope. *New York,* 1933.
    950 copies only. Introduction by Boyd.
The American Historical Scene as Depicted by Stanley Arthurs. *Philadelphia,* 1935.
    Contains Boyd's "The Siege of Boonesboro."
One More Free Man. [*New York*] 1941.
    A play published by The Free Company, March 24, 1941 in an edition of 1,000 copies. Blue printed wrappers. *See next item.*
The Free Company Presents ... *New York* [1941].
    Introduction and "One More Free Man" by Boyd, the latter having appeared pre-·viously in separate form. Sherwood Anderson's "Above Suspicion" contained in this volume was edited by Boyd.

Hugh Henry Brackenridge
1748–1816

A POEM ON THE RISING GLORY OF AMERICA. *Philadelphia*, 1772.
Anonymous. With PHILIP FRENEAU.

A POEM ON DIVINE REVELATION. *Philadelphia*, 1774.
Anonymous.

THE BATTLE OF BUNKERS-HILL. *Philadelphia*, 1776.
Anonymous. By *A Gentleman of Maryland.*

THE DEATH OF GENERAL MONTGOMERY. *Philadelphia*, 1777.
Anonymous. With frontispiece. Also an issue with *Norwich and Providence* imprint.

SIX POLITICAL DISCOURSES. *Lancaster* [1778].

AN EULOGIUM OF THE BRAVE MEN WHO HAVE FALLEN IN THE CONTEST WITH GREAT BRITAIN. *Philadelphia* [1779].

NARRATIVE OF A LATE EXPEDITION AGAINST THE INDIANS. *Philadelphia,* 1773 [1783].

MODERN CHIVALRY. *Philadelphia*, M.DCC.XCII.
Vol. 2, *Philadelphia*, M.DCC.XII(!) [1792].
Vol. 3, *Pittsburgh*, M.DCC.XIII(!) [1793].
Vol. 4, *Philadelphia*, M,DCC,XCVII.
Part 2, Vol. 1, *Carlisle*, 1804.
Part 2, Vol. 2, *Carlisle*, 1805.
Various later revised editions.

POLITICAL MISCELLANY. *New York*, 1793.
Anonymous.

INCIDENTS OF THE INSURRECTION IN THE WESTERN PARTS OF PENNSYLVANIA IN THE YEAR 1794. *Philadelphia*, 1795.

THE STANDARD OF LIBERTY. *Philadelphia* [1802?].
Under the pseudonym *Democritus.*

AN EPISTLE TO WALTER SCOTT ... [*Pittsburgh*] 1811.
Franklin Head Printing-Office, Pittsburgh at foot of p. 8.

LAW MISCELLANIES. *Philadelphia*, 1814.

The Spirit of the Public Journals; or, Beauties of the American Newspapers for 1805. *Baltimore,* 1806.
    Edited.

Gazette Publications. *Carlisle,* 1806.
    Contributions selected from newspapers. Boards, paper label.

Indian Narratives, by Archibald Loudon. *Carlisle,* 1808.
    Contribution.

Essays on the Constitution of the United States. *Brooklyn,* 1892.
    Paul Leicester Ford, editor. Contains "Cursory Remarks," by Brackenridge.

A Bibliography of the Writings of Hugh Henry Brackenridge Prior to 1825.
    Compiled by Charles F. Heartman. *New York,* 1917.
    59 copies only.

The Life and Writings of Hugh Henry Brackenridge, by Claude Milton Newlin. *Princeton,* 1932.

Gamaliel Bradford

1863–1932

TYPES OF AMERICAN CHARACTER. *New York*, 1895.

A PAGEANT OF LIFE. *Boston*, 1904.

THE PRIVATE TUTOR. *Boston*, 1904.
Published October 1904 on the copyright page.

BETWEEN TWO MASTERS. *Boston*, 1906.
Published April 1906 on the copyright page.

MATTHEW PORTER. *Boston*, 1908.

LEE, THE AMERICAN. *Boston*, 1912.
Revised Riverside Edition, *Boston*, 1927.

CONFEDERATE PORTRAITS. *Boston*, 1914.

PORTRAITS OF WOMEN. *Boston*, 1916.

UNION PORTRAITS. *Boston*, 1916.

A NATURALIST OF SOULS. *New York*, 1917.
Revised edition, *Boston*, 1926.

UNMADE IN HEAVEN: A PLAY IN FOUR ACTS. *New York*, 1917.

PORTRAITS OF AMERICAN WOMEN. *Boston*, 1919.

A PROPHET OF JOY. *Boston*, 1920.
Boards, paper label.

SHADOW VERSES. *New Haven*, 1920.

AMERICAN PORTRAITS. *Boston*, 1922.

DAMAGED SOULS. *Boston*, 1923.
Also 200 copies, untrimmed, paper label. Revised edition, 1931.

BARE SOULS. *New York* [1924].

THE SOUL OF SAMUEL PEPYS. *Boston*, 1924.
Also 200 copies with paper label.

WIVES. *New York* [1925].

DARWIN. *Boston*, 1926.

D. L. MOODY: A WORKER IN SOULS. *New York* [1927].
First edition has insignia on copyright page.

LIFE AND I: AN AUTOBIOGRAPHY OF HUMANITY. *Boston*, 1928.

EARLY DAYS IN WELLESLEY. *Wellesley*, 1928.
Paper label. 500 copies only.

AS GOD MADE THEM: PORTRAITS OF SOME NINETEENTH-CENTURY AMER-
ICANS. *Boston*, 1929.
Also 200 copies with paper label.

DAUGHTERS OF EVE. *Boston*, 1930.
Also 200 signed copies.

THE QUICK AND THE DEAD. *Boston*, 1931.
Also 200 signed copies.

SAINTS AND SINNERS. *Boston*, 1932.

BIOGRAPHY AND THE HUMAN HEART. *Boston*, 1932.
Also 150 numbered copies.

PORTRAITS AND PERSONALITIES. *Boston* [1933].
Mabel A. Bessey, editor.

THE JOURNAL OF GAMALIEL BRADFORD, 1883-1932. *Boston*, 1933.
Van Wyck Brooks, editor.

THE LETTERS OF GAMALIEL BRADFORD, 1918-1931. *Boston*, 1934.
Van Wyck Brooks, editor.

ELIZABETHAN WOMEN. [*Boston*] 1936.
Harold Ogden White, editor.

The Founding of the German Empire. *New York* [1890-1898].
7 vols. Co-translator.
Macaulay's Life of Samuel Johnson. *Boston* [1895].
Edited.
A Portrait of General George Gordon Meade. [*New York*, 1915].
Pamphlet.
The Haunted Biographer. *New York*, 1927.
All reprint.
Percy MacKaye: A Symposium on His Fiftieth Birthday. *Hanover, N. H.*, 1928.
Contains an appreciation by Bradford, "The Range and Compass of His
Instrument."
Biography: The Literature of Personality, by James C. Johnston. *New York* [1927].
Introduction.
Gamaliel Bradford: A Memoir, by C. K. Bolton, *Boston*, 1932.
Wrappers.

GAMALIEL BRADFORD

Annals of an Era: Percy MacKaye and the MacKaye Family 1826-1932. *Washington, D. C.*, 1932.
Edited and with an introduction by Edwin Osgood Grover. Prefatory note by Bradford.

"The Lesson of Popular Government," by Gamaliel Bradford. *New York*, 1899, is by the father of the present subject.

Roark Bradford

1896–

OL' MAN ADAM AN' HIS CHILLUN. *New York, 1928.*
First edition so stated on the copyright page. Boards, cloth back.
Marc Connelly's play, "The Green Pastures," *New York* [1929], is based on this title. "Little David," by Marc Connelly, *New York,* 1937, is a one act play suggested by the same book.

THIS SIDE JORDAN. *New York,* 1929.
First edition so stated on copyright page.

OL' KING DAVID AN' THE PHILISTINE BOYS. *New York,* 1930.
First edition so stated on copyright page. Boards, cloth back.

HOW COME CHRISTMAS. *New York,* 1930.
1,400 copies only for private distribution. Trade edition, *New York,* 1934.

JOHN HENRY. *New York,* 1931.
Also Literary Guild edition. First edition so stated on copyright page. Label on spine. Dramatized as "John Henry: A Play," *New York,* 1939, with music by Jacques Wolfe.

KINGDOM COMING. *New York,* 1933.
First edition so stated on copyright page.

LET THE BAND PLAY DIXIE. *New York,* 1934.
First edition so stated on copyright page. Code letters *H-I* on copyright page.

THE THREE HEADED ANGEL. *New York,* 1937.
First edition so stated on copyright page. Code letters *C-M* on copyright page.

The Best Short Stories of 1927. *New York,* 1927.
Edward J. O'Brien, editor. Contains "Child of God," by Bradford; appeared also in "O. Henry Memorial Prize Stories of 1927," *Garden City,* 1928.
O. Henry Memorial Award Prize Stories for 1930. *Garden City,* 1930.
First edition so stated on copyright page. Contains a short story by Roark Bradford.
So Red the Nose. *New York* [1935].
Contribution.
A Southern Harvest. *Boston,* 1937.
Robert Penn Warren, editor. Contribution.

Louis Bromfield
1896–

THE GREEN BAY TREE. *New York*, 1924.
Dramatized as "The House of Women."

POSSESSION. *New York*, 1925.

EARLY AUTUMN. *New York*, 1926.

A GOOD WOMAN. *New York*, 1927.
Also presentation issue in yellow boards.

THE STRANGE CASE OF MISS ANNIE SPRAGG. *New York*, 1928.

AWAKE AND REHEARSE. *New York* [1929].
Also 500 numbered and signed copies in boards.

TWENTY-FOUR HOURS. *New York*, 1930.
Also 500 signed copies. Published serially as "Shattered Glass."

TABLOID NEWS. *New York*, 1930.
875 copies only in "The Random House Prose Quartos." Wrappers, paper label.

A MODERN HERO. *New York*, 1932.
Also 250 signed copies.

THE FARM. *New York*, 1933.
First edition so stated on copyright page.

HERE TODAY AND GONE TOMORROW. *New York*, 1934.
First edition so stated on copyright page.

THE MAN WHO HAD EVERYTHING. *New York*, 1935.
First edition so stated on copyright page. Appeared partially in magazine as "Three Faces in the Mirror."

THE RAINS CAME. *New York*, 1937.
First edition so indicated on copyright page.

IT TAKES ALL KINDS. *New York*, 1939.
First edition so indicated on copyright page.

ENGLAND, A DYING OLIGARCHY. *New York*, 1939.
First edition so indicated on copyright page.

NIGHT IN BOMBAY. *New York*, 1940.
First edition so indicated on copyright page.

The Work of Robert Nathan. *Indianapolis* [n.d.].
 Pamphlet.
Louis Bromfield and His Books, by Ben Ray Redman. *New York* [n.d.].
Bobbed Hair: A Novel by Twenty Authors. *New York,* 1925.
 Contains a chapter by Bromfield.
The House of Women. *New York,* 1927.
 Dramatization of "The Green Bay Tree."
O. Henry Memorial Award Prize Stories of 1927. *Garden City,* 1928.
 Contains "The Scarlet Woman," by Bromfield. The story was also issued in
 separate form by the magazine in which it originally appeared.
Pomp and Circumstance, by E. de Gramont. *New York* [1929].
 Translated by Brian W. Down. Introduction by Bromfield.
Shattered Glass. [*New York, ca.* 1930].
 Pamphlet. Issued by *Cosmopolitan* as an advertisement for the serial publication
 of this title; issued in book form as "Twenty-Four Hours," 1930.
Revolt in the Arts. *New York,* 1930.
 O. M. Sayler, editor. Contains "The Novel in Transition," by Bromfield.
One Heavenly Night. *New York* [1931].
 A novelization by Lynn Farnol of Bromfield's screen play.
American Writers on American Literature. *New York* [1931].
 John Macy, editor. Contains "Hawthorne," by Bromfield.
Spécialité de la Maison. *New York* [1940].
 Preface.

Charles Brockden Brown

1771–1810

ALCUIN. *New York*, 1798.

WIELAND. *New York*, 1798.
Anonymous.

ORMOND. *New York*, 1799.
By the Author of Wieland, etc.

ARTHUR MERVYN. *Philadelphia*, 1799.
By the Author of Wieland, etc. Part 2, *New York*, 1800.

EDGAR HUNTLY. *Philadelphia*, 1799.
By the Author of Arthur Mervyn, etc. 3 volumes.

CLARA HOWARD. *Philadelphia*, 1801.
Published in England, *London*, 1807, as "Philip Stanley."

JANE TALBOT. *Philadelphia*, 1801.
By the Author of Arthur Mervyn, etc.

MEMOIRS OF CARWIN, THE BILOQUIST. *Philadelphia*, 1815.
In: "The Life of Charles Brockden Brown," by William Dunlap, Vol. 2.

Brown was the author of numerous political pamphlets; only three of these are listed in the following list.

Monroe's Embassy; or, The Conduct of the Government. ... *Philadelphia, Baltimore, Washington*, 1803.
Wrappers.
Address to the Government. [*n.p.*] 1803.
A View of the Soil and Climate of the United States of America ... by C. F. Volney ... *Philadelphia*, 1804.
Translated by Brown.
Valerian: A Narrative Poem ... by John Blair Linn, D.D. ... *Philadelphia*, 1805.
Contains a brief biography of Linn by Brown.
Address to Congress. *Philadelphia*, 1809.
The Works of Charles Brockden Brown. *Boston*, 1827.
12 vols.

BIOGRAPHICAL

The Life of Charles Brockden Brown, by William Dunlap. *Philadelphia*, 1815.
2 vols. First printing for Brown's "Memoirs of Carwin, the Biloquist."

William Cullen Bryant

1794–1878

THE EMBARGO; OR, SKETCHES OF THE TIMES: A SATIRE. *Boston,* 1808.
Anonymous. *By A Youth of Thirteen.* Stitched without wrappers. The second edition, *Boston,* 1809, contains added material and bears the author's name; unprinted wrappers.

POEMS. *Cambridge,* 1821.
Boards or wrappers, printed.

POEMS. *New York,* 1832.
Also with *Boston* imprint. Boards, cloth back, paper label on spine. The *London,* 1832, edition is a reprint.

POEMS. *Boston,* 1834.
With added material.

POEMS. *New York,* 1836.
Newly revised and edited; with additions. Some state *Third Edition* (1835) or *Third Edition* (1836).

POEMS. *New York,* 1836.
Fourth Edition. Contains added material.

POEMS. *New York,* 1839.
Fifth Edition. With added material. There seems to have been five subsequent reprints of this edition.

THE FOUNTAIN AND OTHER POEMS. *New York,* 1842.
Boards; or cloth, label on spine; or, cloth with gold stamping on front cover.

THE WHITE-FOOTED DEER AND OTHER POEMS. *New York,* 1844.
No. 1 in "The Home Library." Yellow wrappers. Copies have been noted with a leaf of notes at the end and with blank fly leaves at both back and front.

POEMS. *Philadelphia,* 1847.
Collected and arranged by Bryant. First illustrated edition. Subsequent Philadelphia editions with *D. Appleton* imprint, dated 1848, 1849, 1854.

LETTERS OF A TRAVELLER; OR, NOTES OF THINGS SEEN IN EUROPE AND AMERICA. *New York,* 1850.
Reissued, *New York,* 1851, illustrated, as "The Picturesque Souvenir, Letters of a Traveller."

POEMS. *New York,* 1854.
Collected and arranged by Bryant. London edition of this date contains three added poems.

BRYANT

LETTERS OF A TRAVELLER: SECOND SERIES. *New York,* 1859.

THIRTY POEMS. *New York,* 1864.
Noted on two types of paper, laid and wove, with no known priority. Several types of cloth binding.

HYMNS. [*New York,* 1864].
First state reads, second line, fourth stanza, p. 9, *Dwells on Thy works in deep delight.* Privately printed. *See:* "Hymns," 1869.

VOICES OF NATURE. *New York,* 1865.

LETTERS FROM THE EAST. *New York,* 1869.

HYMNS. [*New York,* 1869?].
Reissue of the 1864 edition with added material. Privately printed.

THE ILIAD OF HOMER. *Boston,* 1870.
2 vols. Translated.

THE ODYSSEY OF HOMER. *Boston,* 1871.
2 vols. Translated.

THE SONG OF THE SOWER. *New York,* 1871.

POEMS. *New York,* 1871.
With added material and revisions. Frequently reprinted.

THE STORY OF THE FOUNTAIN. *New York,* 1872.

THE LITTLE PEOPLE OF THE SNOW. *New York,* 1873.

ORATIONS AND ADDRESSES. *New York,* 1873.

AMONG THE TREES. *New York* [1874].

POETICAL WORKS. *New York* [1876].

A POPULAR HISTORY OF THE UNITED STATES. *New York,* 1876, 1878, 1879, 1880.
With SYDNEY HOWARD GAY. 4 vols., or 51 parts.

POEMS. *New York,* 1878.
R. H. Stoddard, editor.

POETICAL WORKS. *New York,* 1879.
Household Edition.

POETICAL WORKS. *New York,* 1883.
2 vols. Parke Godwin, editor.

PROSE WRITINGS. *New York,* 1884.
2 vols. Parke Godwin, editor.

UNPUBLISHED POEMS BY BRYANT AND THOREAU. *Boston,* 1907.
470 copies only. Boards.

A Collection of Psalms and Hymns for Private Worship. *New York*, 1820.
    Henry D. Sewall, editor. Contains 5 poems by Bryant.

An Oration Delivered at Stockbridge, July 4th, 1820. *Stockbridge*, 1820.
    Stitched without wrappers.

The Idle Man. *New York*, 1821-1822.
    Richard Henry Dana, I, editor. Contains 5 poems by Bryant.

Miscellaneous Poems Selected from the United States Literary Gazette. *Boston*, 1826.
    Contributions by Bryant.

The Atlantic Souvenir. *Philadelphia* [1826].
    Contribution by Bryant.

The Talisman. *New York*, 1828, 1829, 1830.
    3 vols. Edited with G. C. Verplanck and R. C. Sands. 15 poems and 13 prose sketches by Bryant.

The American Landscape, No. 1. *New York*, 1830.
    By Various Authors.

Tales of the Glauber-Spa. *New York*, 1832.
    By Several American Authors. Edited and with an introduction and two poems by Bryant. Noted in both cloth with paper labels or printed cloth; no known priority. 2 vols.

The Jubilee of the Constitution. A Discourse ... *New York*, 1839.
    Contains an ode by Bryant.

Selections from the American Poets. *New York*, 1840.
    No. III in "Harper's Family Library."

Popular Considerations on Homœopathia. *New York* [1841].
    Yellow wrappers.

An Address to the People of the United States, in Behalf of the American Copyright Club. *New York*, 1843.

History of Texas, by A. B. Lawrence [ca. 1846].
    Contains "The Prairies of Texas," by Bryant.

A Funeral Oration ... Death of Thomas Cole. *New York and Philadelphia*, 1848.

International Copyright. [*Washington*, 1848].
    Contribution.

Reminiscences of the Evening Post. *New York*, 1851.
    Anonymous.

Memorial of James Fenimore Cooper. *New York*, 1852.
    Contains "A Discourse on the Life, Character and Genius of Cooper." Reprinted in Cooper's "Precaution," *New York*, 1852.

Gifts of Genius: A Miscellany ... *New York* [1859].
    Contribution by Bryant.

A Discourse on the Life, Character, and Genius of Washington Irving. *New York*, 1860.
    Also large paper edition.

A Forest Hymn. *New York* [1860].
    First state has *C. A. Alvord, Printer, New York* on verso of title page; second state has *Printed by Alvord*.

Only Once. *New York*, 1862.
    Contribution by Bryant.

The Bryant Festival at the Century. *New York*, 1865.
 Also 150 copies in the "Illustrated Edition."
Some Notices of the Life and Writings of Fitz-Greene Halleck. *New York*, 1869.
 Privately printed. Wrappers.
The Green House as a Winter Garden, by F. E. Field. *New York*, 1869.
 Introduction by Bryant.
The Bryant Homestead Book. *New York*, 1870.
 By The Idle Scholar [i.e., Julia Hatfield]. Cloth or publisher's leather, identically stamped.
A Library of Poetry and Song. *New York*, 1871.
 Reissued, as "A New Library of Poetry and Song" [1876], 2 vols.; as "The Family Library of Poetry and Song" [1878]; with revisions as "The New Library of Poetry and Song," 2 vols., [1886].
The Gospel in the Trades, by Alexander Clark. *Philadelphia*, 1871.
 Introduction by Bryant.
A Child's Poems, by Lucy Catlin Ball. *Hartford*, 1872.
 Introduction.
Picturesque America; or, The Land We Live In. *New York* [1872-74].
 2 vols. Edited.
Facsimile Edition of Thanatopsis. *New York*, 1874.
 Wrappers. Reprinted from "Poems," 1821.
To William Cullen Bryant at Eighty Years ... *New York*, 1876.
 Contains an address by Bryant.
Custer's Immortality, by Laura S. Webb. [*New York?*, 1876?].
 Contribution.
Studies in Bryant: A Text Book, by Joseph Alden. *New York*, 1877.
 Introduction by Bryant.
Tribute to William Cullen Bryant, by Robert C. Waterston. *Boston*, 1878.
 Contains Bryant's address on Mazzini.
The Flood of Years. *New York*, 1878.
 Cloth or morocco.
Thoughts on the Religious Life, by Joseph Alden. *New York*, 1879.
 Introduction by Bryant.
Studies of Irving. *New York*, 1880.
 With others.
Complete Works of Shakespeare. *New York* [1886-1896].
 3 vols. Edited in part and with a preface by Bryant.

BIOGRAPHICAL

The Life, Character and Writings of William Cullen Bryant, By George William Curtis. *New York* [1879].
A Biography of William Cullen Bryant, With Extracts From His Private Correspondence. *New York*, 1883.
 Parke Godwin, editor. 2 volumes.
William Cullen Bryant, by John Bigelow. *Boston*, 1890.

Pearl (Sydenstricker) Buck

1892–

EAST WIND: WEST WIND. *New York* [1930].

THE GOOD EARTH. *New York* [1931].
  Also 125 copies in paper wrappers as an advance issue. Early states have *flees* for *fleas*, p. 100, line 17; *For The John Day Publishing Company, Inc.* on copyright page. The first printing consisted of 9,475 copies; the first 2,700 copies issued had the top edges stained brown; the remaining copies in the first printing were issued with the top edges stained green. 150 copies in leather for *Individual Library;* it is questionable that any of these were first run sheets. Modern Library Edition, *New York* [1934], first edition so stated on copyright page, has new introduction by the author.

THE YOUNG REVOLUTIONIST. *New York* [1932].

SONS. *New York* [1932].
  First edition so stated on copyright page. Also 371 de luxe copies, signed by the author, published two days before the trade edition.

THE FIRST WIFE AND OTHER STORIES. *New York* [1933].

THE MOTHER. *New York* [1934].

A HOUSE DIVIDED. *New York* [1935].
  Also 300 copies in wrappers in advance of publication.

THE EXILE. *New York* [1936].

FIGHTING ANGEL. *New York* [1936].

THIS PROUD HEART. *New York* [1938].

THE PATRIOT. *New York* [1939].

OTHER GODS. *New York* [1940].

STORIES FOR LITTLE CHILDREN. *New York* [1940].

TODAY AND FOREVER. *New York* [1941].

OF MEN AND WOMEN. *New York* [1941].

Is There a Case for Foreign Missions? *New York* [1932].
  No. 18 in the "John Day Pamphlets."
All Men Are Brothers. *New York* [1933].
  2 vols. Translated from the Chinese of Shui Hu Chuan by Pearl Buck. There was also issued an elaborate pamphlet prospectus.

BUCK

Molders of American Thought. *Garden City*, 1934.
  William H. Cordell, editor. First edition so indicated on the copyright page. Contains "What Religion Means to Me," by Pearl Buck.
O. Henry Memorial Award Prize Stories of 1934. *Garden City*, 1934.
  Contains "Shanghai Scene."
My Country and My People, by Lin Yutang. *New York* [1935].
  Introduction by Pearl Buck.
House of Earth. *New York* [1935].
  Reprint of "The Good Earth," "Sons," and "A House Divided."
American Points of View: A Reader's Guide. *Garden City*, 1936.
  Edited by William H., and Kathryn Coe Cordell. Contains Pearl Buck's "Advice to Unborn Novelists."
Breaking Into Print. *New York*, 1937.
  Elmer Adler, editor. Contribution.
On Discovering America. [*New York*, 1937].
1937 Essay Annual. *New York* [1937].
  Erich A. Walter, editor. Contribution.
The Chinese Novel. *New York* [1939].
Our Family, by Adet and Anor Lin. *New York* [1939].
  Introduction.
I Believe. *New York*, 1939.
  Clifton Fadiman, editor. Contribution.
A Novel in the Making. *New York* [1940].

BIOGRAPHICAL

A Biographical Sketch of Pearl S. Buck. *New York* [1936].
  Anonymous. By Richard J. Walsh. Wrappers.

H. C. (Henry Cuyler) Bunner
1855–1896

A WOMAN OF HONOR. *Boston*, 1883.

AIRS FROM ARCADY AND ELSEWHERE. *New York*, 1884.
Also 36 large paper copies.

IN PARTNERSHIP: STUDIES IN STORY TELLING. *New York*, 1884.
With BRANDER MATTHEWS.

THE MIDGE. *New York*, 1886.
First state has decorative end papers and imprint of *Grant & Faires* on copyright page; later with the *J. J. Little* imprint.

THE STORY OF A NEW YORK HOUSE. *New York*, 1887.

"SHORT SIXES": STORIES TO BE READ WHILE THE CANDLE BURNS. *New York*, 1891.*
First state, p. 47 so numbered. Several impressions without change of date. It is probable that the earliest copies contain no advertisements at the back of the book. Fore and bottom edges untrimmed. Issued in several colors of boards with cloth back of which the author once wrote "liver colored boards" are first. It seems likely that the author was in error in making the latter statement. A copyright deposit copy at the Library of Congress has all the accepted points of the first edition but is bound in blue boards, green cloth back.

ZADOC PINE AND OTHER STORIES. *New York*, 1891.

THE RUNAWAY BROWNS. *New York*, 1892.*

ROWEN: "SECOND CROP" SONGS. *New York*, 1892.

"MADE IN FRANCE." *New York*, 1893.*

MORE "SHORT SIXES." *New York*, 1894.*

JERSEY STREET AND JERSEY LANE. *New York*, 1896.

THE SUBURBAN SAGE. *New York*, 1896.*

THE POEMS OF H. C. BUNNER. *New York*, 1896.
The Harry B. Smith catalog, "A Sentimental Library," lists this title as 1895. I have been unable to find any record of such publication in any of the contemporary listings, the Library of Congress or the publisher's files. A copy at the Library of Congress, received November 13, 1896, is dated 1896 on the title page.

LOVE IN OLD CLOATHES AND OTHER STORIES. *New York,* 1896.

Title story appeared previously in "Stories by American Authors," No. 4, *New York,* 1884.

THREE OPERETTAS. *New York,* 1897.

With music by Oscar Weil. "The Seven Old Ladies of Lavendartown," *New York* [1910] reprinted from this.

Bunner was for many years the editor of *Puck* and as such compiled or edited numerous compilations of *Puck* material. A representative few of these are included in the following list.

A Masque of Poets. *Boston,* 1878.

Contains "I Love to Dine," by Bunner. For further discussion of this publication see under *Alcott.*

A Bad Case: A Comedy for Amateurs. *New York* [1879].

With Julian Magnus.

Comedies for Amateur Acting. *New York,* 1880.

Brander Matthews, editor. Contribution.

Henry W. Longfellow: A Biography, by W. S. Kennedy. *Cambridge,* 1882.

Poem by Bunner at p. 236.

Stories by American Authors. *New York,* 1884.

No. 1 contains "The Documents in the Case," written in collaboration with Brander Matthews; No. 4 contains "Love in Old Cloathes."

Songs and Ballads, by E. C. Stedman. *New York,* 1884.

100 copies on vellum only. Contains an introductory sonnet by Bunner.

Pen and Ink ... by Brander Matthews. *New York,* 1888.

Contains "An Epistle," by Bunner.

A Portfolio of Players. *New York,* 1888.

110 copies only; of which, 25 with set of proofs.

With My Friends, by Brander Matthews. *New York,* 1891.

Joint author.

Mavericks. *New York,* 1892.

Contains "The Recording Spook," by Bunner.

A Set of [56] Cartoons from *Puck. New York,* 1893.

By Joseph Keppler. Text and introduction by Bunner. Also 300 large paper copies.

Hanks, Assorted from *Puck* ... *New York,* 1893.

Contains "The Senator," by Bunner.

The Modern Poster. *New York,* 1895.

Introduction by Bunner. Also de luxe edition on Japan vellum.

Courtship with Variations: A Comedy in One Act. *Boston,* 1902.

A translation [?] by Bunner.

Recreations of an Anthologist, by Brander Matthews. *New York,* 1904.

Contains "The Uncollected Poems of H. C. Bunner."

The Seven Old Ladies of Lavendartown. *New York* [1910].

See above: "Three Operettas," 1897.

The Stories of H. C. Bunner: First Series. *New York,* 1916.

    Also, "Second Series," same date. Reprints of previously published stories. "Short Sixes" and "More Short Sixes" added in 1917, uniform binding.

BIOGRAPHICAL

The Life and Letters of Henry Cuyler Bunner, by Gerard E. Jensen. *Durham, N. C.,* 1939.

---

   * Various reissues without change of date, appearing in both cloth and wrappers. Inspection of advertisements is necessary to determine first printings. Issued later as a set in half cloth, the bottom portion of the covers being bound in cloth unlike the top portion.

(Frank) Gelett Burgess

1866–

THE PURPLE COW! [*San Francisco,* 1895].

Pamphlet. First state printed on both sides of leaf; second state printed on one side of leaf only, folded. Often collected as a companion piece is *The Lark*, Vol. 1, No. 1, May 1, 1895. The first state of the latter may be determined by the presence of the *Murdock* imprint on the copyright page; later states have the *Doxey* imprint.

Gelett Burgess describes the evolution of his "Purple Cow!" as follows:

1) First printed in *The Lark*, Vol. 1, No. 1, May, 1895. The first copies printed had the *Murdock* imprint on the copyright page.

2) Same as preceding but second state, having the *Doxey* imprint.

3) An experimental printing of "The Purple Cow!" the front cover decorated, top and bottom, with a horizontal ornament of animal figures and scrolls. The dedication on the verso of the front cover is signed: "F. G. B." [Frank Gelett Burgess]. Mr. Burgess knows of but one existing copy.

4) The published edition of "The Purple Cow!" *San Francisco,* 1895, with a large "purple cow," printed in black, on the front cover. Dedication signed: "Gelett Burgess." First printed on a rough China paper but because it caused the type to break the publisher later printed it—

5) —on thinner and smoother paper. Printed on one side only.

6) Of the first printing the author had printed, for presentation, a very few copies on white laid paper and hand colored the illustrations. One known copy of this state.

VIVETTE; OR, THE MEMOIRS OF THE ROMANCE ASSOCIATION. *Boston,* 1897.
Also a few copies in calf for private distribution.

CHANT-ROYAL OF CALIFORNIA. *San Francisco* [1899].

THE LIVELY CITY O' LIGG. *New York,* 1899.

NONSENSE ALMANAC. *New York* [1899].
Wrappers. First state has cover design by the author on dark brown English antique paper. Reissued with revisions, 1901.

GOOPS AND HOW TO BE THEM. *New York* [1900].

A GAGE OF YOUTH. *Boston,* 1901.

THE BURGESS NONSENSE BOOK. *New York* [1901].

THE ROMANCE OF THE COMMONPLACE. *San Francisco* [1902].
Cloth or leather; also 13 copies on vellum and 93 on handmade paper; signed.

THE REIGN OF QUEEN ISYL. *New York*, 1903.
With WILL IRWIN. *Published, November, 1903* on copyright page.

MORE GOOPS AND HOW NOT TO BE THEM. *New York* [1903].

THE PICAROONS. *New York*, 1904.
With WILL IRWIN. *Published, April, 1904* on copyright page.

THE RUBAIYAT OF OMAR CAYENNE. *New York* [1904].
Wrappers or boards.

GOOP TALES ALPHABETICALLY TOLD. *New York* [1904].
Boards.

A LITTLE SISTER OF DESTINY. *Boston*, 1906.

ARE YOU A BROMIDE? *New York*, 1906.
Boards, paper label on front cover. A copy of the fourth printing has been noted
with an inserted slip signed by the author, *American Booksellers' Association
Souvenir Edition, May 15, 1907.*

THE MAXIMS OF METHUSELAH. *New York* [1907].
Boards.

THE WHITE CAT. *Indianapolis* [1907].
March on copyright page.

THE HEART LINE: A DRAMA OF SAN FRANCISCO. *Indianapolis* [1907].
October on copyright page.

LADY MÉCHANTE; OR, LIFE AS IT SHOULD BE. *New York* [1909].
October, 1909 on copyright page.

BLUE GOOPS AND RED. *New York* [1909].

FIND THE WOMAN. *Indianapolis* [1911].

THE MASTER OF MYSTERIES. *Indianapolis* [1912].
Anonymous.

LOVE IN A HURRY. *Indianapolis* [1913].

THE MAXIMS OF NOAH. *New York* [1913].
Boards.

THE CAT'S ELEGY. *Chicago*, 1913.
With BURGES JOHNSON.

THE GOOP DIRECTORY OF JUVENILE OFFENDERS. *New York* [1913].
On Cover: *The Little Goop Books. August 1913* on copyright page.

BURGESS UNABRIDGED. *New York* [1914].
Boards. *September, 1914* on copyright page.

77

WAR THE CREATOR. *New York*, 1916.

THE GOOP ENCYCLOPEDIA. *New York* [1916].

MRS. HOPE'S HUSBAND. *New York*, 1917.
Published September, 1917 on copyright page.

AIN'T ANGIE AWFUL! *Philadelphia* [1923].

HAVE YOU AN EDUCATED HEART? *New York* [1923].

WHY BE A GOOP? *New York*, 1924.

WHY MEN HATE WOMEN. *New York*, 1927.

TWO O'CLOCK COURAGE. *Indianapolis* [1934].
First edition so indicated on copyright page.

TOO GOOD LOOKING. *Indianapolis* [1936].
First edition so indicated on copyright page.

A MURDER AT THE DOME. *Book Club of California*, 1937.
Printed wrappers. 600 copies only.

LOOK ELEVEN YEARS YOUNGER. *New York*, 1937.

SHORT WORDS ARE WORDS OF MIGHT. [*Harrington, Del.*, 1939].
Printed wrappers.

Le Petit Journal des Refusees. Number 1 [All Published]. *San Francisco*, 1896.
Wrappers. Printed on various patterns of wall-paper.
Seen & Unseen, by Yone Noguchi. *San Francisco*, 1897.
Introduction by Burgess. Published by Burgess and Porter Garnett, both of whom edited the work.
Enfant Terrible! Vol. 1, Number 1, April 1, 1898. [All Published]. *New York*, 1898.
Wrappers.
The Love Sonnets of a Hoodlum, by Wallace Irwin. *San Francisco*, 1902.
Introduction by Burgess.
My Maiden Effort. *Garden City*, 1921.
First edition so stated on copyright page. Contains an introduction and contribution by Burgess.
The Stag Cook Book. *New York* [1922].
C. Mac Sheridan, editor. Contains Burgess' recipe for "Pandowdy."
The Bromide and Other Theories. *New York*, 1933.
An omnibus volume of the various "bromides."

John Burroughs

1837–1921

NOTES ON WALT WHITMAN AS POET AND PERSON. *New York, 1867.*
  First copies have trimmed edges. Cloth with gold lettering on the front cover or
  wrappers. Written in part by Whitman. Reissued, revised and enlarged, *New
  York, 1871.*

WAKE-ROBIN. *New York, 1871.*
  With or without pictorial front cover; priority undetermined.
  Reissued with revisions, *New York, 1877.*

WINTER SUNSHINE. *New York, 1876.*

BIRDS AND POETS. *New York, 1877.*

LOCUSTS AND WILD HONEY. *Boston, 1879.*

PEPACTON. *Boston, 1881.*

FRESH FIELDS. *Boston, 1885.*

SIGNS AND SEASONS. *Boston, 1886.*

INDOOR STUDIES. *Boston, 1889.*

RIVERBY. *Boston, 1894.*

WHITMAN: A STUDY. *Boston, 1896.**

THE LIGHT OF DAY. *Boston, 1900.**

LITERARY VALUES. *Boston, 1902.**
  Published December, 1902 on copyright page.

JOHN JAMES AUDUBON. *Boston, 1902.*
  In "The Beacon Biographies." Also 350 large paper copies.

FAR AND NEAR. *Boston, 1904.**

WAYS OF NATURE. *Boston, 1905.**

BIRD AND BOUGH. *Boston, 1906.*
  Also 150 large paper copies.

CAMPING WITH PRESIDENT ROOSEVELT. [*Boston, 1906*].
  Reprinted, *Boston, 1907,* as "Camping and Tramping with Roosevelt," with
  added chapter, of which 250 copies were issued uncut with paper label.

LEAF AND TENDRIL. *Boston, 1908.**

TIME AND CHANGE. *Boston, 1912.**

THE SUMMIT OF THE YEARS. *Boston, 1913.**

THE BREATH OF LIFE. *Boston, 1915.**

UNDER THE APPLE-TREES. *Boston, 1916.**

FIELD AND STUDY. *Boston, 1919.**

ACCEPTING THE UNIVERSE. *Boston, 1920.*

UNDER THE MAPLES. *Boston, 1921.*

THE LAST HARVEST. *Boston, 1922.*

MY BOYHOOD. *Garden City, 1922.*
    First edition so indicated on copyright page. Boards, cloth back, paper label on front cover.

MY DOG FRIENDS. *Boston, 1928.*
    Clara Barrus, editor.

THE HEART OF BURROUGHS's JOURNALS. *Boston, 1928.*
    Clara Barrus, editor. Most of the extracts from the journals are here published for the first time.

THE SLABSIDES BOOK OF JOHN BURROUGHS. *Boston, 1931.*
    H. A. Haring, editor.

COMPLETE WORKS. *Boston, 1904-1922.*
    23 vols.

Essays from *The Critic. Boston,* 1882.
    Contains three essays by Burroughs.
The Art of Authorship. *London,* 1890.
    George Bainton, editor. Contains a letter from Burroughs.
Natural History of Selborne ... by Gilbert White. *New York,* 1895.
    2 vols. Introduction by Burroughs.
Bird Neighbors, by Neltje Blanchan. *New York,* 1897.
    Introduction by Burroughs.
Alaska. Vol. 1. Narrative, Glaciers, Natives. *New York,* 1901.
    By John Burroughs and others. Report of the Harriman Alaska Expedition. Burroughs' "Narrative of the Expedition" was reprinted in revised form in "Far and Near," 1904.
Songs of Nature. *New York,* 1901.
    Edited by Burroughs.
Waiting. *Boston,* 1910.
    Wrappers, label on front cover. Poem and two letters; poem reprinted from "Light of Day," 1900; later, *Roxbury, N. Y.* [1927] with supplementary notes by Clara Barrus.

Theodore Roosevelt: In Memoriam. *New York*, 1919.
>   Contribution by Burroughs.

Harper's Essays. *New York*, 1927.
>   Edited by Henry Seidel Canby. First edition so indicated on copyright page. Contains "The Friendly Rocks," by Burroughs.

Reprints from the Burroughs books have been issued with the following titles: "Squirrels and other Fur-Bearers," "Bird Stories from Burroughs," "A Year in the Fields," "In the Catskills," "Birds and Bees," "Sharp Eyes," "A Bunch of Herbs," "Afoot and Afloat," "Nature Near Home," "Studies in Nature and Literature," "The Wit of a Duck," "Bird Courtships," "The Bluebird," and "Little Nature Studies."

BIOGRAPHICAL

Old John Burroughs, by Fra Elbertus [Elbert Hubbard]. *East Aurora, N. Y.* [1901].
>   Boards, cloth back.

The Retreat of a Poet Naturalist, by Clara Barrus. *Boston*, 1905.
Our Friend John Burroughs, by Clara Barrus. *Boston*, 1914.
John Burroughs: Boy and Man, by Clara Barrus. *New York*, 1920.
The Seer of Slabsides, by Dallas Lore Sharp. *Boston*, 1921.
My Boyhood, by John Burroughs. *Garden City*, 1922.
>   Edited and with conclusion by Julian Burroughs.

John Burroughs Talks, by Clifton Johnson. *Boston*, 1922.
The Real John Burroughs, by William Sloane Kennedy. *New York*, 1924.
The Life and Letters of John Burroughs, by Clara Barrus. *Boston*, 1925.
>   2 vols.

John Burroughs and Ludella Peck. *New York*, 1925.
>   Letters. Boards.

John Burroughs at Troutbeck. *Amenia, N. Y.*, 1926.
>   150 copies only. Printed wrappers.

The Boys' Life of John Burroughs, by Dallas Lore Sharp. *New York* [1928].
With John Burroughs at Slabsides, by Clyde Fisher. *New York*, 1931.
>   Printed wrappers.

Whitman and Burroughs: Comrades, by Clara Barrus. *Boston*, 1931.

* Titles so marked are part of the *Riverside Edition*, all edges untrimmed, cloth, paper label on spine, limited to 1,000 sets. Labels are marked *First Edition*.

(Harold) Witter Bynner

1881–

AN ODE TO HARVARD AND OTHER POEMS. *Boston, 1907.*
> Cloth or leather, with or without the Harvard seal stamped on the front cover.
> Priority, if any, yet to be determined.
> Reprinted with revisions, *New York,* 1925, as "Young Harvard." Reissued without date by Stokes.

TIGER. *New York,* 1913.

THE LITTLE KING. *New York,* 1914.

THE NEW WORLD. *New York,* 1915.

SPECTRA. *New York,* 1916.
> By Emanuel Morgan ₁Bynner₁ and Anne Knish ₁Arthur Davison Ficke₁. *Pseudonyms.*

GRENSTONE POEMS: A SEQUENCE. *New York* ₁1917₁.
> It is presumed that red cloth with no picture on the front cover is a remainder state. Reprinted with additions, *New York,* 1926.

A CANTICLE OF PRAISE. *San Francisco,* 1918.

THE BELOVED STRANGER. *New York,* 1919.

SNICKERTY NICK. *New York,* 1919.
> With JULIA ELLSWORTH FORD.

A CANTICLE OF PAN. *New York,* 1920.

PINS FOR WINGS. ₁*New York,* 1920₁.
> Emanuel Morgan, *pseudonym.* Also 50 copies on handmade paper.

A BOOK OF PLAYS. *New York,* 1922.

CARAVAN. *New York,* 1925.

CAKE: AN INDULGENCE. *New York,* 1926.

ROOTS. *New York,* 1929.
> 475 copies only in "The Random House Poetry Quartos."

INDIAN EARTH. *New York,* 1929.
> Reprints, with other material, "Roots"; see preceding item.

THE PERSISTENCE OF POETRY. *San Francisco,* 1929.

EDEN TREE. *New York,* 1931.
> First edition so stated on copyright page.

AGAINST THE COLD. ₁*New York*, 1933₁.
Wrappers.

GUEST BOOK. *New York*, 1935.
Emanuel Morgan, *pseudonym*.

AGAINST THE COLD AND OTHER POEMS. *New York*, 1940.
The title poem separately issued in wrappers, ₁*New York*, 1933₁.

Iphigenia in Tauris. *New York*, 1915.
Translated and edited by Bynner.
Courage! by Richard Mansfield, 2nd. *New York* ₁1918₁.
Preface by Bynner.
W. B. in California: A Tribute. *Berkeley*, 1919.
Privately printed. 400 copies only.
A Book of Love. *New York* ₁1923₁.
Translated from the French of Charles Vildrac.
Best Poems of 1923. *Boston* ₁1924₁.
Contains "Wistaria," by Bynner.
An Import of China. *Newark*, 1924.
Wrappers.
The Borzoi, 1925. *New York* ₁1925₁.
Also 500 large paper copies. Contains "Kahlil the Gibranite," by Bynner. Also: "The Poetry of Witter Bynner," by James Oppenheim.
Dawn Boy: Blackfoot and Navajo Songs, by Eda Lou Walton. *New York* ₁1926₁.
Preface by Bynner.
Percy MacKaye: A Symposium on His Fiftieth Birthday. *Hanover, N. H.*, 1928.
Contains "Living His Word" by Bynner.
Indian Stories From the Pueblos, by Frank G. Applegate. *Philadelphia*, 1929.
Foreword by Bynner.
The Jade Mountain. *New York*, 1929.
In collaboration with Kiang Kang-Hu. Translated from 300 poems of the T'ang Dynasty.
The Sonnets of Frederick Goddard Tuckerman. *New York*, 1931.
Edited and with an introductory essay by Bynner.
Fifty Poets. *New York* ₁1933₁.
William Rose Benét, editor. Contains a letter by Bynner.
The Smart Set Anthology. *New York* ₁1934₁.
Burton Rascoe and Groff Conklin, editors. Contains "The Shadow" and "A Dead One" by Bynner. *Roscoe* for *Rascoe* on spine.
Designed for Reading. *New York*, 1934.
Contribution.
Best Poems of 1935. *London* ₁1935₁.
Thomas Moult, editor. Contains "Not in Russia" by Bynner.
Selected Poems. *New York*, 1936.
Pictographs of the Southwest. *Cedar Rapids* ₁1937₁.
Contribution.

(Brian Oswald) Donn Byrne

1889–1928

STORIES WITHOUT WOMEN (AND A FEW WITH WOMEN). *New York*, 1915.

THE STRANGERS' BANQUET. *New York* [1919].

M-T on copyright page.

THE FOOLISH MATRONS. *New York* [1920].

I-U on copyright page. Light or dark green cloth with no known priority.

MESSER MARCO POLO. *New York*, 1921.

In the first printing the conjugate of pp. 145-146 is used as the terminal lining paper. In later printings the conjugate of pp. 145-146 is used as a fly-leaf and book has the customary lining paper. The earliest copies have perfect type in the word *of*, last line of p. 10; misspelled *forgetting* (*forgettng*) p. 39, line 3. Copies exist with forged title pages but these have broken type at p. 10.

THE WIND BLOWETH. *New York*, 1922.

First state has misprint, p. 151, line 20, *mouth of money;* later corrected to *mouth of honey.*

CHANGELING AND OTHER STORIES. *New York* [1923].

Two printings in first year with no marks of identification.

BLIND RAFTERY AND HIS WIFE HILÀRIA. *New York* [1924].

Two printings in the first year with no priority as yet established. Issued in both cloth and leather. Noted in two types of cloth: with a diagonal grain, with a vertical rib; no known priority. The earliest copies have perfect type in the last lines of pp. 108 and 138.

O'MALLEY OF SHANGANAGH. *New York* [1925].

Two printings in first year with no known distinction. The earliest published state, preceding trade edition by nine days, is the issue containing a printed notice dated March 5, 1925, stating that the book is for presentation at The Women's National Book Association. Trade edition issued in both cloth and leather. Issued in England as "An Untitled Story."

HANGMAN'S HOUSE. *New York* [1926].

Also 350 large paper copies, signed. *First Printing, March, 1926* on copyright page.

BROTHER SAUL. *New York* [1927].

Also 500 large paper copies, signed. The first trade edition carries notice of second printing on copyright page.

CRUSADE. *Boston*, 1928.

Also 365 large paper copies, signed.

DESTINY BAY. *Boston,* 1928.
Also 365 large paper copies, signed. *Published September, 1928* on copyright page.

IRELAND, THE ROCK WHENCE I WAS HEWN. *Boston,* 1929.
Published July, 1929 on copyright page.

FIELD OF HONOR. *New York* [1929].
Also 500 large paper copies signed by Dorothea Donn-Byrne. Limited edition issued after trade edition. American edition printed July; English edition, as "Power of the Dog," printed September.

A PARTY OF BACCARAT. *New York* [1930].
First printing so stated on copyright page. Issued in both cloth and leather. Issued in England as "The Golden Goat."

RIVERS OF DAMASCUS. *New York* [1931].
First edition so indicated on the copyright page.

A WOMAN OF THE SHEE. *New York* [1932].
First edition so indicated on the copyright page. Previously issued, *London* [1932] under the title, "Sargasso Sea and Other Stories."

THE ISLAND OF YOUTH AND OTHER STORIES. *London* [1932].
New York edition [1933].

AN ALLEY OF FLASHING SPEARS AND OTHER STORIES. *London* [1933].
American edition, *New York,* 1934.

A DAUGHTER OF THE MEDICI. *London* [1933].
American edition, *New York,* 1935.

COLLECTED POEMS. *London,* 1934.

THE HOUND OF IRELAND. *New York,* 1935.
Previously published, *London* [1934].

The Lyric Year. *New York,* 1912.
Contains "The Piper" by Donn Byrne. For further regarding this book see under *Millay.*
Down By The Tan-Yard Side. [*n.p.,* 1914].
Unpublished play. A few sets of galley proofs were pulled, three sheets to the set, for purposes of copyright. A set at The Library of Congress is inscribed by the author with the date January 7, 1914.
War Stories. *New York* [1919].
Contains "Underseaboat F-33" by Byrne.
The Best College Short Stories 1924-1925. *Boston,* 1925.
H. T. Schnittkind and Horace C. Baker, editors. Contains "How I Attained Literary Success" by Donn Byrne.

Dawgs! An Anthology of Dog Stories. *New York*, 1925.
> Contains "Triangle" by Byrne.

Donn Byrne: Bard of Armagh, by Thurston Macauley. *New York* [1929].
> First edition so stated on copyright page.

The Smart Set Anthology. *New York* [1934].
> Burton Rascoe and Groff Conklin, editors. Contains "Réveil" and "The Kingdom of Thule" by Byrne. First state of the binding has *Roscoe* for *Rascoe* on the spine.

Brian Oswald Donn Byrne: A Bibliography, by Winthrop Wetherbee, Jr. *Boston*, 1938.
> Wrappers. The author is preparing an exhaustive revision of this bibliography.

James Branch Cabell (Branch Cabell)

1879–

THE EAGLE'S SHADOW. *New York,* 1904.
First state has dedication *M. L. P. B.;* later: *To Martha Louise Branch.* First state has frontispiece of seated figure.

THE LINE OF LOVE. *New York,* 1905.
Binding in green stamped with white, gold lettering. Revised edition, *New York,* 1921, with two new episodes.

GALLANTRY. *New York,* 1907.
Binding in grey cloth, stamped with white and silver, gold lettering.

THE CORDS OF VANITY. *New York,* 1909.
Cords of Vanity on spine and cover; *The* added later.

CHIVALRY. *New York,* 1909.
Binding is red, stamped with green and white, gold lettering.

THE SOUL OF MELICENT. *New York* [1913].
Binding is dark blue cloth; later black. Revised edition *New York,* 1920, as "Domnei."

THE RIVET IN GRANDFATHER'S NECK. *New York,* 1915.
The seventh printing contains a new preface.

FROM THE HIDDEN WAY. *New York,* 1916.
First state has trimmed edges. Only 620 copies printed, consequently any copy dated 1916 is collectible. With or without short dash under *c* in *McBride* on spine. Mr. Cabell states that "the first ... was that without the short dash ..."

THE CERTAIN HOUR. *New York,* 1916.
Second and later bindings have the kalki stamp on cover.

THE CREAM OF THE JEST. *New York,* 1917.
First state of binding does not have the kalki stamp. Reissued with illustrations and a new preface by the author, *New York,* 1927; first edition so stated on copyright page.

BEYOND LIFE. *New York,* 1919.
Early copies are bound in very dark brown, almost black, cloth. Second printing *Demiurges* corrected to *Démiurges* on title page.

JURGEN. *New York,* 1919.
First state measures about 1¼" across top of covers; second state about ¼" more. Reissued, *New York* [1934] with new introduction by the author.

THE JEWEL MERCHANTS. *New York,* 1921.
One act play. 1,040 copies only. All numbered, first 100 copies signed.

FIGURES OF EARTH. *New York,* 1921.
Also 25 untrimmed copies, signed. Reissued, *New York,* 1925, with new preface.

THE LINEAGE OF LICHFIELD. *New York,* 1922.
365 copies only, numbered and signed.

THE HIGH PLACE. *New York,* 1923.
First edition so stated on copyright page. 2,000 copies only, numbered.

STRAWS AND PRAYER-BOOKS. *New York,* 1924.
First edition so marked. Small paper edition issued October 15; large paper edition, 330 numbered and signed copies, issued November 1.

THE SILVER STALLION. *New York,* 1926.
First edition so marked. Also 850 large paper copies, numbered and signed. Reissued, *New York,* 1928, with new preface.

THE MUSIC FROM BEHIND THE MOON. *New York,* 1926.
3,000 copies only. Of this book Mr. Cabell writes: "... the first state ... has upon the spine a paper label about ⅜ of an inch in width, as opposed to the ½ inch label of later states."

SOMETHING ABOUT EVE. *New York,* 1927.
Marked *First Impression.* Also 850 large paper copies, numbered and signed. Reissued, *New York,* 1929, with new preface.

THE WHITE ROBE. *New York* [1928].
3,290 numbered copies only.

THE WAY OF ECBEN. *New York,* 1929.
First Impression on copyright page. Also 850 large paper signed copies.

SONNETS FROM ANTAN. *New York,* 1929.
718 copies only, signed on the fly-title.

SOME OF US: AN ESSAY IN EPITAPHS. *New York,* 1930.
1,295 signed copies only.

THESE RESTLESS HEADS. *New York,* 1932.
410 signed copies issued three days before Literary Guild and trade editions. The publishers state that the trade edition started with the *Second Printing.*

SPECIAL DELIVERY: A PACKET OF REPLIES. *New York,* 1933.
Also: 7 copies with letter from the author; 26 de luxe copies; 207 large paper copies; all signed. First edition so indicated.

SMIRT. *New York,* 1934.
Also 99 large paper copies, signed. First edition so indicated on the copyright page.

LADIES AND GENTLEMEN. *New York,* 1934.
Also limited and signed copies. First edition so stated on copyright page.

SMITH: A SYLVAN INTERLUDE. *New York*, 1935.
Also 153 large paper copies, signed. First edition so indicated on the copyright page.

PREFACE TO THE PAST. *New York* [1936].
First edition so indicated on the copyright page.

SMIRE: AN ACCEPTANCE IN THE THIRD PERSON. *Garden City*, 1937.
First edition so indicated on the copyright page.

THE KING WAS IN HIS COUNTING HOUSE. *New York* [1938].
Also 125 copies, numbered and signed. First printing has publisher's monogram on copyright page.

HAMLET HAD AN UNCLE. *New York* [1940].
First printing has the publisher's monogram on the copyright page. Also 125 copies, numbered and signed.

The following are genealogical, controversial, or critical. "The Judging of Jurgen" was incorporated in the English edition of "Jurgen." Further details in the bibliographies by I. R. Brussel, Merle Johnson and Guy Holt.

Branchiana. *Richmond, Va.* [1907].
147 copies only.
Branch of Abingdon. *Richmond, Va.* [1911].
The Majors and Their Marriages. *Richmond, Va.* [1915].
The Judging of Jurgen. *Chicago*, 1920.
Wrappers.
Jurgen and the Censor. *New York*, 1920.
458 numbered copies only.
Taboo. *New York*, 1921.
920 numbered copies only, of which 100 are signed. Also a four page leaflet, "The Taboo in Literature" [n.p., n.d.] issued previously.
Joseph Hergesheimer. *Chicago*, 1921.
1,000 in wrappers. The 99 copies in boards constitute a second issue.
Jurgen and the Law, by Guy Holt. *New York*, 1923.
1,080 copies only.
A Round Table in Poictesme. *Cleveland*, 1924.
Limited edition only as follows: 2 copies on handmade paper; 2 copies on handmade paper signed by all the contributors; 248 copies on Japan vellum; 526 copies on paper. Contains "The Author of the Eagle's Shadow," by Cabell. Twelve other authors contributed articles on Cabell.

MISCELLANEOUS

Jamestown Tributes and Toasts. *Lynchburg, Va.*, 1907.
Julia Wyatt Bullard, editor. Contains "The New Virginia," by Cabell.

Johan Bojer, the Man and His Works, by Carl Gad. *New York*, 1920.
   Contains "Critique on the Face of the World," by Cabell.
O. Henry Memorial Award Prize Stories of 1919. *Garden City*, 1920.
   Contains "Porcelain Cups" by Cabell.
The Novel of Tomorrow. *Indianapolis* [1922].
   Contains "A Note on Alcoves" by Cabell.
The Queen Pedauque, by Anatole France. *New York* [1923].
   Modern Library edition. Introduction by Cabell. First edition so stated on copy-
   right page.
Retractions ... 1926.
   Issued by The Cat's Head Club. Reprint material.
The House of Lost Identity, by Donald Corley. *New York*, 1927.
   Introduction by Cabell.
Storisende Edition: The Works of James Branch Cabell. *New York*, 1927-1930.
   18 vols. Definitive edition. 1,590 sets only, numbered and signed by the author.
   The text of each volume revised and with a new introduction for each volume.
   Volume XVIII, "Townsend of Lichfield," is practically all first edition material.
   Certain of the volumes were issued by the publishers as individual volumes.
Breaking Into Print. *New York*, 1937.
   Elmer Adler, editor. Contribution.
The Nightmare Has Triplets. An Author's Note on Smire. [n.p., 1937?]
   Wrappers. 1,700 copies only.
Of Ellen Glasgow, An Inscribed Portrait. By Ellen Glasgow and James Branch
   Cabell. *New York*, 1938.
   109 copies only.

Ballades From the Hidden Way, by James Branch Cabell. *New York*, 1928.
   839 copies only. All reprint material with the exception of the introduction.
Cabellian Harmonics, by Warren A. McNeill. *New York*, 1928.
   1,500 numbered copies only. Foreword by Cabell.
Notes on Jurgen, by J. P. Cover. *New York*, 1928.
   850 copies only.
Notes on Figures of Earth, by J. P. Cranwell and J. P. Cover. *New York*, 1929.
   865 numbered copies only.
Between Dawn and Sunrise. *New York*, 1930.
   An anthology of Cabell's writings edited by John Macy.
The Colophon, No. 7. *New York*, 1931.
   Contains "Recipes For Writers," by Cabell.
The American Spectator Year Book. *New York*, 1934.
   Sherwood Anderson and others, editors. Contribution by Cabell.
The Smart Set Anthology. *New York* [1934].
   Burton Rascoe and Groff Conklin, editors. First state of binding has *Roscoe* for
   Rascoe on the spine. Contains Cabell's "Some Ladies and Jurgen," 'the short
   story out of which Cabell's famous novel "Jurgen" was evolved.'
Books About Poictesme. An Imaginative Bibliography, by Walter Klinefelter.
   Chicago, 1937.
   Boards.

BIOGRAPHICAL AND BIBLIOGRAPHICAL

The Art of James Branch Cabell, by Hugh Walpole. *New York*, 1920.

A Bibliographic Check List of the Works of James Branch Cabell, by Merle Johnson. *New York*, 1921.

Preface by Cabell. Colophon states limited to 250 copies but actually only 214 copies were received by the publisher.

A Bibliography of the Writings of James Branch Cabell, by Guy Holt. *Philadelphia*, 1924.

99 large paper copies, signed. Foreword by Cabell.

James Branch Cabell, by Carl Van Doren. *New York*, 1925.

Revised and reissued, *New York*, 1932.

James Branch Cabell, by H. L. Mencken. *New York*, 1927-1928.

Large paper edition of 110 copies misdated 1928. Small paper edition properly dated 1927. Issued simultaneously.

A Bibliography of the Writings of James Branch Cabell, by I. R. Brussel. *Philadelphia*, 1932.

450 copies only of which 100 were on large paper and signed by compiler and subject. Introduction by Cabell.

George W[ashington] Cable

1844–1925

OLD CREOLE DAYS. *New York,* 1879.

Earliest copies have no advertisements at the back of the book. Later copies have advertisements, the earliest of the latter having no mention of the present title. "Madame Delphine" added after first edition. Reissued *New York,* 1883, 2 vols., paper or cloth.

THE GRANDISSIMES. *New York,* 1880.

MADAME DELPHINE. *New York,* 1881.

THE CREOLES OF LOUISIANA. *New York,* 1884.

Also issued in a de luxe edition, simultaneous publication.

DR. SEVIER. *Boston,* 1885.

Probably preceded by the *Edinburgh,* 1884, edition in 2 vols. First American edition has no table of contents.

THE SILENT SOUTH. *New York,* 1885.

Revised and reissued with additions, *New York,* 1889.

BONAVENTURE. *New York,* 1888.

STRANGE TRUE STORIES OF LOUISIANA. *New York,* 1889.

THE NEGRO QUESTION. *New York,* 1890.

This is a reprint, with additional material, of the pamphlets, "The Negro Question" [*New York,* 1888] and "The Southern Struggle For Pure Government," *Boston,* 1890.

THE BUSY MAN'S BIBLE. *Meadville, Pa.,*1891.

JOHN MARCH: SOUTHERNER. *New York,* 1894.

First binding is light green with gold and green stamping. Second binding dark green with white and blind stamping.

STRONG HEARTS. *New York,* 1899.

THE CAVALIER. *New York,* 1901.

First state of binding front cover has sword and wing design stamped in black with lettering and ornament in gold. Later, white substituted for the gold. Reissued, *New York,* 1903, "Julia Marlowe Edition," with new preface.

BYLOW HILL. *New York,* 1902.

KINCAID'S BATTERY. *New York,* 1908.

Copies with the *Caxton Press* slug on the copyright page published October 31,

1908. Copies with the *Scribner* slug published December 12, 1908. First binding stamped in gold and color; later bindings stamped in white.

"POSSON JONE'" AND PÈRE RAPHAËL. *New York,* 1909.

First title reprinted from "Old Creole Days"; second title, the sequel, here first collected but privately printed, 1901, wrappers, four copies only.

GIDEON'S BAND. *New York,* 1914.

THE AMATEUR GARDEN. *New York,* 1914.

THE FLOWER OF THE CHAPDELAINES. *New York,* 1918.

LOVERS OF LOUISIANA. *New York,* 1918.

Social Statistics of Cities. *Washington,* 1881.
 With George E. Waring.
Historical Sketch Book and Guide to New Orleans. *New York,* 1885.
 Prefatory note by Cable recommending the book and part of the footnote at p. 298. *See:* Hearn checklist for complete description of this item.
The Negro Question. ₍*New York,* 1888₎.
 Wrappers. *See above:* "The Negro Question," 1890.
Shall the Negro Be Educated or Suppressed? *Nashville,* 1889.
 Contains a letter by Cable.
The Southern Struggle for Pure Government. *Boston,* 1890.
 Wrappers. *See above:* "The Negro Question," 1890.
A Memory of Roswell Smith. ₍*New York,* 1892₎.
 Privately printed.
Famous Adventures and Prison Escapes of the Civil War. *New York,* 1893.
 Edited and with an introductory note to the first article, "War Diary of a Union Woman in the South."
The Cable Story Book. *New York,* 1899.
 Mary E. Burt and Lucy Leffingwell Cable, editors. Selections from previously published writings.
A House Party. *Boston,* 1901.
 Contains "Angel of the Lord" by Cable.
The Voice of the Garden, by Lucy Leffingwell Cable Biklé. *London and New York,* 1902.
 Preface by Cable.
Liber Scriptorum. *New York,* 1921.
 "The Second Book of the Author's Club." Contains "Malvina" by Cable.
George W. Cable: His Life and Letters. *New York,* 1928.
 Edited by Lucy Leffingwell Cable Biklé.
The Trail of the Comet, by Mary Cable Dennis. *New York,* 1937.
 Biography. First edition so indicated on the copyright page.

Erskine (Preston) Caldwell

1903–

THE BASTARD. *New York* [1929].
  1,100 numbered copies only. Copies 1-200 signed by author and illustrator.

POOR FOOL. *New York*, 1930.
  1,000 numbered copies only.

AMERICAN EARTH. *New York*, 1931.
  First edition has code letter *A* on copyright page.

TOBACCO ROAD. *New York*, 1932.
  First edition has code letter *A* on copyright page. Dramatization by Jack Kirk-
  land, *New York* [1934]. Reissued with a new introduction by the author, *New
  York*, 1941.

GOD'S LITTLE ACRE. *New York*, 1933.
  The fifth printing contains an appendix. Modern Library Edition, *New York*
  [1934] contains an introduction by the author; first edition so stated on copyright page.

WE ARE THE LIVING. *New York*, 1933.
  Also 250 copies on rag paper, numbered, signed by the author.

JOURNEYMAN. [*New York*, 1935].
  1,475 numbered copies only. Revised edition, *New York*, 1938.

KNEEL TO THE RISING SUN. *New York*, 1935.
  Also 300 copies, numbered and signed, top edges gilt; 285 offered for sale.

SOME AMERICAN PEOPLE. *New York* [1935].
  First edition so stated on copyright page.

YOU HAVE SEEN THEIR FACES. *New York*, 1937.
  With Margaret Bourke-White. De luxe edition with Viking imprint. Reissued in
  a popular edition by Modern Age.

SOUTHWAYS. *New York*, 1938.
  Published in June 1938 on copyright page.

NORTH OF THE DANUBE. *New York* [1939].
  With Margaret Bourke-White.

TROUBLE IN JULY. *New York* [1940].
  First edition indicated on the copyright page.

JACKPOT. *New York* [1940].
  First edition so indicated on the copyright page.

SAY, IS THIS THE U. S. A. *New York* [1941].
  With Margaret Bourke-White. First edition indicated on copyright page.

In Defense of Myself. *Portland, Maine* [1930].
  Broadside. Privately printed.
Mamma's Little Girl. *Mount Vernon, Maine,* 1932.
  Pamphlet. 75 copies only signed by the author.
A Message for Genevieve. *Mount Vernon, Maine,* 1933.
  Pamphlet. 100 numbered copies only, signed by the author; frontispiece signed
  by the artist.
Tenant Farmer. *New York* [1935].
  Said to be but 1,500 copies in the first printing; green wrappers lettered in
  orange. Appears in "Some American People" as "Southern Tenant Farmers."
So Red the Nose. *New York* [1935].
  Contribution.
The Sacrilege of Alan Kent. *Portland, Maine,* 1936.
A Southern Harvest. *Boston,* 1937.
  Robert Penn Warren, editor. Contribution.
The Cock's Funeral, by Ben Field. *New York* [1937].
  Introduction.
The Bedside Esquire. *New York* [1940].
  Arnold Gingrich, editor. Contribution.

Mr. Caldwell is the editor of the "American Folkways" series currently published
by Duell, Sloan & Pearce, New York. As projected the series will comprise six titles.
Already published are "Desert Country," by Edwin Corle, *New York* [1941], first
printing so indicated on copyright page; and "Piñon Country" by Hamill Long, *New
York* [1941], first printing so indicated on copyright page.

(William) Bliss Carman

1861–1929

LOW TIDE ON GRAND PRÉ. *Toronto* [1889? 1890?].

Wrappers. Piracy. Author's name misspelled *Carmen*. All but a few copies destroyed by fire.

LOW TIDE ON GRAND PRÉ: A BOOK OF LYRICS. *New York*, 1893.

Reprints preceding item with additions. Reissued, *Cambridge and Chicago* 1894, of which there were also 50 signed large paper copies.

SONGS FROM VAGABONDIA. *Boston*, 1894.

With RICHARD HOVEY. Boards. 810 copies, of which 60 copies were large paper; ten of the latter not for sale.

BEHIND THE ARRAS: A BOOK OF THE UNSEEN. *Boston*, 1895.

Boards. Later states add the imprint of Briggs (*Toronto*) and Mathews (*London*). It is said that three or four copies were printed with brown ink.

MORE SONGS FROM VAGABONDIA. *Boston*, 1896.

With RICHARD HOVEY. Boards. Also 60 large paper copies.

BALLADS OF LOST HAVEN: A BOOK OF THE SEA. *Boston*, 1897.

BY THE AURELIAN WALL AND OTHER ELEGIES. *Boston*, 1898.

A WINTER HOLIDAY. *Boston*, 1899.

Boards. Title poem separately issued [*New York*, 1898] anonymous, 4to folder.

THE VENGEANCE OF NOEL BRASSARD: A TALE OF THE ACADIAN EXPULSION. *Cambridge*, 1919(!) [1899].

Boards. 100 copies only, privately printed. Title page misdated MDCCCCXIX.

LAST SONGS FROM VAGABONDIA. *Boston*, 1901.

With RICHARD HOVEY. Boards. Also 60 large paper copies of which but 50 were for sale.

CHRISTMAS EVE AT ST. KAVIN'S. *New York*, 1901.

222 copies only of which there were for sale 160 copies on handmade paper, 10 on Japan vellum, 2 on parchment.

BALLADS AND LYRICS. *London*, 1902.

A. H. Bullen, editor. Contains material here first collected. Same title reissued with similar material, *Toronto* [1923] and *Boston*, 1924.

ODE ON THE CORONATION OF KING EDWARD. *Boston*, 1902.

Boards. Preceded by an issue of 9 copies in wrappers titled "A Coronation Ode," *Boston*, 1902; for copyright purposes.

FROM THE BOOK OF MYTHS. *Boston*, 1902.
  The Pipes of Pan. Number One. Cloth or stamped leather; later in limp leather. Reissued, *London* [1903] with added material. With added material, *Boston*, 1904.

FROM THE GREEN BOOK OF THE BARDS. *Boston*, 1903.
  The Pipes of Pan. Number Two. Cloth or stamped leather; later in limp leather.

THE WORD AT ST. KAVIN'S. *Nelson, N.H.* [1903].
  300 copies only.

SONGS OF THE SEA CHILDREN. *Boston*, 1904.
  The Pipes of Pan. Number Three. Some late copies in limp leather.

THE KINSHIP OF NATURE. *Boston*, 1904.

SONGS FROM A NORTHERN GARDEN. *Boston*, 1904.
  The Pipes of Pan. Number Four. Some late copies in limp leather. Verso of title page states that the book was published September, 1903.

SAPPHO: ONE HUNDRED LYRICS. *Boston*, 1904.
  500 copies in boards on deckle edge paper; 200 on Albon handmade paper; 50 signed copies on Japan vellum. Fifteen of the lyrics privately printed [*New York*, 1902], 60 copies only signed by the author.

THE FRIENDSHIP OF ART. *Boston*, 1904.

POEMS. *New York*, 1904.
  2 vols. 500 signed copies only: 350 for America, 150 for England. American edition issued in 1905 with a new title page and additional material; various bindings. English edition: 50 in maroon buckram, balance in wrappers.

FROM THE BOOK OF VALENTINES. *Boston*, 1905.
  The Pipes of Pan. Number Five. Also 150 copies in limp leather.

THE POETRY OF LIFE. *Boston*, 1905.

THE PRINCESS OF THE TOWER. *New York*, 1906.
  62 copies only numbered and signed by the author, of which 4 copies on vellum.

PIPES OF PAN. *Boston*, 1906.
  Definitive edition of the five "Pipes of Pan," issued 1902-3-4-4-5.

THE GATE OF PEACE. *New York*, 1907.
  Boards. 112 copies only of which all but 24 were destroyed by fire. Reissued in an edition of 60 copies, signed, *New Canaan*, 1909.

THE MAKING OF PERSONALITY. *Boston*, 1908.

THE ROUGH RIDER AND OTHER POEMS. *New York*, 1909.

A PAINTER'S HOLIDAY AND OTHER POEMS. *New York*, 1911.

155 copies only, privately printed; 150 on handmade paper, five on vellum. The paper copies on Italian handmade paper are first; copies on French handmade paper issued to replace the original paper copies, most of which were destroyed.

ADDRESS TO THE GRADUATING CLASS ... *New York*, 1911.

250 copies only. Privately printed. Copies remain unbound; copies issued bound in boards.

ECHOES FROM VAGABONDIA. *Boston*, 1912.

First state has Hovey's name on front cover as co-author; second state has Carman's name pasted over original printing; third state has Carman's name properly printed.

DAUGHTERS OF DAWN: A LYRICAL PAGEANT. *New York*, 1913.

With MARY PERRY KING.

EARTH DEITIES AND OTHER RHYTHMIC MASQUES. *New York*, 1914.

With MARY PERRY KING.

APRIL AIRS: A BOOK OF NEW ENGLAND LYRICS. *Boston*, 1916.

Boards.

JAMES WHITCOMB RILEY: AN ESSAY. *New York* [1918].

250 signed copies only. Privately printed for George D. Smith, first state having his imprint.

LATER POEMS. *Toronto* [1921].

Selected and with an appreciation by R. H. Hathaway. Contains material here first collected. First state has misprint *murmer* on front end paper; only about 50 copies so printed. Also 12 copies in full morocco, *Boston* [1922].

FAR HORIZONS. *Boston* [1925].

TALKS ON POETRY AND LIFE. *Toronto*, 1926.

Blanche Hume, editor. 206 copies only of which 6 are on large paper. All signed.

WILD GARDEN. *New York*, 1929.

SANCTUARY: SUNSHINE HOUSE THOUGHTS. *New York*, 1929.

Also 20 copies in yellow cloth.

THE MUSIC OF EARTH. *Toronto*, 1931.

Wrappers. 250 copies only with the Toronto imprint and 50 copies [New York] 1931, for copyright purposes. Lorne Pierce, editor.

BLISS CARMAN'S POEMS. *New York*, 1931.

BROADSHEETS, PAMPHLETS, ETC.

Death in April. ₁*Fredericton, N. B.*, 1888₁.
 Wrappers.
A Woman's Exile, *etc.* ₁*Fredericton, N. B.*, 1888₁.
 Broadsheet. It is believed that the heading was removed from all copies.
Tidings. *Fredericton, N. B.* ₁1889₁.
 Galley proof.
Signal. *Fredericton, N. B.* ₁1889₁.
 Galley proof.
Guendolen ₁and₁ Marjory. *Fredericton, N. B.*, 1889.
 Broadsheet.
The Kelpie Riders. ₁*Windsor, N. S.*₁ 1889.
 Broadsheet.
Marian Drurie. ₁*Windsor, N. S.*, 1889₁.
Pulvis et Umbra, *etc.* ₁*New York*, 1890₁.
 Broadsheet. Some copies in two parts.
A Windflower. ₁*New York*₁ 1890.
 4 pp. leaflet.
The Last Watch. *New York*, 1891.
 Galley proof privately pulled for the author. Blue or white paper.
A Sailor's Wedding. *New York*, 1891.
 Broadsheet.
The Trail of the Bugle. *New York*, 1891.
 Galley proof privately pulled for the author.
The Yule Guest. *New York*, 1891.
 Broadsheet.
A Pagan's Prayer. ₁*New York*₁ 1891.
 4 pp. leaflet.
The Grave Tree, *etc. New York*, 1892.
 Folder.
Marjory Darrow. *New York*, 1892.
 Galley proof privately pulled for the author.
Crispin Hjöward. *New York* ₁1892₁.
 Broadsheet. Privately printed. Suppressed and reprinted in broadsheet form as
 "Olaf Hjöward," *New York*, 1892.
The Vagabonds. *New York*, 1892.
 Galley proof privately pulled for the author.
The Wind and the Tree. *New York*, 1892.
 Broadsheet.
In the Heart of the Hills. *New York*, 1892.
 Galley proof privately pulled for the author.
An April Alibi. *New York* ₁1892₁.
 Broadsheet.
The Master of the Isles, *etc. New York*, 1892.
 Broadsheet.

The White Gull. *New York,* 1892.
  Broadsheet.
Saint Kavin: A Ballad. *Cambridge,* 1894.
  50 copies only including 6 on vellum. Wrappers.
At Michaelmas: A Lyric. [*Wolfville, N. S.*] 1895.
  100 copies only. Wrappers.
A Seamark: A Threnody for Robert Louis Stevenson. *Boston,* 1895.
  Also 50 copies on handmade paper. Wrappers.
Ninety-Six: A Calendar for 1896. *Toronto* [1896].
  With Charles D. G. Roberts. Wrappers.
The Girl in the Poster. [*Springfield, Mass.*] 1897.
  Wrappers. 100 copies only.
The Green Book of the Bards. *Cambridge,* 1898.
  100 copies only. Wrappers.
A Winter Holiday. [*New York,* 1898].
  60 copies only. First published edition, with added poems, *Boston,* 1899.
Moonshine Songs and Ballads. *Twilight Park, N. Y.,* 1901.
  Four broadsheets: "The Spell," "The Sceptics," "Vagabond Song," and "Daisies [and] Marigolds."
Sappho: Lyrics. [*New York*] 1902.
  60 copies only. Wrappers.
A Vision of Sappho. [*New York*] 1903.
  60 copies only. Wrappers. A few copies issued, *Boston,* 1905, for copyright purposes.
The Path of Sankoty. *Siaconset, Mass.,* 1908.
  4 pp. leaflet.
An Apostle of Personal Harmonizing. [*New Canaan, Conn.,* 1911].
  Wrappers.
To Those Who Wear Shoes. *New York,* 1913.
  Wrappers.
Christmas Eve: A Choral. *New Canaan, Conn.,* 1913.
  Folder.
Four Sonnets. *Boston* [1916].
  438 copies only. Wrappers.
The Man of the Marne and Other Poems. *New Canaan, Conn.,* 1918.
  300 copies only. With MARY PERRY KING.
An Open Letter. [*New Canaan, Conn.*] 1920.
  Broadsheet. About 20 copies only.
An Open Letter From Bliss Carman. *Boston* [1920].
  Wrappers.
Bethlehem. [*Toronto,* 1928].
  Folder.
On Bibliomania: A Letter. *New York,* 1931.
  Folder.

BOOKS WITH CONTRIBUTIONS

Northland Lyrics, by W. C. Roberts, *etc. Boston*, 1889.
  Epilogue by Carman.
Silas Marner, by George Eliot. *Boston*, 1895.
  Wrappers. Introduction by Carman.
Nugæ Illiteratæ. [*New York*] 1899.
  150 copies only, privately printed.
The Summer Cloud: Prose Poems, by Yone Noguchi. *Tokyo*, 1905.
  Wrappers. Introduction by Carman.
The Holy Graal and Other Fragments, by Richard Hovey. *New York*, 1907.
  Preface by Carman.
Travelers Five Along Life's Highway, by Annie Fellows Johnston. *Boston*, 1911.
  Foreword by Carman.
Claude Debussy. *Boston*, 1913.
  Wrappers. Translated by Carman.
Album of Six Songs, by Henri Duparc. *Boston*, 1914.
  Wrappers. Translated by Carman.
The Oxford Book of American Verse. *New York*, 1927.
  Edited by Carman.

BIOGRAPHICAL AND BIBLIOGRAPHICAL

Bliss Carman, by Goodridge Bliss Roberts. [*Windsor, N. S.*, 188?].
  Broadsheet.
To the President, Johns Hopkins University. [*Fredericton, N. B.*, 1886].
  Application for a fellowship in English. Testimonials of W. Bliss Carman. Folder.
Bliss Carman: A Study in Canadian Poetry, by H. D. C. Lee. *Buxton* [*England*] 1912.
  Wrappers. With bibliography.
To Bliss Carman: On the Anniversary of His Nativity ... A Little Anthology by Four Admirers [R. H. and E. J. Hathaway, J. D. Logan and Newton Mactavish]. *Toronto*, 1913.
  Privately printed. 100 numbered copies only, signed by the contributors. Wrappers.
A Check List of the First Editions of Bliss Carman, by Frederic Fairchild Sherman. *New York*, 1915.
  Wrappers. 75 copies only.
Bliss Carman, by Odell Shepard. *Toronto* [1923].
  Contains a check list of Carman's works. First state of first edition does not have artist's name on the frontispiece.
The Poetry of Bliss Carman, A Review of Odell Shepard's *Bliss Carman*, by R. H. Hathaway. [*Toronto*, 1925].
  25 copies only. Wrappers.
In The Offing: A Tribute to Bliss Carman. [*Halifax*, 1929].
Bliss Carman: 1861-1929, by Julian Hawthorne. *Palo Alto, Calif.*, 1929.
  20 copies only. Wrappers.

CARMAN

Bliss Carman and the Literary Influences of His Time, by James Cappon. *New York*, 1929.

Preceded by the Toronto edition.

The Prince of Song (Bliss Carman), by Frederic Fairchild Sherman. *New York*, 1930.

50 copies only. Wrappers.

Bliss Carman's Scrap Book ... A Table of Contents ... *Toronto* [1931].

Lorne Pierce, editor. Wrappers. 75 copies only.

Willa (Sibert) Cather
1876–

APRIL TWILIGHTS. *Boston,* 1903.

Boards, paper label. Some copies noted with a tipped in "Literary Note." Revised and reissued, *New York,* 1923, also 450 signed copies. Reissued, *New York,* 1933, with added material.

THE TROLL GARDEN. *New York,* 1905.

McClure Phillips & Co. at foot of spine. All examined copies of the first edition have the subtitle for "The Marriage of Phædra" tipped in on a stub; this was probably done in order to correct an error, but thus far no copy has been noted with error. Later copies have the leaf bound in.

ALEXANDER'S BRIDGE. *Boston,* 1912.

Author's name on the spine: *Willa S. Cather;* later, *Willa Cather.* Copies have been noted in blue, green, beige, lavender and white cloths. Frederick B. Adams, Jr., in his notes on Willa Cather (*The Colophon, New Graphic Series,* Parts 3 and 4, 1939-1940) identifies the first issue as follows: "... blue mesh cloth with gilt stamping, title and author's name contained in one rectangular box on front cover, with preliminaries in correct order," that is, "(i) half-title, (ii) blank, (iii) title page, (iv) copyright notice." Reissued, *Boston,* 1922 and 1933, with new introductions.

O PIONEERS! *Boston,* 1913.

Either tan or cream ribbed cloth; later, brown cloth. The last page of text is printed on the recto of a single inserted leaf. Reissued, *Boston,* 1923, with preface.

MY AUTOBIOGRAPHY, BY S. S. MC CLURE. *New York* [1914].

September, 1914 on the copyright page. "... ostensibly by S. S. McClure, but actually written entirely by Willa Cather." F. B. Adams, Jr.

THE SONG OF THE LARK. *Boston,* 1915.

Ribbed and smooth cloth, priority undetermined. Advertisements appear either opposite the half-title or on the copyright page. It is probable that the earliest copies have the advertisements on the copyright page; a copy of the tenth printing has been noted with the advertisements opposite the half-title. Reissued with new preface, *London,* 1932.

MY ÁNTONIA. *Boston,* 1918.

Although reprints of this title have been noted with the illustrations printed on glazed paper and inserted, as well as on book-stock and integral parts of their respective signatures, all early inscribed copies noted have the illustrations on glazed paper and inserted. It seems highly likely that the earliest copies have inserted illustrations printed on glazed paper. New and revised edition, *Boston,* 1926.

YOUTH AND THE BRIGHT MEDUSA. *New York*, 1920.
Also 25 uncut copies, signed.

ONE OF OURS. *New York*, 1922.
Also 310 large paper copies on handmade paper and 35 copies on Japan vellum; signed. Of the trade issue there were 250 copies bound in boards with a notice "... made for bookseller friends ..."

A LOST LADY. *New York*, 1923.
Also 220 large paper copies; 20 lettered *A-T*, balance numbered 1-200. Trade edition first issued in green cloth, gold stamped; later tan cloth, gold and orange stamped.

THE PROFESSOR'S HOUSE. *New York*, 1925.
Also 225 large paper copies, numbered and signed of which 40 were on Japan vellum.

MY MORTAL ENEMY. *New York*, 1926.
Also 220 copies on Japan vellum numbered and signed. Boards.

DEATH COMES FOR THE ARCHBISHOP. *New York*, 1927.
Also 220 large paper copies: 170 on rag paper and 50 on Japan vellum, signed. Reissued with illustrations, *New York*, 1929; also 170 signed de luxe copies.

SHADOWS ON THE ROCK. *New York*, 1931.
Also 199 copies on Japan vellum and 619 copies on rag paper, all numbered and signed. First edition so stated on copyright page.

OBSCURE DESTINIES. *New York*, 1932.
Also 260 signed copies on Japan vellum. First edition so indicated on the copyright page.

LUCY GAYHEART. *New York*, 1935.
Also 749 large paper copies, numbered and signed by the author. First printing so stated on copyright page.

NOT UNDER FORTY. *New York*, 1936.
First printing indicated on the copyright page. Also 333 copies on Japan vellum, numbered and signed.

SAPPHIRA AND THE SLAVE GIRL. *New York*, 1940.
Also 520 large paper copies, numbered and signed. First edition so indicated on the copyright page. Also copies of the trade edition, issued in advance of publication, with the statement *Complimentary Advance Copy* printed on the preliminary end paper.

The Sombrero. *Lincoln, Neb.* [1894].
Contains "The Fear that Walks by Noonday," written in collaboration with Dorothy Canfield. Reissued in a small separate edition, *New York*, 1931.

The Life of Mary Baker G. Eddy and the History of Christian Science, by Georgine Milmine. *New York,* 1909.
Edited.

The New Poetry. *New York,* 1917.
Harriet Monroe and Alice Corbin Henderson, editors. Contains two poems by Miss Cather.

The Borzoi 1920. *New York,* 1920.
Contains Cather's "On the Art of Writing Fiction."

The Fortunate Mistress, by Daniel Defoe. *New York,* 1924.
Introduction by Miss Cather.

Modern Essays: Second Series. *New York,* 1924.
Edited by Christopher Morley. Contribution.

These United States: Second Series. *New York* [1924].
Contribution.

The Borzoi 1925. *New York* [1925].
Also 500 de luxe copies. Contains "Katherine Mansfield" by Cather. Also an essay on Miss Cather by Thomas Beer. The first printing gives Miss Cather's birthdate as 1867 at p. 246; later corrected to 1876.

The Best Short Stories of Sarah Orne Jewett. *Boston,* 1925.
2 vols. Edited and with an introduction by Miss Cather.

Wagnerian Romances, by Gertrude Hall. *New York,* 1925.
Introduction.

The Work of Stephen Crane. *New York* [1925-1926].
12 vols. Introduction vol. 9 by Miss Cather.

The Best Short Stories of 1929. *New York,* 1929.
Edward J. O'Brien, editor. Contains a short story by Miss Cather.

The Colophon, Part Six. *New York,* 1931.
Contains "My First Novels ... There Were Two," by Miss Cather.

December Night. [*New York,* 1933].
Reprinted from "Death Comes For the Archbishop."

Designed for Reading. *New York,* 1934.
Contribution by Cather.

1940. Alfred A. Knopf: Quarter Century. [*New York,* 1940].
Paper labels. Contribution.

BIOGRAPHICAL

Willa Cather: A Biographical Sketch ... *New York* [ca. 1926].
Pamphlet. Reissued, *New York* [ca. 1933] containing, with other added material, a letter previously published in an 8 pp. leaflet [*London,* 1927?] by Heinemann.

Willa Cather, by René Rapin. *New York,* 1930.

Charles W[addell] Chesnutt

1868–1933

THE CONJURE WOMAN. *Boston*, 1899.
   Also 150 large paper copies with paper label on the spine which, according to the
   author, were issued in advance of the trade edition.

THE WIFE OF HIS YOUTH. *Boston*, 1899.

FREDERICK DOUGLASS. *Boston*, 1899.

THE HOUSE BEHIND THE CEDARS. *Boston*, 1900.

THE MARROW OF TRADITION. *Boston*, 1901.

THE COLONEL'S DREAM. *New York*, 1905.
   Published, September, 1905 on the copyright page.

American Orators and Oratory: Lectures Delivered at Western Reserve University,
   by Thomas Wentworth Higginson. *Cleveland*, 1901.
   "Reported" by Chesnutt. 500 numbered copies only.
The Negro Problem. *New York*, 1903.
   Printed September, 1903 on the copyright page. Contains Chesnutt's "The Disen-
   franchisement of the Negro."
The Colophon: Part Five, *New York*, 1931.
   Contains "Post Bellum—Pre-Harlem" by Chesnutt.

Thomas Holley Chivers
1809–1858

THE PATH OF SORROW. *Franklin, T[enn.]* 1832.

CONRAD AND EUDORA. *Philadelphia,* 1834.

NACOOCHEE. *New York,* 1837.

THE LOST PLEIAD AND OTHER POEMS. *New York,* 1845.

SEARCH AFTER TRUTH. *New York,* 1848.

EONCHS OF RUBY. A GIFT OF LOVE. *New York,* 1851.

MEMORALIA. *Philadelphia,* 1853.
Reissue of the preceding book with new title page and added material.

VIRGINALIA. *Philadelphia,* 1853.

A GIFT OF THE BEAUTIFUL. *Philadelphia,* 1853.

ATLANTA. *Macon, Georgia,* 1853.
Wrappers.

BIRTH-DAY SONG OF LIBERTY. *Atlanta, Georgia,* 1856.
Wrappers.

THE SONS OF USNA: A TRAGI-APOTHEOSIS IN FIVE ACTS. *Philadelphia,* 1858.
Wrappers.

In the Poe Circle, With Some Account of the Poe-Chivers Controversy, by Joel
Benton. *New York* [1899].
Thomas Holley Chivers: A Selection by Lewis Chase. *Oglethorpe University Press,*
1929.
Thomas Holley Chivers ... by S[amuel] Foster Damon. *New York,* 1930.
Poe and Chivers, by Landon C. Bell. *Columbus, Ohio,* 1931.

Winston Churchill

1871–

THE CELEBRITY. *New York*, 1898.

RICHARD CARVEL. *New York*, 1899.
Reissued, 1914, with new preface by the author.

THE CRISIS. *New York*, 1901.
P. 257, line 38, *its head* for *his head*.

MR. KEEGAN'S ELOPEMENT. *New York*, 1903.

THE CROSSING. *New York*, 1904.
Portions appeared serially in *Collier's Weekly*, December 1903, as "The Border-land."

CONISTON. *New York*, 1906.
Also 100 copies on vellum, signed by the author.

MR. CREWE'S CAREER. *New York*, 1908.

A MODERN CHRONICLE. *New York*, 1910.

THE INSIDE OF THE CUP. *New York*, 1913.

A FAR COUNTRY. *New York*, 1915.
Advance copies have been noted with the top edges stained.

THE DWELLING-PLACE OF LIGHT. *New York*, 1917.

A TRAVELLER IN WAR-TIME. *New York*, 1918.

THE UNCHARTED WAY. *Philadelphia* [1940].

The Title-Mart. *New York*, 1905.
Three act comedy.
Anecdotes of the Hour. *New York* [1914].
Contribution.
The Faith of Frances Craniford. [*n.p.*] 1917.
Written and printed for the Church Pension Fund. Loosely inserted, later as an integral part, is a facsimile Churchill letter regarding publication of story. Boards, later wrappers.
Dr. Jonathan. *New York*, 1919.
Three act play.
St. Louis After the War. *St. Louis*, 1918.
Introduction.

The Crisis. *New York,* 1927.
  Four act play. Of this Mr. Churchill states: "I did not write the *Crisis* as a play
  and had nothing to do with it. I do not think it should be set forth as my work."

Winston Churchill: A Sketch of the Author of *Coniston. New York,* 1906.
  Anonymous. 16 pp. pamphlet.

Samuel L[anghorne] Clemens
(Mark Twain)
1835–1910

THE CELEBRATED JUMPING FROG OF CALAVERAS COUNTY AND OTHER SKETCHES. *New York,* 1867.

First state has perfect *i* last line, last page of text. Also, yellow leaf of publisher's advertisements facing title page, inserted. Title story, with revisions and deletions by an unknown editor, appeared previously in "Beadle's Dime Book of Fun," No. 3, *New York* [1866].

THE INNOCENTS ABROAD. *Hartford,* 1869.

First state does not have picture of Napoleon III at p. 129; also, does not have reference numbers, last page of table of contents.

MARK TWAIN'S (BURLESQUE) AUTOBIOGRAPHY. *New York* [1871].

Cloth or wrappers. Copyright notice at center of copyright page, without advertisements for Ball, Black and Company.

ROUGHING IT. *Hartford,* 1872.

Perfect *M,* first word table of contents, p. xi; perfect *My* first word of text, p. 19. Also, first state has no missing words or letters, p. 242, lines 20 and 21.

THE GILDED AGE. *Hartford,* 1873.

In collaboration with Charles Dudley Warner. At p. xvi the list of illustrations must end with *211;* not *212.* No illustration at p. 403. For a full discussion of the bibliographical features of this book see "The Gilded Age: A Collation," in *The Publishers' Weekly,* July 20, 1940.

MARK TWAIN'S SKETCHES: NEW AND OLD. *Hartford,* 1875.

First state prints "From Hospital Days" at p. 299; also, erratum slip at same place. Duplicated note at pp. 119 and 120.

THE ADVENTURES OF TOM SAWYER. *Hartford,* 1876.

First state on calendared paper, with half title and preface versos blank. Measures 1″ across top of covers. English edition published about six months earlier.

A TRUE STORY. *Boston,* 1877.

First binding has *J R O* monogram at center of front cover.

PUNCH, BROTHERS, PUNCH! *New York* [1878].

Cloth or wrappers. First state has *Mark Twain* in Roman type on the title page.

A TRAMP ABROAD. *Hartford,* 1880.

Frontispiece is captioned *Moses;* later, *Titian's Moses.* Engraved portrait frontispiece shows, in the first state, an underlying field of vertically engraved lines;

later states have these lines on the diagonal. A copy, probably an experimental binding, has been noted in blue cloth.

THE PRINCE AND THE PAUPER. *Boston*, 1882.

First state has the imprint of the *Franklin Press* on the copyright page. Also a few copies printed on China paper for presentation.

THE STOLEN WHITE ELEPHANT, etc. *Boston*, 1882.

English edition published four days before the American.

LIFE ON THE MISSISSIPPI. *Boston*, 1883.

First state has picture of Mark Twain in flames at p. 441. Suppressed sheets later issued with a new title page bearing the imprint of *Webster*. English edition issued five days prior to the first American.

THE ADVENTURES OF HUCKLEBERRY FINN. *New York*, 1885.

The first edition exists in varying states; the collector is referred to the exhaustive study at pp. 43-50 of the revised Mark Twain bibliography by Merle Johnson (*Harper, New York*, 1935). Definite first state points are: *was* for *saw*, p. 57, line 23; *Him and Another Man* listed as at p. 88, in the list of illustrations. It is now established that the leaf constituting pp. 283-284 exists in the following states: 1st: bound in; 2nd: bound in but the plate on p. 283 defaced; 3rd: the leaf tipped in, the plate on p. 283 having been reëngraved; 4th: the leaf bound in, the plate on p. 283 in the reëngraved state. For a pictorial explanation of this feature see "A Supplement to *A Bibliography of Mark Twain*," 1939. In the early states the second 5, folio of p. 155, is either missing, or present, and of about the same size as the first; later states have a larger 5 that is in proper position but extends *below* the line of the first five. English edition published a few days before the American.

A CONNECTICUT YANKEE IN KING ARTHUR'S COURT. *New York*, 1889.

Some copies, status undetermined, noted with half title on verso of frontispiece.

THE AMERICAN CLAIMANT. *New York*, 1892.

MERRY TALES. *New York*, 1892.

Decorated end papers. Later states have plain end papers and a portrait frontispiece of the author.

THE £1,000,000 BANK-NOTE. *New York*, 1893.

Also copies in publisher's leather with the same stamping as that used on the cloth.

TOM SAWYER ABROAD. *New York*, 1894.

THE TRAGEDY OF PUDD'NHEAD WILSON. *Hartford*, 1894.

PERSONAL RECOLLECTIONS OF JOAN OF ARC. *New York*, 1896.

In the earliest copies the advertisements at the back list the 3rd and 4th volumes of "Memoirs of Barras" as *just ready;* later the advertisements are changed and the set is offered without the *just ready* statement.

TOM SAWYER ABROAD, TOM SAWYER, DETECTIVE, AND OTHER STORIES. *New York*, 1896.

FOLLOWING THE EQUATOR. *Hartford*, 1897.
Also, about 60 copies on large paper, signed. First state has the single imprint of *The American Publishing Company, Hartford, etc.* Later states have joint imprint.

HOW TO TELL A STORY AND OTHER ESSAYS. *New York*, 1897.
Page 187, line 16, *ciper* for *cipher*. Reissued with additional material, *Hartford*, 1900.

THE MAN THAT CORRUPTED HADLEYBURG AND OTHER STORIES AND ESSAYS. *New York*, 1900.
Probable first state measures 1½" across top of covers.

A DOUBLE BARRELLED DETECTIVE STORY. *New York*, 1902.

MY DEBUT AS A LITERARY PERSON. *Hartford*, 1903.
Limited to 512 copies in the "Autograph Edition." Issued in various types of leather binding.

A DOG'S TALE. *New York*, 1904.
About 250 copies printed, 1903, from the magazine plates; wrappers.

EXTRACTS FROM ADAM'S DIARY. *New York*, 1904.
Reprinted from, with revisions, "The Niagara Book," 1893.

KING LEOPOLD'S SOLILOQUY. *Boston*, 1905.
Wrappers. First state, wrappers are printed in dark green.

WHAT IS MAN? *New York*, 1906.
Anonymous. 250 numbered copies only.

THE $30,000 BEQUEST. *New York*, 1906.
The first printing has no advertisements on the copyright page.

EVE'S DIARY. *London and New York (sic)* 1906.
Reprinted from "Their Husband's Wives," which appeared in the Spring of 1906.

CHRISTIAN SCIENCE. *New York*, 1907.
Several printings without change of date. The earliest states have perfect *W* in *Why*, p. 5, line 14.

A HORSE'S TALE. *New York*, 1907.

IS SHAKESPEARE DEAD? *New York*, 1909.
First state does not have *Publisher's Note* before text. First state has gilt top. Copies with rubber stamped *Printed in U. S. A.* were intended for export to England.

EXTRACT FROM CAPTAIN STORMFIELD'S VISIT TO HEAVEN. *New York,* 1909.
First state measures ¾" across top of covers.

MARK TWAIN'S SPEECHES. *New York,* 1910.
Revised edition, *New York* [1923].

THE MYSTERIOUS STRANGER. *New York* [1916].
K-Q at foot of copyright page.

WHAT IS MAN? AND OTHER ESSAYS. *New York* [1917].
E-R at foot of copyright page.

MARK TWAIN'S LETTERS. *New York* [1917].
2 vols. *L-R* at foot of copyright page. Albert Bigelow Paine, editor. Boards, buckram back, untrimmed, 350 sets. Regular edition in red cloth.

THE CURIOUS REPUBLIC OF GONDOUR. *New York,* 1919.
Boards, cloth back.

THE MYSTERIOUS STRANGER AND OTHER STORIES. *New York,* 1922.
First edition so stated on copyright page.

EUROPE AND ELSEWHERE. *New York* [1923].
First edition so stated on copyright page. Noted with grey and white end papers; no priority established.

MARK TWAIN'S AUTOBIOGRAPHY. *New York,* 1924.
2 vols. First edition so stated on copyright page.

MARK TWAIN'S NOTEBOOK. *New York,* 1935.
Albert Bigelow Paine, editor. First edition so stated on copyright page.

THE WASHOE GIANT IN SAN FRANCISCO. *San Francisco,* 1938.
Franklin Walker, editor. 2,000 copies only.

MARK TWAIN'S TRAVELS WITH MR. BROWN. *New York,* 1940.
Franklin Walker and G. Ezra Dane, editors. 1,795 numbered copies only.

MARK TWAIN IN ERUPTION. *New York* [1940].
Bernard DeVoto, editor. First edition so indicated on the copyright page.

The following list is representative of the many secondary Mark Twain items. For a further listing consult the Johnson bibliography of Mark Twain.

Beadle's Dime Book of Fun, No. 3. *New York* [1866].
Wrappers. First book appearance of "The Jumping Frog."
Sketches No. 1. *New York* [1874].
Back cover blank.

Old Times on the Mississippi. *Toronto*, 1876.
> First state has no mention of "Tom Sawyer" on the title page; no advertisement for "Tom" on verso of half title; and the title is set in Old English type.

Date 1601: Conversation as it was in the Time of Queen Elizabeth. [*n.p., n.d., Cleveland, 1880*].
> Privately printed. Only a few copies (about eight were printed) are known. Dozens of reprints exist, including a facsimile edition of 110 copies.

The Suppressed Chapter of "Life on the Mississippi." [*n.p., n.d.*].
> 250 copies only. 4 pp. leaflet.

New Guide of the Conversation. *Boston*, 1883.
> Preface by Mark Twain.

The Niagara Book. *Buffalo*, 1893.
> First state has no advertisements at the back and carries American copyright only. Later states have advertisements and include Canada in copyright notice. First appearance of "Adam's Diary."

Liber Scriptorum: The First Book of the Author's Club. *New York*, 1893.
> First appearance of "A Californian's Tale."

Pudd'nhead Wilson's Calendar for 1894. [*New York?* 1893].
> Wrappers. Several states of this publication exist.

English As She Is Taught. *Boston* [1900].
> Wrappers or cloth. First state has *fivc* for *five*, p. 16, line 5.

Edmund Burke on Croker and Tammany. [*New York*, 1901].

To the Person Sitting in Darkness. [*New York*, 1901].

Their Husbands' Wives. *New York*, 1906.
> First book appearance of "Eve's Diary."

Mark Twain on Simplified Spelling. [*New York*, 1906].
> Leaflet. P. 1, line beginning *reached*, is clearly printed in the early states.

Queen Victoria's Jubilee. [*New York?* 1909].
> Privately printed. 195 copies only.

Letter to the California Pioneers. *Oakland, Cal.*, 1911.
> First copies have copyright notice.

St. Joan of Arc. *New York* [1919].
> First separate printing. First state has printed end papers and decoration at p. 18 is printed in proper position.

Mark by Mark. [*New York? ca.* 1920].
> Otherwise: "The Yacht Races."

The Sandwich Islands. *New York*, 1920.
> 30 copies only.

S. L. C. to C. T. [*New York*, 1925].
> Wrappers. 100 copies only.

Sketches of the Sixties, by Bret Harte and Mark Twain. *San Francisco*, 1926.
> Also 250 copies on Strathmore paper. Mark Twain material here first collected from old newspapers. Reissued, 1927, with additional material.

The Quaker City Holy Land Excursion. [*New York*] 1927.
> 200 copies printed, about 150 destroyed.

More Maxims [of] Mark. [*n.p., New York*] 1927.
  50 copies only privately printed.
The Adventures of Thomas Jefferson Snodgrass. *Chicago*, 1928.
  375 numbered copies only.
Three Aces. [*Westport, Conn.*, 1929].
  Privately printed, 50 copies only.
A Champagne Cocktail. [*n.p.*, 1930].
  Privately printed.
Slovenly Peter. *New York*, 1935.
  Translated by Mark Twain from Dr. Heinrich Hoffman's "Der Struwwelpeter."
  First edition issued by The Limited Editions Club, 1,500 numbered copies.
  Within a few weeks of the limited edition Harpers issued their edition with
  first edition notice on copyright page.
A Boy's Adventure. [*n.p., n.d.*].
  Originally intended as part of "The Prince and the Pauper." Leaflet, 4 pp.
Letters From Honolulu. *Honolulu*, 1939.
  1,000 copies only.

Many of the Mark Twain stories have been reissued under various titles—among
these, "In Defense of Harriet Shelley," and "The Private Life of Adam and Eve."
The collector is referred to the Johnson bibliography for a complete list and also for
a listing of the many small items too numerous to mention here.

BIOGRAPHICAL

My Mark Twain, by William Dean Howells. *New York*, 1910.
A Bibliography of the Work of Mark Twain, by Merle Johnson. *New York*, 1910.
  500 copies only, signed by the author and publisher. Revised and extended,
  New York, 1935, with material by Mark Twain included.
Mark Twain: A Biography, by Albert Bigelow Paine, *New York*, 1912.
  3 vols. Gilt top, other edges untrimmed. Vol. 1 has *H-M* at foot of copyright
  page; Vols. 2 and 3, *I-M* at foot of copyright pages. This is the so-called "Library
  Edition." Other editions issued in various types of binding.
The Ordeal of Mark Twain, by Van Wyck Brooks. *New York* [1920].
  Revised and reissued, *New York*, 1933.
Abroad With Mark Twain and Eugene Field, by H. W. Fisher. *New York*, 1922.
  Introduction by Merle Johnson. Also, 12 large paper copies signed; 325 large paper
  copies in boards; trade issue in cloth.
A Lifetime With Mark Twain: The Memories of Kate Leary, for Thirty Years
  His Faithful and Devoted Servant, by Mary Lawton. *New York* [1925].
My Father, by Clara Clemens. *New York*, 1931.
Mark Twain the Letter Writer, by Cyril Clemens. *Boston*, 1932.
Mark Twain's Western Years, by Ivan Benson. *Stanford University* [1938].

Irvin S[hrewsbury] Cobb
1876–

BACK HOME. *New York* [1912].
The first printing has the *Plimpton Press* slug on the copyright page, rules (two above and one below) on each page of text. The first binding has the publisher's name at the foot of the spine in three lines; later in one line.

COBB'S ANATOMY. *New York* [1912].

THE ESCAPE OF MR. TRIMM. *New York* [1913].

COBB'S BILL-OF-FARE. *New York* [1913].

ROUGHING IT DE LUXE. *New York* [1914].

EUROPE REVISED. *New York* [1914].
Also 25 de luxe copies with signature of author inserted.

PATHS OF GLORY. *New York* [1915].
Published in London as "The Red Glutton."

"SPEAKING OF OPERATIONS ——." *New York* [1915].
Boards.

OLD JUDGE PRIEST. *New York* [1916].
The first copies have the GHD square-diamond insignia on the title page. In the early copies the dedication is to Margaret Mayo Selwyn; later to Margaret Mayo.

FIBBLE, D. D. *New York* [1916].

LOCAL COLOR. *New York* [1916].

"SPEAKING OF PRUSSIANS ——." *New York* [1917].

THOSE TIMES AND THESE. *New York* [1917].

THE GLORY OF THE COMING. *New York* [1918].

THE THUNDERS OF SILENCE. *New York* [1918].
Boards.

THE LIFE OF THE PARTY. *New York* [1919].
Boards.

EATING IN TWO OR THREE LANGUAGES. *New York* [1919].

FROM PLACE TO PLACE. *New York* [1920].

"OH, WELL, YOU KNOW HOW WOMEN ARE!" *New York* [1920].
An upside down book, the opposing section being Mary Roberts Rinehart's "Isn't That Just Like a Man!"

THE ABANDONED FARMERS. *New York* [1920].

A PLEA FOR OLD CAP COLLIER. *New York* [1921].
Boards.

ONE THIRD OFF. *New York* [1921].

SUNDRY ACCOUNTS. *New York* [1922].
Has GHD insignia on copyright page.

J. POINDEXTER, COLORED. *New York* [1922].
Has GHD insignia on copyright page.

SNAKE DOCTOR. *New York* [1923].
Has GHD insignia on copyright page.

STICKFULS. *New York* [1923].
Has GHD insignia on copyright page. Third edition issued as "Myself—to Date."

A LAUGH A DAY KEEPS THE DOCTOR AWAY. *New York* [1923].
Has GHD insignia on copyright page.

GOIN' ON FOURTEEN. *New York*, 1924.
Code letter *A* on copyright page.

NORTH CAROLINA. *New York* [1924].
Has GHD insignia on copyright page.

NEW YORK. *New York* [1924].
Has GHD insignia on copyright page.

MAINE. *New York* [1924].
Has GHD insignia on copyright page.

KENTUCKY. *New York* [1924].
Has GHD insignia on copyright page.

KANSAS. *New York* [1924].
Has GHD insignia on copyright page.

INDIANA. *New York* [1924].
Has GHD insignia on copyright page. This, and the five preceding titles, issued in the "Cobb's America Guyed Books" series; were reissued, *New York* [1926], as "Some United States," with additional material.

"HERE COMES THE BRIDE ——," AND SO FORTH. *New York* [1925].
Has GHD insignia on copyright page.

MANY LAUGHS FOR MANY DAYS. *New York* [1925].
Has GHD insignia on copyright page.

ALIAS BEN ALIBI. *New York* [1925].
Code letter *A* on copyright page.

PROSE AND CONS. *New York* [1926].
Has publisher's insignia on copyright page.

ON AN ISLAND THAT COST $24.00. *New York* [1926].
Has publisher's insignia on copyright page.

LADIES AND GENTLEMEN. *New York*, 1927.

CHIVALRY PEAK. *New York*, 1927.

ALL ABOARD. *New York*, 1928.

IRVIN COBB AT HIS BEST. *New York*, 1929.

RED LIKKER. *New York*, 1929.
First edition so stated on copyright page. Cloth, paper labels. Also advance copies in printed wrappers.

THIS MAN'S WORLD. *New York*, 1929.

TO BE TAKEN BEFORE SAILING. *New York*, 1930.

BOTH SIDES OF THE STREET. *New York*, 1930.
Includes the preceding title.

INCREDIBLE TRUTH. *New York*, 1931.

DOWN YONDER WITH JUDGE PRIEST AND IRVIN S. COBB. *New York*, 1932.
P. 251, line 11, *quarel* for *quarrel*.

ONE WAY TO STOP A PANIC. *New York*, 1933.

MURDER DAY BY DAY. *Indianapolis* [1933].
First edition so indicated on the copyright page.

FAITH, HOPE, AND CHARITY. *Indianapolis* [1934].
First edition so indicated on the copyright page.

AZAM. *Chicago* [1937].

JUDGE PRIEST TURNS DETECTIVE. *Indianapolis* [1937].
First edition so indicated on the copyright page.

EXIT LAUGHING. *Indianapolis* [1941].
First edition so indicate on the copyright page.

Caleb Conover, Railroader, by Albert Payson Terhune. *New York*, 1907.
    Editorial assistance by Cobb.
Pleiades Club Year Book. [*New York*, 1910].
    Edition de luxe, 600 copies. Contains Cobb's "Hallroumania."
Pleiades Club Year Book. [*New York*, 1911].
    Edition de luxe, 500 numbered copies. Contains Cobb's "Uncle Dud on Ancestors."
The Lost Tribes of the Irish in the South. *New York*, 1917.
    Address by Cobb.
R. H. D. *New York*, 1917.
    Contains an appreciation of Richard Harding Davis by Cobb. 375 copies only.
Daisy Ashford. *New York*, 1920.
    Preface by Cobb.
The Stag Cook Book. *New York* [1922].
    Contains Cobb's recipe for hog jowl and turnip greens.
Il Conte, by Joseph Conrad, with Other Stories. *New York*, 1925.
    Contains Cobb's "Who's Who at the Zoo."
Literary Treasures of 1926. [*Chicago*, 1927].
    Contains Cobb's "Three Wise Men of the East Side."
Percy MacKaye: A Symposium on His Fiftieth Birthday. *Hanover, N. H.*, 1928.
    Contains an appreciation by Cobb, "Dreamer and Mountaineer."
O. Henry Memorial Award Prize Stories for 1930. *Garden City*, 1930.
    First edition so stated on copyright page. Contains a short story by Cobb.
Creeps by Night. *New York* [1931].
    Dashiell Hammett, editor. Contribution by Cobb.
Here They Are ... Amos 'n' Andy, by Charles J. Correll and Freeman F. Gosden. *New York*, 1931.
    Foreword by Cobb.
The Woman Accused. *New York*, 1933.
    Chapter by Cobb.
Many Laughs for Many Days. *Garden City*, 1933.
    Reprint.
Irvin S. Cobb's Own Recipe Book. *Louisville and Baltimore* [1934].
    Wrappers.
The Romance of Truth, by John Bernard Kelly. *New York* [1935].
    Foreword by Cobb.
Four Useful Pups. *Chicago, New York* [etc.] [1940].
Pot Luck ... , by Ed Ainsworth. *Hollywood* [1940].
    Foreword.

BIOGRAPHICAL

Irvin Cobb: His Book. *New York*, 1915.
    "Friendly tributes upon the occasion of a dinner tendered Irvin Shrewsbury Cobb at the Waldorf-Astoria Hotel, New York, April 25, 1915."
Irvin S. Cobb: Story Teller, by Robert H. Davis. *New York* [n.d.].

COBB

Irvin S. Cobb, by F. G. Neuman. *Paducah*, 1924.
  Revised and enlarged, 1926.
Irvin S. Cobb: His Life and Letters. *Emaus, Pa.*, 1938.
  F. G. Neuman, editor.

The following plays by Cobb have not yet been published in book form: "Funabashi," 1907; "Busybody," 1908; "Back Home," with BAYARD VEILLER, 1915; "Sergeant Bagby," with BOZEMAN BULGER, 1913; "Guilty as Charged," with HARRY BURKE, 1915; "Under Sentence," with ROI COOPER MEGRUE, 1916.

John Esten Cooke

1830–1886

LEATHER STOCKING AND SILK. *New York*, 1854.
Anon. Various colors of cloth.

THE VIRGINIA COMEDIANS. *New York*, 1854.
2 vols. *From the MSS. of C. Effingham, Esq.*, p. 249, line 3, vol. 2, *earsed* for *erased*.

THE YOUTH OF JEFFERSON. *New York*, 1854.
Anon. First edition has *Redfield* imprint.

ELLIE. *Richmond*, 1855.

THE LAST OF THE FORESTERS. *New York*, 1856.

HENRY ST. JOHN, GENTLEMAN. *New York*, 1859.
Reissued as "Bonnybel Vane."

THE LIFE OF STONEWALL JACKSON. *Richmond*, 1863.
By A Virginian. First edition has *Ayres and Wade* imprint. Printed wrappers. The New York edition of 1863 followed this. Reissued, *New York*, 1866, revised and with author's name on title page.

SURRY OF EAGLE'S NEST. *New York*, 1866.
First edition has *Bunce and Huntington* imprint. Illustrated by Winslow Homer.

WEARING OF THE GRAY. *New York*, 1867.

FAIRFAX. *New York*, 1868.
Reissued as "Lord Fairfax."

HILT TO HILT. *New York*, 1869.

MOHUN. *New York*, 1869.

HAMMER AND RAPIER. *New York*, 1870.

THE HEIR OF GAYMOUNT. *New York*, 1870.

OUT OF THE FOAM. *New York*, 1871.
Reissued as "Westbrooke Hall."

LIFE OF GENERAL ROBERT E. LEE. *New York*, 1871.

DOCTOR VANDYKE. *New York*, 1872.
Cloth or printed wrappers.

HER MAJESTY THE QUEEN. *Philadelphia*, 1873.

PRETTY MRS. GASTON AND OTHER STORIES. *New York* [1874].

JUSTIN HARLEY. *Philadelphia*, 1875.

LIFE OF SAMUEL J. TILDEN. *New York*, 1876.

CANOLLES. *Detroit*, 1877.

PROFESSOR PRESSENSEE, MATERIALIST AND INVENTOR. *New York*, 1878.
No. 76 in "Harper's Half Hour Series." Cloth or wrappers.

MR. GRANTLEY'S IDEA. *New York*, 1879.
Cloth or wrappers.

STORIES OF THE OLD DOMINION. *New York*, 1879.

THE VIRGINIA BOHEMIANS. *New York*, 1880.

VIRGINIA: A HISTORY OF THE PEOPLE. *Boston*, 1883.

FANCHETTE. *Boston*, 1883.
By One of Her Admirers.

MY LADY POKAHONTAS. *Boston*, 1885.
By Anas Todkill ... With Notes by J. E. Cooke.

THE MAURICE MYSTERY. *New York*, 1885.
Reissued, printed from the original plates, as "Col. Ross of Piedmont."

"Bonnybel Vane," "Lord Fairfax," "Westbrooke Hall," and "Col. Ross of Piedmont" are reissues, with changed titles, of previously published works.

Cooke is said to have issued two pamphlets, one an appeal to support the war; the other, an account of the burning of Charleston. I have been unable to secure definite data on these publications.

Virginia Girls and Gallants Four Score Years Ago: An Excursion into Antiquity. *Richmond*, 1856.
Out At the Elbows, by John Esten Cooke.
A short story in "Gifts of Genius," *New York* [1859].
Confession of J. E. Cooke, One of the Participants in the Harper's Ferry Invasion. *Charleston, Va.*, 1859.
The Grayjackets: How They Lived and Fought and Died for Dixie. *Richmond* ... 1867.

John Esten Cooke, Virginian, by John Owen Beaty. *New York*, 1922.
A Bibliography of John Esten Cooke, by Oscar Wegelin. *Metuchen*, 1925.
50 copies only. Revised, 1941.

James Fenimore Cooper
1789–1851

PRECAUTION: A NOVEL. *New York*, 1820.
 2 vols. Anonymous. Copies have been noted with a leaf of errata at the end of either volume. Bound in printed boards. Revised and reissued, *Philadelphia*, 1839, 2 vols.

THE SPY: A TALE OF THE NEUTRAL GROUND. *New York*, 1821.
 2 vols. *By the Author of "Precaution."* Copies have been noted in boards, paper label on spine. Second and third editions, so marked, contain new introductions. Revised editions, *London*, 1831 and *New York*, 1849.

THE PIONEERS: OR, THE SOURCES OF THE SUSQUEHANNA: A DESCRIPTIVE TALE. *New York*, 1823.
 2 vols. *By the Author of "Precaution."* The earliest state of vol. 1 carries the name of J. Seymour as printer. Copies have been noted with an apology at the end of vol. 1 but the status of such copies has not been determined. Revised and reissued *London*, 1832 and *New York*, 1850.

TALES FOR FIFTEEN. *New York*, 1823.
 Jane Morgan, pseudonym. Printed boards.

THE PILOT: A TALE OF THE SEA. *New York*, 1823.
 2 vols. Boards, paper labels. Revised and reissued, *New York*, 1849.

LIONEL LINCOLN: OR, THE LEAGUER OF BOSTON. *New York*, 1825-1824 [!].
 2 vols. Vol. 2 dated 1824. Boards, paper labels. Revised and reissued. *London*, 1832.

THE LAST OF THE MOHICANS: A NARRATIVE OF 1757. *Philadelphia*, 1826.
 2 vols. Boards, paper label. P. 89 misnumbered 93 in vol. 1. Volume 1, p. 71, has been noted both with and without the folio; no known priority. Also, *Chapter XVI is misnumbered XIV;* no examined copy has this error corrected. Some copies have been noted with p. *vii* of the preface numbered *vi*. Revised and reissued, *London*, 1831, and *New York*, 1850.

THE PRAIRIE: A TALE. *Philadelphia*, 1827.
 2 vols. *By the Author of, etc.* Boards, paper labels. The copyright notice in both volumes is corrected by a pasted slip. Revised and reissued, *London*, 1832, and *New York*, 1851.

THE RED ROVER: A TALE. *Philadelphia*, 1828.
 2 vols. *By the author of, etc.* Boards, paper labels. An author's note has been noted in some copies of Vol. 2. Preceded in time of publication by the Paris edition, November 27, 1827; and the London edition, November 30, 1827. American

edition published January 9, 1828. Revised and reissued, *London*, 1834 and *New York*, 1852.

NOTIONS OF THE AMERICANS: PICKED UP BY A TRAVELLING BACHELOR. *Philadelphia*, 1828.

2 vols. Anonymous. Boards, cloth back, paper labels.

THE WEPT OF WISH TON-WISH: A TALE. *Philadelphia*, 1829.

2 vols. Boards, paper labels. *By the Author of, etc.* Published November 9, 1829, but preceded by the English edition published in September. Reissued with new introduction, *London*, 1833.

THE WATER-WITCH: OR, THE SKIMMER OF THE SEAS. *Philadelphia*, 1831.

2 vols. *By the Author of, etc.* Boards, paper labels. Published in Dresden, September 1830, dated *1830;* London, October 1830, dated *1830;* Philadelphia, December 1830, dated *1831.*

THE BRAVO: A TALE. *Philadelphia*, 1831.

2 vols. *By the Author of, etc.* Boards, paper labels. English edition preceded the American by at least a month in time of publication. Revised and reissued, *London*, 1834.

THE HEIDENMAUER; OR, THE BENEDICTINES: A LEGEND OF THE RHINE. *Philadelphia*, 1832.

2 vols. *By the Author of, etc.* Boards, paper labels. American edition published September; English edition published preceding July. It has been stated that the Paris edition (in English) preceded the American edition.

THE HEADSMAN; OR, THE ABBAYE DES VIGNERONS: A TALE. *Philadelphia*, 1833.

2 vols. *By the Author of, etc.* Boards, paper labels. English edition published in the month preceding the American. One leaf of advertisements in each volume.

THE MONIKINS. *Philadelphia*, 1835.

2 vols. *Edited by the Author of "The Spy."* Boards, cloth back, paper labels.

SKETCHES OF SWITZERLAND. *Philadelphia*, 1836.

2 vols. *By An American.* Paper labels.

SKETCHES OF SWITZERLAND: PART SECOND. *Philadelphia*, 1836.

2 vols. *By An American.* Cloth or boards, paper labels. Errata slip in Vol. 2. The English edition is said to have preceded the American in time of publication by about one month.

GLEANINGS IN EUROPE: [FRANCE]. *Philadelphia*, 1837.

2 vols. *By An American.* Cloth or boards, paper labels. Errata slip before the preface. The English edition is said to have preceded the American in time of publication by about one month.

GLEANINGS IN EUROPE: ENGLAND. *Philadelphia*, 1837.
2 vols. *By An American.* Paper labels. English edition published in May; American edition, September.

GLEANINGS IN EUROPE: ITALY. *Philadelphia*, 1838.
2 vols. *By An American.* Cloth, paper labels. English edition published in February; American edition, May.

HOMEWARD BOUND; OR, THE CHASE: A TALE OF THE SEA. *Philadelphia*, 1838.
2 vols. *By the Author of, etc.* Paper labels on spine. English edition published in May; American edition in August.

HOME AS FOUND. *Philadelphia*, 1838.
2 vols. Cloth, or boards and cloth, with paper labels on spine. *By the Author of, etc.* Copies have been noted with a "notice to the public" before the title page in Vol. 1.

THE HISTORY OF THE NAVY OF THE UNITED STATES OF AMERICA. *Philadelphia*, 1839.
2 vols. Revised and reissued with corrections and additions, *Philadelphia*, 1840; *Philadelphia* [and] *Cooperstown*, 1847; *New York*, 1853, 1856 and 1864.

THE PATHFINDER; OR, THE INLAND SEA. *Philadelphia*, 1840.
2 vols. *By the Author of, etc.* Copyright notice omitted from Vol. 1 and some copies of Vol. 2. Copies exist with the notices pasted in at the usual place. Cloth, or cloth and boards, paper labels.

MERCEDES OF CASTILE; OR, THE VOYAGE TO CATHAY. *Philadelphia*, 1840.
2 vols. *By the Author of, etc.* Cloth, paper labels.

THE DEERSLAYER; OR, THE FIRST WAR-PATH. *Philadelphia*, 1841.
2 vols. *By the Author of, etc.* Some copies with half-title stating that the book is the first of The Leatherstocking Series. Paper labels on spine. Revised and reissued, *New York*, 1850.

THE TWO ADMIRALS: A TALE. *Philadelphia*, 1842.
2 vols. *By the Author of, etc.* Wrappers or cloth, paper label on spine. Revised edition, *New York*, 1851. English edition published in month preceding American publication.

THE WING-AND-WING; OR, LE FEU-FOLLET: A TALE. *Philadelphia*, 1842.
2 vols. Wrappers. Revised edition, *New York*, 1851.

LE MOUCHOIR: AN AUTOBIOGRAPHICAL ROMANCE. *New York* [1843].
Wrappers.

WYANDOTTÉ; OR, THE HUTTED KNOLL: A TALE. *Philadelphia*, 1843.
2 vols. Wrappers.

NED MYERS; OR, A LIFE BEFORE THE MAST. *Philadelphia*, 1843.
Cloth or wrappers.

AFLOAT AND ASHORE; or, THE ADVENTURES OF MILES WALLINGFORD. *Philadelphia,* 1844.
2 vols. Wrappers. *By the Author of, etc.*

AFLOAT AND ASHORE; or, THE ADVENTURES OF MILES WALLINGFORD: [SECOND SERIES]. *Philadelphia,* 1844.
2 vols. (3 and 4 of the series). Wrappers. *By the Author of, etc.*

SATANSTOE; or, THE LITTLEPAGE MANUSCRIPTS: A TALE OF THE COLONY. *New York,* 1845.
2 vols. Printed wrappers. *By the Author of, etc.* English edition preceded the American by about one month.

THE CHAINBEARER; or, THE LITTLEPAGE MANUSCRIPTS. *New York,* 1845.
2 vols. Wrappers. *By the Author of, etc.* English edition preceded the American by a few weeks.

LIVES OF DISTINGUISHED AMERICAN NAVAL OFFICERS. *Philadelphia,* 1846.
2 vols.

THE REDSKINS; or, INDIAN AND INJ[G]IN: BEING THE CONCLUSION OF THE LITTLEPAGE MANUSCRIPTS. *New York,* 1846.
2 vols. Wrappers. *By the Author of, etc.* Title page has *J* spelling of *Injin;* wrapper the *G* spelling.

THE CRATER; or, VULCAN'S PEAK: A TALE OF THE PACIFIC. *New York,* 1847.
2 vols. Wrappers. *By the Author of, etc.* In the first state the preliminary leaves of the preface are misnumbered; later corrected. English edition preceded the American by about two weeks.

JACK TIER; or, THE FLORIDA REEF. *New York,* 1848.
2 vols. *By the Author of, etc.* Printed wrappers.

THE OAK OPENINGS; or, THE BEE-HUNTER. *New York,* 1848.
2 vols. Wrappers. *By the Author of, etc.*

THE SEA LIONS; or, THE LOST SEALERS. *New York,* 1849.
2 vols. *By the Author of, etc.* Printed wrappers.

THE WAYS OF THE HOUR: A TALE. *New York,* 1850.

THE WORKS OF J. FENIMORE COOPER. *New York,* 1849-1851.
32 vols. *Author's Revised Edition.*

Redwood, par M. Cooper. *Paris,* 1824.
A French translation of Catherine Sedgwick's novel attributed to, but not the work of, Cooper.

L'Espion, Drame en Cinq Actes et en Prose, Par MM. Angelot et Mazères. *Paris,* 1829.
 The earliest located published dramatization of "The Spy."

Letter of J. Fenimore Cooper to Gen. Lafayette on the Expenditure of the United States of America. *Paris,* 1831.
 Wrappers.

Contributions for the Poles. ｢*Paris,* 1831｣.
 Leaflet.

A Letter to His Countrymen. *New York,* 1834.
 Boards.

The American Democrat; or, Hints on the Social and Civic Relations of the United States of America. *Cooperstown,* 1838.
 Cloth, paper label.

The Chronicles of Cooperstown. *Cooperstown,* 1838.
 Anonymous. Cloth, paper label.

The Battle of Lake Erie; or, Answers to Messrs. Burges, Duer, and Mackenzie. *Cooperstown,* 1843.
 Wrappers.

Proceedings of the Naval Court Martial in the Case of Alexander Slidell Mackenzie. *New York,* 1844.

The Cruise of the Somers: Illustrative of the Despotism of the Quarter Deck, etc. *New York,* 1844.
 Anonymous.

Elinor Wyllys; or, The Young Folk of Longbridge: A Tale. *Philadelphia,* 1846.
 2 vols. By *Amabel Penfeather,* presumably the pseudonym of Susan Cooper. While Cooper appears as editor of this work it has been argued that he was the author.

The Home Book of the Picturesque. *New York,* 1852.
 Contains Cooper's "American and European Scenery Compared."

Stories of the World; or, Adventures of Leatherstocking. *New York,* 1863.
 Compilation of Cooper writings.

The Seventh Yearbook of the Bibliophile Society. *Boston,* 1908.
 Contains an unpublished letter by Cooper.

The Correspondence of James Fenimore Cooper. *New Haven,* 1922.
 Edited by the author's grandson, James Fenimore Cooper.

New York, by James Fenimore Cooper. *New York,* 1930.
 750 copies only.

The Lake Gun, by James Fenimore Cooper. *New York,* 1932.
 Previous book publication in "Specimens of American Literature," *New York,* 1866.

A Descriptive Bibliography of the Writings of James Fenimore Cooper, by Robert E. Spiller and Philip C. Blackburn. *New York,* 1934.
 500 copies only.

Stephen Crane
1871–1900

MAGGIE: A GIRL OF THE STREETS (A STORY OF NEW YORK). [*New York,* 1893].

Johnston Smith, *pseudonym*. Yellow wrappers. Reissued by Appleton, *New York,* 1896; four issues of this date. It is probable that the first has an eleven line title page printed in Roman type.

THE BLACK RIDERS AND OTHER LINES. *Boston,* 1895.

Issued in both yellow cloth and grey printed boards. Trade edition limited to 500 copies on calendared paper; also 50 copies, printed in green ink, on Japan vellum, bound in plain boards, paper label. A few of the latter, said to be but three, bound in full vellum with the same stamping as the trade copies. A copy of the trade edition in grey boards has been noted without the lettering on the back cover. Since the artist who designed the book intended that the lettering should appear on the front cover only, it seems likely that the copy without the lettering on the back is an experimental state.

THE RED BADGE OF COURAGE. *New York,* 1895.

Exists in two or three states but the earliest has perfect type at p. 225, last line. Later states show the type at this point either broken or repaired with the final letter in *congratulated* out of perpendicular.

THE LITTLE REGIMENT. *New York,* 1896.

First state has 6 pp. advertisements at the back, the first page headed Gilbert Parker's Best Books.

GEORGE'S MOTHER. *New York,* 1896.

THE THIRD VIOLET. *New York,* 1897.

Also printed wrappers.

THE OPEN BOAT AND OTHER TALES OF ADVENTURE. *New York,* 1898.

Three issues, in all about 1,500 copies; priority undetermined. London edition, 1898, contains nine additional stories.

ACTIVE SERVICE. *New York* [1899].

WAR IS KIND. *New York,* 1899.

Boards.

THE MONSTER AND OTHER STORIES. *New York,* 1899.

London edition, 1901, contains four additional stories.

WOUNDS IN THE RAIN. *New York* [1900].

Later states have the number of the issue on the copyright page.

WHILOMVILLE STORIES. *New York,* 1900.

GREAT BATTLES OF THE WORLD. *Philadelphia,* 1901.
Second edition so stated on half title.

LAST WORDS. *London,* 1902.

THE O'RUDDY. *New York* [1903].
With ROBERT BARR. Later editions so stated on title page.

MEN, WOMEN AND BOATS. *New York* [1921].
First edition for three stories. Mr. Vincent Starrett, Crane's bibliographer, states
that the first issue lacks the word *immediately* after *almost,* line 19, p. 69.

THE WORK OF STEPHEN CRANE. *New York* [1925-1926].
A definitive edition. Wilson Follett, editor. 750 sets only. 12 vols.

THE COLLECTED POEMS OF STEPHEN CRANE. *New York,* 1930.
Wilson Follett, editor.

A BATTLE IN GREECE. *Mt. Vernon, N. Y.,* 1936.
425 numbered copies only.

Pike County Puzzle. *Interlaken, Penna.,* 1894.
Burlesque newspaper, 4 pp.
The Members of the Society of the Philistines. *East Aurora,* 1895.
'The Time Has Come.' *East Aurora,* 1895.
Wrappers.
A Souvenir and a Medley: Seven Poems and a Sketch, by Stephen Crane. *East
Aurora,* 1896.
Spanish-American War Songs. *Detroit,* 1898.
Sidney A. Witherbee, editor. Contains Crane's "The Blue Battalions."
The Lanthorn Book. [*New York,* 1898].
Contains "The Wise Men," by Crane. 125 copies only, some signed by Crane.
Best Things from American Literature. *New York,* 1899.
Irving Bacheller, editor. Contains "A Tale of Mere Chance," by Crane and the
first American book appearance of "A Detail."
Stories of Authors, by Edwin Watts Chubbs. *New York,* 1910.
Contains excerpts from two letters.
The Windmill. *London,* 1923.
L. Callender, editor.
Et Cetera: A Collector's Scrap-Book. *Chicago,* 1924.
Vincent Starrett, editor. Boards, cloth back, paper label. 625 numbered copies
only. Contains "At the Pit Door" and "The Great Boer Trek" by Crane.
Two Letters from Stephen Crane to Joseph Conrad. [*London,* 1926].
Wrappers. 220 copies only.
The Colophon: No. 4. [*New York,* 1930].
Contains "A Stephen Crane Letter."

A Lost Poem. ₁*New York,* 1932₁.
100 copies only, signed by Harvey Taylor. Leaflet.

BIOGRAPHICAL AND BIBLIOGRAPHICAL

Stephen Crane: In Memoriam, by A. E. Keats. *New York* ₁*n.d.*₁.
Printed for "fifty appreciative friends."
Stephen Crane, by Thomas L. Raymond. *Newark, N. J.,* 1923.
250 copies only.
Stephen Crane: A Bibliography, by Vincent Starrett. *Philadelphia,* 1923.
335 copies only.
Stephen Crane: A Study in American Letters, by Thomas Beer. *New York,* 1923.
Also 165 copies as follows: 150 numbered, 15 lettered.
Stephen Crane and the Stephen Crane Association, by M. J. Herzberg. *Newark, N. J.,* 1926.
Wrappers. Includes a bibliography.
The Second Twenty-Eight Years, by Wilson Follett. *Newark, N. J.,* 1930.
300 copies only.
Stephen Crane: A List of His Writings and Articles about Him, by B. J. R. Stolper. *Newark, N. J.,* 1930.
Wrappers.
The Colophon: No. 7. *New York,* 1931.
Contains Vincent Starrett's "Stephen Crane," with a bibliography.
A Bibliography of Stephen Crane, by Ames W. Williams and Vincent Starrett.
In preparation.

E[dward] E[stlin] Cummings
1894–

THE ENORMOUS ROOM. *New York* [1922].
 With or without the fifth word, last line of p. 219, blacked out by hand. Reissued, *New York* [1934] with new introduction.

TULIPS AND CHIMNEYS. *New York*, 1923.
 Boards, paper label. Reissued, *Mount Vernon, N. Y.*, 1937 with 84 added poems, in an edition comprising 333 numbered copies and 148 numbered and signed copies.

XLI POEMS. *New York*, 1925.
 Label on front cover.

&. *New York*, 1925.
 111 copies on Vidalon Handmade Paper; 222 copies on De Coverly Rag Laid Paper; consecutively numbered 1-333 and signed by the author.

IS 5. *New York*, 1926.
 Boards, cloth back.

HIM. *New York*, 1927.
 Boards, cloth back. Also 160 numbered and signed copies.

CHRISTMAS TREE. *New York*, 1928.
 Privately printed in limited edition for friends of author and publisher.

[NO TITLE]. *New York*, 1930.
 "The dam thing has no title—the frontispiece is a blank—the illustrations don't make sense—the text is meaningless—its all absolutely crazy!" 491 copies only, illustrated and signed by the author.

CIOPW. *New York*, 1931.
 Also 391 signed copies.

W [VIVA: SEVENTY NEW POEMS]. *New York*, 1931.
 95 signed copies.

EIMI. [*New York*, 1933].
 1,381 signed copies only.

TOM: A BALLET. [*Santa Fe, N. M.*, 1935.]
 Printed for the "Arrow Editions."

NO THANKS. [*New York*, 1935.]
 Holograph Edition on Japan Vellum, signed, numbered I-IX; 90 copies on hand-made paper, numbered 1-90; and 900 copies on Ricardi Japan paper.

CUMMINGS

FIFTY POEMS. *New York,* 1940.

Eight Harvard Poets. *New York,* 1917.
   Contains eight poems by Cummings.
The Best Poems of 1923. *Boston* [1924].
   Contains a poem by Cummings.
Whither, Whither. *New York,* 1930.
   Contains "Anthropos," by Cummings.
The Red Front, by Louis Aragon. *Chapel Hill* [1933].
   Translated by Cummings.
Collected Poems. *New York* [1938].
   First printing so indicated on copyright page.

George William Curtis

1824–1892

NILE NOTES OF A HOWADJI. *New York*, 1851.
Anon. Various colors of cloth; various end papers.

THE HOWADJI IN SYRIA. *New York*, 1852.
Various colors of cloth. 8 pp. advts. at back dated *February 1852*. Published in London as "The Wanderer in Syria."

LOTUS EATING: A SUMMER BOOK. *New York*, 1852.
Various colors of cloth and paper wrappers, the latter untrimmed. 10 pp. undated advts. at back.

THE POTIPHAR PAPERS. *New York*, 1853.
Anon.

PRUE AND I. *New York*, 1856.
Various colors of cloth, two states of spine stamping. It is presumed that the first state does not have *Curtis' Works* on spine. It has been stated that only the first state has the pronoun I repeated, p. 6, lines 19 and 20. The same error remains uncorrected as late as 1858. Revised, *New York*, 1892; also 250 copies in vellum signed by the illustrator.

TRUMPS. *New York*, 1861.
Various colors of cloth. About 12 copies were issued, entirely uncut.

WASHINGTON IRVING: A SKETCH. *New York*, 1891.
347 copies only for members of the Grolier Club. Full leather binding. Three copies on vellum.

FROM THE EASY CHAIR. *New York*, 1892.
With or without *I* on the spine.

OTHER ESSAYS FROM THE EASY CHAIR. *New York*, 1893.
Reissued as "From the Easy Chair: Second Series," *New York*, 1894.

FROM THE EASY CHAIR: THIRD SERIES. *New York*, 1894.

THE ORATIONS AND ADDRESSES OF GEORGE WILLIAM CURTIS. *New York*, 1894.
3 vols. Charles Eliot Norton, editor.

LITERARY AND SOCIAL ESSAYS. *New York*, 1895.

EARLY LETTERS OF GEORGE WM. CURTIS TO JOHN S. DWIGHT. *New York*, 1898.
George Willis Cooke, editor.

CURTIS

The following list is representative, rather than all-inclusive, of the many minor Curtis productions.

The Duty of the American Scholar to Politics and the Times. *New York*, 1856.
An Address Vindicating the Rights of Woman to the Elective Franchise. *New York*, 1858.
Cecil Dreeme, by Theodore Winthrop. *Boston*, 1861.
  Contains a biographical sketch of the author by Curtis.
The Rhode Island Prisoner: A Sonnet ... [*New York*, 1865].
  4to broadside on grayish paper.
[Equal Rights for Women] Reprinted From The Nation, July 11 and November 21, 1867. *Cambridge* [1867?].
  Wrappers.
Fair Play for Women. *Boston*, 1871.
Charles Sumner: A Eulogy. [*Boston*, 1874].
The Puritan Principle, Liberty under the Law. *New York*, 1877.
  Speech.
William Cullen Bryant: A Commemorative Address. *New York* [1879].
Civil Service Reform: An Address. *New York*, 1885.
The Correspondence of John Lothrop Motley. *New York*, 1889.
  2 vols. Edited.
Address Prepared for the Annual Meeting of the New York Civil-Service Reform Association (May 1, 1889). *New York*, 1889.
Modern Ghosts. *New York*, 1890.
  Anthology. Introduction by Curtis.
Party and Patronage: An Address. [*New York*] 1892.
James Russell Lowell. *New York*, 1892.
  Printed wrappers.
Emerson. *New York*, 1896.
  Printed wrappers.
Hawthorne. *New York*, 1896.
  Printed wrappers.
Longfellow. *New York*, 1896.
  Printed wrappers.
Ars Recte Vivendi ... Essays. *New York*, 1898.

BIOGRAPHICAL

George William Curtis, by John White Chadwick. *New York*, 1893.
  In Harper's "Black and White Series."
George William Curtis, by Edward Cary. *Boston*, 1894.
  In "American Men of Letters" series.

Richard Henry Dana, Jr.

1815–1882

TWO YEARS BEFORE THE MAST. *New York,* 1840.

Issued in black and tan cloth. Tan cloth copies are printed on the back cover with publisher's advertisements for *Harper's Family Library;* in the first state this list does not extend beyond No. 105. The spine stamping has been noted in several states with no apparent priority; the series number, however, must be 106. Type evidence reveals several printings without change of date; the earliest copies have the *i* in *in,* first line of copyright notice, dotted and perfect type in the running head of p. 9. For a full collation and discussion of this title see "One Hundred Good Novels" by David A. Randall and John T. Winterich in *The Publishers' Weekly,* September 21, 1940. Various later reissues of this title with revisions, the edition published *Boston,* 1869, having a new preface and an added chapter.

TO CUBA AND BACK: A VACATION VOYAGE. *Boston,* 1859.

The probable first state of the advertisements offers *A New Narrative by the Author of "Two Years Before the Mast"* (*In Press*).

Dana, as a lawyer, published innumerable pamphlets, contributed to legal publications, etc., etc. These are so numerous that only a representative list of his secondary writings is here appended.

The Seaman's Friend. *Boston and New York* [1841].
Lectures on Art and Poems, by Washington Allston. *New York,* 1850.
   Edited.
Remarks before the Committee on Federal Relations, on the Proposed Removal of
   E. G. Loring, Esq., from the Office of Judge Probate. *Boston* [1855].
The Bible in Schools. *Boston* [1855].
The Dalton Divorce Case. *Boston,* 1856.
   In: "The Massachusetts Supreme Judicial Court Proceedings."
Full Report of R. H. Dana's Argument for the Defense in the Case of Rev. I. S.
   Kalloch ... by Dr. I. W. Ayer. *Boston,* 1857.
Argument of Richard H. Dana, Jr., Esq., Counsel for the Town of West Cambridge.
   Boston, 1857.
Argument for the Plaintiffs in the Case of the Golden Rocket before the Supreme
   Court of Maine. *Boston,* 1862.
   Signed jointly by Dana and Horace Gray, Jr.
A Tribute to Judge Sprague ... at a Dinner Given to the Officers of the
   "Kearsarge." *Boston,* 1864.
   Privately printed.
Enemy's Territory and Alien Enemies. *Boston,* 1864.
Points and Authorities in Support of the Price Charity. *Boston,* 1864.

DANA

Speech of R. H. Dana, Jr. ... in Faneuil Hall, June 21, 1865 ... Subject of the Re-organization of the Rebel States. [*Boston*] 1865.

An Address upon the Life and Services of Edward Everett. *Cambridge*, 1865. 50 copies only for presentation.

Speech in the House of Representatives of Massachusetts, February 14, 1867, on the Repeal of the Usury Laws. *Boston*, 1867.

Argument for the Holders of Bonds in the Boston, Hartford and Erie Railroad ... April 14, 1870. *Boston*, 1870.

Unity of Italy: Letter. [*Boston*, 1871].

The Old South: Argument of Richard Henry Dana, Jr. ... *Boston* [1872].

Oration at Lexington, April 19, 1875. *Boston*, 1875.

Speeches in Stirring Times and Letters to a Son. *Boston*, 1910. Edited and compiled by Richard Henry Dana, 3rd.

Richard Harding Davis

1864–1916

ADVENTURES OF MY FRESHMAN. *Bethlehem* [1883].
Wrappers. Printed for the author. Material appeared originally in the *Lehigh Burr.*

GALLEGHER AND OTHER STORIES. *New York*, 1891.
First state does not contain advertisement at the back for "Famous Women of the French Court." Noted in both dark and light green cloths; no established priority. Simultaneous publication for 1,000 copies on wove paper, bound in cloth; and, 3,032 copies on laid paper in printed wrappers.

STORIES FOR BOYS. *New York*, 1891.
The earliest state has perfect type in the running head, p. 91.

VAN BIBBER AND OTHERS. *New York*, 1892.
Cloth, with some copies noted in wrappers. Second state has publisher's advertisements at the back of book. "Episodes in Van Bibber's Life," *New York*, 1899, reprinted from this volume.

THE WEST FROM A CAR-WINDOW. *New York*, 1892.

THE RULERS OF THE MEDITERRANEAN. *New York*, 1894.

THE EXILES AND OTHER STORIES. *New York*, 1894.

OUR ENGLISH COUSINS. *New York*, 1894.

ABOUT PARIS. *New York*, 1895.

THE PRINCESS ALINE. *New York*, 1895.
One copy has been noted in wrappers bearing the following printed notice: "This copy of this book was printed especially for Francis Wilson at the request of the author."

CINDERELLA AND OTHER STORIES. *New York*, 1896.
The first state of binding has no picture of "Cinderella" on the front cover.

THREE GRINGOES IN VENEZUELA AND SOUTH AMERICA. *New York*, 1896.
Cover stamped in gold, silver and green.

SOLDIERS OF FORTUNE. *New York*, 1897.
American News Company edition of the same year is a later issue.

DR. JAMESON'S RAIDERS VS. THE JOHANNESBURG REFORMERS. *New York*, 1897.
Wrappers. Copies have been noted in untrimmed sts

CUBA IN WAR TIME. *New York*, 1897.
> Boards or wrappers, printed. First state has printer's imprint at last page of text. In the first printing there is a reference to Hearst on p. 9; later removed although Hearst's paper is mentioned by name.

A YEAR FROM A REPORTER'S NOTE-BOOK. *New York*, 1898.
> Grey boards. Noted with and without stamping on spine.

THE KING'S JACKAL. *New York*, 1898.
> Later states carry a list of Davis' books on the verso of the half-title.

THE CUBAN AND PORTO RICAN CAMPAIGNS. *New York*, 1898.

THE LION AND THE UNICORN. *New York*, 1899.
> Cloth binding; leather binding later.

WITH BOTH ARMIES IN SOUTH AFRICA. *New York*, 1900.
> First edition published by Scribner's.

IN THE FOG. *New York*, 1901.
> Noted with and without picture on the front cover; printed on thick or thin paper; no priority established.

CAPTAIN MACKLIN. *New York*, 1902.
> Gilt top. Green cloth. In 1907 the publishers issued a remainder of the original sheets in red cloth.

RANSON'S FOLLY. *New York*, 1902.
> First state has p. 345 so numbered; later, folio missing. Advertisements at back of book announce "Captain Macklin" as *nearly ready*.

REAL SOLDIERS OF FORTUNE. *New York*, 1906.
> First edition published by Scribner's. *Published, November, 1906* on copyright page.

THE SCARLET CAR. *New York*, 1907.
> *Published, June, 1907* on copyright page.

THE CONGO AND THE COASTS OF AFRICA. *New York*, 1907.

VERA THE MEDIUM. *New York*, 1908.
> First binding, purple cloth; later, red cloth. *Published June, 1908* on copyright page.

THE WHITE MICE. *New York*, 1909.
> First binding, yellow cloth; later, red cloth.

NOTES OF A WAR CORRESPONDENT. *New York*, 1910.

ONCE UPON A TIME. *New York*, 1910.
> *Published August, 1910* on copyright page.

THE CONSUL. *New York*, 1911.
 Boards, cloth back; some copies in leather. *Published May, 1911* on copyright page.

THE MAN WHO COULD NOT LOSE. *New York*, 1911.
 Published September, 1911 on copyright page.

THE RED CROSS GIRL. *New York*, 1912.

THE LOST ROAD. *New York*, 1913.
 Published October, 1913 on copyright page.

THE BOY SCOUT. *New York*, 1914.
 Reissued, with added material, *New York*, 1917, as "The Boy Scout and Other Stories"; first book printing for "The Boy Who Cried Wolf."

WITH THE ALLIES. *New York*, 1914.

"SOMEWHERE IN FRANCE." *New York*, 1915.
 Published August, 1915 on copyright page.

WITH THE FRENCH IN FRANCE AND SALONIKA. *New York*, 1916.

THE NOVELS AND STORIES OF RICHARD HARDING DAVIS. *New York*, 1916.
 12 vols. Also 256 signed sets.

Great Streets of the World. *New York*, 1892.
 Contribution by Davis.

Troop C in Service. An Account ... of 1898, by Anthony Ziala. *Brooklyn*, 1899.
 Contribution by Davis.

Episodes in Van Bibber's Life. *New York*, 1899.
 Reprint.

Her First Appearance. *New York*, 1901.
 Reprint. First separate.

The Bar Sinister. *New York*, 1903.
 Reprint. First separate. First state of binding gold lettered; later, blue lettered.

The Deserter. *New York*, 1917.
 Reprint. Boards, cloth back. Reprinted in item following as "The Man who Had Everything."

The Lost Road. *New York*, 1920.
 Reprint.

From Gallegher to the Deserter. *New York*, 1927.
 Roger Burlingame, editor. Selected reprints.

Young Winston Churchill. *New York*, 1941.
 First printing has code letter *A* on copyright page. Reprinted from "Soldiers of Fortune," 1906.

Davis was the author of numerous plays or adaptations. The following have been published:

The Littlest Girl. *New York* [1898].

The Orator of Zepata City. *New York* [1899].
    Yellow wrappers.

Miss Civilization. *New York*, 1905.

Farces. *New York*, 1906.
    Includes the preceding item together with "The Galloper," and "The Dictator." *Published, October, 1906* on the copyright page.

The Dictator. *New York*, 1909.
    Reprinted from "Farces," 1906.

Who's Who. *London*, 1913.
    200 copies only.

Peace Manoeuvres. *New York*, 1914.
    250 copies only. Printed wrappers.

The Zone Police. *New York* [1914].
    250 copies only.

Writing for Vaudeville, by Brett Page. *Springfield* [1915].
    Contains "Blackmail," by Davis.

BIOGRAPHICAL AND BIBLIOGRAPHICAL

Adventures and Letters of Richard Harding Davis. *New York*, 1917.
    Charles Belmont Davis, editor.

R. H. D. *New York*, 1917.
    375 copies only. Boards, cloth back, leather label on spine. Appreciations of Davis by various authors.

Richard Harding Davis: A Bibliography, by H. C. Quinby. *New York* [1924].
    1,000 copies only.

Richard Harding Davis: His Day, by Fairfax Downey. *New York*, 1933.
    First printing has the code letter *A* on the copyright page.

Margaret[ta] (Wade Campbell) Deland
1857–

THE OLD GARDEN AND OTHER VERSES. *Boston,* 1886.
A few copies have been noted with vellum back instead of the usual white cloth. Reissued with added material, *Boston,* 1887. Illustrated edition, 1893.

JOHN WARD, PREACHER. *Boston,* 1888.

FLORIDA DAYS. *Boston,* 1889.
Copies in parti-colored cloth binding were probably intended for the English trade.

SIDNEY. *Boston,* 1890.

THE STORY OF A CHILD. *Boston,* 1892.

MR. TOMMY DOVE AND OTHER STORIES. *Boston,* 1893.

PHILIP AND HIS WIFE. *Boston,* 1894.

THE WISDOM OF FOOLS. *Boston,* 1897.

OLD CHESTER TALES. *New York,* 1899.
P. 5, six lines from bottom of page, reads *Chelsea* instead of *Chester;* later corrected.

DR. LAVENDAR'S PEOPLE. *New York,* 1903.
Published October, 1903 on the copyright page.

THE COMMON WAY. *New York,* 1904.

THE AWAKENING OF HELENA RICHIE. *New York,* 1906.
Front cover stamped either white or with gold; it is believed that the white stamping was experimental. First printing does not have a box enclosing the dedication. A copy has been noted in flexible suede binding. Also advance copies, printed from the magazine plates, bound in red boards, paper label on the front cover. Dramatized by C. Thompson, privately printed, 1908.

AN ENCORE. *New York,* 1907.
Published October, 1907 on the copyright page.

R. J.'S MOTHER. *New York,* 1908.
Published May, 1908 on the copyright page.

THE WAY TO PEACE. *New York,* 1910.
Published September, 1910 on the copyright page

DELAND

THE IRON WOMAN. *New York,* 1911.
First printing does not state chapter and verse number of quotation on title page; merely states —*Ezekiel.* Also advance copies printed from the magazine plates, bound in red boards, paper label on the front cover.

THE VOICE. *New York,* 1912.
Code letters *G-M* on copyright page.

PARTNERS. *New York,* 1913.
Code letters *I-N* on copyright page.

THE HANDS OF ESAU. *New York,* 1914.
Published September, 1914 on the copyright page.

AROUND OLD CHESTER. *New York* [1915].

THE RISING TIDE. *New York* [1916].

THE PROMISES OF ALICE. *New York* [1919].
Code letters *G-T* on the copyright page.

SMALL THINGS. *New York,* 1919.
Symbol (1) below last line of text.

AN OLD CHESTER SECRET. *New York* [1920].
Code letters *K-U* on the copyright page. Dramatized version by Sally Kemper, *Boston,* 1924.

THE VEHEMENT FLAME. *New York* [1922].

NEW FRIENDS IN OLD CHESTER. *New York* [1924].
First edition so indicated on the copyright page.

THE KAYS. *New York,* 1926.
First edition so stated on copyright page. Also 250 copies in boards, signed by the publishers.

CAPTAIN ARCHER'S DAUGHTER. *New York,* 1932.
First edition so indicated on the copyright page.

IF THIS BE I, AS I SUPPOSE IT BE. *New York,* 1935.
(1) below last line of text.

OLD CHESTER DAYS. *New York,* 1937.
First edition so indicated on the copyright page.

A Summer Day. *Boston* [1889].
Pictorial wrappers.
From an Old Garden: Six Songs. *New York,* 1887.
Six musical settings by E. A. MacDowell.

Good for the Soul. *New York,* 1899.
Reprinted from "Old Chester Tales."
Short Story Classics. *New York* [1905].
William Patten, editor. Vol. 5 contains "Many Waters."
Where the Laborers Are Few. *New York,* 1909.
Reprinted from "Old Chester Tales."
Miss Maria: Comedy in One Act ... *New York,* 1917.
A dramatization by Maude B. Vosburgh from the story in "Old Chester Tales."
Printed wrappers. The author's name is misspelled *Leland* on the front wrapper; later corrected.
Harper's Essays. *New York,* 1919.
Contains "Beads," reprinted from "Small Things."
The Story of Delia. [*n.p., n.d.*].
16 pp. pamphlet.
The Light Which Is Darkness. [*New York?* 1919].
8 pp. pamphlet. Reprinted from *Harper's Magazine* for June 1919.
The Vanished Friend, By Jules Thiébault. *New York* [1920].
Foreword.
International Thought, by John Galsworthy; The Great Determination, by Margaret Deland. *New York* [1923].
Printed wrappers.
Boston Theatre Guild Plays. *Boston,* 1924.
Boards. Contains "An Old Chester Secret," a dramatization by Sally Kemper.
"Confession." [*n.p., n.d.* Hampton, Va., ca. 1925].
Printed wrappers. Four printings, the first having the pagination at top of page; later at bottom of page.
Harper Essays. *New York,* 1927.
Henry Seidel Canby, editor. Contribution. First edition indicated on the copyright page.
Prejudice Against the Jew ... A Symposium. *New York,* 1928.
Contribution.
"Though Inland Far We Be ——" [*n.p.,* 1932].
Printed wrappers. Originally a contribution to "The Case For and Against Psychical Belief" where it appeared as "A Peak in Darien."

Emily Dickinson
1830–1886

POEMS. *Boston,* 1890.
Mabel Loomis Todd and Thomas Wentworth Higginson, editors. First printing 500 unnumbered copies. Simultaneously issued in two types of binding, grey cloth or green back with white cloth sides.

POEMS: SECOND SERIES. *Boston,* 1891.
Mabel Loomis Todd and Thomas Wentworth Higginson, editors. First printing, 960 unnumbered copies. Simultaneously issued in two types of binding, grey cloth or green back with white cloth sides. Noted also in publisher's half calf with decorated board sides. The combined contents of this edition and the edition of 1890 were issued as one volume, *Boston,* 1893.

LETTERS. *Boston,* 1894.
Mabel Loomis Todd, editor. The order of the bindings and issues are as follows: 1894, 2 vols., green cloth; 1894, 2 vols., brown cloth; 1894, 2 vols., in 1, brown cloth. Reissued in one volume, 1896. The reissue of 1931 is said by the editor to be "not a reprint ... but an entirely new presentation."

POEMS: THIRD SERIES. *Boston,* 1896.
Mabel Loomis Todd, editor. First printing, 1,000 unnumbered copies. *See:* "Poems: Second Series," 1891, for note on bindings.

THE SINGLE HOUND: POEMS OF A LIFETIME. *Boston,* 1914.
First printing 595 unnumbered copies. Boards, cloth back.

SELECTED POEMS. *London,* 1924.
Edited and with an introduction by Conrad Aiken.

COMPLETE POEMS. *Boston,* 1924.
First printing, 2,000 unnumbered copies. Reissued with new introduction by Martha Dickinson Bianchi, 1926. Also a pocket edition, 1926.

FURTHER POEMS OF EMILY DICKINSON. *Boston,* 1929.
Martha Dickinson Bianchi and Alfred Leete Hampson, editors. First printing, 2,000 unnumbered copies. Later in the month of issue there was published a limited edition of 465 numbered copies.

THE POEMS OF EMILY DICKINSON: CENTENARY EDITION. *Boston,* 1930.
Martha Dickinson Bianchi and Alfred Leete Hampson, editors.

POEMS FOR YOUTH. *Boston,* 1934.
Alfred Leete Hampson, editor.

UNPUBLISHED POEMS. *Boston,* 1935.
   Martha Dickinson Bianchi and Alfred Leete Hampson, editors. 525 numbered
   copies, published November 22, 1935. Trade edition, *Boston,* 1936, published
   February 7, 1936.

A Masque of Poets. *Boston,* 1878.
   Contains "Success" at p. 174. See this title under *Alcott* for further discussion.
Sun Prints in Sky Tints. *Boston,* 1893.
   Contains "The Sleeping Flowers," by Dickinson. This item has been catalogued
   as a first printing for Dickinson; the poem, however, had appeared previously.
Six Songs. *Chicago* [1897].
   Six poems set to music by Clarence Dickinson.

BIOGRAPHICAL AND BIBLIOGRAPHICAL

The Life and Letters of Emily Dickinson, by Martha Dickinson Bianchi. *Boston,*
   1924.
   Reissued with revisions and additions, May, 1924; October, 1924; 1925; July,
   1929; November, 1929.
Emily Dickinson, by Louis Untermeyer. *New York,* 1927.
   In "The Pamphlet Poets" series.
The Life and Mind of Emily Dickinson, by Genevieve Taggard. *New York,* 1930.
   Also 200 numbered copies, signed.
Emily Dickinson: The Human Background of Her Poetry, by Josephine Pollitt.
   New York, 1930.
Emily Dickinson, Friend and Neighbor, by MacGregor Jenkins. *Boston,* 1930.
Emily, by MacGregor Jenkins. *Indianapolis,* 1930.
Emily Dickinson: A Bibliography, by Alfred Leete Hampson. *Northampton,* 1930.
Emily Dickinson: A Bibliography. *Amherst,* 1930.
   Foreword by George F. Whicher.
Alison's House, by Susan Glaspell. *New York,* 1930.
   A play based on Emily Dickinson's life.
Emily Dickinson Face to Face, by Martha Dickinson Bianchi. *Boston,* 1932.
   Includes about 150 Dickinson notes and letters.
A Chronological Grouping of Some of Emily Dickinson's Poems, by George F.
   Whicher.
   In: "The Colophon," No. 16.
This Was a Poet, by George F. Whicher. *New York,* 1938.

It is now generally agreed that Emily Dickinson did not collaborate or contribute
to the "Saxe Holms Stories" or to "Mercy Philbrick's Choice" by Helen Hunt
Jackson. In discussing this, Mabel Loomis Todd writes, "She [Emily Dickinson] had
no connection with them, ... and her brother, Austin Dickinson, and her sister,
Lavinia, and I sifted the amusing tales about her writing parts of those stories to
the bottom, so that we could say that there is no truth in those 'imaginings' of the
romantic public."

Mary (Elizabeth) Mapes Dodge

1838–1905

THE IRVINGTON STORIES. *New York,* 1865.
By *M. E. Dodge.* Revised and enlarged. *New York and Chicago* [1898].

HANS BRINKER; or, THE SILVER SKATES. *New York,* 1866.
By *M. E. Dodge.* Noted with the advertisements at back of book in three varying states; priority undetermined.

A FEW FRIENDS AND HOW THEY AMUSED THEMSELVES. *Philadelphia,* 1869.
By *M. E. Dodge.*

RHYMES AND JINGLES. *New York,* 1875.

THEOPHILUS AND OTHERS. *New York,* 1876.
First edition has *Scribner, Armstrong and Company* imprint.

ALONG THE WAY. *New York,* 1879.
Reissued, *New York,* 1904, as "Poems and Verses."

DONALD AND DOROTHY. *Boston,* 1883.

THE LAND OF PLUCK. *New York,* 1894.

WHEN LIFE IS YOUNG. *New York,* 1894.

THE GOLDEN GATE. *Chicago* [1903].

The Treasure Trove Series. *Boston,* 1875.
Contains "The Insanity of Cain."
Baby Days: Stories, Rhymes and Pictures for Little Folks. *New York,* 1883.
Compiled by Mrs. Dodge.
Baby World: Stories, Rhymes, and Pictures for Little Folks. *New York* [1884].
Compiled by Mrs. Dodge. Revised and reissued, *New York* [1891] and [1897].
The Children's Book of Recitations. *New York* [1898].
Compiled by Mrs. Dodge.
Po-No-Kah: An Indian Tale of Long Ago. *Chicago* [1903].
Reprinted from previously published work.

John (Roderigo) Dos Passos
1896–

ONE MAN'S INITIATION ... 1917. *London* [1920].
   First Published in 1920 on copyright page.

THREE SOLDIERS. *New York* [1921].
   The first state reads *signing*, later *singing*, p. 213, line 7 from the bottom. The
   first printing of this book does *not* have the GHD monogram on the copyright
   page. For a full discussion of this see "Exploding the *Three Soldiers* Myth" in
   The Publishers' Weekly, June 18, 1938. Reissued, *New York* [1932], first edition so stated on the copyright page, with a new introduction by the author.

ROSINANTE TO THE ROAD AGAIN. *New York* [1922].
   First state has the *GHD* insignia on the copyright page. Boards, cloth back.

A PUSHCART AT THE CURB. *New York* [1922].
   First state has the *GHD* insignia on the copyright page. Boards, paper label.

STREETS OF NIGHT. *New York* [1923].
   First state has the *GHD* insignia on the copyright page.

MANHATTAN TRANSFER. *New York*, 1925.
   First edition so stated on copyright page. Cloth or pictorial boards.

THE GARBAGE MAN. *New York*, 1926.
   A play produced under the title "The Moon Is a Gong." First edition so stated on
   copyright page. Boards, paper label. Later in cloth.

ORIENT EXPRESS. *New York*, 1927.
   First edition so stated on copyright page. Illustrated by the author. Boards, cloth
   back; later cloth.

AIRWAYS, INC. *New York* [1928].
   A play in "The New Playwrights' Theatre Series." Boards, cloth back.

THE 42ND PARALLEL. *New York*, 1930.
   Boards. First edition so indicated on the copyright page. Reissued by the Modern
   Library, *New York* [1937], first edition so indicated on the copyright page, with
   a new introduction by the author.

1919. *New York* [1932].
   First edition so stated on copyright page.

IN ALL COUNTRIES. *New York* [1934].
   First edition so stated on copyright page.

THREE PLAYS. *New York* [1934].
First edition for "Fortune Heights."

THE BIG MONEY. *New York* [1936].
First edition so stated on copyright page.

JOURNEYS BETWEEN WARS. *New York* [1938].
First edition so indicated on the copyright page. Contains some reprinted material.

ADVENTURES OF A YOUNG MAN. *New York* [1939].
First edition so indicated on the copyright page.

THE GROUND WE STAND ON. *New York* [1941].

Eight Harvard Poets. *New York*, 1917.
Contains seven poems by Dos Passos.
Roger Bloomer: A Play, by John Howard Lawson. *New York*, 1923.
Foreword by Dos Passos. Boards.
John Dos Passos' Manhattan Transfer, by Sinclair Lewis, *New York*, 1926.
975 numbered copies only.
Transatlantic Stories. *New York*, 1926.
Boards, cloth back. Contains "July" by Dos Passos.
Facing the Chair: Story of the Americanization of Two Foreign-born Workmen. *Boston*, 1927.
Wrappers.
America Arraigned. *New York*, 1928.
Lucia Trent and Ralph Cheyney, editors. Contribution.
Metropolis, by Manuel Maples Arce. *New York*, 1929.
Translated by Dos Passos.
Panama; or, The Adventures of My Seven Uncles, by Blaise Cendrars. *New York*, 1931.
Translated. First edition so stated on copyright page. With illustrations by Dos Passos. Trade edition preceded by 300 numbered copies, signed by author and Dos Passos. Limp boards, wallet edges.
Die Literarische Entwicklung von John Dos Passos, by Werner Neuse. *Giessen* [Germany] 1931.
Contains a bibliography.
Harlan Miners Speak. *New York* [1932].
Contributions by Dos Passos. First edition so indicated.
Veterans on the March, by Jack Douglas. *New York*, 1934.
Foreword by Dos Passos.
Gattorno. *Habana*, 1935.
Contains a critical opinion by Dos Passos. Wrappers.
Interregnum: A Series of Sixty Drawings and an Original Colored Lithograph by George Grosz. *New York*, 1936.
With an introduction and comments by Dos Passos. 300 numbered copies only.

Terror in Cuba, by Arthur Pincus. *New York* [1936].
  Printed wrappers. Preface by Dos Passos.
Portraits and Self-Portraits, by Georges Schreiber. *Boston,* 1936.
  Contribution.
U. S. A. *New York* [1937].
  Reprint.
John Dos Passos: A Biographical and Critical Essay, by John Chamberlain. *New York* [1939].
The Living Thoughts of Tom Paine. *New York,* 1940.
  First edition so indicated on copyright page. Edited.
The Bedside Esquire. *New York* [1940].
  Arnold Gingrich, editor. Contribution.

Joseph Rodman Drake

1795–1820

POEMS, BY CROAKER, CROAKER & CO., AND CROAKER, JUN. *New York,* 1819.

With FITZ-GREENE HALLECK. Reissued as "The Croakers," *New York,* 1860, by the Bradford Club, 250 copies only, of which 100 special copies for members.

THE CULPRIT FAY AND OTHER POEMS. *New York,* 1835.

Title poem published separately as a new year's greeting by *The Westchester Republican and Democrat* [*Westchester, Penna.*] 1837 (1836) with text revised.

The Poetry of the Portfolio. *Philadelphia,* 1818.

Oliver Oldschool (Joseph Dennie), editor. Contains three poems signed *Croaker & Co.*

The American Flag ... Illustrated ... By F. O. C. Darley. *New York,* 1861.

Illuminated wrappers. Set to music by George Danskin from Bellini. Reprinted from "The Culprit Fay," 1835, where it appeared without music. It is believed that Fitz-Greene Halleck wrote the final stanza of this poem.

The Life and Letters of Fitz-Greene Halleck, by James Grant Wilson. *New York,* 1869.

Also 100 large paper copies, some extra-illustrated. Contains hitherto uncollected material.

The Poetical Writings of Fitz-Greene Halleck: With Extracts From Those of Joseph Rodman Drake. *New York,* 1869.

James Grant Wilson, editor. Also 150 large paper copies.

The Life and Works of Joseph Rodman Drake. *Boston,* 1935.

Frank Lester Pleadwell, editor. 750 copies only.

Drake, together with Fitz-Greene Halleck, collaborated as *The Croakers.*

Theodore Dreiser

1871–

SISTER CARRIE. *New York*, 1900.
Reissued, 1932, with new preface by the author.

JENNIE GERHARDT. *New York*, 1911.
First state of binding is blue mottled cloth. First state of text reads *is* for *it*, p. 22, line 30.

THE FINANCIER. *New York*, 1912.
Blue mottled cloth. Copyright page states *Published October, 1912* and with code letters *K-M*. Revised edition, *New York*, 1927.

A TRAVELLER AT FORTY. *New York*, 1913.

THE TITAN. *New York*, 1914.
First binding is mottled blue cloth. Later in plain grey-blue cloth.

THE "GENIUS". *New York*, 1915.
White edges, measures 1 ¾" across top of covers. The earliest copies have p. 497 so numbered; later, the folio is lacking.

PLAYS OF THE NATURAL AND THE SUPERNATURAL. *New York*, 1916.
Boards, cloth back, paper label. The second issue is extended by the addition of a signature following p. 228 entitled "The Anaesthetic Revelation."

A HOOSIER HOLIDAY. *New York*, 1916.
Boards, cloth back. Last paragraph, p. 173, in the first state has *The war! The war!* etc.; later deleted. First state binding olive-grey buckram spine.

FREE AND OTHER STORIES. *New York*, 1918.
B-L monogram on the title page.

THE HAND OF THE POTTER. *New York*, 1918.
Light green boards, cloth back, paper label. Examination of a prepublication copy of this book results in the following notes: *Prepublication Copy:* p. 191, last word is *that*. Page 209 has but one speech, that of Berchansky; no advertisements on the verso of the half title. *Published edition:* page 191, last word is *it*. Page 209 has several speeches; the half title is tipped in and has advertisements on the verso of the leaf. A subsequent edition has the half title bound in, with advertisements on the verso. Thus far no copy, save the prepublication copy, has been noted with no advertisements on the verso of the half title. A few of the regular issue were signed by the author. Revised and reissued, *New York*, 1927.

TWELVE MEN. *New York*, 1919.

DREISER

HEY RUB-A-DUB-DUB. *New York*, 1920.

A BOOK ABOUT MYSELF. *New York* [1922].
> Reissued, *New York* [1931], with a new foreword as "Newspaper Days" of which there were also 200 de luxe copies on Van Gelder handmade paper.

THE COLOR OF A GREAT CITY. *New York* [1923].

AN AMERICAN TRAGEDY. *New York*, 1925.
> 2 vols. Also 795 numbered and signed copies issued after the trade edition. The first printing has the *Boni and Liveright* imprint; later issued with the *Horace Liveright* imprint.

MOODS, CADENCED AND DECLAIMED. *New York*, 1926.
> Boards, cloth back. 550 copies, numbered and signed. Trade edition, *New York*, 1928, contains added material. Reissued with revisions and additions, *New York*, 1935, as "Moods, Philosophical and Emotional, Cadenced and Declaimed."

CHAINS. *New York*, 1927.
> Also 440 numbered and signed copies issued after trade edition.

THE CARNEGIE WORKS AT PITTSBURGH. *Chelsea* [N.Y., 1927].
> 177 copies only of which 27 were printed on Marlowe Antique Paper with a sheet of the original manuscript bound in.

DREISER LOOKS AT RUSSIA. *New York*, 1928.

A GALLERY OF WOMEN. *New York*, 1929.
> 2 vols. Also 560 numbered and signed copies.

THE ASPIRANT. *New York*, 1929.
> 475 copies only in "The Random House Poetry Quartos."

MY CITY. *New York* [1929].
> 275 signed copies.

EPITAPH. *New York* [1929].
> 200 copies on Van Gelder numbered 1-200; 200 copies on Keijyo Kami Paper bound in silk and numbered 201-400; copies 401-1,100 on Keijyo Kami Paper and bound in cloth.

FINE FURNITURE. *New York*, 1930.
> 875 copies only in "The Random House Prose Quartos." Wrappers, paper label.

DAWN. *New York* [1931].
> Also 275 numbered and signed copies.

TRAGIC AMERICA. *New York* [1931].
> Before publication of this book the publishers were advised that, in order to avoid legal entanglements, it would be necessary to revise the text. The sheets

had already been printed and all but six [12?] sets were destroyed and bound **for** private use in the same binding as that used in the regularly published edition. This suppressed edition contains, literally, dozens of words and phrases later deleted. For purposes of identification, the suppressed readings in part are here appended:

Suppressed	Published
	p. 49, line 14
filched	*pocketed*
	p. 100, line 13, first word
fraudulent	
	p. 130, line 4
corruption	*subservience*
	p. 380, line 4 up
pirates	*figures*

Spanish-American War Songs. *Detroit,* 1898.
  Sidney A. Witherbee, editor. Contains "Exordium," by Dreiser.
A Princess of Arcady, by Arthur Henry. *New York,* 1900.
  Final chapter supplied by Dreiser.
Life in a Garrison Town, by Lt. Bilse. *New York,* 1914.
  Introduction by Dreiser.
Life, Art and America. *New York,* 1917.
  Pamphlet. Reprinted from *The Seven Arts Magazine,* February, 1917.
Theodore Dreiser: America's Foremost Novelist. *New York* [ca. 1917].
  Pamphlet.
Caius Gracchus, by Odin Gregory. *New York* [1920].
  Introduction by Dreiser. Copies in wrappers are marked *Preliminary Edition.*
  Trade edition, all edges trimmed, cloth.
Jurgen and the Censor. *New York,* 1920.
  Contribution by Dreiser.
Ebony and Ivory, by Llewelyn Powys. *New York,* 1923.
  Preface by Dreiser.
Marriage. *Garden City,* 1923.
  Contains "Marriage for One," by Dreiser. First edition so stated on copyright
  page.
Neurotic America and the Sex Impulse. *Girard, Kansas,* 1924.
  "Little Blue Book" No. 661.
These United States: Second Series. *New York* [1924].
  Contribution by Dreiser.
Little Flowers of Love and Wonder. *London* [1925].
  Sheet music.
For a Moment the Wind Died. *London* [1925].
  Sheet music.
Theodore Dreiser, by Burton Rascoe. *New York,* 1925.
Leonardo 1924. [*New York*] 1925.
  Contains a poem, "The Great Blossom," by Dreiser.

Lilith, by George Sterling. *New York,* 1926.
  Introduction by Dreiser.
Poorhouse Sweeney, by Ed Sweeney. *New York,* 1927.
  Introduction by Dreiser.
Tono-Bungay, by H. G. Wells. *New York,* 1927.
  Sandgate edition. Introduction by Dreiser.
The Songs of Paul Dresser. *New York,* 1927.
  Introduction by Dreiser.
A Bibliography of the Writings of Theodore Dreiser, by Edward McDonald. *Phila-delphia,* 1927.
  335 copies of which 35 only were numbered.
/ The Road to Buenos Ayres, by Albert Londres. *London,* 1928.
  Introduction by Dreiser.
The Crime of Dr. Garine, by Boris Sokoloff. *New York,* 1928.
  Introduction by Dreiser.
Notes to Add to a Bibliography of Theodore Dreiser, by Vrest Orton. [*New York*] 1928.
Dreiserana: A Book about His Books, by Vrest Orton. *New York,* 1929.
Catalogue of an Exhibition of Paintings by Jerome Blum ... *New York,* 1929.
  4 pp. leaflet. Foreword by Dreiser.
The Symbolic Drawings of Hubert Davis for An American Tragedy. [*New York,* 1930].
  Limited to 525 copies signed by Dreiser and Davis. Foreword by Dreiser.
Divorce [by Eight Authors]. *New York,* 1930.
  "Modern Marriage Is a Farce," contributed by Dreiser.
Living Philosophies. *New York,* 1931.
  Contribution by Dreiser.
The Colophon, No. 5. [*New York,* 1931].
  Contains "The Early Adventures of Sister Carrie," by Dreiser.
Forgotten Frontiers: Dreiser and the Land of the Free, by Dorothy Dudley. *New York,* 1932.
Harlan Miners Speak. *New York* [1932].
  Contribution by Dreiser. First edition so indicated on the copyright page.
Forced Labor in the United States, by Walter Wilson. *New York* [1933].
  Introduction by Dreiser.
Molders of American Thought. *Garden City,* 1934.
  William H. Cordell, editor. Contribution by Dreiser. First edition so indicated on the copyright page.
The American Spectator Year Book. *New York,* 1934.
  Contains a contribution by Dreiser.
Mr. President: Free the Scottsboro Boys! [*New York,* 1934].
  Wrappers. Preface by Dreiser.
Waiting for Nothing, by Tom Kromer. *London,* 1935.
  Introduction.
So Red the Nose. *New York* [1935].
  Contribution.

Magnificent Hadrian, by Sulamith Ish-Kishor. *New York* [1935].
    Introduction by Dreiser.
The Way of All Flesh, by Samuel Butler. *New York*, 1936.
    Privately printed for members of the Limited Editions Club, 1,500 copies only.
    Introduction by Dreiser.
Paintings and Drawings by Biala. *New York* [1937].
    4 pp. leaflet. Contains a one-page appreciation of Biala by Dreiser.
Breaking Into Print. *New York*, 1937.
    Elmer Adler, editor. Contribution.
Of Human Bondage, by Somerset Maugham. *New Haven* [New York] 1938.
    1,500 copies only for the Limited Editions Club. Introduction.
The Living Thoughts of Thoreau. *New York*, 1939.
    Edited. First edition so indicated on the copyright page.
The Bedside Esquire. *New York* [1940].
    Arnold Gingrich, editor. Contribution.

"The Stoic," a novel by Dreiser, was announced but not published.

Paul Lau[w]rence Dunbar

1872–1906

OAK AND IVY. *Dayton, Ohio,* 1893.
About 500 copies printed.

MAJORS AND MINORS. [*Toledo,* 1895].
1,000 copies printed. The probable first state of binding has bevelled edges. "When Malindy Sings," *New York,* 1903, reprinted from this volume.

LYRICS OF LOWLY LIFE. *New York,* 1896.
With an introduction by William Dean Howells. The introduction was issued separately as an advertising broadside.

FOLKS FROM DIXIE. *New York,* 1898.

THE UNCALLED. *New York,* 1898.
Originally in *Lippincott's Magazine,* May 1898, which was issued with a separate title page for this work, bound in boards, cloth back.

POEMS OF CABIN AND FIELD. *New York,* 1899.

LYRICS OF THE HEARTHSIDE. *New York,* 1899.

THE STRENGTH OF GIDEON AND OTHER STORIES. *New York,* 1900.

THE LOVE OF LANDRY. *New York,* 1900.

CANDLE-LIGHTIN' TIME. *New York,* 1901.

THE FANATICS. *New York,* 1901.

THE SPORT OF THE GODS. *New York,* 1902.
First edition so indicated on the copyright page. Issued in London as "The Jest of Fate."

LYRICS OF LOVE AND LAUGHTER. *New York,* 1903.
First edition so indicated on the copyright page.

IN OLD PLANTATION DAYS. *New York,* 1903.
Published September, 1903 on the copyright page.

LI'L' GAL. *New York,* 1904.

THE HEART OF HAPPY HOLLOW. *New York,* 1904.

LYRICS OF SUNSHINE AND SHADOW. *New York,* 1905.

HOWDY, HONEY, HOWDY. *New York,* 1905.

JOGGIN' ERLONG. *New York*, 1906.

CHRIS'MUS IS A-COMIN'. *New York*, 1907.

COMPLETE POEMS. *New York*, 1913.
First edition so stated on the copyright page.

Dream Lovers: An Operatic Romance. *London & New York* [1898].
Music by S. Coleridge-Taylor.
"Jes Lak White Fo'ks." [*Brooklyn?*] 1900.
"A one-act Negro operetta by Will Marion Cook ... additional lyrics by Paul Laurence Dunbar."
Uncle Eph's Christmas. [*n.p.*] 1900.
A one-act play with music by W. M. Cook.
When Malindy Sings. *New York*, 1903.
Reprint.
Life and Works of Paul Laurence Dunbar, by Lida Keck Wiggins. *Naperville, Ill., and Memphis, Tenn.* [1907].
Contains a bibliography and an introduction by William Dean Howells.
A Child's History of Dunbar, by Julia L. Henderson. [*Chicago*, 1913].
Speaking o' Christmas. *New York*, 1914.
Reprinted material.
Paul Laurence Dunbar: Poet of His People, by Benjamin Brawley. *Chapel Hill*, 1936.
The Best Stories of Paul Laurence Dunbar. *New York*, 1938.
Benjamin Brawley, editor. Selected reprints.
Little Brown Baby. *New York*, 1940.
Reprint.

Finley Peter Dunne

1867–1936

MR. DOOLEY IN PEACE AND WAR. *Boston*, 1898.
Anonymous. Also 25 copies entirely untrimmed.

MR. DOOLEY IN THE HEARTS OF HIS COUNTRYMEN. *Boston*, 1899.
All copies of the first printing list three printings before publication. See *The Publishers' Weekly*, May 10, 1941, pp. 1961-1962. Also 100 copies entirely untrimmed.

MR. DOOLEY'S PHILOSOPHY. *New York*, 1900.

MR. DOOLEY'S OPINIONS. *New York*, 1901.

OBSERVATIONS BY MR. DOOLEY. *New York*, 1902.

DISSERTATIONS BY MR. DOOLEY. *New York*, 1906.

MR. DOOLEY SAYS ... *New York*, 1910.

MR. DOOLEY ON MAKING A WILL. *New York*, 1919.

What Dooley Says. *Chicago* [1899].
A pirated edition with some doubtful material.
Mr. Dooley on Timely Topics. *New York*, 1905.
Pamphlet reprint of the *Collier's* articles.
Familiar Stories for Children. *New York* [1914].
Contribution.
R. H. D. *New York*, 1917.
375 copies only. Contains an appreciation of Richard Harding Davis by Dunne.
Mr. Dooley at His Best. *New York*, 1938.
Mr. Dooley's America: A Life of Finley Peter Dunne, by Elmer Ellis. *New York*, 1941.
Contains the only printing of Dunne's unfinished memoirs.

Walter D(umaux) Edmonds

1903–

ROME HAUL. *Boston,* 1929.
 Published February, 1929 on the copyright page. Also 1,001 copies, same format
 as regular edition, with notice on the title page: *Special Presentation Edition | To
 Be Published on February 16, 1929.* Modern Library edition, *New York* [1938]
 with new introduction by the author; this edition has first edition statement on the
 copyright page. Dramatized as "The Farmer Takes a Wife."

THE BIG BARN. *Boston,* 1930.
 Published September, 1930 on the copyright page.

ERIE WATER. *Boston,* 1933.
 Published February, 1933 on the copyright page.

MOSTLY CANALLERS. *Boston,* 1934.
 Published February, 1934 on the copyright page.

DRUMS ALONG THE MOHAWK. *Boston,* 1936.
 Published May, 1936 on the copyright page. The second printing has the following statement on the copyright page: *Announced May, 1936, Published June,
 1936.*

MOSES. *Winnipeg, Toronto, Montreal* [1939].
 Privately printed and issued as a Christmas token by Charles Bush, Ltd. The copyright date, 1938, is of the original magazine copyright; the foreword, dated
 Christmas, 1939, is date of issue. This item is not to be confused with a small
 edition (said to be but 50 copies) issued by a Hartford insurance company, made
 by extracting and binding the sheets of the original magazine appearance.

CHAD HANNA. *Boston,* 1940.
 First edition so indicated on the copyright page.

THE MATCHLOCK GUN. *New York,* 1941.
 First edition indicated on copyright page.

The Best College Short Stories, 1924-1925. *Boston,* 1925.
 Contains Edmonds' "The Hanging of Kruscombe Shanks."
Young Pegasus. *New York,* 1926.
 Edited by the Intercollegiate Magazine Conference. Contains the following by
 Edmonds: "The Devil's Angels," "The Sacrament by the River," "The Three
 Wise Men," "The Coast Farmer."
Best Short Stories of 1928. *New York,* 1928.
 Edward J. O'Brien, editor. Contains "The Swamper." First binding dark blue
 cloth, gold stamping. Later, various colors stamped in black.

Best Short Stories of 1929. *New York,* 1929.
  Edward J. O'Brien, editor. Contains "Death of Red Peril."
Best Short Stories of 1931. *New York,* 1931.
  Edward J. O'Brien, editor. Contains "Water Never Hurt a Man."
Best American Love Stories of the Year. *New York* [1932].
  Margaret Widdemer, editor. Contains "Blind Eve."
O. Henry Memorial Prize Stories of 1932. *Garden City,* 1932.
  First edition so indicated on the copyright page. Contains "The Cruise of the Cashalot."
Best Short Stories of 1933. *Boston & New York,* 1933.
  Edward J. O'Brien, editor. Contains "Black Wolfe."
O. Henry Memorial Prize Stories of 1934. *Garden City,* 1934.
  First edition so indicated on the copyright page. Contains "Honor of the County."
Post Stories of 1935. *Boston,* 1936.
  First edition so indicated on the copyright page. Contains "Judge."
Stories for Men. *Boston,* 1936.
  Charles Grayson, editor. *Published August, 1936* on the copyright page. Contains an excerpt from a letter.
O. Henry Memorial Prize Stories of 1936. *Garden City,* 1936.
  First edition so indicated on the copyright page. Contains "Escape From the Mine," an episode from "Drums Along the Mohawk" but in varying form.
Post Stories of 1937. *Boston,* 1938.
  Contains "Delia Borst."
Living Speech. *New York,* 1938.
  Contains excerpts from Edmonds' "Upstate."
Writers Take Sides. *New York* [1938].
  First Printing, May, 1938, on the copyright page. Printed wrappers. Contribution
Post Stories of 1938. *Boston,* 1939.
  Contains "Young Ames Goes Down the River."
The Bedside Esquire. *New York* [1940].
  Arnold Gingrich, editor. Contains "The Resurrection of Solly Moon."

The following volumes, while containing material by Edmonds, are of no first edition interest. The material contained in the following had previous publication in the books described in the checklist above. "World's Best 100 Short Stories for 1929"; "Modern Atlantic Stories," 1933; "Book of the Short Story," 1934; "The World's Best Short Stories," 1934; "Modern College Readings," 1936; "Bedside Book of Famous American Stories," 1938; "American Sketchbook," 1938; "50 Best American Short Stories," 1939; "The Short Story Parade," 1940.

Edward Eggleston

1837–1902

MR. BLAKE'S WALKING-STICK. *Chicago, 1870.*
Wrappers.

THE BOOK OF QUEER STORIES AND STORIES TOLD ON A CELLAR DOOR.
Chicago, 1871.

THE HOOSIER SCHOOLMASTER. *New York* [1871].
First state reads *was out,* line 3, p. 71; later, *is out.* List of illustrations, in the
first state, full page plates are described thus: *(Tinted).* Revised and reissued
with notes, *New York, 1892.*

THE END OF THE WORLD. *New York* [1872].

THE MYSTERY OF METROPOLISVILLE. *New York* [1873].
Copies exist with and without publisher's advertisements; priority undetermined.

THE CIRCUIT RIDER. *New York, 1874.*
First state does not have word *Illustrated* on title page.

THE SCHOOLMASTER'S STORIES FOR BOYS AND GIRLS. *Boston, 1874.*
Mostly reprint material but with some first edition material.

ROXY. *New York, 1878.*

THE HOOSIER SCHOOL-BOY. *New York, 1883.*
The publishers state that of the first printing 105 sets of sheets were prepared with
the *Orange Judd* imprint. Further, according to Scribner, the *Orange Judd*
copies were issued a few days after the *Scribner* copies. The first state has frontispiece of *Sukey and Columbus;* later states have picture of schoolhouse interior.
Reissued, 1890, with a vocabulary as a school reader.

QUEER STORIES FOR BOYS AND GIRLS. *New York, 1884.*
Mostly reprint but with some first edition material.

THE GRAYSONS. *New York* [1888].

THE FAITH DOCTOR. *New York, 1891.*

DUFFELS. *New York, 1893.*

EGGLESTON

HISTORIES, ETC.

A History of the United States and Its People. *New York,* 1888.
  Various reissues with additions. Of these reissues the most important are:
    A First Book in American History. *New York,* 1889.
    The Household History of the United States and its People for Young Americans. *New York,* 1889.
    The Household History of the United States and Its People. *New York,* 1891.
    A History of the United States and Its People for Use of Schools. *New York,* 1899.
    The New Century History of the United States. *New York* [1904].

Stories of American Life and Adventure. *New York* [1895].
  Third grade reader. Issued also as reader for second grade.
Stories of Great Americans for Little Americans. *New York* [1895].
The Beginners of a Nation. *New York,* 1896.
The Transit of Civilization From England to America in the Seventeenth Century. *New York,* 1901.

COLLABORATIONS, ETC.

The Manual: A Practical Guide to the Sunday-School Work. *Chicago,* 1869.
The Infant Class, by Sara J. Timanus. *Chicago,* 1870.
  Edited.
Christ in Art. *New York,* 1875.
  Edited.
Christ in Literature. *New York,* 1875.
  Edited.
Famous American Indians. *New York,* 1878-1880.
  Set. With E. E. SEELYE.
Essays From *The Critic. Boston,* 1882.
  Contains Eggleston's "George Eliot and The Novel."
The Art of Authorship, George Bainton, editor. *London,* 1890.
  Contains a contribution by Eggleston.
The Schoolmaster in Literature, by H. M. Skinner. *New York* [1892].
  Introduction by Eggleston.
Sister Tabea. *New York,* 1896.
  Reprinted from "Duffels." 100 copies only.
Delights of History. *New York,* 1892-1907.
  Set. Edited.
Liber Scriptorum: The First Book of the Author's Club. *New York,* 1893.
  Contains Eggleston's "In Defense of the Dead."
Warner's Library of the World's Best Literature. *New York* [1896-97].
  Contains Eggleston's "Roger Williams: The Prophet of Religious Freedom."
American Historical Association Report for 1900.
  Contains "The New History" by Eggleston.
The First of the Hoosiers. *Philadelphia* [1903].
  Reminiscences of Eggleston by G. C. Eggleston.

Ralph Waldo Emerson
1803–1882

LETTER ... TO THE SECOND CHURCH AND SOCIETY. *Boston* [1832].
Stitched without wrappers.

A HISTORICAL DISCOURSE DELIVERED BEFORE THE CITIZENS OF CONCORD, 12TH SEPTEMBER, 1835. *Concord*, 1835.
Blue wrappers.

NATURE. *Boston*, 1836.
Anonymous. P. 94 misnumbered 92. Various cloth bindings. Reissued as "Miscellanies."

THE AMERICAN SCHOLAR. *Boston*, 1837.
"An Oration Delivered Before the Phi Beta Kappa Society ... August 31, 1837." Terra-cotta wrappers or unlettered cloth. Reprinted in England as "Man Thinking" [1843].

AN ADDRESS DELIVERED BEFORE THE SENIOR CLASS IN DIVINITY COLLEGE, CAMBRIDGE ... 15 JULY, 1838. *Boston*, 1838.
Blue wrappers.

AN ORATION DELIVERED BEFORE THE LITERARY SOCIETIES OF DARTMOUTH COLLEGE, July 24, 1838. *Boston*, 1838.
Wrappers of various colors.

THE METHOD OF NATURE. *Boston*, 1841.
"An Oration Delivered ... in Waterville College ... August 11, 1841." Terra-cotta wrappers.

ESSAYS. *Boston*, 1841.
First binding does not have *First Series* on spine. Binding noted with various stamped decorations on cover; no probable priority. Fourth edition, *Boston*, 1847, with revisions.

MAN THE REFORMER. *London*, 1842.

THE YOUNG AMERICAN. *London*, 1844.
"A Lecture Read Before the Mercantile Library Association, in Boston ... February 7, 1844." Apparently stitched without wrappers.

NATURE: AN ESSAY AND LECTURES OF THE TIMES. *London*, 1844.
Published April 10, 1844, by H. G. Clarke and Company in highly decorated wrappers and maroon boards. First issue has period after first line of title, no pages numbered 41 and 42, no imprint at foot of p. 138. First printing for "Introductory Lecture," "The Conservative" and "The Transcendentalist."

AN ADDRESS DELIVERED IN ... CONCORD ... 1ST AUGUST, 1844, ON THE
ANNIVERSARY OF THE EMANCIPATION OF THE NEGROES IN THE BRITISH
WEST INDIES. *Boston*, 1844.
Fawn wrappers.

ORATIONS, LECTURES AND ADDRESSES. *London*, 1844.
Published August 3, 1844, by H. G. Clarke and Company in highly decorated
wrappers and maroon leather. First book printing for the Phi Beta Kappa,
Divinity College, Dartmouth College, Waterville College, Man the Reformer and
Mercantile Association addresses.

ESSAYS: SECOND SERIES. *Boston*, 1844.
The probable first binding has *2D Series* on spine; probable later binding: *Second
Series* on spine. All examined copies have an error in the pagination, an hiatus
occurring at pp. 256-259, the text in no way being affected. Several types of binding and arrangement of preliminary and terminal blank leaves.

POEMS. *Boston*, 1847.
Cloth, yellow-glazed or grey-green boards, paper label on spine. 4 pp. advts.
Preceded by the English issue with *Chapman Brothers* at foot of spine and
advertisements dated November 16, 1846; should not contain an errata slip and
back cover does not have *Emerson's Poems* thereon.

REPRESENTATIVE MEN: SEVEN LECTURES. *Boston*, 1850.
⅞″ thick, hour glass design on front cover. London edition, 1850, may have
preceded American edition.

ENGLISH TRAITS. *Boston*, 1856.

THE CONDUCT OF LIFE. *Boston*, 1860.
Two states of binding: *Conduct | of | Life | Emerson* and *Emerson's | Writings |
Conduct | Of Life*. The latter is probably second. If advertisements are present
opposite the title page they must be tipped in, not bound in.

MAY-DAY AND OTHER PIECES. *Boston*, 1867.
Copies in white cloth may or may not have been so bound for presentation
purposes; however, the known presentation copies are so bound. *flowers*, for
hours, p. 184, line 4.

SOCIETY AND SOLITUDE. *Boston*, 1870.

LETTERS AND SOCIAL AIMS. *Boston*, 1876.

SELECTED POEMS. *Boston*, 1876.
New and revised edition.

FORTUNE OF THE REPUBLIC. *Boston*, 1878.
Wrappers or cloth.

THE PREACHER. *Boston*, 1880.
Wrappers.

THE CORRESPONDENCE OF THOMAS CARLYLE AND RALPH WALDO EMERSON 1834-1872. *Boston,* 1883.
2 vols. Also 250 large paper copies. Supplementary letters published *Boston,* 1886.

LECTURES AND BIOGRAPHICAL SKETCHES. *Boston,* 1884.
Published November: large paper edition published the following March.

THE SENSES AND THE SOUL, etc. *London,* 1884.
Wrappers.

NATURAL HISTORY OF THE INTELLECT AND OTHER PAPERS. *Boston,* 1893.
Also 250 large paper copies.

TWO UNPUBLISHED ESSAYS. *Boston,* 1896.

A CORRESPONDENCE BETWEEN JOHN STERLING AND RALPH WALDO EMERSON. *Boston,* 1897.

LETTERS FROM RALPH WALDO EMERSON TO A FRIEND. *Boston,* 1899.

TANTALUS. *Canton, Penna.,* 1903.
100 copies only.

CORRESPONDENCE BETWEEN RALPH WALDO EMERSON AND HERMAN GRIMM. *Boston,* 1903.
Frederick William Holls, editor.

THE JOURNALS OF RALPH WALDO EMERSON. *Boston,* 1909-1914.
10 vols. See below, *Complete Works,* 1903-1904.

LETTERS. *New York,* 1939.
6 vols. Ralph L. Rusk, editor.

COLLECTED EDITIONS

THE COMPLETE WORKS OF EMERSON. *London,* 1866.
2 vols.

THE PROSE WORKS OF EMERSON. *Boston,* 1869.
2 vols. Vol. 3 added in 1878.

THE WRITINGS OF EMERSON. *Cambridge,* 1883-1887.
16 vols. Limited to 500 sets on large paper.

THE COMPLETE WORKS OF RALPH WALDO EMERSON. *Boston,* 1903-04.
12 vols. Centenary edition. Notes by Edward Waldo Emerson. "The Journals," 10 vols., 1909-1914, issued in uniform format. Also 600 large paper sets, numbered, signed by the publishers, page of manuscript inserted.

Only separate volumes and the more important
of the separate broadsides, etc., are listed here.
More extended lists may be found in the formal
bibliographies listed at the end of this checklist.

The Offering for 1829. *Cambridge,* 1829.
Contribution by Emerson.
A Sermon Delivered at the Ordination of Hersey Bradford Godwin, etc., by James
Kendall. *Concord,* 1830.
Contribution by Emerson.
A Sermon Delivered at the Ordination of Rev. Chandler Robbins, by Henry Ware.
Boston, 1833.
Contribution by Emerson.
Sartor Resartus, by Thomas Carlyle. *Boston,* 1836.
Edited and with a preface by Emerson.
Original Hymn ₁By The Rude Bridge₎. ₁*n.p.,* 1837₎.
Single 24mo sheet.
Prospectus Soliciting Subscribers to Carlyle's Miscellaneous Writings. *Concord,* 1838.
Single sheet.
Essays, by Thomas Carlyle. *Boston,* 1838-39.
4 vols. Introduction by Emerson.
Essays and Poems, by Jones Very. *Boston,* 1839.
Edited by Emerson.
The Dial, Vols. I-IV, July 1840-April 1844. *Boston,* 1840-44.
4 vols. Edited by Emerson with others.
Two Sermons on the Death of Rev. Ezra Ripley. *Boston,* 1841.
Wrappers. Contribution.
Past and Present, by Thomas Carlyle. *Boston,* 1843.
Edited and with a short notice by Emerson. Boards, paper label on spine.
Our Pastor's Offering: A Compilation From the Writings of the Pastors of the
Second Church. *Boston,* 1845.
Contains three poems by Emerson.
The Diadem for 1846. *Philadelphia,* 1846.
Contains three poems by Emerson including "A Fable."
The Diadem for 1847. *Philadelphia,* 1847.
Contains Emerson's "The World Soul."
Aesthetic Papers. *Boston,* 1849.
Elizabeth P. Peabody, editor. Contains "War" by Emerson. Wrappers.
Prospectus of Town and Country Club. ₁*Boston,* 1849₎.
2 leaves.
Nature: Addresses and Lectures. *Boston,* 1849.
Reprint of the material in the two London volumes.
Memoirs of Margaret Fuller Ossoli. *Boston,* 1852.
2 vols. Co-editor. Emerson wrote about 200 pages.
Letter to Walt Whitman. ₁*Brooklyn?* 1855₎.
16mo broadside printed by Walt Whitman. Later included in the 1856 edition
of Whitman's "Leaves of Grass."

Excursions, by Henry David Thoreau. *Boston*, 1863.
    Edited and with a biographical sketch by Emerson.
Memorial R.G.S. *Cambridge*, 1864.
    Privately printed. Contains "Voluntaries."
The Gulistan or Rose Garden, by Musle-Huddeen Sheik Saadi. *Boston*, 1865.
    Preface by Emerson.
Plutarch's Morals, Translated From the Greek by Several Hands. *Boston*, 1870.
    Introduction by Emerson.
Remarks on the Character of George L. Stearns, at Medford, April 14, 1867. [*n.p.*, 1872].
    4 pp. leaflet.
Dedication of the ... Public Library of Concord. *Boston*, 1873.
    Address by Emerson.
Parnassus. *Boston*, 1875.
    Edited and with a preface by Emerson.
Transcendentalism in New England, by O. B. Frothingham. *New York*, 1876.
    Prints Emerson's sermon on the Lord's Supper and reprints "Letter to the Second Church and Society."
Sermon on the Death of George Adams Sampson. *Boston*, 1903.
    Privately printed, 1903.

BIOGRAPHICAL—BIBLIOGRAPHICAL

Memoir of Ralph Waldo Emerson, by James Elliot Cabot. *Boston*, 1887.
    2 vols. Also 500 large paper copies. Also an unknown number of copies issued in May in advance of publication (September) to Emerson's friends. These are marked *Advance Copy—Confidential* on each title page, and have a printed slip tipped in each volume explaining the reason for the advance copies, i.e., to have them available, but not published, on Emerson's birthday.
The Personality of Emerson, by F. B. Sanborn. *Boston*, 1903.
    Also 25 copies on Japan vellum.
A Bibliography of Ralph Waldo Emerson, by George Willis Cooke. *Boston*, 1908.
    530 copies only.
Uncollected Writings, Essays, Addresses, Reviews and Letters. *New York* [1912].
The Stephen H. Wakeman Collection of Books of Nineteenth Century American Writers. *New York* [1924].
    American Art Association catalog. Contains listing of Emerson ephemera, etc.
The Life of Emerson, by Van Wyck Brooks. *New York* [1932].
Uncollected Lectures. *New York*, 1933.
    Clarence Gohdes, editor.
A Letter of Emerson: Being the First Publication ... *Boston*, 1934.
    Willard Reed, editor.
A Bibliography of Ralph Waldo Emerson, by I. R. Brussel.
    Announced for 1941 publication.

James T(homas) Farrell

1904–

YOUNG LONIGAN: A BOYHOOD IN CHICAGO STREETS. *New York*, 1932.

GAS-HOUSE MC GINTY. *New York*, 1933.

THE YOUNG MANHOOD OF STUDS LONIGAN. *New York* [1934].
Errata slip listing eight typographical errors inserted at fly-title. Of these errors the following are sufficient to identify the first printing:
P. 88, line 18, *Connolly* for *Connell*
P. 94, line 3 from bottom, *Connolly* for *Connell*
P. 199, line 21, *quies* for *qui es*
P. 201, line 10, ... *adore Theel* for ... *adore Him!*

CALICO SHOES AND OTHER STORIES. *New York* [1934].

JUDGMENT DAY. *New York*, 1935.
The following typographical errors noted:
P. 218, line 3, *thay* for *they*
P. 378, line 15, *Shries* for *Shires*
P. 414, line 22, *huged* for *hugged*

GUILLOTINE PARTY AND OTHER STORIES. *New York* [1935].

A NOTE ON LITERARY CRITICISM. *New York* [1936].

A WORLD I NEVER MADE. *New York* [1936].
First edition so indicated on the copyright page.

CAN ALL THIS GRANDEUR PERISH? *New York* [1937].

NO STAR IS LOST. *New York* [1938].

TOMMY GALLAGHER'S CRUSADE. *New York* [1939].

FATHER AND SON. *New York* [1940].

ELLEN ROGERS.
Announced.

Readies for Bob Brown's Machine. *Cagnes Sur Mer*, 1931.
Contains Farrell's "Big Jeff," "Sylvester McGullick," "One of the Men." The last in collaboration with John A. Farrell.
Americans Abroad: An Anthology. *Hague*, 1932.
Peter Neagoe, editor. Contains "Soap" by Farrell.

Best Short Stories of 1933. *Boston*, 1933.
  Edward J. O'Brien, editor. Contains "Helen, I Love You" by Farrell.
A Story Anthology, 1931-1933. *New York*, 1933.
  Whit Burnett and Martha Foley, editors. Contains "A Casual Incident."
American Writer's Congress. *New York*, 1935.
  Henry Hart, editor. Contains "The Short Story" by Farrell.
Studs Lonigan: A Trilogy. *New York* [1935].
  Reprint. Contains the three "Studs" books with an introduction by John Chamberlain. Reissued by the Modern Library, *New York* [1938], with an introduction by Farrell.
Proletarian Literature in the United States. *New York*, 1935.
  Contains "The Buddies" by Farrell.
Stories for Men. *Boston*, 1936.
  Charles Grayson, editor. *Published August, 1936* on the copyright page. Contains "Twenty-Five Bucks" by Farrell.
365 Days: An Anthology. *New York*, 1936.
  Kay Boyle, Laurence Vail, Nina Conarain, editors. Contains "Old Age" and "White Hope of America" by Farrell.
The Short Stories of James Thomas Farrell. *New York* [1937].

William Faulkner

1897–

THE MARBLE FAUN. *Boston* [1924].
About 500 copies only of which approximately 300 were destroyed. Boards.

SOLDIERS' PAY. *New York*, 1926.

MOSQUITOES. *New York*, 1927.

THE SOUND AND THE FURY. *New York* [1929].

SARTORIS. *New York* [1929].

AS I LAY DYING. *New York* [1930].
First printing, 2,500 copies. First binding, 750 copies. First state has misplaced *I*, p. 11.

SANCTUARY. *New York* [1931].
First binding has grey end papers with a magenta all-over design. Boards, cloth back. Reissued, *New York* [1932], "Modern Library Edition," with new introduction by the author.

THESE 13. *New York* [1931].
Also 299 copies signed by the author. All copies examined have *280* for *208* in table of contents.

IDYLL IN THE DESERT. *New York*, 1931.
Boards. 400 signed copies only.

SALMAGUNDI. *Milwaukee*, 1932.
Flexible boards. 525 numbered copies only.

THIS EARTH. *New York*, 1932.
8 pp. pamphlet. 1,000 copies only.

MISS ZILPHIA GANT. [*Dallas, Texas*] 1932.
300 numbered copies only.

LIGHT IN AUGUST. *New York* [1932].
First printing so stated on copyright page. *Jefferson* for *Mottstown*, p. 340, line 1.

A GREEN BOUGH. *New York*, 1933.
Also 360 copies signed by the author, numbered.

DOCTOR MARTINO AND OTHER STORIES. *New York*, 1934.
Also 360 copies signed by the author, numbered.

PYLON. *New York,* 1935.
First printing so indicated on the copyright page. Also 310 copies signed by the author.

ABSALOM, ABSALOM! *New York,* 1936.
Also 300 numbered and signed copies.

THE UNVANQUISHED. *New York* [1938].
First printing so indicated on the copyright page. Also 250 signed copies.

THE WILD PALMS. *New York* [1939].
First printing so indicated on the copyright page. Boards, cloth back. Also 250 copies, numbered and signed.

THE HAMLET. *New York,* 1940.
First edition so indicated on the copyright page. Also 250 de luxe copies.

Ole Miss: The Year Book of the University of Mississippi, 1919-1920.
Contains Faulkner's "To a Co-Ed."
Anthology of Magazine Verse for 1925. *Boston* [1925].
William Stanley Braithwaite, editor. Contains "Lilacs" by Faulkner.
Sherwood Anderson and Other Famous Creoles. *New Orleans,* 1926.
Arranged and with an introduction by Faulkner. On the last page is a note stating that the edition is limited to 250 copies only but the printers state that 400 copies were printed. Some copies carry a slip pasted over this notice stating *Second Issue 150 copies January 1927.* Whether with the slip or not all copies are of the same printing.
On William Faulkner's "The Sound and the Fury," by Evelyn Scott. [*New York,* 1929].
Pamphlet.
O. Henry Memorial Award Prize Stories of 1931. *Garden City,* 1931.
Contains "Thrift" by Faulkner.
Pseudo-Realists, by Junius Junior. *New York* [1931].
A critical and comparative analysis of Faulkner and Ben Hecht.
American Caravan IV. *New York,* 1931.
Contains "Ad Astra" by Faulkner.
Contempo, February, 1932.
Written entirely by Faulkner. Contains "Once Aboard The Lugger" together with other material.
An Anthology of the Younger Poets. *Philadelphia,* 1932.
Oliver Welles, editor. Contains 5 poems by Faulkner. 500 copies only.
Best Short Stories of 1932. *New York,* 1932.
Edward J. O'Brien, editor. Contains "Smoke" by Faulkner.
O. Henry Memorial Award Prize Stories of 1932. *New York,* 1932.
Contains "Turn About" by Faulkner.
Best Short Stories of 1934. *Boston,* 1934.
Edward J. O'Brien, editor. Contains "Beyond."

FAULKNER

Story in America: An Anthology. *New York,* 1934.
  Contribution, "Artist at Home," by Faulkner.
O. Henry Memorial Award Prize Stories of 1934. *Garden City,* 1934.
  Contains "Wash" by Faulkner.
The Colophon, No. 19. *New York,* 1934.
  Contains "An American Comedy: An Introduction to a Bibliography of William
  Faulkner," by Aubrey Starke.
Best Short Stories of 1935. *Boston,* 1935.
  Edward J. O'Brien, editor. Contains "Lo!" by Faulkner.
O. Henry Memorial Award Prize Stories of 1936. *Garden City,* 1936.
  First edition indicated on the copyright page. Contribution.
A Southern Harvest. *Boston,* 1937.
  Robert Penn Warren, editor. Contribution.

Edna Ferber

1887–

DAWN O'HARA: THE GIRL WHO LAUGHED. *New York* [1911].

BUTTERED SIDE DOWN. *New York* [1912].
March, 1912 on copyright page.

ROAST BEEF MEDIUM. *New York* [1913].
March, 1913 on copyright page.

PERSONALITY PLUS. *New York* [1914].
Sequel to preceding. *August, 1914* on copyright page.

EMMA MC CHESNEY & CO. *New York* [1915].
Sequel to preceding.

FANNY HERSELF. *New York* [1917].

CHEERFUL BY REQUEST. *Garden City*, 1918.

HALF PORTIONS. *Garden City*, 1920.

THE GIRLS. *Garden City*, 1921.

GIGOLO. *Garden City*, 1922.
First edition so stated on copyright page.

SO BIG. *Garden City*, 1924.
First edition so stated on copyright page. Published serially as "Selina."

SHOW BOAT. *Garden City*, 1926.
Also 201 large paper copies, numbered and signed; and 1,000 copies in boards, in advance of publication, for presentation, unnumbered and unsigned.

MOTHER KNOWS BEST. *Garden City*, 1927.
First edition so stated on copyright page.

CIMARRON. *Garden City*, 1930.
Also advance issue, 1,000 copies in printed wrappers. First edition so stated on copyright page.

AMERICAN BEAUTY. *Garden City*, 1931.
Also 200 de luxe copies signed by the author. First edition so stated on copyright page.

THEY BROUGHT THEIR WOMEN. *Garden City*, 1933.
First edition so stated on copyright page.

COME AND GET IT. *Garden City*, 1935.
> First edition so stated on copyright page. *Byes* for *Eyes*, p. 403, 5th line from bottom.

NOBODY'S IN TOWN. *Garden City*, 1938.
> First edition so indicated on copyright page.

A PECULIAR TREASURE. *New York*, 1939.
> Also 351 copies, numbered and signed.

SARATOGA TRUNK.
> Announced.

PLAYS

$1200 A Year. *Garden City*, 1920.
> Three-act comedy in collaboration with Newman Levy.

Minick. *Garden City*, 1924.
> First edition so stated on copyright page. In collaboration with George S. Kaufman. Adapted from "Old Man Minick"; a short story appearing in "Gigolo," 1922. Adapted for the English stage by L. Leycester, *London*, 1930.

The Eldest. *New York*, 1925.

The Royal Family. *Garden City*, 1928.
> With George S. Kaufman.

Our Mrs. McChesney.
> Play, in collaboration with George V. Hobart. No record of publication.

Dinner at Eight. *Garden City*, 1932.
> With George F. Kaufman. First edition so stated on copyright page.

Stage Door. *Garden City*, 1936.
> With George S. Kaufman. First edition so indicated on copyright page.

REPRINTS

The Homely Heroine. *Boston* [1926].
> Reprinted from "Buttered Side Down" [1912].

The Man Who Came Back. *Boston* [1926].
> Reprinted from "Buttered Side Down" [1912].

CONTRIBUTIONS

My Maiden Effort. *Garden City*, 1921.
> First edition so stated on copyright page.

My Short Story that I Like Best. *New York*, 1924.
> Contains "The Gay Old Dog," by Miss Ferber; had previous book appearance in "Best Short Stories of 1917."

Heywood Broun as He Seemed to Us. *New York*, 1940.

BIOGRAPHICAL—BIBLIOGRAPHICAL

Edna Ferber, By Rogers Dickinson. *Garden City* [1925].
A ... Bibliography of Edna Ferber's Works. *Garden City*, 1928.
  Wrappers.

Eugene Field

1850–1895

TRIBUNE PRIMER. [*Denver, n.d.* (1881)].
Printed wrappers. "The Model Primer," *Brooklyn* [1882], is a selection from the above; later reissued with *New York* imprint.

THE SYMBOL AND THE SAINT. [*Chicago*] 1886.
Wrappers.

CULTURE'S GARLAND. *Boston*, 1887.
Cloth or printed wrappers. Also six uncut copies, some signed. P. 2 of the four leaves of advertisements at the end were written by Field.

A LITTLE BOOK OF WESTERN VERSE. *Chicago*, 1889.
Also 250 numbered large paper copies. New York edition of 1890 contains four added poems.

A LITTLE BOOK OF PROFITABLE TALES. *Chicago*, 1889.
Also 250 numbered large paper copies.

ECHOES FROM THE SABINE FARM. *New Rochelle*, 1891.
With Roswell Martin Field. 30(?) copies on Japan vellum; 70 on handmade paper. The Chicago edition of 1893 contains three added poems; 500 copies only.

SECOND BOOK OF VERSE. *Chicago*, 1892.
12 numbered copies on Japan paper; 300 numbered copies on Holland paper; also trade edition.

WITH TRUMPET AND DRUM. *New York*, 1892.
250 numbered copies published November 21, 1892. Trade edition published December 3, 1892. Also 12 copies on vellum for the author.

THE HOLY CROSS AND OTHER TALES. *Cambridge and Chicago*, 1893.
20 copies on Japan vellum; 110 copies on large paper, all signed by the publisher. New York edition of 1896 contains added material.

LOVE SONGS OF CHILDHOOD. *New York*, 1894.
15 copies on Japan vellum numbered I-XV; 106 copies on Van Gelder numbered 1-106. Also, trade edition. All states published simultaneously.

AUTO ANALYSIS. *Chicago*, 1894.
Privately printed pamphlet. 8 copies on Japan vellum. Reissued, *Chicago*, 1896. 350 numbered copies in boards.

THE LOVE AFFAIRS OF A BIBLIOMANIAC. *New York*, 1896.
Also 150 numbered copies on Holland paper. Trade edition published January 25, 1896; limited edition published February 8, 1896.

THE HOUSE. *New York,* 1896.
> Also 150 numbered large paper copies published simultaneously with trade edition.

SONGS AND OTHER VERSE. *New York,* 1896.
> Also 150 numbered large paper copies published simultaneously with trade edition.

SECOND BOOK OF TALES. *New York,* 1896.
> Also 150 numbered large paper copies published simultaneously with trade edition.

WORKS. *New York,* 1896.
> 12 vols. Also 100 de luxe sets, numbered.

FLORENCE BARDSLEY'S STORY. *Chicago,* 1897.
> Also 175 copies: 25 on Japan vellum and 150 on paper.

HOW ONE FRIAR MET THE DEVIL AND TWO PURSUED HIM. *Chicago,* 1900.
> 300 copies only. Reprinted as "The Temptation of Friar Gonsol," *Washington,* 1900, of which there were 22 copies on Japan vellum.

SHARPS AND FLATS. *New York,* 1900.
> 2 vols. "Collated by Slason Thompson." The trade edition was published December 15, 1900; the limited edition of 150 numbered copies on Holland paper, dated 1901, published March 3, 1901.

A LITTLE BOOK OF TRIBUNE VERSE. *Denver,* 1901.
> 750 copies only. Joseph G. Brown, editor.

THE STARS. *New York,* 1901.
> Also 210 large paper copies.

A LITTLE BOOK OF NONSENSE. *Boston,* 1901.
> Wrappers.

MY BOOK. [*St. Louis,* 1905].
> Privately printed.

SISTER'S CAKE AND OTHER POEMS. *New York* [1908].

CLIPPINGS FROM THE DENVER TRIBUNE. *New York,* 1909.
> 25 copies only.

PENN-YAN BILL'S WOOING. [*Cedar Rapids, Ia.*] 1914.
> Privately printed for members of The Bibliophile Society.

THE YANKEE ABROAD. [*Boston,* 1917].
> Privately printed for members of The Bibliophile Society.

VERSE AND PROSE. [*Boston*] 1917.
> Privately printed for members of The Bibliophile Society.

"Slug 14." A Doggerel Rhyme (Detailing the Fate of a "Rat" Who Spaced Nonpareil
with Brevier. Read by Eugene Field, Esq., at the Printer's Banquet, January 1st,
1876, at St. Joseph, Missouri. [*St. Joseph, Missouri,* 1875].
Broadside. 15½" x 6⅜".

The Model Primer. *Brooklyn* [1882].
See: Tribune Primer [1881], in main list.

The Journalist: A Pictorial Souvenir. *New York,* 1887.
Contribution by Field.

Little Willie.
The earliest known printing of this poem is 1888, a 4 pp. leaflet measuring
3½" x 5½".

Dibdin's Ghost. [*n.p.,* 1892].
Privately printed leaflet, 25 copies only.

First Editions of American Authors, by Herbert Stuart Stone. *Cambridge,* 1893.
Also 50 large paper copies signed by the publishers. Introduction by Field.

The Book-Lover's Almanac for 1895. *New York* [1894].
Wrappers. Contains "Dr. Rabelais."

Tributes in Memory of Mrs. Ruth C. Gray. [*Cambridge*] 1894.
Privately printed. Contribution by Field.

Songs of Childhood. *New York,* 1896.
Verses by Field, music by Reginald de Koven.

Eugene Field to Francis Wilson: Some Attentions. *New Rochelle,* 1896.
Boards. 100 copies only.

Some Letters of Edgar Allan Poe to E. H. N. Patterson of Oquawka, Illinois, With
Comments by Eugene Field. *Chicago,* 1898.
189 copies only.

Lullaby Land. *New York,* 1897.
Selected by Kenneth Grahame. Reprint.

Author's Readings. *New York* [1897].
A. H. Young, editor. Contains a recitation by and a biography of Field.

The Clink of the Ice. *Chicago* [1905?].
Reprint.

Letter: Eugene Field to Francis Wilson. *Philadelphia,* 1925.
Printed wrappers. 60 numbered copies only of which 10 were on large paper.

Conkey Stiles. *Cleveland,* 1925.
Printed wrappers. 153 numbered copies only.

Nightfall in Dordrecht. [*n.p., n.d.*].
Broadside. Printed by Will Bradley. Three copies only, numbered and signed by
Field.

In Imitation of Robert Herrick. [*n.p., n.d.*].
Pamphlet.

The Morris Book Shop. *Chicago,* 1912.
Wrappers. Contribution by Field.

Verse and Prose From the George H. Yenowine Collection of Books and Manuscripts.
St. Louis, 1917.
Henry H. Harper, editor. 100 copies only. Contains material by Field.

Some Love Letters of Eugene Field. *Buffalo,* 1927.
  110 copies only. Foreword by Thomas B. Lockwood.

"John Smith, U. S. A." is a reprint of previously published material.

BIOGRAPHICAL

Biographical Sketch [of Eugene Field]. [*n.p.,* 1894?].
  8 copies on Japan vellum only, numbered and signed by Field.
The Eugene Field I Knew, by Francis Wilson. *New York,* 1898.
  Also 12 copies on Japan vellum with additional material. Also 216 large paper
  copies.
The Eugene Field Myth, by William Marion Reedy. *St. Louis,* 1901.
Eugene Field, by Slason Thompson. *New York,* 1901.
  2 vols. Also 260 numbered copies on Holland paper.
Abroad With Mark Twain and Eugene Field, by H. W. Fisher. *New York,* 1922.
  Introduction by Merle Johnson. Also 12 copies signed by Merle Johnson and the
  author; 325 large paper copies in boards; trade edition in green cloth.
Life of Eugene Field, by Slason Thompson. *New York,* 1927.

Vardis (Alvero) Fisher

1895–

SONNETS TO AN IMAGINARY MADONNA. *New York*, 1927.
Boards. Paper label.

TOILERS OF THE HILLS. *Boston*, 1928.

DARK BRIDWELL. *Boston*, 1931.

IN TRAGIC LIFE. *Caldwell, Idaho*, 1932.
Also 25 copies in full leather signed by the author. Both this and the following title were also issued with the Garden City imprint of Doubleday-Doran. The publishers state that "the linotype slugs from which these editions were printed were sent to Garden City, and Doubleday-Doran printed their editions."

PASSIONS SPIN THE PLOT. *Caldwell, Idaho*, 1934.
Also 75 copies in full leather signed by the author. See note under preceding title.

WE ARE BETRAYED. *Caldwell, Idaho* [1935].
First edition so stated on copyright page. Also 75 copies in full leather signed by the author. Issued also by Doubleday-Doran with their name preceding *Caxton* on title page and their imprint on spine.

THE NEUROTIC NIGHTINGALE. [*Milwaukee*, 1935].
300 copies, numbered and signed. Also 25 copies for review, unnumbered and unsigned.

NO VILLAIN NEED BE. *Caldwell, Idaho*, 1936.
First edition so stated on copyright page. Also 75 numbered copies in full leather signed by the author. Issued also by Doubleday. See under "We Are Betrayed" for description of the latter.

APRIL. *Caldwell, Idaho & Garden City*, 1937.
First edition so indicated on copyright page. Also 50 signed copies.

TOURS IN EASTERN IDAHO. [*n.p.*, 1937].
Anonymous. Printed wrappers.

ODYSSEY OF A HERO. *Philadelphia*, 1937.
Boards, paper label on front cover. Also 50 copies, numbered and signed.

FORGIVE US OUR VIRTUES. *Caldwell, Idaho*, 1938.
Also 75 copies in full leather, numbered and signed.

CHILDREN OF GOD: AN AMERICAN EPIC. *New York*, 1939.
First edition so indicated on the copyright page. Also 100 copies, numbered and signed.

CITY OF ILLUSION. *New York* [1941].

First edition so indicated on the copyright page. Trade edition published by Harper's. Caxton Printers, Caldwell, Idaho, simultaneously issued two states of the book manufactured from sheets supplied by Harper's: 1,000 copies, limited; 100 copies numbered and signed by the author.

Idaho, A Guide in Word and Picture. *Caldwell, Idaho,* 1937.

Edited.

Vardis Fisher: Challenge to Evasion, by David Rein. *Chicago,* 1938.

400 copies only. Introduction by Vardis Fisher.

The Idaho Encyclopedia. *Caldwell, Idaho,* 1938.

Edited.

Idaho Lore. *Caldwell, Idaho,* 1939.

Paul Leicester Ford

1865–1902

"THE BEST LAID PLANS." [*n.p.*] 1889.

> 50 copies only, a play printed for the author. Second edition, 100 copies only. [*Brooklyn*] 1889. Reprinted in "Tattle-Tales ..." 1898.

THE HONORABLE PETER STIRLING AND WHAT PEOPLE THOUGHT OF HIM. *New York*, 1894.

> First state binding has *Sterling* for *Stirling* on cover; second, original stamping buffed-out and stamped-over with correct spelling; third, no evidence of buffing and correctly stamped.

THE GREAT K. & A. TRAIN ROBBERY. *New York*, 1897.

> Covers of first state 7¼" tall, top edges gilt, other edges untrimmed. Originally in *Lippincott's Magazine*, August, 1896, copies of which were issued with title page for the story and bound in boards, cloth back.

THE STORY OF AN UNTOLD LOVE. *Boston*, 1897.

TATTLE-TALES OF CUPID. *New York*, 1898.

JANICE MEREDITH. *New York*, 1899.

> In the first state, p. 121, line 22, the *l* in *leader* must be present. Examination indicates that the very first copies were printed from type, later copies from plates. The copies printed from type have no dot over the *N* in *REVOLUTION* on the title page. This description applies to the one volume edition published October 10th; the two-volume edition was published November 25th.

WANTED—A MATCH MAKER. *New York*, 1900.

WANTED—A CHAPERON. *New York*, 1902.

> First edition so indicated on the copyright page.

A CHECKED LOVE AFFAIR AND "THE CORTELYOU FEUD." *New York*, 1903.

> *Published October, 1903* on the copyright page.

LOVE FINDS THE WAY. *New York*, 1904.

> *Published In October, 1904* on the copyright page.

The Webster Genealogy. *Brooklyn*, 1882.

> Six copies only.

Bibliotheca Chaunciana: A List of the Writings of Charles Chauncy. *Brooklyn*, 1884.

> Privately printed on one side of paper. 10 copies numbered and signed. Half title: *Elzevir Club Series, No. 6.*

Lines to Mr. Dodson, by Frances Sargent. *Brooklyn*, 1885.

> Edited. 10 copies only.

A List of Treasury Reports and Circulars Issued by Alexander Hamilton, 1789-1795. *Brooklyn*, 1886.
  Compiled by Ford. Printed on one side of leaf, 50 copies numbered and signed.
Bibliotheca Hamiltoniana ... *New York*, 1886.
  Printed on one side of leaf, 500 copies only.
A List of Editions of *The Federalist. Brooklyn*, 1886.
  Printed on one side of leaf, 50 copies, signed.
Bibliography and Reference List of the History and Literature Relating to the Adoption of the Constitution of the United States, 1787-8. *Brooklyn*, 1888.
  250 copies only.
A List of the Members of the Federal Convention of 1787. *Brooklyn*, 1888.
  100 copies only.
Pamphlets on the Constitution of the U. S. *Brooklyn*, 1888.
  Edited. 500 numbered copies only.
Some Materials for a Bibliography of the Official Publications of the Continental Congress, 1774-89. *Brooklyn*, 1888.
  250 copies only.
Franklin Bibliography. *Brooklyn*, 1889.
  500 copies only.
Check Lists of Bibliographies, Catalogues, Reference Lists, Etc. *Brooklyn*, 1889.
  Compiled by Ford. 500 copies only.
Check-List of American Magazines Printed in the Eighteenth Century. *Brooklyn*, 1889.
  Printed on one side of leaf. 250 copies.
Who Was the Mother of Franklin's Son? An Historical Conundrum ... *Brooklyn*, 1889.
  100 numbered and signed copies. 100 copies privately reprinted, *New Rochelle*, 1932.
List of Some Briefs in Appeal Causes Which Relate to America. *Brooklyn*, 1889.
  Printed on one side of leaf. 250 copies.
A Partial Bibliography of the Published Works of Members of the American Historical Association. *Washington*, 1890.
Proceedings of a Council of War Held in Burke Jail, Georgia, June 14, 1779 ... *Brooklyn*, 1890.
  250 numbered copies only.
"The Sayings of Poor Richard," etc. ₁*Brooklyn*₁ 1890.
  100 copies only. Trade edition, *New York*, 1890.
The Origin, Purpose and Result of the Harrisburg Convention of 1788. *Brooklyn*, 1890.
  250 numbered copies only.
Bibliography of the American Historical Association. *New York*, 1890.
  Vol. iv of its "Papers."
Supplementary Bibliography of the Writings of the Members of The American Historical Association. *Washington*, 1891.
  With A. Howard Clarke.
Essays on the Constitution of the U. S. *Brooklyn*, 1892.
  Edited. 500 copies only.

The Writings of Christopher Columbus. *New York*, 1892.
Edited.
A Summary View ... by Thomas Jefferson. *Brooklyn*, 1892.
Edited. 100 copies.
Memorial Volume of the Washington Centennial. *New York*, 1893.
In collaboration with others.
Some Notes Toward an Essay on the Beginnings of American Dramatic Literature,
1606-1789. *New York*, 1893.
25 copies privately printed for the author.
James Lorimer Graham, Jr., January 17, 1894. [*New York*] 1894.
With others.
Notes on Virginia, by Thomas Jefferson. *Brooklyn*, 1894.
Edited. 100 copies.
Josiah Tucker and His Writings. *Chicago* [1894].
Writings of John Dickinson. *Philadelphia*, 1895.
3 vols. Edited.
The True George Washington. *Philadelphia*, 1896.
The New-England Primer. *New York*, 1897.
Edited. 57 copies on Japan vellum and 425 copies on handmade paper.
Great Words From Great Americans. *New York, London* [1898].
Edited.
Washington and the Theatre. *New York*, 1899.
265 copies printed by De Vinne.
The Many-Sided Franklin. *New York*, 1899.
A House Party. *Boston*, 1901.
A collection of 12 anonymous contributions. Introduction and "A Family Tra-
dition" by Ford.
Thomas Jefferson. *Boston* [1904].
500 copies printed for subscribers by the University Press.

His Version of It. *New York*, 1905.
Published October, 1905 on the copyright page. Reprinted from "Tattle-Tales ..."
1898.
A Warning to Lovers and "Sauce for the Goose is Sauce for the Gander." *New
York*, 1906.
Published, September, 1906 on the copyright page. Reprinted from "Tattle-
Tales ..." 1898.

John (William) Fox, Jr.

1862–1919

A CUMBERLAND VENDETTA AND OTHER STORIES. *New York,* 1896.

"HELL FER SARTAIN" AND OTHER STORIES. *New York,* 1897.

THE KENTUCKIANS. *New York,* 1898.

A MOUNTAIN EUROPA. *New York,* 1899.

CRITTENDEN. *New York,* 1900.

BLUE-GRASS AND RHODODENDRON. *New York,* 1901.

THE LITTLE SHEPHERD OF KINGDOM COME. *New York,* 1903.
> First state has *laugh* for *lap,* p. 61, line 14. Published September 12, 1903; advance issue, printed from magazine plates, boards with paper label, published in August. 100 copies in unstamped red cloth, edges untrimmed, printed paper label on spine, for the author and issued in advance of publication. First state of trade edition has no advertisements on verso of half title.

CHRISTMAS EVE ON LONESOME AND OTHER STORIES. *New York,* 1904.
> *Published, September, 1904* on the copyright page.

FOLLOWING THE SUN-FLAG. *New York,* 1905.

A KNIGHT OF THE CUMBERLAND. *New York,* 1906.
> First state cover stamped gold and black; later states white stamped. *Published, October, 1906* on the copyright page.

THE TRAIL OF THE LONESOME PINE. *New York,* 1908.
> First state has the *Scribner* seal on the copyright page; later states have imprint of the *Chelsea Press.* Also, first state of dedication, *F. S.* measures $\frac{3}{16}''$ high; later $\frac{1}{8}''$ high.

THE HEART OF THE HILLS. *New York,* 1913.
> *Published March, 1913* on the copyright page. Also copies in boards printed from the magazine plates, in advance of publication.

IN HAPPY VALLEY. *New York,* 1917.
> *Published October, 1917* on the copyright page.

ERSKINE DALE: PIONEER. *New York,* 1920.
> *Published September, 1920* on the copyright page.

The Blue Grass Cook Book, by Minnie C. Fox. *New York,* 1904.
> Introduction by John Fox, Jr.

FOX

R. H. D. *New York*, 1917.
    375 copies only. Contains an appreciation of Richard Harding Davis by John
Fox, Jr.

Harold Frederic
1856–1898

SETH'S BROTHER'S WIFE. *New York*, 1887.

THE LAWTON GIRL. *New York*, 1890.
Cloth or wrappers.

IN THE VALLEY. *New York*, 1890.
London edition, 1891; priority undetermined.

THE YOUNG EMPEROR: WILLIAM II OF GERMANY. *New York*, 1891.
French translation, *Paris,* 1894.

THE RETURN OF THE O'MAHONY. *New York*, 1892.
No. 71 in both "The Choice" and "The Ledger" libraries.

THE NEW EXODUS; A STUDY OF ISRAEL IN RUSSIA. *New York*, 1892.

THE COPPERHEAD. *New York*, 1893.
Reissued, *London,* 1894, with four added stories.

MARSENA AND OTHER STORIES OF THE WARTIME. *New York*, 1894.

MRS. ALBERT GRUNDY: OBSERVATIONS IN PHILISTIA. *London and New York*, 1896.
Vol. 6 in "The Mayfair Set."

THE DAMNATION OF THERON WARE. *Chicago*, 1896.
Reprints are so stated on copyright page.

MARCH HARES. *New York*, 1896.
George Forth, pseudonym. Reissue same year with author's name.

THE DESERTER AND OTHER STORIES. *Boston* [1898].

GLORIA MUNDI. *Chicago*, 1898.

THE MARKET-PLACE. *New York* [1899].
Noted in both plain and pictorial cloth with no known priority. Later editions have been noted in the pictorial cloth.

Vandyke Brown Poems, by Marc Cooke. *Boston,* 1883.
With preface by Harold Frederic. This item has been noted in two states with no known priority.
Tales of Our Coast. *New York,* 1896.
By various authors. Contains "The Path of Murtogh" by Frederic.

FREDERIC

In The Sixties. *New York*, 1897.
   Reprinted from "The Copperhead" and "Marsena." Contains an introduction
here first printed.

Mary E[leanor] Wilkins Freeman
1852–1930

DECORATIVE PLAQUES. *Boston* [1883].

THE ADVENTURES OF ANN. *Boston* [1886].

A HUMBLE ROMANCE. *New York*, 1887.

A NEW ENGLAND NUN AND OTHER STORIES. *New York*, 1891.

THE POT OF GOLD AND OTHER STORIES. *Boston* [1892].

YOUNG LUCRETIA AND OTHER STORIES. *New York*, 1892.

GILES COREY, YEOMAN. *New York*, 1893.
The copyright deposit copy is in cloth. Copies have been noted in printed paper boards.

JANE FIELD. *New York*, 1893.

PEMBROKE. *New York*, 1894.
Advertisements have no reviews of this title. Biographical edition, *New York*, 1899.

COMFORT PEASE AND HER GOLD RING. *New York and Chicago*, 1895.

MADELON. *New York*, 1896.

JEROME, A POOR YOUNG MAN. *New York*, 1897.

ONCE UPON A TIME, AND OTHER CHILD-VERSES. *Boston* [1897].

SILENCE AND OTHER STORIES. *New York*, 1898.

THE PEOPLE OF OUR NEIGHBORHOOD. *Philadelphia and New York* [1898].

IN COLONIAL TIMES. *Boston* [1899].

THE JAMESONS. *New York and Philadelphia*, 1899.

THE HEART'S HIGHWAY. *New York*, 1900.

THE LOVE OF PARSON LORD AND OTHER STORIES. *New York*, 1900.

UNDERSTUDIES. *New York*, 1901.

THE PORTION OF LABOR. *New York*, 1901.

SIX TREES. *New York*, 1903.
Published February, 1903 on the copyright page.

THE WIND IN THE ROSE-BUSH. *New York*, 1903.
    Published March, 1903 on the copyright page. A later binding has a picture pasted to the front cover.

THE GIVERS. *New York*, 1904.
    Published June, 1904 on the copyright page.

THE DEBTOR. *New York*, 1905.

"DOC." GORDON. *New York*, 1906.

BY THE LIGHT OF THE SOUL. *New York*, 1906.
    Published September, 1906 on the copyright page.

THE FAIR LAVINIA. *New York*, 1907.
    Published October, 1907 on the copyright page.

THE SHOULDERS OF ATLAS. *New York*, 1908.
    Published June, 1908 on the copyright page.

THE WINNING LADY. *New York*, 1909.
    Published October, 1909 on the copyright page.

THE GREEN DOOR. *New York*, 1910.
    Published September, 1910 on the copyright page.

THE BUTTERFLY HOUSE. *New York*, 1912.
    Published, February, 1912 on the copyright page.

THE YATES PRIDE. *New York*, 1912.
    Code letters *G-M* on the copyright page.

THE COPY-CAT AND OTHER STORIES. *New York*, 1914.
    Code letters *H-O* on the copyright page.

AN ALABASTER BOX. *New York*, 1917.
    With FLORENCE MORSE KINGSLEY. (1) below last line of text.

EDGEWATER PEOPLE. *New York* [1918].
    Boards, cloth back. Code letters *K-S* on the copyright page.

Golden Years: Original and Selective Stories. *Boston* [1886].
    Contribution.
The Long Arm [and other Stories]. *London*, 1895.
    Title story by Mrs. Freeman.
In Memory of Sarah Earle Stevens. *Boston*, 1898.
    Contribution. Boards.
Evelina's Garden. *New York*, 1899.
    Reprinted from "Silence," 1898.

The Home-Coming of Jessica.
> A short story in: "Three Short Stories," (cover title). Issued by *The Woman's Home Companion, New York, Springfield, Chicago,* 1901.
> Printed wrappers.

The World's Great Woman Novelists. [*Philadelphia,* 1901].
> Contains "Emily Brontë and Wuthering Heights" by Mrs. Freeman.

Little Lasses. *Akron* [1904].
> Contribution.

Little Lads. *Akron* [1904].
> Contribution.

Short Story Classics. *New York* [1905].
> Vol. 4. Edited by William Patten. Contains "The Hall Bedroom."

The Arabella and Araminta Stories, by Gertrude Smith. *Boston,* 1905.
> Introduction. Also de luxe edition.

The Whole Family: A Novel by Twelve Authors. *New York,* 1908.
> Contribution.

The Pilgrim's Progress Adapted to a Motion Picture Play. *New York,* 1915.
> With William Dinwiddie.

The Best Stories of Mary E. Wilkins. *New York,* 1927.
> Henry Wysham Lanier, editor. First printing so indicated on copyright page.

A Nineteenth Century Puritan: A Biography of Mary E. Freeman, by Thomas S. Shaw.
> Unpublished.

Philip (Morin) Freneau

1752–1832

THE AMERICAN VILLAGE. *New York*, 1772.

A POEM ON THE RISING GLORY OF AMERICA. *Philadelphia*, 1772.
Anon. With H. H. BRACKENRIDGE.

AMERICAN LIBERTY. *New York*, 1775.
Anonymous.

A VOYAGE TO BOSTON. *New York* [1775].
Anonymous. Later issued *Philadelphia*, 1775.

GENERAL GAGE'S CONFESSION. [*New York*] 1775.
Anonymous.

THE BRITISH PRISON-SHIP: A POEM. *Philadelphia*, 1781.
Anonymous.

THE POEMS OF PHILIP FRENEAU. *Philadelphia*, 1786.
Probable first state is on heavy paper with p. 257 unnumbered.

A JOURNEY FROM PHILADELPHIA TO NEW YORK. *Philadelphia*, 1787.
Anonymous. *By Robert Slender, Stocking Weaver.* Reissued with revisions
Philadelphia, 1809.

THE MISCELLANEOUS WORKS OF MR. PHILIP FRENEAU. *Philadelphia*, 1788

THE VILLAGE MERCHANT. *Philadelphia*, 1794.
Anon. Some copies noted with p. 7 unnumbered.

POEMS WRITTEN BETWEEN THE YEARS 1768 & 1794. *Monmouth*, 1795
Copies have been noted with faulty pagination and with last line of text missing

LETTERS ON VARIOUS INTERESTING AND IMPORTANT SUBJECTS. *Philadel
phia*, 1799.
Robert Slender, O. S. M., pseud.

POEMS ... THIRD EDITION. *Philadelphia*, 1809.
2 vols. Contains material here first collected.

A COLLECTION OF POEMS. *New York*, 1815.
2 vols.

SOME ACCOUNT OF THE CAPTURE OF THE SHIP "AURORA." *New York*
[1899].

There are numerous anonymous works which have been attributed to Freneau; among these are the following.

The Last Words, Dying Speech, and Confession of J—s R—g—n, P—t—r ... Executed ... Thirteen ... April, 1775.
 [n.p., n.d.].
Tom Gage's Proclamation Versified. *New York*, June 30, 1775.
General Gage's Soliloquy. *New York*, 1775.
The Probationary Odes of Jonathan Pindar, Esq. *Philadelphia*, 1796.
Negara and Altavola, 1797.

In addition to the following secondary productions, Freneau was also the author of several broadsheets issued as New Year's greetings by eighteenth century newspapers.

The Travels of Imagination ... *Philadelphia*, 1778.
 Contains Freneau's "American Independence."
New Travels Through North America ... by Abbé Robin. *Philadelphia*, 1783.
 Translated by Freneau. Attributed.
The Monmouth Almanac For the Year 1795. *Middletown-Point* [1794].
 Contribution by Freneau.
Poems, by the Late Josias Lyndon Arnold, Esq. *Providence*, 1797.
 Contains "The Last Words of Shalum, or, the Dying Indian," by Freneau.
Poems Relating to the American Revolution, by Philip Freneau. *New York*, 1865.
 E. A. Duyckinck, editor.
Proceedings of the Huguenot Society of America, Vol. II, 1891. *New York*, 1891.
 Contains "Philip Freneau, The Huguenot Poet Patriot of the American Revolution ..." by Edward F. de Lancey.
Philip Freneau: The Poet of the Revolution ... by Mary S. Austin. *New York*, 1901.
 Helen Kearney Vreeland, editor.
The Political Activities of Philip Freneau, by Samuel E. Forman. *Baltimore*, 1902.
 Contains a bibliography.
A Bibliography of the Separate and Collected Works of Philip Freneau, by Victor Hugo Paltsits. *New York*, 1903.
Unpublished Freneauana. *New York*, 1918.
 Boards. 51 copies only.
That Rascal Freneau: A Study in Literary Failure, by Lewis Leary. [*New Brunswick, N. J.*, 1941].
 Contains a bibliography.

Robert (Lee) Frost
1875–

A BOY'S WILL. *London,* 1913.

Four states noted as follows: 1st: bound in pebbled bronze cloth; 2nd: white vegetable parchment, stamped in red; 3d: buff wrappers, black stamped with the *A* decorated with a horizontal rule at the top; 4th: buff wrappers with plain *A*. The first American edition, *New York,* 1915, has *aind* for *and,* p. 14, last line. Reissued with woodcut on title page by T. W. Nason, *New York,* 1935.

NORTH OF BOSTON. *London* [1914].

Issued in four states of binding as follows: 1st: green buckram, gold lettering, blind rule border all around front cover. 2nd: green cloth with blind lettering on front, spine gilt lettered, blind rule border all around front cover; 3d: blue cloth, black lettering, all edges trimmed; 4th: green buckram, gold lettering, blind rule at top and bottom of front cover with either all edges trimmed or top edge only trimmed.

American edition, *New York,* 1914, brown boards, cloth back; made up of the English sheets with new title page tipped in on stub. The first major Frost book to be printed in America was this collection, *New York,* 1915. Reissued with illustrations, *New York* [1919].

MOUNTAIN INTERVAL. *New York* [1916].

Two states: 1st: p. 88, verses 6 and 7, are duplications; 2nd state: duplication corrected by means of a cancel-leaf. Reissued *New York,* 1921.

NEW HAMPSHIRE: A POEM WITH NOTES AND GRACE NOTES. *New York,* 1923.

Also 350 copies numbered and signed by the author. Boards.

WEST-RUNNING BROOK. *New York* [1928].

Also 1,000 numbered and signed copies printed by the Merrymount Press, signed. Trade edition, unsigned, printed by The Plimpton Press; first edition so stated on copyright page. *Roams* for *romps* (p. 38 in the limited edition, p. 44 in the trade edition) occurs in all examined copies.

A WAY OUT. *New York,* 1929.

Boards, cloth back. One-act play. 485 copies only, signed. Previously in: "More One-Act Plays," *New York,* 1927, H. L. Cohen, editor.

THE COW'S IN THE CORN. *Gaylordsville,* 1929.

"A One-Act Irish Play in Rhyme." 91 copies only, numbered and signed. Erratum slip inserted.

THE LOVELY SHALL BE CHOOSERS. *New York,* 1929.

475 copies only in "The Random House Poetry Quartos." Printed wrappers.

COLLECTED POEMS. *New York*, 1930.

1,000 copies with *Random House* imprint, numbered and signed. Trade edition, *Holt* imprint, later; also with imprint of *Longmans* for the English trade. Contains material here first in book form. The Holt edition is undated on the title page [1930] and with notice of first edition on the copyright page. Both large and small paper states on p. 128, print *laces* for *faces*.

TWO LETTERS WRITTEN ON HIS UNDERGRADUATE DAYS AT DARTMOUTH COLLEGE IN 1892. *Hanover*, 1931.

Wrappers. Paper label on front cover. 10 copies only.

THE LONE STRIKER. [*n.p.*, *New York*, 1933].

Pamphlet. No. 8 in the "Borzoi Chap Books."

TWO TRAMPS IN MUD TIME. [*v.p.*] 1934.

Wrappers. Issued as a Christmas greeting by several persons.

NEITHER OUT FAR NOR IN DEEP. [*n.p.*] 1935.

Wrappers. Issued as a Christmas greeting by several persons.

THE GOLD HESPERIDEE. [*Cortland, N. Y.*, 1935].

Wrappers. First state has code letter A on copyright page and next to last line, p. 7, unturned; second state has the line turned and carried over.

THREE POEMS. *Hanover, N.H.* [1935].

125 copies only; privately printed. Wrappers. Early poems here collected for the first time.

A FURTHER RANGE. *New York* [1936].

Also 803 large paper copies, numbered and signed, published May 20. Trade edition, 4,100 copies, unnumbered, first edition so stated on copyright page, published May 29. The order blank issued by the publishers in advance of publication prints the dedication in form other than that in which it finally appeared in the book. "Book of the Month Club" edition published June.

TO A YOUNG WRETCH. [*v.p.*,1937].

Wrappers. Issued with seven varying imprints as a Christmas token.

TRIPLE PLATE. [*v.p.*, 1939].

Wrappers. Issued with eight varying imprints as a Christmas token.

COLLECTED POEMS. *New York*, 1939.

First edition so indicated on the copyright page.

OUR HOLD ON THE PLANET. [*v.p.*, 1940].

Wrappers. Issued with several varying imprints as a Christmas token.

Robert Frost is today so widely read that many critical studies have been published in periodicals and book form. Included in the following list is a representative selection of these comments. For a complete list of the books to which Frost has contributed see "Robert Frost: A Chronological Survey," *Middletown, Conn.*, 1936, and "Robert Frost: A Bibliography" by W. B. S. Clymer and C. R. Green, *Amherst*, 1937. The latter was published in an edition limited to 650 copies of which 150 were signed by the subject.

Twilight. [*Lawrence, Mass.*, 1894].
> Two copies only. 20 pp. bound in leather. Contains five poems, all of which have been uncollected save "My Butterfly" which appears in "A Boy's Will."

The Mosher Books. *Portland, Me.*, 1913.
> Printed wrappers. Contains "Reluctance."

A Treasury of War Poetry. *Boston*, 1917.
> George Herbert Clarke, editor. Issued in cloth, wrappers and leather. Contribution.

Others For 1919: An Anthology of the New Verse. *New York*, 1920.
> Alfred Kreymborg, editor. Contribution.

A Miscellany of American Poetry, 1920. *New York*, 1920.
> Contributions.

American and British Verse from the Yale Review. *New Haven*, 1920.
> Contribution.

The Pilgrim Spirit, by George P. Baker. *Boston* [1921].
> Contains Frost's "The Return of the Pilgrims." Cloth or wrappers. P. 74, line 8, has the name *Brewster;* later removed. Some copies have an erratum slip at the same page.

A Miscellany of American Poetry, 1922. *New York* [1922].
> Contributions.

Selected Poems. *New York*, 1923.
> *March, 1923* on copyright page. Revised, *New York* [1928] first printing so indicated on copyright page. Further revised, *New York* [1934]. Title page marked Third Edition.

Memoirs of the Notorious Stephen Burroughs. *New York*, 1924.
> Preface.

Dartmouth Verse, 1925. *Portland, Me.*, 1925.
> Introduction.

Prose Preferences. *New York*, 1926.
> Sidney Cox and E. Freeman, editors. First edition so indicated on the copyright page. Contribution.

A Miscellany of American Poetry, 1927. *New York* [1927].
> Contributions by Frost. First edition so stated.

Percy MacKaye: A Symposium on His Fiftieth Birthday. *Hanover, N. H.*, 1928.
> Contains "Poet—One of the Truest" by Frost.

The Second American. *New York*, 1928.
> Contribution.

Fifty Poets. *New York* [1933].
> William Rose Benét, editor. Contribution.

Come Christmas. *New York* [1935].
> Lesley Frost, editor. Contains a poem by Frost, "Good Relief," reproduced in facsimile autograph.

King Jasper, by Edwin Arlington Robinson. *New York*, 1935.
Also 250 de luxe copies. Introduction by Frost.
From Snow to Snow. *New York* [1936].
Wrappers. Selected poems, reprint material.
Everybody's Sanity. *Los Angeles*, 1936.
Pamphlet.
Portraits and Self-Portraits, by Georges Schreiber. *Boston*, 1936.
Contribution.
The Stag at Ease, by Marian Squire. *Caldwell*, 1938.
Contribution.
Bread Loaf Anthology. *Middlebury, Vt.*, 1939.
Preface.

BIOGRAPHICAL AND BIBLIOGRAPHICAL

Tendencies in Modern Poetry, by Amy Lowell. *New York*, 1917.
Chapter on Frost.
Fire Under the Andes, by Elizabeth Shepley Sergeant. *New York*, 1927.
Contains a chapter on Frost.
Robert Frost, by Gorham B. Munson. *New York* [1927].
Contemporary American Authors, by J. C. Squire and the Critics of *The London Mercury*. *New York*, 1928.
Chapter on Frost by John Freeman.
Robert Frost: Original "Ordinary Man," by Sidney Cox. *New York* [1929].
1,000 signed copies only. Also reprinted in wrappers.
Robert Frost and His Books, by Frederic G. Melcher.
In: "The Colophon," No. 2, *New York*, 1930. Contains a bibliography.
The White Hills, by Cornelius Weygandt. *New York*, 1934.
Chapter on Frost.
The Less Travelled Road: A Study of Robert Frost, by Caroline Ford. *Cambridge*, 1935.
Robert Frost: A Chronological Survey. *Middletown, Conn.*, 1936.
250 copies only of which 25 were printed on Fabriano handmade paper. All numbered.
Threescore: The Autobiography of Sarah N. Cleghorn. *New York*, 1936.
First edition so stated on copyright page. Introduction.
Robert Frost: A Bibliography, by W. B. Shubrick Clymer and Charles R. Green. *Amherst*, 1937.
650 copies only of which 150 were signed by Mr. Frost.
Recognition of Robert Frost. *New York* [1937].
Edited by Richard Thornton.
Robert Frost: Godfather of Bread Loaf. [*n.p., n.d. (Middlebury, Vt.*, 1939)].
By W. Storrs Lee. Printed wrappers.
A Chat With Robert Frost. *Webster Groves, Mo.*, 1940.
100 copies only.

Henry Blake Fuller

1857–1929

THE CHEVALIER OF PENSIERI-VANI. *Boston* [1890].
Stanton Page, *pseudonym*. Cloth or wrappers, no priority for either. An advertisement in *The Publishers' Weekly*, January 24, 1891, offered the book in "cloth, $1; paper, 50¢". Another edition, with additions *New York*, 1892, with the author's name. Revised and reissued, *New York*, 1899.

THE CHATELAINE OF LA TRINITÉ. *New York*, 1892.

THE CLIFF-DWELLERS. *New York*, 1893.

WITH THE PROCESSION. *New York*, 1895.

THE PUPPET BOOTH: TWELVE PLAYS. *New York*, 1896.

FROM THE OTHER SIDE: STORIES OF TRANSATLANTIC TRAVEL. *Boston*, 1898.

THE LAST REFUGE: A SICILIAN ROMANCE. *Boston*, 1900.

UNDER THE SKYLIGHTS. *New York*, 1901.

WALDO TRENCH AND OTHERS. *New York*, 1908.
Published September 1908 on the copyright page.

LINES LONG AND SHORT: BIOGRAPHICAL SKETCHES IN VARIOUS RHYTHMS. *Boston*, 1917.

ON THE STAIRS. *Boston*, 1918.
Published March 1918 on the copyright page.

BERTRAM COPE'S YEAR: A NOVEL. *Chicago*, 1919.

GARDENS OF THIS WORLD. *New York*, 1929.
2,000 numbered copies only.

NOT ON THE SCREEN. *New York*, 1930.
3,000 numbered copies only.

The New Flag. [*n.p.*, 1899].
Printed wrappers.
The Coffee House, by Carlo Goldoni. *New York*, 1925.
Translated by Fuller.
The Fan, by Carlo Goldoni. *New York* [1925].
Translated by Fuller.
Hamlin Garland: A Son of the Middle Border. [*N. Y.*, 1926?].
Contribution.

Henry B. Fuller, by Carl Van Vechten. *Chicago*, 1929.
Tributes to Henry B——. [*Privately Printed*, 1929].
   Anna Morgan, editor.
Henry Blake Fuller: A Critical Biography, by Constance M. Griffin. *Philadelphia*,
   1939.
   Contains some hitherto unpublished material by Fuller.

(Hannibal) Hamlin Garland

1860–1940

UNDER THE WHEEL: A MODERN PLAY IN SIX SCENES. *Boston,* 1890.
Wrappers. *See:* "Jason Edwards," 1892.

MAIN-TRAVELLED ROADS. *Boston,* 1891.
Wrappers, number of thousand printed at foot of front wrapper. Also copies bound in either blue or grey cloth with various states of stamping. The cloth-bound copies are said to have been for the author's personal use, but contemporary advertisements prove that the book was regularly published in both cloth and wrappers. The first edition measures $\frac{7}{8}$" thick across the pages; an apparent later issue measures $\frac{7}{8}$" at the same place. Reissued with additional material *New York,* 1907.

A MEMBER OF THE THIRD HOUSE. *Chicago* [1892].
Cloth or wrappers.

JASON EDWARDS, AN AVERAGE MAN. *Boston,* 1892.
Cloth or wrappers. The wrappers are dated (misdated?) 1891. A novelized version of "Under The Wheel."

A LITTLE NORSK: OR, OL' PAP'S FLAXEN. *New York,* 1892.
Boards.

A SPOIL OF OFFICE. *Boston,* 1892.
Cloth or wrappers. Revised edition, *New York,* 1897.

PRAIRIE FOLKS. *Chicago,* 1893.
Noted in wrappers. Revised edition *New York,* 1899.

PRAIRIE SONGS. *Chicago and Cambridge,* 1893.
Also de luxe edition of 110 copies. First edition so indicated on the copyright page.

CRUMBLING IDOLS. *Chicago,* 1894.

ROSE OF DUTCHER'S COOLLY. *New York,* 1895.
Revised edition, *New York,* 1899.

WAYSIDE COURTSHIPS. *New York,* 1897.
Later used as material for revised edition of "Main-Travelled Roads" and "Other Main-Travelled Roads."

ULYSSES S. GRANT: HIS LIFE AND CHARACTER. *New York,* 1898.

THE SPIRIT OF SWEETWATER. *Philadelphia and New York* [1898].
Complete version later published with original magazine title, "Witch's Gold," *New York,* 1906, in cloth or publisher's leather.

THE TRAIL OF THE GOLDSEEKERS. *New York*, 1899.

BOY LIFE ON THE PRAIRIE. *New York*, 1899.
  Revised edition, *New York*, 1908.

THE EAGLE'S HEART. *New York*, 1900.

HER MOUNTAIN LOVER. *New York*, 1901.

THE CAPTAIN OF THE GRAY HORSE TROOP. *New York*, 1902.
  Published March, 1902 on the copyright page.

HESPER. *New York*, 1903.
  Published October, 1903 on the copyright page.

THE LIGHT OF THE STAR. *New York*, 1904.
  Published May, 1904 on the copyright page.

THE TYRANNY OF THE DARK. *New York*, 1905.
  Published May, 1905 on the copyright page.

THE LONG TRAIL. *New York*, 1907.
  Published April, 1907 on the copyright page.

MONEY MAGIC. *New York*, 1907.
  Published October, 1907 on the copyright page.

THE SHADOW WORLD. *New York*, 1908.
  Published September, 1908 on the copyright page.

THE MOCCASIN RANCH. *New York*, 1909.
  Published September, 1909 on the copyright page.

CAVANAGH, FOREST RANGER. *New York*, 1910.
  Published March, 1910 on the copyright page.

OTHER MAIN-TRAVELLED ROADS. *New York* [1910].
  See: "Wayside Courtships," 1897.

VICTOR OLLNEE'S DISCIPLINE. *New York*, 1911.
  Published September, 1911 on the copyright page.

THE FORESTER'S DAUGHTER. *New York*, 1914.
  Code letters *A-O* on the copyright page.

THEY OF THE HIGH TRAILS. *New York*, 1916.

A SON OF THE MIDDLE BORDER. *New York*, 1917.
  Also special autograph edition.

A DAUGHTER OF THE MIDDLE BORDER. *New York*, 1921.

A PIONEER MOTHER. *Chicago,* 1922.
  525 copies only as follows: 500 in wrappers, 25 tall paper copies in boards.

THE BOOK OF THE AMERICAN INDIAN. *New York,* 1923.
  First edition so stated on copyright page.

TRAIL-MAKERS OF THE MIDDLE BORDER. *New York,* 1926.

MEMORIES OF THE MIDDLE BORDER. *New York,* 1926.

THE WESTWARD MARCH OF AMERICAN SETTLEMENT. *Chicago,* 1927.

BACK-TRAILERS FROM THE MIDDLE BORDER. *New York,* 1928.

ROADSIDE MEETINGS. *New York,* 1930.

COMPANIONS ON THE TRAIL. *New York,* 1931.

MY FRIENDLY CONTEMPORARIES. *New York,* 1932.

AFTERNOON NEIGHBORS. *New York,* 1934.

LONG TRAIL. *New York,*1935.

FORTY YEARS OF PSYCHIC RESEARCH. *New York,* 1936.

IOWA, O IOWA! *Iowa City,* 1935.

THE MYSTERY OF THE BURIED CROSSES. *New York,* 1939.
  First edition so indicated on the copyright page.

A New Declaration of Rights. [*n.p.,* 1891?].
Out-of-Door Americans. [*Philadelphia,* 1901].
  Contributions.
Witch's Gold. *New York,* 1906.
  See: "The Spirit of Sweetwater," [1898].
The Grand Canyon of Arizona. Published by the Passenger Department of the
  Santa Fé. 1909.
  Contains "The Grand Canyon at Night" and "John Hance: A Study."
For France. *Garden City,* 1917.
  Contains Garland's "Jim Mattison of Wagon Wheel Gap."
Prairie Gold. *Topeka, Kansas* [1917].
  Contains "The Graven Image" by Garland.
My Maiden Effort. *Garden City,* 1921.
  Contribution. First edition so stated on copyright page.
Joseph Crosby Lincoln. [*New York,* 1921?].
  Wrappers.
Proceedings of the American Academy. *New York,* 1922.
  Contains "Commemorative Tribute to James Whitcomb Riley" by Garland.

Hamlin Garland: A Son of the Middle Border. [*New York*, 1926?].
  Wrappers.
Percy MacKaye: A Symposium on His Fiftieth Birthday. *Hanover, N. H.*, 1928.
  300 copies only, privately printed. Contribution by Garland.
Prairie Song and Western Story. *Boston*, 1928.
  Selected reprints. Stella S. Center, editor.
American Writers on American Literature. *New York* [1931].
  Contains Garland's "William Dean Howells." John Macy, editor.
The American Historical Scene. *Philadelphia*, 1935.
  Contains "Osceola's Defiance," by Garland.
Joys of the Trail. *Chicago,* 1935.
  100 signed copies only, privately printed for members of "The Bookfellows."
Old Favorites From the McGuffey Readers. *Cincinnati* [1936].
  Co-editor.
Reflections and Essays, by Leo Tolstoi. *Oxford*, 1937.
  Vol. 21 contains an introduction by Garland.

Ellen (Anderson Gholson) Glasgow

1874–

THE DESCENDANT. *New York*, 1897.

Anon. The first printing has *New York* imprint only; later, *New York & London* imprint. First binding does not have the author's name on the spine.

PHASES OF AN INFERIOR PLANET. *New York*, 1898.

Erratum slip at back regarding error at p. 194.

THE VOICE OF THE PEOPLE. *New York*, 1900.

Copies in green cloth binding with *Author's Edition* stamped at the foot of the spine are a later binding. A reissue appears in a pictorial red cloth binding.

THE FREEMAN AND OTHER POEMS. *New York*, 1902.

Boards.

THE BATTLE-GROUND. *New York*, 1902.

Published March 1902 on the copyright page.

THE DELIVERANCE. *New York*, 1904.

Copies noted with either three or four illustrations. No known priority but copies in smooth red cloth are believed earlier than copies in rough red cloth.

THE WHEEL OF LIFE. *New York*, 1906.

Published, January, 1906 on the copyright page.

THE ANCIENT LAW. *New York*, 1908.

Published, January, 1908 on the copyright page.

THE ROMANCE OF A PLAIN MAN. *New York*, 1909.

THE MILLER OF OLD CHURCH. *Garden City*, 1911.

VIRGINIA. *Garden City*, 1913.

LIFE AND GABRIELLA. *Garden City*, 1916.

THE BUILDERS. *Garden City*, 1919.

ONE MAN IN HIS TIME. *Garden City*, 1922.

First edition so indicated on the copyright page.

THE SHADOWY THIRD AND OTHER STORIES. *Garden City*, 1923.

First edition so stated on copyright page.

BARREN GROUND. *Garden City*, 1925.

First edition so stated on copyright page. Also advance edition of 500 copies in boards. Reissued by the Modern Library with a new introduction, *New York* [1936].

THE ROMANTIC COMEDIANS. *Garden City*, 1926.
  First edition so stated on copyright page. Also 500 copies specially bound for presentation.

THEY STOOPED TO FOLLY. *Garden City*, 1929.
  The first 3,000 copies were printed for "The Old Dominion Edition."

THE SHELTERED LIFE. *Garden City*, 1932.
  Also 300 signed copies. First edition so stated on copyright page.

VEIN OF IRON. *New York* [1935].
  First edition so stated on copyright page.

IN THIS OUR LIFE. *New York* [1941].
  First printing indicated on copyright page.

COLLECTED WORKS

The Old Dominion Edition of the Works of Ellen Glasgow. *Garden City*, 1929-1933.
  Each volume revised and with a new preface. 16 volumes.
The Virginia Edition of the Works of Ellen Glasgow. *New York*, 1938.
  With new prefaces by the author. 12 volumes. 810 sets only, signed.

BIOGRAPHICAL

Ellen Glasgow: Novelist of the Old and the New South: An Appreciation by Louise Maunsell Field. *Garden City* [1923].
  Wrappers.
Ellen Glasgow, by Dorothea Lawrence Mann. *Garden City*, 1927.
Ellen Glasgow: Critical Essays. *Garden City*, 1929.
  First printing indicated on copyright page. Essays by Stuart P. Sherman, Sara Haardt, Emily Clark. Wrappers.
A Memorial Volume of Virginia Historical Portraiture, 1585-1830. *Richmond*, 1930.
  Alexander Wilbourne Weddell, editor. Introduction by Miss Glasgow.
What is a Book? *Boston*, 1935.
  Dale Warren, editor. Contains "Heroes and Monsters" by Miss Glasgow.
Of Ellen Glasgow, An Inscribed Portrait. By Ellen Glasgow and James Branch Cabell. *New York*, 1938.
  109 copies only.

Anna Katharine Green (Rohlfs)

1846–1935

THE LEAVENWORTH CASE. *New York*, 1878.
  A 4to edition in wrappers was published about 1882.

A STRANGE DISAPPEARANCE. *New York*, 1880.

THE SWORD OF DAMOCLES. *New York*, 1881.

THE DEFENSE OF THE BRIDE AND OTHER POEMS. *New York*, 1882.

X.Y.Z. *New York*, 1883.
  Printed wrappers.

HAND AND RING. *New York*, 1883.

THE MILL MYSTERY. *New York*, 1886.
  Printed wrappers.

RISIFI'S DAUGHTER. *New York*, 1887.

7 TO 12: A DETECTIVE STORY. *New York*, 1887.
  Printed wrappers.

BEHIND CLOSED DOORS. *New York*, 1888.

THE FORSAKEN INN. *New York* [1890].

A MATTER OF MILLIONS. *New York*, 1890.

THE OLD STONE HOUSE. *New York*, 1891.

CYNTHIA WAKEHAM'S MONEY. *New York*, 1892.

MARKED "PERSONAL." *New York*, 1893.

MISS HURD: AN ENIGMA. *New York*, 1894.
  Noted with and without advertisements facing title page; no established priority.
  The copyright deposit copy has the advertisements.

THE DOCTOR, HIS WIFE AND THE CLOCK. *New York*, 1895.

DR. IZARD. *New York*, 1895.

THAT AFFAIR NEXT DOOR. *New York*, 1897.

LOST MAN'S LANE. *New York*, 1898.
  Printed wrappers.

AGATHA WEBB. *New York*, 1899.

THE CIRCULAR STUDY. *New York,* 1900.

A DIFFICULT PROBLEM, *etc. New York,* 1900.

ONE OF MY SONS. *New York,* 1901.

THREE WOMEN AND A MYSTERY. [*New York,* 1902].

THE FILIGREE BALL. *Indianapolis* [1903].
March on the copyright page.

THE MILLIONAIRE BABY. *Indianapolis* [1905].
January on the copyright page.

THE AMETHYST BOX. *Indianapolis* [1905].
April on the copyright page.

THE HOUSE IN THE MIST. *Indianapolis* [1905].
April on the copyright page.

THE WOMAN IN THE ALCOVE. *Indianapolis* [1906].

THE CHIEF LEGATEE. *New York,* 1906.

THE MAYOR'S WIFE. *Indianapolis* [1907].

THE HOUSE OF THE WHISPERING PINES. *New York,* 1910.

THREE THOUSAND DOLLARS. *Boston,* 1910.

INITIALS ONLY. *New York,* 1911.

DARK HOLLOW. *New York,* 1914.
Published January, 1914 on the copyright page.

THE GOLDEN SLIPPER. *New York,* 1915.

TO THE MINUTE (*and*) SCARLET AND BLACK. *New York,* 1916.

THE MYSTERY OF THE HASTY ARROW. *New York,* 1917.

THE STEP ON THE STAIR. *New York,* 1923.

Masterpieces of Mystery. *New York,* 1913.
Reprint. Reissued, *New York,* 1919, as "Room Number Three and Other Detective Stories."

Louise Imogen Guiney

1861–1920

SONGS AT THE START. *Boston*, 1884.
Errata slip at p. 110. Cloth; or boards, leather back.

GOOSE-QUILL PAPERS. *Boston*, 1885.
Paper label on the spine.

THE WHITE SAIL AND OTHER POEMS. *Boston* [1887].

BROWNIES AND BOGLES. *Boston* [1888].

"MONSIEUR HENRI": A FOOT-NOTE TO FRENCH HISTORY. *New York*, 1892.
Also 50 copies bound in red and white cloth. Folded chart at [p. 140].

A ROADSIDE HARP. *Boston*, 1893.
Also 100 large paper copies.

A LITTLE ENGLISH GALLERY. *New York*, 1894.

ROBERT LOUIS STEVENSON. *Boston*, 1895.
With Alice Brown. 250 privately printed copies only. Boards.

LOVERS' SAINT RUTH'S AND THREE OTHER TALES. *Boston*, 1895.
Also 30 copies on China paper.

NINE SONNETS WRITTEN AT OXFORD. [*Cambridge, Mass.*] 1895.
Privately printed. Wrappers.

PATRINS. *Boston*, 1897.

"ENGLAND AND YESTERDAY." *London*, 1898.

THE MARTYRS' IDYL AND SHORTER POEMS. *Boston*, 1899.
Also 150 copies in boards.

ROBERT EMMET. *London*, 1904.
Wrappers.

THE PRINCESS OF THE TOWER. *New York*, 1906.
62 copies only privately printed.

BLESSED EDMUND CAMPION. *London*, 1908.
New York, 1908, edition issued later.

HAPPY ENDING. *Boston*, 1909.
"The Collected Lyrics of Louise Imogen Guiney." Also 550 large paper copies.
Boards. Reissued with added material, *Boston*, 1927.

LETTERS. *New York,* 1926.

2 vols. Boards. First edition so stated on copyright page. Preface by Agnes Repplier, edited by Grace Guiney.

RECUSANT POETS. *New York,* 1939.

Edited with Geoffrey Bliss. Final revision by Edward O'Brien.

Lothrop's Annual. *Boston* [1889].

Contribution.

The Divine Comedy of Dante Alighieri. *Boston,* 1893.

Translated by Charles Eliot Norton. Contains a memorial sketch by Guiney.

Three Heroines of New England Romance. *Boston,* 1894.

Contains "Martha Hilton" by Guiney. Also 125 large paper copies. Copies have been noted in both white and grey cloth, with or without a blank leaf at the back; no known priority.

Carmen, by Prosper Merimée. *Boston,* 1896.

Contains a memoir of the author by Guiney. Boards. Also with *Winchester,* 1896, imprint.

Chap-Book Essays. *Chicago,* 1896.

Contributions by Guiney.

The Colours at Cambridge: William Eustis Russell: July 20th, 1896. [*Rockland, Me.,* 1896?].

Anonymous. 50 copies only. Privately printed.

James Clarence Mangan: His Selected Poems. *Boston,* 1897.

Edited and with a study of Mangan by Guiney.

The Secret of Fougereuse. *Boston,* 1898.

Translated from the French.

The Sermon to the Birds and The Wolf of Gubbio. [*n.p.*] 1898.

Translated. Wrappers. Privately printed.

Sohrab and Rustum and Other Poems, by Matthew Arnold. *Boston,* 1899.

Wrappers. "Riverside Literature Series," No. 132. Contains a biographical sketch of the author by Guiney.

The Mount of Olives and Primitive Holiness ... by Henry Vaughan. *London,* 1902.

Edited by Guiney.

Hurrell Froude: Memoranda and Comments. *London* [1904].

Edited by Guiney.

Katherine Philips ... Selected Poems. *Cottingham-near-Hull,* 1904.

250 copies only. Edited by Guiney.

Thomas Stanley ... [Poems]. *Hull,* 1907.

Edited by Guiney.

Some Poems of Lionel Johnson. *London,* 1912.

Introduction by Guiney.

BIOGRAPHICAL

Louise Imogen Guiney, by Alice Brown. *Boston,* 1921.

Also 100 numbered large paper copies.

Louise Imogen Guiney, by E. M. Tenison. *London,* 1923.

Contains a bibliography.

Fitz-Greene Halleck

1790–1867

POEMS BY CROAKER, CROAKER & CO., AND CROAKER, JUN. *New York*, 1819.

With JOSEPH RODMAN DRAKE. Reissued as "The Croakers," *New York*, 1860, by The Bradford Club, 250 copies only, of which 100 special copies for members.

FANNY. *New York*, 1819.

Anon. Reissued with additions, *New York*, 1821, and 1839. Special edition for W. L. Andrews, *New York*, 1866, 75 copies, five on India paper and two on various colored papers.

MARCO BOZZARIS. [*New York*, 1825.]

Supplement to the New York Review. *See:* Chamberlain catalog, No. 271.

ALNWICK CASTLE WITH OTHER POEMS. *New York*, 1827.

Printed wrappers. Noted in two states with cover title printed from solid face or hollow face type; no known priority. A copy has been noted in unprinted boards which may or may not be the original binding. Revised and reissued with additions, *New York*, 1836, of which there was also a large paper edition; and *New York*, 1845.

YOUNG AMERICA: A POEM. *New York*, 1865.

Pictorial wrappers or boards.

LINES TO THE RECORDER. *New York*, 1866.

75 copies only printed for W. L. Andrews, five on India paper and two on various colored papers.

A LETTER ... TO JOEL LEWIS GRIFFING. *Rutland*, 1921.

31 copies only. Wrappers.

The Poetry of the Portfolio. *Philadelphia*, 1818.
Oliver Oldschool (Joseph Dennie), editor. Contains three poems signed *Croaker & Co.*
The Works of Lord Byron. *New York*, 1834.
Contains a life of Byron by Halleck.
Selections from the British Poets. *New York*, 1840.
2 vols. Edited.
The Poetical Works of Fitz-Greene Halleck. *New York*, 1847.
First collected edition. Reissued, 1852 and 1858, each with a new poem.
The American Flag ... Illustrated ... By F. O. C. Darley. *New York*, 1861.
See under: *Joseph Rodman Drake.*

Fitz-Greene Halleck, by E. A. Duyckinck. *New York,* 1868.
  50 copies only. Privately printed.
Poetical Writings: With Extracts from Those of Joseph Rodman Drake. *New York,*
  1869.
  James Grant Wilson, editor. Also 150 large paper copies.
The Life and Letters of Fitz-Greene Halleck, by James Grant Wilson. *New York,*
  1869.
  Also 100 large paper copies, some extra-illustrated.
A Memorial of Fitz-Greene Halleck. *New York,* 1877.
  James Grant Wilson, editor.
Fitz-Greene Halleck, by Nelson Frederick Adkins. *New Haven,* 1930.
  Contains letters and poems here first collected.

Halleck, together with Joseph Rodman Drake, collaborated as *The Croakers.*

Joel Chandler Harris
1848–1908

UNCLE REMUS: HIS SONGS AND HIS SAYINGS. *New York*, 1881.
> The first printing has *presumptive* for *presumptuous*, last line, p. 9. The first state of the advertisements at the back has no mention or review of the present title. Intermediate states exist. Bound in various colors of cloth with various colors of butterfly-design printed end-papers. In the Julia Collier Harris book on Joel Chandler Harris there is a reproduction of an 1880 dated title page; Mrs. Harris states that the reproduction was made from a page that "was not an integral part of a book, but a loose leaf." It is probable that the page so reproduced was printed as either a proof or as a copyright measure. Thus far no copy with an 1880 title page has been recorded. Two copies of the first edition have been noted with title page tipped-in on a stub; status unknown. Reissued *New York*, 1895, with illustrations by A. B. Frost, new preface by the author; also 250 large paper copies, signed.

NIGHTS WITH UNCLE REMUS. *Boston*, 1883.
> The title page of this volume lists Harris as the author of "At Teague Poteet's." I have been unable to find a record of any previous publication of this title save as a magazine contribution; later in "Mingo."

MINGO AND OTHER SKETCHES IN BLACK AND WHITE. *Boston*, 1884.

FREE JOE. *New York*, 1887.

DADDY JAKE THE RUNAWAY. *New York* [1889].
> Glazed pictorial boards.

BALAAM AND HIS MASTER. *Boston*, 1891.

ON THE PLANTATION. *New York*, 1892.
> Published in London as "A Plantation Printer."

UNCLE REMUS AND HIS FRIENDS. *Boston*, 1892.
> Also, "Visitor's Edition," *Boston*, 1914, with a biographical introduction by Myrta Lockett Avary.

LITTLE MR. THIMBLEFINGER AND HIS QUEER COUNTRY. *Boston*, 1894.

MR. RABBIT AT HOME. *Boston*, 1895.

SISTER JANE. *Boston*, 1896.

STORIES OF GEORGIA. *New York*, 1896.
> Also issued with title, "Georgia from the Invasion of De Soto to Recent Times," *New York*, 1896.

THE STORY OF AARON. *Boston,* 1896.

AARON IN THE WILDWOODS. *Boston,* 1897.

TALES OF THE HOME FOLKS IN PEACE AND WAR. *Boston,* 1898.

PLANTATION PAGEANTS. *Boston,* 1899.

THE CHRONICLES OF AUNT MINERVY ANN. *New York,* 1899.
  Noted in three states: (a) top edges gilt, all edges trimmed, printed on wove
  paper; (b) top edges gilt, bottom and fore-edges untrimmed, on wove paper;
  (c) top edges gilt, bottom and fore-edges trimmed, on laid paper. The publisher's
  file copy is state (a), probably the correct issue. All copies of the first edition
  noted have the letter *T* missing at p. 11, second line from bottom; this feature
  persists in late reprints.

ON THE WING OF OCCASIONS. *New York,* 1900.
  The probable first binding is light green cloth, stamped entirely in black with
  sword and wing decoration on the front cover. The copyright deposit copy at The
  Library of Congress is so stamped. It is believed that the following bindings are
  later: light green cloth stamped in black and gilt; and, dark green cloth with no
  stamping on front cover and with *Special | Edition* stamped at base of spine. It
  has been definitely established that copies bound in red cloth with green stamping
  and printed picture pasted to the front cover are later. Reissued, *New York,* 1909,
  as "The Kidnapping of President Lincoln."

GABRIEL TOLLIVER. *New York,* 1902.

THE MAKING OF A STATESMAN. *New York,* 1902.
  Published, March, 1902, R. on the copyright page.

WALLY WANDEROON AND HIS STORY-TELLING MACHINE. *New York,* 1903.

A LITTLE UNION SCOUT. *New York,* 1904.
  Published, April, 1904 on the copyright page.

THE TAR-BABY AND OTHER RHYMES OF UNCLE REMUS. *New York,* 1904.

TOLD BY UNCLE REMUS: NEW STORIES OF THE OLD PLANTATION. *New York,* 1905.

UNCLE REMUS AND BRER RABBIT. *New York,* 1907.
  Boards.

THE BISHOP AND THE BOOGERMAN. *New York,* 1909.

THE SHADOW BETWEEN HIS SHOULDER-BLADES. *Boston* [1909].

UNCLE REMUS AND THE LITTLE BOY. *Boston* [1910].

UNCLE REMUS RETURNS. *Boston,* 1918.

213

THE WITCH WOLF. *Cambridge*, 1921.
Boards.

BOOKS EDITED OR TRANSLATED BY HARRIS

Life of Henry W. Grady. *New York* [1890].
The first edition has 628 pp.; second edition, 645 pp.
Evening Tales, by Frédéric Ortoli. *New York*, 1893.
Translated.
The Book of Fun and Frolic. *Boston* [1901].
Reissued [1902] as "The Merry-Maker." Edited.
American Wit and Humor. *New York*, 1907.
Introduction.
Library of Southern Literature. *New Orleans* [1908-1913?].
16 vols. Co-editor.

BOOKS WITH HARRIS CONTRIBUTIONS

The Young Marooners, by F. R. Goulding. *New York* [1887].
Poems, by Irwin Russell. *New York* [1888].
First edition has figured end papers; later editions contain added poems, have plain white end papers and are printed on heavier paper. Introduction by Harris.
Songs of a Day, by Frank L. Stanton. *Atlanta*, 1893.
Introduction.
Stories of the South. *New York*, 1893.
Contains Harris's "Aunt Fountain's Prisoner." Reprinted from "Free Joe," 1887.
Songs of the Soil, by Frank L. Stanton. *New York*, 1894.
Introduction.
Thought Blossoms from the South. [*Atlanta*, 1895].
Contribution.
Bandanna Ballads, by Howard Weeden. *New York*, 1899.
Exists in two states, 8vo and 12mo, with no known priority. Introduction.
Down South, by Rudolf Eickemeyer, Jr. *New York*, 1900.
First state has *RHR* monogram on the front cover, the *R's* having short tails, not long, in the first state.
A Book of Drawings, by A. B. Frost. *New York*, 1904.
Introduction.
Complete Works of Eugene Field. *New York*, 1907.
Introduction to Vol. VIII by Harris.
Reminiscences of Famous Georgians, by L. L. Knight. *Atlanta*, 1907.
Songs of the South. *New York*, 1913.
Jennie T. Clark, editor.
Complete Works of James Whitcomb Riley. *Indianapolis* [1913].
Introduction to Vol. V by Harris.

BIOGRAPHICAL

"Uncle Remus": Joel Chandler Harris as Seen and Remembered by a Few of His
    Friends [by Ivy Lee]. [*n.p.*] 1908.
    300 copies only for private distribution.
The Life and Letters of Joel Chandler Harris, by Julia Harris. *Boston*, 1918.
    With a bibliography.
The Life of Joel Chandler Harris, by Robert Lemuel Wiggins. *Nashville*, 1918.
Joel Chandler Harris: Editor and Essayist. Miscellaneous Political and Social Writings. *Chapel Hill, N. C.*, 1931.
    Julia Collier Harris, ed.

(Francis) Bret Harte

1836 (1839?)–1902

THE LOST GALLEON AND OTHER TALES. *San Francisco,* 1867.

CONDENSED NOVELS. *New York,* 1867.

Commonly referred to as a piracy, this publication was authorized by Bret Harte who received payment therefor. See Nathan Van Patten's "Concerning Condensed Novels," *Stanford University,* 1929. Reissued with added material, *Boston,* 1871. Issued in London as "Sensation Novels."

THE LUCK OF ROARING CAMP. *Boston,* 1870.

Second edition adds "Brown of Calaveras." Illustrated edition, *Boston,* 1872.

PLAIN LANGUAGE FROM TRUTHFUL JAMES [THE HEATHEN CHINEE]. *Chicago,* 1870.

Nine lithographed cards in envelope, front of envelope printed with title, etc. Exists in various states none of which have been exactly placed but it is probable that in the first state the folios on each card (*e.g. No. 1*) in no case exceed 6/16″ at the widest points; and that in later states the folios are never less than $\frac{7}{16}$″. The lithographed cards were available before January 16, 1871, as evidenced by an advertisement in the *American Literary Gazette,* p. 108, of that date, announcing the cards as *now ready.* The same magazine, May 15, 1871, refers to the illustrated Eytinge edition of 1871 as "the only illustrated edition published with the author's sanction." A complete discussion of the various states appears at pp. 71-75 of Merle Johnson's "You Know These Lines!" (*New York, G. A. Baker and Company,* 1935). The poem was issued in a facsimile edition, *San Francisco,* 1871; also various broadsheet editions of unknown dates.

POEMS. *Boston,* 1871.

Fields, Osgood imprint on title page. First state has *F O & Co.* monogram at base of spine and has *S. T. K* for *T. S. K.* at head of poem, p. 136. Later bindings have *Jas. R. Osgood* on spine. Printed on both thick and thin paper; no known priority. A copy on thick paper has been noted with a *January 1, 1871* inscription.

EAST AND WEST POEMS. *Boston,* 1871.

STORIES OF THE SIERRAS. *London* [1872].

THE LITTLE DRUMMER. *London* [1872].

MRS. SKAGGS'S HUSBANDS. *Boston,* 1873.

The *London* [1873] edition contains added material.

TALES OF THE ARGONAUTS. *Boston,* 1875.

The title story previously issued as a *New York Tribune* "Extra" *ca.* 1873.

ECHOES OF THE FOOT-HILLS. *Boston,* 1875.

WAN LEE: THE PAGAN. *London* [1876].

TWO MEN OF SANDY BAR. *Boston,* 1876.
Acting version, *New York,* 1876, printed on one side of the sheet only; said to be but six, or less, copies printed for Stuart Robson.

GABRIEL CONROY. *London* [1875-6].
30 parts. American edition, *Hartford,* 1876, issued later. First state of latter has small bear on spine. It has been asserted that some of the early copies were issued in wrappers.

THANKFUL BLOSSOM. *Boston,* 1877.
First state of binding has *James R. Osgood & Co.* at foot of spine.

THE STORY OF A MINE. *Boston,* 1878.
Preceded by the London edition of [1877].

DRIFT FROM TWO SHORES. *Boston,* 1878.
Preceded by the London publications "Jinny" [1878] and "The Man on the Beach" [1878].

THE TWINS OF TABLE MOUNTAIN. *Boston,* 1879.
Preceded by the *London* [1879] edition.

POETICAL WORKS. *Boston,* 1880.

FLIP AND FOUND AT BLAZING STAR. *Boston,* 1882.

IN THE CARQUINEZ WOODS. *London,* 1883.
American edition, *Boston,* 1884.

ON THE FRONTIER. *Boston,* 1884.
Preceded by the *London,* 1884, edition.

BY SHORE AND SEDGE. *Boston,* 1885.

MARUJA. *Boston,* 1885.

THE QUEEN OF THE PIRATE ISLE. *London* [1886].
Gilt edges. American edition, *Boston,* 1887, printed at same time and place.

SNOW-BOUND AT EAGLE'S. *Boston,* 1886.

THE CRUSADE OF THE EXCELSIOR. *Boston,* 1887.
London edition has a two-page foreword dated January, 1888.

A MILLIONAIRE OF ROUGH-AND-READY. *Boston,* 1887.
First state has 299 pp. only.

A PHYLLIS OF THE SIERRAS. *Boston,* 1888.

THE ARGONAUTS OF NORTH LIBERTY. *Boston*, 1888.

CRESSY. *Boston*, 1889.

THE HERITAGE OF DEDLOW MARSH. *Boston*, 1889.
Probably preceded by the English edition.

A WARD OF THE GOLDEN GATE. *Boston*, 1890.
Preceded by the *London*, 1890, edition.

A WAIF OF THE PLAINS. *Boston*, 1890.
Preceded by the English edition.

A SAPPHO OF GREEN SPRINGS. *Boston*, 1891.
Preceded by the *London*, 1891 edition.

A FIRST FAMILY OF TASAJARA. *London*, 1891.
2 vols. American edition, *Boston*, 1892.

COLONEL STARBOTTLE'S CLIENT. *Boston*, 1892.

SUSY: A STORY OF THE PLAINS. *Boston*, 1893.
Preceded by the *London*, 1893 edition.

SALLY DOWS. *Boston*, 1893.
Preceded by the *London*, 1893 edition.

A PROTÉGÉE OF JACK HAMLIN'S. *Boston*, 1894.

THE BELL-RINGER OF ANGEL'S. *Boston*, 1894.

CLARENCE. *Boston*, 1895.
Preceded by the *London*, 1895 edition.

IN A HOLLOW OF THE HILLS. *Boston*, 1895.
Preceded by the *London*, 1895 edition.

POETICAL WORKS OF BRET HARTE. *London*, 1896.
"A New Edition, Revised."

BARKER'S LUCK AND OTHER STORIES. *London*, 1896.
Published *Boston*, 1896, in month following.

THREE PARTNERS. *Boston*, 1897.
Preceded by the *London*, 1897 edition.

SOME LATER VERSES. *London*, 1898.
Green cloth, gold stamping, top edges gilt, other edges untrimmed. Later (1905?) issued for "The Times Book Club."

TALES OF TRAIL AND TOWN. *Boston*, 1898.
Preceded by the *London*, 1898 edition.

STORIES IN LIGHT AND SHADOW. *Boston*, 1898.

MR. JACK HAMLIN'S MEDIATION. *Boston*, 1899.
Preceded by the *London*, 1895 edition.

FROM SAND HILL TO PINE. *Boston*, 1900.
Preceded by the *London*, 1895 edition.

UNDER THE REDWOODS. *Boston*, 1901.

CONDENSED NOVELS: SECOND SERIES. *Boston*, 1902.
Preceded by the English edition of the same date.

SUE: A PLAY IN THREE ACTS. *London*, 1902.
With T. EDGAR PEMBERTON. Dramatization of "The Judgment of Bolinas Plain."

OPENINGS IN THE OLD TRAIL. *Boston*, 1902.

TRENT'S TRUST. *Boston*, 1903.
Also uncut copies with leather labels on the spine. Preceded by the *London*, 1903, edition.

STORIES AND POEMS AND OTHER UNCOLLECTED WRITINGS. *Boston*, 1914.
Charles Meeker Kozlay, editor. 525 copies only.

THE STORY OF ENRIQUEZ. *San Francisco*, 1924.
100 copies only.

SKETCHES OF THE SIXTIES. *San Francisco*, 1926.
Early newspaper writings now first collected. Also 250 copies on Japan vellum. Reissued with additional material, 1927.

In Memoriam: Thomas Starr King. [*n.p., n.d.*].
Published *ca.* 1864. Contains "Relieving Guard," later included in "Poems," 1871.
Fourteenth Anniversary of the Society of California Pioneers. *San Francisco*, 1864.
Wrappers. Contains a poem by Bret Harte.
Outcroppings. *San Francisco*, 1866.
Edited and with a preface by Harte. No tail piece at the foot of p. 102. An inscribed presentation copy from the author has been noted, bound in half roan and purple cloth, all edges marbled, and taller than the regularly published edition. There is no definite proof regarding this last but it is quite possible that it was bound for the author.
The Natural Wealth of California, by Titus Fey Cronise. *San Francisco*, 1868.
Harte "aided in the preparation of the material for this volume."
To the Pliocene Skull. [*Washington, D. C.*, 1871].
First separate edition. Wrappers. It is said that a second state has an added page of burlesque introduction.
Proceedings of the Third Anniversary of the Army of the Potomac. *New York*, 1872.
Contains "The Old Major Explains," by Harte.

HARTE

An Episode of Fiddletown and other Sketches. *London,* 1873.
> According to R. H. Shove ("Cheap Book Production in the United States, 1870-1891," *Urbana, Ill.,* 1937) the title story was issued as an extra in the *New York Tribune Novels,* No. 2, *ca.* 1873.

M'liss. *New York* [1873].
> First separate printing of a story originally collected in "The Luck of Roaring Camp," with additional material not by Harte. At least three states of this book are known, with some question as to the earlier. For a discussion of this see "The Question of Bret Harte's "M'liss," in *The Publishers' Weekly,* November 28, 1936, and March 20, 1937. "The Waif of Smith's Pocket," *San Francisco,* 1878, is a dramatization of the story by Kate M. Widmer. Dramatized by C. M. Greene and A. S. Thompson, *Philadelphia* [1878].

West Point Tic Tacs. *New York,* 1878.
> Contains "Cadet Grey," by Harte. Issued in both cloth and leather. The Harte contribution exists in contemporary(?) broadside form.

Excelsior. *New York* [1879].
> Advertisement for "Sapolio." No title page. Wrappers or pictorial cloth.

The Life and Public Services of James A. Garfield ... by Capt. F. H. Mason ... *London,* 1881.
> Preface by Harte.

St. Nicholas Songs. *New York* [1885].
> Contains "Jessie," by Harte.

The Art of Authorship. *London,* 1890.
> George Bainton, editor. Contribution by Harte.

The Bret Harte Birthday Book. *London,* 1892.
> Reprinted material selected by Mme. Van de Velde.

The Lectures of Bret Harte. *Brooklyn, N. Y.,* 1909.
> Also 100 copies in leather. Includes also "The Piracy of Bret Harte's Fables," by Charles Meeker Kozlay.

Fables, by George Washington Æsop. *London* [n.d.].
> Pseudonym.

BIOGRAPHICAL

Bret Harte, by T. Edgar Pemberton. *London,* 1900.
The Life of Bret Harte, by T. Edgar Pemberton. *London,* 1903.
> Contains a brief bibliography.

Bret Harte, by Henry Walcott Boynton. *New York,* 1903.
The Life of Bret Harte, by Henry Childs Merwin. *Boston,* 1911.
> 200 copies, paper label.

Letters of Bret Harte. *Boston,* 1926.
> Geoffrey Bret Harte, editor.

Bret Harte: Argonaut and Exile, by George R. Stewart, Jr. *Boston,* 1931.

BIBLIOGRAPHICAL

There is no formal bibliography of the writings of Bret Harte. The collector is referred to the sales catalog of the Charles Meeker Kozlay Collection of Bret Harte, issued by the American Art Association, the only known listing of the variants and minutiæ. Much of Bret Harte's writing was first published in England, very often preceding American books in time of publication. For information regarding this see . R. Brussel's "Anglo-American First Editions: West to East," *London and New York,* 1936.

Nathaniel Hawthorne
1804–1864

FANSHAWE: A TALE. *Boston*, 1828.

Anonymous. Boards, paper label. *See:* "Fanshawe and other Pieces," Boston, 1876.

PETER PARLEY'S UNIVERSAL HISTORY. *Boston*, 1837.

2 vols. Anonymous.

TWICE-TOLD TALES. *Boston*, 1837.

Table of contents lists fifth story as beginning at p. 78, an error which remained uncorrected so far as I know. Various colors of cloth, two heights, but both these features are without apparent bibliographical significance. 2 leaves advts. at front; 8 at back. Reissued, *Boston*, 1842, 2 vols., vol. 1 being a reprint of the 1837 edition with the exception of one added tale; vol. 2 is new material. Reissued, *Boston*, 1851, with new preface. "The Gentle Boy," Boston, 1839, is reprinted from the 1837 edition but first appeared in "The Token" for 1832.

GRANDFATHER'S CHAIR. *Boston*, 1841.

Label on front cover.

FAMOUS OLD PEOPLE, BEING THE SECOND EPOCH OF GRANDFATHER'S CHAIR. *Boston*, 1841.

Label on front cover.

LIBERTY TREE, WITH THE LAST WORDS OF GRANDFATHER'S CHAIR. *Boston*, 1841.

The first state, line two, p. 24, ends *in a Con-*. Line 13, p. 30, reads: *half burned out* etc. Reissued with tipped in title page dated 1851. Label on front cover.

BIOGRAPHICAL STORIES FOR CHILDREN. *Boston*, 1842.

Reissued in 1842, with the 3 preceding titles, as "Historical Tales for Youth," and in 1851 as "True Stories from History and Biography." "The Sunday School Society's Gift" [*Boston*, 1842] is a reprint of "The Biography of Samuel Johnson," which appeared in this publication; issued 16 pp. stitched, without wrappers.

THE CELESTIAL RAIL-ROAD. *Boston*, 1843.

Wrappers. Pirated. This has been noted with two different imprints: (a) *Wilder and Co.*, (b) *James F. Fish*. The Wilder imprint is probably earlier, but the Fish imprint is scarcer. Also a *Lowell*, 1847, imprint. "A Visit to the Celestial City," *Philadelphia* [1844] is a reprint of the same material with one anecdote deleted.

MOSSES FROM AN OLD MANSE. *New York*, 1846.

2 vols. First state has the name of the printer, *Craighead*, and name of stereotyper, on versos of both title pages. Cloth or printed wrappers. The paper covered copies should not have advertisements beyond "Mosses" on the back cover. Cloth bound edition is usually 2 volumes in 1. Reissued, *Boston*, 1854, 2 vols., with three added stories.

THE SCARLET LETTER. *Boston*, 1850.

Distinguished from the second edition of the same year by the word *reduplicate,* line 20, p. 21; *characterss,* line 5, p. 41; *Catechism,* line 29, p. 132; *known of it,* line 4, p. 199. Numerous other changes but these are sufficient for purposes of identification. Late 1850 editions contain an introduction that does not appear in the first edition.

TRUE STORIES FROM HISTORY AND BIOGRAPHY. *Boston*, 1851.

Verso of title page has following imprint: *Cambridge: Printed by Bolles and Houghton.* It is probable that the earliest copies do not have a comma after *way,* first page of preface, third line from the bottom. First state has 335 pp. only. *See:* "Biographical Stories for Children," 1842.

THE HOUSE OF THE SEVEN GABLES. *Boston*, 1851.

Advertisements variously dated March, and on, 1851, appearing at the front end paper. Some presentation copies have no advertisements.

A WONDER-BOOK FOR GIRLS AND BOYS. *Boston*, 1852.

Gilt decoration should cover only top third of spine. No advertisements.

THE SNOW-IMAGE AND OTHER TWICE-TOLD TALES. *Boston*, 1852.

The title story first appeared in a "Memorial" for Mrs. Osgood, *New York,* 1851. London edition is dated 1851. American edition has 4 pp. advertisements dated *January 1852.*

THE BLITHEDALE ROMANCE. *Boston*, 1852.

4 pp. advertisements, sometimes lacking in presentation copies. Preceded in time of publication by the two-volume English edition.

LIFE OF FRANKLIN PIERCE. *Boston*, 1852.

Cloth or wrappers, the latter possibly later. 4 pp. advertisements dated July or September 1852 with no apparent priority as to sheets of book. Spine noted with slightly varying differences in stamping but must have *Ticknor & Co.* at foot; title page imprint: *Ticknor, Reed & Fields.* P. 1 of advertisements lists "Golden Legend" as *Just Published.*

TANGLEWOOD TALES FOR GIRLS AND BOYS. *Boston*, 1853.

In the earliest state of the advertisements this title is described as *in press;* later: *just out;* still later, *Price, 88 cts.*

THE MARBLE FAUN. *Boston*, 1860.

2 vols. 16 pp. advertisements bound in at the end of vol. 1 dated March or February 1860. Issued in London as "The Transformation; or, The Romance of Monte Beni," 3 vols. First state, both English and American, lacks the *Conclusion.*

OUR OLD HOME. *Boston*, 1863.

It is possible that the very earliest copies have no advertisements but copies with one page of advertisements, verso blank, preceded copies with 22 pages of advertisements. Probably preceded by the English edition of the same date.

PANSIE: A FRAGMENT. *London* [1864].
Wrappers. Pirated.

PASSAGES FROM THE AMERICAN NOTE-BOOKS. *Boston,* 1868.
Base of spine reads *Ticknor & Co.;* later, *Fields, Osgood & Co.*

PASSAGES FROM THE NOTE-BOOKS OF THE LATE NATHANIEL HAWTHORNE.
London, 1869.
Pirated. Previously in "The Atlantic Almanac" for 1868. Cloth or wrappers.

PASSAGES FROM THE ENGLISH NOTE-BOOKS. *Boston,* 1870.
2 vols. *Fields, Osgood & Co.,* imprint. See preceding item.

PASSAGES FROM THE FRENCH AND ITALIAN NOTE-BOOKS. *Boston,* 1872.
2 vols. English edition is dated 1871.

SEPTIMIUS FELTON; or, THE ELIXIR OF LIFE. *Boston,* 1872.
London edition published as "Septimius: A Romance." Copies on large paper without the publisher's imprint on the spine are remainders of a later binding.

THE DOLLIVER ROMANCE AND OTHER PIECES. *Boston,* 1876.

FANSHAWE AND OTHER PIECES. *Boston,* 1876.

DR. GRIMSHAWE'S SECRET. *Boston,* 1883.
A few copies issued with untrimmed edges. Also 250 large paper copies. Edited by Julian Hawthorne.

COMPLETE WORKS. *Boston,* 1883.
12 vols. Riverside edition. Also 250 large paper sets.

COMPLETE WRITINGS. *Boston,* 1900.
22 vols. Autograph edition. With a bibliography by Horace E. Scudder.

THE GHOST OF DOCTOR HARRIS. *New York,* 1900.
Wrappers.

The following is a selection of broadsides, pamphlets, books with contributions, etc., etc. A complete list requires more space than is available here and the collector is therefore referred to the bibliographies listed at the end of this section.

Nevertheless, "The Tokens" must be given special mention. These gift annuals practically supported Hawthorne up to the time of "Twice-Told Tales." In the 1837 "Token" Hawthorne, with eight contributions, fills 110 pages. The piece in the 1828 "Token," "The Adventures of a Raindrop," attributed to Hawthorne, is not his work but the product of Lydia Maria Francis (Child). Hawthorne's contributions to this annual are as follows: 1830, one; 1831, two; 1832, four; 1833, three; 1835, three; 1836, three; 1837, eight; and 1838, five.

Time's Portraiture. *Salem* [1838].
The Salem Gazette's carrier's address for January 1, 1838. Reprinted [Salem, 1853], as an 8 pp. pamphlet without wrappers, disclosing the authorship.

The Sister Years. *Salem*, 1839.
The Salem Gazette's carrier's address for January 1, 1839. 8 pp. stitched, without wrappers.
The Gentle Boy: A Thrice-Told Tale. *Boston*, 1839.
Wrappers. Reprinted from "Twice-Told Tales," *q.v.*
Journal of an African Cruiser, [by Horatio Bridge]. *New York*, 1845.
Edited by Hawthorne. First state has both printer's and stereotyper's name; copyright notice in four lines. Printed wrappers.
A Rill from the Town Pump. *London*, 1857.
Anonymous. First separate edition.
The Philosophy of the Plays of Shakspere Unfolded, by Delia Bacon. *London*, 1857.
Introduction by Hawthorne.
The Weal Reaf. *Salem*, 1860.
Issued as a daily record of the Essex Institute Fair, Salem, September 4 to 8; issued also, an "Extra" and two supplementary numbers dated September 10 and 11.
Contains a letter and a contribution by Hawthorne.
The Snow Image. *New York*, 1864.
First separate edition.
Legends of New England. *Boston*, 1877.
First separate edition.
Tales of the White Hills. *Boston*, 1877.
First separate edition.
Legends of the Province House. *Boston*, 1877.
First separate edition.
A Virtuoso's Collection. *Boston*, 1877.
First separate edition.
Sketches and Studies. *Boston* [1883].
Practically all reprint material.

BIOGRAPHICAL

Memoir of Nathaniel Hawthorne, by H. A. Page (A. H. Japp). *London*, 1872.
First book printing for "The Duston Family," "April Fools" and "A Prize from the Sea," which last is printed as "Sir William Phips" in "Fanshawe, *etc.*," 1876.
A Study of Hawthorne, by George Parsons Lathrop. *Boston*, 1876.
Nathaniel Hawthorne and His Wife, by Julian Hawthorne. *Cambridge*, 1884.
2 vols. 250 copies only published a year in advance of the trade edition, *Boston*, 1885.
Personal Recollections of Nathaniel Hawthorne, by Horatio Bridge. *New York*, 1893.
Memories of Hawthorne, by Rose Hawthorne Lathrop. *Boston*, 1897.
Hawthorne's First Diary with an Account of Its Discovery. *Boston*, 1897.
The diary has proved a forgery.
Nathaniel Hawthorne, by George E. Woodberry. *Boston*, 1902.
600 numbered copies only.
Hawthorne's Love Letters. *Chicago*, 1907.
2 vols. 62 copies only.

Hawthorne and His Publisher, by Caroline Ticknor. *Boston*, 1913.
The Heart of Hawthorne's Journals. *Boston*, 1929.
  Newton Arvin, editor. Contains previously uncollected material.
The American Note Books of Nathaniel Hawthorne. *New Haven*, 1932.
  Randall Stewart, editor. "This is a first authentic edition of Hawthorne's note-
  books as he wrote them."

BIBLIOGRAPHICAL WORKS

First Editions of the Works of Nathaniel Hawthorne [by J. C. Chamberlain]. *New
  York*, 1905.
Bibliography of Hawthorne, by Nina E. Browne. *Boston*, 1905.
  550 copies only, designed by Bruce Rogers.
Bibliography of Hawthorne, by Wallace Hugh Cathcart. *Cleveland*, 1905.
  91 copies only, printed for members of the Rowfant Club by Bruce Rogers.
Letters of Hawthorne to William Ticknor, 1851-1864. *Newark*, 1910.
  2 vols. 100 copies only.
The Stephen H. Wakeman Collection of Books of Nineteenth Century American
  Writers. *New York* [1924].
  Issued as a sales catalog by the American Art Association.

John Hay
1838–1905

JIM BLUDSO OF THE PRAIRIE BELLE, AND LITTLE BREECHES. *Boston*, 1871.
Orange wrappers. Reissued in grey wrappers with no title page change. "Little Breeches," was issued separately in wrappers. *New York*, 1871.

CASTILIAN DAYS. *Boston*, 1871.
Reissued, "Pennell Edition," *Cambridge*, 1903; also 350 de luxe copies.

PIKE COUNTY BALLADS. *Boston*, 1871.
Cloth or wrappers.

THE BREAD-WINNERS. *New York*, 1884.
Anonymous. Exists with and without *The End* at the end of the last page of text. A copyright deposit copy at The Library of Congress does not have the words present. A sequel, "Drafted In," by Faith Templeton, published *New York*, 1888.

ABRAHAM LINCOLN: A HISTORY. *New York*, 1890.
10 vols. With JOHN G. NICOLAY.

POEMS. *Boston*, 1890.
Reported, but not seen: a copy printed on handmade paper, de luxe.

IN PRAISE OF OMAR. *Portland, Me.,* 1898.
Boards. 925 copies on Van Gelder paper; 50 numbered copies on Japan vellum; four copies on parchment, numbered and signed.

ADDRESSES OF JOHN HAY. *New York*, 1906.
Many of the speeches contained herein were issued separately previous to this publication.

LETTERS OF JOHN HAY AND EXTRACTS FROM DIARY. *Washington*, 1908.
3 vols. Privately printed.

A POET IN EXILE. *Boston*, 1910.
440 copies only. Caroline Ticknor, editor. Boards.

THE COMPLETE POETICAL WORKS OF JOHN HAY. *Boston*, 1916.
Also large paper edition of 1,000 copies.

A COLLEGE FRIENDSHIP. A SERIES OF LETTERS ... *Boston*, 1938.
350 copies only.

LINCOLN AND THE CIVIL WAR IN THE DIARIES AND LETTERS OF JOHN HAY. *New York*, 1939.
Tyler Dennett, editor.

The following list of secondary items does not include the innumerable political speeches.

Brown University Class of 1858. *Providence*, 1858.
  Contains "Erato," by Hay.
The Pioneers of Ohio. *Cleveland*, 1879.
Amasa Stone. [*New York*, 1883].
  95 copies only.
Appleton's Cyclopedia of American Biography. *New York*, 1886-89.
  6 vols. "Lincoln," by Hay.
The Enchanted Shirt. *New York and Chicago* [1889].
  Pictorial wrappers.
Lincoln's Complete Works. *New York*, 1894.
  Edited by Hay and Nicolay.
Speech ... at the Unveiling of the Bust of Sir Walter Scott. *London*, 1897.

BIOGRAPHICAL

Life and Letters. *Boston*, 1915.
  2 vols. William Roscoe Thayer, editor. 300 large paper copies.
John Hay, by Tyler Dennett. *New York*, 1933.

Lafcadio Hearn
1850–1904

STRAY LEAVES FROM STRANGE LITERATURE. *Boston,* 1884.
Must have the *Osgood* imprint at foot of spine.

SOME CHINESE GHOSTS. *Boston,* 1887.
Bound in several colors of cloth with various colors of ink used in stamping; no priority established. A copy has been noted in figured cloth.

CHITA. *New York,* 1889.

TWO YEARS IN THE FRENCH WEST INDIES. *New York,* 1890.

YOUMA. *New York,* 1890.
First binding is white calico with blue printed all-over design; five patterns noted with no probable priority. Top edges trimmed, otherwise untrimmed. Paper label on spine. Copies have been noted in plain red cloth.

GLIMPSES OF UNFAMILIAR JAPAN. *Boston,* 1894.
2 vols. Black or green cloth with no priority established.

"OUT OF THE EAST." *Boston,* 1895.
First state measures 1⅝" thick across top of covers.

KOKORO. *Boston,* 1896.
Reissued with additional material, *Tokyo,* 1921.

GLEANINGS IN BUDDHA-FIELDS. *Boston,* 1897.

EXOTICS AND RETROSPECTIVES. *Boston,* 1898.

JAPANESE FAIRY TALES. *Tokyo* [1898-1903].
4 vols. *The Boy Who Drew Cats* [1898]; *The Goblin Spider* [1899]; *The Old Woman Who Lost Her Dumpling[s]* [1902]; *Chin Chin Kobakama* [1903]. Issued also in large paper and crepe paper states. First edition issued in at least three states with no probable priority as to time of issue. For more detailed description see American Art Association catalog, January 20, 1914, and the Perkins' bibliography, 1934.

IN GHOSTLY JAPAN. *Boston,* 1899.

SHADOWINGS. *Boston,* 1900.

A JAPANESE MISCELLANY. *Boston,* 1901.
It has been asserted that the first state does not have *October 1901* on the copyright page. In the ordinary course of publisher's events the first would have such a notice; later printings would either lack it or supplement it with a reprint notice. Thus far no definite priority has been established for either state.

KOTTŌ. *New York,* 1902.

First state has background of title page upside down, showing artist's monogram at upper right; second state corrected by means of a cancel leaf; third state corrected and with title page an integral part of signature.

KWAIDAN. *Boston,* 1904.

Blue, green or tan cloth; the publishers state that blue is first. *Published April 1904* on the copyright page.

JAPAN: AN ATTEMPT AT INTERPRETATION. *New York,* 1904.

Fourth printing has added material.

WRITINGS. *Boston,* 1922.

16 vols. Also 750 large paper sets signed in vol. 1 by Mrs. Hearn and containing a page of Hearn manuscript.

The following posthumous works are compilations of Hearn's early newspaper writings, lectures as recorded by his students and similar material. Similar material is being constantly published.

THE ROMANCE OF THE MILKY-WAY. *Boston,* 1905.

Grey linen binding; later in olive green.

LEAVES FROM THE DIARY OF AN IMPRESSIONIST. *Boston,* 1911.

575 numbered copies only.

EDITORIALS FROM THE KOBE CHRONICLE. [*New York,* 1913].

100 copies only. Wrappers.

FANTASTICS AND OTHER FANCIES. *Boston,* 1914.

550 copies only. Boards.

JAPANESE LYRICS. *Boston,* 1915.

Wrappers. In the first state the title page is pasted in on a stub; no advertisement for *The New Poetry Series* in the preliminary matter.

INTERPRETATIONS OF LITERATURE. *New York,* 1915.

2 vols.

APPRECIATIONS OF POETRY. *New York,* 1916.

LIFE AND LITERATURE. *New York,* 1917.

KARMA. *New York,* 1918.

Boards.

BOOKS AND HABITS. *New York,* 1921.

John Erskine, editor. Reprint together with first edition material.

PRE-RAPHAELITES AND OTHER POETS. *New York,* 1922.

John Erskine, editor.

ESSAYS IN EUROPEAN AND ORIENTAL LITERATURE. *New York*, 1923.
Albert Mordell, editor.

CREOLE SKETCHES. *New York*, 1924.
Charles Woodward Hutson, editor. Reprint together with first edition material.

AN AMERICAN MISCELLANY. *New York*, 1924.

OCCIDENTAL GLEANINGS. *New York*, 1925.
2 vols.

SOME NEW LETTERS AND WRITINGS. *Tokyo*, 1925.
Sanki Ichikawa, editor. 200 sets of sheets imported by Greenberg and issued with their New York imprint.

EDITORIALS. *Boston*, 1926.
Charles Woodward Hutson, editor. Also 250 untrimmed copies. Portions previously published in "Editorials from the Kobe Chronicle," [1913].

INSECTS AND GREEK POETRY. *New York*, 1926.
550 copies only. Boards.

A HISTORY OF ENGLISH LITERATURE. *Tokyo*, 1927.
2 vols Reissued, *Toyko*, 1930, one volume, revised.

SOME STRANGE ENGLISH LITERARY FIGURES OF THE EIGHTEENTH AND NINETEENTH CENTURIES. *Tokyo* [1927].
R. Tanabé, editor.

LECTURES ON SHAKESPEARE. *Tokyo* [1928]
Popular edition [*Tokyo*, 1931].

ESSAYS ON AMERICAN LITERATURE. *Tokyo*, 1929.
Albert Mordell, editor.

LECTURES ON PROSODY. [*Tokyo*, 1929].

VICTORIAN PHILOSOPHY. [*Tokyo*, 1930].

GIBBETED. *Los Angeles*, 1933.
200 numbered copies only.

COMPLETE LECTURES. *Tokyo* [1932].

LETTERS FROM SHIMANE AND KYUSHU. *Kyoto*, 1934.
100 numbered copies only.

BARBAROUS BARBERS AND OTHER STORIES. [*Tokyo*, 1939].

BUYING CHRISTMAS TOYS AND OTHER ESSAYS. [*Tokyo*, 1939].

LITERARY ESSAYS. [*Tokyo*, 1939].

231

COMPILATIONS BY HEARN

Historical Sketch Book and Guide to New Orleans. *New York*, 1885.
  First state does not have Hearn's name at foot of p. 299. 1,000 copies in red wrappers of which about 500 were stripped and reissued in grey wrappers carrying an advertisement for D. H. Holmes. Status of copies in cloth is undetermined.

"Ghombo Zhèbes." *New York*, 1885.

La Cuisine Creole. *New York* [1885].
  First state has *Brùlot*, line 9 of introduction. Later corrected to *Brùlot*.

TRANSLATIONS BY HEARN

One of Cleopatra's Nights, by Théophile Gautier. *New York*, 1882.
  The first book to bear Hearn's name on a title page. The publisher's name has been noted in three states on the spine, with no established priority; (a) all capital letters; (b) small capital letters; (c) capital and lower case letters. "Clarimonde," *New York* [1899] reprinted from this volume.

Tales Before Supper. *New York*, 1887.
  Although Hearn's name is not mentioned in this book, there is a possibility that the translation of "Avatar" herein contained was his work. See "Avatar—Hearn or Saltus?" in *The Publishers' Weekly*, June 19, 1937 and June 26, 1937.

The Crime of Sylvestre Bonnard, by Anatole France. *New York*, 1890.
  Wrappers. No. 665 in the "Franklin Square Library." The first edition lists this in the publisher's advertisements; later states carry additional titles beyond the 665 figure. Untrimmed copies in cloth with paper label on spine are probably of a later issue as indicated by the advertisement for "Two Years in the French West Indies," which is priced; first state copies in paper announced the latter as *in press*.

The Temptation of Saint Anthony, by Gustave Flaubert. *New York*, 1910.
  Reissued, *New York*, 1911, with addenda containing passages omitted from the first edition.

Saint Anthony and Other Stories, by Guy de Maupassant. *New York*, 1924.

The Adventures of Walter Schnaffs and Other Stories, by Guy de Maupassant. [*Tokyo*, 1931].

BOOKS WITH HEARN CONTRIBUTIONS

La Nouvelle Atala ou la Fille de l'Esprit, par Chahta-Ima. *Nouvelle-Orlèans*, 1879.
  Various colored wrappers. Contribution.

Harper's Fifth Reader. *New York*, 1889.
  Contains "The Coming of the Hurricane."

A Handbook for Travellers in Japan: Third Edition. *London*, 1891.
  Contribution. American edition, *New York*, 1893.

Things Japanese: Second Edition. *London*, 1891.
  Contribution. Also a large paper edition.

Letters from the Raven. *New York,* 1907.
  Milton Bronner, editor.
Japanese Letters. *Boston,* 1910.
  Also 200 copies signed by the editor, Elizabeth Bisland.
Studies by Members of the English Club. *Tokyo,* 1923.
  Vol. 5 contains Hearn's "The Value of the Imaginative Faculty."
Et Cetera: A Collector's Scrap Book. *Chicago,* 1924.
  Vincent Starrett, editor. 625 numbered copies only. Boards, cloth back, paper label. Contains Hearn's translation of Palma's "The Chemise of Margarita Pareja."
Stories and Sketches, by Lafcadio Hearn. *Tokyo* [1925].
  Reprint together with some first edition material.
Poets and Poems, by Lafcadio Hearn. *Tokyo* [1926].
  R. Tanabé, editor. Reprint together with some first edition material.
Romance and Reason, by Lafcadio Hearn. *Tokyo* [1928].
  R. Tanabé, editor. Contains material here first collected together with reprinted items.
Facts and Fancies, by Lafcadio Hearn. *Tokyo* [1929].
  R. Tanabé, editor. Reprint together with some first edition material.
Letters to a Pagan. *Detroit,* 1933.
  550 numbered copies only.

For a more complete and detailed listing of the Hearn first editions and ephemera the collector is referred to the following work:

Lafcadio Hearn: A Bibliography of His Writings, by P. D. and Ione Perkins. *Tokyo,* 1934.
  Also 200 copies in full cloth with numbered colophon tipped in at the copyright page.

The following are representative of the many separate and other reprints of the Hearn writings:

"Talks to Writers," 1920; "On Composition," 1920; "On Reading, etc.," 1921; "Kimiko," 1923; "Kusa-Hibari," 1924; "The Tale of a Fan," 1928; "On Art, Literature and Philosophy," 1932.

BIOGRAPHICAL

Life and Letters, by Elizabeth Bisland. *Boston,* 1906.
  2 vols. Also 200 copies with page of Hearn manuscript.
Concerning Lafcadio Hearn, by George M. Gould. *Philadelphia* [1908].
  Contains a bibliography by Laura Stedman. Top edges either gilt or stained.
Lafcadio Hearn in Japan, by Yone Noguchi. *London,* 1910.
  Contains Mrs. Hearn's "Reminiscences."
Lafcadio Hearn, by Nina H. Kennard. *London,* 1911.

Lafcadio Hearn, by Edward Thomas. *London,* 1912.
Reminiscences of Lafcadio Hearn, by [Mrs.] Setsuko Hearn. *Boston,* 1918.
    See above: "Lafcadio Hearn in Japan," 1910.
Glimpses of Authors, by Caroline Ticknor. *Boston,* 1922.
    Contains material by and about Hearn.
Lafcadio Hearn's American Days, by Edward L. Tinker. *New York,* 1924.
    Also 150 large paper copies, signed. Revised edition, 1925.
Hearn and His Biographers, by Oscar Lewis. *San Francisco,* 1930.
    350 copies only. Contains several letters by Hearn.
Lafcadio Hearn: A Bibliography, by Martha Howard Sisson. *Boston,* 1933.
Father and I: Memories of Lafcadio Hearn, by Kazuo Koizumi. *Boston,* 1935.

Ernest Hemingway
1898–

THREE STORIES & TEN POEMS. *[Dijon, 1923].*
  Wrappers. 300 copies only. Printed at Dijon; published by Contact Publishing Company, Paris.

IN OUR TIME. *Paris, 1924.*
  Printed boards. Reissued, *New York, 1925,* with so many additions that it is virtually a new book. The original material, for the most part, is used as chapter headings. Reissued, *New York,* 1930, with further revisions and one added story.

THE TORRENTS OF SPRING. *New York, 1926.*

TODAY IS FRIDAY. *[Englewood, N. J., 1926].*
  300 numbered copies only. Wrappers. Later in "Men Without Women."

THE SUN ALSO RISES. *New York, 1926.*
  First state has *stoppped* for *stopped,* p. 181, line 26. Issued in England as "Fiesta."

MEN WITHOUT WOMEN. *New York, 1927.*
  First state printed on paper heavier than that of later issues. For a full discussion of this feature see the Cohn-Hemingway bibliography listed at the end of this list.

A FAREWELL TO ARMS. *New York, 1929.*
  Also 510 numbered copies, signed. First state does not have a notice that "none of the characters in this book is a living person."

DEATH IN THE AFTERNOON. *New York, 1932.*
  First edition has code letter *A* on copyright page.

GOD REST YOU MERRY GENTLEMEN. *New York, 1933.*
  300 numbered copies only. Reprinted in expurgated form in "Winner Take Nothing."

WINNER TAKE NOTHING. *New York, 1933.*
  First edition has code letter *A* on copyright page.

GREEN HILLS OF AFRICA. *New York, 1935.*
  First edition has code letter *A* on copyright page.

TO HAVE AND HAVE NOT. *New York, 1937.*
  First edition has code letter *A* on copyright page.

THE SPANISH EARTH. *Cleveland,* 1938.

1,000 numbered copies only. The first issue has pictorial end papers showing a large F. A. I. banner. These were recalled and the books were reissued with plain end papers, the terminal lining paper carrying a note by the publishers explaining the reason for the change.

THE FIFTH COLUMN AND THE FIRST FORTY-NINE STORIES. *New York,* 1938.

The first printing has the code letter *A* on the copyright page. The title story was separately reprinted, *New York,* 1940.

FOR WHOM THE BELL TOLLS. *New York,* 1940.

The first printing has the code letter *A* on the copyright page. The publishers bound fifteen copies of the regular edition wholly untrimmed for the author's use.

The following list of the secondary Hemingway items in no way purports to be complete. Collectors are referred to the exhaustive "Bibliography of the Writings of Ernest Hemingway," by Louis Henry Cohn, *New York,* 1931.

Senior Tabula June, 1917. *Oak Park, Ill.* [1917].

Printed wrappers. Contains "Class Prophecy" at pp. 57-62.

The Best Poems of 1923. *Boston* [1924].

L. A. G. Strong, editor. Contribution.

The Best Short Stories of 1923. *Boston* [1924].

Edward J. O'Brien, editor. Contains Hemingway's "My Old Man." First state misspells Hemingway's name in the dedication.

The Best Short Stories of 1926. *New York,* 1927.

Edward J. O'Brien, editor. Contains "The Undefeated," by Hemingway.

The American Caravan. *New York* [1927].

Also Literary Guild Edition. Contains "An Alpine Idyll," by Hemingway.

The Best Short Stories of 1927. *New York,* 1927.

Edward J. O'Brien, editor. Contains Hemingway's "The Killers."

Kiki's Memoirs. *Paris,* 1930.

Samuel Putnam, translator. Introduction by Hemingway. For purposes of copyright the introduction was privately printed [*New York,* 1929] in an edition of 25 copies only.

The "Bastard" Note. [*n.p., n.d., New York,* 1931].

4to broadside. 93 numbered copies only. Facsimile of printer's proof of notice added to second edition of "A Farewell to Arms," with Hemingway's comments.

Salmagundi, by William Faulkner. *Milwaukee,* 1932.

Flexible boards. 525 numbered copies only. Contains "Ultimately," a poem by Hemingway.

Active Anthology. *London* [1933].

Ezra Pound, editor. Contains "They All Made Peace ... What Is Peace?"

This Must Be the Place ... by Jimmie the Barman [James Charters]. *London* [1934].

Introduction.

attorno. *Habana*, 1935.
Preliminary essay by Hemingway.

merican Big Game Fishing. *New York* [1935].
Eugene Connett, editor. Contribution by Hemingway. Limited edition: 950 copies and 56 de luxe copies in full leather.

o Red the Nose. *New York* [1935].

ortraits and Self-Portraits, by Georges Schreiber. *Boston*, 1936.
Contribution.

merican Points of View: A Reader's Guide, 1935. *Garden City*, 1936.
William H. Cordell and Kathryn Cordell, editors. Contains Hemingway's "Notes on the Next War."

he Writer in a Changing World. [*New York*, 1937].
Henry Hart, editor. Contribution.

tlantic Game Fishing, by S. Kip Farrington, Jr. *New York*, 1937.
Introduction.

he Yachtsman's Reader. Blow the Man Down. *Garden City*, 1937.
Eric Devine, editor. Contains Hemingway's "On the Blue Water."

ll Good Americans, by Jerome Bahr. *New York*, 1937.
First printing has code letter *A* on copyright page. Introduction.

he Spanish War. [*London*, 1938].
In "Fact," July, 1938. Printed wrappers.

n Exhibition of Sculpture by Jo Davidson. [*New York*, 1938].
Printed wrappers. Contribution.

uintanilla: An Exhibition of Drawings ... [*New York*, 1938].
Leaflet. Preface.

ll the Brave, by Luis Quintanilla. *New York* [1939].
Also 440 copies, numbered and signed by the publishers. Preface. Originally announced as "Guns and Castanets."

en in the Ranks, by Joseph North. [*New York*, 1939].
Wrappers. Foreword.

he Great Crusade, by Gustav Regler. *New York*, 1940.
The preface by Hemingway was previously issued in pamphlet form.

Davidson: Spanish Portraits. [*n.p., n.d.*].
Printed wrappers. Contribution.

he Bedside Esquire. *New York* [1940].
Arnold Gingrich, editor. Contribution.

Henry William Herbert
(Frank Forester)
1807–1858

NOVELS AND HISTORICAL WORKS

THE BROTHERS. *New York*, 1835.
2 vols. Anonymous. Cloth, paper labels.

CROMWELL. *New York*, 1838.
2 vols. Anonymous. Revised and reissued, *New York*, 1856, as "Oliver Cromwell."

RINGWOOD THE ROVER. *Philadelphia*, 1843.
Copyright 1841. Wrappers. First state title page states author as *W. H. Herbert*.

MARMADUKE WYVIL. *New York* [1843].
Wrappers.

THE VILLAGE INN. *New York*, 1843.
Wrappers.

GUARICA: THE CARIB BRIDE. *Philadelphia*, 1844.
Wrappers.

THE LORD OF THE MANOR. *Philadelphia*, 1844.
Wrappers.

RUTH WHALLEY; or, THE FAIR PURITAN. *Boston*, 1844.
Wrappers.

THE INNOCENT WITCH: A CONTINUATION OF RUTH WHALLEY. *Boston*, 1845.
Wrappers.

THE REVOLT OF BOSTON: A CONTINUATION OF RUTH WHALLEY. *Boston*, 1845.
Wrappers.

THE ROMAN TRAITOR. *New York and Baltimore*, 1846.
Wrappers. 2 vols.

INGLEBOROUGH HALL AND THE LORD OF THE MANOR. *New York*, 1847.
Wrappers.

THE MILLER OF MARTIGNÈ. *New York* [1847].
Wrappers.

ISABEL GRAHAM. *New York*, 1848.
Wrappers.

PIERRE THE PARTISAN. *New York*, 1848.
Wrappers. Reissued, [*New York*, 1880] as "The Silent Rifleman."

DERMOT O'BRIEN. *New York*, 1849.
Wrappers.

THE CAPTAINS OF THE OLD WORLD. *New York*, 1851.

KNIGHTS OF ENGLAND, FRANCE AND SCOTLAND. *New York*, 1852.

THE CAVALIERS OF ENGLAND. *New York*, 1852.

THE CHEVALIERS OF FRANCE. *New York*, 1853.

THE CAPTAINS OF THE ROMAN REPUBLIC. *New York*, 1854.

PERSONS AND PICTURES FROM THE HISTORIES OF FRANCE AND ENGLAND.
New York, 1854.

MEMOIRS OF HENRY THE EIGHTH OF ENGLAND. *New York*, 1855.

WAGER OF BATTLE. *New York*, 1855.

POEMS OF "FRANK FORESTER." *New York*, 1888.
250 copies only. Morgan Herbert, editor.

SPORTING BOOKS

THE WARWICK WOODLANDS. *Philadelphia*, 1845.
Wrappers. Reissued, *New York*, 1851, cloth or wrappers, with illustrations by
the author.

MY SHOOTING BOX. *Philadelphia*, 1846.
Wrappers. Vol. 3 in "Carey and Hart's Library of Humorous American Works."
P. 35, last line has *mattter* for *matter*. A copy has been noted with the advertise-
ments at the back dated *May, 1845*.

FIELD SPORTS IN THE UNITED STATES AND BRITISH PROVINCES OF AMERICA.
London, 1848.
2 vols. Issued in New York, 1849, 2 vols., as "Frank Forester's Field Sports of
the United States, *etc.*," first binding having *Burgess, Stringer* at foot of spine;
later: *Stringer, Townsend*.

FRANK FORESTER'S FISH AND FISHING OF THE UNITED STATES AND BRITISH
PROVINCES OF NORTH AMERICA. *London*, 1849.
Issued in New York, 1850; also a supplement, *New York*, 1850. The two revised
and reissued in one volume, *New York*, 1850.

THE DEERSTALKERS. *Philadelphia*, 1849.
Wrappers. There are various undated Peterson reprints with spurious copyright dates. Previously in "Frank Forester and His Friends," *London*, 1849, 3 vols.

THE QUORNDON HOUNDS. *Philadelphia*, 1852.
Wrappers or cloth.

AMERICAN GAME IN ITS SEASONS. *New York*, 1853.
Illustrated by the author.

THE COMPLETE MANUAL FOR YOUNG SPORTSMEN. *New York*, 1856.
Illustrated by the author.

FRANK FORESTER'S HORSE AND HORSEMANSHIP OF THE UNITED STATES AND BRITISH PROVINCES OF NORTH AMERICA. *New York and London*, 1857.
2 vols.

FISHING WITH HOOK AND LINE. *New York* [*ca.* 1858].
Anonymous. Printed wrappers. *Brother Jonathan Office* imprint.

HINTS TO HORSE-KEEPERS. *New York*, 1859.
Posthumous. First thirteen chapters by Herbert; balance edited and written from his notes.

FRANK FORESTER'S FUGITIVE SPORTING SKETCHES. [*Westfield, Wis.*] 1879.
Cloth or wrappers. Edited by F. E. Pond, *Will Wildwood*, pseudonym.

TROUTING ALONG THE CATASAUQUA. *New York*, 1927.
Boards. 423 copies only.

COLLECTED SETS

FRANK FORESTER AND HIS FRIENDS. *London*, 1849.
3 vols. Comprises: "My Shooting Box," "The Warwick Woodlands," and "The Deerstalkers." The last named preceded the Philadelphia 1849 edition in time of publication.

THE HITCHCOCK EDITION OF FRANK FORESTER. *New York*, 1930.
4 vols. Comprises: "The Warwick Woodlands," "My Shooting Box," "The Quorndon Hounds," and "The Deerstalkers." Contains a checklist and appendix by Harry Worcester Smith.

TRANSLATIONS, ETC., ETC.

Dr. Goldsmith's History of Rome. *New York*, 1840.
Edited.

Sporting Scenes and Sundry Sketches, by J. Cypress, Jr. *New York*, 1842.
2 vols. Edited and with a biographical sketch of the author. Later bindings add the name, *Forester*, to the spine.

Matilda, by Eugene Sue. *New York,* 1843.
   3 parts in wrappers. Translated. Reissued in one volume, *New York,* 1844.
The Salamander, by Eugene Sue. *New York* [1844].
   Wrappers. Translated.
The Wandering Jew, by Eugene Sue. *New York* [n.d.]—1845.
   19 parts in wrappers, or two volumes. Vol. 1 undated; vol. 2 dated 1845.
Atar Gull, by Eugene Sue. *New York,* 1846.
   Wrappers. Translated.
The Fair Isabel, by Eugene Sue. *New York,* 1846.
   Wrappers. Translated and illustrated by Herbert.
Genevieve, by Alexandre Dumas. *New York,* 1846.
   Wrappers. Translated.
Diana of Méridor, by Alexandre Dumas. *New York,* 1846.
   2 parts in wrappers. Translated.
Tales of the Spanish Seas. *New York,* 1847.
   All reprint material.
The Countess of Morion, by Frederick Soulié. *New York,* 1847.
   Wrappers. Translated.
Acté of Corinth, by Alexandre Dumas. *New York,* 1847.
   Wrappers. Translated.
History of the Consulate and Empire, by Louis Thiers. *Philadelphia,* 1847-[1849].
   2 vols. Also 12 paper parts [1845]-[1852]. Translated with D. FORBES CAMPBELL.
The Apple Stand. *Newark,* 1848.
   Pamphlet.
The Prometheus and Agamemnon of Æschylus. *Cambridge,* 1849.
   Translated.
The Sportsman's Vade Mecum, by Dinks. *New York,* 1850.
   Edited. Revised and reissued, *New York,* 1856.
The Old Forest Ranger, by Maj. Walter Campbell. *New York,* 1853.
   Preface by Herbert.
History of the French Protestant Refugees, by Charles Weiss. *New York,* 1854.
   2 vols. Translated.
Mr. Sponge's Sporting Tour. *New York,* 1856.
   Edited.
The Dog, by Dinks, Mayhew and Hutchinson. *New York,* 1857.
   Illustrated and edited by Herbert.

BIOGRAPHICAL AND BIBLIOGRAPHICAL

The Life and Writings of Frank Forester. *New York,* 1882.
   2 vols. David W. Judd, editor.
The First Editions of Henry William Herbert "Frank Forester" 1807-1858, by Paul S[pencer] Seybolt. *Boston,* 1932.
   60 numbered copies only, privately printed.
Frank Forester (Henry William Herbert): A Tragedy in Exile, by William S. Hunt. *Newark, N. J.,* 1933.

HERBERT

Henry William Herbert (Frank Forester): A Bibliography of His Writings, 1832-1858. Compiled by William Mitchell Van Winkle and David A. Randall. *Portland, Me., 1936.*
   250 copies only.

Oliver Herford
1863–1935

ARTFUL ANTICKS. *New York*, 1888.

PEN AND INKLINGS. *New York* [1893].
  waived for *waved*, p. 21, 18th line of poem.

THE BASHFUL EARTHQUAKE. *New York*, 1898.
  Boards.

AN ALPHABET OF CELEBRITIES. *Boston*, 1899.
  Boards.

A CHILD'S PRIMER OF NATURAL HISTORY. *New York*, 1899.
  Boards.

MC ADAM AND EVE. *New York*, 1900.

OVERHEARD IN A GARDEN. *New York* [1900].
  Boards.

MORE ANIMALS. *New York*, 1901.

WAGNER FOR INFANTS. *Boston*, 1901.

THE RUBAIYAT OF A PERSIAN KITTEN. *New York*, 1904.
  Boards.

TWO IN A ZOO. *Indianapolis* [1904].
  With CURTIS DUNHAM.

THE FAIRY-GOD-MOTHER-IN-LAW. *New York* [1905].
  Boards. *Published, November, 1905* on copyright page.

MOTHER'S GEESE. *New York*, 1906.
  With G. B. BAKER and GEORGE C. CHAPPELL.

A LITTLE BOOK OF BORES. *New York* [1906].
  Boards.

BOLD BAD BUTTERFLY, *etc. London*, 1906.

THE ASTONISHING TALE OF A PEN AND INK PUPPET. *New York*, 1907.

THE PETER PAN ALPHABET. *New York*, 1907.

CUPID'S ALMANAC AND GUIDE TO HEARTICULTURE. *Boston* [1908].
  With JOHN CECIL CLAY.

THE SIMPLE JOGRAPHY. *Boston* [1908].
Reissued, *New York* [1919] as "This Giddy Globe."

THE SMOKER'S YEAR BOOK. *New York*, 1908.

CUPID'S CYCLOPEDIA. *New York*, 1910.
With JOHN CECIL CLAY. Boards.

THE KITTEN'S GARDEN OF VERSES. *New York*, 1911.

HAPPY DAYS. *New York*, 1911.
With JOHN CECIL CLAY.

CUPID'S FAIR WEATHER BOOKE. *New York* [1911].
With JOHN CECIL CLAY.

THE MYTHOLOGICAL ZOO. *New York*, 1912.

THE BISHOP'S PURSE. *New York*, 1913.
With CLEVELAND MOFFETT.

THE JINGLE-JUNGLE BOOK. *New York*, 1913.

CAPERS. *New York*, 1914.

CONFESSIONS OF A CARICATURIST. *New York*, 1917.

THE LAUGHING WILLOW. *New York* [1918].
Boards.

THE HERFORD ÆSOP. *Boston* [1921].

NEITHER HERE NOR THERE. *New York* [1922].
First edition has *GHD* insignia on copyright page.

WHAT'LL YOU HAVE. *New York*, 1925.
With KARL SCHMIDT.

EXCUSE IT PLEASE. *Philadelphia* [1929].
First edition so stated on copyright page.

SEA LEGS. *Philadelphia* [1931].
Boards.

THE DEB'S DICTIONARY. *Philadelphia*, 1931.
First edition so stated on copyright page.

THE "CYNIC" BOOKS

In Collaboration With ETHEL WATTS MUMFORD (GRANT) and ADDISON MIZNER.

Cynic's Calendar of Revised Wisdom for 1903. *San Francisco* [1902].
The "Calendar" for 1904 contains no new material by Herford.

Entirely New Cynic's Calendar of Revised Wisdom, 1905. *San Francisco* [1904].
Complete Cynic's Calendar of Revised Wisdom, 1906. *San Francisco* [1905].
  Contains no new material by Herford.
Altogether New Cynic's Calendar for 1907. *San Francisco* [1906].
Quite New Cynic's Calendar of Revised Wisdom for 1908. *San Francisco* [1907].
Perfectly Good Cynic's Calendar with Astronomical Attachment. *San Francisco*
  [1908].
Complete Cynic. *San Francisco* [1910].
  Reissue of material in preceding "Calendars."
Revived Cynic's Calendar. *San Francisco* [1917].

PLAYS, TRANSLATIONS, ETC.

The Love Cure, by Leo Stein and Carl Lindau. *New York,* 1906.
  Operetta. Translated.
The Devil, by Ferenc Molnar. *New York* [1908].
  Adapted by Herford. Must have *Kennerley* imprint.
The Florist Shop, by Alexander Engel and Julius Horst, 1909.
  Translated from the German. No record of publication.
Con and Co., by Paul Gavault, Zuros Nancey, Petroccochino Armont, 1910.
  Translated from the French. No record of publication.

SOME BOOKS ILLUSTRATED BY HERFORD

The following list is representative of the many books illustrated by Herford.

Behind Time, by G. P. Lathrop. *New York* [1886].
New Waggings of Old Tales. *Boston,* 1888.
  Anon. By John Kendrick Bangs and Frank Dempster Sherman.
Little Mr. Thimblefinger and His Queer Country, by Joel Chandler Harris. *Boston,*
  1894.
Allegretto, by Gertrude Hall. *Boston,* 1894.
Mr. Rabbit at Home, by Joel Chandler Harris. *Boston,* 1895.
The Story of Aaron, by Joel Chandler Harris. *Boston,* 1896.
Aaron in the Wildwoods, by Joel Chandler Harris. *Boston,* 1897.
The Jingle Book, by Carolyn Wells. *New York,* 1899.
Dream Fox Story Book, by Mrs. Mabel Osgood Wright. *New York,* 1900.
Her Majesty the King, by J. J. Roche. *Boston,* 1902.
A Phenomenal Fauna, by Carolyn Wells. *New York,* 1902.
Folly for the Wise, by Carolyn Wells. *Indianapolis* [1904].
Con the Wizard, by J. H. Jewett. *New York* [1905].
Monologues, by Beatrice Herford. *New York,* 1908.
Bible Rimes for the Not-Too-Young, by Clare Beecher-Kummer. *New York,* 1909.
Gambolling with Galatea, by Curtis Dunham. *Boston,* 1909.
Mouse-Colored Road, by Vance Thompson. *New York,* 1913.
Epilogue ... Closing of Wallack's Theatre, May 1, 1915. [*New York*] 1915.
  4 pp. folder.

HERFORD

The Spoon River Anthology, by Edgar Lee Masters. *New York,* 1916.
  For further regarding this see under Masters.
Alice's Adventures in Wonderland, by Lewis Carroll. *Boston* [1917].
Bird's Nest Boarding House, by Verbena Reed. *New York* [1922].

BOOKS WITH CONTRIBUTIONS, ETC.

The Literary Guillotine, by Mark Twain, Oliver Herford, etc. *New York,* 1903.
  Variously attributed to Mark Twain, Herford, and others but believed to be by
  William Wallace Wheelock.
Poems from "Life." *New York,* 1923.
  Edited by, and with contribution by, Herford.
This Giddy Globe. *New York* [1919].
  Reissue of "Simple Jography," *Boston* [1908].

Joseph Hergesheimer

1880–

THE LAY ANTHONY. *New York,* 1914.
Revised and reissued, *New York,* 1919.

MOUNTAIN BLOOD. *New York,* 1915.

THE THREE BLACK PENNYS. *New York,* 1917.
In the first state the lower portion of the medallion on the fly-title page is approximately 2" from the bottom of the page. In later states it is about ½" from the bottom of the page. It has been stated that the first issue may be distinguished by the repeated running head at p. 363 but since this feature persists in reprints, it is of no value as a distinguishing point. A number, variously stated as ten and twenty-five, were bound untrimmed; not signed or numbered.
Reissued with a new preface, 1930, of which there was also a de luxe signed edition.

GOLD AND IRON. *New York,* 1918.
Top edges stained black.

THE HAPPY END. *New York,* 1919.
Also 60 large paper copies, numbered and signed.

LINDA CONDON. *New York,* 1919.
Also 60 large paper copies, numbered and signed. Bound in smooth blue cloth.

JAVA HEAD. *New York,* 1919.
Also 100 large paper copies, numbered and signed.

SAN CRISTÓBAL DE LA HABANA. *New York,* 1920.
Boards. Also 110 large paper copies, numbered and signed; 10 copies lettered A to J.

CYTHEREA. *New York,* 1922.
Also 270 large paper copies in red cloth with paper label, numbered and signed. Also 100 copies in printed boards, numbered, for presentation to "bookseller friends."

THE BRIGHT SHAWL. *New York,* 1922.
Published, October, 1922 on the copyright page. Also 225 large paper copies, numbered and signed, and 10 copies lettered A to J. Also, 200 copies in advance of publication for presentation to "bookseller friends."

THE PRESBYTERIAN CHILD. *New York,* 1923.
950 copies only, numbered and signed.

BALISAND. *New York,* 1924.
  Also 50 copies on Japan vellum; 175 on Borzoi All-Rag paper. All numbered and signed.

FROM AN OLD HOUSE. *New York,* 1925.
  1,050 numbered copies on large paper signed by the author. Trade edition dated 1926.

TAMPICO. *New York,* 1926.
  Also 55 copies on Japan vellum; 200 on Borzoi All-Rag paper; numbered and signed by the author.

QUIET CITIES. *New York,* 1928.
  Also 55 copies on Japan vellum, 210 copies on Borzoi All-Rag paper, numbered and signed by the author.

SWORDS AND ROSES. *New York,* 1929.
  Also 70 copies on Japan vellum, 225 on Borzoi All-Rag paper, numbered and signed by the author.

TRIALL BY ARMES. *London,* 1929.
  500 copies only, numbered and signed.

THE PARTY DRESS. *New York,* 1930.
  Also 60 copies in full vellum, top edges gilt, untrimmed, signed. 225 copies with vellum back, signed.

THE LIMESTONE TREE. *New York,* 1931.
  Also 75 copies on Shidzuoka Japan vellum, 225 on Borzoi All-Rag paper, numbered and signed.

SHERIDAN: A MILITARY NARRATIVE. *Boston,* 1931.
  Also 350 untrimmed copies, numbered and signed.

BERLIN. *New York,* 1932.
  First edition so stated on copyright page. Also 110 signed copies.

LOVE IN THE UNITED STATES AND THE BIG SHOT. *London* [1932].
  Wrappers. *First Published September 1932* on verso of title page.

TROPICAL WINTER. *New York,* 1933.
  First edition so stated on copyright page.

THE FOOLSCAP ROSE. *New York,* 1934.
  First edition so stated on copyright page.

BOOKS WITH CONTRIBUTIONS

Hugh Walpole: An Appreciation. *New York* [1919].
First state has no mention of Marshall Field as publisher.

Pleiades Year Book, 1918-1919. [*New York, 1919*].
  600 copies on Japan vellum.
Tales of My Native Town, by Gabriel D'Annunzio. *Garden City,* 1920.
Domnei, by James Branch Cabell. *New York,* 1920.
The Borzoi, 1920. *New York,* 1920.
My Maiden Effort. *Garden City,* 1921.
  First edition so stated on copyright page.
The Novel of Tomorrow. *Indianapolis,* 1922.
The Best Short Stories of 1922. *Boston* [1923].
  Edward J. O'Brien, editor. Contains Hergesheimer's "The Token." The edition
  for 1919, *Boston* [1920] contains a story also.
Marriage. *Garden City,* 1923.
Et Cetera. *Chicago,* 1924.
The Borzoi, 1925. *New York* [1925].
  For further regarding this see under *Cather.*
Hagar's Hoard, by George Kibbe Turner. *New York,* 1925.
The Work of Stephen Crane. *New York* [1925-1926].
  12 vols. Vol. I contains an introduction by Hergesheimer.
Interiors of Virginia Houses of Colonial Times, by Edith D. T. Sale. *Richmond,*
  1927.
The Colophon, No. 8.
  Contains Hergesheimer's "Biography and Bibliographies."
Colonial Houses, Philadelphia, Pre-Revolutionary Period, by Philip B. Wallace
  and W. Luther Miller. *New York* [1931].
Breaking into Print. *New York,* 1937.
  Elmer Adler, editor. Contribution.

BIOGRAPHICAL AND BIBLIOGRAPHICAL

Joseph Hergesheimer, the Man and His Books, by Llewellyn Jones. *New York,* 1920.
Joseph Hergesheimer, an Essay in Interpretation, by James Branch Cabell. *Chicago,*
  1921.
  For further regarding this item see under Cabell.
A Bibliography of Joseph Hergesheimer, by H. L. R. Swire. *Philadelphia,* 1922.
  335 copies only.

"Wild Oranges," "Tubal Cain" and "The Dark Fleece" are separate reprints from
"Gold and Iron."
"Wild Oranges" was also issued in a de luxe edition of 85 numbered copies, *New
York,* 1918.

Du Bose Heyward

1885–1940

CAROLINA CHANSONS. *New York,* 1922.
With HERVEY ALLEN. Boards, cloth back.

SKYLINES AND HORIZONS. *New York,* 1924.

PORGY. *New York* [1925].
First printing has the publisher's monogram on the copyright page. First binding gold-stamped; later, black-stamped. Dramatization with Dorothy Heyward, *Garden City,* 1927.

ANGEL. *New York* [1926].
First printing has publisher's monogram and code letter *A* on copyright page.

MAMBA'S DAUGHTERS. *Garden City,* 1929.
First edition so stated on copyright page. Dramatized with Dorothy Heyward, *New York* [1939] the first printing having publisher's monogram on the copyright page.

THE HALF PINT FLASK. *New York,* 1929.

JASBO BROWN AND SELECTED POEMS. *New York* [1931].
First printing has publisher's monogram on copyright page. Reprints, together with first edition material, "Skylines and Horizons," 1924.

BRASS ANKLE. *New York* [1931].
Also 100 large paper copies, numbered and signed. First edition so stated. Also an edition, without the first edition notice, in yellow wrappers: *Special First Night Presentation Edition ... Compliments of James W. Elliott.*

PETER ASHLEY. *New York* [1932].
First printing has publisher's monogram on copyright page.

PORGY AND BESS: AN OPERA IN THREE ACTS. *New York,* 1935.
250 large paper copies signed by the author, composer, illustrator and director.

LOST MORNING. *New York* [1936].
First printing has the publisher's monogram on the copyright page.

STAR SPANGLED VIRGIN. *New York* [1939].
First printing has publisher's monogram on the copyright page. Noted in both black and orange cloths; copies deposited for copyright are bound in black cloth.

THE COUNTRY BUNNY AND THE LITTLE GOLD SHOES. *Boston,* 1939.

Du Bose Heyward: A Critical and Biographical Sketch. *New York* [1926].
    Wrappers.
Spiritual Songs From the Guild Production Porgy. *New York* [1928].
The Lyric South. *New York,* 1928.
    Addison Hibbard, editor. Contains several contributions.
The Emperor Jones: From the Stage Play by Eugene O'Neill. [*n.p., n.d.*].
    Screen version by Du Bose Heyward. 98 page scenario, mimeographed, for
    private use.
Fort Sumter. *New York* [1938].
    With Herbert Ravenel Sass. Adapted from previously collected writings.
Cordially Yours. [*Boston*] 1939.
    Contribution.

Charles Fenno Hoffman

1806–1884

A WINTER IN THE WEST. *New York,* 1835.
By a New Yorker. 2 vols. Reissued with notes, *Chicago,* 1882.

WILD SCENES IN THE FOREST AND PRAIRIE. *London,* 1839.
2 vols. Reissued in *New York,* 1843, 2 vols.

GREYSLAER: A ROMANCE OF THE MOHAWK. *New York,* 1840.
Anonymous. 2 vols. Label on spines. Errata slip in Vol. 1. Revised and reissued, *Philadelphia,* 1841.

THE VIGIL OF FAITH AND OTHER POEMS. *New York,* 1842.
Boards. Label on spine. Reissued as "Songs and other Poems," *New York,* 1846.

THE ECHO; OR, BORROWED NOTES FOR HOME CIRCULATION. *Philadelphia,* 1844.
Printed wrappers.

LAYS OF THE HUDSON. *New York,* 1846.

LOVE'S CALENDAR, LAYS OF THE HUDSON, AND OTHER POEMS. *New York,* 1847.

THE PIONEERS OF NEW YORK. *New York,* 1848.

THE POEMS OF CHARLES FENNO HOFFMAN. *Philadelphia,* 1873.
Edward Fenno Hoffman, editor.

The New York Book of Poetry. *New York,* 1837.
Edited by and with contributions by Hoffman. The title page occurs in two states.
The Wintergreen. *New York* [1843].
Contribution.
The Opal. *New York,* 1844.
Contribution. Hoffman also contributed to the editions of 1846 and 1847.
The Gift. *Philadelphia,* 1844.
Contribution.
Proceedings of the New York Historical Society. *New York,* 1844.
Contains "The Distinctive Character of the People of New York."
Charles Fenno Hoffman, by Homer F. Barnes. *New York,* 1930.

Oliver Wendell Holmes
1809–1894

ILLUSTRATIONS OF THE ATHENAEUM GALLERY OF PAINTINGS. *Boston*, 1830.
Stitched without wrappers. Of the 18 anonymous poems included, nine are by Holmes. About five copies known.

THE HARBINGER: A MAY-GIFT. *Boston*, 1833.
Contains 17 poems by Holmes. A joint production with other poems by J. O. Sargent and Park Benjamin. Cloth, paper label on spine. A few copies known with untrimmed edges.

POEMS. *Boston*, 1836.
Various cloth bindings, paper label. Some copies have the *New York and Boston* imprint.

BOYLSTON PRIZE DISSERTATIONS FOR ... 1836 AND 1837. *Boston*, 1838.
Wholly by Holmes. Folding colored map of New England. The last of the three dissertations had been printed in a similar volume in 1836.

PRINCIPLES OF THE THEORY AND PRACTICE OF MEDICINE. *Boston*, 1839.
Sheep. First American edition of a text-book by Marshall Hall, "revised and much enlarged by" Holmes and Dr. Jacob Bigelow, who added about a third to the book, including six new chapters, placing these additions in brackets.

HOMOEOPATHY, AND ITS KINDRED DELUSIONS. *Boston*, 1842.
Boards, paper label.

THE CONTAGIOUSNESS OF PUERPERAL FEVER. [*Boston*, 1843].
Wrappers. A pioneer treatise on this subject anticipating Semmelweiss. Reissued, *Boston*, 1855, with 24 pp. of new material and an introduction, as "Puerperal Fever As A Private Pestilence," wrappers.

THE POSITION AND PROSPECTS OF THE MEDICAL STUDENT. *Boston*, 1844.
Wrappers.

URANIA: A RHYMED LESSON. *Boston*, 1846.
Printed wrappers. A variant of unknown status has been noted in unprinted wrappers with a star appearing over *Urania* on the title page.

POEMS. *London*, 1846.
Boards, paper label or cloth. Contains nine poems not in the 1836 edition.

INTRODUCTORY LECTURE, DELIVERED ... [at] HARVARD UNIVERSITY, NOV. 3, 1847. *Boston*, 1847.
Wrappers. The first state misprints the date as *Nov. 13* on the cover. Holmes continued as Parkman Professor of Anatomy until 1882.

POEMS. *Boston*, 1849.
Boards, paper label, or cloth; various colors and types of stamping. A copy has been noted with *Pomes* for *Poems* on the label. First printing has 272 pages; imprint of *William D. Ticknor and Company; Perpsichore* for *Terpsichore*, running head, p. 187. Second printing, 286 pages, 5 added poems; *Ticknor, Reed and Fields* imprint. Earliest state of second issue does not have printer's imprint on copyright page.

ASTRÆA: THE BALANCE OF ILLUSIONS. *Boston*, 1850.
Yellow glazed boards or rough cloth. Smooth cloth bindings are remainder.

A POEM ... DELIVERED AT ... THE PITTSFIELD CEMETERY, SEPT. 9, 1850. [*Pittsfield*, 1850].
Wrappers. A separate printing. The formal address at the occasion, and Holmes' poem, were also printed together in a pamphlet in the same year.

THE BENEFACTORS OF THE MEDICAL SCHOOL OF HARVARD UNIVERSITY. *Boston*, 1850.
Wrappers. A biography of George Parkman is included.

THE POETICAL WORKS OF OLIVER WENDELL HOLMES. *London*, 1852.
First book appearance of three poems.

SONGS OF THE CLASS OF MDCCCXXIX. *Boston*, 1854.
Wrappers. About six copies known. Three of the five poems are by Holmes; the other two are by S. F. Smith, including "America."

ORATION DELIVERED BEFORE THE NEW ENGLAND SOCIETY. [*New York*,?] 1856].

VALEDICTORY ADDRESS, *etc.*, MARCH 10th, 1858. *Boston*, 1858.
Wrappers.

THE AUTOCRAT OF THE BREAKFAST-TABLE. *Boston*, 1858.
Engraved decorative half-title. Third and fourth end papers headed *Poetry and the Drama* and *School Books* respectively. Bound in various colors of cloth, all except tan being uncommon. The possible first binding has five ring decorations on the spine instead of the usual four. Large paper copies are later and dated 1859, may be with or without illustrations, but must read *Boston* and not *Ticknor & Co* at the base of spine. Reissued, *Boston*, 1883, with new introduction.

SONGS AND POEMS OF THE CLASS OF 1829: SECOND EDITION. *Boston*, 1859.
Various bindings. Eight of the seventeen poems are by Holmes. Some copies contain frontispiece portrait and have red edges; priority undetermined.

THE PROFESSOR AT THE BREAKFAST TABLE. *Boston*, 1860.
Some copies have two imprints. Later on large paper. Reissued, *Boston*, 1883, with new introduction.

ELSIE VENNER: A ROMANCE OF DESTINY. *Boston,* 1861.
2 vols. Vol. 1 has leaf of advertisements at front. Vol. 2 has no half-title. Vol. 1 has *richer,* first page of text; later, the *r* dropped out; still later, probably re-inserted. Reissued, *Boston,* 1883, with new introduction.

CURRENTS AND COUNTER-CURRENTS IN MEDICAL SCIENCE. *Boston,* 1861.
First state has no advertisements, no publisher's stamp on spine. Second state has advertisements and *T & F* on the spine.

SONGS IN MANY KEYS. *Boston,* 1862.
Advertisements dated *November 1861* announcing this title as *in press.*

THE POEMS OF OLIVER WENDELL HOLMES. *Boston,* 1862.
"Blue and Gold Series." Contains two poems here first collected.

BORDER LINES OF KNOWLEDGE IN ... MEDICAL SCIENCE. *Boston,* 1862.

ORATION ... ON THE FOURTH OF JULY, 1863. *Boston,* 1863.
First three issues are 4to in leather. First two issues are 71 pp. 12 copies were so done, the first issue lacking the half-title and leaf of alterations. It is stated that 50 copies were done of the 3rd issue, 75 pp. 8vo issues in cloth and wrappers with imprint of both *Ticknor and Fields* and the *City of Boston,* followed. The 8vo Philadelphia issue is probably still later. Entitled when collected: "The Inevitable Trial."

SOUNDINGS FROM THE ATLANTIC. *Boston,* 1864.

HUMOROUS POEMS. *Boston,* 1865.
Three poems here first collected. Cloth or printed wrappers. Portrait frontispiece.

THE GUARDIAN ANGEL. *Boston,* 1867.
Reissued, *Boston,* 1883, with new introduction.

TEACHING FROM THE CHAIR AND THE BEDSIDE. *Boston,* 1867.
Wrappers.

SONGS AND POEMS OF THE CLASS OF EIGHTEEN HUNDRED AND TWENTY-NINE: THIRD EDITION. *Boston,* 1868 [1881] [1889].
3 vols. Continuous pagination, containing respectively 20, 17, and 8 poems by Holmes.

THE MEDICAL PROFESSION IN MASSACHUSETTS. *Boston,* 1869.
Wrappers.

MECHANISM IN THOUGHT AND MORALS. *Boston,* 1871.

VALEDICTORY ADDRESS ... MARCH 2, 1871. *New York,* 1871.
Wrappers.

THE CLAIMS OF DENTISTRY. *Boston,* 1872.
Wrappers.

THE POET AT THE BREAKFAST TABLE. *Boston,* 1872.
First state has *Talle* for *Table,* running head, p. 9. Reissued, *Boston,* 1883, w
new introduction.

SONGS OF MANY SEASONS, 1862-1874. *Boston,* 1875.

POETICAL WORKS. *Boston,* 1877.
"Household Edition." About 20 poems here first collected.

AN ADDRESS DELIVERED AT ... THE BOSTON MICROSCOPICAL SOCIETY. *B*
ton, 1877.
Wrappers.

JOHN LOTHROP MOTLEY: A MEMOIR. *Boston,* 1879.
Also large paper copies. The small pamphlet published by John Wilson a
Son, 1879, is later.

THE SCHOOL-BOY. *Boston,* 1879.
Flowered or black end-papers. Cloth or morocco. Also printed in large type, s
copies only.

THE IRON GATE AND OTHER POEMS. *Boston,* 1880.

ADDRESS DELIVERED AT ... THE BOSTON MEDICAL LIBRARY ASSOCIATIC
DECEMBER 3, 1878. *Cambridge,* 1881.
Wrappers. Holmes gave his medical library to this association.

POETICAL WORKS. *Boston,* 1881.
2 vols. "Handy Volume Edition." Five poems here first collected.

MEDICAL HIGHWAYS AND BY-WAYS. *Cambridge,* 1882.
Wrappers.

FAREWELL ADDRESS ... TO THE MEDICAL SCHOOL OF HARVARD UNIVERSIT
November 28, 1882. *Cambridge,* 1882.
Wrappers.

MEDICAL ESSAYS 1842-1882. *Boston,* 1883.

PAGES FROM AN OLD VOLUME OF LIFE. *Boston,* 1883.

A MORTAL ANTIPATHY. *Boston,* 1885.

RALPH WALDO EMERSON. *Boston,* 1885.
A few copies, untrimmed, in buckram. P. 350, line 1, reads *eighthieth* f
seventy-ninth.

ILLUSTRATED POEMS. *Boston,* 1885.
First printing for "Ave."

OUR HUNDRED DAYS IN EUROPE. *Boston,* 1887.

Dark green or pictorial olive green cloth bindings; no priority. Large paper edition printed in England, 1888.

BEFORE THE CURFEW AND OTHER POEMS. *Boston,* 1888.

Grey boards, white cloth back; white cloth with green cloth back; three-quarter leather, uncut; and 250 copies in blue cloth, uncut, with paper label on spine stating *First Edition,* of which there is no proof. A copy has been noted with an inserted presentation label.

OVER THE TEACUPS. *Boston,* 1891.

Dark green or pictorial olive green cloth bindings; no priority. First state has no price after *Teacups* in advertisements facing title page and lists "The Breakfast-Table Series" as *10 Vols. $17.00* instead of *11 Vols. $18.50.* When in pictorial cover the word *Tea-cups* is hyphenated on front cover, all edges stained yellow, yellow or white end papers. Reissued in the same year with a second preface.

MEMOIR OF HENRY JACOB BIGELOW. *Cambridge,* 1891.

Wrappers.

COLLECTED WORKS. *Boston,* 1891.

13 vols. "Riverside Edition." 300 numbered sets on large paper; each of the first nine volumes contains a new preface. Three poems are here first collected. A fourteenth volume was added in 1892: "Memoirs of Motley and Emerson." The first state erroneously entitles the poem, in volume twelve, concerning Benjamin Pierce *1819-1891.*

COLLECTED POEMS: CAMBRIDGE EDITION. *Boston,* 1895.

Contains ten poems here first collected.

A DISSERTATION ON ACUTE PERICARDITIS. *Boston,* 1937.

500 copies only.

BROADSIDES AND LEAFLETS

No American author was so prone as Holmes to the first printing of his work in leaflet or broadside form. It is by no means certain that the list below even approaches completeness. It does not include programs, orders of exercises, etc., etc., in which Holmes productions are combined with other matter; or the leaflets such as "Hymn of Peace," which were preceded by publication in some other form.

A Scintilla. [*Cambridge,* 1849].
Affecting Ballad of the Oysterman. *Boston,* 1849.
  Sheet music. 8 pp.
A Song of '29. [*Boston,* 1851].
Response of Oliver Wendell Holmes, M. D., *etc. New York* [1853].
The Old Man Dreams. [*Boston,* 1854].
The New Eden. [*Pittsfield,* 1854].
Poem ["A Sentiment"]. [*n.p.*] 1855.

Mare Rubrum. [Boston, 1858].

The Promise ... March 20, 1859. Boston, 1859.

Boston Common: Three Pictures. [Boston, 1859].
Printed in facsimile on Holmes' personal stationery.

Lecture: 1863. [Boston, 1863].
Six copies only; printed from large types.

New England's Master-Key. [Boston, 1864].
Six copies only; printed from large types.

Hymn ... For the Great Central Fair. Philadelphia, 1864.

Lecture ["The Poetry of the War"] 1865. [Boston, 1865].

Lines Read ... At a Farewell Dinner Given to Longfellow ... May 27, 1868. Boston [1868].
Holmes gave the original MS. to Longfellow; now preserved at Craigie House, Cambridge.

Tribute ... to Christian Gottfried Ehrenberg ... November 5, 1868. Berlin [1868].
4 pp. 4to leaflet. Holmes' poem together with German translation. Only one copy known.

Class Poem, '29, January 6, 1869. [Boston] 1869.

In Memory of Fitz-Greene Halleck. [Boston] 1869.

Bonaparte ... Humboldt ... 1769. [Boston] 1869.

Nearing the Snow Line. [Boston, 1869].

Professor Jeffries Wyman: A Memorial Outline. [Boston, 1874].

Crime and Automatism. [Boston, 1875].

The Brave Old South. Boston [1876].

The First Fan. [Boston] 1877.

A Family Record, Woodstock, Connecticut, July 4, 1877. [Cambridge, 1877].
Wrappers. 11 pp.

Harvard ... February 21, 1878. [Boston] 1878.

Letter to the Rabelais Club. [Boston, 1880].

Jonathan Edwards: An Essay. New York [1880].
Stitched, without wrappers.

The Pulpit and the Pew. [Boston, 1881].

Benjamin Pierce. [Cambridge, 1881].

Alma Mater ... February 21, 1882. [Boston, 1882].

A Welcome to Dr. Benjamin Apthorp Gould. [Boston, 1885].

Hymn: The Word of Promise. [Boston] 1886.

New Hail Columbia! Philadelphia [1887].

Poem ... For the Dedication of the Fountain ... at Stratford-on-Avon. [Boston (and England?)] 1887.
There is a 4 pp. leaflet, printed in Boston, and one of 8 pp. which, from internal evidence, was printed in England; Boston leaflet is earlier.

Leaflet Concerning Holmes' Eyesight. Boston, 1887.
Reissued, 1889 and 1893, with added material.

"Proudly Beneath Her Glittering Dome." [Boston, 1888].
Holmes public library poem in large type; two known copies, one being nerstone of the Boston Public Library.

James Russell Lowell, 1819-1891. [Boston, 1891].
Lines ... on the Presentation of His Portrait ... April 30, 1892. [Philadelphia? 1892].
Hymn ... Written For ... The Twenty-Fifth Anniversary ... of The Boston Y. M. C. U. [Boston, 1893].
"Teacher of Teachers! Yours the Task." [Boston, 1893].
Francis Parkman. [Boston, 1894].

The following are of unknown date.

An Unpublished Poem.
8 pp. Though stated to have been "read at a medical supper party in the year 1845" it was certainly not printed until much later.
"For Private Circulation Only."
Broadside. Contains "A Cluster of Crimes," "Inscription for a Gin Palace," and "From Goethe." Probably dates from 1870 to 1890.
Dorothy Q.
Exists as a broadside signed by Holmes in 1884; as a folio 8 pp. leaflet, presented in 1887. The latter is the Wakeman-Huntington copy, erroneously catalogued at the time of sale as 4to. 4 pp. leaflet. The poem first appeared in the *Atlantic Monthly*, January, 1871.

BOOKS CONTAINING HOLMES' CONTRIBUTIONS

Only the most important of these are here listed. For further listing consult the bibliographical works at the end of this list.

The Collegian. *Cambridge*, 1830.
This Harvard College Magazine contains 26 poems by Holmes, some 14 of which remain uncollected.
Youth's Keepsake. *Boston*, 1831.
Contains "Crossing the Ford," and "The Fairy World."
The Mariner's Library or Voyager's Companion. *Boston*, 1833.
First book printing for "Old Ironsides."
The Laurel: A Gift For All Seasons. *Boston*, 1836.
Contains nine poems by Holmes.
Library of Practical Medicine ... Vol. VII. *Boston*, 1836.
Contains Holmes' first Boylston Prize Dissertation, 100 pp.
Report of the Dinner Given to Charles Dickens. *Boston*, 1842.
Wrappers. Holmes sang the song here first printed.
The Berkshire Jubilee. *Albany*, 1845.
Contains an address and a poem by Holmes.
Some Account of the Letheon, by Edward Warren, Second Edition. *Boston*, 1847.
Wrappers. Contains Holmes' letter dated November 21, 1846, not in the first edition, to Dr. W. T. G. Morton, discoverer of ether, suggesting the terms *anaesthesia* and *anaesthetic*, both of which words Holmes invented.
The Seventy-Fourth Anniversary of the Birth-Day of Daniel Webster. *Boston*, 1856.
Wrappers. Contains a poem by Holmes.

HOLMES

Speeches at the Annual Dinner of the Massachusetts Medical Society. *Boston*, 1856.
  Wrappers. Contains a speech by Holmes.
Report of the 24th National Anti-Slavery Festival. *Boston*, 1858.
  Wrappers. Contains first book appearance of "The Chambered Nautilus."
Celebration of the Hundredth Anniversary of ... Burns, Jan. 25, 1859. *Boston*, 1859.
  Contains two poems by Holmes, one never collected by him.
Memorial of the ... Fiftieth Birthday of James Freeman Clarke. *Boston*, 1860.
  Contains a poem in honor of his classmate.
Current and Counter Currents in Medical Science. *Boston*, 1860.
  Wrappers. The separate address with this title. First issue has 48 pp.; second has, adding two obituaries by Holmes, 55 pp.
Life of John Collins Warren, by Edward Warren. *Boston*, 1860.
  2 vols. Contains Holmes' long prose tribute to Warren; never collected
Proceedings in Behalf of the Morton Testimonial. *Boston*, 1861.
The Address of Mr. Everett and the Poem of Dr. O. W. Holmes ... to ... the Prince Napoleon: September 25, 1861. *Cambridge*, 1861.
  Yellow glazed boards.
Pansie: A Fragment, by Nathaniel Hawthorne. *London* [1864].
  Wrappers. Pirated. The unsigned Holmes introduction, from the *Atlantic*, July, 1864, was never reprinted.
The Boatswain's Whistle. November 9-19, 1864. *Boston*, 1864.
  Ten numbers.
Tribute ... to the Memory of Edward Everett. *Boston*, 1865.
  Wrappers or cloth. Contains a long poem by Holmes.
The Atlantic Almanac. *Boston* [1867].
  Contains a long prose article, "The Seasons."
History of the American Stereoscope. [*Boston*, 1869].
  Wrappers. Nearly all by Holmes.
Reception and Entertainment of the Chinese Embassy by the City of Boston. *Boston*, 1868.
The Atlantic Almanac. *Boston* [1868].
  Contains a long prose article, "Talk Concerning the Human Body and its Management."
Centennial of the Boston Pier. *Cambridge*, 1873.
  Wrappers. Contains a poem by Holmes who was one of the "proprietors" of the pier.
In Memoriam .... Gardner Brewer. *Boston*, 1874.
  Wrappers. Contains Holmes' prose tribute to his friend; not elsewhere printed.
Memorial, Bunker Hill, June 17, 1875. *Boston*, 1875.
  Printed wrappers. Contains "Grandmother's Story of Bunker Hill." The earliest copies contain an inserted slip *To The Press*. Also six copies printed from large types; one copy known and that in the Boston Public Library.
Cambridge in the "Centennial." *Cambridge*, 1875.
  First printing of the long poem, "Old Cambridge."
Parks For the People. *Boston*, 1876.
  Wrappers. Contains a speech by Holmes on the subject; not elsewhere printed.

Golden Songs of Great Poets. *New York*, 1877.
   Contains six poems by six American poets, one by Holmes. All first printing.
Visions: A Study of False Sight (Pseudopia). *Boston*, 1878.
   Holmes wrote the long introduction to this posthumous book by his classmate, Edward H. Clarke, also the memorial sketch therein.
The Huguenots in the Nipmuck Country, by George F. Daniels. *Boston*, 1880.
   Introduction by Holmes.
Seventieth Birthday of James Freeman Clarke. *Boston*, 1880.
   Contains Holmes' poem to his classmate.
The Poets' Tribute to Garfield. *Cambridge*, 1881.
   Wrappered copies precede those in cloth. Contains Holmes' poem to Garfield.
Proceedings at a Dinner Given by the Medical Profession of the City of New York, April 12, 1883, to Oliver Wendell Holmes. *New York*, 1883.
   Contains a long poem by Holmes and biographical material. Holmes distributed at the dinner, reproduced on a telegraph blank, a message to the diners and a self-caricature.
Memoir of Jonathan Mason Warren, M. D., by Howard Payson Arnold. *Boston*, 1886.
   Only book printing of the Holmes' tribute to the subject of the memoir, and of his lines to John Collins Warren.
The Last Leaf. *Cambridge*, 1886.
   First separate printing, illustrations on India Paper by George Wharton Edwards and F. Hopkinson Smith. Also 100 copies, folio, half vellum, linen sides. Contains an introduction by Holmes.
Typical Elms and Other Trees of Massachusetts, by Lorin L. Dame. *Boston*, 1890.
   Introduction.
The One-Hoss Shay. *Boston*, 1892.
   First separate printing. Undressed leather binding. Illustrations by Howard Pyle.
Dorothy Q. *Boston*, 1893.
   First separate printing except for broadsides of unknown date. Cloth; 250 copies in vellum, silk ties, uncut edges. Illustrations by Howard Pyle.
Horatian Echoes, by J. D. Sargent. *Boston*, 1893.
   Introduction. Copies have been noted uncut with paper labels.
The Poet Among the Hills, by J. E. A. Smith. *Pittsfield*, 1895.
   First printing of four Holmes poems and two addresses.
The Cornhill Booklet, February, 1901. *Boston*, 1901.
   First printing in other than magazine form of the original two "Autocrat" articles, from *Buckingham's New England Magazine*, November, 1831, and February, 1832.
The History of Woodstock, Connecticut, by Clarence W. Bowen. *Norwood, Mass.*, 1926.
   Introduction by Holmes, written in 1891.
At Dartmouth. The Phi Beta Kappa Poem ... Introduction by Miss Eleanor H. Tilton. *New York*, 1940.
   100 copies printed. First complete printing of this poem, delivered July 24, 1839. The introduction treats fully Holmes' Dartmouth professorship of anatomy and physiology.

HOLMES

BIOGRAPHICAL AND BIBLIOGRAPHICAL WORKS

Oliver Wendell Holmes, by William Sloane Kennedy. *Boston*, 1883.

Life of Oliver Wendell Holmes, by E. E. Brown. *Boston* [1884].

Oliver Wendell Holmes, by Walter Jerrold. *London*, 1893.

Life and Letters of Oliver Wendell Holmes, by John T. Morse, Jr. *Boston*, 1896.
2 vols. Also 275 numbered sets on large paper.

Oliver Wendell Holmes. The Autocrat and His Fellow-Boarders, by Samuel McChord Crothers. *Boston*, 1907.
Also 300 large paper copies.

A Bibliography of Oliver Wendell Holmes, by George B. Ives. *Boston and New York*, 1907.
530 copies only.

Holmes of the Breakfast-Table, by M. A. De Wolfe Howe. *New York*, 1939.

Emerson Hough

1857–1923

THE SINGING MOUSE STORIES. *New York*, 1895.
Revised edition, *Indianapolis* [1910].

THE STORY OF THE COWBOY. *New York*, 1897.

THE GIRL AT THE HALFWAY HOUSE. *New York*, 1900.

THE MISSISSIPPI BUBBLE. *Indianapolis* [1902].
April on copyright page. First binding has *Hough* on spine, not *Emerson Hough*.
Several states of frontispiece with no definite priority. Later bindings, either green
or red cloth, have the author's full name on spine and are less highly decorated
on front cover.

THE WAY TO THE WEST. *Indianapolis* [1903].
October on copyright page.

THE LAW OF THE LAND. *Indianapolis* [1904].
October on copyright page.

HEART'S DESIRE. *New York*, 1905.

THE KING OF GEE-WHIZ. *Indianapolis* [1906].
Lyrics by Wilbur D. Nesbit.

THE STORY OF THE OUTLAW. *New York*, 1907.
First state has rule at top of page v.

THE WAY OF A MAN. *New York*, 1907.

THE YOUNG ALASKANS. *New York*, 1908.

54-40 OR FIGHT. *Indianapolis* [1909].
January on copyright page.

THE SOWING. *Chicago*, 1909.

THE PURCHASE PRICE. *Indianapolis* [1910].

THE YOUNG ALASKANS ON THE TRAIL. *New York*, 1911.
Published October, 1911 on copyright page.

JOHN RAWN. *Indianapolis* [1912].
Also copies in boards, cloth back, for presentation.

THE LADY AND THE PIRATE. *Indianapolis* [1913].

THE YOUNG ALASKANS ON THE TRAIL. *New York*, 1911.

OUT OF DOORS. *New York*, 1915.
First printing has the symbol (1) below last line of text.

GETTING A WRONG START. *New York*, 1915.
Anon.

LET US GO AFIELD. *New York*, 1916.

THE MAGNIFICENT ADVENTURE. *New York*, 1916.
The symbol (1) appears below the last line of text.

THE MAN NEXT DOOR. *New York*, 1917.
The symbol (1) appears below the last line of text.

THE BROKEN GATE. *New York*, 1917.
The symbol (1) appears below the last line of text.

THE YOUNG ALASKANS IN THE FAR NORTH. *New York* [1918].

THE PASSING OF THE FRONTIER. *New Haven*, 1918.
In the Yale University Press "Chronicles of America" series. Vol. 26.

THE WAY OUT. *New York*, 1918.
The symbol (1) appears below the last line of text.

THE SAGEBRUSHER. *New York*, 1919.
The symbol (1) appears below the last line of text.

THE WEB. *Chicago* [1919].

MAW'S VACATION. *St. Paul*, 1921.

THE YOUNG ALASKANS ON THE MISSOURI. *New York* [1922].
First edition so stated on copyright page.

THE COVERED WAGON. *New York*, 1922.
First edition has (1) below last line of text. All examined copies of the first
edition have the table of contents leaf tipped in. Regarding this the publishers
state "when originally printing after coming off press we discovered there were
two transposed lines in the Contents. We immediately had cancels printed for
the entire edition and tipped in before any copies were sent out."

NORTH OF 36. *New York*, 1923.
The symbol (1) appears below the last line of text.

MOTHER OF GOLD. *New York*, 1924.
The symbol (1) appears below the last line of text.

THE SHIP OF SOULS. *New York*, 1925.
The symbol (1) appears below the last line of text.

Madre d'Oro.
   A play. Believed to have been published about 1885-1890.
Comedy ... Stories From McClure's. *New York*, 1901.
   Contains "The Horse Thief."
The Morris Book Shop. *Chicago*, 1912.
   Contribution.
The Firefly's Light. ₍*New York*, 1916₎.
The Indefinite American Attitude Toward the War and When Shall it Change?
   New York ₍1917₎.
My Lady's Plumes. *Providence* ₍*R. I., n.d.*₎.
   4 pp. leaflet. Issued by The Humane Education Society.
A Good Book—Brothers. A Review by Emerson Hough. ₍*Indianapolis*(?), *ca.* 1922₎.
   4 pp. leaflet review of Herbert Quick's "Vandemark's Folly."
Emerson Hough: His Place in American Letters, by Lee Alexander Stone. ₍*Chicago?*₎
   1925.

Richard Hovey

1864–1900

POEMS. *Washington,* 1880.
Privately printed. Cloth or wrappers.

THE LAUREL: AN ODE. *Washington,* 1889.
Privately printed. Cardboard wrappers. Printed on one side of sheet only.

LAUNCELOT AND GUENEVERE: A POEM IN DRAMAS. *New York* [1891].
Contains "The Quest of Merlin" and "The Marriage of Guenevere."

SEAWARD. *Boston,* 1893.

SONGS FROM VAGABONDIA. *Boston,* 1894.
Boards. 810 copies, of which 60 were large paper; ten of the latter not for sale.
With BLISS CARMAN.

MORE SONGS FROM VAGABONDIA. *Boston,* 1896.
Boards. Also 60 large paper copies of which but 50 were for sale. With BLISS
CARMAN.

ALONG THE TRAIL: A BOOK OF LYRICS. *Boston,* 1898.

THE BIRTH OF GALAHAD. *Boston,* 1898.
Boards.

TALIESIN: A MASQUE. *Boston,* 1900.
Boards.

THE HOLY GRAAL AND OTHER FRAGMENTS. *Boston,* 1900.

LAST SONGS FROM VAGABONDIA. *Boston,* 1901.
Boards. Also 60 large paper copies of which but 50 were for sale. With BLISS
CARMAN.

TO THE END OF THE TRAIL. *New York,* 1908.
Edited and with notes by Mrs. Hovey.

DARTMOUTH LYRICS. *Boston* [1924].
Edwin Osgood Grover, editor.

A POEM AND THREE LETTERS. [*Hanover, N.H.*] 1935.
125 numbered copies only. Printed wrappers.

Harmonics. [*n.p., n.d.*].
In format and design this is similar to the first two items here listed. Further
information is wanting.

266

Dartmouth Lyrics. *Hanover, N. H.,* 1893.
    Edited by Bertrand A. Small. Contains seven poems by Hovey. Do not confuse this publication with Hovey's book of the same title published in 1924.

The Plays of Maurice Maeterlinck. *Chicago,* 1894.
    Translated by Hovey. Also, second series, *Chicago,* 1896.

The Marriage of Guenevere. *Chicago,* 1895.
    Reprinted from "Launcelot and Guenevere."

The Daily Tatler, Vol. 1, Nos. 1-13. November 7-21, 1896. *New York,* 1896.
    Contributions.

See: "Echoes From Vagabondia," 1912, under Bliss Carman.

William Dean Howells

1837–1920

FICTION

SUBURBAN SKETCHES. *Boston*, 1871.
Revised and enlarged, *Boston*, 1872.

THEIR WEDDING JOURNEY. *Boston*, 1872.
First state has a period after "... & Co." on the title page, next to the last line.
With added chapter, "Niagara Revisited," 1884, *q.v., Boston*, 1887.

A CHANCE ACQUAINTANCE. *Boston*, 1873.
With or without gilt edges. "Glimpses of Quebec," *Boston* [1884], is a series of
twelve photographs illustrating this title.

A FOREGONE CONCLUSION. *Boston*, 1875.
First state has no advertisements opposite title page.

A DAY'S PLEASURE AND OTHER SKETCHES. *Boston*, 1876.

THE LADY OF THE AROOSTOOK. *Boston*, 1879.

THE UNDISCOVERED COUNTRY. *Boston*, 1880.
In the first state the binding (front cover and spine) is decorated with an all-
over black floral stamp.

DOCTOR BREEN'S PRACTICE. *Boston*, 1881.

A FEARFUL RESPONSIBILITY AND OTHER STORIES. *Boston*, 1881.

A MODERN INSTANCE. *Boston*, 1882.
It is probable that the first state is 1¼" across top of covers.

A WOMAN'S REASON. *Boston*, 1883.

NIAGARA REVISITED. *Chicago*, 1884.
All but a few copies destroyed. Included in the *Boston*, 1888, edition of "Their
Wedding Journey."

THE RISE OF SILAS LAPHAM. *Boston*, 1885.
Bound in various colors of cloth. There are two states of the advertisements
facing the title page. One reads: *Mr. Howells' Latest Works;* the other, *Mr.
Howells' Latest Novels.* The former advertisement measures scant 3¾" in
height and is most probably the first state of the advertisements. Numerous letters
are lacking throughout the book and while no definite evidence of priority has as
yet been deduced from these it is certain that the earliest printed copies have
unbroken type, foot of p. 176, words *thick* and *sojourner.*

268

INDIAN SUMMER. *Boston,* 1886.
Some copies issued wholly untrimmed, white cloth, label on spine.

THE MINISTER'S CHARGE. *Boston,* 1887.

APRIL HOPES. *New York,* 1888.

ANNIE KILBURN. *New York,* 1889.

A BOY'S TOWN. *New York,* 1890.
First state has illustration at p. [iv]; later removed to p. 44.

A HAZARD OF NEW FORTUNES. *New York,* 1890.
Copies in wrappers were received at The Library of Congress November 27, 1889; copies in cloth January 27, 1890.

THE SHADOW OF A DREAM. *New York,* 1890.
Wrappers or cloth.

AN IMPERATIVE DUTY. *New York,* 1892.

THE QUALITY OF MERCY. *New York,* 1892.
Copies in cloth were received at The Library of Congress March 26, 1892; copies in wrappers October 1, 1892.

CHRISTMAS EVERY DAY AND OTHER STORIES TOLD FOR CHILDREN. *New York,* 1893.

THE WORLD OF CHANCE. *New York,* 1893.

THE COAST OF BOHEMIA. *New York,* 1893.
Reissued with a new introduction *New York,* 1899.

A TRAVELER FROM ALTRURIA. *New York,* 1894.

THE DAY OF THEIR WEDDING. *New York,* 1896.

A PARTING AND A MEETING. *New York,* 1896.

THE LANDLORD AT LION'S HEAD. *New York,* 1897.

AN OPEN-EYED CONSPIRACY: AN IDYL OF SARATOGA. *New York,* 1897.

THE STORY OF A PLAY. *New York,* 1898.

RAGGED LADY. *New York,* 1899.

THEIR SILVER WEDDING JOURNEY. *New York,* 1899.
2 vols. Reissued, *New York,* 1900, 1 vol.

A PAIR OF PATIENT LOVERS. *New York,* 1901.
Boards, cloth back.

THE KENTONS. *New York*, 1902.
Published April, 1902 on the copyright page.

THE FLIGHT OF PONY BAKER. *New York*, 1902.

LETTERS HOME. *New York*, 1903.
Published September, 1903 on the copyright page.

QUESTIONABLE SHAPES. *New York*, 1903.
Published May, 1903 on the copyright page.

THE SON OF ROYAL LANGBRITH. *New York*, 1904.
Published October, 1904 on the copyright page.

MISS BELLARD'S INSPIRATION. *New York*, 1905.
Published June, 1905 on the copyright page.

THROUGH THE EYE OF THE NEEDLE. *New York*, 1907.

BETWEEN THE DARK AND THE DAYLIGHT. *New York*, 1907.
First binding: green cloth with gold stamping; second binding, red cloth with black stamping.

FENNEL AND RUE. *New York*, 1908.
Published March, 1908 on the copyright page.

NEW LEAF MILLS. *New York*, 1913.
Published January, 1913 on the copyright page.

THE DAUGHTER OF THE STORAGE. *New York* [1916].
First state has *D-Q* on copyright page.

THE LEATHERWOOD GOD. *New York*, 1916.
Published, October, 1916 on the copyright page.

THE VACATION OF THE KELWYNS. *New York* [1920].
Published September, 1920 on the copyright page; also code letters *H-U*.

MRS. FARRELL. *New York* [1921].
Code letters *G-V* on the copyright page.

POETRY

POEMS OF TWO FRIENDS. *Columbus, Ohio*, 1860.
With John James Piatt.

NO LOVE LOST: A ROMANCE OF TRAVEL. *New York*, 1869.

POEMS. *Boston*, 1873.
With four additional poems, *Boston*, 1886.

STOPS OF VARIOUS QUILLS. *New York,* 1894.
> 50 copies only, large paper, signed. Illustrated by Howard Pyle. Trade edition, *New York,* 1895.

THE MOTHER AND THE FATHER: DRAMATIC PASSAGES. *New York,* 1909.

TRAVEL, CRITICISM, BIOGRAPHY, ETC.

LIVES AND SPEECHES OF ABRAHAM LINCOLN AND HANNIBAL HAMLIN. *Columbus, Ohio,* 1860.
> With John L. Hayes. Printed wrappers or cloth, the latter existing in several states. Various imprints but the earliest does not have a period following the O₍hio₎ after *Columbus.* For further regarding this book see Ernest James Wessen's "Campaign Lives of Abraham Lincoln, 1860" ₍n.p., n.d. (*Chicago,* 1938?)₎.

VENETIAN LIFE. *New York,* 1866.
> Revised and enlarged editions *Boston* 1872 and 1892. Of the latter there were also 250 large paper copies. Further revised, *Boston,* 1907.

ITALIAN JOURNEYS. *New York,* 1867.
> Revised edition, *Boston,* 1872. De luxe edition, *Boston,* 1901, with illustrations by Joseph Pennell. Of the latter there were also 300 large paper copies.

SKETCH OF THE LIFE AND CHARACTER OF RUTHERFORD B. HAYES ₍etc.₎. *New York,* 1876.
> Some copies have been noted with an errata slip.

THREE VILLAGES. *Boston,* 1884.

A LITTLE GIRL AMONG THE OLD MASTERS. *Boston,* 1884.
> Also de luxe edition.

TUSCAN CITIES. *Boston,* 1886.

MODERN ITALIAN POETS. *New York,* 1887.

CRITICISM AND FICTION. *New York,* 1891.
> Copies have been noted in white cloth with top edges gilt.

A LITTLE SWISS SOJOURN. *New York,* 1892.

MY YEAR IN A LOG CABIN. *New York,* 1893.

MY LITERARY PASSIONS. *New York,* 1895.

IMPRESSIONS AND EXPERIENCES. *New York,* 1896.

STORIES OF OHIO. *New York* ₍etc.₎, 1897.

LITERARY FRIENDS AND ACQUAINTANCE. *New York,* 1900.
> Also limited signed edition.

HEROINES OF FICTION. *New York*, 1901.
2 vols.

LITERATURE AND LIFE. *New York*, 1902.

LONDON FILMS. *New York*, 1905.

CERTAIN DELIGHTFUL ENGLISH TOWNS. *New York*, 1906.

ROMAN HOLIDAYS AND OTHERS. *New York*, 1908.

SEVEN ENGLISH CITIES. *New York*, 1909.
Copies have been noted with a rubber stamped *Printed In U. S. A.* Such copies were probably intended for export by the publishers.

IMAGINARY INTERVIEWS. *New York*, 1910.

MY MARK TWAIN. *New York*, 1910.
Gilt top. Copies bearing a rubber stamped *Printed In U. S. A.* on the copyright page were probably intended for export by the publishers.

FAMILIAR SPANISH TRAVELS. *New York*, 1913.

THE SEEN AND THE UNSEEN AT STRATFORD-ON-AVON. *New York*, 1914.

YEARS OF MY YOUTH. *New York* [1916].
Code letters *F-Q* on the copyright page; received at The Library of Congress November 7, 1916. *Illustrated Edition*, code letters *K-R* on the copyright page copyrighted in 1917.

EIGHTY YEARS AND AFTER. [*New York*] 1921.
Pamphlet.

LIFE IN LETTERS OF WILLIAM DEAN HOWELLS. *Garden City*, 1928.
2 vols. Mildred Howells, editor. First edition so indicated on the copyright page

PLAYS

THE PARLOR CAR. *Boston*, 1876.

OUT OF THE QUESTION. *Boston*, 1877.

A COUNTERFEIT PRESENTMENT. *Boston*, 1877.

THE SLEEPING CAR. *Boston*, 1883.

THE REGISTER. *Boston*, 1884.

THE ELEVATOR. *Boston*, 1885.

THE GARROTERS. *New York*, 1886.

A SEA-CHANGE; or, LOVE'S STOWAWAY. *Boston*, 1888.

THE MOUSE-TRAP AND OTHER FARCES. *New York*, 1889.

THE ALBANY DEPOT. *New York*, 1892.

A LETTER OF INTRODUCTION. *New York*, 1892.

THE UNEXPECTED GUESTS. *New York*, 1893.

EVENING DRESS. *New York*, 1893.

A LIKELY STORY. *New York*, 1894.

A PREVIOUS ENGAGEMENT. *New York*, 1897.
Printed wrappers.

ROOM FORTY-FIVE. *Boston*, 1900.

BRIDE ROSES. *Boston*, 1900.

THE SMOKING CAR. *Boston*, 1900.

AN INDIAN GIVER. *Boston*, 1900.

PARTING FRIENDS. *New York*, 1911.

Howells contributed writings to innumerable works by other authors. A full listing of such material may be found in "William Dean Howells: A Critical Study," by Delmar Gross Cooke, *New York* [1922]. The following are representative of the type of material here discussed.

Jubilee Days: An Illustrated Record of the Humorous Features of the World's Peace Jubilee. *Boston*, 1872. [See under *Aldrich* for further discussion of this publication].
Samson. A Tragedy ... by Ippolito d'Aste. *New York* [1889].
Translation by Howells.
The Art of Authorship. *London*, 1890.
George Bainton, editor. Contribution by Howells.
The Whole Family: A Novel by Twelve Authors. *New York*, 1908.
Contribution.

The following titles are reprints from previously published books: "Doorstep Acquaintance and other Sketches" [1900]; "Buying a Horse," 1916; "Hither and Thither in Germany" [1920]; "Five O'Clock Tea," 1894.

BIOGRAPHICAL

William Dean Howells, A Study ... by Alexander Harvey. *New York*, 1917.
William Dean Howells, A Study, by Oscar W. Firkins. *Cambridge*, 1924.

James (Gibbons) Huneker

1860–1921

MEZZOTINTS IN MODERN MUSIC. *New York*, 1899.

CHOPIN: THE MAN AND HIS MUSIC. *New York*, 1900.

MELOMANIACS. *New York*, 1902.

OVERTONES. *New York*, 1904.

ICONOCLASTS. *New York*, 1905.
First state has *Norwood Press* imprint on copyright page.

VISIONARIES. *New York*, 1905.
Top edges gilt. *Published October, 1905.* on the copyright page.

EGOISTS. *New York*, 1909.

PROMENADES OF AN IMPRESSIONIST. *New York*, 1910.
Boards.

FRANZ LISZT. *New York*, 1911.
It has been stated that the first binding is silk-like cloth with top edges gilt; second binding, red cloth.

THE PATHOS OF DISTANCE. *New York*, 1913.
Published May, 1913 on the copyright page.

OLD FOGY. *Philadelphia* [1913].
First binding has figured end papers. Boards. *Old Fogy* was a pseudonym.

IVORY, APES AND PEACOCKS. *New York*, 1915.
Published September, 1915 on the copyright page.

NEW COSMOPOLIS. *New York*, 1915.

THE DEVELOPMENT OF PIANO MUSIC. *New York*, 1915-16.

UNICORNS. *New York*, 1917.
Published September, 1917 on the copyright page.

THE PHILHARMONIC SOCIETY OF NEW YORK. [*New York*, 1917].
Privately printed. Copies have been noted with printed presentation slip at the front.

THE STEINWAY COLLECTION OF PAINTINGS. [*New York*] 1919.

BEDOUINS. *New York*, 1920.

STEEPLEJACK. *New York*, 1920.
2 vols. *Published September, 1920* on the copyright page.

PAINTED VEILS. *New York* [1920].

 1,200 signed copies only, numbered. The genuine first edition is printed on laid paper watermarked *Blandford Book U. S. A.* A forged edition is printed on laid paper with no maker's name. As part of their sales-promotion the publishers issued an unknown number of copies of the book in page-proof form, laid in printed wrappers.

VARIATIONS. *New York*, 1921.

LETTERS OF JAMES GIBBONS HUNEKER. *New York*, 1922.

 Also 260 copies in boards, numbered. Edited by Josephine Huneker. *Published October, 1922* on the copyright page.

INTIMATE LETTERS OF JAMES GIBBONS HUNEKER. *New York*, 1924.

 Josephine Huneker, editor. 2,050 numbered copies only. Boards, cloth back, paper label on spine.

Nassau: Island of New Providence, Bahamas. *New York* [1877?].
 Contains "An Isle of June" by Huneker.
Anton Seidl. *New York*, 1899.
 1,000 copies only. Contribution by Huneker.
The Standard Opera Glass, by Charles Annesley [*pseud.* for: Charles and Anna Tittman]. *New York*, 1899.
 Contains a prelude by Huneker.
Modern Masters of Music. [*Philadelphia*, 1901].
 Contribution.
Forty Songs by Johannes Brahms. *Boston* [1903].
 Edited.
Frédéric Chopin: Forty Piano Compositions.
 Edited. Further definite information wanting.
Tales. *New York*, June, 1905.
 Magazine. Contains "Pan" by Huneker. No other record of publication found.
Dramatic Opinions and Essays, by G. Bernard Shaw. *New York*, 1906.
 2 vols. Contribution by Huneker. The contribution, "A Work on the Dramatic Opinions and Essays of G. Bernard Shaw," was separately issued in wrappers, *New York*, 1906.
The Works of Henrik Ibsen. *New York*, 1911-12.
 13 vols. Vol. 13 contains an essay on Ibsen by Huneker.
Joseph Conrad, by A. A. Knopf. [*Garden City*, 1913].
 Contains a pen portrait by Huneker.
Poems and Prose of Charles Baudelaire. *New York*, 1919.
 Introduction by Huneker. Boards.
James Gibbons Huneker, by Benjamin de Casseres. *New York* [1925].
 Includes a bibliography by Joseph Lawren. Printed boards.
Essays by James Huneker. *New York*, 1929.
 Selected and with an introduction by H. L. Mencken.

Washington Irving
1783–1859

SALMAGUNDI; OY, THE WHIM-WHAMS AND OPINIONS OF LAUNCELOT LANG-
STAFF, ESQ., AND OTHERS. *New York*, 1807-1808.
2 vols. or 20 parts in wrappers. In collaboration with William Irving and J. K.
Paulding. Regarding the authorship of the individual contributions see "The
Authorship of Salmagundi," in *The Publishers' Weekly*, November 28, 1936.
The first edition exists in several states, identification requiring complete and
careful collation. For a list of the variances consult the American Art Association
catalog 4201 (Dean Sage, et al.) November 13-14, 1935; and, the Langfeld-
Blackburn bibliography.

A HISTORY OF NEW YORK FROM THE BEGINNING OF THE WORLD TO THE
END OF THE DUTCH DYNASTY. *New York*, 1809.
2 vols. Diedrich Knickerbocker, *pseudonym*. Vol. 1 contains an engraved folding
plate of New Amsterdam.

THE SKETCH BOOK OF GEOFFREY CRAYON, GENT. *New York*, 1819-1820.
Seven parts in wrappers. Parts 1-5 dated 1819; parts 6-7 dated 1820. Second
editions so stated on wrappers. Copies in wrappers are so seldom met with that
rebound [?] copies in leather, usually lacking the wrappers, have been found ac-
ceptable. There are literally hundreds of textual and other changes in the early
issues and the collector is referred to the Langfeld-Blackburn bibliography of
Irving for a complete list.

BRACEBRIDGE HALL; OY, THE HUMORISTS. *New York*, 1822.
2 vols. Geoffrey Crayon, *pseudonym*.

LETTERS OF JONATHAN OLDSTYLE, GENT. *New York*, 1824.
By the Author of the Sketch Book.

TALES OF A TRAVELLER. *Philadelphia*, 1824.
Four parts. Geoffrey Crayon, *pseudonym*. The first state of part 2, p. 99, 3rd line
of 2d paragraph reads *at housand;* later corrected to *a thousand.* Imprint on the
wrapper of Part 1 reads: *H. C. Cary and I. Lee;* later corrected to *H. C. Carey and
I. Lea.*

A HISTORY OF THE LIFE AND VOYAGES OF CHRISTOPHER COLUMBUS. *New
York*, 1828.
3 vols. Boards, paper labels.

A CHRONICLE OF THE CONQUEST OF GRANADA. *Philadelphia*, 1829.
2 vols. Fray Antonio Agapida, *pseudonym*. Boards, paper labels. Also a large
paper edition.

VOYAGES AND DISCOVERIES OF THE COMPANIONS OF COLUMBUS. *Philadelphia,* 1831.

Boards, cloth back, paper label.

THE ALHAMBRA. *Philadelphia,* 1832.

2 vols. Boards, cloth back, paper labels.

A TOUR ON THE PRAIRIES. *Philadelphia,* 1835.

Paper label on spine. Vol. 1 of "The Crayon Miscellany." First state does not have *No. I.* on label.

ABBOTSFORD AND NEWSTEAD ABBEY. *Philadelphia,* 1835.

Paper label on spine. Vol. 2 of "The Crayon Miscellany."

LEGENDS OF THE CONQUEST OF SPAIN. *Philadelphia,* 1835.

Papel label on the spine. Vol. 3 of "The Crayon Miscellany."

ASTORIA. *Philadelphia,* 1836.

2 vols. Contains a map, usually in Vol. 2 but occasionally in Vol. 1.

THE ROCKY MOUNTAINS. *Philadelphia,* 1837.

2 vols. "Digested From the Journal of Captain B. L. E. Bonneville ... by Washington Irving." Folding map in each volume.

THE LIFE OF OLIVER GOLDSMITH WITH SELECTIONS FROM HIS WRITINGS. *New York,* 1840.

Various types of cloth binding with no established priority. *See:* "Oliver Goldsmith's Works," section two of this checklist.

BIOGRAPHY AND POETICAL REMAINS OF THE LATE MARGARET MILLER DAVIDSON. *Philadelphia,* 1841.

MAHOMET AND HIS SUCCESSORS. *New York,* 1850.

2 vols.

THE LIFE OF GEORGE WASHINGTON. *New York,* 1855-1859.

5 vols. 1-2: 1855; 3: 1856; 4: 1857; 5: 1859. Also a quarto edition limited to 110 copies with Vol. 2 dated 1856. The publishers issued, in uniform binding, a set of engraved plates to go with the text. The volume of engraved plates was issued in two states: either for the first four volumes, or for the complete set. Copies in paper parts are presumed to be later.

WOLFERT'S ROOST AND OTHER PAPERS. *New York,* 1855.

SPANISH PAPERS AND OTHER MISCELLANIES. *New York,* 1866.

2 vols.

ABU HASSAN. *Boston,* 1924.

455 copies only printed for members of the Bibliophile Society.

THE WILD HUNTSMAN. *Boston,* 1924.
455 copies only printed for members of the Bibliophile Society.

COMPLETE WORKS. *New York,* 1897.
40 vols. Joseph Jefferson Edition, limited to 250 sets. Author's Autograph Edition, 500 sets. Holly Edition, 1,000 sets. Trade Edition: New Knickerbocker Edition. All printed from the same plates.

The following list is representative of the secondary Irving items; complete listing is given in the Langfeld-Blackburn bibliography.

A Voyage to the Eastern Part of Terra Firma, by François Depons. *New York,* 1806. 3 vols. *Translated by An American Gentleman.* Translated by Irving together with George Caines.
A Fragment of a Journal of a Sentimental Philosopher. *New York,* 1809.
Anonymous. Often attributed to Irving.
The Poetical Works of Thomas Campbell ... To Which is Prefixed a Biographical Sketch of the Author. By A Gentleman of New York [Irving]. [*Various Places*] 1810.
2 volumes or two volumes in one; no established priority. Noted with several places of publication with no probable priority.
Biography of James Lawrence, Esq. ... *New Brunswick,* 1813.
Charles II: A Play, by John Howard Payne. *London,* 1824.
Irving is said to have collaborated with the author.
Oliver Goldsmith's Works. *Paris,* 1825.
4 vols. Vol. 1 contains a brief life of Goldsmith by Irving. Republished, *Philadelphia,* 1830. Revised and reissued, *New York,* 1840. With further revisions, added preface, *New York,* 1849. *See:* "The Life of Oliver Goldsmith, etc." 1840. listed above.
Richelieu: A Play, by John Howard Payne. *New York,* 1826.
Irving is said to have collaborated with the author.
Poems of William Cullen Bryant. *London,* 1832.
Edited and with an introduction by Irving.
Harvey's Scenes of the Primitive Forest of America. *New York,* 1841.
Edited by Irving. Printed wrappers.
The Poetry and History of Wyoming. *New York,* 1841.
Contribution by Irving.
A Book of the Hudson: Collected From the Various Works of Diedrich Knickerbocker. *New York,* 1849.
Selections from his own writings edited and with a preface by Irving. Exists in various states with no established priority.
The Home Book of the Picturesque. *New York,* 1852.
Contains a contribution by Irving.
Memorial of James Fenimore Cooper. *New York,* 1852.
Contains a contribution by Irving.
The Knickerbocker Gallery. *New York,* 1855.
Contains a contribution by Irving.

An Unwritten Drama of Lord Byron. *Metuchen, New Jersey,* 1925.
    51 copies only. Reprinted from "The Gift," 1836.
Notes While Preparing the Sketch Book, 1817. *New Haven,* 1927.
    525 copies only. Stanley T. Williams, editor.
Tour of Scotland, 1817. *New Haven,* 1927.
    525 copies only. Stanley T. Williams, editor.
Poems of Washington Irving. *New York,* 1931.
    William R. Langfeld, editor. Wrappers.

BIOGRAPHICAL AND BIBLIOGRAPHICAL

Irvingiana: A Memorial of Irving. *New York,* 1860.
    Boards. Issued in at least two states as regards number of illustrations; no established priority.
The Life and Letters of Washington Irving, by Pierre M. Irving. *New York,* 1862-1864.
    4 vols.
The Letters of Washington Irving to Henry Brevoort. *New York,* 1915.
    2 vols. Brevoort's replies to Irving published, *New York,* 1916, 2 vols.
Journals of Washington Irving. *Boston,* 1919.
    3 vols. Edited by William P. Trent and George S. Hellman. Privately printed for members of the Bibliophile Society.
Letters From Washington Irving to Mrs. William Renwick ... [*n.p., n.d.*].
    Privately printed. Wrappers.
Notes and Journal of Travel in Europe 1804-1805. *New York,* 1921.
    3 vols. Privately printed in an edition of 230 copies only for members of the Grolier Club.
Washington Irving Diary: Spain, 1828-1829. *New York,* 1926.
    Clara Louise Penney, editor.
Letters From Sunnyside and Spain. *New Haven,* 1928.
    Stanley T. Williams, editor.
Journal of Washington Irving, 1823-1824. *Cambridge,* 1931.
    Stanley T. Williams, editor.
Washington Irving and the Storrows: Letters 1821-1828. *Cambridge,* 1933.
    Stanley T. Williams, editor.
Washington Irving: A Bibliography, by William R. Langfeld and Philip C. Blackburn. *New York,* 1933.
    450 copies only.
A Bibliography of the Writings of Washington Irving: A Checklist by Stanley T. Williams and Mary Allen Sage. *New York,* 1936.
Washington Irving on the Prairie; or, a Narrative of a Tour of the Southwest in the Year 1832, by Henry Leavitt Ellsworth. *New York,* 1937.
    Edited by Stanley Williams and Barbara Simison. First printing has *W. P. 1* on the copyright page.
Journal of Washington Irving, 1828, and Miscellaneous Notes on Moorish History and Legend. *New York,* 1937.
    1,500 copies only.

Helen (Maria Fiske) Hunt Jackson

1831–1885

VERSES. *Boston,* 1870.
> Anon. *By H. H.* Considerably enlarged and revised, *Boston,* 1874. The editions of 1877, 1879, 1885, 1886, 1887, 1888, although marked "revised and enlarged" are but reprints of the 1874 edition.

BITS OF TRAVEL. *Boston,* 1872.

BITS OF TALK ABOUT HOME MATTERS. *Boston,* 1873.

SAXE HOLM'S STORIES: FIRST SERIES. *New York,* 1874.
> Anon.

THE STORY OF BOON. *Boston,* 1874.
> Reprinted in "Sonnets and Lyrics," 1886.

MERCY PHILBRICK'S CHOICE. *Boston,* 1876.
> Anon. In "The No Name Series."

BITS OF TALK, IN VERSE AND PROSE, FOR YOUNG FOLKS. *Boston,* 1876.

HETTY'S STRANGE HISTORY. *Boston,* 1877.
> Anon. In "The No Name Series."

BITS OF TRAVEL AT HOME. *Boston,* 1878.

SAXE HOLM'S STORIES: SECOND SERIES. *New York,* 1878.
> Anon.

NELLY'S SILVER MINE. *Boston,* 1878.
> Anon. *By H. H.*

LETTERS FROM A CAT. *Boston,* 1879.
> See: "The Hunter Cats of Connorloa," 1884.

MAMMY TITTLEBACK AND HER FAMILY. *Boston,* 1881.
> See: "The Hunter Cats of Connorloa," 1884.

A CENTURY OF DISHONOR. *New York,* 1881.
> Revised and enlarged, *Boston,* 1885.

RAMONA. *Boston,* 1884.
> Dramatized, "Ramona: A Play in Five Acts," by Ina Dillaye, *Syracuse,* 1887.

EASTER BELLS. *New York* [1884].

THE HUNTER CATS OF CONNORLOA. *Boston,* 1884.

This, together with "Letters From a Cat" and "Mammy Tittleback and Her Family," reissued in one volume, *Boston* [1884] as "Cat Stories."

ZEPH: A POSTHUMOUS STORY. *Boston,* 1885.

GLIMPSES OF THREE COASTS. *Boston,* 1886.

See: "Glimpses of California," 1902.

SONNETS AND LYRICS. *Boston,* 1886.

BETWEEN WHILES. *Boston,* 1887.

MY LEGACY. *Boston,* 1888.

POEMS. *Boston,* 1892.

Complete edition. Also 250 de luxe copies. A reprint of "Sonnets and Lyrics" and "Verses" with the addition of two poems: "Cheyenne Mountain," and "With Them That Do Rejoice." Not included in the reprint is "Mordecai" which was collected in "Sonnets and Lyrics."

PANSY BILLINGS AND POPSY. *Boston* [1898].

GLIMPSES OF CALIFORNIA AND THE MISSIONS. *Boston,* 1902.

Reprint of "Glimpses of Three Coasts" with added material.

Bathmendi: A Persian Tale. *Boston,* 1867.

Translated from the French by Jackson.

Nathan The Wise, A Dramatic Poem by G. E. Lessing. *New York,* 1868.

Translated by Ellen Frothingham. Contains a biography of the author by Jackson.

The Training of Children. *New York,* 1882.

Report on the Condition and Needs of the Mission Indians of California. *Washington,* 1883.

With Abbott Kinney. An "Abbreviated" edition, *Boston,* 1887.

The Procession of Flowers in Colorado. *Boston,* 1886.

100 numbered copies only signed by the illustrator.

A Calendar of Sonnets. *Boston,* 1891.

The Helen Jackson Yearbook. *Boston,* 1895.

Harriet T. Perry, editor. Reprint.

Father Junipero and the Mission Indians of California. *Boston,* 1902.

The True Story of Ramona. Its Facts and Fictions, Inspiration and Purpose, by Carlyle Channing Davis and William A. Alderson. *New York* [1914].

Helen Hunt Jackson, by Ruth Odell. *New York,* 1939.

Henry James
1843–1916

A PASSIONATE PILGRIM AND OTHER TALES. *Boston*, 1875.

TRANSATLANTIC SKETCHES. *Boston*, 1875.

RODERICK HUDSON. *Boston*, 1876.
First edition has the *Osgood* imprint, not *Houghton Mifflin*.

THE AMERICAN. *Boston*, 1877.

WATCH AND WARD. *Boston*, 1878.

FRENCH POETS AND NOVELISTS. *London*, 1878.

THE EUROPEANS. *Boston*, 1879.
London edition dated 1878, but both editions appeared in the Fall, 1878.

DAISY MILLER. *New York*, 1879.
Cloth or wrappers. No. 82 in "Harper's Half Hour Series." It is probable that the earliest state of the advertisements lists only 79 titles. Issued in play form, *Boston*, 1883. English edition includes "An International Episode" and "Four Meetings."

AN INTERNATIONAL EPISODE. *New York*, 1879.
Cloth or wrappers.

THE MADONNA OF THE FUTURE AND OTHER TALES. *London*, 1879.
2 vols.

HAWTHORNE. *New York*, 1880.
Reprinted from "English Men of Letters," *London*, 1879, John Morley, editor.

THE DIARY OF A MAN OF FIFTY, AND A BUNDLE OF LETTERS. *New York*, 1880.
First book appearance for the second title; later, separately issued, *Boston* [1880].

CONFIDENCE. *Boston*, 1880.

WASHINGTON SQUARE. *New York*, 1881.

WASHINGTON SQUARE: THE PENSION BEAUREPAS: A BUNDLE OF LETTERS. *London*, 1881.
First book appearance for the second title.

THE PORTRAIT OF A LADY. *Boston*, 1882.
London edition, 3 vols., dated 1881.

THE SIEGE OF LONDON: THE PENSION BEAUREPAS: THE POINT OF VIEW. *Boston*, 1883.
First book appearance for first and third titles.

PORTRAITS OF PLACES. *Boston*, 1884.
London edition dated 1883.

TALES OF THREE CITIES. *Boston*, 1884.

A LITTLE TOUR IN FRANCE. *Boston*, 1885.
Reissued, illustrated, new introduction, *Boston*, 1900; also 250 large paper copies.

STORIES REVIVED. *London*, 1885.
Some reprint but largely first edition. "The Author of Beltraffio ..." *Boston*, 1885, "A Landscape Painter," *New York*, 1919 and "Master Eustace," *New York*, 1920 are partial reissues of "Stories Revived."

THE BOSTONIANS. *London*, 1886.
3 vols.

THE PRINCESS CASAMASSIMA. *London*, 1886.
3 vols.

PARTIAL PORTRAITS. *London*, 1888.

THE ASPERN PAPERS: LOUISA PALLANT: THE MODERN WARNING. *London*, 1888.
2 vols. Later, 2 vols. in one.

THE REVERBERATOR. *London*, 1888.
2 vols. Later, 1 vol. edition, either 7⅛" or 7⅜" tall, with no known priority. Bound in rough blue cloth. A probable remainder state is bound in smooth blue cloth with black stamping.

A LONDON LIFE: THE PATAGONIA: THE LIAR: MRS. TEMPERLEY. *London*, 1889.
2 vols.

THE TRAGIC MUSE. *Boston*, 1890.
2 vols.

THE LESSON OF THE MASTER: THE MARRIAGES, *etc. New York*, 1892.

THE PRIVATE LIFE, *etc. New York*, 1893.

THE WHEEL OF TIME, *etc. New York*, 1893.

THE REAL THING AND OTHER TALES. *New York*, 1893.

PICTURE AND TEXT. *New York*, 1893.

ESSAYS IN LONDON AND ELSEWHERE. *New York*, 1893.

THEATRICALS: TWO COMEDIES: TENANTS [and] DISENGAGED. *London,* 1894.
New York edition English sheets with new title page.

THEATRICALS: SECOND SERIES. *London,* 1895.
American edition English sheets with new title page.

TERMINATIONS: THE DEATH OF THE LION, *etc. New York,* 1895.

EMBARRASSMENTS. *New York,* 1896.

THE OTHER HOUSE. *New York,* 1896.

THE SPOILS OF POYNTON. *Boston,* 1897.

WHAT MAISIE KNEW. *Chicago,* 1897.

THE TWO MAGICS: THE TURN OF THE SCREW: COVERING END. *New York,* 1898.

IN THE CAGE. *Chicago,* 1898.

THE AWKWARD AGE. *New York,* 1899.

THE SOFT SIDE. *New York,* 1900.

THE SACRED FOUNT. *New York,* 1901.
Noted with or without a sub-title leaf inserted before p. 1. No known priority.

THE WINGS OF THE DOVE. *New York,* 1902.
2 vols. *Published, August, 1902* on the copyright page.

WILLIAM WETMORE STORY AND HIS FRIENDS. *Edinburgh,* 1903.
2 vols. American edition Edinburgh sheets with new title page.

THE BETTER SORT. *New York,* 1903.
The binding has been noted in varying colors of cloth and with the publisher's name at foot of spine in differing sizes of type; no known priority. *Published, February, 1903* on the copyright page.

THE AMBASSADORS. *New York,* 1903.
Published November, 1903 on the copyright page.

THE GOLDEN BOWL. *New York,* 1904.
2 vols.

THE QUESTION OF OUR SPEECH: THE LESSON OF BALZAC. *New York,* 1905.
Boards.

ENGLISH HOURS. *Boston,* 1905.
Also 400 numbered copies.

THE AMERICAN SCENE. *New York,* 1907.

VIEWS AND REVIEWS. *Boston*, 1908.

JULIA BRIDE. *New York*, 1909.
 Published, September, 1909 on the copyright page.

ITALIAN HOURS. *Boston*, 1909.
 Some reprint material with other writings here first collected.

THE FINER GRAIN. *New York*, 1910.
 Published October, 1910 on the copyright page.

THE OUTCRY. *New York*, 1911.
 Published September, 1911 on the copyright page.

A SMALL BOY AND OTHERS. *New York*, 1913.

NOTES ON THE NOVELISTS. *New York*, 1914.

NOTES OF A SON AND BROTHER. *New York*, 1914.

THE IVORY TOWER. *New York*, 1917.
 Published October, 1917 on the copyright page.

THE MIDDLE YEARS. *New York*, 1917.

THE SENSE OF THE PAST. *New York*, 1917.
 Published October, 1917 on the copyright page.

WITHIN THE RIM AND OTHER ESSAYS. 1914-1915. *London* [1918].

GABRIELLE DE BERGERAC. *New York*, 1918.
 Boards.

TRAVELLING COMPANIONS. *New York*, 1919.

THE LETTERS OF HENRY JAMES. *New York*, 1920.
 2 vols.

NOTES AND REVIEWS. *Cambridge, Mass.*, 1921.

A MOST UNHOLY TRADE. *Cambridge*, 1923.
 Printed boards. 100 copies only.

THE LETTERS OF HENRY JAMES TO WALTER BERRY. *Paris*, 1928.
 4 copies, *hors de commerce*, numbered I-IV; 16 copies on Japan vellum, each with an original letter, lettered A-P; 100 copies on Van Gelder numbered 1-100.

LETTERS TO A. C. BENSON AND AUGUSTE MONOD. *London*, 1930.
 E. F. Benson, editor. 1,050 copies only.

THEATRE AND FRIENDSHIP. *New York*, 1932.

THE ART OF THE NOVEL: CRITICAL PAPERS. *New York*, 1934.
 First edition has code letter *A* on copyright page.

HENRY JAMES

The following list of James' minor items is representative. A more complete list of similar material is given in "A Bibliography of the Writings of Henry James," by LeRoy Phillips, *Boston*, 1906, 250 copies only. Revised and extended edition, *New York*, 1930, 525 copies only.

Notes (No. 15 of Series) On a Collection of Drawings by Mr. George du Maurier ... *London*, 1884.

The Author of Beltraffio. *Boston*, 1885.
   See: "Stories Revived," 1885.

The Odd Number: Thirteen Tales by Guy de Maupassant. *New York*, 1889.
   Jonathan Sturges, translator. Introduction by James.

The Art of Authorship. *London*, 1890.
   George Bainton, editor. Contribution by James.

Port Tarascon ... by Alphonse Daudet. *New York*, 1891.
   Translated by James.

Catalogue of a Collection of Drawings by Alfred Parsons. *London*, 1891.
   Prefatory note by James.

The Quest and Achievement of the Holy Grail: A Series of Paintings by Edwin Austin Abbey. *London*, 1895.
   Pamphlet. Later, *New York*, 1895. There were also printed 30 copies, sm. 2 pp. folio, for The Boston Public Library.

The Vicar of Wakefield, by Oliver Goldsmith. *New York*, 1900.
   Introduction.

The Whole Family: A Novel by Twelve Authors. *New York*, 1908.
   Contains a chapter by James.

The Ambulance Volunteer ... *London*, 1914.
   Pamphlet.

The Book of France. *London*, 1915.
   Winifred Stevens, editor. Contains "France" by James and his translation of Maurice Barrès' "Les Saints de France."

England at War, by Clifton Brock. *London* [1915].
   Pamphlet. Contains an excerpt from the James writings.

The Book of the Homeless. *Paris*, 1915.
   Contains "The Long Wards" by James.

A Landscape Painter. *New York*, 1919.
   See: "Stories Revived," 1885.

Master Eustace. *New York*, 1920.
   See: "Stories Revived," 1885.

Alice James: Her Brothers, Her Journal. [*n.p.*, 1934].
   Anna Robeson Burr, editor.

Publishing as he did, on both sides of the Atlantic, Henry James presents a difficult bibliographical problem as to priority of the American and English editions. I. R. Brussel's "Anglo-American First Editions: West to East," *London* and *New York*, 1936, establishes publication dates for many of the James items.

Will (William Roderick) James

1892–

COWBOYS NORTH AND SOUTH. *New York*, 1924.

THE DRIFTING COWBOY. *New York*, 1925.
Boards, cloth back.

SMOKY: THE COWHORSE. *New York*, 1926.
"The Illustrated Classics Edition," *New York* [1929].

COW COUNTRY. *New York*, 1927.

SAND. *New York*, 1929.

LONE COWBOY. *New York*, 1930.
First printing has the code letter *A* on the copyright page. The trade edition was published August 1, 1930; the de luxe edition of 250 signed copies was published October 29, 1930. Reissued, *New York*, 1932, with seven added plates.

SUN UP. *New York*, 1931.

BIG-ENOUGH. *New York*, 1931.
First printing has the code letter *A* on the copyright page.

UNCLE BILL. *New York*, 1932.
First edition has code letter *A* on copyright page.

ALL IN THE DAY'S RIDING. *New York*, 1933.
First edition has code letter *A* on copyright page.

THE THREE MUSTANGEERS. *New York*, 1933.
First edition has code letter *A* on copyright page.

HOME RANCH. *New York*, 1935.
First edition has code letter *A* on copyright page.

IN THE SADDLE WITH UNCLE BILL. *New York*, 1935.
First edition has code letter *A* on copyright page.

SCORPION. *New York*, 1936.
First printing has the code letter *A* on the copyright page.

FLINT SPEARS. *New York*, 1938.
All examined copies of the first printing lack the customary *A* on the copyright page, the symbol indicating this publisher's first printings.

LOOK-SEE WITH UNCLE BILL. *New York*, 1938.
First printing has the code letter *A* on the copyright page.

WILL JAMES

THE DARK HORSE. *New York*, 1939.
   First printing has the code letter *A* on the copyright page.

HORSES I'VE KNOWN. *New York*, 1940.
   First printing has the code letter *A* on the copyright page.

MY FIRST HORSE. *New York*, 1940.
   First printing has the code letter *A* on the copyright page.

Tombstone, by Walter Noble Burns. *Garden City*, 1929.
   Illustrated by James.
Young Cowboy. *New York*, 1935.
   First edition has code letter *A* on copyright page. Reprinted material, arranged for children.
Cowboy in the Making. *New York*, 1937.
   First printing has code letter *A* on the copyright page. Reprinted from "Lone Cowboy."
The Will James Cowboy Book. *New York* [1938].
   Edited by Alice Dalgleish. First printing has code letter *A* on the copyright page.

Thomas A[llibone] Janvier

1849–1913

COLOR STUDIES. *New York*, 1885.
Various cloths. Reissued, *New York*, 1891, as "Color Studies and a Mexican Campaign," the second title being added.

THE MEXICAN GUIDE. *New York*, 1886.
Reissued with added material, *New York*, 1887.

THE AZTEC TREASURE HOUSE. *New York*, 1890.

STORIES OF OLD NEW SPAIN. *New York*, 1891.
Printed wrappers.

THE UNCLE OF AN ANGEL. *New York*, 1891.
Also in printed wrappers.

AN EMBASSY TO PROVENCE. *New York*, 1893.

THE WOMEN'S CONQUEST. *New York*, 1953 [*sic.*] [1894].
Anon. Printed wrappers.

IN OLD NEW YORK. *New York*, 1894.
12mo, brown cloth. Later, 8vo, green cloth.

SAINT ANTONIO OF THE GARDENS. *Avignon*, 1895.
160 copies only of which 10 were on Orlando handmade paper, numbered. Contains also, a translation into Provençal by Mary Girard.

IN THE SARGASSO SEA. *New York*, 1898.

THE PASSING OF THOMAS. *New York*, 1900.

IN GREAT WATERS. *New York*, 1901.
November, 1901 on the copyright page.

THE CHRISTMAS KALENDS OF PROVENCE. *New York*, 1902.

THE DUTCH FOUNDING OF NEW YORK. *New York*, 1903.

SANTA FE'S PARTNER. *New York*, 1907.
Published September, 1907 on the copyright page.

HENRY HUDSON. *New York*, 1909.
Cloth, paper label.

LEGENDS OF THE CITY OF MEXICO. *New York*, 1910.

JANVIER

FROM THE SOUTH OF FRANCE. *New York*, 1912.
Published May, *1912* on the copyright page.

AT THE CASA NAPOLEON. *New York*, 1914.

Maria: A South American Romance, by Jorge Issaacs. *New York*, 1890.
Translated by Rollo Ogden. Introduction.
Flower o' the Vine, by William Sharp. *New York*, 1892.
Introduction by Janvier.
The Armies of Today. *New York*, 1893.
Contribution.
The Reds of the Midi, by Félix Gras. *New York*, 1896.
Introduction by Janvier.

(John) Robinson Jeffers

1887–

FLAGONS AND APPLES. *Los Angeles,* 1912.
500 unnumbered copies only. Boards, paper labels.

CALIFORNIANS. *New York,* 1916.

TAMAR AND OTHER POEMS. *New York* [1924].
500 unnumbered copies only.

ROAN STALLION, TAMAR AND OTHER POEMS. *New York,* 1925.
Boards. Also 12 copies in marbled boards, printed after the trade edition, for presentation. Reissued in the Modern Library, *New York* [1935] with added material.

THE WOMEN AT POINT SUR. *New York,* 1927.
Also 265 copies, *New York* [1927], numbered and signed, published after issue of the trade edition.

POEMS. *San Francisco,* 1928.
310 signed and numbered copies. Also 10 [?] copies, out of series, bound in half leather.

AN ARTIST. [*Austin, Texas,* 1928].
Colophon states that edition consists of 96 copies only. The publisher informs me that this is an error, that it should have read *196* and that about 200 copies were printed; bulk of edition is said to be either wholly destroyed or damaged by fire. Wrappers, paper label on the front cover.

CAWDOR. *New York,* 1928.
Also 375 copies, numbered and signed.

DEAR JUDAS AND OTHER POEMS. *New York,* 1929.
Also 375 copies, numbered and signed. Boards, cloth back.

STARS. [*Pasadena*] 1930.
Boards, paper label, 80 numbered copies only. Reissued in printed wrappers in an edition limited to 110 numbered copies [*Pasadena*] 1930.

APOLOGY FOR BAD DREAMS. *Paris,* 1930.
Wrappers. 30 numbered copies only.

DESCENT TO THE DEAD. *New York* [1931].
500 copies only, numbered and signed. Boards.

THURSO'S LANDING. *New York* [1932].
Also 200 copies, numbered and signed.

GIVE YOUR HEART TO THE HAWKS. *New York*, 1933.
Also 200 copies, numbered and signed.

RETURN: AN UNPUBLISHED POEM. *San Francisco*, 1934.
253 copies only as follows: 250 numbered copies in wrappers over flexible boards, three copies printed on vellum.

SOLSTICE AND OTHER POEMS. *New York*, 1935.
Also 320 large paper copies, signed.

THE BEAKS OF EAGLES. *San Francisco*, 1936.
Printed wrappers.

SUCH COUNSELS YOU GAVE TO ME. *New York* [1937].
Also 300 copies, numbered and signed, in boards.

THE HOUSE-DOG'S GRAVE—HAIG'S GRAVE. [*San Mateo*, 1939].
30 numbered copies only, bound in morocco.

TWO CONSOLATIONS. [*San Mateo*] 1940.
250 copies only. Rose or grey boards.

As with Robert Frost, the writings of Robinson Jeffers have appeared in numerous anthologies; the collector is referred to the excellent and exhaustive Jeffers bibliography by S. S. Alberts (1933), listed below.

Continent's End. An Anthology. *San Francisco*, 1925.
600 numbered copies only. Boards.
A Miscellany of American Poetry, 1927. *New York* [1927].
Contributions by Jeffers. First edition so stated.
Winter Sundown. [*San Francisco*, 1930].
Broadside. The poem appeared in a shorter form in "Cawdor," 1928.
The Colophon, No. 10. *New York*, 1932.
Contains "First Books," by Jeffers.
Fifty Poets. *New York* [1933].
William Rose Benét, editor. Contribution by Jeffers.
Rock and Hawk. [*n.p.*] 1934.
20 copies only. Printed on various types of paper. Wrappers.
Four Poems and a Fragment. [*n.p.*] 1936.
Typewritten. A few numbered copies in wrappers for copyright purposes.
Breaking Into Print. *New York*, 1937.
Elmer Adler, editor. Contribution.
Selected Poetry. *New York* [1938].
First printing so indicated on the copyright page.
Fire and Other Poems, by D. H. Lawrence. [*San Francisco*] 1940.
300 copies only. Foreword by Jeffers.

BIOGRAPHICAL

Robinson Jeffers: The Man and the Artist, by George Sterling. *New York*, 1926.

Robinson Jeffers: Tragic Terror, by Benjamin De Casseres. ₁*Austin, Texas,* 1928₁.
Privately printed. 49 copies only. Printed wrappers.

Robinson Jeffers: A Portrait, by Louis Adamic. *Seattle*, 1929.
Wrappers.

An Introduction to Robinson Jeffers, by Lawrence Clark Powell. *Dijon*, 1932.
Wrappers. *University of Dijon* ... at top of title page. Later issued in a trade edition.

A Bibliography of the Works of Robinson Jeffers, by S. S. Alberts. *New York*, 1933.
487 numbered copies only. With material here first printed.

Robinson Jeffers: The Man and His Work. ₁*Los Angeles*, 1934₁.
By Lawrence Clark Powell. *See above:* "An Introduction to Robinson Jeffers."

Robinson Jeffers and the Sea, by Melba Berry Bennett. *San Francisco*, 1936.
Foreword by Una Jeffers and an unpublished poem by Robinson Jeffers. 300 copies only. Boards.

Shine, Perishing Republic. Robinson Jeffers and the Tragic Sense in Modern Poetry, by Rudolf Gilbert. *Boston* ₁1936₁.

Robinson Jeffers, by William Van Wyck. *Los Angeles*, 1938.
250 copies only. Boards.

Sarah Orne Jewett
1849–1909

DEEPHAVEN. *Boston*, 1877.
> Reissued, *Boston*, 1894, with new preface and illustrations; also 250 large pape copies.

PLAY DAYS: A BOOK OF STORIES FOR CHILDREN. *Boston*, 1878.
> Reissued, *Boston* [1906].

OLD FRIENDS AND NEW. *Boston*, 1879.

COUNTRY BY-WAYS. *Boston*, 1881.

A COUNTRY DOCTOR. *Boston*, 1884.

THE MATE OF THE DAYLIGHT AND FRIENDS ASHORE. *Boston*, 1884.

A MARSH ISLAND. *Boston*, 1885.

A WHITE HERON AND OTHER STORIES. *Boston*, 1886.
> Pictorial boards, gilt top, cloth back.

THE STORY OF THE NORMANS. *New York*, 1887.

THE KING OF FOLLY ISLAND AND OTHER PEOPLE. *Boston*, 1888.

BETTY LEICESTER. *Boston*, 1890.
> List of advertisements opposite title page with "Betty Leicester" at end. Also copies on large paper.

STRANGERS AND WAYFARERS. *Boston*, 1890.

A NATIVE OF WINBY AND OTHER TALES. *Boston*, 1893.

BETTY LEICESTER'S ENGLISH CHRISTMAS, *etc. Baltimore*, 1894.
> Privately printed for Bryn Mawr. Reissued, *Boston*, 1899, as "Betty Leicester's Christmas."

THE LIFE OF NANCY. *Boston*, 1895.

THE COUNTRY OF THE POINTED FIRS. *Boston*, 1896.
> The first printing was issued in both plain and silk-like cloths. Reissued with two added stories, 1910.

THE QUEEN'S TWIN AND OTHER STORIES. *Boston*, 1899.

THE TORY LOVER. *Boston*, 1901.
> First printing, p. 278, first line of chapter heading, reads: *Lackynge, my love, I goe from place to place.* Copyright page has notice: *Published September 1901.*

THE NORMANS. *New York*, 1901.

LETTERS OF SARAH ORNE JEWETT. *Boston*, 1911.
  Annie Fields, editor.

VERSES. *Boston*, 1916.
  Privately printed. Boards.

Katy's Birthday, by Sarah Orne Jewett, With Other Stories by Famous Authors.
  Boston [1883].
  Contribution.
Plucky Boys, By ... [Several Authors]. *Boston* [1884].
  Contains "The Church Mouse" by Jewett.
Tales of New England. *Boston*, 1890.
  Reprint. The first printing of this edition has no mention of this title in the ad-
  vertisements. Also a large paper edition. Reissued in 1912 with one added story.
The Art of Authorship. *London*, 1890.
  George Bainton, editor. Contribution by Jewett.
A Memorial of the One Hundredth Anniversary of the Founding of Berwick
  Academy, South Berwick, Maine. *Cambridge* [1891].
  Printed wrappers. Preface by Jewett.
A House Party. *Boston*, 1901.
  Contains "The Green Bowl" by Jewett.
An Empty Purse. *Boston*, 1905.
  Privately printed.
The Best Stories of Sarah Orne Jewett. *Boston*, 1925.
  Selected and with an introduction by Willa Cather.
Sarah Orne Jewett, by Francis Otto Matthiessen. *Boston*, 1929.

Mary Johnston

1870–1936

PRISONERS OF HOPE. *Boston,* 1898.
London edition as "The Old Dominion."

TO HAVE AND TO HOLD. *Boston,* 1900.
Also 250 untrimmed copies, paper label on spine. The trade edition was reprinted numerous times with no known textual changes. The cover stamping has been noted in several colors; no known priority. Issued in England [*London*] 1900, as "By Order of the Company."

AUDREY. *Boston,* 1902.
Also 1,000 untrimmed copies, signed, paper label on spine. *Published February, 1902* on the copyright page.

SIR MORTIMER. *New York,* 1904.
Published March, 1904 on the copyright page. A copy has been noted in printed boards; status unknown.

LEWIS RAND. *Boston,* 1908.
Also 500 untrimmed copies, signed, paper label on spine.

THE LONG ROLL. *Boston,* 1911.
Also 500 untrimmed copies, signed, paper label on spine. *Published May 1911* on the copyright page.

CEASE FIRING. *Boston,* 1912.
Also 500 untrimmed copies, signed, paper label on spine. *Published November 1912* on the copyright page.

HAGAR. *Boston,* 1913.
Published October 1913 on the copyright page.

THE WITCH. *Boston,* 1914.
Published October 1914 on the copyright page.

THE FORTUNES OF GARIN. *Boston,* 1915.
Published October 1915 on the copyright page.

THE WANDERERS. *Boston* [1917].
Published September 1917 on the copyright page.

FOES. *New York* [1918].
Boards. Code letters *I-S* on the copyright page. London edition as "The Laird of Glenfernie."

PIONEERS OF THE OLD SOUTH. *New Haven*, 1918.
In "The Chronicles of America Series."

MICHAEL FORTH. *New York* [1919].
Code letters *L-T* on the copyright page.

SWEET ROCKET. *New York* [1920].
Code letters *I-U* on the copyright page.

SILVER CROSS. *Boston*, 1922.
Published March, 1922 on the copyright page.

1492. *Boston*, 1922.
Published October, 1922 on the copyright page. Issued in England as "Admiral of the Ocean-Sea," *London* [1923].

CROATAN. *Boston*, 1923.
Published October, 1923 on the copyright page.

THE SLAVE SHIP. *Boston*, 1924.
Published November, 1924 on the copyright page.

THE GREAT VALLEY. *Boston*, 1926.
Published April, 1926 on the copyright page.

THE EXILE. *Boston*, 1927.
Published September, 1927 on the copyright page.

HUNTING SHIRT. *Boston*, 1931.
Published October, 1931 on the copyright page.

MISS DELICIA ALLEN. *Boston*, 1933.
Published March, 1933 on the copyright page.

DRURY RANDALL. *Boston*, 1934.
Published October, 1934 on the copyright page.

The Goddess of Reason. *Boston*, 1907.
A play. Cloth or wrappers.
An Address Read at Vicksburg ... *Boston*, 1907.
Privately printed.
The Status of Woman [and] The Reason Why.
Two pamphlets issued by The Suffrage Press, *Richmond, Va., ca.* 1910.
Historic Gardens of Virginia. *Richmond*, 1923.
Compiled by the James River Garden Club. Introduction by Miss Johnston.
The Old Virginia Omnibus. *London*, 1932.
Reprints: "Prisoners of Hope" (*The Old Dominion*); "To Have and To Hold" (*By Order of the Company*); and "Audrey."
The American Historical Scene as Depicted by Stanley Arthurs. *Philadelphia*, 1935.
Contains Miss Johnston's "Jefferson at Monticello."

John Pendleton Kennedy

1795–1870

THE RED BOOK. *Baltimore,* 1818-1819.
2 vols. With PETER HOFFMAN CRUSE.

SWALLOW BARN. *Philadelphia,* 1832.
2 vols. Boards, cloth back, paper labels on spine. Revised and reissued, 1851.

HORSE-SHOE ROBINSON. *Philadelphia,* 1835.
Anon. 2 vols. Revised and reissued, *New York,* 1852.

ROB OF THE BOWL. *Philadelphia,* 1838.
Cloth, paper labels on spine. 2 vols. Revised and reissued, *New York,* 1852.

QUODLIBET. *Philadelphia,* 1840.
Solomon Secondthoughts, pseudonym. Title on cover: "Annals of Quodlibet."

MEMOIRS OF THE LIFE OF WILLIAM WIRT. *Philadelphia,* 1849.
2 vols. Revised and reissued, *Philadelphia,* 1850.

THE BORDER STATES. *Philadelphia,* 1861.

MR. AMBROSE'S LETTERS ON THE REBELLION. *New York,* 1865.

COLLECTED WORKS OF JOHN PENDLETON KENNEDY. *New York,* 1870-72.
10 vols. Vol. 10 is a life of Kennedy by H. T. Tuckerman.

AT HOME AND ABROAD: A SERIES OF ESSAYS: WITH A JOURNAL IN EUROPE
IN 1867-68. *New York,* 1872.

The following is a representative selection of Kennedy's secondary or political productions.

An Address Before the American Institute ... October 17th, 1833. *New York,* 1833.
Address ... Before the Horticultural Society of Maryland ... June 12, 1833. *Baltimore,* 1833.
A Discourse on the Life and Character of William Wirt. *Baltimore,* 1834.
Letter of J. P. Kennedy to His Constituents. [*Baltimore,* 1842].
Defence of the Whigs. *New York,* 1844.
Anon. *By a Member of the Twenty-Seventh Congress.*
Discourse on the Life and Character of George Calvert, First Lord Baltimore. *Baltimore,* 1846.
Wrappers.
The Blackwater Chronicle. *New York,* 1853.
Authorship in doubt.

298

KENNEDY

Letter of Mr. Paul Ambrose on the Great Rebellion in the United States. ₍n.p., ca. 1865₎.
  Leaflet.
The Great Drama: An Appeal to Maryland. *Baltimore* ₍1861₎.
The Privilege of the Writ of Habeas Corpus under the Constitution of the United States. *Philadelphia,* 1862.
  Anon. *By Common Sense.*
Slavery: The Mere Pretext for the Rebellion, Not Its Cause. *Philadelphia,* 1863.
  Anon. *By A Southern Man.*

BIOGRAPHICAL AND BIBLIOGRAPHICAL

The Life of John Pendleton Kennedy, by Henry T. Tuckerman. *New York,* 1871.
John Pendleton Kennedy, by Edward M. Gwathmey. *New York,* 1931.
Horse-Shoe Robinson. *Cincinnati* ₍1937₎.
  Edited by E. E. Leisy. Contains a bibliography of Kennedy's writings.

Rockwell Kent

1882–

BOOKS BY ROCKWELL KENT

WILDERNESS: A JOURNAL OF QUIET ADVENTURE IN ALASKA. *New York,* 1920.

With 69 illustrations. The first binding is grey linen with gilt stamping. Second binding, tan boards with decorative stamping. Reissued by The Modern Library, 1930, with new introduction by the author.

VOYAGING SOUTHWARD FROM THE STRAIT OF MAGELLAN. *New York,* 1924.

Bound in tan buckram with decorative stamping. Also 110 signed copies with one extra illustration.

ELMER ADLER. *New York,* 1929.

25 copies only for private distribution.

N BY E. *New York,* 1930.

Trade edition issued after the following: 100 copies in linen with an extra page, for presentation. Also 900 signed and numbered, the so-called limited edition.

HOW I MAKE A WOOD CUT. *Pasadena,* 1934.

1,000 copies in boards. Also a popular edition in wrappers.

SALAMINA. *New York,* 1935.

First edition so stated on copyright page.

THIS IS MY OWN. *New York* [1940].

First edition so indicated on copyright page.

COLLECTED ILLUSTRATIONS

THE SEVEN AGES OF MAN. *New York,* 1918.

100 copies only. Portfolio of four signed reproductions.

THE GOLDEN CHAIN. [*n.p.*] 1922.

Eight copies only. Privately printed.

DRAWINGS. *New York,* 1924.

Privately printed. 30 copies only. Portfolio of 28 signed reproductions.

THE BOOKPLATES AND MARKS OF ROCKWELL KENT. *New York,* 1929.

1,250 signed copies only.

A BIRTHDAY BOOK. *New York*, 1931.
1,850 numbered and signed copies only.

ROCKWELLKENTIANA: FEW WORDS AND MANY PICTURES. *New York*, 1933.
Contains a bibliography by Carl Zigrosser. First edition so stated on copyright
page.

FORTY DRAWINGS ... TO ILLUSTRATE THE WORKS OF WILLIAM SHAKESPEARE.
[*Garden City*, 1936].
1,000 boxed sets only.

LATER BOOKPLATES & MARKS OF ROCKWELL KENT. *New York*, 1937.
1,250 copies only, numbered and signed.

SOME BOOKS ILLUSTRATED BY ROCKWELL KENT

The following list contains only the more important of the items in this classification.

ARCHITEC-TONICS: THE TALES OF TOM THUMTACK. *New York*, 1914.
By *Tom Thumtack*, pseudonym for Frederick Squires.

THE MODERN SCHOOL, by Carl Zigrosser. [*New York*. 1917].

ROLLO IN SOCIETY. *New York*, 1922.
By George S. Chappell. "Embellished with Cuts by Hogarth, Jr."

CHRONICLES OF KENNEBUNK, by William E. Barry. [*Privately Printed*]
1923.

A BASKET OF POSES. *New York*, 1924.
By George S. Chappell. "Pictures by Hogarth, Jr." Boards.

CASANOVA'S MEMOIRS. [*Privately Printed*] 1925.
12 vols. 1,026 numbered sets of which 150, numbered 1-150 are in half morocco; 26 full levant, lettered A-Z and with a portfolio of Kent plates. Reprinted,
2 vols., *New York*, 1932, with a few slight expurgations and minor changes.

DREAMS AND DERISIONS. *New York*, 1927.
Anon. Privately printed. 200 copies only of which the first hundred contain an
extra plate and one added poem.

AMERICANA ESOTERICA. *New York*, 1927.
Carl Van Doren, editor. 3,000 copies only.

BURNING BUSH, by Louis Untermeyer. *New York*, 1928.
Later printings have numeral 2 under copyright notice.

ON THE DUTY OF CIVIL DISOBEDIENCE, by H. D. Thoreau. *New Haven*
[1928].
300 numbered copies only.

THE BALLAD OF YUKON JAKE. *New York,* 1928.
By Edward E. Paramore, Jr. "Illustrations by Hogarth, Jr." Boards.

MOSES, by Louis Untermeyer. *New York,* 1928.

UNSER KENT, by W[aldo] P[ierce]. *New York,* 1928.
The colophon states that "one hundred copies were privately printed by C. G. and and F. W." but this edition was withdrawn after 13 copies had been distributed. Reprinted, 1930, 85 copies only.

CANDIDE, by Voltaire. *New York,* 1928.
1,470 numbered copies in gold embossed buckram. 95 copies, numbered and signed, in linen and morocco with the illustrations colored in the studio of the artist. Later issued by The Random House and Literary Guild.

THE DECORATIVE WORK OF T. M. CLELAND, by Alfred E. Hamill. *New York,* 1929.
1,200 numbered copies of which 55 were de luxe with an added signed plate.

THE BRIDGE OF SAN LUIS REY, by Thorton Wilder. *New York,* 1929.
1,100 copies only signed by author and artist. Although the colophon states that the publishers were issuing 100 sets of proofs, such a publication was not issued.

GABRIEL: A POEM IN ONE SONG, by Alexander Pushkin. *New York,* 1929.
Max Eastman, translator. 750 copies only.

THE CANTERBURY TALES, by Chaucer. *New York,* 1930.
2 vols. Limited editions only; 75 copies on Crane's Old Book Paper, numbered 1-75; 925 copies on Worthy Rag paper. All signed. Reissued [1934] with added illustrations.

MOBY DICK. *Chicago,* 1930.
3 vols. 1,000 sets. Trade edition, re-set type, 1 vol., same illustrations, *New York,* 1930.

VENUS AND ADONIS, by Shakespeare. *Rochester,* 1931.
1,250 copies only numbered and signed; first 75 copies printed on English hand-made paper.

CITY CHILD, by Selma Robinson. *New York,* 1931.
300 copies only with signature of author and thumbmark of Kent. Later issued with Farrar and Rinehart imprint.

BEOWULF. *New York,* 1932.
William Ellery Leonard, translator. Also 950 numbered copies.

CANDY, by L. M. Alexander. *New York,* 1934.

EREWHON, by Samuel Butler. *New York,* 1934.
Issued in a limited edition for members of The Limited Editions Club.

LEAVES OF GRASS, by Walt Whitman. *New York & London* [1936].
  Also 1,000 signed copies.

COMPLETE WORKS OF WILLIAM SHAKESPEARE. *Garden City*, 1936.
  2 vols., 750 signed copies. Also trade edition in one volume. The plates were
  issued in a separate portfolio, 1,000 sets only [*Garden City*, 1936].

THE SAGA OF GISLI. *New York* [1936].
  Translated by Ralph B. Allen. First edition indicated on the copyright page.

Alaska Drawings. *New York*, 1919.
  Art gallery catalog of Kent exhibition. First edition so marked.
Fifty Prints of the Year. *New York*, 1927.
  500 copies only. Contribution by Kent.
Recent Gains in American Civilization. *New York*, 1928.
  Kirby Page, editor. Contribution.
Down With The Gang: A Message to Republican Voters. [*n.p., n.d.*].
  Unillustrated. A leaflet issued as political propaganda by Kent, *Au Sable Forks,
  New York*, 1930.
Eskimo, by Peter Freuchen. *New York* [1931].
  Contribution.
Rockwell Kent, by Merle Armitage. *New York*, 1932.
  550 copies only, numbered and signed.
So Red the Nose. *New York* [1935].
State of Vermont Marble Company Workers. [*New York*, 1936].
  Wrappers. Contribution.
What is an American? *Los Angeles* [1936].
  Wrappers.
Breaking into Print. *New York*, 1937.
  Elmer Adler, editor. Contribution.

  "Greenland," announced in 1932, has not been published.

(Alfred) Joyce Kilmer
1886–1918

SUMMER OF LOVE. *New York*, 1911.

TREES AND OTHER POEMS. *New York* [1914].
The first state is bound in grey boards, paper labels on the cover, has top edges gilt; does not have *Printed in U. S. A.* on the copyright page. The title poem was first collected in Braithwaite's "Anthology of Magazine Verse for 1913," *Cambridge* [1913], boards or wrappers.

THE CIRCUS AND OTHER ESSAYS. *New York*, 1916.
Gomme imprint; boards, cloth back. Later issued with an inserted slip stating that the publication had been taken over by Mitchell Kennerley.

MAIN STREET AND OTHER POEMS. *New York* [1917].
Three bindings as follows: first, brown boards, gilt top; second, tannish boards, plain top; third, green cloth.

LITERATURE IN THE MAKING. *New York* [1917].
Publisher's code letters *D-R* on copyright page. First binding brown cloth, gilt lettering, 2nd binding, brown boards.

The Younger Choir. *New York*, 1910.
500 copies only of which fifty were signed by the contributors. Contributions.
The Lyric Year. *New York*, 1912.
Contains "Martin." For further regarding this book see under *Millay.*
The Mayor of Casterbridge, by Thomas Hardy. *New York* [1917].
Modern Library edition. Introduction.
Verses, by Hilaire Belloc. *New York*, 1916.
Introduction by Kilmer.
Dreams and Images. *New York*, 1917.
Edited by Kilmer.
The Courage of Enlightenment. [*Prairie du Chien, Wis.?* 1917].
Address to the graduating class of Campion College.
Yanks: A Book of A. E. F. Verse. [*Somewhere-in-France*] 1918.
First state in tan wrappers; first edition so stated. Later states are in grey wrappers and in addition to the first edition notice add *Peace Edition,* or *Victory Edition* or both. Contains Kilmer's "L'Envoi."
Joyce Kilmer. *New York* [1918-1921].
3 vols. Edited and with a memoir by Robert Cortes Holliday. Vol. 1 [1918] "Memoir and Poems"; Vol. 2 [1918] "Prose Works"; Vol. 3 "The Circus and Other Essays" [1921].

Father Duffy's Story. *New York* [1919].
    Contains an historical appendix by Kilmer.
The Catholic Anthology. *New York,* 1927.
    Thomas Walsh, editor. Contains "Daw's Dinner" by Kilmer.
The Smart Set Anthology. *New York* [1934].
    Edited by Burton Rascoe and Groff Conklin. Contains "Whitemail," by Kilmer.
    First state of the binding has *Roscoe* for *Rascoe* on the spine.

"Joyce Kilmer's Anthology of Catholic Poets" is a reissue of "Dreams and Images."

BIOGRAPHICAL

Memories of My Son, Sergeant Joyce Kilmer, by Annie Kilburn Kilmer. *New York* [1920].
    Contains hitherto unpublished Kilmer material.
Leaves from My Life, by Annie Kilburn Kilmer. *New York* [1925].

Sidney Lanier

1842–1881

TIGER-LILIES. *New York,* 1867.

FLORIDA: ITS SCENERY, CLIMATE, AND HISTORY, etc. *Philadelphia,* 1876.
Copyright date 1875. Later states lack the 1876 date on the title page, have a
footnote at p. 130 referring to the first edition; advertisements at the back referring to a railroad to be completed about January 1, 1881. It is not known whether
or not all the reissues had these last two features.

POEMS. *Philadelphia,* 1877.

THE SCIENCE OF ENGLISH VERSE. *New York,* 1880.

THE ENGLISH NOVEL AND THE PRINCIPLE OF ITS DEVELOPMENT. *New York,*
1883.
Revised and reissued as "The English Novel: A Study in the Development of
Personality," *New York,* 1897.

POEMS OF SIDNEY LANIER. *New York,* 1884.
Edited by Mrs. Lanier. Green or grey cloth with no known priority. Errata
slip at p. xlii. Reissued with additions, *New York,* 1891 and *New York,* 1916.

MUSIC AND POETRY. *New York,* 1898.

BOB: THE STORY OF OUR MOCKING-BIRD. *New York,* 1899.
Pictorial boards.

LETTERS 1866-1881. *New York,* 1899.

RETROSPECTS AND PROSPECTS. *New York,* 1899.

SHAKSPERE AND HIS FORERUNNERS. *New York,* 1899.
Also 102 copies on Van Gelder handmade paper.

POEM OUTLINES. *New York,* 1908.
Published September, 1908 on the copyright page.

Catalogue of the Trustees, Faculty, Alumnae and Students of Furlow Masonic
Female College, Americus, Ga., 1868-1869. *Macon, Ga.,* 1869.
Contains a commencement address by Lanier.
The Centennial Meditation of Columbus: A Cantata. *New York* [1876].
Red printed boards. Set to music by Dudley Buck.
Sketch of the Life of J. F. D. Lanier: Second Edition. [*New York?*] 1877.
Privately printed. The second edition of the title but the first to contain a letter
by Sidney Lanier.

The Hard Times in Elfland: A Story of Christmas Eve, by Sidney Lanier. *Baltimore,* 1877.
Supplement to *Every Saturday* (Baltimore) Christmas, 1877.
Some Highways and Byways of American Travel. *Philadelphia,* 1878.
Material is reprinted from "Florida," 1876.
A Masque of Poets. *Boston,* 1878.
First printing for Lanier's "The Marshes of Glynn." For further discussion of this publication see under *Alcott.*
Charlotte Cushman, by Emma Stebbins. *Boston,* 1879.
Contains a poem by Lanier.
The Boy's Froissart ... *New York,* 1879.
Edited and with an introduction by Lanier. First state has *Boys'* and not *Boy's* on the title page.
The Boy's King Arthur ... *New York,* 1880.
Edited and with an introduction by Lanier.
Sunrise. [*Baltimore,* 1880].
4 pp. pamphlet.
The Boy's Mabinogion ... *New York,* 1881.
Edited and with an introduction by Lanier. Reissued, *New York,* 1884, as "Knightly Legends of Wales; or, The Boy's Mabinogion."
The Boy's Percy ... *New York,* 1882.
Edited and with an introduction by Lanier.
The Forty-Sixth Birthday of Sidney Lanier. *Baltimore,* 1888.
Printed wrappers.
San Antonio de Bexar. *San Antonio, Texas,* 1890.
William Corner, editor. Contains an essay on San Antonio by Lanier; later reprinted in "Retrospects and Prospects."
From Dixie. *Richmond, Va.,* 1893.
Kate Pleasants Minor, editor. Contains a poem by Lanier.
Select Poems of Sidney Lanier. *New York,* 1895.
Morgan Callaway, Jr., editor. Contains a Lanier Checklist.
Southern Writers, by W. M. Baskervill. *Nashville, Tenn.,* 1897.
Contains a poem and an outline by Lanier.
The Lanier Book: Selections ... *New York* [1904].
Mary E. Burt, editor. First printing for a story for children and a brief essay on King Arthur.
Hymns of the Marshes. *New York,* 1907.
Reprint of the four "Marsh Hymns" with photographic illustrations by Henry Troth.
Stratford on the Potomac, by Ethel Armes. *Greenwich, Conn.,* 1928.
Contains "An Address on Robert E. Lee," by Lanier.

BIOGRAPHICAL

Sidney Lanier, by Edward Mims. *Boston,* 1905.
Also 150 large paper copies.

LANIER

Some Reminiscences and Early Letters of Sidney Lanier, by George Herbert Clarke. *Macon, Ga.,* 1907.

Sidney Lanier at Rockingham Springs, by John W. Wayland. *Dayton, Va.,* 1912.

Sidney Lanier: A Biographical and Critical Study, by Aubrey H. Starke. *Chapel Hill,* 1933.

The Life of Sidney Lanier, by Lincoln Lorenz. *New York,* 1935.

Some New Facts Concerning Sidney Lanier in Florida, by John S. Mayfield. *Baltimore,* 1935.

Originally in *The Johns Hopkins Alumni Magazine,* November, 1935. 28 separate reprints made.

Sidney Lanier's Immoral Bird, by John S. Mayfield. *Metuchen, N. J.,* 1935.

Originally in *The American Book Collector,* May-June, 1935. 35 separate reprints made, numbered. Contains an hitherto unpublished poem.

Sidney Lanier at Oglethorpe University, by Leola Selman Beeson. *Macon,* 1936.

150 copies only.

Ring (Ringold Wilmer) Lardner

1885–1933

BIB BALLADS. *Chicago* [1915].

YOU KNOW ME AL. *New York* [1916].
Revised and reissued, *New York*, 1925.

GULLIBLE'S TRAVELS. *Indianapolis* [1917].
Revised and reissued, *New York*, 1925.

MY FOUR WEEKS IN FRANCE. *Indianapolis* [1918].

TREAT 'EM ROUGH. *Indianapolis* [1918].
Paper labels.

OWN YOUR OWN HOME. *Indianapolis* [1919].

REGULAR FELLOWS I HAVE MET. *Chicago*, 1919.

THE REAL DOPE. *Indianapolis* [1919].

THE YOUNG IMMIGRUNTS. *Indianapolis* [1920].
Boards.

SYMPTOMS OF BEING 35. *Indianapolis* [1921].
Boards.

THE BIG TOWN. *Indianapolis* [1921].
Reissued with new introduction, *New York*, 1925.

SAY IT WITH OIL. *New York* [1923].
An "upside-down" book. Contains also Nina Wilcox Putnam's "Say It with Bricks." First edition has *GHD* insignia on copyright page.

HOW TO WRITE SHORT STORIES (WITH SAMPLES). *New York*, 1924.

WHAT OF IT? *New York*, 1925.

THE LOVE NEST AND OTHER STORIES. *New York*, 1926.

THE STORY OF A WONDER MAN. *New York*, 1927.

LOSE WITH A SMILE. *New York*, 1933.
First edition has code letter *A* on copyright page.

March 6th, 1914: The Home Coming of Charles A. Comiskey, John J. McGraw and James J. Callahan. [*Chicago*, 1914].

LARDNER

Funny Stories About The Ford. *Hamilton* [1915].
   Wrappers. Contains "Phil and His 4D."
The Best Short Stories of 1922. *Boston* [1923].
   Edward J. O'Brien, editor. Contains Lardner's "The Golden Honeymoon."
Charles Scribner's Sons Present Ring W. Lardner in The Golden Honeymoon and
   Haircut, American Booksellers Association. *St. Louis*, May 13, 1926.
   Reprinted from "The Love Nest" and "How to Write Short Stories." First edition
   for the preface. Boards, cloth back.
Round Up: The Stories of Ring Lardner. *New York*, 1929.
   Reprint. Issued in green cloth but copies have been noted in red. The copyright
   deposit copy is bound in green cloth.
Not for Children, by Roland Young. *Garden City*, 1930.
   Introduction.
The Timid Soul, by H. T. Webster. *New York*, 1931.
   Introduction.
June Moon. *New York*, 1930.
   Play. In collaboration with GEORGE S. KAUFMAN.
The Sixth New Yorker Album. *New York*, 1933.
   Foreword by Lardner.
First and Last. *New York*, 1934.
   First printing has code letter *A* on the copyright page.
Ring Lardner's Best Short Stories. *Garden City* [1938].
The Bedside Esquire. *New York* [1940].
   Arnold Gingrich, editor. Contribution.

(Harry) Sinclair Lewis

1885–

HIKE AND THE AEROPLANE. *New York* [1912].
Tom Graham, *pseud. August, 1912* on the copyright page.

OUR MR. WRENN. *New York,* 1914.
M-N on copyright page.

THE TRAIL OF THE HAWK. *New York* [1915].
H-P on copyright page.

THE JOB. *New York* [1917].
B-R on copyright page. Copies containing an inserted leaf advertising "Main Street" and other titles are presumed to be remainders.

THE INNOCENTS. *New York* [1917].
F-R on copyright page.

FREE AIR. *New York,* 1919.

MAIN STREET. *New York,* 1920.
Bound in several shades of blue cloth with no known priority. The earliest printed copies have perfect folio, p. 54; perfect type lower right corner of p. 387. Reissued in 1937 by The Limited Editions Club with a new introduction by the author.

BABBITT. *New York* [1922].
First state, p. 49, line 4, reads *Purdy* for *Lyte;* p. 49, line 5, *my fellow* for *any fellow.*

ARROWSMITH. *New York* [1925].
Also 500 large paper copies, signed. The first trade edition is marked *Second Printing* [first trade edition] *January, 1925* on the copyright page.

MANTRAP. *New York* [1926].

ELMER GANTRY. *New York* [1927].
First binding (20,000 copies) of first edition (100,000 copies) has *G* on spine strongly resembling *C.*

THE MAN WHO KNEW COOLIDGE. *New York* [1928].

DODSWORTH: A NOVEL. *New York* [1929].
Also advance issue, 500 copies, in orange cloth binding. *Published, March, 1929* on the copyright page. Dramatized, *New York* [1934], first edition so stated on copyright page. Dramatization by Sidney Howard.

ANN VICKERS. *Garden City*, 1933.

Also 2,350 unnumbered copies printed on laid paper; first edition so stated on copyright page.

WORK OF ART. *Garden City*, 1934.

First edition so stated on copyright page.

JAYHAWKER: A PLAY IN THREE ACTS. *Garden City*, 1935.

With LLOYD LEWIS. First edition so stated on copyright page.

SELECTED SHORT STORIES. *Garden City*, 1935.

First edition so stated on copyright page.

IT CAN'T HAPPEN HERE. *Garden City*, 1935.

First edition so stated on copyright page. The first 32 pp. were issued in pamphlet form as advance publicity. Dramatized by Lewis in collaboration with John C. Moffitt [New York] 1938; first edition so indicated on copyright page.

THE PRODIGAL PARENTS. *Garden City*, 1938.

First edition so indicated on copyright page.

BETHEL MERRIDAY. *New York*, 1940.

First edition so indicated on copyright page.

Yale Verse: 1898-1908. *New Haven*, 1909.

Contains seven poems by Lewis.

Dad, by Albert Payson Terhune. *New York* [1914].

Contains three chapters written by Lewis.

Hugh Walpole. *New York* [1915].

Contribution.

Hobohemia: A Play.

Produced in New York, 1919. No record of publication found.

These United States. *New York*, 1924.

Contains "Minnesota," by Lewis.

Irvin S. Cobb: His Book. [New York, 1925].

Contains "C-O-B-B!" by Lewis.

Four Days on the Webutuck River, by Charles E. Benton. *Amenia, N. Y.*, 1925.

200 privately printed copies only. Introduction by Lewis.

Short Stories. *New York* [1925].

H. C. Schweikert, editor. Contribution by Lewis.

American Criticism. 1926. *New York* [1926].

W. A. Drake, editor. Contribution.

John Dos Passos' Manhattan Transfer, by Sinclair Lewis. *New York*, 1926.

975 copies only. Boards.

Cheap and Contented Labor. *New York* [1929].

Pamphlet. First state lacks the quotation marks before *Dodsworth* on the title page; said to be about 300 copies only in this state.

A Letter to Critics. *Brattleboro, Vt.* [n.d., 1931].
  Broadside. 375 copies only.
The 1930 American Scrap Book. *New York* [1930].
  First edition so stated on copyright page. Contribution by Lewis.
Nobel Prize Address. *New York* [1931].
  Pamphlet. First edition has no mention of "The Man Who Knew Coolidge" in
  list of books at back; no footnote at p. 1 of text. Second edition, revised and with
  additions.
O-Sa-Ge Annual. *Sauk Center, Minn.,* 1931.
  350 copies only. Contribution by and about Lewis.
Launcelot, by Sinclair Lewis. [*New York,* 1932].
  Pamphlet. Lewis' first published writing as originally published in *The Yale
  Literary Review.* 100 copies only, numbered and signed by Harvey Tayor.
Sinclair Lewis on the Valley of the Moon. [*New York,* 1932].
  Pamphlet. A review of Jack London's novel. 100 copies only, numbered and
  signed by Harvey Taylor.
An American Omnibus. *Garden City,* 1933.
  Contains Lewis' "Ring-Around-A-Rosy."
The Panorama of Modern Literature. *Garden City,* 1934.
  First edition indicated on the copyright page.
Samples: A Book Containing Many Fine Pages from the Books to Be Published by
  the Limited Editions Club. [*n.p., n.d.*].
  Contains a note on book-collecting by Lewis.
The Yale Literary Magazine. *New Haven,* 1936.
  Centennial number. Boards or wrappers. Contribution by Lewis.
Portraits and Self-Portraits, by Georges Schreiber. *Boston,* 1936.
  Contribution.
The Limited Editions Club ... Eighth Series. *New York* [1936].
  Contains "An Opinion."
In New England Fields and Woods, by Rowland E. Robinson. *Rutland* [1937].
  Foreword by Lewis.
Breaking into Print. *New York,* 1937.
  Elmer Adler, editor. Contribution.
American Points of View. *Garden City,* 1937.
  W. H. and K. C. Cordell, editors. Contribution.
The Good Old Days, by David L. Cohn. *New York,* 1940.
  Introduction.

BIOGRAPHICAL AND BIBLIOGRAPHICAL

The Significance of Sinclair Lewis, by Stuart P. Sherman. *New York* [1922].
  First state is in stiff paper wrappers.
Sinclair Lewis, by Oliver Harrison. *New York* [1925].
  Pamphlet. Limited issue of 500 copies in boards for presentation at the American
  Booksellers' Convention issued later.
Sinclair Lewis: Our Own Diogenes, by Vernon Louis Parrington. *Seattle* [*Wash.*],
  1927.

LEWIS

Half a Loaf, by Grace Hegger Lewis. *New York, 1931.*
  Biographical material in fictionized form.
Sinclair Lewis, by Carl Van Doren. With a Bibliography by Harvey Taylor. *Garden City, 1933.*
  First edition so stated on copyright page.
Sinclair Lewis Interprets America, by E. M. Forster. [*New York, 1932*].
  Pamphlet. 100 copies only.

(Nicholas) Vachel Lindsay

1879–1931

THE TRAMP'S EXCUSE AND OTHER POEMS. [*n.p., n.d. (Springfield, Ohio,* 1909)].
Printed wrappers.

GENERAL WILLIAM BOOTH ENTERS INTO HEAVEN AND OTHER POEMS. *New York,* 1913.

ADVENTURES WHILE PREACHING THE GOSPEL OF BEAUTY. *New York,* 1914.

THE CONGO AND OTHER POEMS. *New York,* 1914.

THE ART OF THE MOVING PICTURE. *New York,* 1915.
Revised and with added material, *New York,* 1922.

A HANDY GUIDE FOR BEGGARS. *New York,* 1916.

THE CHINESE NIGHTINGALE AND OTHER POEMS. *New York,* 1917.

THE GOLDEN WHALES OF CALIFORNIA, AND OTHER RHYMES IN THE AMERICAN LANGUAGE. *New York,* 1920.

THE GOLDEN BOOK OF SPRINGFIELD. *New York,* 1920.

GOING-TO-THE-SUN. *New York,* 1923.

COLLECTED POEMS. *New York,* 1923.
Also 400 signed large paper copies.

COLLECTED POEMS. *New York,* 1925.
Illustrated by the author. Also 350 signed large paper copies.

GOING-TO-THE-STARS. *New York,* 1926.

THE CANDLE IN THE CABIN: A WEAVING TOGETHER OF SCRIPT AND SINGING. *New York,* 1926.

THE LITANY OF WASHINGTON STREET. *New York,* 1929.
Half cloth, decorated boards. Reissued, *New York,* 1932.

RIGAMAROLE, RIGAMAROLE. *New York,* 1929.
475 copies only in the "Random House Poetry Quartos."

EVERY SOUL IS A CIRCUS. *New York,* 1929.

LINDSAY

Lindsay issued numerous pamphlets and broadsides, usually decorated with his own drawings. Some were used for distribution "while preaching the gospel of beauty."

PAMPHLETS

The Tree of Laughing Bells. *New York*, 1905.
  8 pp.
To the Sweet Singer of Israel. [*n.p., n.d. (Springfield*, 1908?)].
The Last Song of Lucifer. *New York*, 1908.
God Help Us To Be Brave. *New York*, 1908.
The Heroes of Time. [*n.p., n.d. (Springfield*, 1908?)].
  12 pp.
The Village Improvement Parade. *Springfield* [1908?].
  Revised edition, 1930.
"The Future of Springfield." [*n.p., n.d. (Springfield*, 1908?)].
  4 pp.
War Bulletin No. One. *Springfield*, 1909.
  4 pp.
War Bulletin No. Two. *Springfield*, 1909.
  4 pp.
War Bulletin No. Three. *Springfield*, 1909.
  6 pp.
War Bulletin No. Five. *Springfield*, 1909.
The Village Magazine. [*Springfield*, 1910].
  All material, prose, poetry and illustrations, by Lindsay. 700 copies only, 76 unnumbered pages. Revised and enlarged [1920] 1,000 copies and third and fourth impressions [1925].
Rhymes to Be Traded for Bread. [*n.p., n.d. (Springfield*, 1912)].
  16 pp.
Vision, A Quarterly Journal of Aesthetic Appreciation of Life, Spring Number, 1912. *Johnsville, Pa.*, 1912.
  Contains "The New Localism, an Illustrated Essay for Statesmen."
The Wedding of the Rose and the Lotus. [*Springfield*, 1912].
  3 pp.
The Soul of the City Receives the Gift of the Holy Spirit. [*Springfield*, 1913].
  20 pp. Wrappers.
A Letter for Your Wicked Ear Only. *Springfield*, 1921.
  28 pp. Expanded from broadside of earlier date.
I Know All This When Gypsy Fiddles Cry. *San Francisco*, 1922.

BROADSIDES

I Heard Immanuel Singing. [*n.p., n.d. (Springfield*, 1908?)].
Map of the Universe. [*Springfield*, 1909].
  Reissued *Spokane*, 1924.

The Moon Worms. [*Springfield*] 1910.

To the United States Senate. [*Springfield*, 1911].

Proclamation of the Gospel of Beauty. [*Springfield*, 1912].

A Letter for Your Wicked Private Ear Only. *Springfield* [1912?].
    Reissued as a pamphlet, 28 pp., 1921, and with revisions, as "The Kind of Visit I Like to Make."

The Golden Whales California. 1919.
    Place of publication unknown.

So Keep Going to the Sun. *Gulfport* [1922?].

When the Stuffed Prophets Quarrel. [*Spokane?*] 1924.

Our Little Cave-Man. *Spokane*, 1927.

Hamlet in Springfield. *Spokane*, 1927.

Under Spokane's Brocaded Sun. *Spokane* [*n.d.*].

The Virginians Are Coming Again. *Springfield*, 1928.

The Ezekiel's Chant. [*Springfield*, 1930].

BIOGRAPHICAL AND CRITICAL

Tramping with a Poet in the Rockies, by Stephen Graham. *New York*, 1922.

Vachel Lindsay: Adventurer, by A. E. Trombly. *Columbia, Mo.*, 1929.

Vachel Lindsay: A Poet in America, by Edgar Lee Masters. *New York*, 1935.

The Elementary English Review, May 1932.
    Vachel Lindsay Memorial Number.

"Daniel Jazz and Other Poems," *London*, 1920, is a selection of previously published poems. "Johnny Appleseed and Other Poems," *New York*, 1928, selected reprint in "Macmillan's Children's Classics."

Numerous Lindsay poems appeared in "A Miscellany of American Poetry," 1922, 1925 and 1927, published *New York* [1922] [1925] and [1927]. The last two have first edition statements on the copyright page. Lindsay contributed an introduction to "John Burroughs at Troutbeck," *Amenia, N. Y.*, 1926, 150 copies only in printed wrappers.

Jack (John Griffith) London
1876–1916

THE SON OF THE WOLF. *Boston,* 1900.
First binding is slate black with silver stamping. A trial binding, located at the Library of Congress, is bound in *rough* green cloth with the first state stamping. Later issued in *smooth* green cloth with pictorial stamping.

THE GOD OF HIS FATHERS AND OTHER STORIES. *New York,* 1901.

A DAUGHTER OF THE SNOWS. *Philadelphia,* 1902.

CHILDREN OF THE FROST. *New York,* 1902.

THE CRUISE OF THE DAZZLER. *New York,* 1902.
Published October, 1902 on the copyright page.

THE CALL OF THE WILD. *New York,* 1903.
First binding is vertically ribbed cloth.

THE KEMPTON-WACE LETTERS. *New York,* 1903.
Anon. With ANNA STRUNSKY.

THE PEOPLE OF THE ABYSS. *New York,* 1903.

THE FAITH OF MEN AND OTHER STORIES. *New York,* 1904.

THE SEA-WOLF. *New York,* 1904.
Lettering on spine in either gold or white; the former probably first.

WAR OF THE CLASSES. *New York,* 1905.
"The Tramp" [*New York,* 1904], wrappers, reprinted here.

THE GAME. *New York,* 1905.
First state does not have rubber stamped notice on copyright page.

TALES OF THE FISH PATROL. *New York,* 1905.
Two states of binding; no established priority.

MOON-FACE AND OTHER STORIES. *New York,* 1906.
An advance copy at the Library of Congress has no month of publication on the copyright page.

WHITE FANG. *New York,* 1906.
An advance copy has been noted dated 1905. See note at end of this list.

SCORN OF WOMEN. *New York,* 1906.
White spine.

LOVE OF LIFE AND OTHER STORIES. *New York*, 1907.
An advance copy has been noted dated 1906. See note at end of this list.

BEFORE ADAM. *New York*, 1907.
An advance copy has been noted dated 1906.

THE ROAD. *New York*, 1907.
Reported in various bindings; details not available.

THE IRON HEEL. *New York*, 1908.
An advance copy has been noted in printed wrappers, dated 1907, no month of publication on the copyright page.

MARTIN EDEN. *New York*, 1909.

REVOLUTION. *Chicago* [1909].
Wrappers. First edition has union seal and number 284 on front wrapper.

REVOLUTION AND OTHER ESSAYS. *New York*, 1910.
First binding is red. Includes preceding title.

LOST FACE. *New York*, 1910.

BURNING DAYLIGHT. *New York*, 1910.
Two states of binding noted. (a) with *Macmillan* at foot of spine; (b) with *The | Macmillan | Company*. Earliest known presentation copies are of the latter state.

THEFT. *New York*, 1910.
First state has white spine.

WHEN GOD LAUGHS AND OTHER STORIES. *New York*, 1911.

ADVENTURE. *New York*, 1911.

THE CRUISE OF THE SNARK. *New York*, 1911.
All examined copies of the first edition have the title page tipped in.

SOUTH SEA TALES. *New York*, 1911.

A SON OF THE SUN. *Garden City*, 1912.

THE HOUSE OF PRIDE AND OTHER TALES OF HAWAII. *New York*, 1912.

SMOKE BELLEW. *New York*, 1912.
Blue pictorial cloth. A copy has been noted in plain grey-blue cloth; status unknown.

THE NIGHT-BORN. *New York*, 1913.
Published, February, 1913 on the copyright page.

THE ABYSMAL BRUTE. *New York*, 1913.
Published, May, 1913 on the copyright page. First binding is stamped in yellow and dark green; later binding is stamped in black.

JOHN BARLEYCORN. *New York,* 1913.

THE VALLEY OF THE MOON. *New York,* 1913.

THE STRENGTH OF THE STRONG [AND OTHER PIECES]. *New York,* 1914.
Title story published in pamphlet form, *Chicago* [1911] with cover illustrations
by Groesbeck. This pamphlet has been noted in both wove paper and glazed paper
covers; no known priority.

THE MUTINY OF THE ELSINORE. *New York,* 1914.

THE SCARLET PLAGUE. *New York,* 1915.

THE STAR ROVER. *New York,* 1915.

THE LITTLE LADY OF THE BIG HOUSE. *New York,* 1916.

THE TURTLES OF TASMAN. *New York,* 1916.

THE ACORN-PLANTER. *New York,* 1916.
First state of binding has white spine.

THE HUMAN DRIFT. *New York,* 1917.

JERRY OF THE ISLANDS. *New York,* 1917.

MICHAEL, BROTHER OF JERRY. *New York,* 1917.

THE RED ONE. *New York,* 1918.
Boards.

ON THE MAKALOA MAT. *New York,* 1919.

HEARTS OF THREE. *New York,* 1920.
Published *London,* 1918.

DUTCH COURAGE AND OTHER STORIES. *New York,* 1922.

COMPLETE WORKS. *New York,* 1919-1920.

There have been several compilations of the Jack London stories, issued with titles
supplied by the publishers. Those which contain reprint material only have not
been included in the above list.

The Tramp. [*New York,* 1904].
Pamphlet.
The Apostate: A Parable of Child Labor. *Girard, Kansas,* 1906.
Argonaut Stories. *San Francisco,* 1906.
Contains "Moon Face." First edition does not contain press notices. Most of edi-
tion destroyed by San Francisco earthquake and fire.

Sea Stories. *New York,* 1907.
  Contains "To Repel Boarders."
The Spinners' Book of Fiction. *San Francisco* ₁1907₁.
  All London material contained is reprint.
A Book of Verses. ₁*Oakland*₁ 1910.
  Wrappers. Contains "The Worker and the Tramp."
The Red Hot Dollar, by Herman D. Umbstaetter. *Boston,* 1911.
  Preface by London.
Wonder of Woman: A Smoke Bellew Story. *New York* ₁1912₁.
  Wrappers.
The Cry for Justice. *Philadelphia,* 1915.
  Upton Sinclair, editor. Contribution by London.
What Do You Know About a Horse? by Francis A. Cox. *London,* 1916.
  Preface by London.
The Sea Sprite and the Shooting Star. ₁*n.p.,* 1932₁.
  4 pp. leaflet.

"The Scab," "A Dream of Debs," and "What Life Means to Me," are first separate
printings only.
  "The Good Soldier" is a pamphlet often attributed to Jack London. This, and the
printed denial, appeared in numerous forms and was printed almost (and probably)
simultaneously in several parts of the country.

BIOGRAPHICAL AND BIBLIOGRAPHICAL

Jack London: His Life and Literary Work. *New York* ₁1908₁.
  Wrappers. Also contains a contribution by Jack London.
Through the South Seas with Jack London, by Martin Johnson. *New York,* 1913.
Jack London, by Himself. *New York* ₁*ca.* 1913₁.
  Wrappers.
The Log of the Snark, by Charmian K. London (Mrs. Jack London). *New York,*
  1915.
Our Hawaii, by Charmian K. London. *New York,* 1917.
  Published: *London* ₁1918₁ as "Jack London and Hawaii," reissued, *New York,*
  1923, with "My Hawaiian Aloha." The latter published separately, *London*
  ₁1923₁.
The Book of Jack London, by Charmian K. London. *New York,* 1921.
  2 vols. With bibliography. English edition contains added material.
The Twenty-Fifth Man: The Strange Story of Ed Morrell, The Hero of Jack Lon-
  don's "Star Rover" ... *Montclair, N. J.* ₁1924₁.
The Mystery of Jack London, by Georgia Loring Bamford. *Oakland,* 1931.
Sailor on Horseback, by Irving Stone. ₁*Boston*₁ 1938.
  As advance publicity the publishers issued a four-page facsimile of a typed Jack
  London letter dated *Oakland, California, Jan. 31, 1900.* The letter is addressed
  to Houghton Mifflin in reply to their request for biographical information.

LONDON

Jack London and His Times, by Joan London. *New York,* 1939.
    First edition so indicated on the copyright page.
Footloose in Arcadia: A Personal Record ... , by Joseph Noll. *New York* [1940].

Note: "White Fang" and "Love of Life" occur with the title page tipped in on a
stub; all examined copies of the first edition are so distinguished. This may be ac
counted for by the fact that the copyright deposit copies are dated *one year earlie*
than published copies. It would seem that while the books were printed in the yea
preceding publication, issuance was delayed and a cancel title page with the correc
year of publication inserted.

Henry Wadsworth Longfellow
1807–1882

ELEMENTS OF FRENCH GRAMMAR. *Brunswick, Maine,* 1830.

Cloth, paper label. Five errata slips, in two forms, with or without folios. Anonymous.

FRENCH EXERCISES. *Brunswick,* 1830.

Anon. Cloth, paper label. 2 errata slips. Later in 1830 this and the preceding title were bound as a single volume, boards, cloth back, paper label. Combined with the above again, 1831, the first book to bear Longfellow's name on the title page.

NOVELAS ESPANOLAS. *Portland,* 1830.

Anon. Boards, cloth back or unlettered blue wrappers. First state has seven words in the last line of *A: Lector* leaf.

MANUEL DE PROVERBES DRAMATIQUES. *Brunswick,* 1830.

Anon. 156 pp. only. No table of contents or errata slips. Reissued, 1830, with 288 pp. The last page is misnumbered *188* and has seven added pieces not in the first edition. A second edition in 1832 omits two of the old pieces and adds eight others.

SYLLABUS DE LA GRAMMAIRE ITALIENNE. *Boston,* 1832.

First state has *la traite* for *le traite,* line 13 of advertisement. First state also has rule under *Bowdoin College* on title page. Various bindings.

SAGGI DE' NOVELLIERI ITALIANI. *Boston,* 1832.

Cloth, paper label.

COPLAS DE DON JORGE MANRIQUE. *Boston,* 1833.

Red and purple cloths noted. Paper label on spine.

OUTRE-MER: A PILGRIMAGE BEYOND THE SEA. *Boston,* 1833-1834.

No. 1 published by Hilliard, Gray and Company, 1833. Marbled paper wrappers, the earlier omitting the quotation from Maundeville which appears on the title page. No. 2 published by Lilly, Wait and Company, 1834. Blue or grey paper wrappers or boards, also in tan boards, cloth back, lettered in gilt on spine. Wrappered copies have quotation on front wrappers.

Also issued, two volumes in one, with no title page for part two, cloth, paper or leather label, reading *Part I.* Published in 1835 by Harper's, New York, in 2 vols., various cloths, all of vol. 2 being new material. Volume one contains either 18 pp. advertisements or 28 pp. (omitting pp. 12-13), in each case followed by two unnumbered leaves dated *May, 1835.*

London, 1835, edition, 2 vols., boards, cloth back, paper labels, prints "Old English Prose Romances," not in the American editions.

London, 1851, edition, is first book printing of "The Ladder of St. Augustine," and "The Phantom Ship."

HYPERION: A ROMANCE. *New York,* 1839.

2 vols. Boards, paper labels. It is highly probable that the earliest copies were issued with plain white end papers, several presentation or contemporaneously inscribed copies being so bound. The Longfellow family copies are with the white end papers while two copies have been noted with 1841 inscriptions that are with brown papers pasted over the white. Issued also, in black cloth with no imprint on spine, 2 vols. or 2 in 1; this is undoubtedly a remainder binding.

VOICES OF THE NIGHT. *Cambridge,* 1839.

First edition consisted of 900 copies. Boards, paper label. First state, p. 78, line 10, reads "His, Hector's arm; and his the might." Large paper edition issued 1840.

BALLADS AND OTHER POEMS. *Cambridge,* 1842.

Boards, paper label. First state has quotation marks at end of first line, p. 34. P. 88, last line, *teacher* spelled with lower case initial; later, capital initial. Large paper edition issued 1842. Copies have been noted with fore-edges untrimmed; status unknown.

"The Skeleton in Armor," *Boston,* 1877, reprinted from this title.

POEMS ON SLAVERY. *Cambridge,* 1842.

Wrappers. 31 pp. followed by 8 pp. advertisements. Large paper edition, 1842, has not been noted in original state. Second edition is so marked.

THE SPANISH STUDENT: A PLAY IN THREE ACTS. *Cambridge,* 1843.

Boards, paper label. Also large paper edition, 1843.

POEMS. *Philadelphia,* 1845.

Cloth or various types of leather binding. First printing in book form for 19 poems including "The Bridge."

THE BELFRY OF BRUGES. *Cambridge,* 1846.

Wrappers, with a few noted in boards. First edition consisted of 1,000 copies, the earliest state dated 1845 on the front cover, 1846 on title page. Large paper edition issued 1846, *Fourth Edition* on title page, *Third Edition* on spine label.

EVANGELINE: A TALE OF ACADIE. *Boston,* 1847.

Grey or yellow glazed boards, paper label; the former probably having priority. 4 pp. advertisements may be sewn in, tipped in, or absent, dated *October 1847.* Presentation copies have been noted in either grey boards or three quarter black morocco and cloth sides. Forged copies exist which either omit the printer's diamond-rule on the title page, have short pages at pp. 61-68 and elsewhere or both. Large paper edition published 1848. Argument persists as to the first state of p. 61 which at line 1 reads either *Long* or *Lo,* the final letters of the word being absent. Presentation copies exist in both states. It is claimed that the very first copies printed have the word in its entirety, a plausible contention in view of the fact that the *Lo* reading has been noted in second, third, and other subsequent editions.

KAVANAGH: A TALE. *Boston,* 1849.

First state omits word *end* at foot of p. 188; p. 173, last line, reads: *older than when they left. At the sight of him.* Second state reads: *older than when they left him there. To Cecilia.* Third state reads: p. 180, line 6, *less than* instead of *now only.* The word *end* now appears at the bottom of p. 188. Fourth state, p. 25, line 12, reads *Wainwright* instead of *Cartwright;* p. 96, line 14, *Arius* instead of *Arian;* p. 132, line 2, *golden* instead of *yellow.* A freak state has been noted that has all the first edition points, but the last signature has the third state points.

THE SEASIDE AND THE FIRESIDE. *Boston,* 1850.

Several types of cloth, or boards, paper label. Noted advertisements are October, November or December 1849. Longfellow's presentation copies have December advertisements. Large paper edition issued but believed to be later than trade edition; noted in grey or yellow glazed boards. "The Building of the Ship," *Boston,* 1870, reprinted from this volume.

THE GOLDEN LEGEND. *Boston,* 1851.

First printing consisted of 3,500 copies. Edition of 1854 is first to have supplementary notes.

THE SONG OF HIAWATHA. *Boston,* 1855.

Exists in four variant states. Variant 1: p. 27, line 9, ... *heron;* p. 32, line 11, *In the Moon* ... ; p. 39, line 11 (and elsewhere) ... *Wahonomin;* p. 96, line 7, *Dove* ... Variant 2: p. 27, same; p. 32, *To the melancholy* ...; p. 39 (and elsewhere) ... *Wahonowin;* p. 96, *Dove.* Variant 3: p. 27, same; pp. 32 and 39, same as Variant 2; p. 96, *Dived.* Variant 4: p. 27, ... *curlew;* otherwise as variant 3. The earliest printed copies have the *n* in *one* present, p. 279, line 5 from the bottom. Study of this last will show the letter present wearing away, and later replaced. Most copies with first state reading have *November 1855* advertisements but it is claimed that copies exist with *October 1855* advertisements, but no point of issue can be made of this feature.

American edition published November 10, 1855; English edition, cloth or wrappers, published November 1, 1855. In the earliest cloth copies the text varies.

PROSE WORKS. *Boston,* 1857.

2 vols. "Blue and Gold Series."

THE COURTSHIP OF MILES STANDISH AND OTHER POEMS. *Boston,* 1858.

Copies have been noted with or without a publisher's slip advertising Scott's "Waverley Novels" tipped in at the front; this same slip has been noted, however, in editions of this book and other titles published during 1859. It has been claimed that the first edition exists in two states as to the reading of line 3, p. 124; that in the first state it reads *treacherous* and not *ruddy.* Thus far no copy of the 1858 edition has appeared with the revised reading.

Issued with 12 pp. advertisements at the back dated October 1858. Also with September advertisements listing a *new poem* as *in press.*

THE NEW ENGLAND TRAGEDY. *Boston*, 1860.
Prose. Privately printed. Two copies known.

TALES OF A WAYSIDE INN. *Boston*, 1863.
Earliest state of advertisements, p. 11, *nearly ready* for this title. Several types of cloth, top edges gilt.

NOËL. *Cambridge*, 1864.
In French. Privately printed. 8 pp. unbound. An English translation by J. E. Norcross, 50 copies only, privately printed pamphlet, *Philadelphia*, 1867.

THE DIVINE COMEDY OF DANTE ALIGHIERI. *Boston*, 1865-66-67.
3 vols. Ten sets only bound in three-quarter turkey-red morocco; some with top edges uncut. No notes, and with one Longfellow sonnet in each volume; other differences (as compared with trade edition described below) too numerous to state here. Published edition has all three volumes dated 1867 and contains about 100 pp. notes in each volume together with two sonnets.

HOUSEHOLD POEMS. *Boston*, 1865.
Cloth or wrappers.

FLOWER-DE-LUCE. *Boston*, 1867.

THE NEW ENGLAND TRAGEDIES. [*Cambridge*] 1868.
Privately printed. Half green morocco, gilt top. Anon. Part 1 is titled "Wenlock Christison." Only 10 copies printed. In the published state issued by Ticknor and Fields, *Boston*, 1868, Part 1 is titled "John Endicott." Later states of the published edition have two unfilled diamonds under the monogram on the spine and defective type, notably at p. 12, line 14 and p. 71.

THE ALARM-BELL OF ATRI. *Boston*, 1871.
4 pp. leaflet.

THE DIVINE TRAGEDY. *Boston*, 1871.
12mo small type edition preceded 8vo edition.

THREE BOOKS OF SONG. *Boston*, 1872.
Contains Part II, "Tales of a Wayside Inn."

CHRISTUS: A MYSTERY. *Boston*, 1872.
3 vols. Vol. 2, p. 171, line 20, reads *set sail*. Contains "The Divine Tragedy," "The Golden Legend," "The New England Tragedies," and is first printing for the four introductory, intercalary and terminal poems.

AFTERMATH. *Boston*, 1873.
Part third of "Tales of a Wayside Inn."

THE HANGING OF THE CRANE. *Boston*, 1874.
Privately issued, only 3 copies known. Published edition, 1875, p. 37, line 5, reads in first state: *A Princess from the Fairy Tales*. All edges gilt.

THE MASQUE OF PANDORA AND OTHER POEMS. *Boston,* 1875.
First page of contents, one line from last, reads: *Cadenabria;* later, *Cadenabbia.*

KERÁMOS. *[Cambridge,* 1877].
Leaflet. Privately printed. 6 copies only.

KERÁMOS AND OTHER POEMS. *Boston,* 1878.
Houghton, Osgood & Co at base of spine.

THE EARLY POEMS OF HENRY WADSWORTH LONGFELLOW. *London,* 1878.
First book printing for four poems.

BAYARD TAYLOR. *[Cambridge,* 1879].
2 leaves.

FROM MY ARM-CHAIR. *[Cambridge,* 1879].
Leaflet, 2 leaves. Two states noted, the earliest reading *are wrought,* next to the last stanza.

ULTIMA THULE. *Boston,* 1880.
Various colors of cloth. Also in limp cloth. English edition preceded the American.

IN THE HARBOR: ULTIMA THULE—PART II. *Boston,* 1882.

MICHAEL ANGELO. *London,* 1882-3.
3 parts. Part 1, 1882; parts 2 and 3, 1883. A single copy of part 2 has been noted with 1882 date. Published edition, 1884.

THERE WAS A LITTLE GIRL. *New York* [1883].
Pirated and here offered in a garbled version. Another version previously published in "The Home Life of Henry Wadsworth Longfellow," by Blanche Roosevelt Tucker-Macchetta, *New York,* 1882. A still different version appeared anonymously in *The Balloon Post,* Boston, April 1871, and was copied therefrom, still anonymous, in an undated pamphlet issued by a cosmetic manufacturer, in New York, not before January, 1877.

THE COMPLETE WORKS OF HENRY WADSWORTH LONGFELLOW. *Boston,* 1886.
7 vols. Also 100 large paper sets.

COMPLETE POETICAL AND PROSE WORKS. *Boston,* 1886.
11 vols. "Riverside Edition." Also 500 large paper sets.

FINAL MEMORIALS. *Boston,* 1887.
Several poems here first printed. Also 300 large paper copies, untrimmed, in boards.

The following are representative of the secondary Longfellow items. A more complete listing may be found in the Livingston bibliography (*see below*) and the

"Stephen H. Wakeman Collection of Books of Nineteenth Century American Writers ..." *New York,* 1924.

Boston Prize Poems. *Boston,* 1824.
  Printed or plain boards. Contain Longfellow's anonymous contribution "Ode II."
Miscellaneous Poems, Selected from the United States Literary Gazette. *Boston,* 1826.
  Half cloth, board sides, paper label.
Le Ministre de Wakefield. *Boston,* 1831.
  Edited. Boards, cloth back, paper label.
The Token.
  Volumes for 1832, 1833, 1834, 1835 and 1842 contain first printings of Longfellow contributions.
The Boston Book.
  Editions of 1836, 1841, and 1850 contain Longfellow contributions, the edition of 1841, containing the first book appearance of "The Wreck of the Hesperus."
The Poets of America: Second Volume of the Series. *New York,* 1842.
  John Keese, editor. Contains "The Village Blacksmith," later published in "Ballads and Other Poems."
The Poets and Poetry of Europe. *Philadelphia,* 1845.
  Edited and with voluminous notes by Longfellow. First printing of some thirty translations by him. First state has imprint of *Cambridge, Metcalf & Co., etc.;* second state has imprint of *T. K. & P. G. Collins, Philadelphia.* A second edition, 1871, contains a supplement of 140 pages by Longfellow and ten additional translations. The 1871 edition appears in two states, one with a portrait frontispiece of Longfellow, the other with a head of Goethe, and with other differences. Priority undetermined.
The Waif: A Collection of Poems. *Cambridge,* 1845.
  Edited and with a proem, "The Day Is Done," later in "Poems," *Philadelphia,* 1845. "The Waif" appears in various types of cloth, board bindings, and yellow or illuminated wrappers. When found with paper label on spine, label must not have Longfellow's name present.
The Estray: A Collection of Poems. *Boston,* 1847.
  Edited and with a proem by Longfellow. In illuminated wrappers, yellow glazed boards, with paper label on spine; also in cloth.
Poems of Places, 1876-1879.
  31 vols. Edited by Longfellow. Twenty poems are here first printed.
Poems of the "Old South," by Henry. Wadsworth Longfellow [and others]. *Boston,* 1877.
  First for "A Ballad of the French Fleet" and for all other poems contained.
Autograph Birthday Book. *Boston* [1881].
  Amanda B. Harris, editor. Contribution by Longfellow.
"On Account of Illness ..." *Cambridge* [1882].
  A printed notice written by Longfellow in reply to correspondents.
Origin and Growth of the Languages of Southern Europe, etc. *Brunswick,* 1907.
  250 copies only.

Longfellow's Boyhood Poems. *Saratoga Springs, 1925.*
  By George Thomas Little. 500 copies only. Contains 11 juvenile poems, reprinted for the most part from the Portland, Maine, newspapers.
The Leap of Roushan Beg. *New York, 1931.*
  First separate printing. 500 copies only, printed by Rudge, with facsimile of original MS.

BIOGRAPHICAL AND BIBLIOGRAPHICAL WORKS

Life and Works of Henry W. Longfellow, by D. Gilbert Dexter. *Cambridge, 1882.*
  Wrappers or cloth.
The Home Life of Henry W. Longfellow, by Blanche Roosevelt Tucker-Macchetta. *New York, 1882.*
Henry Wadsworth Longfellow: A Biographical Sketch, by Francis H. Underwood. *Boston, 1882.*
Henry Wadsworth Longfellow, by W. Sloane Kennedy. *Cambridge, 1882.*
Henry Wadsworth Longfellow ... by George Lowell Austin. *Boston, 1883.*
The Longfellow Collectors' Hand-Book, by W. E. Benjamin. *New York, 1885.*
  Boards.
Life of Henry Wadsworth Longfellow, by Samuel Longfellow. *Boston, 1886.*
  2 vols. Also 300 large paper copies, untrimmed.
Life of Henry Wadsworth Longfellow, by Eric S. Robertson. *London, 1887.*
  In the "Great Writers Series."
Final Memorials of Longfellow, by Samuel Longfellow. *Boston, 1887.*
  Also 300 large paper copies in boards, paper label.
American Men of Letters, Henry Wadsworth Longfellow, by Thomas Wentworth Higginson. *Boston, 1902.*
A Bibliography of the First Editions in Book Form of the Writings of H. W. Longfellow, by L. S. Livingston. *New York, 1908.*
  550 copies only.
New Light on Longfellow, by James Taft Hatfield. *Boston, 1933.*
Literary Pioneers, by Orie W. Long. *Cambridge, 1935.*
  Six Americans fully discussed, one of them Longfellow, who went early to Germany for their education.
Young Longfellow (1807-1843), by Lawrance Thompson. *New York, 1938.*
  Definitive for the period covered.
Uncle Sam Ward and His Circle, by Maud Howe Elliot. *New York, 1938.*
  First printing of about 50 biographical letters from Longfellow to Ward.

Amy Lowell

1874–1925

DREAM DROPS; or, STORIES FROM FAIRY LAND. *Boston* [1887].
Anonymous. "By A Dreamer." 250 copies only, cloth or wrappers.

A DOME OF MANY-COLORED GLASS. *Boston, 1912.*
Boards, cloth back, paper labels.

SWORD BLADES AND POPPY SEED. *New York, 1914.*
Boards, cloth back, paper labels.

SIX FRENCH POETS. *New York, 1915.*
Boards, cloth back, paper labels.

MEN, WOMEN AND GHOSTS. *New York, 1916.*
Boards, cloth back, paper labels.

TENDENCIES IN MODERN AMERICAN POETRY. *New York, 1917.*

CAN GRANDE'S CASTLE. *New York, 1918.*
Boards, cloth back, paper labels.

PICTURES OF THE FLOATING WORLD. *New York, 1919.*
Boards, cloth back, paper labels.

LEGENDS. *Boston, 1921.*
Boards, cloth back, paper labels.

A CRITICAL FABLE. *Boston, 1922.*
Wrappers. Anonymous. "By A Poker of Fun."

WHAT'S O'CLOCK. *Boston, 1925.*
Boards, cloth back, paper labels.

JOHN KEATS. *Boston, 1925.*
2 vols.

EAST WIND. *Boston, 1926.*
Boards, cloth back, paper labels.

BALLADS FOR SALE. *Boston, 1927.*
Boards, cloth back, paper labels.

THE MADONNA OF CARTHAGENA. [*n.p.*] 1927.
Wrappers. 50 copies only.

FOOL O' THE MOON. [*Austin, Texas, 1927*].
Wrappers. 41 copies only.

POETRY AND POETS: ESSAYS. *Boston*, 1930.
Boards, cloth back, paper labels.

Weeping Pierrot and Laughing Pierrot: Pierrot Qui Pleure et Pierrot Qui Rit. *Boston* [1914].
Translated from the French of Edmond Rostand by Amy Lowell. Set to music and published by the Boston Music Company.

Some Imagist Poets. *Boston*, 1915.
Wrappers. Contains six poems and a prose article by Amy Lowell

Diaries of Court Ladies of Old Japan. *Boston*, 1920.
Translated by Annie Shepley Amori and Kochi Doi. Foreword by Amy Lowell.

A Miscellany of American Poetry, 1920. *New York*, 1920.
Contributions by Lowell.

Fir-Flower Tablets. *Boston*, 1921.
Translations from the Chinese. By Florence Ayscough. English versions by Amy Lowell.

A Miscellany of American Poetry, 1922. *New York* [1922].
Contributions by Lowell.

A Miscellany of American Poetry, 1925. *New York* [1925].
Contributions by Lowell. First edition so stated.

The Work of Stephen Crane. *New York* [1925-26].
12 vols. Introduction to vol. 6 by Amy Lowell.

Percy Mackaye: A Symposium on His Fiftieth Birthday. *Hanover, N. H.*, 1928.
Privately printed. 300 copies only. Foreword by Amy Lowell.

Selected Poems. *Boston*, 1928.
John Livingston Lowes, editor.

Designed For Reading. *New York*, 1934.
Contribution.

BIOGRAPHICAL — BIBLIOGRAPHICAL

Amy Lowell, by W. Bryher. *London*, 1918.
Amy Lowell, by Royall H. Snow. [*n.p.*, 1921].
Amy Lowell, by Clement Wood. *New York*, 1926.
Amy Lowell: A Mosaic, by George H. Sargent. *New York*, 1926.
Boards. 450 copies only.
Amy Lowell: A Chronicle, With Extracts From Her Correspondence, by S. Foster Damon. *Boston*, 1935.

331

James Russell Lowell

1819–1891

CLASS POEM. [*Cambridge*] 1838.
Anonymous. Wrappers.

A YEAR'S LIFE. *Boston,* 1841.
Some copies, not necessarily the first issued, noted with an errata slip. Boards, paper label.

POEMS. *Cambridge,* 1844.
Brown boards, paper label. Also a few copies on large paper.

CONVERSATIONS ON SOME OF THE OLD POETS. *Cambridge,* 1845.
Wrappers or decorated boards. A copy has been noted in gold-stamped blue cloth and one in red watered silk. Erratum, p. 127, line 10. Revised and reissued, *Cambridge,* 1846. Reissued, 1893, with 50 pp. reprinted from *The Pioneer, q.v.,* 1843.

POEMS: SECOND SERIES. *Cambridge,* 1848.
Boards. Large paper state in cloth. It has been stated that small paper copies bound in white cloth were for purposes of presentation but at least one copy in the board binding is known to exist with a presentation inscription.

A FABLE FOR CRITICS, etc. *New York* [18]48.
Must not have *A Vocal and Musical Medley* on the title page. In the first state pp. 63 and 64 are misnumbered; second state: p. 64 misnumbered; third state: p. 63 misnumbered; fourth state: pagination at pp. 63-64 in correct order. Anonymous. Issued cloth, or boards with paper label.

THE BIGLOW PAPERS. *Cambridge,* 1848.
Issued also with *New York and Cambridge* and *Cambridge and London* imprints. *Homer Wilbur,* pseudonym. 12 pp. advertisements written by Lowell preceding text.

THE VISION OF SIR LAUNFAL. *Cambridge,* 1848.
Printed glazed yellow boards. Copies have been noted in brown boards, status undetermined. All examined copies have *Galabad* for *Galahad* in the note opposite the copyright notice, lines 10 and 12.

POEMS. *Boston,* 1849.
2 vols. With additional poems here first collected. Grey boards, brown cloth and in various "gift" bindings.

IL PESCEBALLO. [*Cambridge,* 1862].
In Italian by Prof. F. J. Child and with English translation by Lowell. First state has four signatures and without date or wrappers, printed on wove paper. At p. 4, line 4, misprinted *piacier.* P. 8, line 1, *pocco* instead of *poco.*

THE BIGLOW PAPERS: SECOND SERIES. *London, 1862.*

Part 1 comes in two states, the first has gray-green wrappers and no price at bottom; second state has pink wrappers (like parts 2 and 3) and *Price One Shilling* at bottom. Parts 2 and 3 have *Originally Published in the Atlantic Monthly* at top and price at bottom. Reissued, *London, 1864*, with 13 added pages. First state of 1864 edition has imprint at pp. 52 and 90. Third edition, *London, 1865*, green or blue wrappers, with added "paper," "Mr. Hosea Biglow to the Editor of the Atlantic Monthly," at pp. 134-141. American edition, *Boston, 1867*, first state measures about ⅞" across top of covers, but less than 1"; later states measure a full inch or more. Also 12 large paper copies.

FIRESIDE TRAVELS. *Boston, 1864.*

ODE RECITED AT THE COMMEMORATION OF THE LIVING AND DEAD SOLDIERS OF HARVARD UNIVERSITY. *Cambridge, 1865.*

Privately printed. 50 numbered copies only. Grey boards, paper label on side.

UNDER THE WILLOWS AND OTHER POEMS. *Boston, 1869.*

Errata slip at p. 286. First word, p. 224, line 7, *Thy.*

POEMS. *Boston, 1869.*

2 vols.

THE CATHEDRAL. *Boston, 1870.*

AMONG MY BOOKS. *Boston, 1870.*

MY STUDY WINDOWS. *Boston, 1871.*

First state has FO monogram on spine.

AMONG MY BOOKS: SECOND SERIES. *Boston, 1876.*

Earliest state has 1875 copyright date; *Belles-Letters* on title page under author's name.

THREE MEMORIAL POEMS. *Boston, 1877.*

ON DEMOCRACY. *Birmingham* [1884].

Wrappers. Also a few copies printed on one side of the leaf only. Privately printed for members of The Birmingham and Midland Institute. First state does not have *Price Sixpence* at top of first leaf. Published edition has the price.

DEMOCRACY AND OTHER ADDRESSES. *Boston, 1887.*

Blue cloth, paper label, edges untrimmed.

POLITICAL ESSAYS. *Boston, 1888.*

In addition to the regular trade edition there were some copies (said to be but 75) bound in blue cloth, all edges untrimmed and with paper label on the spine stating *First Edition.*

HEARTSEASE AND RUE. *Boston, 1888.*

Also 250 copies, untrimmed, paper label. First state omits last line, p. 63, but thus far copies with this feature have been noted only in unlettered wrapper binding. Boards, cloth back.

J. R. LOWELL

WRITINGS. *Boston,* 1890-92.
Riverside edition. 12 vols. Large paper edition, 11 volumes (12 in 11). First 10 volumes issued 1890; vol. 11 1891; vol. 12 1892. Later the last two were issued as one.

LAST LITERARY ESSAYS AND ADDRESSES. *Cambridge,* 1891.
300 large paper copies only, numbered. Trade edition, 1892.

THE OLD ENGLISH DRAMATISTS. *Cambridge,* 1892.
Also 300 large paper copies, numbered.

AMERICAN IDEAS FOR ENGLISH READERS. *Boston* [1892].
An unauthorized publication of speeches made in England.

LETTERS. *New York,* 1894.
2 vols. Charles Eliot Norton, editor.

LAST POEMS. *Boston,* 1895.

THE POWER OF SOUND. *New York,* 1896.
Privately printed, 75 copies only, of which 25 were on Japan vellum; balance on handmade paper.

LECTURES ON ENGLISH POETS. *Cleveland,* 1897.
224 copies only printed for members of the Rowfant Club. Cloth, leather back.

ANTI-SLAVERY PAPERS. *Boston,* 1902.
500 numbered copies only. Boards, paper label.

EARLY PROSE WRITINGS. *London* [1902].
Edward Everett Hale, editor. Boards.

FOUR POEMS. *Hingham,* 1906.
Boards. 50 numbered copies only, printed for private distribution.

NEW LETTERS OF JAMES RUSSELL LOWELL. *New York,* 1932.
M. A. De Wolfe Howe, editor.

The following list is representative of the secondary Lowell items. For a more complete list the collector is referred to the bibliographies listed at the end of this section.

Harvardiana. *Cambridge,* 1838.
Vol. 4 contains 24 Lowell contributions; 11 in prose.
Valedictory Exercises of the Senior Class of 1838. [*Cambridge?* 1838].
Broadside.
The Pioneer. *Boston,* 1843.
Lowell edited and contributed to the three numbers printed, January, February and March. See: "Conversations ..." 1845.
Lines on the Reading of the Capture of Certain Fugitive Slaves. *Boston,* 1845.

The American Anti-Slavery Almanac for 1847. *New York* [1846].
  First printing for any of the "Biglow Papers."
The Liberty Bell, by Friends of Freedom. *Boston*, 1847.
  Wrappers. Contains Lowell's "Extreme Unction."
Water Celebration. *Boston*, October 25, 1848.
  Broadside. Contains a poem by Lowell. This poem also appears in a pamphlet
  report of the celebration, *Boston*, 1848.
Memory and Hope. *Boston*, 1851.
  First book printing for Lowell's "The First Snowfall."
Thalatta: A Book for the Sea-Side. *Boston*, 1853.
  Contributions by Lowell.
The Poetical Works of William Wordsworth. *Boston*, 1854.
  7 vols. Contains a brief biography of Wordsworth by Lowell.
The Poetical Works of John Keats. *Boston*, 1854.
  Contains a memoir of Keats by Lowell.
The Poetical Works of John Donne. *Boston*, 1855.
  Edited by Lowell. Also a 2 volume edition, *New York*, 1895, limited to 383 copies
  for members of the Grolier Club.
The Poetical Works of Percy Bysshe Shelley. *Boston*, 1855.
  3 vols. Contains a memoir of Shelley by Lowell. In the first state the memoir is
  unsigned.
The Poems of Maria Lowell. *Cambridge*, 1855.
  50 copies only privately printed. Edited by Lowell.
Poetical Works of Andrew Marvell. *Boston*, 1857.
  Edited by Lowell.
To Mr. John Bartlett Who Sent Me a Seven Pound Trout. *Elmwood*, 1858.
  Sq. 12mo. 4 pp. leaflet.
The Victoria Regina: A Volume of Original Contributions in Poetry and Prose.
  London, 1861.
  Adelaide A. Proctor, editor. Contains "The Fatal Curiosity" by Lowell.
Mason and Slidell: A Yankee Idyll. [*Boston*, 1862].
  Anonymous.
Only Once: Original Papers by Various Contributors. *New York*, 1862.
  Contribution by Lowell.
The President's Policy. [*Philadelphia*, 1864].
  First state has *crisises* for *crises* first line of text.
Autograph Leaves of Our Country's Authors. [*Baltimore*, 1864].
  First complete printing of "The Courtin'."
The Spirit of the Fair. *New York*, 1864.
  17 numbers. Wrappers. Contributions by Lowell.
The Courtin'. *Boston*, 1874.
  Illustrated by Winslow Homer. First separate edition, reprinted from "The
  Biglow Papers: Second Series."
A Masque of Poets. *Boston*, 1878.
  Contains "My Heart, I Cannot Still It" and "Red Tape" by Lowell. For further
  description of this item see under *Alcott*.

Death of President Garfield ... *London*, 1881.
  6 copies only printed on vellum.
A Record of the 250th Anniversary ... Harvard College. *Cambridge*, 1887.
  Contains two speeches by Lowell.
The Independent in Politics, etc. *New York*, 1888.
  In "Questions of the Day" series, No. XLVIII.
The Forty-Sixth Birthday of Sidney Lanier. *Baltimore*, 1888.
  Wrappers. Contains a letter.
Address Before the Modern Language Association of America. [Baltimore?] 1889
The Complete Angler, by Izaak Walton. *Boston*, 1889.
  2 vols. Introduction by Lowell. 500 numbered copies only.
Areopagitica, by John Milton. *New York*, 1890.
  Privately issued, 325 copies only, for members of the Grolier Club. Introduction
  by Lowell.
My Brook. *New York*, 1890.
  Issued as a supplement to *The New York Ledger*, December 13, 1890.
Impressions of Spain. *Boston*, 1899.
  Compiled by Joseph B. Gilder.

BIOGRAPHICAL AND BIBLIOGRAPHICAL WORKS

James Russell Lowell and His Friends, by Edward Everett Hale. *Boston*, 1899.
James Russell Lowell, by Horace E. Scudder. *Cambridge*, 1901.
  2 vols. Also 300 large paper copies.
James Russell Lowell: His Life and Work, by Ferris Greenslet. *Boston*, 1905.
  Also 160 copies, totally untrimmed, cloth, paper label.
Bibliography of James Russell Lowell, by George Willis Cooke. *Boston*, 1906.
  530 copies only.
Bibliography of ... James Russell Lowell, From the Collection of ... J. C. Chamberlain
  ... by Luther S. Livingston. *New York*, 1914.
The Stephen H. Wakeman Collection of Books of Nineteenth Century American
  Writers ... *New York* [1924].
  Issued as a sales catalog by The American Art Association. Facsimile edition, pub-
  lished *New York* [1930?]. Contains numerous listings of Lowell items.

George Barr McCutcheon

1866–1928

GRAUSTARK. *Chicago, 1901.*
Noble for *Lorry*, p. 150, line 6.

CASTLE CRANEYCROW. *Chicago, 1902.*
Usually found in green cloth, pictorially stamped in green, yellow and white. The author's personal copy is so bound. A copy, probably trial binding, is red cloth stamped in green and gold.

BREWSTER'S MILLIONS. *Chicago, 1903.*
Richard Greaves, *pseud.* In either smooth or rough red cloth with no known priority.

THE SHERRODS. *New York, 1903.*

BEVERLY OF GRAUSTARK. *New York, 1904.*
With or without the *O* in *Harrison* (on the title page) present; no known priority.

THE DAY OF THE DOG. *New York, 1904.*
Published March, 1904 on the copyright page. Reissued, *New York,* 1916, with added material.

THE PURPLE PARASOL. *New York, 1905.*
Published April, 1905 on the copyright page.

NEDRA. *New York, 1905.*

JANE CABLE. *New York, 1906.*

COWARDICE COURT. *New York, 1906.*
First state of binding has *Coward | Ice* on spine; later: *Cowardice.*

THE FLYERS. *New York, 1907.*
Published March, 1907 on the copyright page.

THE DAUGHTER OF ANDERSON CROW. *New York, 1907.*

THE HUSBANDS OF EDITH. *New York, 1908.*

THE MAN FROM BRODNEY'S. *New York, 1908.*
Published September, 1908 on copyright page.

THE ALTERNATIVE. *New York, 1909.*
Published, April, 1909 on the copyright page.

TRUXTON KING. *New York, 1909.*

THE BUTTERFLY MAN. *New York*, 1910.
  Published, May, 1910 on the copyright page.

THE ROSE IN THE RING. *New York*, 1910.

WHAT'S-HIS-NAME. *New York*, 1911.

MARY MIDTHORNE. *New York*, 1911.

HER WEIGHT IN GOLD. *Indianapolis* [1911].
  Privately printed for members of the Indiana Society of Chicago. Trade edition,
  New York, 1912. Reissued, *New York*, 1914, with added material.

THE HOLLOW OF HER HAND. *New York*, 1912.
  Also 25 large paper copies, numbered and signed.

A FOOL AND HIS MONEY. *New York*, 1913.
  Also 50 large paper copies, numbered and signed.

BLACK IS WHITE. *New York*, 1914.

THE PRINCE OF GRAUSTARK. *New York*, 1914.
  Published, September, 1914 on copyright page. Also 40 large paper copies,
  numbered and signed and an advance issue in wrappers.

MR. BINGLE. *New York*, 1915.

FROM THE HOUSETOPS. *New York*, 1916.

THE LIGHT THAT LIES. *New York*, 1916.

GREEN FANCY. *New York*, 1917.

SHOT WITH CRIMSON. *New York*, 1918.

THE CITY OF MASKS. *New York*, 1918.

SHERRY. *New York*, 1919.

ANDERSON CROW, DETECTIVE. *New York*, 1920.

WEST WIND DRIFT. *New York*, 1920.

QUILL'S WINDOW. *New York*, 1921.

YOLLOP. *New York*, 1922.

VIOLA GWYN. *New York*, 1922.
  Also 50 large paper copies, numbered and signed.

OLIVER OCTOBER. *New York*, 1923.

EAST OF THE SETTING SUN. *New York*, 1924.

ROMEO IN MOON VILLAGE. *New York*, 1925.

KINDLING AND ASHES. *New York*, 1926.
  Also 25 large paper copies, numbered.

THE INN OF THE HAWK AND RAVEN. *New York*, 1927.

BLADES. *New York*, 1928.

THE MERIVALES. *New York*, 1929.

BOOKS ONCE WERE MEN. *New York*, 1931.
  1,000 copies only.

Brood House: A Play in Four Acts. *New York*, 1910.
  Privately printed. 75 copies only.
The Morris Book Shop. *Chicago*, 1912.
  Wrappers. Contribution.
My Pictures. [*n.p.*] 1916.
  15 numbered copies only.
One Score and Ten: A Comedy in Four Acts. *New York*, 1919.
  Privately printed. 30 copies only.
Three Yarns. [*Chicago*, 1924].
  Contains "Anthony, The Joker," by McCutcheon.
The Renowned Collection of First Editions of Charles Dickens and William Make-
  peace Thackeray Formed by George Barr McCutcheon. *New York* [1931].
  Facsimile edition of sales catalog issued by American Art Association-Anderson
  Galleries, part 1, 1925; part 2, 1926.

William (Morley Punshon) McFee
1881–

LETTERS FROM AN OCEAN TRAMP. *London,* 1908.
First state has *Cassell & Co.* at foot of spine. Reissued as "An Ocean Tramp," *Garden City,* 1921, with new preface.

ALIENS. *London,* 1914.
First state of the advertisements dated 1915. First American edition, *New York,* 1916, printed in England with the *Doubleday, Page* imprint.

CASUALS OF THE SEA. *London,* 1916.
First American edition printed in England with Doubleday imprint.

A PORT SAID MISCELLANY. *Boston* [1918].
Wrappers. No. 6 in "The Atlantic Readings" series. The first state carries a list of seven titles on the back cover; later states have extended lists.

CAPTAIN MACEDOINE'S DAUGHTER. *Garden City,* 1920.
First state has yellow stamping on blue cloth cover. Later issues stamped with gold. On the spine in the first state there is a scroll-flourish decoration; later replaced by a group of four horizontal rules.

A SIX-HOUR SHIFT. *Garden City,* 1920.
377 copies only, numbered and signed. Boards.

HARBOURS OF MEMORY. *Garden City,* 1921.
First edition so stated on copyright page.

AN OCEAN TRAMP. *Garden City,* 1921.
See: "Letters From an Ocean Tramp," 1908.

AN ENGINEER'S NOTE BOOK. *New York,* 1921.
First state has *By William McFee* on front wrapper. Second state has redrawn cover design, is relettered and omits the word *By.* The illustration used in the first state later used for dust-jacket and spine label of "Swallowing the Anchor."

COMMAND. *Garden City,* 1922.
Also 377 copies, numbered and signed. Noted in both smooth and ribbed cloths; no known priority. First edition so indicated on the copyright page.

THE GATES OF THE CARIBBEAN. [*n.p.* 1922].
Issued by the United Fruit Co. First state does not have *Printed in the U. S. A.* on the back cover, no dotted sailing route on map. Wrappers.

RACE. *Garden City,* 1924.
Also 100 copies in advance of publication for presentation purposes. First edition so stated on copyright page.

SWALLOWING THE ANCHOR. *Garden City*, 1925.
First edition so stated on copyright page. Boards, cloth back, paper labels. Extended material contained in "An Engineer's Note Book."

SUNLIGHT IN NEW GRANADA. *Garden City*, 1925.
First edition so stated on the copyright page.

THE LIFE OF SIR MARTIN FROBISHER. *New York*, 1928.
First edition so indicated on the copyright page.

PILGRIMS OF ADVERSITY. *Garden City*, 1928.
First edition so stated on copyright page. Two types of paper noted; it is probable that the earliest printed copies (if not the first published) have perfect type at p. 43, last line.

SAILORS OF FORTUNE. *Garden City*, 1929.
First edition so stated on copyright page.

NORTH OF SUEZ. *Garden City*, 1930.
Also 350 large paper copies, signed. First edition so stated on the copyright page.

BORN TO BE HANGED. *Gaylordsville*, 1930.
91 signed copies only. Boards, cloth back, paper label.

THE HARBOURMASTER. *Garden City*, 1932.
First edition so stated on copyright page. Also 377 de luxe copies dated 1931.

THE REFLECTIONS OF MARSYAS. *Gaylordsville*, 1933.
300 numbered copies only, signed at p. 43 by the author. Boards paper label.

NO CASTLE IN SPAIN. *Garden City*, 1933.
First edition so stated on copyright page.

MORE HARBOURS OF MEMORY. *Garden City*, 1934.
First edition so stated on copyright page.

THE BEACHCOMBER. *Garden City*, 1935.
First edition so stated on copyright page.

SAILOR'S WISDOM. *London* [1935].

SAILOR'S BANE. *Philadelphia*, 1936.
250 numbered copies only.

DERELICTS. *Garden City*, 1938.
First edition so indicated on the copyright page.

WATCH BELOW. *New York* [1940].
First edition so indicated on the copyright page. Also 250 numbered copies, signed.

The following does not purport to be a complete list of the minor McFee items; a fuller listing is given in the bibliographies below.

Iron Men and Wooden Ships. *New York,* 1920.
　Frank Shay, editor. Contains McFee's "Sea Library."
Spindrift, by Milton Raison. *New York* (1922).
　Introduction.
Lord Jim, by Joseph Conrad. *Garden City,* 1922.
　Introduction.
Ocean Echoes, by Arthur Mason. *New York,* 1922.
　Introduction.
Black'erchief Dick, by Margery Allingham. *New York,* 1923.
　Introduction.
Songs of the Sea and Sailors' Chanteys. *Boston,* 1924.
　Robert Frothingham, editor. Contributions by McFee.
Almayer's Folly, by Joseph Conrad. *New York,* 1925.
　Introduction.
The Purple Land, by W. H. Hudson. *New York,* 1926.
　Introduction.
Tom Cringle's Log, by Michael Scott. *New York,* 1927.
　Introduction.
Innocents Aloft, by Henry Justin Smith. *Chicago,* 1927.
　Introduction.
Deep Waters. *New York,* 1928.
　Charles W. Gray, editor. Contribution by McFee.
"Harold the Webbed," by Alfred Aloysius (Trader) Horn. *London* [1928].
　Also, *New York,* 1928.
　Introduction.
Moby-Dick, by Herman Melville. *Philadelphia* [1931].
　Introduction.
All Sail Set: A Romance of the "Flying Cloud," by Armstrong Sperry. *Philadelphia*
　[1935].
　Introduction.
The American Historical Scene as Depicted by Stanley Arthurs. *Philadelphia,* 1935.
　Contribution by McFee, "The Clermont."
Full and By, by David Stanley Livingston. *New York* [1936].
　First edition so stated on copyright page. Introduction by McFee.
Breaking Into Print. *New York,* 1937.
　Elmer Adler, editor. Contribution.
Ring Lardner's Best Stories. *Garden City* [1938].
The Bedside Esquire. *New York* [1940].
　Arnold Gingrich, editor. Contribution.

BIOGRAPHICAL AND BIBLIOGRAPHICAL

William McFee: A Note on His Life and Works. Containing a Complete Chronological Bibliography, by Harry E. Maule. *Garden City* [1923].
　First edition so stated on the copyright page.

MC FEE

A Bibliography of the Writings of William McFee, by James T. Babb. *Garden City*, 1931.

With an introduction and notes by McFee. Introduction signed by McFee. 360 numbered copies only.

343

Archibald MacLeish
1892–

SONGS FOR A SUMMER DAY. *[New Haven]* 1915.
Wrappers.

TOWER OF IVORY. *New Haven,* 1917.
Boards, paper label.

THE HAPPY MARRIAGE AND OTHER POEMS. *Boston,* 1924.
Boards, paper label.

THE POT OF EARTH. *Cambridge,* 1925.
100 copies on handmade paper. Trade edition, *Boston,* 1925. Both states bound in boards.

NOBODADDY. *Cambridge,* 1926.
750 copies only of which 50 were on large paper, numbered.

STREETS IN THE MOON. *Boston,* 1926.
540 copies, and 60 numbered copies on handmade paper.

THE HAMLET OF A. MACLEISH. *Boston* [1928].
Boards.

NEW FOUND LAND. *Paris,* 1930.
100 numbered copies on Van Gelder paper; 35 on Japan vellum, numbered and signed; 500 copies printed at the Black Sun Press, *Paris,* with *Boston* imprint.

CONQUISTADOR. *Boston,* 1932.

POEMS. *Boston,* 1933.

PANIC. *Boston,* 1935.

PUBLIC SPEECH. *New York* [1936].
Also 275 de luxe copies in leather, numbered and signed.

THE FALL OF THE CITY. *New York* [1937].
Boards. First printing has the publisher's monogram on the copyright page.

AIR RAID: A VERSE PLAY FOR RADIO. *New York* [1938].

LAND OF THE FREE. *New York* [1938].

AMERICA WAS PROMISES. *New York* [1939].

THE IRRESPONSIBLES: A DECLARATION. *New York* [1940].
First edition so indicated on the copyright page.

A TIME TO SPEAK. *Boston*, 1941.

THE AMERICAN CAUSE. *New York* [1941].
First edition so indicated on the copyright page.

The following is a selection of the secondary MacLeish productions. No attempt has been made to describe the innumerable documents and publications issued by Mr. MacLeish in his capacity as Librarian of Congress.

History of the Class of Nineteen Hundred & Fifteen. *New Haven*, 1915.
Albert H. Ely, Jr., editor. Contribution.
The Yale Book of Student Verse, 1910-1919. *New Haven*, 1919.
Contribution.
American Criticism, 1926. *New York* [1926].
W. A. Drake, editor. Contribution.
A Miscellany of American Poetry, 1927. *New York* [1927].
Contributions by MacLeish. First edition so stated.
Einstein. *Paris*, 1929.
100 large paper copies on Van Gelder; 50 large paper copies on Japan vellum. Reprinted from "Streets in the Moon."
Before March. [*New York*, 1932].
8 pp. pamphlet.
An Anthology of the Younger Poets. *Philadelphia*, 1932.
Oliver Wells, editor. 500 copies only. Preface by MacLeish.
Frescoes For Mr. Rockefeller's City. *New York* [1933].
Permit Me Voyage, by James Agee. *New Haven*, 1934.
Foreword by MacLeish.
What is a Book? *Boston*, 1935.
Dale Warren, editor. Contains "Emotion and Form in Poetry" by MacLeish.
Portraits and Self-Portraits, by Georges Schreiber. *Boston*, 1936.
Contribution.
Jews in America. *New York*, 1936.
Contribution.
American Points of View: A Reader's Guide. *Garden City*, 1936.
William H., and Kathryn Coe Cordell, editors. Contains MacLeish's "The Writer and the Revolution."
Yale Literary Magazine. *New Haven*, 1936.
Centennial number. Boards or wrappers. Contribution.
The Writer in a Changing World. [*New York*, 1937].
Henry Hart, editor. Contains "Spain and American Writers."
A Catalogue of the First Editions of Archibald MacLeish, by Arthur Mizener. [*New Haven*] 1938.
Printed wrappers.

MAC LEISH

Law and Politics. Occasional Papers of Felix Frankfurter, 1913-1918. *New York* [1939].
   Co-editor and with a foreword by MacLeish.
The American Experience. [*Washington, D. C.*] 1939.
   Printed wrappers.
Post-War Writers and Pre-War Readers. [*New York*, 1940].
   Wrappers.
Freedom of the Press Today. *New York* [1941].
   Contribution.
The Free Company Presents ... *New York* [1941].
   Contains "The States Talking." Previously issued as a separate pamphlet.

(Charles) Edwin Markham

1852–1940

THE MAN WITH THE HOE. *San Francisco*, 1899.
  1,000 copies printed. Pamphlet. The publisher stated "... part of the edition was printed on white and part on toned paper ... they ₍the toned paper copies₎ are original issues same as the white." The poem was previously issued as a supplement to the San Francisco *Examiner*, January 15, 1899.

THE MAN WITH THE HOE AND OTHER POEMS. *New York*, 1899.
  P. 35, line 5, *fruitless* for *milkless*. Reissued with notes, 1900.

LINCOLN AND OTHER POEMS. *New York*, 1901.

CHILDREN IN BONDAGE. *New York*, 1914.
  Prose. With Ben B. Lindsey and George Creel.

CALIFORNIA THE WONDERFUL. *New York* ₍1914₎.
  Prose.

THE SHOES OF HAPPINESS AND OTHER POEMS. *New York*, 1915.

GATES OF PARADISE AND OTHER POEMS. *Garden City*, 1920.

OUR ISRAFEL: IN MEMORY OF EDGAR ALLAN POE. ₍*New York*, 1925₎.

NEW POEMS: EIGHTY SONGS AT EIGHTY. *Garden City*, 1932.
  First edition so indicated on the copyright page.

THE STAR OF ARABY. ₍*Privately Printed*₎ 1937.
  Stamped imitation leather wrappers. 98 copies of the regular edition numbered and signed.

Markham edited and contributed to numerous books. Among these is the following group:

The Works of Edgar Allan Poe. *New York* ₍1904₎.
  10 vols. Introduction.
Modern Poets and Christian Teaching. *New York & Cincinnati* ₍1906₎.
  With Richard Watson Gilder and E. R. Sill.
The Real America in Romance. *New York*, 1907.
  15 vols. Edited.
The Burt-Markham Primer. *Boston* ₍1907₎.
  With Mary E. Burt.
The Struggle Between Graft and Democracy, by William H. Langdon. *New York*, 1908.
  Contribution.

The Marvelous Year, by William Churchill. *New York,* 1909.
   Introduction.
The Younger Choir. *New York,* 1910.
   500 copies only. Introduction by Markham. Also fifty copies signed by all the contributors.
₍Imagination. *New York,* 1912₎.
   Pamphlet. Issued by the New York Browning Society. Reported, not seen.
What and Why and When to Read. ₍*New York,* 1916₎.
Sir Oliver Lodge's "Raymond." A Review by Rev. John Whitehead. *Boston* ₍*n.d., ca.* 1917₎.
   Printed wrappers. Contribution.
Archibald Henderson: An Appreciation of the Man. ₍*Sewanee, Tenn.,* 1918₎.
   Printed wrappers.
A Wreath for Edwin Markham. *Chicago,* 1922.
   300 copies only issued by The Bookfellows. Boards.
A Talk With Edwin Markham, by Fred Lockley. ₍*Portland, Ore.,* (1923) *n.d.*₎.
Oration ... at the Funeral of Adam Willis Wagnall. *Lithopolis,* 1924.
   Printed wrappers.
Edwin Markham on Swedenborg and other Papers. ₍*n.p., n.d., Boston*(?) *ca.* 1925₎.
   Printed wrappers.
Campbell Meeker. *New York,* 1925.
   147 copies only, signed by Markham.
The Book of Poetry, Collected From the Whole Field of British and American Poetry. *New York,* 1926.
   Edited and with an introduction by Markham. 3 vols.
Sarpedon. ₍*n.p., n.d., ca.* 1927₎.
   4 pp.
Boston. ₍*n.p., n.d., Boston*(?) *ca.* 1930₎.
   8 pp. First printing is headed *Boston.* Reprints headed *Ode to Boston.*
How The Great Guest Came, A Play by Lionel Adams. *New York* ₍1930₎.
   Based on Markham's poem of the same name.
Songs and Stories ... of ... California. *Los Angeles* ₍1931₎.
   Edited and with an introduction by Markham.
Washington, The Nation-Builder.
   Broadside. Also issued as part of the program for "Celebration of the Bi-Centenary of the Birth of Washington ... ," New York University, February 22, 1932.
Edwin Markham, by William L. Stidger. *New York* ₍*etc.*₎ ₍1933₎.
The Book of Modern English Poetry. *New York,* 1934.
   Edited.
The Testimony of Genius. ₍*Hawthorne, N. J.*₎ 1934.
   Wrappers. Contribution.
How the Great Guest Came. ₍*n.p., n.d.* (*New York,* 1935)₎.
   Broadside. Reprinted from "The Shoes of Happiness."
Poetry of Youth. *New York,* 1935.
   Edited.
Collected Poems of John Jerome Rooney. *New York,* 1938.
   Introduction.

Don (Robert Perry) Marquis
1878–1937

DANNY'S OWN STORY. *Garden City*, 1912.
Green and grey cloths; no known priority.

DREAMS AND DUST. *New York* [1915].
"This is Another Day" [*n.p., n.d. New York*, 1936], 100 unnumbered copies only, single sheet, French fold, reprinted from this title.

THE CRUISE OF THE JASPER B. *New York*, 1916.
First printing has the symbol (1) below last line of text.

HERMIONE AND HER LITTLE GROUP OF SERIOUS THINKERS. *New York*, 1916.
First printing has the symbol (1) below last line of text.

PREFACES. *New York*, 1919.
First printing has the symbol (1) below last line of text.

CARTER AND OTHER PEOPLE. *New York*, 1921.
First printing has the symbol (1) below last line of text. "Words and Thoughts," *New York*, 1924, reprinted from this volume, being issued in both cloth and wrappers, the first printing having the symbol (1) below the last line of text.

NOAH, AN' JONAH, AN' CAP'N JOHN SMITH. *New York*, 1921.
First edition has the symbol (1) below last line of text. Reported but not examined: a previously issued pamphlet edition of the title poem.

THE OLD SOAK, AND HAIL AND FAREWELL. *Garden City*, 1921.
Boards, cloth back. "A Certain Club," broadside, privately printed [*New York*, 1936], reprinted from this volume. It is stated that no more than 50 copies of the broadside were printed.

POEMS AND PORTRAITS. *Garden City*, 1922.
Boards, cloth back. First edition so indicated on the copyright page.

SONNETS TO A RED-HAIRED LADY ... AND FAMOUS LOVE AFFAIRS. *Garden City*, 1922.
Boards, cloth back, paper label on the front cover. First edition so indicated on the copyright page.

THE REVOLT OF THE OYSTER. *Garden City*, 1922.
Boards, cloth back. First printing so indicated on the copyright page.

MR. HAWLEY BREAKS INTO SONG. *New York*, 1923.
Boards, paper label on front cover. 200 unnumbered copies only, privately printed.

THE OLD SOAK'S HISTORY OF THE WORLD. *Garden City*, 1924.
Boards, paper label on front cover. First printing so indicated on copyright page.

PANDORA LIFTS THE LID. *New York* [1924].
With Christopher Morley. First printing has the *GHD* monogram on the copyright page.

THE AWAKENING AND OTHER POEMS. *London*, 1924.
American edition, *Garden City*, 1925, made of the English sheets with tipped-in title page.

THE ALMOST PERFECT STATE. *Garden City*, 1927.
Boards, cloth back, paper label on the spine. First printing so indicated on the copyright page.

ARCHY AND MEHITABEL. *Garden City*, 1927.
First printing so indicated on the copyright page.

LOVE SONNETS OF A CAVE MAN AND OTHER POEMS. *Garden City*, 1928.
Cloth, paper labels. First printing so indicated on the copyright page.

WHEN THE TURTLES SING AND OTHER UNUSUAL TALES. *Garden City*, 1928.
Cloth, paper labels. First printing so indicated on the copyright page.

A VARIETY OF PEOPLE. *Garden City*, 1929.
Cloth, paper labels. First printing so indicated on the copyright page.

OFF THE ARM. *Garden City*, 1930.
First printing so indicated on the copyright page.

ARCHY'S LIFE OF MEHITABEL. *Garden City*, 1933.
Cloth, paper labels. First printing so indicated on the copyright page.

CHAPTERS FOR THE ORTHODOX. *Garden City*, 1934.
First printing so indicated on the copyright page.

ARCHY DOES HIS PART. *Garden City*, 1935.
Paper labels. First printing so indicated on the copyright page.

SUN DIAL TIME. *Garden City*, 1936.
First printing indicated on the copyright page.

SONS OF THE PURITANS. *New York*, 1939.
First printing indicated on the copyright page.

PLAYS

THE DARK HOURS. *Garden City*, 1924.
Boards, cloth back, paper labels. First printing indicated on the copyright page.

WORDS AND THOUGHTS. *New York*, 1924.
See above under "Carter ... ," 1921.

THE OLD SOAK: A COMEDY IN THREE ACTS. *New York*, 1926.
   The publishers stated (in 1937) that the book went into three printings with no changes.

OUT OF THE SEA. *Garden City*, 1927.
   Boards, cloth back, paper label on spine. First printing indicated on the copyright page.

MASTER OF THE REVELS. *Garden City*, 1934.
   First printing indicated on the copyright page.

The following is representative of Marquis' secondary productions.

The Shadow-Eater, by Benjamin de Casseres. *New York*, 1923.
   Preface.
Full and By. *Garden City*, 1925.
   Cameron Rogers, editor. Preface by Marquis. Also 209 de luxe copies.
An Ode to Hollywood. ₍n.p.₎ 1929.
   Anonymous. Wrappers. 100 copies only, privately printed.
Her Foot is on the Brass Rail. ₍New York₎ 1935.
   500 numbered copies only.
The Lives and Times of Archy and Mehitabel. *New York*, 1940.
   Reprint.

BIOGRAPHICAL

Don Marquis, by Benjamin de Casseres. ₍New York, 1938₎.

Edgar Lee Masters

1869–

A BOOK OF VERSES. *Chicago,* 1898.
Boards. First binding, grey; later, green or greenish grey.

MAXIMILIAN: A PLAY. *Boston,* 1902.
Boards, paper labels. A copy has been reported in printed wrappers.

THE NEW STAR CHAMBER AND OTHER ESSAYS. *Chicago,* 1904.
Boards, paper label.

THE BLOOD OF THE PROPHETS. *Chicago,* 1905.
Dexter Wallace, *pseudonym.*

ALTHEA: A PLAY. *Chicago,* 1907.

THE TRIFLER: A PLAY. *Chicago,* 1908.

SONGS AND SONNETS. *Chicago,* 1910.
Webster Ford, *pseudonym.*

EILEEN: A PLAY. *Chicago,* 1910.

THE LEAVES OF THE TREE: A PLAY. *Chicago,* 1910.

THE LOCKET: A PLAY. *Chicago,* 1910.

THE BREAD OF IDLENESS: A PLAY. *Chicago,* 1911.

SPOON RIVER ANTHOLOGY. *New York,* 1915.
First state measures ⅞″ across top of covers. Reissued, *New York,* 1916, with additional poems; illustrated.

SONGS AND SATIRES. *New York,* 1916.

THE GREAT VALLEY. *New York,* 1916.

TOWARD THE GULF. *New York,* 1918.

STARVED ROCK. *New York,* 1919.

MITCH MILLER. *New York,* 1920.
First state measures 7¾″ tall.

DOMESDAY BOOK. *New York,* 1920.

THE OPEN SEA. *New York,* 1921.

CHILDREN OF THE MARKET PLACE. *New York,* 1922.

SKEETERS KIRBY. *New York*, 1923.

THE NUPTIAL FLIGHT. *New York* [1923].

MIRAGE. *New York* [1924].

THE NEW SPOON RIVER. *New York*, 1924.
  Also 300 signed copies.

SELECTED POEMS. *New York*, 1925.

LEE: A DRAMATIC POEM. *New York*, 1926.
  Also 250 signed copies.

KIT O'BRIEN. [*New York*] 1927.

LEVY MAYER AND THE NEW INDUSTRIAL ERA. *New Haven*, 1927.
  1,500 copies only.

JACK KELSO: A DRAMATIC POEM. *New York*, 1928.

THE FATE OF THE JURY: AN EPILOGUE TO DOMESDAY BOOK. *New York*,
  1929.

LICHEE NUTS. *New York*, 1930.

GETTYSBURG, MANILA, ÁCOMA. *New York*, 1930.
  Three plays. 375 numbered and signed copies only.

LINCOLN, THE MAN. *New York*, 1931.
  Also 150 signed copies.

GODBEY: A DRAMATIC POEM. *New York*, 1931.
  347 numbered and signed copies only.

THE SERPENT IN THE WILDERNESS. *New York* [1933].
  400 numbered and signed copies only; copies 1-84 have an inserted page of the
  manuscript.

THE TALE OF CHICAGO. *New York*, 1933.

DRAMATIC DUOLOGUES: FOUR SHORT PLAYS ... *New York*, 1934.
  120 numbered copies only.

RICHMOND: A DRAMATIC POEM. *New York*, 1934.
  First printing indicated on copyright page.

INVISIBLE LANDSCAPES. *New York*, 1935.

VACHEL LINDSAY: A POET IN AMERICA. *New York*, 1935.
  First printing has code letter *A* on copyright page.

POEMS OF PEOPLE. *New York*, 1936.
  First edition has (1) under last line of text.

MASTERS

ACROSS SPOON RIVER. *New York* [1936].

THE GOLDEN FLEECE OF CALIFORNIA. *Weston, Vt.* [1936].
550 signed copies only. Trade edition, *New York* [1937].

WHITMAN. *New York*, 1937.
First printing has the code letter *A* on the copyright page.

THE TIDE OF TIME. *New York* [1937].
First printing has the publisher's monogram on the copyright page.

THE NEW WORLD. *New York*, 1937.

MARK TWAIN, A PORTRAIT. *New York*, 1938.
First printing has the code letter *A* on the copyright page.

MORE PEOPLE. *New York*, 1939.
First printing has the symbol (1) below last line of text.

Theodore Dreiser: America's Foremost Novelist. *New York* [ca. 1917].
Pamphlet. Contains "Theodore Dreiser—A Portrait" by Masters.
Commemoration of the Centenary of the Birth of James Russell Lowell ... *New York*, 1919.
Contribution.
American Criticism. 1926. *New York* [1926].
W. A. Drake, editor. Contribution.
Portraits and Self-Portraits, by Georges Schreiber. *Boston*, 1936.
Contribution.
The Living Thoughts of Emerson. *New York*, 1940.
Edited. First printing so indicated on the copyright page.

Referring to the many poems that have appeared in anthologies Mr. Masters writes: "... no use to list stray poems, etc. They are innumerable and have gone in few of my books—and never will be included."

Herman Melville

1819–1891

TYPEE. *New York, 1846.*

Issued in England as "Narrative of a Four Months' Residence Among the Natives of a Valley of the Marquesas," *London, 1846.* Both editions either one volume in cloth, or two volumes wrappers. The chronology of publication is as follows: February 28: Part 1, wrappers, issued in London. March 1-7: 2 volumes in 1, cloth, London. March 17: All American forms issued. April 1: Part II, wrappers, issued in London. Revised and reissued, *New York, 1846,* containing an added story, "The Story of Toby."

OMOO. *New York, 1847.*

Various types of cloth binding, the probable first being smooth cloth with a gilt stamped ship on the side; later, rough cloth with or without ship decoration. Also 2 vols. in wrappers.

MARDI. *New York, 1849.*

2 vols. Cloth or wrappers.

REDBURN. *New York, 1849.*

Contains pages of Harper's "Book List" dated October, 1849. The *To* in the dedication is not centered; this feature has been noted in an obvious reprint. Issued in both cloth and paper. A book issued, "Redburn: Or The Schoolmaster of a Morning," *New York, 1845,* is of doubtful authorship.

WHITE-JACKET. *New York, 1850.*

2 vols., wrappers or 1 vol. in cloth.

MOBY-DICK. *New York, 1851.*

Issued in various colors of cloth. It is probable that the first binding does not have blind, grolieresque stamping on the sides. First binding has publisher's name blind-stamped at the center of the sides. It has been stated without authority that the first state has orange-yellow end papers but it is almost certain that following the binding custom of the period, various end papers were used. The American edition was preceded by the London edition in three volumes with the title, "The Whale." The American edition contains 35 passages not included in the English.

PIERRE. *New York, 1852.*

Cloth or wrappers.

ISRAEL POTTER. *New York, 1855.*

Fifty Years Exile on cover. The probable first state has perfect type, p. 113, line 1. A pirated edition as "The Refugee," *Philadelphia* [1865].

THE PIAZZA TALES. *New York, 1856.*

THE CONFIDENCE-MAN. *New York*, 1857.

BATTLE-PIECES. *New York*, 1866.

The copyright notice misspells *hundred, hnndred*. Noted in two types of cloth binding with no known priority: blue cloth, gold monogram on the sides; green cloth, blind-stamped monogram on the sides.

CLAREL: A POEM AND A PILGRIMAGE IN THE HOLY LAND. *New York*, 1876.

2 vols. Red or green cloth.

JOHN MARR AND OTHER SAILORS. *New York*, 1888.

Privately printed in an edition of 25 copies only. Printed wrappers. Reissued with other stories, *Princeton*, 1922, of which there were also 175 copies on French handmade paper.

TIMOLEON. *New York*, 1891.

Privately printed in an edition of 25 copies only. Printed wrappers.

THE APPLE-TREE TABLE. *Princeton*, 1922.

Also 175 numbered copies on French handmade paper. Boards, cloth back.

WORKS OF HERMAN MELVILLE. *London*, 1922-1924.

16 vols. Contains hitherto unpublished material. *See:* two items following.

BILLY BUDD AND OTHER PROSE PIECES. *London*, 1924.

Raymond W. Weaver, editor. 750 copies only. Issued as part of preceding entry.

POEMS. *London*, 1924.

Some reprint but "the other poems in this volume have not previously been printed." Issued as part of the "Works," *London*, 1922-1924.

JOURNAL UP THE STRAITS. *New York*, 1935.

Raymond W. Weaver, editor. 650 copies only.

The History of Pittsfield, ... Massachusetts ... by J. E. A. Smith ... Springfield, 1876.
Contribution.
Herman Melville: Mariner and Mystic, by Raymond W. Weaver. *New York*, 1921.
Some Personal Letters of Herman Melville. *New York*, 1923.
Meade Minnigerode, editor. With bibliography.
Benito Cereno. *London*, 1926.
1,650 numbered copies only. First separate edition. Reprinted from "Piazza Tales," 1856.
Herman Melville, by Lewis Mumford. *New York* [1929].
Journal of Melville's Voyage in a Clipper Ship. [*n.p.*] 1929.
Wrappers.
A Book Review by Herman Melville, by John Howard Birss. [*n.p.*] 1932.
Wrappers.
Journal of a Cruise to the Pacific Ocean, 1842-44 ... With Notes on Herman Melville. *Durham, N. C.*, 1937.
Charles Robert Anderson, editor.

Herman Melville ... Selections, With Introduction, Bibliography and Notes. *New York* [1938].
  Willard Thorp, editor.
Melville in the South Seas, by Charles Robert Anderson. *New York,* 1939.
The Encantadas; or, Enchanted Isles. *Burlingame,* 1940.
  Edited by Victor Wolfgang Von Hagen. Boards, cloth back, 550 copies only.
A Complete Bibliography of the Writings of Herman Melville, by John Howard Birss and Robert S. Forsythe.
  Announced.

H[enry] L[ouis] Mencken
1880–

VENTURES INTO VERSE. *Baltimore,* 1903.
> Published in an edition of 100 (200?) copies. Copies have been noted in brown paper wrappers, boards and one copy in limp ooze calf; all with printed label on front cover. Mr. Mencken states: "The number of copies ... that were bound in printer's boards with printed labels was probably twenty or twenty-five. How many copies of the book were printed altogether I simply don't recall. My impression is that it was a little over 100, but much less than 200."

GEORGE BERNARD SHAW: HIS PLAYS. *Boston,* 1905.
> Cloth, paper labels.

THE PHILOSOPHY OF FRIEDRICH NIETZSCHE. *Boston,* 1908.
> First state of binding omits *Friedrich* from spine.

WHAT YOU OUGHT TO KNOW ABOUT YOUR BABY. *New York,* 1910.
> In collaboration with Dr. L. K. Hirshberg, whose name appears as author.

MEN VERSUS THE MAN. *New York,* 1910.
> A correspondence with Robert Rives La Monte. First binding in vertical ribbed cloth.

THE ARTIST. *Boston,* 1912.
> Wrappers over boards, paper label. *A Drama Without Words* does not appear on title page of first printing.

EUROPE AFTER 8:15. *New York,* 1914.
> With George Jean Nathan and Willard Huntington Wright. Mencken wrote the introduction, "Munich," and the first and last parts of "London." First binding has blue stamping.

A LITTLE BOOK IN C MAJOR. *New York,* 1916.

A BOOK OF BURLESQUE. *New York,* 1916.
> Various later revisions.

A BOOK OF PREFACES. *New York,* 1917.
> A few copies issued with untrimmed edges, signed by the author.

DAMN! A BOOK OF CALUMNY. *New York,* 1918.
> Reissued with the *Damn!* deleted from the title.

IN DEFENSE OF WOMEN. *New York,* 1918.
> Publisher's name on title page misspelled *Ppilip.* Revised and reissued, *New York,* 1922.

THE AMERICAN LANGUAGE. *New York,* 1919.
  1,500 numbered copies only; 25 signed by the author. Reissued, 1921, 1923, 1926, 1936 with additions and revisions.

PREJUDICES: FIRST SERIES. *New York* [1919].
  Also 50 untrimmed copies signed by the author.

PREJUDICES: SECOND SERIES. *New York* [1920].
  Also a few untrimmed copies signed by the author.

THE AMERICAN CREDO. *New York,* 1920.
  With George Jean Nathan. In 1921 the authors issued 50 copies of a 4 pp. addition, paged 193-196, for private circulation.

HELIOGABALUS. *New York,* 1920.
  With George Jean Nathan. 2,000 numbered copies. Also 60 copies on special paper, numbered and signed by the authors. Also 200 copies of a so-called acting edition in light brown wrappers.

PREJUDICES: THIRD SERIES. *New York* [1922].
  Also 25 signed copies but in no other way distinguished from the trade edition. Some copies noted with errata slip following copyright page. The author later issued a sheet of corrections to be inserted.

PREJUDICES: FOURTH SERIES. *New York* [1924].
  Also 110 large paper copies, numbered and signed. 3,610 copies only. Errata slip.

NOTES ON DEMOCRACY. *New York* [1926].
  Also 235 signed copies as follows: 200 on rag paper and 35 on Japan vellum.

PREJUDICES: FIFTH SERIES. *New York* [1926].
  Also 200 large paper copies numbered and signed.

PREJUDICES: SIXTH SERIES. *New York* [1927].
  Also 50 copies on vellum, 140 on rag paper, all numbered and signed. Has been noted with a tipped-in errata slip.

TREATISE ON THE GODS. *New York,* 1930.
  Also 375 large paper copies, signed.

MAKING A PRESIDENT. *New York,* 1932.
  First edition so stated on copyright page.

TREATISE ON RIGHT AND WRONG. *New York,* 1934.
  First edition so stated on copyright page.

HAPPY DAYS. *New York* [1940].
  First printing indicated on the copyright page.

NEWSPAPER DAYS.
  Announced.

MENCKEN

A NEW DICTIONARY OF QUOTATIONS ON HISTORICAL PRINCIPLES.
Announced.

The following list does not purport to be a complete checklist of the many minor and fugitive Mencken productions. Mr. Mencken issued numberless pamphlets and contributed introductions and prefaces to so many books that it is impossible to list them all here. The collector is referred to the Frey Bibliography and similar works.

The Gist of Nietzsche. *Boston*, 1910.
    Edited.
Pistols For Two, by Owen Hatteras. *New York*, 1917.
    Owen Hatteras, pseudonym for Nathan and Mencken.
Literary Capital of the United States. *Chicago*, 1920.
    Later included in "Our American Books," Francis Hackett, editor. *New York*,
    1920.
The Free Lance Books. *Boston*, 1919-1920.
    5 vols. Edited and with prefaces by Mencken.
The Borzoi 1920. *New York*, 1920.
    Contribution.
Youth and Egolatry, by Pio Baroja. *New York*, 1920.
    Introduction.
The Line of Love, by James Branch Cabell. *New York*, 1921.
    Preface.
A Round Table in Poictesme. *Cleveland*, 1924.
    Contribution. See under *Cabell* for further discussion.
The Borzoi 1925. *New York* [1925].
    Contribution. Also large paper edition signed by the editors. See under *Cather*.
Americana 1925 [also] 1926. *New York*, 1925 [and] 1926.
    Edited. Of the 1925 edition there were also 50 signed copies. A copy of the 1926
    edition has been noted in boards, cloth back, paper label, signed.
The Work of Stephen Crane. *New York* [1925-1926].
    12 vols. Introduction for vol. x.
George Sterling: A Memorial. *San Francisco*, 1926.
    4 pp. leaflet.
American Criticism. 1926. *New York* [1926].
    W. A. Drake, editor. Contribution.
A Statement to Friends of the American Mercury. *New York*, 1926.
    6 pp. pamphlet. Mr. Mencken issued various similar pamphlets and broadsides
    while editor of *The Mercury* and *Smart Set*.
James Branch Cabell. *New York*, 1927.
    See under *Cabell* for further discussion of this item.
Selected Prejudices. *New York*, 1927.
    With new preface. Issued in England with varying text.
Essays by James Gibbons Huneker. *New York*, 1929.
    Edited and with an introduction.

Lo, The Poor Bookseller. [*Hollywood*, 1930].
  Privately printed. Wrappers.
You Know These Lines! by Merle Johnson. *New York*, 1935.
  Introduction. 1,000 copies only signed by the author.
Eleven Plays of Hendrik Ibsen. *New York* [1935].
  Introduction.
Southern Album, by Sara Haardt. *Garden City*, 1936.
  First edition so stated on copyright page. Edited and with a preface by Mencken.
Portraits and Self-Portraits, by Georges Schreiber. *Boston*, 1936.
  Contribution.
The Sunpapers of Baltimore. *New York*, 1937.
  Edited. First printing indicated on copyright page.
Baltimore Yesterdays, by Meredith Janvier. *Baltimore*, 1937.
  Preface.
1937 Essay Annual. *New York* [1937].
  Erich A. Walter, editor. Contribution.
The Charlatanry of the Learned, by Johann Burkhard Mencken. *New York*, 1937.
  Notes and introduction by H. L. Mencken. 1,475 copies only.
Breaking Into Print. *New York*, 1937.
  Elmer Adler, editor. Contribution.
In American: The Collected Poems of John V. A. Weaver. *New York*, 1939.
  Introduction.
1940. Alfred A. Knopf: Quarter Century. [*New York*, 1940].
  Cloth, paper labels. Contribution.

Mr. Mencken contributed prefaces to numerous translations of Ibsen, Brieux and the Modern Library publications.

BIOGRAPHICAL, BIBLIOGRAPHICAL, AND CRITICAL

A Bibliography of the Writings of H. L. Mencken, by Carroll Frey. *Philadelphia*, 1924.
  Foreword by Mencken. Also 85 large paper copies, signed.
The Man Mencken, by Isaac Goldberg. *New York*, 1925.
H. L. Mencken, by Ernest Boyd. *New York*, 1925.
The Reincarnation of H. L. Mencken, by G. L. Roosebroeck. *New York*, 1925.
H. L. Mencken, by Walter Lippmann. [*New York*?] 1926.
  8 pp. pamphlet reprinted from *The Saturday Review of Literature*.
Menckeniana: A Schimpflexikon. *New York*, 1928.
  Also 230 large paper copies, signed by Mencken. A collection of adverse criticism edited by the subject, Mencken.
Mencken and Shaw, by Benjamin de Casseres. *New York* [1930].

Edna St. Vincent Millay

1892–

RENASCENCE. *New York*, 1917.
Also 17 copies on Japan vellum, bound in boards. First regular edition, black cloth binding, paper watermarked *Glaslan*. Second issue paper watermarked *Ingres d'Arches*.

A FEW FIGS FROM THISTLES. *New York*, 1920.
First state may or may not have a "wallet" edge on back wrapper. Issued in several colors of wrapper. Reissued with additional material 1921 and [1922]. Of the latter there were also 250 large paper copies, numbered, one of which has been noted with a frontispiece.

THE LAMP AND THE BELL. *New York*, 1921.
Wrappers, later in boards.

ARIA DA CAPO. *New York*, 1921.
The Chapbook, No. 14 [*London*] August, 1920, is composed entirely of this work.

SECOND APRIL. *New York*, 1921.
First state on paper watermarked *Glaslan*.

TWO SLATTERNS AND A KING. *Cincinnati* [1921].
Wrappers.

THE BALLAD OF THE HARP WEAVER. *New York*, 1922.
Various colors of wrappers. First edition so stated on copyright page. Also 5 copies on Japan vellum.

THE HARP-WEAVER AND OTHER POEMS. *New York*, 1923.
Has code letters *K-X* on copyright page. First edition so stated on copyright page.

DISTRESSING DIALOGUES. *New York* [1924].
Nancy Boyd, *pseudonym*. First edition so stated on copyright page. Code letters *G-Y* on copyright page.

THE KING'S HENCHMAN. *New York*, 1927.
Harper and Fischer editions issued simultaneously; Fischer edition printed first. The latter has the Deems Taylor score, but the special edition containing the cast of singers came later. Harper edition: 31 copies on vellum, 26 lettered A-Z; 158 on handmade paper, numbered and signed; trade edition, first edition so stated on copyright page. Harper's later issued "The Artist's Edition," 500 numbered copies on handmade paper, signed. A libretto was issued for the performance, February 17, 1927. The latter has been noted in five states as follows: 1: Rullman advertisement inside front cover, Harper advertisement on the last page facing inner back wrapper; 2: Same as preceding but inside front cover is blank;

3: Same as first state but the Harper advertisement faces the last page of text; 4: in the Knabe advertisement the address is given as *Fifth Avenue at Thirty-ninth Street;* 5: Same as the preceding but the Knabe address is changed to *Fifth Avenue at Fifty-second Street.*

THE BUCK IN THE SNOW AND OTHER POEMS. *New York,* 1928.
First edition so stated on copyright page. Also 36 copies on Japan vellum, 479 copies on d'Arches handmade paper, numbered and signed.

POEMS SELECTED FOR YOUNG PEOPLE. *New York,* 1929.
First edition so stated on copyright page. Also 1,050 large paper copies. First book appearance of seven poems after appearance in "American Poetry, 1925: A Miscellany," *New York* [1925], first edition so stated on copyright page.

FATAL INTERVIEW. *New York,* 1931.
Also 36 copies on Japan vellum, 479 on d'Arches handmade paper, numbered and signed. The first copies of the trade edition had top edges yellow stained. Boards. First edition so stated on copyright page. Announced originally as "Twice Required."

THE PRINCESS MARRIES THE PAGE. *New York,* 1932.
First edition so stated on copyright page. Boards, cloth back.

WINE FROM THESE GRAPES. *New York,* 1934.
2 vols. [with] "Epitaph For The Race of Man," 36 on Japan vellum and 299 on Worthy Charta Paper; vol. 1 of each set numbered and signed by the author. Trade edition, 1 vol., first edition so stated on copyright page, issued in cloth or leather.

CONVERSATION AT MIDNIGHT. *New York,* 1937.
Cloth, board sides, paper label on spine, first edition indicated on the copyright page. Also 36 copies on Japan vellum, signed, numbered 1-36; and copies on handmade paper numbered 37-615, signed.

HUNTSMAN, WHAT QUARRY? *New York,* 1939.
First edition indicated on the copyright page. Also 551 copies, numbered and signed.

MAKE BRIGHT THE ARROWS. *New York,* 1940.
First edition indicated on the copyright page. Also 1,550 copies in leather.

Many of Miss Millay's poems have appeared in the various anthologies. The following is a representative list of the secondary items.

The Lyric Year. *New York,* 1912.
First state measures 1" across top of covers. P. 25, line 13, *careful gentlemen;* later, *polite gentleman.* Contains first book appearance of "Renascence."
A Book of Vassar Verse. [Poughkeepsie, N. Y.] 1916.
First state, line 7, p. 130, has misprint *fcultily.* Contains three poems by Millay. Boards, cloth back.

Defenders of Democracy. *New York*, 1918.
Contains "Defenders of Democracy."
A Miscellany of American Poetry, 1922. *New York* [1922].
Contributions by Millay.
Renascence. *New York*, 1924.
100 copies only, printed and initialled by Frederic Goudy. First separate printing.
American Poetry: A Miscellany. *New York* [1925].
Contains "From a Very Little Sphinx."
Reflections on the Sacco-Vanzetti Tragedy. *Boston* [n.d., 1927?].
Pamphlet. Contains "Fear" by Millay, separately published [n.d., 1929?].
A Miscellany of American Poetry, 1927. *New York* [1927].
Contributions by Millay. First edition so stated.
Outcrop, by Abbie Huston Evans. *New York*, 1928.
Preface.
A Day on Skates: The Story of a Dutch Picnic, by Hilda Van Stockum. *New York*, 1934.
Foreword.
Flowers of Evil, by Charles Baudelaire. *New York*, 1936.
First edition so stated on copyright page. Translated from the French. George Dillon, co-translator.
Vacation Song. *Hanover, N. H.*, 1936.
Pamphlet. 85 numbered copies only.
... and Spain Sings. Fifty Loyalist Ballads. *New York*, 1937.
Contribution.
To the Maid of Orleans. [n.p.] 1940.
Broadside. The first printing has no advertisement on the verso. Later in "Make Bright the Arrows."
"There Are No Islands, Any More." *New York*, 1940.
Boards or wrappers. First edition indicated on the copyright page. Preceded by a broadside published by the British War Relief Society, New York.

BIOGRAPHICAL AND BIBLIOGRAPHICAL

Edna St. Vincent Millay: An Essay and a Bibliography, by Harold Lewis Cook. *New York*, 1935.
Announced but not published. The publishers issued a dummy of this book together with a few of the preliminary leaves. Included in the latter was an otherwise unpublished note by Miss Millay.
A Bibliography of Edna St. Vincent Millay, by Karl Yost. *New York*, 1937.
First edition indicated on the copyright page. Contains three poems and other Millay material here first collected. 1,500 copies only.

For further regarding certain of Miss Millay's early ephemera see "Some Undergraduate Printings of Edna St. Vincent Millay," by John S. Van E. Kohn, in *The Publishers' Weekly*, November 30, 1940.

Joaquin (Cincinnatus Heine [Hiner]) Miller
1841 (?)–1913

SPECIMENS. [*Canyon City, Oregon, 1868*].
   Preface dated *Canyon City, Oregon, April, 1868*. Signed *C. H. Miller*.

JOAQUIN, ET AL. *Portland, Oregon, 1869*.
   By *Cincinnatus H. Miller*. Reissued, *London, 1871*, with a new introduction.

PACIFIC POEMS. *London, 1871*.
   Miller states in the *London, 1871*, edition of "Songs of the Sierras" that "less than half a dozen copies of this book were issued" and in the preface to "Complete Poetical Work," *San Francisco, 1897*, "that one hundred copies were printed bearing the name of the printer as publisher." In 1915, Walter M. Hill of Chicago issued a brochure giving an interesting account of the publication and suppression of the book.

SONGS OF THE SIERRAS. *London, 1871*.
   An unknown number of copies issued with a cancel title page bearing an American imprint; possibly for purposes of copyright. Also a *Toronto, 1871*, edition; status unknown. Reissued with three added poems, *Boston, 1871*; the first binding has *R. B.* at foot of spine and not the full name of the publisher.

SONGS OF THE SUN-LANDS. *London, 1873*.
   Also large paper edition. A variant edition has been noted without place or date on the title page. Reissued, *Boston, 1873*.

LIFE AMONGST THE MODOCS: UNWRITTEN HISTORY. *London, 1873*.
   Reissued as "Unwritten History: Life Among the Modocs," *Hartford, 1874*. Reissued as "Paquita: The Indian Heroine. A True Story," *Hartford, 1881*. Revised and abridged, as "My Own Story," *Chicago, 1890*.

ARIZONIAN. *Baltimore, 1874*.

FIRST FAM'LIES IN THE SIERRAS. *London, 1875*.
   Materially extended and reissued as "First Fam'lies of the Sierras," *Chicago, 1876*. Reissued, *Chicago, 1878* and *1881*, as "Danites in the Sierras."

THE SHIP IN THE DESERT. *London, 1875*.
   Revised and reissued with added material, *Boston, 1875*.

THE ONE FAIR WOMAN. *London, 1876*.
   3 vols. Reissued, *New York, 1876*, 1 vol.

THE BARONESS OF NEW YORK. *New York, 1877*.

SONGS OF ITALY. *Boston, 1878*.

MILLER

SONGS OF FAR-AWAY LANDS. *London*, 1878.

HOW TO WIN IN WALL STREET. *New York*, 1881.
Anonymous. *By A Successful Operator.*

SHADOWS OF SHASTA. *Chicago*, 1881.

FORTY NINE: A CALIFORNIA DRAMA. *San Francisco*, 1882.
Contains also "Danites in the Sierras, A Drama."

WILLIAM BROWN OF OREGON. *Cleveland*, 1883.
Wrappers.

"TALLY-HO!" A MUSICAL DRAMA. [*n.p.*, 1883].
Printed wrappers.

THE SILENT MAN: A COMEDY DRAMA. [*n.p.*, 1883].
Printed wrappers.

OREGON IDYL. [*n.p.?* 1883?].
Details not available.

MEMORIE AND RIME. *New York*, 1884.
Cloth, or printed wrappers.

'49, THE GOLD-SEEKER OF THE SIERRAS. *New York*, 1884.
Cloth, wrappers, or boards with cloth back.

THE DESTRUCTION OF GOTHAM. *New York*, 1886.
Cloth, or printed wrappers.

SONGS OF THE MEXICAN SEAS. *Boston*, 1887.

IN CLASSIC SHADES AND OTHER POEMS. *Chicago*, 1890.

SONGS OF SUMMER LANDS. *Chicago*, 1892.

THE BUILDING OF THE CITY BEAUTIFUL. *Chicago*, 1893.
50 large paper copies in boards. 500 small paper copies in cloth.

AN ILLUSTRATED HISTORY OF THE STATE OF MONTANA. *Chicago*, 1894.
2 vols.

SONGS OF THE SOUL. *San Francisco*, 1896.
Also a de luxe edition in padded morocco.

CHANTS FOR THE BOER. *San Francisco*, 1900.
Printed wrappers.

TRUE BEAR STORIES. *Chicago* [1900].

AS IT WAS IN THE BEGINNING. [*San Francisco*, 1903].
Printed wrappers.

LIGHT: A NARRATIVE POEM. *Boston*, 1907.
  Published, March, 1907 on copyright page.

TRELAWNEY WITH SHELLEY AND BYRON. *Pompton Lakes, N. J.*, 1922.
  300 copies only. Wrappers.

OVERLAND IN A COVERED WAGON. *New York*, 1930.
  Sidney A. Firman, editor. The first printing has the symbol (1) below last line of text.

A ROYAL HIGHWAY OF THE WORLD. *Portland, Ore.*, 1932.
  245 numbered copies only.

COLLECTED WORKS

POETICAL WORKS: HOUSEHOLD EDITION. *Boston*, 1882.
COMPLETE POETICAL WORKS. *San Francisco*, 1897.
  Reissued, *San Francisco*, 1902.
JOAQUIN MILLER'S POEMS. *San Francisco*, 1909-1910.
  6 vols. 250 sets only.
POETICAL WORKS. *New York*, 1923.
  Stuart P. Sherman, editor.

Stories of the Sierras, by Bret Harte. *London* [1872?].
  Contains "The Last Man of Mexican Camp" by Miller.
Mae Madden, by Mary Murdock Mason. *Chicago*, 1876.
  Contribution.
Song of the Centennial. [*n.p., ca.* 1876].
  4 pp.
The Danites and other Choice Selections. *New York*, 1878.
  Reprint.
Beyond the River. [*n.p., n.d., ca.* 1880?].
  Broadside.
For the Right. [*New York*, 1883].
  Broadside.
Katy's Birthday by Sarah O[rne] Jewett. With Other Stories by Famous Authors.
  Boston [1883].
  Contains "Mr. Tennyson's Fairies" by Miller.
The Tree by the Well. [*Oregon University*, 1884?].
  Broadside.
The Little Gold Miners of the Sierras. *Boston* [1886].
  Title story by Joaquin Miller.
The Battle of Castle Crages. [*n.p., n.d.,* 1894?].
  Printed wrappers.
Spanish-American War Songs. *Detroit*, 1898.
  Sidney A. Witherbee, editor. Contribution.

The River of Rest. *New York* [1898].

Joaquin Miller's Romantic Life Amongst the Indians. *London* [1898?].
  Reprint.

Japan of Sword and Love. *Tokyo,* 1905.
  With Yone Noguchi. Wrappers.

Kindergarten Gems. *Akron* [1907].
  Contribution.

The Grand Canyon of Arizona. *[n.p.]* 1909.
  Published by the Passenger Department of the Santa Fé. Boards. Contains "A
  New Wonder of the World."

Christmas Wishes. *[n.p., n.d.]*.

About "The Hights" With Juanita Miller. *[Oakland,* 1917].
  Printed wrappers.

Joaquin Miller and His Other Self, by Harr Wagner. *San Francisco* [1929].

The Joaquin Miller Cabin. *Lansdale, Penna.* [1931].
  Privately printed. Wrappers.

Joaquin Miller, Frontier Poet, by Merritt Parmelee Allen. *New York,* 1932.
  First printing indicated on the copyright page.

Joaquin Miller, His California Diary Beginning in 1855 and Ending in 1857. *Seattle,*
  1936.
  John S. Richards, editor. 700 numbered copies only.

Joaquin Miller, Literary Frontiersman, by M. S. Peterson. *Stanford University*
  [1937].

"Chez le Peaux Rougus," supposedly published at Paris in 1879, is nothing more
than an extract from the *Revue Britannique* and not a separate publication.

Donald G[rant] Mitchell
(Ik Marvel)
1822–1908

FRESH GLEANINGS. *New York*, 1847.

2 vols. wrappers, or 1 vol. in cloth. Reissued, *New York*, 1851, with new preface.

THE BATTLE SUMMER. *New York*, 1850.

First state has *1850* at foot of engraved title page.

THE LORGNETTE. *New York* [1850].

24 paper covered parts. Anonymous. *By An Opera Goer*. Later issued as a 2 vol. cloth set, marked Second Edition on title page. Fourth edition, *New York*, 1851, has preface acknowledging authorship. Issued in *London*, 1852, as "The Opera Goer," by Ike Marvell(!).

THE REVERIES OF A BACHELOR. *New York*, 1850.

Issued in several types of cloth and leather bindings with no established priority. Three copies in three quarter leather have been noted with contemporary inscriptions by the author. There were numerous printings without change of title page but the copies measuring 7½" tall (in the sheets) seem typographically best. The earliest printed copies have the type in *sleep,* p. 29, last line, unbroken. The earliest state of the cloth binding shows the stem of the leaves in the top panel on the spine pointing to the right; later to the left. "A Bachelor's Reverie," *Wormsloe (Ga.,)* 1850, 12 copies only, privately printed, is reprinted in this volume. Reissued with new prefaces *New York*, 1863, 1884 and 1889.

DREAM LIFE. *New York*, 1851.

First state has stereotyper's slug on copyright page. Noted with or without title page tipped-in; no known priority. Reissued with new prefaces, *New York*, 1863, 1884 and 1889.

FUDGE DOINGS. *New York*, 1855.

2 vols. Various colors of cloth.

MY FARM OF EDGEWOOD. *New York*, 1863.

Noted with either gilt stamping or paper label on spine; no known priority. Pirated in London [1873] as "A Freehold Villa For Nothing."

SEVEN STORIES. *New York*, 1864.

Anonymous. Noted in the following bindings: two types of brown cloth; maroon cloth; black cloth with paper label on the spine. The advertisements at the back occur in two states. In one "My Farm of Edgewood" and "Dream Life" are priced at $1.75 and $1.50 respectively; in the other state the books are priced at $1.60 and $1.30. No priority as yet determined.

D. G. MITCHELL

WET DAYS AT EDGEWOOD. *New York*, 1865.
> Anonymous. Reissued with new preface, *New York*, 1883.

DR. JOHNS. *New York*, 1866.
> 2 vols. or 2 vols. in 1. Reissued, *New York*, 1884, in one volume. With or without decorated spines; priority unknown.

RURAL STUDIES. *New York*, 1867.
> With or without the publisher's name on the spine; no established priority. Reissued, *New York*, 1884, as "Out-of-Town Places."

PICTURES OF EDGEWOOD. *New York*, 1869.
> 300 copies only. Anonymous.

ABOUT OLD STORY-TELLERS. *New York*, 1878.
> Issued in various cloths.

THE WOODBRIDGE RECORD. [*n.p.*, 1883].
> Anon. 200 copies only.

BOUND TOGETHER. *New York*, 1884.

ENGLISH LANDS, LETTERS AND KINGS: FROM CELT TO TUDOR. *New York*, 1889.

ENGLISH LANDS, LETTERS AND KINGS: FROM ELIZABETH TO ANNE. *New York*, 1890.

ENGLISH LANDS, LETTERS AND KINGS: QUEEN ANNE AND THE GEORGES. *New York*, 1895.

AMERICAN LANDS AND LETTERS: THE MAYFLOWER TO RIP VAN WINKLE. *New York*, 1897.

ENGLISH LANDS, LETTERS AND KINGS: THE LATER GEORGES TO VICTORIA. *New York*, 1897.

AMERICAN LANDS AND LETTERS: LEATHERSTOCKING TO POE'S RAVEN. *New York*, 1899.

Poem by Guy Bryant Schott ... Valedictory Oration by Donald Grant Mitchell. *New Haven*, 1841.
> Wrappers. The oration, "The Dignity of Learning," was also issued as a separate pamphlet.

Report of the Proceedings of the 25th Anniversary of the Brotherhood of the Alpha Delta Phi ... *New York*, 1858.
> Contains a speech by Mitchell.

The Atlantic Almanac, 1869. *Boston* [1868].
> Edited.

Sayings Wise and Otherwise. *New York*, 1871.
  Introduction.
Description of Lafayette College and Vicinity. [*Easton, Pa., ca.* 1880].
  Wrappers. Anonymous.
A Report to the Commission on Lay-Out of East Rock Park. *New Haven*, 1882.
  Wrappers.
The Woodbridge Record. *New Haven*, 1883.
  200 numbered copies only. Co-editor.
Daniel Tyler: A Memorial Volume. *New Haven*, 1883.
  Edited. 200 copies only.
Readings From Macaulay. *Boston*, 1885.
  Introduction.
Homes in City and Country. *New York*, 1893.
  Contains "The Country House" by Mitchell.
Capital Stories by American Authors. *New York* [1895].
  Contribution.
The International Library of Famous Literature. *New York* [1898].
  Contributor.

COLLECTED WORKS

The Works of Donald G. Mitchell. *New York*, 1888.
  8 vols.
The Edgewood Edition of the Works ... *New York*, 1907.
  15 vols. With an introduction by the author.

BIBLIOGRAPHICAL

The Life of Donald G. Mitchell, by Waldo H. Dunn. *New York*, 1922.
The First Editions of Donald G. Mitchell: "Ik Marvel": A Checklist Compiled by
  Paul S[pencer] Seybolt. *Boston*, 1930.
  Wrappers. 100 numbered copies only.

S[ilas] Weir Mitchell
1829–1914

THE CHILDREN'S HOUR. *Philadelphia*, 1864.
Anon. *By E. W. S.* [Elizabeth W. Sherman] *and S. W. M.* [S. Weir Mitchell].

THE WONDERFUL STORIES OF FUZ-BUZ THE FLY AND MOTHER GRABEM, THE
SPIDER. *Philadelphia*, 1867.
Anon. Also 170 large paper copies. Boards.

HEPHZIBAH GUINNESS: THEE AND YOU: AND A DRAFT ON THE BANK OF
SPAIN. *Philadelphia*, 1880.

THE HILL OF STONES AND OTHER POEMS. *Boston*, 1883.
Also large paper edition.

IN WAR TIME. *Boston*, 1885.

ROLAND BLAKE. *Boston*, 1886.
Preceded by a privately printed edition of six copies with the imprint *Phila
delphia: Printed, Not Published*, 1886.

A MASQUE AND OTHER POEMS. *Boston*, 1887.
Boards, cloth back, label on spine.

PRINCE LITTLE BOY AND OTHER TALES OUT OF FAIRY-LAND. *Philadelphia*,
1888.

THE CUP OF YOUTH. *Boston*, 1889.
Boards, cloth back, label on spine.

FAR IN THE FOREST. *Philadelphia*, 1889.

A PSALM OF DEATHS AND OTHER POEMS. *Boston*, 1890.
Boards, cloth back, label on spine.

CHARACTERISTICS. *New York*, 1892.

THE MOTHER AND OTHER POEMS. *Boston*, 1893.
Also a preliminary edition [n.p., n.d., ca. 1892] in sheets, for the author's use, 20
numbered copies only. The published edition of 1893 is extensively revised.

FRANCIS DRAKE. *Boston*, 1893.

MR. KRIS KRINGLE. *Philadelphia*, 1893.
Boards, cloth back.

WHEN ALL THE WOODS ARE GREEN. *New York*, 1894.

A MADEIRA PARTY. *New York*, 1895.
Publisher's leather.

PHILIP VERNON. *New York*, 1895.

COLLECTED POEMS. *New York*, 1896.

HUGH WYNNE: FREE QUAKER. *New York*, 1897 (1896).
First state is trimmed all around, no gilt top, and red stamped decorations on front cover. Vol. 1, p. 54, last word is *in*. Vol. 2, p. 260, line 16, reads ... *before us*, ... Later states have different readings, gilt top, fore and bottom edges untrimmed, decoration on front cover blind stamped.
The first state has been noted in light brown cloth instead of the usual grey; probably an experimental binding. There is also an edition of 60 large paper copies, plates separate, but with the revised reading.
One of the editors of the publishing house informs us that the book was printed with the title page dated 1896 but that on his insistence the story was serially published and that book publication was consequently delayed until after the story had its run in the magazine. This accounts for the fact that a few copies have appeared with the 1896 title page and that copies of the 1897 edition appear with the title page tipped in.

THE ADVENTURES OF FRANÇOIS. *New York*, 1898.

ODE ON A LYCIAN TOMB. [*New York*] 1899.
Privately printed.

DR. NORTH AND HIS FRIENDS. *New York*, 1900.

THE WAGER AND OTHER POEMS. *New York*, 1900.

THE AUTOBIOGRAPHY OF A QUACK. *New York*, 1900.

CIRCUMSTANCE. *New York*, 1901.

A COMEDY OF CONSCIENCE. *New York*, 1903.
Published March, 1903 on copyright page.

LITTLE STORIES. *New York*, 1903.
Published, October, 1903 on copyright page.

NEW SAMARIA AND THE SUMMER OF ST. MARTIN. *Philadelphia*, 1904.
A few copies printed from the magazine plates were deposited for copyright in 1902. The story appeared originally in *Lippincott's Magazine*, 1902, copies of which were issued with special title page. The regularly published edition of 1904 has the following on the copyright page: *Published September, 1904.*

THE YOUTH OF WASHINGTON. *New York*, 1904.
Also 100 large paper copies.

CONSTANCE TRESCOT. *New York*, 1905.
Published March, 1905 on copyright page.

S. W. MITCHELL

A DIPLOMATIC ADVENTURE. *New York*, 1906.
Published April, 1906 on copyright page.

PEARL. *New York*, 1906.

THE RED CITY. *New York*, 1908.

A VENTURE IN 1777. *Philadelphia* [1908].

THE COMFORT OF THE HILLS. [*New York*] 1909.
Privately printed. Flexible cloth. 50 numbered copies only.

THE COMFORT OF THE HILLS AND OTHER POEMS. *New York*, 1910.
Published February, 1910 on copyright page.

THE GUILLOTINE CLUB AND OTHER STORIES. *New York*, 1910.
Published October, 1910 on copyright page.

JOHN SHERWOOD, IRONMASTER. *New York*, 1911.
Published, May, 1911 on copyright page. Also advance issue in printed paper
wrappers.

WESTWAYS: A VILLAGE CHRONICLE. *New York*, 1913.
Published, September, 1913 on the copyright page.

COMPLETE POEMS. *New York*, 1914.

Five Essays, by John Kearsley Mitchell. *Philadelphia*, 1859.
  Edited.
The Mother. *Boston*, 1893.
  Reprinted from "The Mother and other Poems," *Boston*, 1893.
The Year Book of Pegasus, No. 1. *Philadelphia*, 1895.
  Contains "The Passing of Tennyson."
The Birth and Death of Pain. [*New York*, 1896?].
  Also in "The Semi-Centennial of Anæsthesia," *Boston*, 1897.
Addresses at the Dinner Given to Dr. T. Gaillard Thomas. *New York* [1901].
  Contains a speech by Mitchell.
Washington in His Letters. [*Philadelphia*, 1903].
Cooking in Old Creole Days, by Célestine Eustis. *New York*, 1904.
  Introduction.
The Proceedings of the Charaka Club, Vols. I and II. *New York*, 1906-1910.
  Contributions.

Dr. Mitchell was the author of innumerable monographs and non-technical
medical essays. The following is a representative selection.

Gunshot Wounds, And Other Injuries of Nerves. *Philadelphia*, 1864.
  With others.
Wear and Tear, or, Hints for the Overworked. *Philadelphia*, 1871.

Rest in the Treatment of Nervous Diseases. *New York*, 1875.
 Wrappers.
Fat and Blood: And How to Make Them. *Philadelphia*, 1877.
Nurse and Patient, and Camp Cure. *Philadelphia*, 1877.
Doctor and Patient. *Philadelphia*, 1888.

BIBLIOGRAPHICAL—BIOGRAPHICAL

A Catalogue of the Scientific and Literary Work of S. Weir Mitchell. [*Philadelphia*, 1894].
Weir Mitchell: His Life and Letters, by Anna Robeson Burr. *New York*, 1929.
 Contains a bibliography.

William Vaughn Moody

1869–1910

THE MASQUE OF JUDGMENT. *Boston,* 1900.
Noted with both gold and silver stamping; no priority established. Also 150 copies, boards, paper label.

POEMS. *Boston,* 1901.
Also 150 copies, boards, paper label. Republished as "Gloucester Moors and Other Poems," *New York* [1910].

A HISTORY OF ENGLISH LITERATURE. *New York,* 1902.
With ROBERT MORSS LOVETT. Condensations of this title are: "A First View of English Literature," *New York,* 1905, with LOVETT; and, "A First View of English and American Literature," *New York,* 1909, with LOVETT and PERCY H. BOYNTON.

THE FIRE-BRINGER. *Boston,* 1904.
Also 150 copies in boards, paper label.

THE GREAT DIVIDE: A PLAY. *New York,* 1909.

THE FAITH HEALER: A PLAY. *Boston,* 1909.

THE POEMS AND PLAYS OF WILLIAM VAUGHN MOODY. *Boston,* 1912.
2 vols.

SOME LETTERS OF WILLIAM VAUGHN MOODY. *Boston,* 1913.
Daniel Gregory Mason, editor.

SELECTED POEMS. *Boston,* 1931.
Robert Morss Lovett, editor.

LETTERS TO HARRIET. *Boston,* 1935.
Percy MacKaye, editor.

William Vaughn Moody, by Edwin Herbert Lewis. [Chicago] 1914.
275 copies only.
William Vaughn Moody: A Study, by David D. Henry. *Boston* [1934].

Moody edited and wrote introductions to numerous school editions. The following is a representative selection.

The Pilgrim's Progress, by John Bunyan. *Boston* [1896].
The Rime of the Ancient Mariner, by S. T. Coleridge. *Chicago,* 1898.
The Lay of the Last Minstrel, by Sir Walter Scott. *Chicago,* 1899.
The Poems of Trumbull Stickney. *Boston,* 1905.

Christopher (Darlington) Morley

1890–

THE EIGHTH SIN. *Oxford and London,* 1912.
Wrappers. 250 copies only. *By C. D. Morley.* Some copies have been noted with
a printed presentation slip.

PARNASSUS ON WHEELS. *Garden City,* 1917.
First state is misprint Y *ears* for *Years,* p. 4, line 8. Boards, cloth back. A variant
binding has been noted with grayish-brown cloth spine instead of the usual light
tan.

SONGS FOR A LITTLE HOUSE. *New York* [1917].
First state has quotation from Southwell facing title page. Boards, paper labels.

SHANDYGAFF. *Garden City,* 1918.
First binding is dark blue cloth with gold stamping. Poem facing copyright page
not removed until fourth or fifth printing.

THE ROCKING HORSE. *New York* [1919].
First state has Burns quotation facing title page. Boards, paper labels.

THE HAUNTED BOOKSHOP. *New York,* 1919.
First state has numeral 76 at bottom of proper page, type above it, *Burroughs,*
is unbroken; p. 100, line one, reads *Sty,* later corrected to *Styx;* p. 163, line 1,
footfalls, later *foo tfalls.* Subsequent states have the numeral 76 lacking, still later
replaced in a position varying slightly from the original. In these replaced states,
however, the type immediately above is broken. Reissued, *Garden City,* 1920,
with an inserted leaf containing "P. S. to the Fifth Edition."

IN THE SWEET DRY AND DRY. *New York,* 1919.
With **BART HALEY.**

MINCE PIE. *New York* [1919].
First state, last work on p. vii, is *of;* later corrected to *on.* Boards, cloth back.

KATHLEEN. *Garden City,* 1920.
Boards, cloth back.

TRAVELS IN PHILADELPHIA. *Philadelphia* [1920].
First state has *along* for *among,* p. 202, line 13. Noted in two types of green cloth
binding with no priority established for either.

HIDE AND SEEK. *New York* [1920].
Bound in dark gray or smooth brown boards, with no priority established. First
state, p. 41, line 2, has *damsel,* later corrected to *damosel.*

PIPEFULS. *Garden City*, 1920.
Boards, cloth back.

TALES FROM A ROLLTOP DESK. *Garden City*, 1921.
Boards, cloth back.

PLUM PUDDING. *Garden City*, 1921.
First edition so stated on copyright page. Boards, cloth back.

CHIMNEYSMOKE. *New York* [1921].
First edition has *GHD* insignia on copyright page. Earliest state measures 9″ x 6″.
Later states, 7¼″ x 4¾″.

THE STORY OF GINGER CUBES. [*n.p.* (*New York?*), 1922].
Wrappers.

TRANSLATIONS FROM THE CHINESE. *New York* [1922].
First edition has *GHD* insignia on copyright page. Boards, cloth back. Reissued,
Garden City, 1927, "with additions and a few scholarly redactions, from four
previous books, viz.: *The Rocking Horse ... Hide and Seek ... Translations from
the Chinese ... Parsons' Pleasure.*"

WHERE THE BLUE BEGINS. *Garden City*, 1922.
First edition so stated on copyright page. Boards, cloth back. Rackham illustrated
edition, *Garden City* [1924] of which there were also 100 copies signed by artist
and author. Dramatised by the author in collaboration with E. S. Colling, *Garden
City*, 1925, wrappers, "... 100 advance copies for production purposes and for
private circulation ..."

THE POWDER OF SYMPATHY. *Garden City*, 1923.
First edition so stated on copyright page. Boards, cloth back. Noted in pale
orange boards, brown cloth back, and brilliant orange boards, black cloth back.

INWARD HO! *Garden City*, 1923.
First edition so stated on copyright page.

PARSONS' PLEASURE. *New York* [1923].
First edition has *GHD* insignia on copyright page. Boards. First state of labels
on cover misplaces apostrophe thus: *Parson's*.

PANDORA LIFTS THE LID. *New York* [1924].
First edition has *GHD* insignia on copyright page. In collaboration with DON
MARQUIS.

ONE ACT PLAYS. *Garden City*, 1924.
First edition so stated on copyright page. Boards, cloth back.

RELIGIO JOURNALISTICI. *Garden City*, 1924.
First edition so stated on copyright page. Boards.

FORTY-FOUR ESSAYS. *New York* [1925].
Cloth, paper labels. Issued in England as: "Safety Pins and Other Essays."

HOSTAGES TO FORTUNE. *Haverford* [1925].
Juvenilia written for a college magazine, 1908-1910. Boards. Second issue has double rule border on title page.

THUNDER ON THE LEFT. *Garden City*, 1925.
First edition so stated on copyright page. Also 100 copies, numbered and signed.

THE ROMANY STAIN. *Garden City*, 1926.
First edition so stated on copyright page. Boards, cloth back. Also 365 signed copies with three added essays.

THE ARROW. *Garden City*, 1927.
First edition so stated on copyright page. Also 30 copies in ornamented boards for presentation.

PLEASED TO MEET YOU. *Garden City*, 1927.
First edition so stated on copyright page. Boards. Also 30 copies in ornamented boards for presentation.

HAVERFORD EDITION [COLLECTED WORKS]. *Garden City*, 1927.
12 vols. 1,001 sets only. Vol. 1 signed. Contains some new material.

I KNOW A SECRET. *Garden City*, 1927.
First edition so stated on copyright page.

TOULEMONDE. *Garden City*, 1928.
First edition so stated on copyright page. 1,250 copies only.

OFF THE DEEP END. *Garden City*, 1928.
First edition so stated on copyright page. Boards, cloth back.

ESSAYS. *Garden City*, 1928.
First edition so stated on copyright page.

SEACOAST OF BOHEMIA. *Garden City*, 1929.
First edition so stated on copyright page. First printing has *raerly* for *rarely*, p. 20, line 19. Also 50 large paper copies.

BORN IN A BEER GARDEN; or, SHE TROUPES TO CONQUER. *New York*, 1930.
With others. Limited edition: "... 1 to 50 are for hilarity, and copies 51 to 999 are for sale. Copies 51 to 71 on imported paper and signed by all the contributors."

APOLOGIA PRO SUA PREOCCUPATIONE. *New York*, 1930.
225 copies only. Boards.

RUDOLPH AND AMINA. *New York* [1930].

MORLEY

JOHN MISTLETOE. *Garden City*, 1931.
First edition so stated on copyright page. Chapter number at p. 199 is 23; later corrected to 22.

SWISS FAMILY MANHATTAN. *Garden City*, 1932.
First edition so stated on copyright page. Also advance issue of 250 copies in decorated boards.

EX LIBRIS CARISSIMIS. *Philadelphia*, 1932.

HUMAN BEING. *Garden City*, 1932.
First edition so stated on copyright page. Also 250 copies with reproductions of the manuscript on covers.

MANDARIN IN MANHATTAN. *Garden City*, 1933.
First edition so stated on copyright page.

FIFTH AVENUE BUS. *Garden City*, 1933.
First edition so stated on copyright page. Reprinted material but with added first edition "translations."

SHAKESPEARE AND HAWAII. *Garden City*, 1933.
First edition so stated on copyright page. Also 500 copies with tipped-in title page having the University of Hawaii imprint.

INTERNAL REVENUE. *Garden City*, 1933.
First edition so stated on copyright page.

HASTA LA VISTA. *Garden City*, 1935.
First edition so stated on copyright page.

FOOTNOTES FOR A CENTENNIAL. *New York*, 1936.
400 copies only.

STREAMLINES. *Garden City*, 1936.
First printing indicated on copyright page.

CHRISTOPHER MORLEY'S BRIEFCASE. [*Philadelphia*, 1936].
Cloth or printed wrappers. *PLAza* for *PLaza*, p. 64, penultimate line.

THE TROJAN HORSE. [*Philadelphia*] 1937.
First printing indicated on the copyright page.

HISTORY OF AN AUTUMN. *Philadelphia & New York*, 1938.

KITTY FOYLE. *Philadelphia* [1939].
First printing indicated on the copyright page. The preliminary leaves, including some text, issued in advance of publication in pamphlet form as an advertisement.

LETTERS OF ASKANCE. *Philadelphia* [1939].

The secondary productions of Christopher Morley are so numerous that lack of space prevents a complete listing here. The more thorough collector is referred to the excellent and exhaustive "A Bibliography of Christopher Morley," by Alfred P. Lee, *Garden City*, 1935. The following are representative of the secondary items.

Record of the Class of 1910 of Haverford College. [*Haverford, Penna.*, 1910].
  Edited.
American Rhodes Scholars, 1910-1913. [*n.p., n.d.*, 1913].
  Contains material by and about Morley.
War Manual. *Garden City*, 1914.
  Contains "What America Thinks of War."
The Bookseller's Blue Book: February-August ... *Garden City*, 1914.
  Also, October-February, *Garden City*, 1915. Edited with others.
The Kaiser: A Book About the Most Interesting Man in Europe. *Garden City*, 1914.
  Co-editor and contributor.
Making Books and Magazines ... *Garden City* [1916].
  Wrappers. Edited.
Christopher Morley on the Amenities of Book Collecting. [*Boston*, 1919].
  Wrappers. Issued as an advertisement by the Atlantic Monthly Press.
The Gentle Art of Columning ... by C. L. Edson. *New York*, 1920.
  Introductory essay by Morley.
Best Short Stories. *Garden City*, 1918.
  Thomas L. Masson, ed. Contains: "The Arrival of Wilhelm," an anonymous contribution by Morley.
Modern Essays. *New York*, 1921.
  Edited. First state has *now* for *not*, last word, p. 50. School edition, *New York* [1922].
Folk Songs of Many Peoples. *New York* [1921].
  Florence Hudson Botsford, editor. Contribution.
Casuals of the Sea, by William McFee. *Garden City*, 1922.
  Lambskin Library Edition. Preface.
Explorers of the Dawn, by Mazo de la Roche. *New York*, 1922.
  Foreword by Morley.
A Treasury of Plays for Women. *Boston*, 1922.
  Frank Shay, ed. Contains: "Rehearsal," issued separately, *Garden City*, 1925.
The Child and the Book. [*Chicago*, 1922].
  Leaflet.
Thursday Evening. *Cincinnati* [1922].
  Play. Wrappers.
Parodies on Walt Whitman. *New York*, 1923.
  Compiled by Henry S. Saunders. Preface by Morley.
Nine Answers by George Bernard Shaw. [*n.p.*, 1923].
  62 copies only. Introduction by Morley.
An Apology for Boccaccio. *Philadelphia*, 1923.
  18 copies printed for James Shields; also 4 large paper copies.
Conrad and the Reporters. *Garden City*, 1923.
  815 copies only. Boards.

Justice of the Peace, by Frederic Niven. *New York*, 1923.
    Introduction by Morley.
Recitations Old and New for Boys and Girls, by Grace Gaige. *New York*, 1924.
    Introduction by Morley. First edition has (1) at foot of last printed page.
Outward Bound. *Grand Rapids, Michigan*, 1924.
    377 numbered copies only, printed for Oliver Wallace.
Modern Essays: Second Series. *New York*, 1924.
    Edited.
A Round Table in Poictesme. *Cleveland*, 1924.
    Samuel Loveman, editor. For further regarding this publication see under Cabell.
    Contribution by Morley.
The Bowling Green. *Garden City*, 1924.
    First edition so stated on copyright page. Edited.
A Daughter of the Samurai, by Etsu Inagaki Sugimoto. *Garden City*, 1925.
    Introduction by Morley.
Full and By. *Garden City*, 1925.
    Cameron Rogers, ed. Boards. Also 200 de luxe copies. Preface by Morley.
Forty-Four Essays. *New York*, 1925.
    Contribution by Morley.
Two Fables. *Garden City*, 1925.
    Translated by Morley from the French of De Musset and the German of Hauff.
    First edition so stated on copyright page.
'Twixt Land and Sea, by Joseph Conrad. *Garden City*, 1925.
    Vol. XIII of the Memorial Edition of the Writings of Joseph Conrad. Introduction by Morley.
Two Prefaces by Walt Whitman. *Garden City*, 1926.
    First edition so stated on copyright page. Introduction by Morley.
Good Theatre: A Fancy in One Scene. *New York*, 1926.
    Boards. 105 copies with Rudge imprint; later published by Doubleday, Page and Company.
Paumanok. *Garden City*, 1926.
    107 privately printed copies only. Boards.
The Jessamy Bride, by F. Frankfort Moore. *New York*, 1926.
    Introduction by Morley.
Serenade, by Hugh Western. *Chicago*, 1926.
    Preface by Morley. Boards.
The Century. [*New York?*, 1927].
    Wrappers. Issued as an advertisement for the New York Central Railroad.
Epigrams in a Cellar. [*Oxford*, 1927].
    Leaflet.
The Case of Bouck White. *Philadelphia*, 1927.
    72 copies only, privately printed. Wrappers.
My One Contribution to Seventeenth Century Scholarship. *New York*, 1927.
    Wrappers. 100 copies only.
A Letter to Leonora. [*Chicago*] 1928.
    Issued by Marshall Field and Company as an advertisement. Also 125 copies, in boards, numbered and signed.

The Sea and the Jungle, by H. M. Tomlinson. *New York* [1928].
  Modern Library edition. Introduction by Morley.
Really, My Dear ... : A Play in One Act. *New York*, 1928.
  300 copies only. Boards.
A Ride in the Cab of the Twentieth Century Limited. *Lancaster, Penna.*, 1928.
  250 copies in either boards or wrappers. Issued as an advertisement by the
  Hamilton Watch Company.
The House of Dooner: The Last of the Friendly Inns. *Philadelphia*, 1928.
  With THOMAS AUGUSTIN DALY. 1,000 numbered copies in boards only.
Thoughts at the Bottom of a Mug of Cider. *Northampton* [1928].
  Wrappers.
The Worst Christmas Story. [*New York*] 1928.
  365 copies only.
In Modern Dress: A One Act Play. *Larchmont*, 1929.
  500 copies only. Boards, paper label.
Poems. *Garden City*, 1929.
  First edition so stated on copyright page. Cloth or red leather. Contains some first
  edition material.
The Palette Knife. *New York*, 1929.
  450 copies only, numbered and signed. Reprinted from "Off the Deep End."
The Goldfish Under the Ice. *London*, 1929.
  530 copies. Boards. Dated 1929 but not published until 1930. American edition,
  Garden City, 1932, with imprint of Doubleday Doran or The Junior Literary
  Guild.
Sun Cured: A Peccadillo. *New York* [1930].
  53 copies only, privately printed. Leaflet.
The Complete Sherlock Holmes. *Garden City*, 1930.
  Foreword by Morley.
Second Mate. *New York*, 1930.
  Announced but not published. In collaboration with FELIX RIESENBERG.
The Short Stories of Saki (H. H. Munro). *New York*, 1930.
  Introduction by Morley.
Whisky, by Aeneas MacDonald. *Garden City*, 1930.
  Boards. 307 copies only.
The Blue and the Gray; or, War Is Hell ... By Judson Kilpatrick and J. Owen
  Moore. *Garden City*, 1930.
  Revised and edited by Morley. First edition so stated on copyright page. Also
  100 special copies with inserted leaf signed by Morley.
Wanderer's End, by Dennis Clough. *Garden City*, 1930.
  Foreword by Morley.
A Book of Days, For 1931. *New York* [1930].
  Selected by Morley. Revised and reissued [1931], "A Book of Days, For 1932."
The Adventures of Tom Sawyer, by Mark Twain. *Philadelphia* [etc.] [1931].
  Introduction by Morley.
Don't Open Until Christmas. *Garden City*, 1931.
  First printing so stated. Boards. Reprint of "Slow Gin," in: "The Romany Stain,"
  Garden City, 1926.

MORLEY

Notes on Bermuda. *New York*, 1931.
 Boards.
"When We Speak of a Tenth ——." ₁*Lancaster, Penna.*, 1931₁.
 Also 260 large paper copies in boards. Ordinary edition, in wrappers, issued simul-
 taneously, marked "second printing."
Blythe Mountain, Vermont. *Brattleboro* ₁1931₁.
 500 copies.
Max and Moritz. *New York*, 1932.
 Translated from the German of Wilhelm Busch and with a foreword by Morley.
 Boards.
England, Their England, by A. G. MacDonell. *New York*, 1933.
"Effendi" Frank Nelson Doubleday 1862-1934. ₁*Privately Printed, Garden City?*₁
 1934.
Old Loopy: A Love Letter for Chicago. *Chicago*, 1935.
BR's Secret Passion. ₁*New York*(?) 1935₁.
 Wrappers.
The Life and Opinions of Tristram Shandy ... by Laurence Sterne. *New York*, 1935.
 2 vols. 1,500 copies only for members of the Limited Editions Club. Introduction
 by Morley.
America's Town Meeting of the Air, No. 9, Literature and Life. *New York* ₁1935₁.
 Lyman Bryson, editor. Contribution by Morley.
Rare Books: An Essay. *New York*, 1935.
 Privately printed pamphlet. 75 copies only.
A Christmas Salute. *New York*, 1935.
 Wrappers. 300 copies only.
Portraits and Self-Portraits, by Georges Schreiber. *Boston*, 1936.
 Contribution.
The Complete Works of William Shakespeare. *Garden City*, 1936.
Selected Poems of Thomas Augustin Daly. *New York* ₁1936₁.
Ex Libris. Compiled for the First New York Times National Book Fair. *New York*,
 1936.
 Title page in red and black. *Helen* for *Helm* on the back cover.
Thomas Bird Mosher. ₁*Privately Printed*₁ 1936.
 Wrappers.
Preface to "Bartlett." *Boston*, 1937.
 Boards. A separate printing of Morley's preface to "Bartlett's Familiar Quota-
 tions," *Boston*, 1937, edited by Morley and Louella D. Everett.
"It's a Kind of a Memorabilia." *Philadelphia*, 1937.
 Wrappers.
Sir Kenelm Reads in Bed. *New York* ₁1937₁.
 Wrappers. 400 copies only.
Goodbye to Spring. *New York*, 1937.
 200 copies only. All but 12 copies have a cancel title page bearing the *Philadelphia*
 imprint. The first state of the book has a *New York* imprint and the title page is
 not a cancel. Boards.

Morley's Magnum. *Philadelphia*, 1938.
    Mainly reprint but with some first edition material.
Friends of the Library. *New York* [1937].
    Wrappers.
Christopher Morley's Scrapbook. [*n.p., n.d.*].
    1,000 copies only. Wrappers.
On the Return of a Book Lent to a Friend. [*Chicago*] 1938.
    Wrappers. 50 copies only.
Esoterica Viniani. [*Muscatine, Iowa*] 1938.
    Wrappers. 100 copies only.
No Crabb, No Christmas. *Chicago*, 1938.
    225 copies only.
The Stag at Ease. *Caldwell, Idaho*, 1938.
    Marian Squire, editor.
Sons of the Puritans, by Don Marquis. *New York*, 1939.
    Introduction.
Passivity Program. *Chicago*, 1939.
Friends, Romans, ——. *Minneapolis and St. Paul*, 1940.
    535 copies only.
Leaves of Grass, by Walt Whitman. *New York*, 1940.
    Edited and with an introduction by Morley.

BIOGRAPHICAL

Christopher Morley: His History. *Garden City*, 1922.
    Wrappers.
Christopher Morley: Multi ex Uno, by Babette Hughes. *Seattle*, 1927.
    Pamphlet.
A Bibliography of Christopher Morley, by Alfred P. Lee. *Garden City*, 1935.

John Muir

1838–1914

THE MOUNTAINS OF CALIFORNIA. *New York*, 1894.
Also revised and enlarged edition with illustrations by the author, *New Yor*
1911.

OUR NATIONAL PARKS. *Boston*, 1901.
Revised and enlarged, *Boston*, 1909.

STICKEEN. *Boston*, 1909.

EDWARD HENRY HARRIMAN. *Garden City*, 1911.

MY FIRST SUMMER IN THE SIERRA. *Boston*, 1911.

THE YOSEMITE. *New York*, 1912.

THE STORY OF MY BOYHOOD AND YOUTH. *Boston*, 1913.

LETTERS TO A FRIEND ... MRS. EZRA C. CARR. *Boston*, 1915.
300 copies only.

TRAVELS IN ALASKA. *Boston*, 1915.

THE WRITINGS OF JOHN MUIR. *Boston*, 1916.
10 vols. Edited by W. F. Badè. Also, Manuscript Edition limited to 750 copies.

A THOUSAND-MILE WALK TO THE GULF. *Boston*, 1916.
Also 550 large paper copies.

THE CRUISE OF THE CORWIN. *Boston*, 1917.
Edited by W. F. Badè. See below, 1883.

STEEP TRAILS. *Boston*, 1918.
Edited by W. F. Badè.

JOHN OF THE MOUNTAINS. *Boston*, 1938.
Hitherto unpublished journals edited by Linne Marsh Wolfe.

Cruise of the Revenue Steamer Corwin. *Washington*, 1883.
Contribution.
Picturesque California and the Region West of the Rocky Mountains from Alaska
to Mexico. *San Francisco*, 1888.
Edited and with contributions by Muir. 30 paper covered parts or "Artist's Edi-
tion," 100 copies only on Japan vellum with illustrations signed by the artists.
There were numerous other states in various formats and bindings; no probable
priority.

Reference List to Published Writings of John Muir, by Cornelius B. Bradley. [Berke-
ley, Cal., 1897].
    Wrappers.
Let Every One Help to Save the Famous Hetch-Hetchy Valley. [San Francisco, 1909].
    Pamphlet.
Two California Neighbors. [Sacramento, 1912].
The Boyhood of a Naturalist. Boston [1913].
    Reprinted from "The Story of my Boyhood and Youth."
Alaska Days With John Muir, by S. Hall Young. New York and Chicago [1915].
John Muir in Yosemite, by William F. Badè. [New York?, 1920].
John Muir, A Picturesque Biography ... Compiled by the Pupils of the John Muir
School, Seattle, Washington. [Seattle, Wash., 1938].

George Jean Nathan

1882–

THE ETERNAL MYSTERY. *New York,* 1913.

EUROPE AFTER 8:15. *New York,* 1914.
With H. L. MENCKEN and WILLARD HUNTINGTON WRIGHT.

ANOTHER BOOK ON THE THEATRE. *New York,* 1915.

BOTTOMS UP. *New York,* 1917.

MR. GEORGE JEAN NATHAN PRESENTS. *New York,* 1917.
Black cloth with gold stamping. Also some copies with untrimmed edges.

A BOOK WITHOUT A TITLE. *New York,* 1918.
First edition has *Philip Goodman* imprint.

THE POPULAR THEATRE. *New York,* 1918.
Reissued with new introduction, *New York* [1923].

COMEDIANS ALL. *New York,* 1919.

HELIOGABALUS. *New York,* 1920.
With H. L. MENCKEN. For further regarding this publication see under the latter.

THE AMERICAN CREDO. *New York,* 1920.
With H. L. MENCKEN. In 1921 the authors issued a supplementary leaflet, uniform in size and format with the published book; the pagination was continuous and the entire edition was limited to 50 privately printed copies. Revised and enlarged editions, *New York,* 1921, 1927 and 1935.

THE THEATRE, THE DRAMA, THE GIRLS. *New York,* 1921.

THE CRITIC AND THE DRAMA. *New York,* 1922.

THE WORLD IN FALSEFACE. *New York,* 1923.

MATERIA CRITICA. *New York,* 1924.
Also 100 copies, uncut and signed.

THE AUTOBIOGRAPHY OF AN ATTITUDE. *New York,* 1925.
Also a few untrimmed copies.

THE HOUSE OF SATAN. *New York,* 1926.
Also 100 signed copies.

THE NEW AMERICAN CREDO. *New York,* 1927.
Also 50 copies, numbered and signed.

LAND OF THE PILGRIMS' PRIDE. *New York,* 1927.
Also 140 signed large paper copies, numbered.

ART OF THE NIGHT. *New York,* 1928.
Also 150 signed copies.

MONKS ARE MONKS: A DIAGNOSTIC SCHERZO. *New York,* 1929.
Also 110 signed copies.

TESTAMENT OF A CRITIC. *New York,* 1931.

THE INTIMATE NOTE BOOKS OF GEORGE JEAN NATHAN. *New York,* 1932.
First edition so stated on the copyright page.

SINCE IBSEN. *New York,* 1933.
First edition so stated on the copyright page.

PASSING JUDGMENTS. *New York,* 1935.
First edition so stated on the copyright page.

THE THEATRE OF THE MOMENT. *New York,* 1936.
First printing indicated on the copyright page.

THE AVON FLOWS. *New York* [1937].
First printing indicated on the copyright page.

THE MORNING AFTER THE FIRST NIGHT. *New York,* 1938.
First printing indicated on the copyright page.

ENCYCLOPEDIA OF THE THEATRE. *New York,* 1940.
First printing indicated on the copyright page.

THE BACHELOR LIFE. *New York* [1941].

THE ENTERTAINMENT OF A NATION.
Announced.

Pistols for Two, by Owen Hatteras. *New York,* 1917.
Pamphlet. Owen Hatteras, pseudonym for Nathan and H. L. Mencken; joint authors.
How's Your Second Act? by Arthur Hopkins. *New York,* 1918.
Foreword.
The Borzoi, 1920. *New York,* 1920.
Contains an essay on Mencken by Nathan.
Suggestions to Our Visitors. *New York* [1922].
Leaflet. With H. L. MENCKEN.
Civilization in the United States. *New York,* 1922.
Contribution.
The Moon of the Caribbees, by Eugene O'Neill. *New York,* 1923.
Preface.

The Borzoi, 1925. *New York* [1925].

    Contains "Hergey," by Nathan. Also "Fender Fishing with Mr. Nathan," by Carl van Doren. Also 500 large paper copies signed by the editors.

The Theatre of Today. *New York,* 1927-28.

    4 vols. Edited and with prefaces by Nathan.

Living Philosophies. *New York,* 1931.

    Contains a chapter by Nathan.

Encyclopedia Britannica. *New York* [1929].

    Vol. 7 contains "The American Drama," by Nathan.

The Vanity Fair Book. *New York* [1931].

    Contains "The Theatre," by Nathan.

American Spectator Year Book. *New York,* 1934.

    Edited by Nathan with others.

The Bedside Esquire. *New York* [1940].

    Arnold Gingrich, editor. Contribution.

Five Great Modern Irish Plays. *New York* [1941].

    Foreword.

Britannica Book of the Year.

    Issues for 1939, 1940, 1941 contain Nathan's survey of the American theatre.

BIOGRAPHICAL

George Jean Nathan: A Critical Study, by Isaac Goldberg. *Girard, Kansas* [1925].

    Wrappers. The item following is "an extension" of this publication.

The Theatre of George Jean Nathan, by Isaac Goldberg. *New York,* 1926.

    Also 12 copies signed by author and Nathan.

The Quintessence of Nathanism, by Vladimir Kozlenko. *New York,* 1930.

While a student at Bologna, Mr. Nathan wrote a book of sonnets in Italian; information unavailable.

Robert (Gruntal) Nathan
1894–

PETER KINDRED. *New York*, 1919.

AUTUMN. *New York*, 1921.
It is said that the first binding is light green. *Published, 1921* on copyright page. Reissued, *New York* [1935].

YOUTH GROWS OLD. *New York*, 1922.
Published March, 1922 on copyright page.

THE PUPPET MASTER. *New York*, 1923.
Issued in various colored boards with cloth back. *First Published 1923* on copyright page.

JONAH. *New York*, 1925.
The first binding is green-stamped; later binding is gold-stamped. Illustrated edition, with new preface, *New York*, 1934. Issued in England as "The Son of Amittai."

THE FIDDLER IN BARLY. *New York*, 1926.
First Published, October, 1926 on copyright page.

THE WOODCUTTER'S HOUSE. *Indianapolis* [1927].
Apparently two or more printings without change of title page. No definite priority established.

THE BISHOP'S WIFE. *Indianapolis* [1928].
First edition so stated on copyright page.

A CEDAR BOX. *Indianapolis* [1929].
1,500 numbered copies only. Paper boards. At least two types of paper were used on the covers; no known priority.

THERE IS ANOTHER HEAVEN. *Indianapolis* [1929].
Also a very few large paper copies for private use. It has been asserted that the earliest copies do not have the first edition notice on the copyright page; the copyright deposit copies do not have it.

THE ORCHID. *Indianapolis* [1931].
First edition so stated on copyright page. Also a few copies issued untrimmed.

ONE MORE SPRING. *New York*, 1933.
First edition so stated on copyright page. Reissued, *Stamford, Conn.*, 1935, in a de luxe edition of 750 copies only.

ROBERT NATHAN

ROAD OF AGES. *New York,* 1935.

First edition so stated on copyright page. The first printing has a 1934 copyright notice and the colophon credits the paper to *Warren;* later printings have a 1935 copyright notice, paper credited to *Glatfelter.*

SELECTED POEMS. *New York,* 1935.

First edition, so stated on copyright page. First binding, 250, is blue decorated cloth, paper label on spine; second binding, wood veneer sides, cloth back, paper label.

THE ENCHANTED VOYAGE. *New York,* 1936.

First edition so stated on copyright page.

WINTER IN APRIL. *New York,* 1938.

First edition so indicated on copyright page. Also advance copies in printed wrappers.

JOURNEY OF TAPIOLA. *New York,* 1938.

First printing indicated on copyright page.

PORTRAIT OF JENNIE. *New York,* 1940.

First printing indicated on copyright page, has copyright notice dated 1939 and 1940, the latter date in some copies inked out by hand. Also the following typographical errors: p. 29, line 5, *Stuart* for *Steuart;* p. 171, 7th line from the bottom of page, *onght* for *ought.* Later printings have the errors corrected and the copyright date is 1939 only.

THE CONCERT. *New York,* 1940.

250 copies only, numbered and signed.

A WINTER TIDE: SONNETS AND POEMS. *New York,* 1940.

First printing indicated on the copyright page. Also advance copies in stiff wrappers with paper label on the front cover.

THEY WENT ON TOGETHER. *New York,* 1941.

First printing indicated on the copyright page. Also advance copies with the statement *Complimentary Advance Copy* on the preliminary end paper.

The Barly Fields. *New York,* 1928.
Reprint of previously collected works with an introduction by the author.
Tina-Mina, by Dorothy Mayer. *Boston,* 1930.
Illustrated by Nathan.
The Work of Robert Nathan, by Louis Bromfield. *Indianapolis* [n.d.].
Pamphlet. Contains a bibliographical checklist.
Best Poems of 1933. *London* [1933].
Thomas Moult, editor. Contains "Atque Vale," by Nathan.
Designed for Reading. *New York,* 1934.
Contribution.

Best Poems of 1935. *London* [1935].
Thomas Moult, editor. Contains "Answer to Millay," by Nathan.

"Atoms" and "The Coward" are one-act plays, first printed in *The Harvard Monthly*, Cambridge, November 1913 and March 1914, respectively. "It," written under the pseudonym, Richard Florance, in *The Smart Set*, December 1915, also remains uncollected.

John G[neisenau] Neihardt

1881–

A BUNDLE OF MYRRH. [*n.p.*] MCIII [! 1903].
Limp leather binding. 5 copies only. See "A Bundle of Myrrh," 1907.

THE DIVINE ENCHANTMENT. *New York*, 1900.

THE LONESOME TRAIL. *New York*, 1907.

A BUNDLE OF MYRRH. *New York*, 1907.
Boards. A revised reissue of the author's first book with added material.

MAN-SONG. *New York*, 1909.
Label on front cover.

THE RIVER AND I. *New York*, 1910.
Revised and reissued, 1927.

THE DAWN-BUILDER. *New York*, 1911.

THE STRANGER AT THE GATE. *New York*, 1912.

LIFE'S LURE. *New York*, 1914.

THE SONG OF HUGH GLASS. *New York*, 1915.
Annotated edition, *New York*, 1919. Published with "The Song of Three Friends," 1924.

THE QUEST. *New York*, 1916.

THE SONG OF THREE FRIENDS. *New York*, 1919.
Published in an annotated edition with "The Song of Hugh Glass," 1924.

THE SPLENDID WAYFARING. *New York*, 1920.

TWO MOTHERS. *New York*, 1921.
Contains two plays: "The Death of Agrippina" and "800 Rubles."

LAUREATE ADDRESS. *Chicago*, 1921.
500 signed copies only.

POETIC VALUES: THEIR REALITY AND OUR NEED OF THEM. *New York*, 1925.

THE SONG OF THE INDIAN WARS. *New York*, 1925.
Also 500 numbered and signed copies. Annotated edition, 1928.

INDIAN TALES AND OTHERS. *New York*, 1926.

COLLECTED POEMS. *New York,* 1926.
  Also 500 signed copies. 2 vols.

BLACK ELK SPEAKS. *New York,* 1932.

SONG OF THE MESSIAH. *New York,* 1935.

The Poet's Pack. *Chicago,* 1921.
  Edited. Vol. 3 in "The Bookfellow's Series." 500 copies only.
John G. Neihardt: Man and Poet, by J. T. House. *Wayne, Neb.,* 1920.
Fifty Poets. *New York* [1933].
  Contribution.

A[lfred] Edward Newton
1863–1940

THE AMENITIES OF BOOK COLLECTING AND KINDRED AFFECTIONS. *Boston,* 1918.

Boards. An erratum slip is usually found at p. 268; 9th word from the left, line three, should be *Piccadilly.* The second edition has an index; the second and third new prefaces by the author. A caricature plate of Dr. Johnson, omitted from this book by the publishers, was privately circulated by Mr. Newton. Reissued, *New York* [1935] with new introduction.

A MAGNIFICENT FARCE AND OTHER DIVERSIONS OF A BOOK COLLECTOR. *Boston* [1921].

Boards. Also 265 numbered large paper copies, signed; and a preissue with all edges trimmed in unprinted brown wrappers. Mr. Newton privately circulated a caricature of Woodrow Wilson, omitted from this book.

DOCTOR JOHNSON: A PLAY. *Boston,* 1923.

Boards. Also 585 copies on handmade paper, signed. Paraphrases of lines by Johnson and his contemporaries with additional lines by Newton.

THE GREATEST BOOK IN THE WORLD. *Boston* [1925].

Boards. Also 470 large paper copies, signed. Later issues are so designated on copyright page; p. xvi lists the autograph of Cruikshank as on p. 341; later corrected to p. 334.

THIS BOOK COLLECTING GAME. *Boston,* 1928.

Also 990 large paper copies, numbered and signed. Boards. The running head at p. 49 reads *Childhood* for *Boyhood.*

THE FORMAT OF THE ENGLISH NOVEL. *Cleveland,* 1928.

289 copies only.

A TOURIST IN SPITE OF HIMSELF. *Boston,* 1930.

Also 525 large paper copies, signed. "A Tourist in Spite of Himself in Egypt," *Boston,* 1929, 300 numbered copies only, later included in this volume.

ON BOOKS AND BUSINESS. [*New York*] 1930.

Boards. 325 signed copies only.

END PAPERS. *Boston,* 1933.

Also 1,351 large paper copies, signed.

DERBY DAY AND OTHER ADVENTURES. *Boston,* 1934.

Also 1,129 large paper copies, signed.

BIBLIOGRAPHY AND PSEUDO-BIBLIOGRAPHY. *Philadelphia*, 1936.
Boards.

NEWTON ON BLACKSTONE. *Philadelphia*, 1937.
2,000 copies only, numbered and signed.

Some years before the appearance of his first book of essays Mr. Newton wrote some advertising material for his electrical concern. The first two listed below are among these. As *A. Edward Newton and Company* he published the books of other authors, at least one of his own and edited several others. A full list of these publications is given in John T. Winterich's "The Imprints of A. Edw. Newton & Co.," in "The Colophon," Vol. 1, No. 4, *New York*, Spring, 1936. Newton was also the author of numerous Christmas "cards," a representative few of these are listed below. Practically all of these Christmas publications were later incorporated into the books in the main list above.

Who's Who and What's What. *Philadelphia* [1913].
Experience Is Master. *Philadelphia* [1926].
Designed ... More Especially. *Oak Knoll*, 1910.
Trollopeana. *Oak Knoll*, 1911.
Oscar Wilde. *Oak Knoll*, 1912.
   Errata slip.
A Ridiculous Philosopher. *Oak Knoll*, 1913.
A Leech Drawing. *Oak Knoll*, 1923.
My Library. *Oak Knoll*, 1926.
A Reprimand and What Came of It. *Oak Knoll*, 1927.
Nelson. *Oak Knoll*, 1928.

The eight preceding are representative of Mr. Newton's Christmas "cards."

A Slogan for Booksellers. *Boston* [1920].
A Noble Fragment. *New York*, 1921.
   A leaf from the Gutenberg Bible with an essay. Also a few unbound preliminary copies without the leaf.
Sales Catalog of Dr. Johnson's Library. *New York* [1925].
   250 signed copies only with an essay.
A Peregrination of Philadelphia. [*Philadelphia*, 1926].
Prime Pickwicks in Parts, by John C. Eckel. *New York*, 1928.
   440 copies only signed by Eckel and Newton. Foreword by Newton.
Mr. Strahan's Dinner Party. *San Francisco*, 1930.
   Play. Boards.
Introductions to the Ashley Library Catalog. *New York*, 1934.
   Contribution.
A Doctor's Odyssey, by A. Gaylord Beaman. *Baltimore*, 1935.
   Introduction.
The American Senator, by Anthony Trollope. *New York* [1940].
   Contribution.

NEWTON

BIBLIOGRAPHICAL

The Writings of A. Edward Newton ... by George H. Sargent. *Philadelphia, 1927.*
110 copies only signed by the compiler. Supplementing this bibliography are:
"The Eminent A. Edward Newton Collection Formed by George H. Sargent,"
Metuchen, N. J., 299 copies only; American Art Association Anderson Galleries,
Inc., sales catalog 4098, April 4 and 5, 1924 (*Bixby et al.*) which contains many
of the Newton books.

A Busted Bibliophile and His Books, by George H. Sargent. *Boston, 1928.*
600 copies only. Boards.

A Tribute to A. Edward Newton. Christmas 1940. [*Washington, D. C.,* 1940].
Printed wrappers. Issued by the Library of Congress. Exists in four states as follows: 1: The text printed on mixed papers; suppressed. 2: Text printed on white
wove paper, limited to 1,000 copies. 3: Same as preceding but marked *Second
Issue, January 1941;* 490 copies printed. 4: Second edition, so marked on reverse
of title page.

Lack of space prevents a greater listing of the many publication to which Mr.
Newton contributed introductions.

(Benjamin) Frank[lin] Norris
1870–1902

YVERNELLE. *Philadelphia*, 1892.
Cloth or full leather.

MORAN OF THE LADY LETTY. *New York*, 1898.
With or without top edges stained; no known priority. Issued in England as "Shanghaied."

MC TEAGUE. *New York*, 1899.
Last word, p. 106, is *moment*.

BLIX. *New York*, 1899.

A MAN'S WOMAN. *New York*, 1900.
Light red cloth, decorative stamping, publisher's name on the spine. Green cloth binding stamped *Special Edition* at foot of spine is later.

THE OCTOPUS. *New York*, 1901.
Later states lack many of the signature numbers. Publisher's name on spine noted in two states.

THE PIT. *New York*, 1903.
First Edition on the copyright page. Boards, paper label on spine, for presentation purposes. First trade edition is bound in red cloth.

THE RESPONSIBILITIES OF THE NOVELIST. *New York*, 1903.
First state has untrimmed edges.

A DEAL IN WHEAT. *New York*, 1903.
Noted in varying shades of red cloth binding with no known priority.

THE JOYOUS MIRACLE. *New York*, 1906.
Boards.

THE THIRD CIRCLE. *New York*, 1909.

VANDOVER AND THE BRUTE. *Garden City*, 1914.
Boards, paper label. Also advance issue, boards, cloth back.

THE SURRENDER OF SANTIAGO. *San Francisco*, 1917.
Wrappers.

COMPLETE WORKS. *Garden City*, 1928.
"The Argonaut Edition," 10 vols., 500 sets only. Vol. I of each set contains a half page of the original "McTeague" manuscript. Vol. X is first edition material

with the exception of "Travis Hallet's Half-Back," "The Surrender of Santiago," and "A Lost Story." Trade edition, *Garden City*, 1929.

"The Golden Gate Edition," *New York*, 1903, 7 vols., 100 sets only.

FRANK NORRIS OF "THE WAVE." STORIES AND SKETCHES. *San Francisco*, 1931.

500 numbered copies only. Foreword by Charles G. Norris. Introduction by Oscar Lewis.

CONTRIBUTIONS, ETC.

Blue and Gold: The University of California Annual, Class of 1893. *San Francisco*, 1892.

Contains both prose and illustrations by Norris.

Blue and Gold: The University of California Annual, Class of 1894. *San Francisco*, 1893.

Contains "Two Pair: A Play," by Norris, with his illustrations. Reprinted in "California Play and Pageant" [*Berkeley, Cal.*, 1913] without the illustrations.

The Story of the Files, by Ella Sterling Cummings. *San Francisco*, 1893.

Contains a poem, "Crespusculum," later reprinted in "Frank Norris: Two Poems and 'Kim' Reviewed," 1930.

Under the Berkeley Oaks. *San Francisco*, 1901.

First book appearance for "Travis Hallet's Half-Back."

The Author's Year Book for 1902. *New York*, 1902.

First book appearance for "The Volunteer Manuscript."

The Panic Episode. [*New York*, 1903].

Reprinted from "The Pit" for William A. Brady. Wrappers.

Argonaut Stories. *San Francisco*, 1906.

First book appearance for "A Caged Lion." First state does not have press notices at the back.

The Spinners' Book of Fiction. *San Francisco* [1907].

First book appearance for "The Lost Story." First binding is rough buckram-like grass cloth.

The California Story Book. *Berkeley, Cal.*, 1909.

Contains "The Passing of Cockeye Blakelock" reprinted from "A Deal in Wheat."

BIBLIOGRAPHICAL AND BIOGRAPHICAL

Frank Norris: Two Poems and 'Kim' Reviewed. With a Bibliography by Harvey Taylor. *San Francisco*, 1930.

200 copies only signed by Harvey Taylor and the illustrator, Clairice Collins. The first 25 copies contained an original Charles G. Norris letter, inserted.

Frank Norris: A Biography, by Franklin Walker. *Garden City*, 1932.

First printing indicated on the copyright page.

Eugene (Gladstone) O'Neill

1888–

THIRST AND OTHER ONE ACT PLAYS. *Boston* [1914].
Boards, cloth back, paper labels.

BOUND EAST FOR CARDIFF. *New York,* 1916.
In "The Provincetown Plays," first series. Printed wrappers.

BEFORE BREAKFAST. *New York,* 1916.
Printed wrappers. In "The Provincetown Plays," third series. Also separately issued a few days later, printed from the same type, with *Frank Shay* imprint on front cover.

THE MOON OF THE CARIBBEES, AND SIX OTHER PLAYS OF THE SEA. *New York,* 1919.
Boards, cloth back. First state is $\frac{7}{8}''$ thick.

BEYOND THE HORIZON. *New York* [1920].
Two states noted. The probable first is the one with the capital letters on the front cover measuring $\frac{9}{16}''$ high.

GOLD. *New York* [1920].
Boards, cloth back.

THE EMPEROR JONES: DIFF'RENT: THE STRAW. *New York* [1921].
Boards, cloth back. "The Emperor Jones" issued later, *Cincinnati* [1921], with textual changes.

THE HAIRY APE: ANNA CHRISTIE: THE FIRST MAN. *New York* [1922].
Boards, cloth back. "Anna Christie" separately issued, *London* [1923]. "The Hairy Ape" separately issued, *New York* [1929].

THE DREAMY KID. *Cincinnati* [1922].
In "Contemporary One Act Plays of 1921."

ALL GOD'S CHILLUN GOT WINGS, AND WELDED. *New York* [1924].
Boards, cloth back.

DESIRE UNDER THE ELMS. *New York,* 1925.
Reprinted from "Complete Works," 1924.

THE GREAT GOD BROWN: THE FOUNTAIN: THE MOON OF THE CARIBBEES AND OTHER PLAYS. *New York,* 1926.
First for "The Great God Brown" and "The Fountain." The former separately issued *London* [1926].

MARCO MILLIONS. *New York*, 1927.

Also 450 numbered copies, signed, issued in the month following the trade.

LAZARUS LAUGHED. *New York*, 1927.

Also 775 copies, numbered and signed, issued after the trade edition; both issued November 1927. Previously in "The American Caravan," published September 1927.

STRANGE INTERLUDE. *New York*, 1928.

Also 775 copies, numbered and signed, printed from type other than that used in the trade edition; issued after the trade edition. A pamphlet, "Extracts from 'The [sic] Strange Interlude,'" issued [Boston, 1929].

DYNAMO. *New York*, 1929.

Also 775 numbered copies, signed, issued after trade edition.

MOURNING BECOMES ELECTRA. *New York*, 1931.

Issued simultaneously with the Theatre Guild edition. Also 550 copies numbered and signed issued after the trade edition.

AH, WILDERNESS! *New York* [1933].

Also 325 numbered and signed copies issued several weeks after trade edition. First edition so stated on copyright page.

DAYS WITHOUT END. *New York* [1934].

Also 325 numbered and signed copies issued in month following publication of trade edition. First edition so stated on copyright page.

COMPLETE WORKS. *New York*, 1924.

2 vols. 1,200 sets only, numbered and signed. First for "Desire Under the Elms." Contains many revisions. Reissued, 4 vols., 1925. "Wilderness Edition," *New York*, 1934-35, 12 vols., with new preface for each. Contains all the O'Neill plays save those in "Thirst" [1914].

Pleiades Club Year Book. [*New York*, 1912].

500 copies only. Contains "Free," a poem by O'Neill.

The Seven Arts Magazine, June 1917. [*New York*] 1917.

Contains "Tomorrow," O'Neill's only known published short story.

The Theatre of George Jean Nathan, by Isaac Goldberg. *New York*, 1926.

Contains several O'Neill letters.

Eugene O'Neill, by Barrett H. Clark. *New York*, 1926.

Contains a bibliography. Revised, *New York* [1936].

Anathema! Litanies of Negation, by Benjamin de Casseres. *New York*, 1928.

1,250 copies only. Foreword by O'Neill.

A Bibliography of the Works of Eugene O'Neill, by Ralph Sanborn and Barrett H. Clark. *New York*, 1931.

500 copies only. Contains 51 pages of unpublished poetry.

Eugene O'Neill: A Critical Study, by S. Keith Winther. *New York*, 1934.

The American Spectator Year Book. *New York,* 1934.
  Contribution by O'Neill.
Eugene O'Neill, A Poet's Quest, by Richard Dana Skinner. *New York,* 1935.
  First printing indicated on copyright page.

"Nine Plays," 1933, is a reprint collection offered as a book club premium.

Thomas Nelson Page

1853–1922

IN OLE VIRGINIA. *New York,* 1887.
Noted with three sets of inserted advertisements, the first of these having no advertisement for "Free Joe" on the last page. Illustrated edition, *New York,* 1896.

BEFO' DE WAR. *New York,* 1888.
With A. C. GORDON.

TWO LITTLE CONFEDERATES. *New York,* 1888.

ON NEWFOUND RIVER. *New York,* 1891.
Reissued with new introduction, *New York,* 1906.

AMONG THE CAMPS. *New York,* 1891.

ELSKET AND OTHER STORIES. *New York,* 1891.

THE OLD SOUTH. *New York,* 1892.
Reissued with new introduction, *Chautauqua, N. Y.,* 1919.

THE BURIAL OF THE GUNS. *New York,* 1894.
Two states of binding. The publishers state that the first is **cream cloth**, but this statement has been questioned.

PASTIME STORIES. *New York,* 1894.

THE OLD GENTLEMAN OF THE BLACK STOCK. *New York,* 1897.
Illustrated edition, *New York,* 1900, the first printing having the *Merrymount Press* slug on the page *opposite* the last page of text.

SOCIAL LIFE IN OLD VIRGINIA. *New York,* 1897.
Maroon and green cloths, priority undetermined, although the publishers once stated that maroon was first.

TWO PRISONERS. *New York,* 1898.

SANTA CLAUS'S PARTNER. *New York,* 1899.

RED ROCK. *New York,* 1898.
First state of binding has gilt, maroon and black stamped decoration on front cover. First state of sheets has *Trow* imprint on copyright page; *Illustrated* on title page, not *Illustrated by B. West Clinedinst.* A presentation copy has been noted with top edges gilt, other edges untrimmed.

GORDON KEITH. *New York,* 1903.
Published May, 1903 on copyright page.

BRED IN THE BONE. *New York*, 1904.
Published, May, 1904 on the copyright page. First binding, green cloth; later, red cloth.

THE NEGRO: THE SOUTHERNER'S PROBLEM. *New York*, 1904.
Published, November, 1904 on the copyright page.

THE COAST OF BOHEMIA. *New York*, 1906.

UNDER THE CRUST. *New York*, 1907.
Published, November, 1907 on copyright page.

THE OLD DOMINION: HER MAKING AND HER MANNERS. *New York*, 1908.
Published February, 1908 on copyright page.

ROBERT E. LEE: THE SOUTHERNER. *New York*, 1908.
Published October, 1908 on copyright page.

TOMMY TROT'S VISIT TO SANTA CLAUS. *New York*, 1908.
Published October, 1908 on copyright page.

JOHN MARVEL: ASSISTANT. *New York*, 1909.
Published October, 1909 on copyright page.

ROBERT E. LEE: MAN AND SOLDIER. *New York*, 1911.
Published December, 1911 on copyright page.

THE LAND OF THE SPIRIT. *New York*, 1913.
Published April, 1913 on copyright page. One of the stories contained herein, "The Shepherd Who Watched by Night," previously published, *New York* [1913], printed from the magazine plates; issued in wrappers. "The Stranger's Pew," *New York*, 1914, reprinted from this book. "The Shepherd Who Watched by Night," *New York*, 1916, boards, a few in leather, is a late reprint.

ITALY AND THE WORLD WAR. *New York*, 1920.
Published November, 1920 on copyright page.

DANTE AND HIS INFLUENCE. *New York*, 1922.
Published October, 1922 on copyright page.

WASHINGTON AND ITS ROMANCE. *New York*, 1923.

THE RED RIDERS. *New York*, 1924.

COMPLETE WORKS. *New York*, 1906-1912.
18 vols. "Plantation Edition." 12 vols. in 1906; 4 in 1909; 2 in 1912. Limited to 230 sets.

Many of Page's short stories were issued separately after appearance in the above books. Among these: "A Captured Santa Claus"; "Polly"; "Unc' Edinburg"; "Meh

Lady"; and "Marse Chan." The last named appeared in "Stories by American Authors," *New York*, 1885, and later in Page's first book, "In Ole Virginia."

The following is a partial list of the many secondary items issued by Page, and books containing his contributions.

The Parnell Movement ... by T. P. O'Connor. *New York* [1891].
  Contains a biography of O'Connor by Page.
The Old Virginia Lawyer. *Richmond, Va.,* 1891.
  Pamphlet.
Address on the Necessity of a History of the South. *Roanoke,* 1892.
From Dixie. *Richmond,* 1893.
  Contribution.
Stories of the Railway. *New York,* 1893.
  Contains "Run to Seed," reprinted from "Elsket," 1891.
Stories of the South. *New York,* 1893.
  Contains "No Haid Pawn," reprinted from "In Ole Virginia," 1887.
Thought Blossoms from the South. [*Atlanta,* 1895].
  Louise Threete Hodges and Gertrude Eloise Bealer, editors. Contribution, "Sleep," by Page.
Spanish-American War Songs. *Detroit,* 1898.
  Sidney A. Witherbee, editor. Contains "The Dragon of the Sea," a poem by Page.
Modern Eloquence. *Philadelphia,* 1900.
  Vol. 3 contains "The Torch of Civilization," by Page.
The Page Story Book. *New York,* 1906.
  Frank E. Spaulding and Catherine T. Bryce, editors. Selections from previously published material.
The Loss of the Fiduciary Principle.
  Originally in "The New York State Bar Association Report," 1907; later issued as a separate pamphlet.
Address at Three Hundredth Anniversary of the Settlement of Jamestown. *Richmond,* 1907.
Mount Vernon and Its Preservation. [*New York,* 1910].
The Old Virginia Gentleman, by George Bagby. *New York,* 1910.
  Introduction by Page.
Greetings to the American Soldiers in Italy. [*n.p., n.d.*].
  Pamphlet. Probably printed in Italy.
The Shepherd Who Watched by Night. *New York,* 1916.
  See: "The Land of the Spirit," 1913.
Tommaso Jefferson. *Florence* [*Italy,* 1918?].
  Written in Italian.
Address at the Three Hundredth Anniversary of the Settlement of Jamestown. *Richmond, Va.,* 1919.
  Wrappers.
From the Rapidan to Richmond, by W. M. Dame. *Baltimore,* 1920.
  Introduction by Page.

BIOGRAPHICAL

Thomas Nelson Page: A Memoir of a Virginia Gentleman, by Rosewell Page. *New York,* 1923.

Commemorative Tributes to Page, by Robert Underwood Johnson [and Others]. [*New York*] 1925.

Dorothy (Rothschild) Parker
1893–

MEN I'M NOT MARRIED TO. *Garden City,* 1922.
: First edition so stated on copyright page. Boards. Bound in, inverted and with separate title page: "Women I'm Not Married To," by Franklin P. Adams.

ENOUGH ROPE. *New York,* 1926.
: Boards.

SUNSET GUN. *New York,* 1928.
: Boards, cloth back.

CLOSE HARMONY; or, THE LADY NEXT DOOR. *New York,* 1929.
: Three act play. Elmer Rice, collaborator. Copyrighted in 1924 as "Soft Music," wrappers, copyright notice on title page.

LAMENTS FOR THE LIVING. *New York,* 1930.

DEATH AND TAXES. *New York,* 1931.
: Also 250 de luxe copies, signed.

AFTER SUCH PLEASURES. *New York,* 1933.
: Also 250 de luxe copies, signed. Dramatized and presented, New York, 1934.

NOT SO DEEP AS A WELL. *New York,* 1936.
: *Published, December 1, 1936* on the copyright page. Also 485 signed copies.

COLLECTED POEMS. *New York,* 1936.

HERE LIES. *New York,* 1939.

Among the many books containing contributions by Miss Parker are:

High Society: Advice as to Social Campaigning ... *New York* [1920].
: With others.

Nonsensorship. *New York,* 1922.
: Contains "A Hymn of Hate" by Miss Parker.

The Second Conning Tower Book. *New York* [1927].
: Edited by Franklin P. Adams.

The Smart Set Anthology. *New York* [1934].
: Burton Rascoe and Groff Conklin, editors. First state of binding has *Roscoe* for *Rascoe* on the spine.

Thunder Over the Bronx, by Arthur Kober. *New York,* 1935.
: Introduction.

An Exhibition of Sculpture by Jo Davidson. [*New York,* 1938].
: Printed wrappers. Contribution. This publication preceded "Jo Davidson: Spanish Portraits" [*n.p., n.d.*] which reprints the same text.

Francis Parkman

1823–1893

THE CALIFORNIA AND OREGON TRAIL. *New York*, 1849.
One volume in cloth, or two volumes in printed wrappers. The book occurs in two forms: with one leaf of advertisements preceding the frontispiece and with four leaves of advertisements at the back of the book; or, no advertisements at the front, advertisements at the back paginated 1-6, 8, the verso of 8 blank. Question exists as to the first state.

HISTORY OF THE CONSPIRACY OF PONTIAC AND THE WAR OF THE NORTH AMERICAN TRIBES ... *Boston*, 1851.
Various later reissues with additions and revisions.

VASSALL MORTON: A NOVEL. *Boston*, 1856.

THE BOOK OF ROSES. *Boston*, 1866.
Botany.

The following titles are known as the "France and England in North America" series. Of each title there was also issued a limited edition of 75 copies.

PIONEERS OF FRANCE IN THE NEW WORLD. *Boston*, 1865.

THE JESUITS IN NORTH AMERICA IN THE SEVENTEENTH CENTURY. *Boston*, 1867.

THE DISCOVERY OF THE GREAT WEST. *Boston*, 1869.
Reissued, *Boston*, 1879, as "La Salle and the Discovery of the Great West."

THE OLD RÉGIME IN CANADA. *Boston*, 1874.

COUNT FRONTENAC AND NEW FRANCE UNDER LOUIS XIV. *Boston*, 1877.

MONTCALM AND WOLFE. *Boston*, 1884.
2 vols.

A HALF CENTURY OF CONFLICT. *Boston*, 1892.
2 vols.

Among the important minor items are:

Historical Handbook of the Northern Tour. *Boston*, 1865.
Material reprinted from "History of the Conspiracy of Pontiac."
Historical Account of Boquet's Expedition Against the Ohio Indians in 1764. *Cincinnati*, 1868.
Preface by Parkman. Also large paper edition.

Some of the Reasons Against Woman's Suffrage. [n.p., 1887?].

The Romance of Dollard, by Mary H. Catherwood. *New York* [1889].
 Preface.

Champlain and His Associates. *New York* [1890].
 Reprinted from "The Pioneers of France in the New World."

Braddock's Defeat. *New York* [1890].
 Reprinted from "Montcalm and Wolfe."

Our Common Schools. *Boston* [1890].
 Pamphlet.

Letters From Francis Parkman to E. G. Squier, With Biographical Note and a Bibliography of E. G. Squier by Don Seitz. *Cedar Rapids, Iowa*, 1911.

The Boy's Parkman. *Boston*, 1912.
 Selected reprints. Louise S. Hasbrouck, editor.

Rivals For America. *Boston*, 1915.
 Selected reprints from "France and England in North America" series. Louise S. Hasbrouck, editor.

Letters of Francis Parkman to Pierre Margry, With an Introductory Note by Spencer Bassett. *Northampton, Mass.* [1923].

BIOGRAPHICAL AND BIBLIOGRAPHICAL

Proceedings of the Massachusetts Historical Society, October and November 1893. [*Boston*, 1893].
 Contains an autobiography by Parkman.

A Life of Francis Parkman. *Boston*, 1900.
 By Charles Haight Farnham. Contains a bibliography.

Francis Parkman, by Henry Dwight Sedgwick. *Boston*, 1904.
 Also 150 large paper copies.

James Kirke Paulding

1778 (1779?)–1860

SALMAGUNDI; OR, THE WHIM-WHAMS AND OPINIONS OF LAUNCELOT LANG-STAFF, ESQ., AND OTHERS. *New York, 1807-1808.*
See: under *Washington Irving.*

THE DIVERTING HISTORY OF JOHN BULL AND BROTHER JONATHAN. *New York and Philadelphia, 1812.*
By Hector Bull-Us. Printed boards.

THE LAY OF THE SCOTTISH FIDDLE: A TALE OF HAVRE DE GRACE. SUPPOSED TO BE WRITTEN BY WALTER SCOTT, ESQ. *New York and Philadelphia, 1813.*
Printed boards.

LETTERS FROM THE SOUTH. *New York, 1817.*
2 vols. *By The Author of John Bull and Brother Jonathan.* Printed boards.

THE BACKWOODSMAN: A POEM. *Philadelphia, 1818.*

SALMAGUNDI: SECOND SERIES. *Philadelphia, 1819-1820.*
By Launcelot Langstaff, esq. 2 vols.

A SKETCH OF OLD ENGLAND. *New York, 1822.*
2 vols. *By A New England Man.*

KONINGSMARKE: THE LONG FINNE, A STORY OF THE NEW WORLD. *New York, 1823.*
2 vols. Anonymous.

JOHN BULL IN AMERICA; OR, THE NEW MUNCHAUSEN. *New York, 1825.*
Anonymous.

THE MERRY TALES OF THE THREE WISE MEN OF GOTHAM. *New York, 1826.*
Edited by the Author of The Backwoodsman. Boards, cloth back, paper label.

THE NEW MIRROR FOR TRAVELLERS, AND A GUIDE TO THE SPRINGS. *New York, 1828.*
By An Amateur. Boards, cloth back, paper label. Title later changed to "The New Pilgrims' Progress." Reissued, *New York,* 1868, as "A Book of Vagaries," edited by W. I. Paulding, with eight added tales.

PAULDING

TALES OF THE GOOD WOMAN. *New York, 1829.*
> By *A Doubtful Gentleman*. Boards, paper label. Reissued as vols. x and xi of the collected works, *New York, 1836*, with added material. Reissued, *New York, 1867*, edited by W. I. Paulding, with added material.

CHRONICLES OF THE CITY OF GOTHAM FROM THE PAPERS OF A RETIRED COMMON COUNCILMAN. *New York, 1830.*
> Edited by the Author of *The Backwoodsman*.

THE DUTCHMAN'S FIRESIDE: A TALE. *New York, 1831.*
> 2 vols. By *the Author of Letters From the South*. Publisher's advertisement on the back cover of Vol. 1 dated *New-York, May, 1831*.

WESTWARD HO! *New York, 1832.*
> 2 vols. By *The Author of the Dutchman's Fireside*. Anonymous.

A LIFE OF WASHINGTON. *New York, 1835.*
> 2 vols.

SLAVERY IN THE UNITED STATES. *New York, 1836.*

THE BOOK OF SAINT NICHOLAS. *New York, 1836.*
> Anonymous. *Translated ... from the Dutch of ... Nicholas Ægidius Oudenarde*.

A GIFT FROM FAIRY-LAND. *New York* [1838].
> Anonymous. Also published as "A Christmas Gift From Fairy-Land."

THE OLD CONTINENTAL: OR, THE PRICE OF LIBERTY. *New York, 1846.*
> 2 vols. Also 2 vols. in 1. Anonymous.

AMERICAN COMEDIES. *Philadelphia, 1847.*
> The first story is by J. K. Paulding, other material by W. I. Paulding.

THE PURITAN AND HIS DAUGHTER. *New York, 1849.*
> 2 vols. *Baker and Scribner* imprint.

The United States and England: Being a Reply to the Criticism on Inchiquin's Letters, Contained in the *Quarterly Review* for January, 1814. *New York, 1815.*
Lectures on the History of Literature, by F. Schlegel. *Philadelphia, 1818.*
> Translated.
Tales of the Glauber-Spa, by Several American Authors. *New York, 1832.*
> Contains two stories by Paulding. 2 vols.
The Atlantic Souvenir, 1826-1832 [inclusive]. *Philadelphia* [1826]-1832.
> Contributions by Paulding.
The Atlantic Club Book. *New York, 1834.*
> With others.
The Token and Atlantic Souvenir. *Boston, 1836.*
> Contains "The Magic Spinning Wheel," by Paulding.

Mr. Douglas and the Doctrine of Coercion. [*Charleston,* 1860].
  Anon. Pamphlet. Also issued, with the author's name, as "State Sovereignty and the Doctrine of Coercion" [*Charleston,* 1860].

Literary Life of James Kirke Paulding, by William Irving Paulding. *New York,* 1867.

A Book of Vagaries. *New York,* 1868.
  See above, "The New Mirror," 1828.

A Bibliography of the Separate Publications of James Kirke Paulding, by Oscar Wegelin. [*Chicago,* 1918].
  Wrappers.

James Kirke Paulding: Versatile American, by Amos L. Herold. *New York,* 1926.
  Contains a bibliography.

Allan Pinkerton

1819–1884

THE EXPRESSMAN AND THE DETECTIVE. *Chicago*, 1874.

CLAUDE MELNOTTE AS A DETECTIVE AND OTHER STORIES. *Chicago*, 1875.

THE DETECTIVE AND THE SONAMBULIST. *Chicago*, 1875.
First state of the advertisements has no mention of this title.

THE MODEL TOWN AND THE DETECTIVES: BYRON AS A DETECTIVE. *New York*, 1876.

THE SPIRITUALISTS AND THE DETECTIVES. *New York*, 1877.
Advertisements, when present, must be dated 1876.

THE MOLLIE MAGUIRES AND THE DETECTIVES. *New York*, 1877.
First state has no advertisements at the back and measures 1 ¾" thick; later states are on appreciably thinner paper and have advertisements.

STRIKERS, COMMUNISTS, TRAMPS AND DETECTIVES. *New York*, 1878.

MISSISSIPPI OUTLAWS AND THE DETECTIVES. *New York*, 1878.

THE GYPSIES AND THE DETECTIVES. *New York*, 1878.

CRIMINAL REMINISCENCES AND DETECTIVE SKETCHES. *New York*, 1879.

BUCHOLZ AND THE DETECTIVES. *New York*, 1880.

PROFESSIONAL THIEVES AND THE DETECTIVES. *New York & Philadelphia*, 1881.
Reported but not examined: this title with a *Chicago*, 1880, imprint.

THE RAIL-ROAD FORGER AND THE DETECTIVES. *New York*, 1881.

BANK-ROBBERS AND THE DETECTIVES. *New York*, 1883.

THE SPY OF THE REBELLION. *New York*, 1883.

THE BURGLAR'S FATE AND THE DETECTIVES. *New York*, 1884.
First state of the advertisements dated 1883.

THIRTY YEARS A DETECTIVE. *New York & Boston*, 1884.
Also issued with single *Boston* or *New York* imprints.

The History and Evidence of the Passage of Abraham Lincoln From Harrisburgh, Pa., to Washington, D. C., on the 22nd and 23rd of February, 1861. *Chicago* [1868].
  18 pp.
Tests on Passenger Conductors Made by the National Detective Agency. *Chicago,* 1870.
The Pinkertons: A Detective Dynasty, By R. W. Rowan. *Boston,* 1931.

Edgar Allan Poe

1809–1849

TAMERLANE AND OTHER POEMS. *Boston,* 1827.

Anon. *By A Bostonian.* Printed wrappers. Exact facsimiles exist which require expert inspection to distinguish them from the original.

AL AARAAF, TAMERLANE AND MINOR POEMS. *Baltimore,* 1829.

Blue or brown boards. Some copies misdated 1820 on title page.

POEMS. *New York,* 1831.

First edition marked *Second Edition* on title page.

THE NARRATIVE OF ARTHUR GORDON PYM. *New York,* 1838.

Anon. Cloth, paper label on spine.

THE CONCHOLOGISTS FIRST BOOK. *Philadelphia,* 1839.

Pictorial boards. First state has the snail plates in color. An adaptation, rather than the work of Poe. Revised, *Philadelphia,* 1840.

TALES OF THE GROTESQUE AND ARABESQUE. *Philadelphia,* 1840.

2 vols. Cloth, paper label on spines. Copies have been noted with p. 213 misnumbered 231 in vol. 2.

THE MURDERS IN THE RUE MORGUE, AND THE MAN THAT WAS USED UP. *Philadelphia,* 1843.

Wrappers. "Prose Romances of Edgar A. Poe, No. I." No record has ever been found of the second number in this series; *No. I* suggests a proposed second part. Two states known with no established priority.

THE RAVEN AND OTHER POEMS. *New York,* 1845.

Printed wrappers. The slug of *T. B. Smith, Stereotyper* appears on copyright page. Later issued in one cloth-bound volume together with the following title.

TALES. *New York,* 1845.

Printed wrappers. The earliest copies have the slug of *H. Ludwig* on the copyright page; later the slug of *Craighead's Power Press* still later without either slug. Reissued in cloth together with "The Raven and other Poems."

MESMERISM: "IN ARTICULO MORTIS." *London,* 1846.

16 pp. pamphlet, self-wrapper. It has been asserted that a pamphlet edition of this item was issued in New York, 1845.

EUREKA: A PROSE POEM. *New York,* 1848.

WORKS. *New York,* 1850-1856.

    4 vols. Rufus Wilmot Griswold, editor. The first three volumes are dated 1850; 4th, 1856. Noted in various types of cloth binding; no known priority. First book appearance for some of material here collected.

WORKS. *Chicago,* 1894-95.

    10 vols. Also 250 large paper sets. With material here first collected. George E. Woodberry and Edmund Clarence Stedman, editors. With revisions. Vol. x contains a brief bibliography.

The following list of the minor Poe items is representative, not inclusive. Collectors are referred to the Robertson and Heartman-Canny bibliographies listed below.

The Gift ... For 1836. *Philadelphia* [1835].

    Contains "Ms. Found in a Bottle."

The Philosophy of Animal Magnetism, by a Gentleman of Philadelphia. *Philadelphia,* 1837.

    At one time attributed to Poe. It has been established beyond any doubt that this is not by Poe.

English Notes by Quarles Quickens. *Boston,* 1842.

    Attributed to Poe.

The Gift ... 1843. *Philadelphia* [1842].

    Also large paper edition. Contains the "Pit and the Pendulum."

Some Letters of Edgar Allan Poe to E. H. N. Patterson ... *Chicago,* 1898.

    189 copies only. Eugene Field, editor.

The Last Letters of Edgar Allan Poe to Sarah Helen Whitman. *New York,* 1900.

Edgar Allan Poe Letters Till Now Unpublished. *Philadelphia,* 1925.

    Introductory essay and comments by Mary Newton Stanard. Also large paper edition.

Doings of Gotham. *Pottsville,* 1929.

    Poe's contributions to *The Columbia Spy*. Includes a poem. Jacob E. Spannuth and Thomas Ollive Mabbott, editors. 749 copies only. Copies 1-36 signed by editors and publisher.

BIOGRAPHICAL

Edgar Poe and His Critics, by Sarah Helen Whitman. *New York,* 1860.

A Defense of Edgar Poe ... An Official Account of His Death by His Attending Physician, John J. Moran. *Washington,* 1885.

Edgar Allan Poe, by George E. Woodberry. *Boston,* 1885.

The Life of Edgar Allan Poe, by George E. Woodberry. *Boston,* 1909.

    2 vols. Also 150 sets with paper label.

Edgar Allan Poe, by Joseph Wood Krutch. *New York,* 1926.

Edgar Allan Poe, by Mary Elizabeth Phillips. *Philadelphia,* 1926.

    2 vols.

POE

Israfel: The Life of Poe, by Hervey Allen. *New York*, 1926.
> 2 vols. First state of first edition has wine glass on table in Longfellow portrait, p. 529. Also untrimmed copies in three quarter leather.

Thomas Holley Chivers: Friend of Poe, by S. Foster Damon. *New York*, 1930.

Edgar Allan Poe and the *Philadelphia Saturday Courier*, by John Grier Varner, Jr. *University of Virginia*, 1933.
> 500 numbered copies only. Contains "five of Poe's tales not hitherto reprinted."

Bibliography of the Writings of Edgar Allan Poe, by E. A. Robertson. *San Francisco*, 1934.
> 2 vols.

Poe and the *Southern Literary Messenger*, by David K. Jackson. *Richmond*, 1934.
> 500 numbered copies only.

Edgar Allan Poe, by Edward Shanks. *New York*, 1937.

A Bibliography of First Printings of the Writings of Edgar Allan Poe, by Charles F. Heartman and James R. Canny. *Hattiesburg, Miss.*, 1940.

Katherine Anne Porter

1894–

OUTLINE OF MEXICAN POPULAR ARTS AND CRAFTS. [*Los Angeles*] 1922.

FLOWERING JUDAS. *New York* [1930].
  Boards. 600 unnumbered copies only. Republished, *New York* [1935], with four added stories. The reissue has indication of first printing on the copyright page.

HACIENDA. [*New York, 1934*].
  895 numbered copies only.

NOON WINE. *Detroit, 1937.*
  Boards, paper label on front cover. 250 numbered copies only, signed.

PALE HORSE, PALE RIDER. *New York* [1939].
  First printing indicated on the copyright page.

The Second American Caravan. *New York,* 1928.
  Alfred Kreymborg, Lewis Mumford and Paul Rosenfeld, editors. Contains "Rope" by Miss Porter. Also 250 leather-bound copies signed by the editors.
Best Short Stories of 1930. *New York,* 1931.
  Edward J. O'Brien, editor. Contains "Theft" by Miss Porter.
French Song Book. [*Paris,* 1933].
  Translations. Boards, cloth back. 610 copies only as follows: 15 copies on Guarro Spanish paper numbered I-XV; 595 copies numbered 1-595. All signed by the author.
Best Short Stories of 1933. *Boston,* 1933.
  Edward J. O'Brien, editor. Contains Porter's "The Cracked Looking Glass."
Best Short Stories of 1936. *Boston,* 1936.
  Edward J. O'Brien, editor. Contains Porter's "The Grave."

William Sydney (Sidney) Porter
(O. Henry)
1862–1910

CABBAGES AND KINGS. *New York*, 1904.
> *McClure, Phillips & Co.* on the spine. Copies have been noted with the "Walrus and the Carpenter" quotation and the table of contents leaf in varying positions; this difference, probably without significance, may have been caused by binder's error in folding. For further discussion of this title see Paul S. Clarkson's complete bibliography, 1938.

THE FOUR MILLION. *New York*, 1906.
> *McClure Phillips* imprint on spine.

THE TRIMMED LAMP. *New York*, 1907.
> *Published April, 1907* on the copyright page. Contains numerous typographical errors which remain uncorrected even as late as the "Authorized Edition."

HEART OF THE WEST. *New York*, 1907.

THE VOICE OF THE CITY. *New York*, 1908.
> First state has the *McClure* imprint at base of spine; second binding, with no change of title page, has *Doubleday Page* imprint on spine.

THE GENTLE GRAFTER. *New York*, 1908.
> The misprint *of* for *as*, p. 226, line 2, hitherto offered as the identifying point of this book has proved valueless since the error remains uncorrected as late as 1935.

ROADS OF DESTINY. *New York*, 1909.
> Numerous typographical errors occur in the first printing, including missing *h*, line 6, p. 9.

OPTIONS. *New York*, 1909.

STRICTLY BUSINESS. *New York*, 1910.

WHIRLIGIGS. *New York*, 1910.
> *Published, September, 1910* on the copyright page. Numerous misprints but none with any apparent value as indications of first printing. Originally announced as "In Divers Tones," later as "Whirlygigs," eventually "Whirligigs."

LET ME FEEL YOUR PULSE. *New York*, 1910.
> *Published, October, 1910* on the copyright page. Exists in at least two states with no known priority.

SIXES AND SEVENS. *Garden City*, 1911.

ROLLING STONES. *Garden City,* 1912.
With or without two fly leaves following front end paper; no known priority.

WAIFS AND STRAYS. *Garden City,* 1917.
200 copies only as stated in colophon on verso of half title. With publisher's device or *First Edition* on spine; no known priority. Trade edition published, 1919.

O. HENRYANA. *Garden City,* 1920.
Contains seven short stories and poems here first collected. 377 copies only.

POSTSCRIPTS. *New York,* 1923.
First binding is red cloth stamped with gilt.

O. HENRY ENCORE. *New York,* 1939.
Preceded by a privately printed edition of five copies only [*n.p.,* 1935]. Mary S. Harrell, editor. First edition so indicated on the copyright page.

THE COMPLETE WORKS OF O. HENRY. *New York,* 1912.
Limp leather edition issued November, 1912, separately or as a twelve volume set. "Authorized Edition," published, 1913, consisting of *Doubleday-Page* sheets with *Review of Reviews* binding. "The Complete Writings of O. Henry," *Garden City,* 1917, 14 vols. First one volume edition (containing biographical notes), "Special Literary Digest Edition," 1926; reissued, *Doubleday-Page* imprint, 1927. "Biographical Edition," *New York,* 1929, 18 volumes.

A Little Nonsense. *New York,* 1906.
Contribution.
Lo: A Musical Comedy. *New York,* 1909.
With Franklin P. Adams. 14 pieces of music, large 4to.
Golden Stories. *New York,* 1909.
Contains "The Gold That Glittered," later in "Strictly Business."
The Two Women. *Boston* [1910].
Dark green printed wrappers, lettered in black. First book appearance for "A Fog in Santone." The other story here included, "A Medley of Moods," had appeared three months before as "Blind Man's Holiday" in "Whirligigs."
The Wind of Destiny, by Sarah Lindsay Coleman. *Garden City,* 1916.
Contains letters by O. Henry. 125 copies only.
Il Conte, by Joseph Conrad ... *New York,* 1925.
Formerly listed as first book appearance of "The Snow Man"; this story appeared previously in "Waifs and Strays," 1917.
Letters to Lithopolis from O. Henry to Mabel Wagnalls. *Garden City and Toronto,* 1922.
427 copies only.

BIOGRAPHICAL

My Friend, O. Henry, by Seth Moyle. *New York* [1914].
O. Henry Biography, by Charles Alphonso Smith. *Garden City,* 1916.
An authorized biography.

W. S. PORTER

Through the Shadows With O. Henry, by Al Jennings. *New York* [1921].
  Also limited edition.
Bill Porter: A Drama of O. Henry in Prison, by Upton Sinclair. *Pasadena* [1925].
  Cloth or wrappers. Fiction.
O. Henry Papers. *Garden City,* 1925.
  Wrappers. Contains "O. Henry's Only Autobiographia," by George MacAdam.
The Dimity Sweetheart, by Frances Goggin Maltby. *Richmond,* 1930.
  Contains first book appearance for some of O. Henry's earliest known writings.
The Caliph of Bagdad, by Robert H. Davis and Arthur Bartlett Maurice. *New York,*
  1931.
The Quiet Lodger of Irving Place, by William Wash Williams. *New York,* 1937.
A Bibliography of William Sydney Porter, by Paul S. Clarkson. *Caldwell, Idaho,*
  1938.
  600 copies only, numbered and signed by the compiler.

Many of O. Henry's stories have been issued in separate form or in anthologies. Among these are: "The Ransom of Red Chief"; "The Gift of the Wise Men"; "A Lickpenny Lover"; "Hostages to Momus"; "The Hiding of Black Bill" and "The Man Higher Up."

"My Tussle With the Devil," by O. Henry's Ghost, is alleged to be a collection of stories received by a medium in contact with O. Henry. It has been said that no more than a dozen copies were bound and issued; actually many more have appeared on the market and it is reported on good authority that the entire edition of several hundred copies was remaindered, in the original binding, soon after publication.

Howard Pyle

1853–1911

THE MERRY ADVENTURES OF ROBIN HOOD. *New York,* 1883.
Stamped full leather binding.

WITHIN THE CAPES. *New York,* 1885.
3,000 copies printed; 1,000 copies in cloth published May 9, 1885, 2,000 copies in printed paper wrappers published August 8, 1885.

PEPPER & SALT. *New York,* 1886.

THE WONDER CLOCK. *New York,* 1888.
Leather back. With KATHERINE PYLE.

THE ROSE OF PARADISE. *New York,* 1888.

OTTO OF THE SILVER HAND. *New York,* 1888.
Leather back.

MEN OF IRON. *New York,* 1892.
Measures 1$\frac{1}{16}$″ across top of covers.

A MODERN ALADDIN. *New York,* 1892.

THE STORY OF JACK BALLISTER'S FORTUNES. *New York,* 1895.

THE GARDEN BEHIND THE MOON. *New York,* 1895.

TWILIGHT LAND. *New York,* 1895.
Leather back.

THE PRICE OF BLOOD. *Boston,* 1899.
Boards, cloth back. Second binding has title on cloth spine.

REJECTED OF MEN. *New York,* 1903.
Published June, 1903 on copyright page.

THE STORY OF KING ARTHUR. *New York,* 1903.

THE STORY OF THE CHAMPIONS OF THE ROUND TABLE. *New York,* 1905.

STOLEN TREASURE. *New York,* 1907.
Published May, 1907 on copyright page.

THE STORY OF SIR LAUNCELOT AND HIS COMPANIONS. *New York,* 1907.

THE RUBY OF KISHMOOR. *New York,* 1908.

THE STORY OF THE GRAIL AND THE PASSING OF ARTHUR. *New York,* 1910.

HOWARD PYLE'S BOOK OF PIRATES. *New York*, 1921.

Boards, cloth back. *D-V* at foot of copyright page. Also 50 copies signed by the editor, Merle Johnson. Includes most of "Stolen Treasure" and "The Ruby of Kishmoor."

HOWARD PYLE'S BOOK OF THE AMERICAN SPIRIT. *New York*, 1923.

Boards, cloth back. *B-X* on copyright page. Compiled by Merle Johnson. Edited by Francis J. O'Dowd. Also 50 copies signed by editor and compiler.

SABBATH THOUGHTS. [*New York*, 1928].

Pamphlet. 26 copies only of which 6 were on large paper.

The following are some of the principal works, written by others, illustrated by Pyle. Some important histories are omitted from this list as the pictures are collected in "Howard Pyle's Book of the American Spirit." *See:* "Howard Pyle: A Record of His Illustrations and Writings," by Willard S. Morse and Gertrude Brincklé, *Wilmington, Del.*, 1921.

McGuffey's Fifth Eclectic Reader. *Cincinnati and New York* [1879].

Yankee Doodle. *New York*, 1881.

The Lady of Shalott, by Tennyson. *New York* [1881].

The Story of Siegfried, by James Baldwin. *New York*, 1882.

A Story of the Golden Age, by James Baldwin. *New York*, 1887.

Storied Holidays, by Elbridge S. Brooks. *Boston* [1887].

In The Valley, by Harold Frederic. *New York*, 1890.

Flute and Violin, by James Lane Allen. *New York*, 1891.

The Buccaneers and Marooners of America, by Esquemeling. *London*, 1891.

Edited and with a long introduction by Pyle, which was later included in "Howard Pyle's Book of Pirates."

The One-Hoss Shay, by Oliver Wendell Holmes. *Boston*, 1892.

Undressed calf binding.

Dorothy Q, by Oliver Wendell Holmes. *Cambridge*, 1893.

Also 250 copies in parchment binding.

The Autocrat of the Breakfast Table, by Oliver Wendell Holmes. *Cambridge*, 1894.

2 vols. 250 large paper sets. Small paper edition has *Boston* imprint.

Stops of Various Quills, by William Dean Howells. *New York*, 1895.

Also, 50 copies on large paper dated 1894, signed.

The First Christmas Tree, by Henry Van Dyke. *New York*, 1897.

Quo Vadis, by Henryk Sienckiewicz. *Boston*, 1897.

2 vols. Also 250 large paper sets.

Hugh Wynne: Free Quaker, by S. Weir Mitchell. *New York*, 1897.

2 vols. *See:* under *S. Weir Mitchell* for full description.

The Story of the Revolution, by Henry Cabot Lodge. *New York*, 1898.

2 vols.

Old Chester Tales, by Margaret Deland. *New York*, 1899.

Chelsea for *Chester*, p. 5, six lines from the foot of page.

The Man With The Hoe, by Edwin Markham. *New York,* 1900.
Prospectus for the Christmas Century. [*N. Y.*] 1902.
    4 pp.
The Island of Enchantment, by Justus Miles Forman. *New York,* 1905.
The Line of Love, by James Branch Cabell. *New York,* 1905.
    See: under *Cabell* for full description.
Gallantry, by James Branch Cabell. *New York,* 1907.
    See: under *Cabell* for full description.
Chivalry, by James Branch Cabell. *New York,* 1909.
    See: under *Cabell* for full description.
The Soul of Melicent, by James Branch Cabell. *New York,* 1913.
    See: under *Cabell* for full description.
Saint Joan of Arc, by Mark Twain. *New York* [1919].
    See: under *Clemens* for full description.

BIOGRAPHICAL AND BIBLIOGRAPHICAL

Howard Pyle: A Record of His Illustrations and Writings, by Willard S. Morse and Gertrude Brincklé. *Wilmington,* 1921.
Howard Pyle: A Chronicle, by Charles D. Abbott. *New York,* 1925.
    Contains many illustrations here first collected or printed.
American Book Illustrators, by Theodore Bolton. *New York,* 1938.
    Contains a detailed checklist of Pyle's works.

Frederic (Sackrider) Remington

1861–1909

PONY TRACKS. *New York*, 1895.
Cloth or publisher's leather.

DRAWINGS. *New York*, 1897.
Boards. Also 250 copies in leather with inserted certificate of issue.

A ROGERS RANGER IN THE FRENCH AND INDIAN WAR. [*New York*] 1897.
Printed wrappers. Later collected in "Crooked Trails."

FRONTIER SKETCHES. *Chicago* [etc.] [1898].
Pictorial boards.

CROOKED TRAILS. *New York*, 1898.
Reissued, *New York* [1923] with an introduction by Zane Grey.

SUNDOWN LEFLARE. *New York*, 1899.

MEN WITH THE BARK ON. *New York*, 1900.
The earliest copies measure about ⅞″ thick; later copies about 1⅛″ thick.

JOHN ERMINE OF THE YELLOWSTONE. *New York*, 1902.
All known copies, including reprint editions, misspell the author's name on the spine: *Reminigton*.

DONE IN THE OPEN. *New York*, 1902.
Pictorial boards, some copies misspelling the author's name *Frederick* on the front cover, or (at the same place) using an outline type rather than a solid type. First issued with the *Russell* imprint, later with the *Collier* imprint. 250 copies in publisher's leather, with inserted certificate of issue. Illustrations by Remington, accompanying verses by Owen Wister.

THE WAY OF AN INDIAN. *New York*, 1906.
The earliest state of the sheets has p. 9 so numbered. The first binding has yellow lettering, with *Fox, Duffield & Company* on the spine.

A full list of the books to which Remington contributed illustrations would run into a list of at least two hundred entries; only the most important are here given.

Army Sacrifices, by James B. Fry. *New York*, 1879.
Two states of the binding; no known priority.
Tenting on the Plains, by Elizabeth B. Custer. *New York*, 1887.
Juan and Juanita, by Frances Courtenay Baylor [Barnum]. *Boston*, 1888.
Although Remington's name doesn't appear on the title page the two first illustrations are his.

Ranch Life and the Hunting Trail, by Theodore Roosevelt. *New York* [1888].
  See: under *Roosevelt* for a full description.
Sport, or Fishing and Shooting. *Boston* [1889].
  A. C. Gould, editor.
Following the Guidon, by Elizabeth B. Custer. *New York*, 1890.
The Aztec Treasure House, by Thomas A. Janvier. *New York*, 1890.
The Song of Hiawatha, by Longfellow. *Boston*, 1891.
  Also 250 copies in vellum binding.
The Oregon Trail, by Francis Parkman. *Boston*, 1892.
  An unknown number issued in full leather binding with same stamping as that
  of cloth edition.
On Canada's Frontier, by Julian Ralph. *New York*, 1892.
The Jonah of Lucky Valley, by Howard Seeley. *New York*, 1892.
  Printed wrappers.
Armies of Today. *New York*, 1893.
Our Great West, by Julian Ralph. *New York*, 1893.
Riders of Many Lands, by Theodore A. Dodge. *New York*, 1894.
Wayside and Fireside Rambles, by Almon Gunnison. *Boston*, 1894.
A Sporting Pilgrimage, by Caspar W. Whitney. *New York*, 1895.
Red Men and White, by Owen Wister. *New York*, 1896.
Personal Recollections and Observations of General Nelson A. Miles. *Chicago*,
  1896.
  Cloth or leather. First state, caption of frontispiece reads *General Miles;* later,
  Major-General Miles.
Wolfville, by Alfred Henry Lewis. *New York* [1897].
  Later printings so stated on title page.
The Old Santa Fe Trail, by Henry Inman. *New York*, 1897.
Cuba in War Time, by Richard Harding Davis. *New York*, 1897.
  See: under *Davis* for fuller description.
Lin McLean, by Owen Wister. *New York*, 1898.
The Book of the American Indian, by Hamlin Garland. *New York*, 1923.

"Stories of Peace and War," *New York*, 1899, is reprinted from previously collected works. All examined copies have the misprint *Frederick* on the binding.

In addition to the above listed collections of Remington's drawings and paintings,
various publishers have assembled and issued collections of plates in portfolios. Certain of these have not as yet been included in book form.

For a more detailed list of Frederic Remington's work see Theodore Bolton's
"American Book Illustrators," *New York*, 1938.

Agnes Repplier

1858–

BOOKS AND MEN. *Boston*, 1888.

POINTS OF VIEW. *Boston*, 1891.

ESSAYS IN MINIATURE. *New York*, 1892.
    With added material, *Boston*, 1895.

ESSAYS IN IDLENESS. *Boston*, 1893.

IN THE DOZY HOURS AND OTHER PAPERS. *Boston*, 1894.

VARIA. *Boston*, 1897.

PHILADELPHIA: THE PLACE AND THE PEOPLE. *New York*, 1898.

THE FIRESIDE SPHINX. *Boston*, 1901.

COMPROMISES. *Boston*, 1904.

IN OUR CONVENT DAYS. *Boston*, 1905.
    Published October 1905 on copyright page.

A HAPPY HALF CENTURY. *Boston*, 1908.

AMERICANS AND OTHERS. *Boston*, 1912.

COUNTER CURRENTS. *Boston*, 1916.

J. WILLIAM WHITE, M.D. A BIOGRAPHY. *Boston*, 1919.

POINTS OF FRICTION. *Boston*, 1920.

UNDER DISPUTE. *Boston*, 1924.

THE PROMISE OF THE BELL. *Boston*, 1924.
    Wrappers.

PÈRE MARQUETTE, PRIEST, PIONEER AND ADVENTURER. *Garden City*, 1929.
    First printing indicated on copyright page.

MÈRE MARIE OF THE URSULINES. *New York*, 1931.
    First edition so stated on copyright page. Also edition for The Literary Guild.

TIMES AND TENDENCIES. *Boston*, 1931.

TO THINK OF TEA! *Boston*, 1932.

JUNÍPERO SERRA: PIONEER COLONIST OF CALIFORNIA. *Garden City*, 1933.
First edition so stated on copyright page.

AGNES IRWIN. *Garden City*, 1934.
First edition so stated on copyright page.

IN PURSUIT OF LAUGHTER. *Boston*, 1936.

EIGHT DECADES. *Boston*, 1937.

A Book of Famous Verse. *Boston*, 1892.
Edited.
Syllabus of a Course of Six Lectures on Books and Reading, by Henry Morse .
Stephens. *Philadelphia*, 1899.
Counsel Upon the Reading of Books. *New York*, 1900.
Contribution.
The World's Great Women Novelists. ₍*Philadelphia*, 1901₎.
Contains "The Immortal Three" by Repplier.
For Remembrance. *Philadelphia*, 1901.
Edited.
Epistolæ Ho-Elianæ, The Familiar Letters of John Howell. *Boston*, 1907.
4 vols. Introduction. 220 numbered copies only, designed by Bruce Rogers.
Appreciations of Horace Edward Furness. *Cleveland*, 1912.
Privately printed. Contribution.
The Cat. *New York*, 1912.
Anthology. Edited.
The Book of the Homeless. *Paris*, 1915.
Contains "The Russian Bogeyman."
The Stranger Within Our Gates. ₍*New York*, 1916₎.
Published by The Travelers' Aid Society.
A Book of Drawings by William Makepeace Thackeray ... Made in ... 1853 for
the Children of William B. Reed. ₍*Philadelphia*₎ 1925.
110 copies only, numbered and signed. Contains a note by Repplier.
Letters of Louise Imogen Guiney. *New York*, 1926.
2 vols. Grace Guiney, editor. Preface by Repplier. First edition so stated on copy-
right page.
Miss Repplier's "Père Marquette," A Review ... by the Rev. Francis Borgia Steck.
₍*Quincy, Ill.,?* 1929₎.

James Whitcomb Riley

1849–1916

"THE OLD SWIMMIN'-HOLE," AND 'LEVEN MORE POEMS. *Indianapolis*, 1883.

> *By Benj. F. Johnson of Boone.* A facsimile reprint issued in 1909, lacks the *W* in *William* at p. 41, next to the last line. Another facsimile was issued in 1920.

CHARACTER SKETCHES, THE BOSS GIRL, A CHRISTMAS STORY, AND OTHER SKETCHES. *Indianapolis*, 1886.

> Cloth or printed wrappers. The first printing has the copyright notice in the name of Riley, an exclamation point appears after *sir*, p. 9, line 5.

AFTERWHILES. *Indianapolis*, 1888.

> Boards, later cloth. P. 27, 4th line from the bottom, *and* for *till*.

NYE AND RILEY'S RAILWAY GUIDE. *Chicago*, 1888.

> With EDGAR W. (BILL) NYE.

OLD-FASHIONED ROSES. *London*, 1888.

> Issued by Bowen-Merrill, 1889.

PIPES O' PAN AT ZEKESBURY. *Indianapolis*, 1889.

> Various bindings with no definitely established priority. Noted with and without the printer's slug on the copyright page.

RHYMES OF CHILDHOOD. *Indianapolis*, 1891.

> First state is stamped with a decoration of child's head on the front cover. P. 64, line 12, *sometimes*, later *sometime*.

NEGHBORLY POEMS. *Indianapolis*, 1891.

> *By Benj. F. Johnson.* A reprint of "The Old Swimmin'-Hole" with additions. Also a few signed copies in silk binding. It is highly probable that the first state does not list "The Flying Islands of the Night" in the list of books on the verso of the half-title.

THE FLYING ISLANDS OF THE NIGHT. *Indianapolis*, 1892.

> Copies in flexible white boards with silver lettering were issued in advance of publication for the benefit of The Flower Mission.

POEMS HERE AT HOME. *New York*, 1893.

> Cloth or full vellum binding with no known priority. P. 50, line 5, *girls*, later *gyrls*. There is an early record of a limited and signed edition but I have not seen such a copy.

GREEN FIELDS AND RUNNING BROOKS. *Indianapolis*, 1893.

> P. 16, line 1, *miles on mile*; later, *mile on mile*.

ARMAZINDY. *Indianapolis*, 1894.
Several states noted, the probable first being as follows: inserted frontispiece printed in sepia; p. ii so numbered; table of contents at pp. vii-viii; p. 110 lacks one line of text, the total number of lines on the page being twenty-six; no advertisements at the back of the book; no illustrations save the frontispiece.

THE DAYS GONE BY AND OTHER POEMS. *Chicago* [1895].
Piracy, suppressed. Contains some material here first collected.

A TINKLE OF BELLS AND OTHER POEMS. *Chicago* [1895].
Piracy, suppressed. Contains some material here first collected.

A CHILD-WORLD. *Indianapolis and Kansas City*, 1897.
Noted with various imprints: *Indianapolis and London; London, Indianapolis and Kansas City*. In the first printing the *Proem* is listed as at p. 15; later, no page number is given. Preceded by the London edition.

RUBÁIYÁT OF DOC SIFERS. *New York*, 1897.
Also 100 signed copies.

RILEY LOVE-LYRICS. *Indianapolis* [1899].
Bowen-Merrill imprint. At p. xvi *The Passing of a Heart* is listed as at p. 71.

HOME-FOLKS. *Indianapolis* [1900].
First printing has repeated caption at p. 59; second state has p. 59 on a stub; third state has p. 59 bound in but with the error corrected as in the second state.

THE BOOK OF JOYOUS CHILDREN. *New York*, 1902.
Published October, 1902 on copyright page.

HIS PA'S ROMANCE. *Indianapolis* [1903].
November on copyright page.

A DEFECTIVE SANTA CLAUS. *Indianapolis* [1904].
December on copyright page.

RILEY SONGS O' CHEER. *Indianapolis* [1905].

WHILE THE HEART BEATS YOUNG. *Indianapolis* [1906].

MORNING. *Indianapolis* [1907].
October on copyright page.

THE BOYS OF THE OLD GLEE CLUB. *Indianapolis* [1907].
November on the copyright page.

OLD SCHOOL DAY ROMANCES. *Indianapolis* [1909].

A HOOSIER ROMANCE, 1868. *New York*, 1910.
Published October, 1910 on copyright page.

COMPLETE WORKS. *Indianapolis*, 1913.
    6 vols. Biographical edition, with bibliography. "Memorial Edition," 1916, with added material.

FUGITIVE PIECES. *New York*, 1914.

EARLY POEMS. *New York*, 1914.

Christmas Carols and Midsummer Songs. *Boston* [1881].
    Contains "The Land of Used to Be."
The Poet and the Children. *Boston* [1882].
    Contains two poems by Riley.
Life's Verses. *New York* [1885].
    Contribution.
Gems From an Old Drummer's Grip, by N. R. Streeter. [*Groton, N. Y.*] 1889.
    Contains "The Old Man and Jim," by Riley.
Lothrop Annual. *Boston* [1889].
    Contains "The Little Pixey People" by Riley.
Golden Rod: The Magazine of the Indianapolis Flower Mission. "The Riley Booth." [*Indianapolis*, 1891].
    Contains "Going to the Fair."
Armazindy. [*n.p.*, 1893].
    Broadside. Probably printed for copyright purposes.
The Army Mule and other War Sketches, by H. A. Castle. *Indianapolis*, 1898.
    Contribution.
Spanish American War Songs. *Detroit, Mich.*, 1898.
    Sidney A. Witherbee, editor. Contains Riley's "On Every Soldier's Grave."
The Soldier ... A Poem. *Indianapolis* [1902].
    Printed wrappers. Possibly printed for copyright purposes.
Early Recollections of James Whitcomb Riley, by Major Ridgeway [pseud. **for** W. Ross Hartpence]. *Harrison, Ohio*, 1902.
In Honor of James Whitcomb Riley. *Indianapolis* [1906].
    Grey wrappers over **b**oards. Contains a speech by Riley.
Abe Martin's Almanac, by Kin Hubbard. *Garden City* [1911].
    Contribution.
The Lockerbie Book. *Indianapolis* [1911].
    Hewitt Hanson Howland, editor.
The Morris Book Shop. *Chicago*, 1912.
    Wrappers. Contribution by Riley.
All The Year Round. *Indianapolis* [1912].
Away. [*Indianapolis*, 1913].
The Riley Baby Book. *Indianapolis* [1913].
The Old Soldier's Story. *Indianapolis* [1915].
[The Apology. *New Castle, Penna.*, 1915].
    Broadside. Privately printed.
The Name of Old Glory. *Indianapolis* [1917].

James Whitcomb Riley: An Essay. by Bliss Carman. *New York* [1918].

    250 signed copies only. First state has the imprint of George D. Smith.

The Youth of James Whitcomb Riley, by Marcus Dickey. *Indianapolis* [1919].

The Maturity of James Whitcomb Riley, by Marcus Dickey. *Indianapolis* [1922].

Love Letters of a Bachelor Poet. *Boston, 1922.*

    475 copies only for members of the Bibliophile Society. Letters from Riley to Miss Elizabeth Kahle.

Letters. *Indianapolis* [1930].

    William Lyon Phelps, editor.

Suppressed Poems. [*n.p., n.d.*].

Among the books composed of reprinted material are: "The Eccentric Mr. Clark"; "The Hoosier Book of Riley Verse"; "The Riley Baby Book"; "Riley Child Verse"; "An Old Sweetheart of Mine," of which there was also a limited edition signed by the author; "The Old Man and Jim"; "The Riley Reader"; "The Girl I Loved"; "When She Was About Sixteen"; "Sketches in Prose and Occasional Verses"; "A Summer's Day and other Poems"; "Down Around the River and other Poems"; "Riley Roses"; "A Discouraged Model"; "The Rose"; "When the Frost is on the Punkin' "; "The Golden Year"; "Mrs. Miller"; "The Prayer Perfect"; "Riley Child Rhymes"; "Riley Farm Rhymes"; "The Runaway Boy"; "Home Again With Me"; "Riley Songs of Home," etc.

Elizabeth Madox Roberts
1886–1941

IN THE GREAT STEEP'S GARDEN. [*Colorado Springs,* 1915].

UNDER THE TREE. *New York,* 1922.
Boards. Enlarged edition, *New York,* 1930.

THE TIME OF MAN. *New York,* 1926.
First state has title printed in dark blue, *on title page.*

MY HEART AND MY FLESH. *New York,* 1927.
First edition so indicated on copyright page.

JINGLING IN THE WIND. *New York,* 1928.
Boards, cloth back.

THE GREAT MEADOW. *New York,* 1930.
Also 295 large paper copies, numbered and signed. In addition to the trade issue,
Literary Guild edition.

A BURIED TREASURE. *New York,* 1931.
Also 200 large paper copies, numbered and signed. In addition to the trade
issue, a Literary Guild edition. "A greatly abridged rendering of this work appeared in *Harper's Magazine.*"

THE HAUNTED MIRROR. *New York,* 1932.

HE SENT FORTH A RAVEN. *New York,* 1935.
First Published March 1935 on copyright page.

BLACK IS MY TRUELOVE'S HAIR. *New York,* 1938.
First Published In October 1938 on the copyright page. Also 175 copies, numbered and signed.

SONG IN THE MEADOW. *New York,* 1940.
Also 135 copies, numbered and signed.

NOT BY STRANGE GODS. *New York,* 1941.

Elizabeth Madox Roberts: A Personal Note by Glenway Wescott. *New York,* 1930.
Pamphlet.
O. Henry Memorial Award Prize Stories, 1930. *Garden City,* 1930.
Contains a short story by Roberts. First edition so stated on copyright page.
A Southern Harvest. *Boston,* 1937.
Robert Penn Warren, editor. Contribution.

Kenneth (Lewis) Roberts

1885–

EUROPE'S MORNING AFTER. *New York* [1921].
Code letters *B-V* on copyright page.

WHY EUROPE LEAVES HOME. [*Indianapolis*, 1922].

SUN HUNTING. *Indianapolis* [1922].

THE COLLECTOR'S WHATNOT. *Boston*, 1923.
Published pseudonymously: *By Cornelius Obenchain, Milton Kilgallen, Cornelius Murgatroyd Van Loot, i.e.,* Kenneth Roberts, Booth Tarkington and Hugh Mac-Nair Kahler. Boards, paper label.

BLACK MAGIC. *Indianapolis* [1924].

CONCENTRATED NEW ENGLAND: A STUDY OF CALVIN COOLIDGE. *Indianapolis* [1924].
Boards, paper label; or, red cloth. No known priority.

FLORIDA LOAFING. *Indianapolis* [1925].
Boards, paper label.

FLORIDA. *New York*, 1926.
First printing indicated on copyright page. Code letters *C-A* on copyright page.

ANTIQUAMANIA. *Garden City*, 1928.
First edition indicated on the copyright page.

ARUNDEL. *Garden City*, 1930.
First edition indicated on copyright page. Numerous changes in the second printing, the following being sufficient for identification: p. 28, line 35, *them* for *then;* p. 84, line 6, *had* for *has;* p. 196, line 1, *protected* for *protested;* p. 299, line 17, *cheeries* for *cherries;* p. 357, line 11, *Arundel* for *Arnold.* Various reissues of first edition interest: 5th edition, *Garden City*, 1931, of which 15 copies have an inserted 8 pp., biography of the Nason family; 6th edition, *Garden City*, 1933, entirely revised; English edition, *London*, 1936, further revised.

THE LIVELY LADY. *Garden City*, 1931.
First edition indicated on the copyright page. The fifth edition, *Garden City*, 1935, was revised.

RABBLE IN ARMS. *Garden City*, 1933.
First edition indicated on the copyright page.

KENNETH ROBERTS

CAPTAIN CAUTION. *Garden City*, 1934.
First edition indicated on the copyright page.

THE BROTHERHOOD OF MAN. *New York*, 1934.
One-act play. With Robert Garland. Wrappers.

FOR AUTHORS ONLY. *Garden City*, 1935.
First edition indicated on the copyright page.

IT MUST BE YOUR TONSILS. *Garden City*, 1936.
First edition indicated on the copyright page.

NORTHWEST PASSAGE. *Garden City*, 1937.
First edition indicated on the copyright page. Also 1,050 sets, numbered, signed, 2 vols., Vol. 1 being the novel, Vol. 2 being an appendix citing the author's sources.

TRENDING INTO MAINE. *Boston*, 1938.
Also 1,075 copies, numbered and signed. First trade edition states *Published June 1938* on copyright page.

MARCH TO QUEBEC. *New York*, 1938.
First printing indicated on copyright page. Third edition, *New York*, 1940, with revisions and the hitherto unpublished journal of John Pierce, Arnold's official surveyor on his march to Quebec. The latter also issued as a separate publication in wrappers.

OLIVER WISWELL. *New York*, 1940.
Also 1,050 de luxe copies, 2 vols., numbered and signed. The first trade edition, one volume, so indicated on copyright page.

Songs of Cornell. *Ithaca* [1909].
Contains Roberts' "Fight for Cornell" and "Carnelian and White."
"Long Live the Kaiser ——!" *Boston* [1917].
Boards, paper labels. Contains "A Prayer" by Roberts.
Wit and Humor of the World. *New York* [n.d., 1917?].
Contributions.
The American Historical Scene as Depicted by Stanley Arthurs and Interpreted by Fifty Authors. *Philadelphia*, 1935.
Contains "Morgan's March Through Maine" by Roberts.
Kenneth Roberts: A Biographical Sketch. *Garden City* [1936].
Wrappers. Anon. By Chilson H. Leonard. First printing indicated on copyright page.
Modern Book Collecting for the Impecunious Amateur, by Herbert Faulkner West. *Boston*, 1936.
Contains a letter by Kenneth Roberts. *Published September, 1936* on copyright page.

"Let Me Show You New Hampshire," by Ella Shannon Bowles. *New York*, 1938.
  First printing indicated on copyright page. Introduction by Roberts.
Kenneth Roberts, An American Novelist. *New York* [1938].
  Wrappers. Also contains material by Roberts.
The Happy End, by Ben Ames Williams. *New York* [1939].
  1,250 numbered copies only. Foreword by Roberts.
Our Cornell. *Ithaca* [1939].
  Contains "Far Above Cayuga's Waters" by Roberts.
Good Maine Food, by Marjorie Mosser. *New York*, 1939.
  First printing indicated on copyright page. Introduction and notes by Roberts.
  Reissued, *New York*, 1940 (*Reprinted April, 1940* on copyright page) with
  additional material by Roberts.
A Bibliography of the Works of Kenneth Roberts, by Frank Stone.
  In preparation.

Edwin Arlington Robinson

1869–1935

THE TORRENT AND THE NIGHT BEFORE. *Gardiner, Maine,* 1896.

Blue wrappers. Privately printed. Reissued, *New York,* 1928, boards, in an edition of 110 signed copies only.

THE CHILDREN OF THE NIGHT. *Boston,* 1897.

50 copies on Japan vellum; 500 copies on Batchworth laid paper.

CAPTAIN CRAIG. *Boston,* 1902.

Also 125 untrimmed copies, with colophon on copyright page, paper label on spine. Of this state 67 copies were trimmed and issued in the trade binding. Revised and reissued *New York,* 1915; in the first binding the rules and lettering on the front cover are in gold.

THE TOWN DOWN THE RIVER. *New York,* 1910.

VAN ZORN. *New York,* 1914.

First state has top edges gilt. In the first binding the rules and lettering on the front cover are in gold.

THE PORCUPINE. *New York,* 1915.

First state has top edges gilt. Erratum slip at pp. [2]-3. In the first binding the rules and lettering on the front cover are in gold.

THE MAN AGAINST THE SKY. *New York,* 1916.

First state has top edges gilt.

MERLIN. *New York,* 1917.

P. 79, line 8 reads: ... *with only philosophy;* later corrected to: *one philosophy.*

THE THREE TAVERNS. *New York,* 1920.

Several states of spine stamping with no known priority.

LANCELOT. *New York,* 1920.

Also limited issue of 450 copies for the Lyric Society. Trade edition issued simultaneously. First binding green; later red.

AVON'S HARVEST. *New York,* 1921.

Boards, cloth back, label on side.

ROMAN BARTHOLOW. *New York,* 1923.

Also 750 numbered and signed copies. The limited edition preceded the trade edition.

THE MAN WHO DIED TWICE. *New York,* 1924.

Also 500 numbered and signed copies. The limited edition preceded the trade edition.

E. A. ROBINSON

DIONYSUS IN DOUBT. *New York*, 1925.

Also 350 numbered large paper copies, signed. The limited edition preceded the trade edition. The first trade issue has grey labels, later white labels.

TRISTRAM. *New York*, 1927.

First state has *rocks* for *rooks*, p. 86, line 2. Also 350 large paper copies, numbered and signed. Trade and Literary Guild editions issued simultaneously. The limited edition preceded the trade editions.

SONNETS 1889-1927. *New York*, 1928.

Also 561 copies, and 9 printed on green paper; numbered and signed. Boards, cloth back, label on side. The limited edition preceded the trade edition.

THREE POEMS. *Cambridge*, 1928.

15(?) copies only. Pirated.

FORTUNATUS. *Reno* [Nev.] 1928.

171 copies, signed, of which 12 were printed on brown paper for presentation. Boards, paper label.

MODRED: A FRAGMENT. *New York*, 1929.

250 signed copies only. Boards, cloth back. Previously in "Three Poems," 1928.

THE PRODIGAL SON. *New York*, 1929.

475 copies only in "The Random House Poetry Quartos." Wrappers.

CAVENDER'S HOUSE. *New York*, 1929.

Also 500 numbered copies, signed, large paper. The limited edition preceded the trade edition.

THE GLORY OF THE NIGHTINGALES. *New York*, 1930.

Also 500 numbered copies, signed, large paper. The limited edition preceded the trade edition.

MATTHIAS AT THE DOOR. *New York*, 1931.

Also 500 large paper copies, signed. First state has no punctuation at end of fifth line from bottom, p. 97. The limited edition preceded the trade edition.

NICODEMUS. *New York*, 1932.

Also 235 numbered copies, large paper, signed. The limited edition preceded the trade edition.

TALIFER. *New York*, 1933.

Also 273 numbered copies, large paper, signed. The limited edition preceded the trade edition.

AMARANTH. *New York*, 1934.

Also 226 numbered copies, large paper, signed. The limited edition preceded the trade edition.

E. A. ROBINSON

KING JASPER. *New York*, 1935.

Also 250 large paper copies, numbered. Introduction by Robert Frost. The limited edition preceded the trade edition.

SELECTED LETTERS. *New York*, 1940.

First printing indicated on copyright page.

COLLECTED POETRY

COLLECTED POEMS. *New York*, 1921.

Also 200 signed and numbered copies, 2 vols. The trade issue was reissued, 1922, with minor revisions.

COLLECTED POEMS. *Cambridge* [1927].

5 vols. 300 sets on large paper, signed. Trade edition *New York* [1927].

COLLECTED POEMS. *New York*, 1929.

Same as preceding but with addition of "Cavender's House." Also a one-volume edition on thin paper.

EDWIN ARLINGTON ROBINSON: POEMS. *New York*, 1931.

Bliss Perry, editor. First appearance for Robinson's notes on his own poetry. Two forms issued simultaneously: with Charles Cestre's "Introduction to Edwin Arlington Robinson" or without this feature. The introduction was separately issued, *New York*, 1930.

COLLECTED POEMS. *New York*, 1937.

BOOKS WITH CONTRIBUTIONS

The great number of books falling into this classification makes complete listing here impossible. Collectors are referred to the complete bibliography by Charles Beecher Hogan listed below.

Spanish-American War Songs. *Detroit*, 1898.
    Sidney A. Witherbee, editor. Contains a reprint of "The One Chord."
Harvard Lyrics. *Boston*, 1899.
    Contribution.
Our Phonographic Poets. *New York*, 1904.
    Wrappers. Contribution.
The Peterborough Idea. *Peterborough, N. H.*, 1917.
    Wrappers.
The Masque of Poets. *New York*, 1918.
    Edward J. O'Brien, editor. Foreword by Robinson.
American and British Verse from *The Yale Review*. *New Haven*, 1920.
    The Robinson material herein contained is reprinted.
The Pilgrim Spirit, by George P. Baker. *Boston* [1921].
    Contains Robinson's "The Pilgrims' Chorus." *See:* under *Robert Frost* for full description.

The Year Book of the Poetry Society of South Carolina, 1921. *Charleston,* 1921.
  Contains a letter from Robinson.
A Wreath for Edwin Markham. *Chicago,* 1922.
  Contribution.
The Peterborough Anthology. *New York,* 1923.
  The Robinson material herein contained is reprinted.
A Miscellany of American Poetry, 1925. *New York* [1925].
  First edition so stated on copyright page. Contribution.
Thoreau's Last Letter. *Amenia, N. Y.,* 1925.
  Wrappers. 200 copies only.
Percy MacKaye: A Symposium on His Fiftieth Birthday. *Hanover, N. H.,* 1928.
  Contains an appreciation of MacKaye by Robinson, "Unquestionable Genius."
Selections From the Letters of Thomas Sergeant Perry. *New York,* 1929.
  Edited and with an introduction by Robinson.
Wind in the Grass, by Christy MacKaye. *New York,* 1931.
  Introductory letter by Robinson.
Fifty Poets. *New York* [1933].
  Contribution by Robinson.
Breaking Into Print. *New York,* 1937.
  Elmer Adler, editor.

BIOGRAPHICAL AND CRITICAL

The Poetry of Edwin Arlington Robinson, by Lloyd Morris. *New York* [1923].
  With a bibliography by W. Van R. Whitall. First edition has *GHD* insignia on copyright page.
Edwin Arlington Robinson, by Ben Ray Redman. *New York,* 1926.
  Contains a bibliography.
Edwin Arlington Robinson, by Mark Van Doren. *New York,* 1927.
Edwin Arlington Robinson and the Arthurian Legend, by Lucius Beebe. *Cambridge,* 1927.
  100 copies only. Boards.
Aspects of the Poetry of Edwin Arlington Robinson, by Lucius Beebe. *Cambridge,* 1928.
  225 copies only of which 25 were signed by the author.
An Introduction to Edwin Arlington Robinson, by Charles Cestre. *New York,* 1930.
  Later in "Edwin Arlington Robinson: Poems," 1931, *q.v.*
A Bibliography of the Writings of Edwin Arlington Robinson, by Lucius Beebe and Robert Johns Bulkley, Jr. *Cambridge,* 1931.
  300 copies only of which 50, numbered I to L, are on large paper. Boards.
Edwin Arlington Robinson: A Collection of His Works From the Library of Bacon Collamore. *Hartford,* 1936.
  Privately printed.
E. A. R., by Laura E. Richards. *Cambridge,* 1936.
The Edwin Arlington Robinson Memorial. *Gardiner, Me.,* 1936.
A Bibliography of Edwin Arlington Robinson, by Charles Beecher Hogan. *New Haven,* 1936.

E. A. ROBINSON

Next Door to a Poet, by Rollin Walter Brown. *New York*, 1937.
  Biography.
A Bibliography of the Writings and Criticisms of Edwin Arlington Robinson, by
  Lillian Lippincott. *Boston,* 1937.
Edwin Arlington Robinson, by Hermann Hagedorn. *New York,* 1938.
Philosophy in the Poetry of Edwin Arlington Robinson, by Estelle Kaplan. *New
  York,* 1940.

Robinson's poems were also first printed in various anthologies including "The
Best Poems of 1929," *London,* 1929; the Braithwaite anthologies for 1913-1916,
1919, 1923-1924, etc., etc.

Rowland E[vans] Robinson
1833–1900

FOREST & STREAM FABLES. *New York* [1886].
  Anonymous. *By Awahsoose the Bear.* Printed wrappers.

UNCLE LISHA'S SHOP. *New York,* 1887.

SAM LOVEL'S CAMPS: UNCLE LISHA'S FRIENDS UNDER BARK AND CANVAS.
  New York, 1889.

VERMONT: A STUDY OF INDEPENDENCE. *Boston,* 1892.

DANVIS FOLKS. *Boston,* 1894.

IN NEW ENGLAND FIELDS AND WOODS. *Boston,* 1896.

UNCLE LISHA'S OUTING. *Boston,* 1897.

A HERO OF TICONDEROGA. *Burlington,* 1898.

IN THE GREEN WOOD. *Burlington,* 1899.

A DANVIS PIONEER. *Boston,* 1900.

SAM LOVEL'S BOY. *Boston,* 1901.

OUT OF BONDAGE. *Boston,* 1905.
  Published February 1905 on the copyright page.

HUNTING WITHOUT A GUN. *New York,* 1905.
  First state of binding has *Forest and Stream* imprint at the foot of spine.

SILVER FIELDS. *Boston.* 1921.

Katy's Birthday, by Sarah O[rne] Jewett. With Other Stories by Famous Authors.
  Boston [1883].
  Contains "The Story of Maple Sugar" by Robinson.
The Collected Works of Rowland E. Robinson. *Rutland, Vermont* [1933-37].
  Centennial Edition. Llewellyn R. Perkins, editor. 7 volumes with added material.

Theodore Roosevelt
1858–1919

NAVAL WAR OF 1812. *New York*, 1882.
Second edition so stated on the title page.

HUNTING TRIPS OF A RANCHMAN. *New York*, 1885.
Medora Edition, 500 large paper copies, untrimmed, bound in buckram.

THOMAS HART BENTON. *Boston*, 1887.

ESSAYS ON PRACTICAL POLITICS. *New York*, 1888.

GOUVERNEUR MORRIS. *Boston*, 1888.

RANCH LIFE AND THE HUNTING-TRAIL. *New York* [1888].
All edges gilt, bound in light colored, coarse weave, tan buckram. Cover design stamped in green and gold. Later bindings are brown linen, designs stamped in brown and gold.

THE WINNING OF THE WEST. *New York*, 1889-1896.
4 vols. Vol. 1: 1889; Vol. 2: 1889; Vol. 3: 1894; Vol. 4: 1896. Uniform bindings. Vol. 1, last word, p. 160, is *diame-*. P. 161, first word, first line, is *ter*.

NEW YORK. *New York*, 1891.

THE WILDERNESS HUNTER. *New York* [1893].
Chapter headings in brown. Tan or brown cloth binding. Some copies have inserted slip announcing a large paper state of this title, to be issued in a limited signed edition "in the early autumn." The latter refers to the limited edition of 200 signed copies.

HERO TALES FROM AMERICAN HISTORY. *New York*, 1895.
With HENRY CABOT LODGE.

AMERICAN IDEALS AND OTHER ESSAYS. *New York*, 1897.

SOME AMERICAN GAME. *New York*, 1897.
Wrappers.

BIG GAME HUNTING. *New York*, 1899.
Full tan buckram, black leather label, frontispiece signed. Also issued in various types of publisher's leather binding.

CUBA'S STRUGGLE AGAINST SPAIN. *New York*, 1899.
With LEE, WHEELER and WAINWRIGHT.

THE ROUGH RIDERS. *New York*, 1899.

THE PUBLIC PAPERS OF THEODORE ROOSEVELT, GOVERNOR. *Albany,* 1899-1900.

2 vols. Should have a presentation slip in each volume.

OLIVER CROMWELL. *New York,* 1900.

THE STRENUOUS LIFE. *New York,* 1900.

First state has 225 pp. Second edition has added material.

THE NAVAL OPERATIONS OF THE WAR BETWEEN GREAT BRITAIN AND THE UNITED STATES. 1812-1815. *Boston,* 1901.

10 copies only for copyright purposes, reprinted from Clowe's "The Royal Navy: A History," *London,* 1897, Vol. vi, pp. 1-180. Regular edition from the same sheets, *London,* 1901.

THE DEER FAMILY. *New York,* 1902.

With VAN DYKE, ELLIOT and STONE. Also 100 large paper copies.

THE PHILIPPINES. *New York,* 1902.

With WILLIAM HOWARD TAFT.

CALIFORNIA ADDRESSES. *San Francisco,* 1903.

Boards, cloth back, label on front cover.

THE SHIP OF STATE. *Boston,* 1903.

With others. Blue cloth, full rigged ship on cover in green, title in orange, lettered in gold on spine.

ADDRESSES AND PRESIDENTIAL MESSAGES. *New York,* 1904.

Green cloth.

OUTDOOR PASTIMES OF AN AMERICAN HUNTER. *New York,* 1905.

Also 260 large paper copies, signed, bound in three-quarter pigskin issued later.

SQUARE DEAL. *Allandale, New Jersey* [1906].

GOOD HUNTING. *New York,* 1907.

ADDRESSES AND PAPERS. *New York,* 1908.

Willis Fletcher Johnson, editor.

OUTLOOK EDITORIALS. *New York,* 1909.

Wrappers.

AFRICAN AND EUROPEAN ADDRESSES. *New York,* 1910.

AFRICAN GAME TRAILS. *New York,* 1910.

Two states issued simultaneously although printed from two different sets of plates with numerous differences in the illustrations: (a) one volume in light brown cloth, 2 elephant heads on front cover in gold, and with *Scribner Press* seal on copyright page. (b) Subscriber's Edition, pictorial binding, with *Conkey-*

445

Hammond press seal on copyright page. A later state: two volumes, 500 copies, large paper, signed, bound in three-quarter pigskin.

AMERICAN PROBLEMS. *New York*, 1910.
Wrappers.

BIOLOGICAL ANALOGIES IN HISTORY. *London*, 1910.

THE NEW NATIONALISM. *New York*, 1910.
Cloth or paper.

APPLIED ETHICS. *Cambridge*, 1911.

THE CONSERVATION OF WOMANHOOD AND CHILDHOOD. *New York*, 1912.

REALIZABLE IDEALS. *San Francisco*, 1912.

HISTORY AS LITERATURE. *New York*, 1913.

PROGRESSIVE PRINCIPLES. *New York*, 1913.

THEODORE ROOSEVELT: AN AUTOBIOGRAPHY. *New York*, 1913.

THROUGH THE BRAZILIAN WILDERNESS. *New York*, 1914.

LIFE-HISTORIES OF AFRICAN GAME ANIMALS. *New York*, 1914.
With EDMUND HELLER. 2 vols.

WHY AMERICA SHOULD JOIN THE ALLIES. *London* [1915].
Wrappers.

AMERICA AND THE WORLD WAR. *New York*, 1915.

A BOOK-LOVER'S HOLIDAY IN THE OPEN. *New York*, 1916.

FEAR GOD AND TAKE YOUR OWN PART. *New York* [1916].
Red cloth, top edges gilt or plain, other edges untrimmed.

AMERICANISM AND PREPAREDNESS. *New York*, 1917.

THE FOES OF OUR OWN HOUSEHOLD. *New York* [1917].
First state has monogram ⅜" in diameter in the printer's device on title page. Later states have device redrawn with monogram measuring $\frac{5}{16}$" in diameter.

NATIONAL STRENGTH AND INTERNATIONAL DUTY. *Princeton*, 1917.

THE GREAT ADVENTURE. *New York*, 1918.

THEODORE ROOSEVELT'S LETTERS TO HIS CHILDREN. *New York*, 1919.
First state has *twenty* for *dozen* in third line of introduction.

THEODORE ROOSEVELT AND HIS TIME SHOWN IN HIS OWN LETTERS. *New York*, 1920.
2 vols. J. B. Bishop, editor.

THEODORE ROOSEVELT IN THE KANSAS CITY STAR. *Boston, 1921.*
Also 375 large paper copies.

LETTERS TO ANNA ROOSEVELT COWLES, 1870-1918. *New York, 1924.*

SELECTIONS FROM THE CORRESPONDENCE OF THEODORE ROOSEVELT AND
HENRY CABOT LODGE. 1884-1918. *New York, 1925.*

WHO SHOULD GO WEST? *New York, 1927.*
73 copies only, privately printed.

THEODORE ROOSEVELT'S DIARIES OF BOYHOOD AND YOUTH. *New York, 1928.*

THE VALUE OF AN ATHLETIC TRAINING. *New York, 1929.*
51 copies only, privately printed.

COLLECTED EDITIONS

Of the many important collected editions the most inclusive are the following:

The Sagamore Edition. *New York, 1900.* 15 vols.
The first collected edition.
The Uniform Edition. *Philadelphia, 1902-03.* 22 vols.
The Elkhorn Edition. *New York, 1906-20.* 28 vols.
The National Edition. *New York, 1926.* 20 vols.
The Memorial Edition. *New York, 1923-25.* 24 vols.
1,000 sets only containing hitherto uncollected material.

BIOGRAPHICAL AND BIBLIOGRAPHICAL

Bibliography of Theodore Roosevelt, by John Hall Wheelock. *New York, 1920.*
500 copies only.
The Letters and Friendships of Sir Cecil Spring Rice. *Boston, 1929.*
2 vols. Stephen Gwynn, editor. Includes no less than 25,000 words of hitherto
unpublished Roosevelt letters.
Taft and Roosevelt: The Intimate Letters of Archie Butt, Military Aide. *Garden City,*
1930.
2 vols.
Roosevelt: The Story of a Friendship, by Owen Wister. *New York, 1930.*
See: under *Wister* for full description.

It has been estimated that a complete list of Roosevelt's writings would number
well over five thousand items; consequently, this list covers only the most important
titles. The Roosevelt Memorial Association, New York City, has a completely catalogued collection of the Roosevelt publications. Among the minor Roosevelt items,
chiefly desirable because of their scarcity are:

ROOSEVELT

The Summer Birds of the Adirondacks in Franklin County, New York, by Theodore Roosevelt, Jr., and H. D. Minot, October, 1877.
   4 pp. Roosevelt's first separately published work.
Notes on Some of the Birds of Oyster Bay, Long Island, by Theodore Roosevelt, March, 1879.
   Broadside.
By-Laws of the Little Missouri River Stockman's Association, Theodore Roosevelt, chairman; Henry S. Boice, vice-chairman. *New York*, 1885.
   6 pp.

Susan (Susanna Haswell) Rowson
1762–1824

VICTORIA. *London*, 1786.
  2 vols.

THE INQUISITOR. [*London*] 1788.
  3 vols. American edition, *Philadelphia*, 1793, 3 vols.

MENTORIA; OR, THE YOUNG LADY'S FRIEND. *London* [1791].
  2 vols. American edition, *Philadelphia*, 1794, 2 vols.

CHARLOTTE: A TALE OF TRUTH. *Philadelphia*, 1794.
  2 vols. The page of advertisements preceding the title page appears in two forms: either pasted or printed on the first leaf. The second edition is so marked on the title page. There is presumed to be a *London*, 1791, edition.

[REBECCA] THE FILLE DE CHAMBRE. *Philadelphia*, 1794.
  There is said to be a *London*, 1792, edition.

SLAVES IN ALGIERS. *Philadelphia*, 1794.

TRIALS OF THE HUMAN HEART. *Philadelphia*, 1795.
  4 vols. or 4 vols. in 2.

REUBEN AND RACHEL. *Boston*, 1798.
  2 vols. or 2 vols. in 1. There is said to be a *London*, 1792, edition.

MISCELLANEOUS POEMS. *Boston*, 1804.

A PRESENT FOR YOUNG LADIES. *Boston*, 1811.

SARAH; OR, THE EXEMPLARY WIFE. *Boston*, 1813.
  Printed boards.

CHARLOTTE'S DAUGHTER; OR, THE THREE ORPHANS. *Boston*, 1828.
  Boards, cloth back, paper label. Reissued as "Lucy Temple ..."

Contemporary records indicate that there are several books and plays by this author that have disappeared. A list of these together with other bibliographical information is contained in R. W. G. Vail's "Susanna Haswell Rowson ... A Bibliographical Study," *Worcester*, 1933.

Elegy. *Boston*, 1804.
An Abridgment of Universal Geography ... *Boston* [1805].
A Spelling Dictionary. *Boston*, 1807.

ROWSON

Youth's First Step in Geography ... *Boston*, 1818.
Biblical Dialogues ... *Boston*, 1822.
   2 vols.
Exercises in History, Chronology and Biography ... *Boston*, 1822.
A Memoir of Mrs. Susanna Rowson, by Elias Nason. *Albany*, 1870.

Edgar (Evertson) Saltus

1855–1921

BALZAC. *Boston*, 1884.

THE PHILOSOPHY OF DISENCHANTMENT. *Boston*, 1885.

THE ANATOMY OF NEGATION. *London*, 1886.
   Printed in England; issued with both New York and English imprints. Saltus said
   that the English edition preceded the American.

MR. INCOUL'S MISADVENTURE. *New York*, 1887.
   First state has green end papers. Publisher's advertisements "title page" has blank
   verso; no advertisements for "Sea Spray."

THE TRUTH ABOUT TRISTREM VARICK. *Chicago* [1888].
   Belford Clarke & Co. at foot of spine. Wrappers and cloth.

EDEN. *Chicago* [1888].
   Wrappers and cloth.

A TRANSACTION IN HEARTS. *New York* [1889].
   Printed wrappers or cloth.

A TRANSIENT GUEST AND OTHER EPISODES. *Chicago* [1889].
   Belford Clarke & Co. at foot or spine. Press of E. B. Sheldon & Co. on verso
   title page. Wrappers or cloth.

THE PACE THAT KILLS. *Chicago* [1889].
   Wrappers or cloth.

LOVE AND LORE. *New York* [1890].
   Wrappers.

MARY MAGDALEN. *New York* [1891].
   In the "Belford American Novels Series." Cloth or wrappers.

IMPERIAL PURPLE. *Chicago*, 1892.

FACTS IN THE CURIOUS CASE OF H. HYRTLE, ESQ. *New York*, 1892.

MADAME SAPPHIRA. *New York* [1893].
   Cloth or wrappers.

ENTHRALLED. *London*, 1894.
   Wrappers.

WHEN DREAMS COME TRUE. *New York* [1894].
   Wrappers.

THE GREAT BATTLES OF ALL NATIONS. *New York*, 1898.
2 vols. *Edited by Archibald Wilberforce.*

PURPLE AND FINE WOMEN. *New York*, 1903.
Wrappers.

THE POMPS OF SATAN. *London*, 1904.
New York, 1906.

THE PERFUME OF EROS. *New York*, 1905.
Appeared in *Tales From Town Topics*, December 1904, as "The Yellow Fay."

VANITY SQUARE. *Philadelphia*, 1906.
Pictorial covers. *Published in May, 1906* on copyright page.

HISTORIS AMORIS. *New York*, 1906.
Red lettering on title page.

THE LORDS OF THE GHOSTLAND. *New York*, 1907.
Gilt top. Leaf 7¼" tall. Red lettering on title page.

DAUGHTERS OF THE RICH. *New York* [1909].

THE MONSTER. *New York*, 1912.
Issued untrimmed and trimmed.

OSCAR WILDE: AN IDLER'S IMPRESSION. *Chicago*, 1917.
474 copies. 49 de luxe signed copies.

THE PALISER CASE. *New York*, 1919.

THE IMPERIAL ORGY. *New York*, 1920.

THE GARDENS OF APHRODITE. *Philadelphia*, 1920.
Privately printed. 68 numbered copies only.

THE GHOST GIRL. *New York* [1922].

PARNASSIANS PERSONALLY ENCOUNTERED. *Cedar Rapids*, 1923.
200 copies only.

THE UPLANDS OF DREAM. *Chicago*, 1925.
750 copies only. Contains a bibliography by Charles Honce.

VICTOR HUGO AND GOLGOTHA. *Chicago*, 1925.
310 copies. Printed on Inomachi vellum. 80 copies contain an original cancelled check with Saltus autograph. Half calf, decorated boards, uncut.

POPPIES AND MANDRAGORA. *New York*, 1926.
300 copies on Georgian Laid Paper; 500 on Etherington Novel Laid Paper.

American Sonnets. *London* [1889].
  William Sharp, editor. Contains a sonnet by Saltus.
The Capitals of the Globe. *New York*, 1894.
  Edited by Archibald Wilberforce. The latter one of Saltus' pseudonyms.
Spain and Her Colonies. *New York*, 1898.
  Compiled by Archibald Wilberforce, *pseud*. Later issues have either *Saltus's Spain*
  or *Saltu's Spain* on the spine.
Russia, by Alfred Rambaud. *New York*, 1898.
  2 vols. Supplementary chapter by Saltus.
Germany, by Wolfgang Menzel. *New York*, 1899.
  2 vols. Supplementary chapter by Saltus.
India, by J. Talboys Wheeler. *New York*, 1899.
  2 vols. Supplementary chapter by Saltus.
Wit and Wisdom From Edgar Saltus. *London*, 1903.
  By G. F. Monkshood and George Gamble.
What the Victory or Defeat of Germany Means to Every American. [*n.p., n.d.*].
  12mo broadside.
For France. *Garden City*, 1917.
  Contains a sonnet by Saltus.
A Bed of Roses, by W. L. George. *New York* [1919].
  Introduction.
Salomé, The Importance of Being Earnest, Lady Windermere's Fan, by Oscar Wilde.
  New York, 1919.
  Introduction.
Intentions, by Oscar Wilde. *Garden City*, 1923.
  Vol. v of the "Complete Works of Oscar Wilde." Introduction by Saltus.
Et Cetera. *Chicago*, 1924.
  For further regarding this see under Stephen Crane.

BIOGRAPHICAL

Edgar Saltus: The Man, by Marie Saltus. *Chicago*, 1925.
Edgar Saltus Bibliography, by Charles Honce.
  See: "Uplands of Dream," 1925.

TRANSLATIONS

After-Dinner Stories From Balzac. *New York*, 1886.
  Myndart Verelst, *pseud*.
Tales Before Supper From Théophile Gautier and Prosper Mérimée. *New York*,
  1887.
  Cloth or wrappers. "Told in English ... and Delayed With a Proem by Edgar
  Saltus." For further regarding this publication see "Avatar: Hearn or Saltus" in
  The Publishers' Weekly, June 19 & 26, 1937.
The Story Without a Name, by Jules Barbey d'Aureyilly. *New York* [1891].
  No. 1 in "The Bel-Esprit Series," dated September 28, 1891. Reissued with new
  introduction, *New York*, 1919.

SALTUS

Shorter Stories from Balzac. *London* [1890?].

English versions by William and Count Stenbock, the latter presumed to be Saltus. Charles Honce writes: "When Saltus was asked about the production he smiled without committing himself. Suspect."

BIBLIOGRAPHICAL

A Complete Bibliography of Edgar Saltus, by Charles Honce. Since appearance of his original bibliography in "Uplands of Dream," 1925, Mr. Honce has made extensive additions and revisions; unpublished.

Carl (Charles August) Sandburg

1878–

IN RECKLESS ECSTASY. *Galesburg,* 1904.
Privately printed pamphlet. *By Charles A. Sandburg.*

CHICAGO POEMS. *New York,* 1916.
First page of publisher's advertisements at back dated *3'16.*

CORNHUSKERS. *New York,* 1918.
Boards. The first state has p. 3 so numbered at foot of page. Also, list of books opposite the title page states price of "Chicago Poems" at $1.30. Later states lack the folio at p. 3 and the price here mentioned is changed to $1.35.

SMOKE AND STEEL. *New York,* 1920.
Boards.

SLABS OF THE SUNBURNT WEST. *New York* [1922].
In the earliest copies the text ends at the foot of p. 75; in later copies the text ends at p. 76.

ROOTABAGA STORIES. *New York* [1922].

ROOTABAGA PIGEONS. *New York* [1923].

ABRAHAM LINCOLN: THE PRAIRIE YEARS. *New York* [1926].
2 vols. Also 260 large paper sets, numbered and signed. Trade edition has first edition notice on copyright page. The very earliest state of the large paper edition, vol. 1, p. 175, line 9, reads *ears;* later corrected to *eyes.* It is said that only 12 copies with the error were circulated. Abridged edition, *New York,* 1929. The first twenty-seven chapters were issued as a juvenile as "Abe Lincoln Grows Up," *New York* [1925-28].

THE AMERICAN SONGBAG. *New York* [1927].

GOOD MORNING, AMERICA. *New York,* 1928.
Also 811 copies, numbered and signed; a few copies printed on blue paper.

STEICHEN, THE PHOTOGRAPHER. *New York* [1929].
925 copies only signed by author and subject.

POTATO FACE. *New York* [1930].
First edition so stated on copyright page.

EARLY MOON. *New York* [1930].
The introduction, "Short Talk on Poetry," is here first printed. First printing indicated on the copyright page.

MARY LINCOLN, WIFE AND WIDOW. *New York* [1932].
Also 260 large paper copies, numbered and signed. First printing of the trade edition indicated on the copyright page.

THE PEOPLE, YES. *New York* [1936].
Also 270 copies, numbered and signed. The first printing of the trade edition so indicated on the copyright page.

A LINCOLN AND WHITMAN MISCELLANY. *Chicago*, 1938.
250 copies only.

ABRAHAM LINCOLN: THE WAR YEARS. *New York* [1939].
4 vols. Also 525 copies, numbered and signed. The trade edition carries the following notice: *First Edition After Printing 525 De Luxe Copies.*

Incidentals. *Galesburg*, 1904.
Privately printed pamphlet.
You and Your Job. *Chicago* [n.d., ca., 1905].
Pamphlet. *By Charles Sandburg.*
The Dreamer, by P. G. Wright. [*Galesburg*, 1906].
Foreword.
The Chicago Race Riots. *New York*, 1919.
With an introduction by Walter Lippmann. Wrappers.
A Miscellany of American Poetry, 1920. *New York*, 1920.
Contributions.
Many Moons, by Lew Sarett. *New York*, 1920.
Introduction.
A Miscellany of American Poetry, 1922. *New York* [1922].
Contributions.
Proceedings of the Celebration of the 50th Anniversary of the Opening ... *Chicago Public Library*, 1923.
Contribution.
Carl Sandburg, the Man and His Poetry, by Harry Hansen. *Girard, Kansas* [1925].
Printed wrappers.
A Miscellany of American Poetry, 1925. *New York* [1925].
Contributions. First Edition so stated.
Selected Poems. *London* [or] *New York*, 1926.
Rebecca West, editor.
Abraham Lincoln: The Prairie Years. *New York*, 1926.
A prospectus issued by Harcourt, Brace in an edition limited to 2,500 copies. Contains material by Sandburg.
A Miscellany of American Poetry, 1927. *New York* [1927].
Contributions. First edition so stated.
Better Angels, by Richard Henry Little. *New York*, 1928.
Introduction.
Rootabaga Country. *New York* [1929].
Selected material from the two "Rootabaga" books.

On Parade. *New York, 1929.*
    Erich Posselt, editor. Contribution by Sandburg.
Dining in Chicago, by John Drury. *New York* [1931].
    Foreword.
Fifty Poets. *New York* [1933].
    Contribution.
Best Poems of 1933. *London* [*n.d.*].
    Thomas Moult, editor. Contribution.
If Lincoln Had Lived: Addresses by Llewellyn Ranley, Lloyd Lewis, Carl Sandburg, William E. Dodd. *Chicago* [1935].
Amy Lowell: A Chronicle, by S. Foster Damon. *Boston, 1935.*
    Contribution.
Modern American Poetry, 5th Revised Edition. *New York* [1936].
    Louis Untermeyer, editor. First book printing for "Elephants are Different to Different People."
Rootabaga Stories. *New York* [1936].
    Reprinted material.
The Letters of Lincoln Steffens. *New York* [1938].
    2 vols. Edited by Ella Winter and Granville Hicks. Contribution.
Myths After Lincoln, by Lloyd Lewis. *New York* [1940].
Abe Lincoln in Illinois, by Robert E. Sherwood. *New York, 1939.*
    Foreword.
Poems Between Wars, by Paul Scott Mowrer. *Chicago* [1941].
    Contribution.

George Santayana
1863–

Note: *Cambridge* in the following list, unless otherwise specified, is understood to be *Cambridge, Massachusetts.*

SONNETS AND OTHER VERSES. *Cambridge and Chicago,* 1894.
  500 copies only: 450 in cloth (three states of stamping with no known priority), and 50 large paper in vellum binding. Cloth copy has been noted with *John Dickinson & Co Ltd New York* stamped on front cover. The latter is "presumably ... from the files of the firm which supplied Stone & Kimball ₍the publishers of this book₎ with paper, and has no ... significance."—Kramer's bibliography of Stone & Kimball. Revised and reissued, 1906.

THE SENSE OF BEAUTY. *New York,* 1896.

LUCIFER: A THEOLOGICAL TRAGEDY. *Chicago and New York,* 1899.
  Revised and reissued with a new introduction by the author, 450 copies only, *Cambridge,* 1924.

INTERPRETATIONS OF POETRY AND RELIGION. *New York,* 1900.

A HERMIT OF CARMEL AND OTHER POEMS. *New York,* 1901.
  Published October, 1901 on copyright page.

THE LIFE OF REASON. *New York,* 1905-1906.
  5 vols. Vols. 1-4, 1905; vol. 5, 1906.

THREE PHILOSOPHICAL POETS: LUCRETIUS, DANTE AND GOETHE. *Cambridge,* 1910.

WINDS OF DOCTRINE. *London,* 1913.
  New York edition published later in same year.

EGOTISM IN GERMAN PHILOSOPHY. *London* ₍1916₎.
  New York edition later in same year. Reissued, *London* ₍1939₎.

CHARACTER AND OPINION IN THE UNITED STATES. *London,* 1920.

SOLILOQUIES IN ENGLAND AND LATER SOLILOQUIES. *London* ₍1922₎.

POEMS. *London* ₍1922₎.
  Also 100 large paper copies, signed. New York edition, 1923.

SCEPTICISM AND ANIMAL FAITH. *London* ₍1923₎.

DIALOGUES IN LIMBO. *London,* 1925.

PLATONISM AND THE SPIRITUAL LIFE. *London*, 1927.

THE REALM OF ESSENCE. *New York*, 1927.

THE REALM OF MATTER. *London*, 1930.

THE GENTEEL TRADITION AT BAY. *New York*, 1931.
First printing has code letter *A* on copyright page. A copy has been noted with an inserted printed presentation slip.

FIVE ESSAYS. *Cambridge, England*, 1933.
Published later in same year, *New York*, 1933, as "Some Turns of Thought in Modern Philosophy."

THE LAST PURITAN. *London*, 1935.
American edition, *New York*, 1936; first state has publisher's code letter *A* on copyright page.

OBITER SCRIPTA. *New York*, 1936.
James Buchler and Benjamin Schwartz, editors. Contains a checklist of Santayana's writings. First state has publisher's code letter *A* on copyright page.

THE REALM OF TRUTH. *London*, 1937.
Also *New York*, 1938.

THE REALM OF SPIRIT. *New York*, 1940.
First printing has code letter *A* on copyright page.

WORKS. [*New York*, 1936-1937].
14 vols. 940 sets, numbered and signed.

Lines on Leaving the Bedford Street Schoolhouse. *Boston*, 1880.
4 pp. leaflet. Privately printed.
Lotze's System of Philosophy. *Cambridge*, 1889.
Platonism in the Italian Poets. *Buffalo*, 1896.
Warner's Library of the World's Best Literature. *New York* [1896].
Contains "Cervantes" by Santayana.
Reminiscences and a List of the Editors of the Harvard Lampoon. *Cambridge*, 1901.
Contains Santayana's "The Lampoon From 1883-1886."
The Complete Writings of Alfred de Musset. *New York*, 1907.
8 vols. Co-translator.
The Harper Edition of Shakespeare's Works. *New York*, 1908.
"Hamlet" contains an introduction by Santayana.
Ethics and De Intellectus Emendatione, by Spinoza. *London*, 1910.
Everyman edition. Introduction by Santayana.
Philosophical Opinion in America. *Oxford* [1918].
Reprinted from "The Proceedings of the British Academy," 1917-1918.
Essays in Critical Realism. *London*, 1920.
Contains Santayana's "Three Proofs of Realism."

SANTAYANA

Little Essays Drawn From the Writings of George Santayana. *London*, 1920.
  By Logan Pearsall Smith, with the collaboration of Santayana.
The Unknowable. *Oxford*, 1923.
Septimana Spinozana. *Hague*, 1933.
  Contains "Ultimate Religion" by Santayana.
Giacomo Leopardi: A Biography, by Iris Origo. *Oxford*, 1935.
  Foreword by Santayana.
The Thought and Character of William James, by Ralph Barton Perry. *Boston*, 1935.
  Pulitzer Prize Winner. Contains several letters by Santayana to William James.
The Philosophy of Santayana. *New York*, 1936.
  Irwin Edman, editor. First printing has code letter *A* on copyright page.
George Santayana, by George W. Howgate. *Philadelphia*, 1938.
The Moral Philosophy of Santayana. *New York*, 1939.
  By Milton K. Munitz.

Ernest (Evan) Thompson Seton (Thompson)

1860–

STUDIES IN THE ART ANATOMY OF ANIMALS. *New York,* 1896.

WILD ANIMALS I HAVE KNOWN. *New York,* 1898.
First state, p. 265, last paragraph, omits: *The Angel whispered don't go.* This line was added to later states.

THE TRAIL OF THE SANDHILL STAG. *New York,* 1899.
Also 250 copies on Japan vellum, published about one month after trade edition.

THE BIOGRAPHY OF A GRIZZLY. *New York,* 1900.

THE WILD ANIMAL PLAY FOR CHILDREN. *Philadelphia & New York* [1900].

LIVES OF THE HUNTED. *New York,* 1901.

HOW TO PLAY INDIAN. *Philadelphia,* 1903.
An annual republication of essentially the same material but with revisions and additions. First published in 1902 for members of the Woodcraft Indians, a forerunner of the Boy Scouts of America. A partial list of the publications is as follows, issued as "The Birch Bark Rolls." 1: "American Woodcraft," in: *Ladies' Home Journal,* May-November, 1902; 2: "How to Play Indian," 1903; 3: "The Red Book," 1904; 4: "Laws of the Seton Indians," in "Camp Conference Secretary's Report," *Boston,* 1905; 5: Reprint of the preceding in *Association Boys,* published by the Boston Y. M. C. A., 1905; 6: "The Birch Bark Roll of the Woodcraft Indians," 1906; 7: Reprint of the preceding, 1907; 8: Reprint of the preceding, 1907; 9: "The American Boy Scout," 1910; 10: "Boy Scouts of America," 1910, etc., etc.

TWO LITTLE SAVAGES. *New York,* 1903.

MONARCH: THE BIG BEAR OF TALLAC. *New York,* 1904.

WOODMYTH AND FABLE. *New York,* 1905.

ANIMAL HEROES. *New York,* 1905.
Noted in printed wrappers; status unknown.

THE NATURAL HISTORY OF THE TEN COMMANDMENTS. *New York,* 1907.
Boards.

LIFE HISTORIES OF NORTHERN ANIMALS. *New York,* 1909.
2 vols. Some copies, not the earliest issued, have corrections in ink on p. 53, Vol. 1; p. 795, Vol. 2.

THE BIOGRAPHY OF A SILVER-FOX. *New York,* 1909.

ROLF IN THE WOODS. *Garden City*, 1911.

THE ARCTIC PRAIRIES. *New York*, 1911.

THE FORESTER'S MANUAL. *Garden City*, 1912.

WILD ANIMALS AT HOME. *Garden City*, 1913.

WILD ANIMAL WAYS. *Garden City*, 1916.

THE PREACHER OF CEDAR MOUNTAIN. *Garden City*, 1917.

SIGN TALK. *Garden City*, 1918.

WOODLAND TALES. *Garden City*, 1921.

BANNERTAIL: THE STORY OF A GRAY SQUIRREL. *New York*, 1922.

LIVES OF GAME ANIMALS. *Garden City*, 1925-1928.
   4 vols. 177 sets. Each set contains an original drawing by the author. Reissued
   from the same plates in a popular edition, 1929, in 8 vols.

THE GOSPEL OF THE RED MAN; AN INDIAN BIBLE. *Garden City*, 1936.
   First edition so stated on copyright page.

THE BIOGRAPHY OF AN ARCTIC FOX. *New York*, 1937.

GREAT HISTORIC ANIMALS. *New York*, 1937.

TRAIL AND CAMPFIRE STORIES. *New York*, 1940.

THE TRAIL OF AN ARTIST-NATURALIST ... AN AUTOBIOGRAPHY. *New York*,
   1940.
   First printing has code letter *A* on copyright page.

Seton is well known as an illustrator and in this capacity has contributed to innumerable books, some of these are listed below. He was also one of the chief illustrators of the Century Dictionary. Before 1898 his writings were almost exclusively
studies in natural history and were printed mainly as contributions to scientific
journals. Among these early works are "The Striped Gopher," "Pediocetes Phasianel-
lus," "Prairie Fires," "The Mammals of Manitoba," "How to Catch Wolves." The
following is a selection.

A List of the Mammals of Manitoba, by Ernest E. Thompson(!). [*Toronto*, 1886].
   Printed wrappers.
How to Catch Wolves. *Oneida Community*, 1894.
   Printed wrappers.
Bird-Life, by Frank M. Chapman. *New York*, 1897.
Four-Footed Americans and Their Kin, by Mabel Osgood Wright. *New York*, 1898.
Lobo, Rag and Vixen. *New York*, 1899.
   Reprint.

A Woman Tenderfoot, by Grace Seton-Thompson. *New York*, 1900.
   Contains illustrations by Seton.
First Across the Continent, by Noah Brooks. *New York*, 1901.
   Contains illustrations by Seton.
Pictures of Wild Animals. *New York*, 1901.
   12 large pictures without text.
Bird Portraits. *Boston*, 1901.
   20 large drawings with text by Ralph Hoffmann.
Krag and Johnny Bear. *New York*, 1902.
   Reprint.
Nimrod's Wife, by Grace Gallatin Seton. *New York*, 1907.
   Illustrated by Seton.
Bird Records from Great Slave Lake Region. [*n.p.*, 1908].
   Printed wrappers.
Fauna of Manitoba. [*n.p.*, 1909].
   Printed wrappers.
The War Dance and the Fire-Fly Dance. *New York*, 1910.
The Red Lodge. *New York*, 1912.
   Privately printed. Wrappers. 100 copies only.
On the Popular Names of Birds. [*n.p.*, 1919].
   Printed wrappers.
Ernest Thompson Seton, A Biographical and Bibliographical Sketch. [*Garden City*]
   1925.
The Rhythm of the Red Man, by Julia M. Buttree. *New York*, 1930.
   Illustrated and with an introduction by Seton.
Famous Animal Stories, Animal Myths, Fables, Fairy Tales, Stories of Real Animals. *New York* [1932].
   Edited by Seton.
Johnny Bear, Lobo and Other Stories. *New York* [1935].
   Reprint.
Pictographs of the Southwest. *Cedar Rapids* [1937].
   With others.
The Indian Costume Book, by Julia M. Seton. *Santa Fe*, 1938.
   500 copies only, 100 of which are hand-colored and signed by Ernest Thompson Seton.
The Buffalo Wind. *Santa Fe*, 1938.
   200 numbered copies only.

William Gilmore Simms

1806–1870

THE BOOK OF MY LADY. *Philadelphia,* 1833.
Anon. *By A Bachelor Knight.*

MARTIN FABER: THE STORY OF A CRIMINAL. *New York,* 1833.
Anon. Reissued, *New York,* 1837, 2 vols. with added material.

GUY RIVERS: A TALE OF GEORGIA. *New York,* 1834.
2 vols. Anon. Cloth, paper labels.

THE YEMASSEE: A ROMANCE OF CAROLINA. *New York,* 1835.
2 vols. Cloth, paper labels. Anon. Copies have been noted with the copyright notice pasted in vol. 1.

THE PARTISAN: A TALE OF THE REVOLUTION. *New York,* 1835.
2 vols. Anon. Cloth, paper labels.

MELLICHAMPE: A LEGEND OF THE SANTEE. *New York,* 1836.
2 vols. Cloth, paper labels.

RICHARD HURDIS; OI, THE AVENGER OF BLOOD. *Philadelphia,* 1838.
2 vols. Cloth, paper labels.

PELAYO: A STORY OF THE GOTH. *New York,* 1838.
2 vols. Anon. Cloth, paper labels.

CARL WERNER, AN IMAGINATIVE STORY. *New York,* 1838.
2 vols. Anonymous.

THE DAMSEL OF DARIEN. *Philadelphia,* 1839.
2 vols. Anon. Errata slip preceding first page of text, vol. 1. Boards or wrappers, labels on spine.

BORDER BEAGLES: A TALE OF MISSISSIPPI. *Philadelphia,* 1840.
2 vols. Anon. Cloth, paper labels.

THE KINSMEN; OI, THE BLACK RIDERS OF CONGAREE. *Philadelphia,* 1841.
2 vols. Anon. Reissued with revisions as "The Scout," *New York,* 1854.

CONFESSION; OI, THE BLIND HEART. *Philadelphia,* 1841.
2 vols. Anon.

BEAUCHAMPE; OI, THE KENTUCKY TRAGEDY. *Philadelphia,* 1842.
2 vols. Anon.

DONNA FLORIDA. *Charleston,* 1843.
Anon.

CASTLE DISMAL; or, THE BACHELOR'S CHRISTMAS. *New York, 1844.*
Anon. Boards.

THE PRIMA DONNA: A PASSAGE FROM LIFE. *Philadelphia, 1844.*
No. 1 in "Godey's Library of Elegant Literature."

HELEN HALSEY; or, THE SWAMP STATE OF CONELACHITA. *New York, 1845.*
Reissued, 1869, as "The Island Bride."

COUNT JULIAN; or, THE LAST DAYS OF THE GOTH. *Baltimore and New York, 1845.*
Anon.

THE WIGWAM AND THE CABIN: FIRST SERIES. *New York, 1845.*
Anon. Printed wrappers. "Second Series" issued *New York, 1845,* printed wrappers.

FATHER ABBOTT; or, THE HOME TOURIST. *Charleston, 1849.*

THE CASSIQUE OF ACCABEE. *Charleston, 1849.*
Boards. Another issue, *New York, 1849.*

THE LILY AND THE TOTEM; or, THE HUGUENOTS IN FLORIDA. *New York, 1850.*
Anon.

FLIRTATION AT THE MOULINE HOUSE. *Charleston, 1850.*

KATHERINE WALTON; or, THE REBEL OF DORCHESTER. *Philadelphia, 1851.*
Anon.

NORMAN MAURICE; or, THE MAN OF THE PEOPLE. *Richmond, 1851.*

THE GOLDEN CHRISTMAS: A CHRONICLE OF ST. JOHN'S, BERKELEY. *Charleston, 1852.*
Anon. Cloth or printed wrappers.

THE SWORD AND THE DISTAFF; or, "FAIR, FAT, AND FORTY." *Charleston, 1852.*
Reissued, *Philadelphia, 1852.* Reissued as "Woodcraft," *New York, 1854.*

MICHAEL BONHAM: OR, THE FALL OF BEXAR. *Richmond, 1852.*
Anon. *By A Southron.*

AS GOOD AS A COMEDY; or, THE TENNESSEEAN'S STORY. *Philadelphia, 1852.*
Anon. *By An Editor.*

MARIE DE BERNIERE. *Philadelphia, 1853.*
Reissued, *Philadelphia, 1855,* as "The Maroon." Reissued, *New York* [1866], as "The Ghost of My Husband."

VASCONSELOS: A ROMANCE OF THE NEW WORLD. *New York*, 1853.
Frank Cooper, *pseud.*

EGERIA; or, VOICES OF THOUGHT AND COUNSEL FOR THE WOODS AND WAY-
SIDE. *Philadelphia*, 1853.

SOUTHWARD HO! A SPELL OF SUNSHINE. *New York*, 1854.

THE FORAYERS; or, THE RAID OF THE DOG-DAYS. *New York*, 1855.

CHARLEMONT; or, THE PRIDE OF THE VILLAGE. *New York*, 1856.

EUTAW. *New York*, 1856.
Sequel to "The Forayers."

THE CASSIQUE OF KIAWAH. *New York*, 1859.

THE QUAKER PARTISANS. *Philadelphia*, 1869.
Anon. Authorship in doubt.

THE SWAMP ROBBERS. *New York*, 1870.
Anon.

POETRY

LYRICAL AND OTHER POEMS. *Charleston*, 1827.

EARLY LAYS. *Charleston*, 1827.

THE VISION OF CORTES, CAIN, AND OTHER POEMS. *Charleston*, 1829.

THE TRI-COLOR; or, THREE DAYS OF BLOOD IN PARIS. *London*, 1830.
Anon. Mention is made of a *Charleston*, 1830, edition.

ATALANTIS. *New York*, 1832.
Anon. Reissued with added material, 1848. "Eye and Wing," *New York*, 1848,
reprinted from the latter.

POEMS. *Richmond*, 1833.
Anon. *By A Collegian*. Attributed to Simms; doubtful authorship.

SOUTHERN PASSAGES AND PICTURES. *New York*, 1839.
Anon.

GROUPED THOUGHTS AND SCATTERED FANCIES. *Richmond*, 1845.
Anon.

AREYTOS; or, SONGS OF THE SOUTH. *Charleston*, 1846.
Reissued, *Charleston*, 1860, with additional material as "Simms' Poems."

LAYS OF THE PALMETTO. *Charleston*, 1848.

SABBATH LYRICS; or, SONGS FROM SCRIPTURE. *Charleston*, 1849.

THE CITY OF THE SILENT. *Charleston*, 1850.

POEMS: DESCRIPTIVE, DRAMATIC, LEGENDARY AND CONTEMPLATIVE. *Charleston*, 1853.
2 vols. Also New York issue from the same type. The latter, probably the first printed, but not necessarily the first issued.

HISTORICAL, BIOGRAPHICAL, ETC.

MEMOIR OF MAYNARD DAVIS RICHARDSON. *Charleston*, 1833.
Anon. *By A Friend.*

THE MORALS OF SLAVERY: BEING A BRIEF REVIEW OF THE WRITINGS OF MISS MARTINEAU. *Charleston*, 1838.
Reissued, 1852, in "The Pro-Slavery Argument."

SLAVERY IN AMERICA. *Richmond*, 1838.
Anon. *By A South Carolinian.* Probably same as preceding item.

THE HISTORY OF SOUTH CAROLINA. *Charleston*, 1840.
Also large paper state. Reissued, 1842 and 1860, with added material.

THE GEOGRAPHY OF SOUTH CAROLINA. *Charleston*, 1843.

THE LIFE OF FRANCIS MARION. *New York*, 1844.

VIEWS AND REVIEWS IN AMERICAN LITERATURE, HISTORY, AND FICTION. *New York*, 1845.
Anon. "Second Series" later in same year.

THE LIFE OF CAPTAIN JOHN SMITH. *New York* [1846].

THE LIFE OF CHEVALIER BAYARD. *New York*, 1847.

CHARLESTON AND HER SATIRISTS. *Charleston*, 1848.
Anon. *By A City Bachelor.*

THE LIFE OF NATHANAEL GREENE. *New York*, 1849.

SOUTH CAROLINA IN THE REVOLUTIONARY WAR. *Charleston*, 1853.
Anon. *By A Southron.*

SACK AND DESTRUCTION OF THE CITY OF COLUMBIA, S. C. *Columbia*, 1865.
Wrappers.

MISCELLANEOUS

A Monody on the Death of General Cotesworth Pinckney. *Charleston*, 1825.
Doubtful as to whether in book form.

The Oration of William Drayton. *Charleston*, 1831.
  Contains an ode by Simms.
The Cosmopolitan: An Occasional, No. 1. *Charleston* [1834].
The Social Principle. *Tuscaloosa*, 1843.
  Oration.
The Sources of American Independence. *Aiken, S. C.*, 1844.
  Oration.
The Charleston Book. *Charleston*, 1845.
  Edited.
The Missionary Memorial. *New York*, 1846.
  Contains "Pocahontas," a poem by Simms.
Self Development. *Milledgeville* [Ga.] 1847.
  Oration.
A Supplement to the Plays of William Shakespere. *New York*, 1848.
The Pro-Slavery Argument. *Charleston*, 1852.
  Reprints Simms' "The Morals of Slavery."
The Spartanburg Female College Oration. *Spartanburg*, 1855.
The Power of Cotton. *New York*, 1856.
  Doubtful authorship; attributed to Simms.
War Poetry of the South. *New York*, 1866.
  Edited.
The Army Correspondence of Colonel John Laurens ... *New York*, 1867.
  Edited. 80 numbered copies only.
A Succinct Memoir of the Life and Public Services of Colonel John Laurens. [*Albany*]
  1867.
  Contains a memoir by Simms. Reprinted from the preceding.
The Sense of the Beautiful. *Charleston*, 1870.
  Oration.
Sumter. [*n.p.,n.d.*].
  Ca. 1870. Doubtful authorship; attributed to Simms.
William Gilmore Simms, by William P. Trent. *Boston*, 1892.
A List of the Separate Writings of William Gilmore Simms, by Oscar Wegelin.
  [*Greenwich, Conn.*] 1906.
  110 numbered copies only.

F[rancis] Hopkinson Smith

1838–1915

OLD LINES IN NEW-BLACK-AND-WHITE. *Boston*, 1885.
Also large paper state.

A BOOK OF THE TILE CLUB. *Boston*, 1886.
With Edward Strahan, *pseudonym* for Earl Shinn. Also 100 de luxe copies.

WELL-WORN ROADS OF SPAIN, HOLLAND, AND ITALY. *Boston*, 1887.
Also large paper state.

A WHITE UMBRELLA IN MEXICO. *Boston*, 1889.
Boards, cloth back.

COLONEL CARTER OF CARTERSVILLE. *Boston*, 1891.
In the first state a picture of a staircase appears at p. 1; later states at p. 3. Early copies have been noted with an apostrophe in *Cartersville* on the spine, the apostrophe appearing either before or after the *s*. It is noteworthy that the dedication of the book is dated *May 1891* and an inscribed presentation copy from the author to his sister, dated May 9, 1891, has the apostrophe thus: *Carter's*. The advertisements have no mention of this title.

A DAY AT LAGUERRE'S. *Boston*, 1892.
Also 250 numbered copies, signed. Copies have been noted in red cloth with printed paper label on spine.

A GENTLEMAN VAGABOND AND SOME OTHERS. *Cambridge*, 1895.
Also 250 large paper copies.

VENICE OF TODAY. *New York*, 1895.
Paper parts. Reissued in book form, *New York*, 1896.

TOM GROGAN. *Boston*, 1896.
Also 100 large paper copies.

GONDOLA DAYS. *Boston*, 1897.

CALEB WEST, MASTER DIVER. *Boston*, 1898.
Pictorial cloth binding preceded by 100 copies in plain cloth, untrimmed, paper lable on spine.

THE OTHER FELLOW. *Boston*, 1899.
Also 300 numbered/large paper copies.

THE FORTUNES OF OLIVER HORN. *New York*, 1902.
Noted in two types of cloth: dullish grey-green, and polished green, no known priority. The publisher's file copy is in the polished green. *Published, August, 1902* on the copyright page.

THE UNDER DOG. *New York*, 1903.
> *Published, May, 1903* on the copyright page.

COLONEL CARTER'S CHRISTMAS. *New York*, 1903.
> Also 500 copies in flexible parchment-boards, signed. *Published, October, 1903* on the copyright page. The trade edition occurs with the spine stamped in either gold or white; priority undetermined.

THE WOOD FIRE IN NO. 3. *New York*, 1905.
> *Published, October, 1905* on copyright page.

AT CLOSE RANGE. *New York*, 1905.

THE TIDES OF BARNEGAT. *New York*, 1906.
> *Published August, 1906* on copyright page. Also advance copies printed from the magazine plates in either boards, paper label or printed wrappers.

OLD FASHIONED FOLK. *Boston*, 1907.
> 750 copies only, privately printed.

THE ROMANCE OF AN OLD-FASHIONED GENTLEMAN. *New York*, 1907.
> *Published, October, 1907* on copyright page.

THE VEILED LADY. *New York*, 1907.
> *Published, March, 1907* on copyright page.

PETER. *New York*, 1908.
> *Published August, 1908* on copyright page.

CAPTAIN THOMAS A. SCOTT, MASTER DIVER. *Boston*, 1908.

FORTY MINUTES LATE AND OTHER STORIES. *New York*, 1909.
> *Published September, 1909* on copyright page.

KENNEDY SQUARE. *New York*, 1911.
> *Published August, 1911* on copyright page.

THE ARM-CHAIR AT THE INN. *New York*, 1912.
> *Published August, 1912* on copyright page.

CHARCOALS OF NEW AND OLD NEW YORK. *New York*, 1912.
> Also 125 de luxe copies.

IN THACKERAY'S LONDON. *New York*, 1913.
> Also 110 large paper copies, signed.

IN DICKENS'S LONDON. *New York*, 1914.
> Boards, cloth back.

FELIX O'DAY. *New York*, 1915.
> *Published September, 1915* on copyright page.

ENOCH CRANE. *New York,* 1916.
First three chapters written by Smith before his death. Book finished by F.
Berkeley Smith from notes. *Published September, 1916* on copyright page.

The Vision of Sir Launfal, by James Russell Lowell. *Boston,* 1888.
Contains some illustrations by Smith.
American Illustrators. *New York,* 1892.
Portfolio. 1,000 copies only.
Readings From A Day at Laguerre's. *Cambridge,* 1893.
Privately printed. One copy only.
Stories of Italy. *New York,* 1893.
Contains "Espero Gorgoni," by Smith.
Some Artists at the Fair. *New York,* 1893.
Contributions.
The Last Leaf, by Oliver Wendell Holmes. *Cambridge,* 1895.
Illustrated with George Wharton Edwards. Also de luxe editions.
Ramblings Among Art Centres. [*Philadelphia,* 1901].
The Gentle Art of Dining. *New York,* 1906.
Reprinted from "The Wood Fire" stories. Boards.
Outdoor Sketching. *New York,* 1915.
Illustrated by the author.

John (Ernst) Steinbeck

1902–

CUP OF GOLD: A LIFE OF HENRY MORGAN, BUCCANEER, WITH OCCASIONAL REFERENCE TO HISTORY. *New York,* 1929.
First Published, August, 1929 on copyright page.

THE PASTURES OF HEAVEN. *New York,* 1932.
First edition has imprint of *Brewer, Warren & Putnam.* Reissued with cancel title page bearing *Robert O. Ballou* imprint. Third issue, also with cancel title page, bears *Covici-Friede* imprint.

TO A GOD UNKNOWN. *New York* [1933].
First edition has imprint of *Robert O. Ballou.* Reissued with cancel title page bearing *Covici-Friede* imprint.

TORTILLA FLAT. *New York* [1935].
Approximately 500 copies in printed wrappers were issued in advance of publication. Reprints are so indicated on the copyright page. Modern Library edition contains new preface.

IN DUBIOUS BATTLE. *New York* [1936].
Also 99 de luxe copies, numbered, signed by the author.

SAINT KATY THE VIRGIN. [*New York,* 1936].
199 signed copies only, signed. Issued as a Christmas token by Covici-Friede with loosely inserted greeting slip.

OF MICE AND MEN. *New York* [1937].
First state has *and only moved because the heavy hands were* | *pendula.* at p. 9, lines 2 and 3 from the bottom of the page; this reading removed from later printings.

THE RED PONY. *New York,* 1937.
699 signed copies only.

"THEIR BLOOD IS STRONG." *San Francisco,* 1938.
Printed wrappers.

THE LONG VALLEY. *New York,* 1938.

THE GRAPES OF WRATH. *New York* [1939].
Regarding this book the publishers state: "Purchasers ... will have three ways of discovering whether or not they own a first edition of the work. First: a yellow top stain is used on the first edition; subsequent printings are stained blue. Second: first edition copies carry as the last line of the copyright page the notice,

First published in April, 1939; subsequent printings carry appropriate additional notice. Third, the jackets on the first edition have a notice of that fact printed on the front flap, this statement being omitted from later printings."

THE FORGOTTEN VILLAGE. *New York,* 1941.
First Published In May 1941 on copyright page.

SEA OF CORTEZ.
With Edward F. Ricketts. Announced.

O. Henry Memorial Award Prize Stories. *Garden City,* 1934.
Harry Hansen, editor. Contains "The Murder," by Steinbeck.
"Nothing So Monstrous: A Story." ₁*New York*₁ 1936.
Boards. Reprinted from "The Pastures of Heaven."
Famous Recipes by Famous People. *Del Monte, California* ₁1936₁.
Pamphlet. First printing so indicated on the copyright page. Contribution.
The Novels of John Steinbeck, by H. T. Moore. *Chicago,* 1939.
1,000 copies only.
The Wrath of John Steinbeck, or, St. John Goes to Church, by Robert Bennett. *Los Angeles,* 1939.
1,000 numbered copies only, signed by the author.
John Steinbeck: Personal and Bibliographical Notes, by Lewis Gannett. *New York* ₁1939₁.
The Bedside Esquire. *New York* ₁1940₁.
Arnold Gingrich, editor. Contribution.
John Steinbeck Replies. ₁*New York,* 1940₁.
4 pp. leaflet. Later reprinted in a de luxe limited edition.
They Die to Live, by Tom Collins.
Announced. Foreword by Steinbeck.

George Sterling
1869–1926

THE TESTIMONY OF THE SUNS AND OTHER POEMS. *San Francisco*, 1903.
Title poem reissued, *San Francisco*, 1927, in a facsimile ms. edition with comments by Ambrose Bierce.

THE TRIUMPH OF BOHEMIA: A FOREST PLAY. [*San Francisco*, 1907].
Printed wrappers.

A WINE OF WIZARDRY AND OTHER POEMS. *San Francisco*, 1909.
The first binding has gilt decoration on the front cover.

THE HOUSE OF ORCHIDS AND OTHER POEMS. *San Francisco*, 1911.
P. 31, line 9, *languorous* is misspelled *langourous*. P. 48, line 12, *omnipotent* is misspelled *omniponent*.

BEYOND THE BREAKERS AND OTHER POEMS. *San Francisco*, 1914.
P. 24, line 7, *stand* spelled *stands*. P. 140, line 13, should read *Stood alert, with an roving eye*.

ODE ON THE OPENING OF THE PANAMA-PACIFIC INTERNATIONAL EXPOSITION ... *San Francisco*, 1915.
525 copies only. Boards, cloth back.

THE EVANESCENT CITY. *San Francisco*, 1915.

YOSEMITE: AN ODE. *San Francisco*, 1916.
Boards.

THE CAGED EAGLE AND OTHER POEMS. *San Francisco*, 1916.
P. 34, line 5, *To* for *Too*. P. 162, line 2, *scourse* for *source*.

SONGS. *San Francisco* [1916].
Some of the music composed by Sterling.

THE PLAY OF EVERYMAN. *San Francisco*, 1917.
With RICHARD ORDYNSKI.

THE BINDING OF THE BEAST AND OTHER WAR VERSE. *San Francisco*, 1917.
Flexible leather.

THIRTY-FIVE SONNETS. [*San Francisco*, 1917].
300 numbered copies, privately printed. Boards, cloth back.

LILITH: A DRAMATIC POEM. *San Francisco*, 1919.
300 copies only, numbered and signed by the author. Wrappers. Reissued, *San Francisco*, 1920, boards, cloth back, 350 numbered copies only.

ROSAMUND. *San Francisco,* 1920.
Also 500 copies numbered and signed by the author.

TO A GIRL DANCING. [*San Francisco,* 1921].
120 copies only. Boards.

SAILS AND MIRAGE AND OTHER POEMS. *San Francisco,* 1921.

TRUTH. *Chicago,* 1923.
285 numbered copies only, signed. Reissued in printed wrappers with revisions, *San Francisco,* 1926.

ROBINSON JEFFERS: THE MAN AND THE ARTIST. *New York,* 1926.

STRANGE WATERS. [*San Francisco,* 1926].
150 privately printed copies, only. Printed wrappers.

FIVE POEMS. [*San Francisco*] 1927.
25 copies only for private circulation.

SONNETS TO CRAIG. *New York,* 1928.
Presumably issued simultaneously by Upton Sinclair and A. C. Boni.

POEMS TO VERA. *New York,* 1938.

AFTER SUNSET. [*San Francisco,* 1939].
Boards, paper label. 250 copies numbered 1-250; 25 copies numbered i-xxv with a page of manuscript.

Sterling contributed to various books and issued a number of minor items, both of which are too numerous to list here. The collector is referred to the formal bibliography by Cecil Johnson.

The Spinners' Book of Fiction. *San Francisco* [1907].
Contribution.
To Ambrose Bierce. *Washington, D. C.,* 1910.
4 pp. leaflet. Reprinted from "A Wine of Wizardry."
An Account of the Closing Ceremonies of the Panama-Pacific International Exposition. [*San Francisco,* 1915].
Contribution.
Lilies of Stone. [*San Francisco,* 1916].
4 pp. leaflet.
The Twilight of the Kings. *San Francisco,* 1918.
Wrappers. Contains a group of lyrics by Sterling.
Odes and Sonnets, by Clark Ashton Smith. *San Francisco,* 1918.
Boards, cloth back. 300 numbered copies only. Introduction.
In Memoriam: Bret Harte. [*San Francisco,* 1920].
4 pp. leaflet.
Selected Poems. *New York,* 1923.

STERLING

The Lake Isle of Innisfree, by William Butler Yeats. ₁San Francisco₁ 1924.
  Privately printed. Contribution.
Continent's End. *San Francisco,* 1925.
  600 numbered copies only. Co-editor.
An Invocation, by Ambrose Bierce. *San Francisco,* 1928.
  300 numbered copies only. Introduction by Sterling.
Together. ₁*n.p.,* 1930₁.
  Leaflet. 25 copies only.
A Bibliography of the Works of George Sterling, by Cecil Johnson. *San Francisco,*
  1931.
  300 copies only.
The Smart Set Anthology. *New York* ₁1934₁.
  Burton Rascoe and Groff Conklin, editors. Contains Sterling's "The Rabbit
  Hutch." First binding has *Roscoe* for *Rascoe* on the spine.
George Sterling, With Comment by Robinson Jeffers. ₁San Francisco₁ 1935.
  4 pp. Contains an inserted A. L. s. in facsimile.
Footloose in Arcadia: A Personal Record, by Joseph Noel. *New York* ₁1940₁.
  Contribution.

Frank R. (Francis Richard) Stockton

1834–1902

TING-A-LING. *New York*, 1870.

ROUND-ABOUT RAMBLES IN LANDS OF FACT AND FANCY. *New York* [1872].

THE HOME. *New York*, 1873.
With MARIAN E. [MRS.] STOCKTON.

WHAT MIGHT HAVE BEEN EXPECTED. *New York* [1874].

TALES OUT OF SCHOOL. *New York*, 1876.

RUDDER GRANGE. *New York*, 1879.
First state does not contain reviews or advertisements of this title. First edition has 18 chapters; 2nd edition, also dated 1879, has 20 chapters. Attempts have been made to insert the date (1879) on the title page. These forgeries are crudely printed with numerals about half the size of the genuine.

A JOLLY FELLOWSHIP. *New York*, 1880.

THE FLOATING PRINCE AND OTHER FAIRY TALES. *New York*, 1881.

THE LADY, OR THE TIGER? AND OTHER STORIES. *New York*, 1884.
"Stockton Stories: First Series," is a reprint of this title. "A Piece of Red Calico," herein printed, appeared previously in "Dick's Recitations and Readings," No. 8 [1878].

THE STORY OF VITEAU. *New York*, 1884.

THE CASTING AWAY OF MRS. LECKS AND MRS. ALESHINE. *New York* [1886].
Cloth or wrappers. In the first state signatures are present at pp. 9, 25, 49, 57, 73, 81, 97, 105, 121, 125. The first state of the wrappers has advertisements for *The Century Magazine* and *St. Nicholas*, announcing material to be published therein during the season 1886-1887. Copies with *reviews* of "The Hundredth Man" are later.

THE LATE MRS. NULL. *New York*, 1886.
First state has *mattrass* for *mattress*, p. 150, line 23. Several states of advertisements at the back with no known priority.

STOCKTON'S STORIES: SECOND SERIES. THE CHRISTMAS WRECK AND OTHER STORIES. *New York*, 1886.
Later states omit *Stockton's Stories*, etc., from title page and binding. "Stockton's Stories: First Series," *New York*, 1886, is a reprint of "The Lady, or the Tiger?" 1884.

THE HUNDREDTH MAN. *New York* [1887].
Cloth with leather labels, or wrappers.

THE BEE-MAN OF ORN, *etc. New York*, 1887.
First state printed on laid paper; later on wove paper.

AMOS KILBRIGHT. *New York*, 1888.
Cloth or printed wrappers.

THE DUSANTES. *New York* [1888].
Sequel to "The Casting Away of Mrs. Lecks, *etc.*" Cloth or printed wrappers.

PERSONALLY CONDUCTED. *New York*, 1889.

THE GREAT WAR SYNDICATE. *New York*, 1889.
Printed wrappers. *Collier* imprint.

THE STORIES OF THE THREE BURGLARS. *New York* [1889].
First state is 12mo. Several later reprints in 16mo size.

ARDIS CLAVERDEN. *New York* [1890].

THE MERRY CHANTER. *New York* [1890].
Cloth or wrappers. Cloth bound copies have been noted with and without *Century Series* (appearing in two varying forms) on spine. The copyright deposit copies have *Century Series* on spine.

THE HOUSE OF MARTHA. *Boston*, 1891.

THE RUDDER GRANGERS ABROAD AND OTHER STORIES. *New York*, 1891.
Wrappers or cloth. First state does not mention this title in the list of books preceding the title page.

THE SQUIRREL INN. *New York*, 1891.
Cover blind or gold-stamped; priority unestablished.

THE CLOCKS OF RONDAINE AND OTHER STORIES. *New York*, 1892.

MY TERMINAL MORAINE. *New York*, 1892.
Printed wrappers. Vol. IX, No. 2, in "Once-A-Week Library," dated April 26, 1892.

THE WATCHMAKER'S WIFE AND OTHER STORIES. *New York*, 1893.

POMONA'S TRAVELS. *New York* [1894].
First binding is green cloth, gold and black stamping, and with publisher's morogram on spine. Later issued in cream-yellow cloth, black and gold stamping, and picture of house stamped in color on both front and back covers, and with *Scribners* on the spine.

THE ADVENTURES OF CAPTAIN HORN. *New York*, 1895.

MRS. CLIFF'S YACHT. *New York*, 1896.

STORIES OF NEW JERSEY. *New York,* 1896.
American Book Company, school edition. Same year, Appleton issue, as: "New Jersey From the Discovery of Scheyichbi to Recent Times."

CAPTAIN CHAP. *Philadelphia,* 1897.

A STORY-TELLER'S PACK. *New York,* 1897.

THE GREAT STONE OF SARDIS. *New York,* 1898.
Biographical edition, *New York,* 1899.

BUCCANEERS AND PIRATES OF OUR COASTS. *New York,* 1898.

THE GIRL AT COBHURST. *New York,* 1898.

THE VIZIER OF THE TWO-HORNED ALEXANDER. *New York,* 1899.
Cloth or wrappers. Copies exist with a prefatory note; status unknown. Cover lettered in gold or white; priority unknown.

THE ASSOCIATE HERMITS. *New York,* 1899.

AFIELD AND AFLOAT. *New York,* 1900.

THE YOUNG MASTER OF HYSON HALL. *Philadelphia,* 1900.

A BICYCLE OF CATHAY. *New York,* 1900.

KATE BONNET. *New York,* 1902.
February, 1902 on copyright page.

JOHN GAYTHER'S GARDEN, *etc. New York,* 1902.
Published November, 1902 on copyright page.

THE CAPTAIN'S TOLL-GATE. *New York,* 1903.
Also 160 large paper copies, with inserted autograph of the author. Contains a bibliography. First printing has the symbol (1) below the text at p. 359.

THE QVEEN'S MVSEVM AND OTHER FANCIFUL TALES. *New York,* 1906.

THE MAGIC EGG AND OTHER STORIES. *New York,* 1907.

THE LOST DRYAD. *Riverside, Conn.,* 1912.
1,000 copies only.

THE POOR COUNT'S CHRISTMAS. *New York,* 1927.

THE NOVELS AND STORIES OF FRANK R. STOCKTON. *New York,* 1899-1904.
23 vols. Also 204 sets on Japan vellum, signed. Bibliography in vol. xxiii.

A Northern Voice For the Dissolution of the Union. [*Philadelphia,* 1860].
Anon. Pamphlet.
Poems, With Autobiographic and Other Notes, by T. H. Stockton. *Philadelphia,* 1862.
Cloth or publisher's three quarter leather. Some illustrations engraved by Frank Stockton.

STOCKTON

Short Stories for Spare Moments. Second Series. *Philadelphia,* 1869.
  Printed wrappers. Contains "Mahala's Drive."
Stories by American Authors. *New York,* 1884.
  Vol. 2 contains "The Transferred Ghost," by Stockton.
The Art of Authorship. *London,* 1890.
  George Bainton, editor. Contribution.
Eleven Possible Cases. *New York* [1891].
  Contains Stockton's "A Thing That Glistens."
Fanciful Tales. *New York,* 1894.
  Julia Elizabeth Langworthy, editor. All reprint.
A Chosen Few. *New York,* 1895.
  All reprint material.
The Spirit of Washington. [*Morristown*] 1895.
  A "paper read to the Washington Association of New Jersey, February 22, 1895."
  Wrappers. Privately printed.
Masterpieces of the World's Literature. *New York,* 1898-1899.
  20 vols. Co-editor.
American Vacations in Europe. [*Philadelphia,* 1901].
  Co-editor.
A House Party. *Boston,* 1901.
  "Aunt Nancy's Annuity" contributed by Stockton.
My Favorite Novelist. *Cleveland, Ohio,* 1908.
  With others. 225 copies only.
Pomona's Club. [*n.p., n.d.*].
  Pamphlet. Also in "The First Book of the Author's Club: Liber Scriptorum."
  New York, 1893.
Return of Frank R. Stockton, by Miss Etta de Camp. *New York,* 1913.
  Alleged to have been written by Stockton's ghost.
Stocktoniana: An Essay by Walter L. Pforzheimer. Prefatory Note by William Lyon
  Phelps. *Purchase* [N. Y.] 1936.
  145 privately printed copies only.
Stocktoniana. No. 2, by Walter L. Pforzheimer. *Purchase, N. Y.* [1936].
  Contains an original Stockton engraving.
Frank R. Stockton, by Martin J. Griffin. *Philadelphia,* 1939.

Harriet (Elizabeth) Beecher Stowe

1811–1896

PRIZE TALE: A NEW ENGLAND SKETCH. *Lowell*, 1834.
Wrappers.

AN ELEMENTARY GEOGRAPHY. *Boston*, 1835.

THE MAYFLOWER; or, SKETCHES OF SCENES AND CHARACTERS AMONG THE DESCENDANTS OF THE PILGRIMS. *New York*, 1843.
Reissued, *Boston*, 1855, with additions.

UNCLE TOM'S CABIN. *Boston*, 1852.
2 vols. Cloth copies have *J. P. Jewett & Co.*, at foot of spine. Certain bindings with additional gilt stamping known as presentation bindings, have no definite position. Similar bindings with the revised lettering at the foot of the spine have been seen on late editions. The first printing has the slug of *Hobart and Robbins, New England Type and Stereotype Foundery, Boston*, on the copyright pages. Later printings have the slug of *George C. Rand*. Also issued in printed wrappers. The 1878 edition contains an introduction relating to the genesis of the book; separately published in wrappers [*Boston*, 1896].

A KEY TO UNCLE TOM'S CABIN. *Boston*, 1853.
Cloth or wrappers.

UNCLE SAM'S EMANCIPATION, *etc. Philadelphia*, 1853.

SUNNY MEMORIES OF FOREIGN LANDS. *Boston*, 1854.
2 vols.

GEOGRAPHY FOR MY CHILDREN. *Boston*, 1855.

DRED: A TALE OF THE GREAT DISMAL SWAMP. *Boston*, 1856.
2 vols. Noted with two states of end papers: (a) with printed publisher's lists; (b) plain, without printed lists. There is a supplied leaf preceding the title page, and it appears that in copies with the printed lists this leaf is tinted. No known priority. Reissued as "Nina Gordon," *Boston*, 1866.

OUR CHARLEY AND WHAT TO DO WITH HIM. *Boston*, 1858.

THE MINISTER'S WOOING. *New York*, 1859.
Noted also with imprint *Boston and New York* with no known priority. The English edition was issued with illustrations by Phiz; cloth or paper covered parts.

THE PEARL OF ORR'S ISLAND. *Boston*, 1862.

AGNES OF SORRENTO. *Boston*, 1862.

STOWE

A REPLY ... IN BEHALF OF THE WOMEN OF AMERICA, *etc. London,* 1863.

THE RAVAGES OF A CARPET. *Boston,* 1865.

HOUSE AND HOME PAPERS. *Boston,* 1865.
Christopher Crowfield, *pseud.*

LITTLE FOXES. *Boston,* 1866.
Christopher Crowfield, *pseud.*

STORIES ABOUT OUR DOGS. *Edinburgh* [1865].

RELIGIOUS POEMS. *Boston,* 1867.

QUEER LITTLE PEOPLE. *Boston,* 1867.

DAISY'S FIRST WINTER AND OTHER STORIES. *Boston,* 1867.

THE CHIMNEY-CORNER. *Boston,* 1868.
Christopher Crowfield, *pseud.* Includes "Little Foxes."

MEN OF OUR TIMES. *Hartford,* 1868.
Reissued as "Lives and Deeds of Our Self-Made Men," *Hartford,* 1872.

OLDTOWN FOLKS. *Boston,* 1869.

THE AMERICAN WOMAN'S HOME. *New York and Boston,* 1869.
With CATHARINE E. BEECHER.

LADY BYRON VINDICATED. *Boston,* 1870.

LITTLE PUSSY WILLOW. *Boston,* 1870.

MY WIFE AND I. *New York,* 1871.

PINK AND WHITE TYRANNY. *Boston,* 1871.

SAM LAWSON'S OLDTOWN FIRESIDE STORIES. *Boston,* 1872.

PALMETTO-LEAVES. *Boston,* 1873.

WOMAN IN SACRED HISTORY. *New York,* 1873.
Reissued as "Bible Heroines," *New York* [1878].

WE AND OUR NEIGHBORS. *New York* [1875].
Sequel to "My Wife and I."

BETTY'S BRIGHT IDEA, *etc. New York,* 1876.
A similar collection issued in London, 1875, as "Deacon Pitkin's Farm, etc."

FOOTSTEPS OF THE MASTER. *New York,* 1876.

POGANUC PEOPLE. *New York* [1878].

A DOG'S MISSION. *New York,* 1881.

OUR FAMOUS WOMEN. *Hartford*, 1884.

WRITINGS OF HARRIET BEECHER STOWE. *Cambridge*, 1896.
  16 vols. Also 250 large paper sets signed by the author.

The following is a representative selection of Mrs. Stowe's secondary productions.

The Christian Souvenir: An Offering for Christmas and the New Year. *Boston*, 1843.
  Edited by Isaac F. Shepard. Contribution.
Works of Charlotte Elizabeth (Tonna). *New York*, 1844-45.
  2 vols. Introduction by Stowe.
Earthly Care, a Heavenly Discipline. *Boston* [n.d., ca. 1845].
  Glazed yellow wrappers, printed. Issued by the American Tract Society. Another
  issue: *Boston and Cleveland*, 1853. Appeared in the 1855 edition of "The May-
  flower."
The Incarnation; or, Pictures of the Virgin and Her Son, by Charles Beecher. *New
  York*, 1849.
  Contains an introductory poem and an essay by Stowe.
Let Every Man Mind His Own Business. *London* [ca. 1850].
  Wrappers. Reprinted from "The Mayflower."
Uncle Tim. *London*, 1852.
  Reprinted from "Prize Tale," 1834.
Pictures and Stories From Uncle Tom's Cabin. *Boston* [1853].
  Printed wrappers, both yellow and red noted.
The Edmondson Family. *Cincinnati*, 1854.
  Boards. Reprinted from "A Key to Uncle Tom's Cabin."
The Two Altars. [*New York*, 1852].
  Pamphlet. Also: [*Boston*] 1852. No known priority.
The Colored Patriots of the American Revolution, by William C. Nell. *Boston*, 1855.
  Introduction.
The Christian Slave. *Boston*, 1855.
  A dramatization by the author of passages from "Uncle Tom's Cabin."
Mrs. Harriet Beecher Stowe on Dr. Monood and the American Tract Society ...
  [*Edinburgh?* 1858].
Father Henson's Story of His Own Life. *Boston*, 1858.
  Introduction by Stowe.
My Expectation. *London*, 1858.
  Pamphlet.
Things That Cannot Be Shaken. *London*, 1858.
  Pamphlet.
My Strength. *London*, 1858.
  Pamphlet.
A Word to the Sorrowful. *London*, 1858.
  Pamphlet.
Strong Consolation. *London*, 1858.
  Pamphlet.

STOWE

Golden Fruits in Silver Baskets. *London*, 1859.
  Reprint.
Tales and Sketches. *London*, 1859.
  Selections from "The Mayflower," 1855.
The Elder's Feast. *London* [n.d., 1859?].
  Wrappers. Reprinted from "The Mayflower," 1855.
Aunt Mary, and other Tales. *London*, 1859.
  Wrappers. Reprinted from "The Mayflower," 1855.
The Canal Boy. *London* [n.d., 1859?].
  Wrappers. Reprinted from "The Mayflower," 1855.
William and Mary; and, Florence, or the Tea Rose. *London*, 1859.
  Wrappers. Reprinted from "The Mayflower," 1855.
The Sabbath; or, Four Ways of Keeping It. *London* [n.d., 1859?].
  Wrappers. Reprinted from "The Mayflower," 1855.
The New Year's Gift; or, "Our Ally." *London* [n.d., 1859?].
  Wrappers. Reprinted from "The Mayflower," 1855.
Helen Ruthven Waterston. *Boston*, 1860.
Chimes of Freedom and Union. *Boston*, 1861.
  Contributions.
Autobiography of Lyman Beecher. *New York*, 1864.
  2 vols. Contributions.
Lyra Americana. *London*, 1865.
  Contribution.
Medora Leigh. *New York*, 1870.
  Charles Mackay, editor. Wrappers. Introduction and commentary by Stowe.
Six of One by Half a Dozen of the Other. *Boston*, 1872.
  With others.
Library of Famous Fiction. *New York*, 1873.
  Introduction.
Tell It All, by Mrs. Stenhouse. *Hartford*, 1874.
  Introduction.
Nelly's Heroines. *Boston* [1883].
Flowers and Fruit From the Writings of Harriet Beecher Stowe. *Boston*, 1888.
  Abbie H. Fairfield, editor.
Dialogues and Scenes From the Writings of Harriet Beecher Stowe. *New York*, 1889.
The Life of Harriet Beecher Stowe, Composed From Her Letters and Journals by Her Son, Charles Edward Stowe. *Boston*, 1889.
Harriet Beecher Stowe, by Catherine Gilbertson. *New York*, 1937.

Certain of the English publications are reprints of material previously published in the United States. Among these are "The Ghost of the Mill and Other Stories," *London*, 1876; and "Captain Kidd's Money and Other Stories," *London*, 1876.

Ernest Wessen, author of "The Campaign Lives of Abraham Lincoln," reports discovery of an advertisement indicating that Mrs. Stowe, in collaboration with her sister Catharine, wrote and published a "Primary Geography for Children," in 1832. Thus far no copy has been located.

T(homas) S(igismund) Stribling

1881–

THE CRUISE OF THE DRY DOCK. *Chicago* [1917].
The author states that no more than 250 copies were published.

BIRTHRIGHT. *New York*, 1922.
P. 168, lines 11-12 transposed.

FOMBOMBO. *New York & London*, 1923.
The copyright notice occurs in two states: *The Century Company and The Ridg-way Company;* and, *The Century Company and T. S. Stribling.* The copyright deposit copies are in the former style.

RED SAND. *New York* [1924].

TEEFTALLOW. *Garden City*, 1926.
First printing indicated on copyright page.

EAST IS EAST. *New York* [1928].
Cloth binding first; later in pictorial boards.

BRIGHT METAL. *Garden City*, 1928.
First printing indicated on copyright page.

CLUES OF THE CARIBBEES. *Garden City*, 1929.
First printing indicated on copyright page. Cloth, paper labels.

STRANGE MOON. *Garden City*, 1929.
First printing indicated on copyright page.

BACKWATER. *Garden City*, 1930.
First printing indicated on copyright page.

THE FORGE. *Garden City*, 1931.
First printing indicated on copyright page.

THE STORE. *Garden City*, 1932.
First printing indicated on copyright page. Cloth, paper labels.

UNFINISHED CATHEDRAL. *Garden City*, 1934.
First printing indicated on copyright page. Also 350 unnumbered copies in boards.

THE SOUND WAGON. *Garden City*, 1935.
First printing indicated on copyright page. Also 250 unnumbered copies in boards, signed by the author.

THESE BARS OF FLESH. *Garden City*, 1938.
First printing indicated on copyright page.

The Panorama of Modern Literature. *Garden City,* 1934.
   First printing indicated on copyright page. Contains "The Mating of Pampalone"
   by Stribling.
O. Henry Prize Stories of 1934. *Garden City,* 1934.
   First printing indicated on copyright page. Contains "Guileford" by Stribling.
Portraits and Self-Portraits, by Georges Schreiber. *Boston,* 1936.
   Contribution.
Post Stories of 1935. *Boston,* 1936.
   First printing indicated on the copyright page.
Press Time, A Book of *Post* Classics. *New York,* 1936.
The Stag at Ease. *Caldwell, Idaho,* 1938.
   Marian Squire, editor. Contribution.
A Bibliography of the Writings of T. S. Stribling, by Frank Stone.
   In preparation.

John B[annister] Tabb
1845–1909

POEMS. [*Baltimore, 1882*].

Publication date of this has been in dispute. In the author's "Some Notes of My Life" in *The Borromean*, December, 1936, Tabb states "my first book [was] privately printed in 1883." However, in June 1882 Tabb wrote a letter to William Hand Browne, at the same time presenting a copy of the book. Further, a presentation copy has been noted with the author's 1882 inscription. It is clear, therefore, that the book was issued in 1882.

AN OCTAVE TO MARY. *Baltimore,* 1893.

POEMS. *Boston,* 1894.

10 copies in boards on China paper, 50 copies in boards on handmade paper, 500 copies in cloth.

BONE RULES; or, SKELETON OF ENGLISH GRAMMAR. *New York and Cincinnati,* 1897.

LYRICS. *Boston,* 1897.

500 copies only in addition to 50 copies on handmade paper in boards and 5 on China paper.

CHILD VERSE. *Boston,* 1899.

TWO LYRICS. [*Boston,* 1900].

50 copies on Japan paper, extra illustrated, numbered and signed by the author, illustrator and designer. 375 copies on Arnold paper, in boards, numbered.

LATER LYRICS. *New York,* 1902.

THE ROSARY IN RHYME. [*Cambridge*] 1904.

350 copies only, vellum boards.

QUIPS AND QUIDDITS. *Boston,* 1907.

LATER POEMS. *New York,* 1910.

THE POETRY OF FATHER TABB. *New York,* 1928.

Collected edition. Contains material here first collected.

The Forty-Sixth Birthday of Sidney Lanier. *Baltimore,* 1888.
Contains a sonnet by Tabb.
A Study, by T. R. Price. *Cambridge,* 1891.
50 copies only.
From Dixie. *Richmond,* 1893.
Contains three poems by Tabb.

TABB

The Children's Wonder Book. *Boston,* 1895.
    Contains a 10-line poem by Tabb.
John Bannister Tabb, by Thomas R. Price. [*Boston*] 1896.
    Boards, 50 copies only.
A Selection From The Verses of John Bannister Tabb. *London* [1906].
    Alice Meynell, editor.
John Bannister Tabb: The Priest-Poet, by M. S. Pine [pseud. for Sister Mary Paulina Finn]. *Washington, D. C.,* 1915.
Father Tabb, His Life and Work, by Jennie Masters Tabb. *Boston,* 1921.
Father Tabb, by Francis A. Litz. *Baltimore,* 1923.
The Poetry of Father Tabb. *New York,* 1928.
    Francis A. Litz, editor.

(Newton) Booth Tarkington

1869–

THE GENTLEMAN FROM INDIANA. *New York,* 1899.

P. 245, line 12, last word, *eye;* line 16, *so pretty.* P. 291, line 7, reads *brainy bumps.* P. 342, line 23, reads *brain of Zeus.* Copies have been noted with ear-of-corn decoration on spine either right side up or upside down; there is no known priority, the decoration having been noted in both states on second states.

MONSIEUR BEAUCAIRE. *New York,* 1900.

Publisher's seal after last page of text is ½ ″ in diameter.

THE TWO VANREVELS. *New York,* 1902.

Also 500 de luxe copies, signed; and 500 copies in brown boards, numbered 501-1000. The latter noted in two states but must have a first edition notice. These were both issued in the month following trade edition publication. Trade edition variant bindings in dispute; probable first state of advertisements states "Monsieur Beaucaire," p. 1, as *80th Thousand* and at p. 3 as *70th Thousand.*

CHERRY. *New York and London,* 1903.

Published October, 1903 on copyright page. Second state has *London and New York* imprint. Third state has date removed .

IN THE ARENA. *New York,* 1905.

Published January, 1905 on copyright page.

THE BEAUTIFUL LADY. *New York,* 1905.

Published May, 1905 on copyright page.

THE CONQUEST OF CANAAN. *New York,* 1905.

Preceded by a special edition, printed from the magazine plates, bound in red boards, paper label. Copies have been noted with and without the letter *R* in the copyright notice box; priority unknown. A copy has been noted in publisher's leather binding.

THE GUARDIAN. *New York,* 1907.

With HARRY LEON WILSON. Black cloth. Revised and reissued, *New York,* 1908, as "The Man From Home."

HIS OWN PEOPLE. *New York,* 1907.

Published October, 1907 on copyright page.

THE GUEST OF QUESNAY. *New York,* 1908.

THE MAN FROM HOME. *New York,* 1908.

See above: "The Guardian."

BEASLEY'S CHRISTMAS PARTY. *New York,* 1909.

Noted with holly or scroll decoration on spine; no known priority. *Published October, 1909* on copyright page.

BEAUTY AND THE JACOBIN. *New York, 1912.*
I-M at foot of copyright page.

THE FLIRT. *Garden City, 1913.*

PENROD. *Garden City, 1914.*
First state of sheets has p. viii so numbered; *sence* for *sense,* p. 19, third line from bottom. First binding: blue mesh cloth; second binding: blue ribbed cloth.

THE TURMOIL. *New York, 1915.*
A-P at foot of copyright page. Preceded by edition printed from magazine plates, red boards, paper label.

THE SPRING CONCERT. *New York* [1916].
Wrappers.

PENROD AND SAM. *Garden City, 1916.*
Various states noted but the earliest printed copies have perfect type at pp. 86, 141, 144, 149, and 210. A copy has been noted bound in blue ribbed cloth, similar to second state "Penrod" binding; probably an experimental binding.

SEVENTEEN. *New York* [1916].
B-Q at foot of copyright page. Cloth or leather. Reissued, *New York, 1932,* with new introduction.

THE OHIO LADY. [*New York, 1916*].
Wrappers. Play, with Julian Street. 60 copies only, "printed, but not published." Revised and reissued as "The Country Cousin," *New York, 1921.*

THE MAGNIFICENT AMBERSONS. *Garden City, 1918.*
First state printed on white paper; second state, white paper and dirty-white of the War period, mixed; third state on War period paper. Binding noted in three states: (a) light brown; (b) maroon; (c) dark brown cloth but measuring 1″ across sheets as against 1⅛″ in state (a) which is probably first.

RAMSEY MILHOLLAND. *Garden City, 1919.*

THE GIBSON UPRIGHT. *Garden City, 1919.*
With HARRY LEON WILSON. Paper labels. Previously issued in wrappers by the Eastman Kodak Company as an advertisement.

THE INTIMATE STRANGERS. *New York, 1921.*
Brown wrappers.

CLARENCE. *New York* [1921].
Brown wrappers.

THE COUNTRY COUSIN. *New York* [1921].
First state has *in* for *is,* p. 3, line 1. Printed wrappers. *See above:* "The Ohio Lady."

ALICE ADAMS. *Garden City, 1921.*
First state reads, p. 419, line 14, *I can't see you why* etc.

490

HARLEQUIN AND COLUMBINE. *Garden City*, 1921.
Boards, cloth back. First edition so stated on copyright page.

GENTLE JULIA. *Garden City*, 1922.
First binding has no silhouette on front cover. First edition so stated on copyright page.

THE WREN. *New York*, 1922.
Printed wrappers.

THE GHOST STORY. *Cincinnati* [1922].
Printed wrappers.

THE TRYSTING PLACE. *Cincinnati* [1923].
Printed wrappers.

THE FASCINATING STRANGER AND OTHER STORIES. *Garden City*, 1923.
377 large paper copies, numbered and signed. Trade edition states *"first edition after the printing of 377 De Luxe Copies."* Published simultaneously.

THE COLLECTOR'S WHATNOT. *Boston*, 1923.
With KENNETH L. ROBERTS and HUGH M. KAHLER. Boards. Published pseudonymously as by Cornelius Obenchain Van Loot, Milton Kilgallen, Murgatroyd Elphinstone.

THE MIDLANDER. *Garden City*, 1923.
377 large paper copies, numbered and signed. Trade edition dated 1924 and published in month following.

TWEEDLES. *New York*, 1924.
With HARRY LEON WILSON. Printed wrappers.

WOMEN. *Garden City*, 1925.
First edition so stated on copyright page.

BIMBO, THE PIRATE. *New York*, 1926.
No. 11 in the "Little Theatre Plays." Has (1) after last line of text. Printed wrappers. Previously printed in "The Ladies' Home Journal's One Act Plays," *Garden City*, 1925.

LOOKING FORWARD AND OTHERS. *Garden City*, 1926.
First edition so stated on copyright page.

THE PLUTOCRAT. *Garden City*, 1927.
Also 1,000 copies in boards. First state reads *Platocrat* for *Plutocrat*, running head, p. 26. First edition so stated on copyright page.

GROWTH. *Garden City*, 1927.
"The Magnificent Ambersons," "The Turmoil," and "The Midlander," rewritten and issued in one volume. First edition so stated on copyright page.

STATION YYYY. *New York*, 1927.
No. 19 in "Appleton Short Plays." (1) after last line of text. Printed wrappers.

THE TRAVELERS. *New York*, 1927.
No. 20 in "Appleton Short Plays." (1) after last line of text. Printed wrappers.

CLAIRE AMBLER. *Garden City*, 1928.
First edition so stated on copyright page. Also 500 copies bound in American Japan vellum, signed by author and publishers.

THE WORLD DOES MOVE. *Garden City*, 1928.
First edition so stated on copyright page. Boards, cloth back.

YOUNG MRS. GREELEY. *Garden City*, 1929.
First edition so stated on copyright page.

PENROD JASHBER. *Garden City*, 1929.
First edition so stated on copyright page.

MIRTHFUL HAVEN. *Garden City*, 1930.
First edition so stated on copyright page.

HOW'S YOUR HEALTH? *New York*, 1930.
A comedy in three acts. With HARRY LEON WILSON. Printed wrappers.

MARY'S NECK. *Garden City*, 1932.
First edition so stated on copyright page.

WANTON MALLY. *Garden City*, 1932.
First edition so stated on copyright page.

PRESENTING LILY MARS. *Garden City*, 1933.
First edition so stated on copyright page.

LITTLE ORVIE. *Garden City*, 1934.
First edition so stated on copyright page.

THE HELP EACH OTHER CLUB. *New York*, 1934.
One act play. Printed wrappers. First printing has symbol (1) below last line of text.

MR. ANTONIO: A COMEDY IN FOUR ACTS. *New York*, 1935.
Printed wrappers.

MR. WHITE, THE RED BARN, HELL AND BRIDEWATER. *Garden City*, 1935.
First edition so stated on copyright page.

THE LORENZO BUNCH. *Garden City*, 1936.
First edition so stated on copyright page.

RUMBIN GALLERIES. *Garden City*, 1937.
First printing indicated on copyright page.

SOME OLD PORTRAITS. *New York*, 1939.
> First printing indicated on copyright page. Also 247 de luxe copies, numbered and signed.

THE HERITAGE OF HATCHER IDE. *New York*, 1941.
> First printing indicated on copyright page.

COLLECTED WORKS

THE WORKS OF BOOTH TARKINGTON. *Garden City*, 1918-1919.
> 14 vols. "Autograph Edition." Vol. 8 contains first book appearance of "Harlequin and Columbine" and seven short stories. Vol. 9 contains first book appearance of "Mr. Brooke" and "Lord Jerningham."

Newton Booth. [*n.p., n.d.*, 1892].
> Contains a poem by Tarkington.

Bric à Brac. [*Princeton, N. J.*, 1893].
> Co-edited and illustrated by Tarkington. Boards, paper label.

A November Leaf. [*Indianapolis*] 1896.
> Wrappers. Contains "Dance Music" by Tarkington.

Mother Goose for All. [*Indianapolis*] 1898.
> May Louise Shipp, editor. Wrappers. Contains "To a Golf Orphan" by Tarkington.

Once A Year. [*Indianapolis*] 1899.
> May Louise Shipp, editor. Wrappers. Contains Tarkington's "The Serious Moment."

Samuel Brohl and Company, by Victor Cherbuliez. *New York* [1902].
> Introduction.

Decennial Record of Class of 1893, Princeton University. *New York* [1903].
> Introduction.

Poe's Run and Other Poems, by M'Cready Sykes. *Princeton*, 1904.
> Illustrated by Tarkington and others.

Werner's Readings and Recitations. *New York*, 1905.
> Contains Tarkington's "The Kisses of Marjorie."

I Knew Him When ——, by George Ade. *Chicago* [1910].
> Illustrations by, and photographs of, Tarkington.

Abe Martin's Almanac, by Kin Hubbard. *Garden City* [1911].
> Contribution.

An Overwhelming Saturday: A "Penrod" Story. *New York* [1913].
> Pamphlet. A reprint from the magazine of one of the "Penrod" episodes.

Monsieur Beaucaire, a Dramatization by Ethel Hale Freeman. *Boston*, 1916.
> Printed wrappers.

The Name of Old Glory, by James Whitcomb Riley. *Indianapolis* [1917].
> Introduction.

R. H. D. *New York*, 1917.
> 375 copies only. Contains an appreciation of Richard Harding Davis by Tarkington.

For France. *Garden City,* 1917.
  Contains "The Destroyers of Nuremberg."
Literature in the Making, by Joyce Kilmer. *New York* [1917].
  Contains an interview mainly by Tarkington. First edition has *D-R* on copyright page. See under *Kilmer* for full description.
Booth Tarkington, by Robert Cortes Holliday. *Garden City,* 1918.
Just Princeton. *Princeton, N. J.,* 1918.
  Contains "Just Princeton" by Tarkington.
War Stories. *New York* [1919].
  Contribution.
Report of the Proceedings at a Dinner Given by the Lotos Club of New York City to Mr. George Ade. *New York,* 1920.
  Contribution.
Best Plays of 1919-1920. *Boston* [1920].
  Burns Mantle, editor. Contains "Clarence."
The Wanderer. *New York* [1920].
  Contains "Why Does a Dog Wag Its Tail" by Tarkington.
Penrod: A Comedy in Four Acts. *New York* [1921].
  Adapted by Edward E. Rose.
My Maiden Effort. *Garden City,* 1921.
  First edition so stated on copyright page. Contribution.
Dulcy, by George Kaufman and Marc Connelly. *New York,* 1921.
  Prologue by Tarkington. Boards.
My Years on the Stage, by John Drew. *New York,* 1922.
  Introduction.
Longer Plays by Modern Authors. *New York* [1922].
  Helen Louise Cohen, editor. Contains "The Intimate Strangers."
"Stay Me With Flagons." [*New York,* 1922].
  Privately printed for members of the Lotos Club. Contribution.
A World Worth While ... by W. A. Rogers. *New York,* 1922.
  Introduction.
The Stag Cook Book. *New York* [1922].
  Contribution. C. MacSheridan, editor.
New Lands, by Charles Fort. *New York* [1923].
  Introduction.
Marriage. *Garden City,* 1923.
  Contains "Us" by Tarkington. First edition so stated on copyright page.
Definitive Edition of the Works of Mark Twain. *New York,* 1923.
  Introduction.
Three Yarns. [*Chicago,* 1924].
  Contains "A Great Man's Wife." Later, separately issued, *Chicago* [1924].
The Wisdom of Laziness, by Fred C. Kelly. *Garden City,* 1924.
  Introduction by Tarkington; later issued as a 12″ x 7¾″ broadside.
Dawgs! An Anthology of Stories About Them. *New York,* 1925.
  Charles W. Gray, editor. Contains "Fox Terrier or Something" by Tarkington.

The *World's* Best Short Stories of 1926. *New York* [1926].
Contains "Thea Zell" by Tarkington.
O. Henry Memorial Award Prize Stories of 1925. *Garden City*, 1926.
First edition so stated on copyright page. Contains "Cornelia's Mountain." Edition for 1926, *Garden City*, 1927, contains "Stella Crozier."
Antiquamania, by Kenneth L. Roberts. *Garden City*, 1928.
Illustrated by Tarkington. First edition so stated on copyright page.
Pen Portraits of Mark Twain, Thomas Hardy, Margaret Deland, William Dean Howells. *New York* [n.d.].
"Howells" by Tarkington.
Tributes to Henry B. [*Privately Printed*, 1929].
Anna Morgan, editor. Contribution.
Commemorative Tributes to Albert J. Beveridge. [*New York*] 1929.
The Tiger's Family Album. *Princeton*, 1931.
Introduction.
Penrod: His Complete Story. *Garden City*, 1931.
Reissue of the three "Penrod" books. First edition so stated on copyright page.
Upheaval, by Olga Woronoff. *New York*, 1932.
Introduction.
Booth Tarkington: A Bibliography by Barton Currie. *Garden City*, 1932.
First edition so stated on copyright page.
The Adventures of Huckleberry Finn, by Mark Twain. *New York*, 1933.
1,500 copies only for members of the Limited Editions Club. Introduction by Tarkington.
Whatever Goes Up, by George C. Tyler and J. C. Furnas. *Indianapolis* [1934].
Introduction.
My Poetry Book. *Philadelphia* [1934].
Grace Thompson Huffard and Laura Mae Carlisle, editors. Introduction.
Horses, Dogs and Men. *New York* [1935].
Charles W. Gray, editor. Contains "Teach Me, My Dog!"
A Mind That Found Itself, by Clifford W. Beers. *Garden City*, 1935.
Introductory letter by Tarkington.
Epernon of Old France, by Leo Mouton. *Garden City*, 1935.
Foreword.
The Rise of Silas Lapham, by William Dean Howells. *Boston*, 1937.
Foreword by Tarkington.
Youth: Adrift or Alert? by Wendell S. Brooks. *Boston*, 1937.
Foreword.
Dutch Paintings, Etchings and Drawings ... February 27 to April 11, 1937, John Herron Art Museum, Indianapolis, Indiana. [*Indianapolis*, 1937].
Preface.

Sara Teasdale

1884-1933

SONNETS TO DUSE AND OTHER POEMS. *Boston*, 1907.
Boards, paper labels.

HELEN OF TROY AND OTHER POEMS. *New York*, 1911.
Reissued with revisions, *New York*, 1922.

RIVERS TO THE SEA. *New York*, 1915.

LOVE SONGS. *New York*, 1917.

FLAME AND SHADOW. *New York*, 1920.
Revised edition, *London*, 1924.

DARK OF THE MOON. *New York*, 1926.
Cloth or flexible leather. Also 250 signed copies.

STARS TO-NIGHT. *New York*, 1930.
Also 150 signed copies.

A COUNTRY HOUSE. *New York* [1932].
Pamphlet. "Borzoi Chap Book" No. 4.

STRANGE VICTORY. *New York*, 1933.

COLLECTED POEMS. *New York*, 1937.
First printing indicated on copyright page.

The Answering Voice: One Hundred Love Lyrics by Women. *Boston*, 1917.
Edited and with an introduction by Teasdale. Revised and enlarged, *New York*, 1928, with new introduction.
Vignettes of Italy. *Boston*, 1919.
Songs set to music by Wintter Watts.
A Miscellany of American Poetry, 1920. *New York*, 1920.
Contributions by Teasdale.
A Miscellany of American Poetry, 1922. *New York* [1922].
Contributions by Teasdale.
Rainbow Gold: Poems Old and New. *New York*, 1922.
"Selected For Boys and Girls."
A Miscellany of American Poetry, 1925. *New York* [1925].
Contributions by Teasdale. First edition so stated.
Percy MacKaye: A Symposium on His Fiftieth Birthday. *Hanover, N. H.*, 1928.
Contains "Poetry in the Hearts of the Multitude," by Teasdale.

Fifty Poets. *New York* [1933].
William Rose Benét, editor. Contribution.
The Smart Set Anthology. *New York* [1934].
Burton Rascoe and Groff Conklin, editors. Contains "The Sentimentalist." First binding has *Roscoe* for *Rascoe* on the spine.
Designed for Reading. *New York,* 1934.
Contribution by Teasdale.

Daniel Pierce Thompson

1795–1868

THE ADVENTURES OF TIMOTHY PEACOCK, ESQUIRE. *Middlebury*, 1835.
> Anon. *By A Member of the Vermont Bar.*

MAY MARTIN. *Montpelier*, 1835.
> Revised, *Boston*, 1852.

THE GREEN MOUNTAIN BOYS. *Montpelier*, 1839.
> 2 vols. Anon. Boards, paper labels. It is probable that the earliest state of Vol. 2 has the publisher's name misspelled *Waltton* in the copyright notice.

LOCKE AMSDEN. *Boston*, 1847.
> Anon. It is claimed that an edition dated 1845 exists but I have never seen it. Copyright notice is dated 1847.

THE SHAKER LOVERS AND OTHER TALES. *Burlington*, 1848.
> Printed wrapper dated 1848.

LUCY HOSMER. *Burlington*, 1848.
> Also issue with Boston imprint.

THE RANGERS. *Boston*, 1851.
> 2 vols. Anon. Also noted 2 vols. in 1.

TALES OF THE GREEN MOUNTAINS. *Boston*, 1852.

GAUT GURLEY. *Boston*, 1857.
> Reissued as "The Demon Trapper of Umbagog."

THE DOOMED CHIEF. *Philadelphia*, 1860.
> Anon.

CENTEOLA AND OTHER TALES. *New York*, 1864.
> Anon.

Thompson was also the author of numerous legal papers; the following are representative.

The Laws of Vermont, 1824-34, Inclusive ... A Continuation of Slade's Compilation. *Montpelier*, 1835.
> Edited.

An Address ... Before the Vermont Historical Society. *Burlington*, 1850.
History of the Town of Montpelier ... *Montpelier*, 1860.
The Novelist of Vermont, by John E. Flitcroft. *Cambridge*, 1929.
> Contains a bibliography of Thompson.

(James) Maurice Thompson
1844–1901

HOOSIER MOSAICS. *New York*, 1875.

THE WITCHERY OF ARCHERY. *New York*, 1878.
Revised and enlarged, *New York* [1879].

HOW TO TRAIN IN ARCHERY. *New York* [1879].
With WILL H. THOMPSON.

A TALLAHASSEE GIRL. *Boston*, 1882.
Anon. In "Round-Robin Series."

HIS SECOND CAMPAIGN. *Boston*, 1883.
Anon. In "Round-Robin Series."

SONGS OF FAIR WEATHER. *Boston*, 1883.
Boards.

AT LOVE'S EXTREMES. *New York*, 1885.
Reissued as "Milly."

A RED-HEADED FAMILY. *New York* [1885].

BY-WAYS AND BIRD NOTES. *New York*, 1885.
First edition has *John B. Alden* imprint.

A BANKER OF BANKERSVILLE. *New York* [1886].

SYLVAN SECRETS. *New York*, 1887.

A FORTNIGHT OF FOLLY. *New York*, 1888.

THE STORY OF LOUISIANA. *Boston* [1888].

POEMS. *Boston*, 1892.

THE KING OF HONEY ISLAND. *New York* [1893].
Printed wrappers.

THE ETHICS OF LITERARY ART. *Hartford*, 1893.

SWEETHEART MANETTE. *Philadelphia* [1894].
Originally in *Lippincott's Magazine*, 1894, copies of which were issued with
printed title page for this story. Regular edition, *Philadelphia*, 1901.

LINCOLN'S GRAVE. *Cambridge and Chicago*, 1894.
450 copies. Also 50 large paper copies with *Cambridge* imprint only.

MAURICE THOMPSON

THE OCALA BOY: A STORY OF FLORIDA. *Boston,* 1895.

STORIES OF THE CHEROKEE HILLS. *Boston,* 1898.

STORIES OF INDIANA. *New York,* 1898.

ALICE OF OLD VINCENNES. *Indianapolis* [1900].
First state does not have a page of *Acknowledgments* following last page of text.
First printing has the running heads printed in bold-face capital letters; later, in a lighter face, using both capital and lower case letters.
Also first state has folio present, first page of text. Various colors of cloth and colors of decorative stamping, no known priority.

MY WINTER GARDEN. *New York,* 1900.

ROSALYNDE'S LOVERS. *Indianapolis* [1901].

The Boys' Book of Sports and Outdoor Life. *New York,* 1886.
Edited.
Indiana ... Department of Geology and Natural History Report[s] [for] 1886, 1888, 1891.
Each contains material by Thompson.
Eleven Possible Cases. *New York,* 1891.
Contribution.
Two Tales. *Boston,* 1892.
Contribution.
How to Study History, Literature, the Fine Arts. *Meadville, Penna.,* 1895.
In collaboration with others.
When Knighthood Was in Flower, by Charles Major. *Indianapolis* [1901].
Contains "The Author and the Book" by Thompson.
The Witchery of Archery ... With an Added Chapter by Will H. Thompson. *Pinehurst, N. C.* [1928].
Contains a bibliography.
Genius and Morality. [*Ridley Park, Penna.*] 1934.
Wrappers. Privately printed.

Henry David Thoreau
1817–1862

A WEEK ON THE CONCORD AND MERRIMACK RIVERS. *Boston and Cambridge*, 1849.
  Said to be about 1,000 copies printed. P. 396, three lines dropped from foot of page; often supplied in pencil by Thoreau. The missing text occurs in *all* copies and does not result in a blank space. The lines of type were removed *before* printing and not during or after the run. There are no copies with a space caused by the missing text. Remaindered sheets issued in 1862 with new title page.

WALDEN; or, LIFE IN THE WOODS. *Boston*, 1854.
  Advertisements at the back in various states, dated March to October, do not necessarily indicate different printings of the book.

EXCURSIONS. *Boston*, 1863.
  Ralph Waldo Emerson and Sophia Thoreau, editors.

THE MAINE WOODS. *Boston*, 1864.
  List of books opposite title page, some printing price of "A Week on the Concord." With or without advertisements at back. Preferred advertisements headed (on the last page) *The Thirteenth Volume.*

CAPE COD. *Boston*, 1865.

LETTERS TO VARIOUS PERSONS. *Boston*, 1865.
  Ralph Waldo Emerson, editor.

A YANKEE IN CANADA, WITH ANTI-SLAVERY AND REFORM PAPERS. *Boston*, 1866.

EARLY SPRING IN MASSACHUSETTS. *Boston*, 1881.
  H. G. O. Blake, editor.

SUMMER. *Boston*, 1884.
  H. G. O. Blake, editor.

WINTER. *Boston*, 1888.
  H. G. O. Blake, editor.

AUTUMN. *Boston*, 1892.
  H. G. O. Blake, editor.

MISCELLANIES. *Boston*, 1894.
  Vol. 10 in "The Riverside Edition." Also 150 large paper copies.

THOREAU

FAMILIAR LETTERS OF HENRY DAVID THOREAU. *Boston*, 1894.
> With new letters. F. B. Sanborn, editor. Uniform with "Riverside Edition." Also 150 large paper copies.

POEMS OF NATURE. *London and Boston*, 1895.

JOURNAL. *Boston*, 1906.
> 14 vols. Bradford Torrey, editor. "Manuscript Edition," 600 copies. This is the *Journal* printed *in extenso* and includes material contained in "Early Spring," "Summer," "Autumn," and "Winter." Part of 20 volume set.

THE MOON. *Boston*, 1927.
> 500 copies only. Part of this essay from the *Journal* appeared in "Excursions" as "Night and Moonlight."

COLLECTED WORKS

RIVERSIDE EDITION. *Boston*, 1894.
> 10 vols. Also 150 large paper sets, numbered. "Familiar Letters," *Boston*, 1894, added as 11th volume, though lacking half-title with volume number.

MANUSCRIPT EDITION. *Boston*, 1906.
> 20 vols. With sheet of *ms.* bound in before frontispiece of vol. 1. 600 numbered sets, paper watermarked *Thoreau*.

WALDEN EDITION. *Boston*, 1906.
> 20 vols. Printed from plates of "Manuscript Edition"; published later.

WORKS. *Boston*, 1937.
> Edited and selected by Henry Seidel Canby.

MISCELLANEOUS

Some Unpublished Letters of Henry D. and Sophia E. Thoreau: A Chapter in the History of a Still-Born Book. *Jamaica, N. Y.,* 1899.
> Samuel Arthur Jones, editor. Boards. 150 numbered copies only.

The Service. *Boston,* 1902.
> Franklin Benjamin Sanborn, editor. 500 copies only.

The First and Last Journeys of Thoreau. *Boston,* 1905.
> 2 vols. Franklin Benjamin Sanborn, editor. Half vellum and boards. 489 copies only of which 10 were printed on Japan vellum.

Sir Walter Raleigh. *Boston,* 1905.
> Henry Aiken Metcalf, editor. Introduction by F. B. Sanborn. 489 copies only.

Unpublished Poems by Bryant and Thoreau. *Boston,* 1907.
> F. B. Sanborn, editor. 470 copies only. Contains "Godfrey of Boulogne."

The Seasons. ₁*Mesa, Ariz.,* 1916₁.
> 250 copies only printed for Edwin B. Hill.

Thoreau's Last Letter. *Amenia, N. Y.,* 1925.
> Wrappers. Privately printed. 200 copies only.

The Transmigration of the Seven Brahmans. *New York*, 1932.
Boards. 1,200 copies only of which 200 were on handmade paper.
The Living Thoughts of Thoreau, Presented by Theodore Dreiser. *New York*, 1939.
First printing indicated on copyright page. *

BOOKS WITH FIRST EDITION MATERIAL

Aesthetic Papers. *Boston*, 1849.
Elizabeth P. Peabody, editor. Contains "Resistance to Civil Government."
Thalatta: A Book for the Seaside. *Boston*, 1853.
Echoes of Harper's Ferry, by James Redpath. *Boston*, 1860.
Contains "A Plea For Capt. John Brown" and "Remarks at Concord ..."
Transactions of the Middlesex Agricultural Society. *Concord*, 1860.
A Masque of Poets. *Boston*, 1878.
Contains Thoreau's "Pilgrims." For complete description of this book see under
Alcott.
Concord Lectures on Philosophy. *Cambridge* [1883].
R. L. Bridgman, editor. Contains "The Service: Qualities of the Recruit."
Daniel Ricketson and His Friends. *Boston*, 1902.
Anna and Walton Ricketson, editors. Contains Thoreau letters.
Fifth Year Book of the Bibliophile Society. *Boston*, 1906.
Contains an early Thoreau letter; "Aphorisms"; fragments of early unpublished
journals.
Vermont Botanical Club, Bulletin No. 3. *Burlington*, 1908.
Contains biographical material and extracts from three unpublished Thoreau
letters.

The following are reprints: "The Succession of Forest Trees"; "Wild Apples,
and Sounds"; "Life and Friendship"; "A Happy Life"; "Notes on New England
Birds"; "Anti-Slavery and Reform Papers"; "On The Duty of Civil Disobedience";
"Katahdin and Chesuncook"; "Walking and Canoeing"; "Life Without Principle";
"Of Friendship"; "The Essay on Friendship"; "Thoreau's Bird-Lore"; "The Heart
of Thoreau's Journals"; "Canoeing in the Wilderness"; "Epigrams"; "Air Castles";
"An Ideal."

BIOGRAPHICAL AND BIBLIOGRAPHICAL

Thoreau, The Poet-Naturalist, by William Ellery Channing. *Boston*, 1873.
Contains loosely quoted extracts from the *Journal*. Revised and enlarged, *Boston*,
1902; also 250 de luxe copies.
Henry D. Thoreau, by F. B. Sanborn. *Boston*, 1882.
Contains "To My Brother," a poem by Thoreau.
The Personality of Thoreau, by F. B. Sanborn. *Boston*, 1901.
Contains a poem, "Pray To What Earth," with a paragraph of prose; "Our
Country," poem, written about 1841; and an excerpt from a junior forensic on
"The Comparative Moral Policy of Severe and Mild Punishments." Also 500
copies on handmade paper.

THOREAU

A Bibliography of Henry David Thoreau, by Francis H. Allen. *Boston,* 1908.

The Life of Henry David Thoreau, by F. B. Sanborn. *Boston,* 1917.
  Including unpublished essays. Also 200 untrimmed copies.

Henry Thoreau, by Léon Bazalgette. *New York* [1924].
  Translated by Van Wyck Brooks.

Henry Thoreau, Cosmic Yankee, by J. Brooks Atkinson. *New York,* 1927.

Thoreau, by Henry Seidel Canby. *Boston,* 1939.

A Henry David Thoreau Bibliography, 1908-1937, by William White. *Boston,* 1939.
  Printed wrappers.

The Concord Saunterer, by Reginald Lansing Cook. *Middlebury, Vt.,* 1940.
  600 copies only. Contains some uncollected material.

John Townsend Trowbridge

1827–1916

KATE THE ACCOMPLICE; or, THE PREACHER AND THE BURGLAR. *Boston*, 1849.
Paul Creyton, *pseud*. Wrappers.

HEARTS AND FACES. *Boston*, 1853.
Paul Creyton, *pseud*.

FATHER BRIGHTHOPES. *Boston*, 1853.
Paul Creyton, *pseud*. Revised, *Boston*, 1892.

BURRCLIFF. *Boston*, 1854.
Paul Creyton, *pseud*.

MARTIN MERIVALE; HIS X MARK. *Boston*, 1854.
Paul Creyton, *pseud*. 15 paper parts or 1 vol. cloth. The cloth binding occurs in two states: first, *Creyton*, not *Trowbridge*, on the spine. Also, must have the stereotyper's slug on the copyright page; second, *Trowbridge*, not *Creyton*, on the spine, no stereotyper's slug on copyright page.

IRONTHORPE: THE PIONEER PREACHER. *Boston*, 1855.
Paul Creyton, *pseud*.

THE DESERTED FAMILY. *Boston*, 1856[?].
Paul Creyton, *pseud*.

NEIGHBOR JACKWOOD. *Boston*, 1857.
By Paul Creyton, *pseud*. Revised and enlarged, *Boston*, 1895. Dramatized, *Boston*, 1857, wrappers.

THE OLD BATTLE-GROUND. *New York*, 1860.

THE DRUMMER BOY. *Boston*, 1863.
Anon. "By The Author of *Father Brighthopes*." Reissued as "Frank Manly."

THE VAGABONDS. *New York*, 1863.
Cloth or printed boards.

THE REBEL. *Boston*, 1864.
Anon.

CUDJO'S CAVE. *Boston*, 1864.
First printing lists the *L' Envoy*, in table of contents, as beginning at p. 503. Second state has table of contents re-set and with error listing *L' Envoy* as starting at p. 501. The error continues until the 1890 period. No indication of authorship on spine.

TROWBRIDGE

THE FERRY-BOY AND THE FINANCIER. *Boston*, 1864.
Anon. "By A Contributor to the *Atlantic*."

THE THREE SCOUTS. *Boston*, 1865.

LUCY ARLYN. *Boston*, 1866.

THE SOUTH: A TOUR OF ITS BATTLEFIELDS AND RUINED CITIES. *Hartford*, 1866.
Reissued with added material, *Hartford*, 1868, as "A Picture of the Desolated States."

COUPON BONDS. *Boston*, 1866.
Wrappers. With other stories, *Boston*, 1873. As a four act play, *Boston*, 1876.

NEIGHBORS' WIVES. *Boston*, 1867.

THE VAGABONDS AND OTHER POEMS. *Boston*, 1869.

THE STORY OF COLUMBUS. *Boston*, 1870.
Wrappers.

LAWRENCE'S ADVENTURES. *Boston*, 1871.
Reissued with Philadelphia imprint, printed from same plates, new title page, un-dated [1870].

JACK HAZARD AND HIS FORTUNES. *Boston*, 1871.

A CHANCE FOR HIMSELF. *Boston*, 1872.

DOING HIS BEST. *Boston*, 1873.

THE COUPON BONDS AND OTHER STORIES. *Boston*, 1873.
See: "Coupon Bonds," 1866.

WHO WON AT LAST. *London* [1874].

FAST FRIENDS. *Boston*, 1875.

THE EMIGRANT'S STORY AND OTHER POEMS. *Boston*, 1875.

THE YOUNG SURVEYOR. *Boston*, 1875.

THE BOOK OF GOLD AND OTHER POEMS. *New York*, 1878.
Illuminated boards.

BOUND IN HONOR. *Boston*, 1878.

HIS OWN MASTER. *Boston*, 1878.

YOUNG JOE. *Boston*, 1880.

BIDING HIS TIME. *Boston* [1880].

A HOME IDYLL AND OTHER POEMS. *Boston*, 1881.

THE SILVER MEDAL. *Boston*, 1881.

THE POCKET RIFLE. *Boston*, 1882.

THE JOLLY ROVER. *Boston*, 1883.

PHIL AND HIS FRIENDS. *New York*, 1884.

THE TINKHAM BROTHERS TIDE-MILL. *Boston*, 1884.
I have been unable to find any copy bearing date earlier than 1884 although the copyright notice is dated 1882. The copyright deposit copy is dated 1884. Appeared serially in 1882 and 1883.

FARNELL'S FOLLY. *Boston*, 1885.

THE SATIN-WOOD BOX. *Boston*, 1886.

HIS ONE FAULT. *Boston*, 1887.

THE LITTLE MASTER. *Boston*, 1887.

THE LOST EARL AND OTHER POEMS. *Boston* [1888].

PETER BUDSTONE: THE BOY WHO WAS HAZED. *Boston*, 1888.
Front cover reads: *The Boy That Was Hazed*.

A START IN LIFE. *Boston*, 1889.

THE ADVENTURES OF DAVID VANE AND DAVID CRANE. *Boston* [1889].

THE KELP-GATHERERS. *Boston*, 1891.

THE SCARLET TANAGER. *Boston*, 1892.

THE FORTUNES OF TOBY TRAFFORD. *Boston*, 1893.

WOODIE THORPE'S PILGRIMAGE AND OTHER STORIES. *Boston*, 1893.

THE PRIZE CUP. *New York*, 1896.

THE LOTTERY TICKET. *Boston*, 1896.

A QUESTION OF DAMAGES. *Boston*, 1897.

THE MAN WHO STOLE A MEETING HOUSE. *Boston*, 1897.

TWO BIDDICUT BOYS. *New York*, 1898.

POETICAL WORKS. *Boston*, 1903.
Also large paper edition with paper label.

MY OWN STORY. *Boston*, 1903.
Cloth or boards with paper label on the spine stating *First Edition*.

A PAIR OF MADCAPS. *Boston* [1909].

TROWBRIDGE

A Masque of Poets. *Boston*, 1878.
    Contains "Guy Vernon" and "The Robin's Song" by Trowbridge. For further regarding this book see under *Alcott*.
The Art of Authorship. *London*, 1890.
    George Bainton, editor. Contribution.
A Book of Brave Deeds. *Boston*, 1901.
    Edited.

"Midsummer," *Boston*, 1887, and "Darius Green and His Flying Machine," *Boston*, 1910, are reprinted from "The Vagabonds and Other Poems," 1869.

Hendrik Willem Van Loon

1882–

THE FALL OF THE DUTCH REPUBLIC. *Boston,* 1913.
Reissued, *Boston,* 1924, with illustrations by the author.

THE RISE OF THE DUTCH KINGDOM. *Garden City,* 1915.

THE GOLDEN BOOK OF THE DUTCH NAVIGATORS. *New York,* 1916.
Reissued as "The Romance of Discovery." *New York* [1937].

HISTORY WITH A MATCH. *Philadelphia* [1917].

A SHORT HISTORY OF DISCOVERY. *Philadelphia* [1917].

ANCIENT MAN. *New York,* 1920.

THE STORY OF MANKIND. *New York,* 1921.
School edition, *New York,* 1923. Revised and enlarged [New York, 1926].

THE STORY OF THE BIBLE. *New York* [1923].

THE STORY OF WILBUR THE HAT. *New York* [1925].

TOLERANCE. *New York,* 1925.
Published in England as "The Liberation of Mankind." Revised and enlarged
edition, *New York,* 1927.

AMERICA. [*New York*] 1927.
Reissued, *New York,* 1934, as "The Story of America."

LIFE AND TIMES OF PIETER STUYVESANT. *New York* [1928].

MAN, THE MIRACLE MAKER. [*New York,* 1928].
Reissued as "The Story of Inventions." Issued in England as "Multiplex Man."

R. V. R. *Nieuw Amsterdam* [*New York*] 1930.
Also an edition with imprint of the Literary Guild. Revised edition, *New York*
[1939].

VAN LOON'S GEOGRAPHY. *New York,* 1932.
Issued in England as "The Home of Mankind."

AN INDISCREET ITINERARY. *New York* [1933].
First edition so stated on copyright page.

RE: AN ELEPHANT UP A TREE. [*New York,* 1933].
Also copies in wrappers in advance of publication.

SHIPS AND HOW THEY SAILED THE SEVEN SEAS. *New York*, 1935.

AIR STORMING. *New York* [1935].
First edition so stated on copyright page.

AROUND THE WORLD WITH THE ALPHABET. [*New York*, 1935].

THE ARTS. *New York*, 1937.

HOW TO LOOK AT PICTURES. *New York* [1938].

OUR BATTLE. *New York*, 1938.

THE LAST OF THE TROUBADOURS, CARL MICHAEL BELI MAN, 1740-1795.
[*New York*, 1939].
With GRACE CASTAGNETTA.

INVASION. *New York* [1940].
First printing indicated on copyright page.

THE STORY OF THE PACIFIC. *New York* [1940].
First printing indicated on copyright page.

THE LIFE AND TIMES OF JOHANN SEBASTIAN BACH. *New York*, 1940.

Adriaen Block: Skipper, Trader, Explorer. *New York*, 1928.
Privately printed for members of Block Hall, Inc. In addition there were 84 numbered copies printed for Edgar A. Eyre.
To Have or To Be ... *New York* [1932].
Wrappers. First edition so stated. Reprinted from "Addresses and Proceedings of the National Education Association of the United States," 1932.
How To Do It: A Book For Children ... [*New York*, 1933].
Reprinted from the Encyclopedia Britannica.
This Changing World, by Samuel S. Fels. *Boston*, 1933.
Illustrated by Van Loon.
A World Divided is a World Lost. [*New York*, 1935].
Boards or wrappers.
The Wonder Book of Traveller's Tales, by H. C. Adams. *New York* [1936].
Introduction and illustrations by Van Loon.
The Songs We Sing. [*New York*, 1936].
With GRACE CASTAGNETTA.
Portraits and Self-Portraits, by Georges Schreiber. *Boston*, 1936.
Contribution.
Observations on the Mystery of Print and the Work of Johann Gutenberg. [*New York*] 1937.
Christmas Carols. *New York* [1937].
With GRACE CASTAGNETTA.
Folk Songs of Many Lands. *New York*, 1938.
With GRACE CASTAGNETTA.

Our Cornell. *Ithaca* [1939].
  With others.
The Life of Napoleon Bonaparte, by William M. Sloane. *New York,* 1939.
  2 vols. Introduction.
My School Books. [*Newburgh, N. Y.,* 1939].
  Wrappers.
The Songs America Sings. *New York* [1939].
  With GRACE CASTAGNETTA.
The New Inquisition, by Konrad Heiden. *New York* [1939].
  Introduction.
The Book of Fairs, by Helen Augur. *New York* [1939].
  Introduction.
Morals for Moderns, by Ralph A. Habas. *New York* [1939].
  Introduction.
Good Tidings. *New York* [1941].
  Boards. With Grace Castagnetta.

Lew[is] Wallace
1827–1905

THE FAIR GOD. *Boston,* 1873.
Noted on two weights of paper; no known priority.

COMMODUS: AN HISTORICAL PLAY. ₁*Crawfordsville,* 1876₁.
Printed wrappers. Reissued with revisions, printed wrappers ₁*Crawfordsville,* 1877₁.

BEN-HUR. *New York,* 1880.
Either light blue pictorial or brown cloth. It has been asserted that the pictorial cloth was first but it is known that the cloth and tools were used on books other than "Ben-Hur" and that the binding was probably a stock feature of the publisher. The first dedication reads: *To The Wife of My Youth,* which reading persists through several printings. The first edition occurs in several colors of cloth.

THE BOYHOOD OF CHRIST. *New York,* 1888.

LIFE OF GEN. BEN HARRISON ... *Philadelphia* ₁1888₁.
Publisher's half morocco, half russia or cloth.

THE PRINCE OF INDIA. *New York,* 1893.
2 vols. First state has no dedication in vol. 1. Cloth; or in publisher's leather, top edges gilt, other edges untrimmed. The probable first cloth binding has the rosary on the front cover stamped in red.

THE WOOING OF MALKATOON: COMMODUS. *New York,* 1898.

LEW WALLACE: AN AUTOBIOGRAPHY. *New York,* 1906.
2 vols. Also 250 signed copies.

The Stolen Stars. ₁*n.p., n.d., ca.* 1864₁.
Broadside. Issued at the Great Western Sanitary Fair and dedicated to the Soldiers of the Union.
Sport With Rod and Gun. *New York* ₁1883₁.
Alfred M. Mayer, editor. Contains Wallace's "A Buffalo Hunt in Northern Mexico."
Ginèvra; or, The Old Oak Chest: A Christmas Story, by Susan E. Wallace. *New York,* 1887.
Pictorial boards. Illustrated by Lew Wallace.
The Land of the Pueblos, by Susan E. Wallace. *New York,* 1888.
Illustrated by Wallace.

Battles and Leaders of the Civil War, by Robert Underwood Johnson, and Clarence Clough Buel. *New York,* 1887-89.

    4 vols., 1887-89 or 32 parts, 1887-88. Contributions by Wallace.

The Art of Authorship. *London,* 1890.

    George Bainton, editor. Contribution by Wallace.

Ben-Hur in Tableaux and Pantomime. [*Crawfordsville, Indiana*(?) 1890].

    Printed wrappers. "Arranged By Thr[!] Author for Messrs. Clark & Cox." Reissued by Harpers, *New York,* 1891, "Ben-Hur in Dramatic Tableaux and Pantomime ... Arranged By The Author For Messrs. Clark & Cox." Printed wrappers. Inserted before the title page is a printed slip calling attention to the copyright laws.

Famous Paintings of the World. *New York,* 1894.

    Edited.

Constantinople, by Edwin A. Grosvenor. *London,* 1895.

    Introduction.

The First Christmas. *New York,* 1899.

    Reprinted from "Ben-Hur."

Tarry Thou Till I Come, by George Croly. *New York,* 1901.

    Introduction.

The Chariot Race from Ben-Hur. *New York,* 1908.

    Published October, 1908 on the copyright page. Reprint.

Glenway Wescott

1901–

THE BITTERNS. *Evanston, Ill.* [1920].
Wrappers.

THE APPLE OF THE EYE. *New York,* 1924.
The publisher's name on spine occurs in either italics or roman; no known priority.

NATIVES OF ROCK, XX POEMS. *New York,* 1925.
575 copies only, of which 25 on vellum; all numbered. Boards.

LIKE A LOVER. *Villefranche-sur-Mer,* 1926.
Privately printed. 200 copies only.

THE GRANDMOTHERS. *New York,* 1927.
Also 250 large paper copies, numbered and signed. Code letters *F-B* on copyright page; also, first printing indicated on copyright page.

GOOD-BYE, WISCONSIN. *New York,* 1928.
Also 250 large paper copies, numbered and signed. Code letters *H-C* on copyright page; also, first printing indicated on copyright page.

THE BABE'S BED. *Paris,* 1930.
18 copies on Madagascar parchment; 375 on Pannekoek paper, all numbered and signed.

A CALENDAR OF SAINTS FOR UNBELIEVERS. *Paris,* 1932.
6 copies on China paper, lettered; 40 on Pannekoek rag paper, signed by author and illustrator; 695 numbered copies on Pannekoek paper and 15 copies on Japan vellum. American edition, *New York,* 1933, first edition so stated on copyright page.

FEAR AND TREMBLING. *New York,* 1932.
First edition so stated on copyright page. Also 40 copies on deckle-edge paper, numbered.

THE PILGRIM HAWK. *New York* [1940].
First printing indicated on copyright page.

O. Henry Memorial Award Prize Stories of 1928.
Contains "Prohibition" by Wescott.
Elizabeth Madox Roberts: A Personal Note, by Glenway Wescott. *New York,* 1930.
Pamphlet.

Miss Moore's Observations. [*n.p. (London?)*, *n.d.*].

    4 pp. leaflet review of Marianne Moore's poems. Issued by The Egoist Press.

Fifty Photographs by George Platt Lynes. *New York*, 1934.

    Broadsheet. Foreword by Wescott.

Tonny: A Biography and Impression. *New York* [1936].

    4 pp.

Murals by Jared French: A Contemporary. *New York*, 1939.

    6 pp.

The Deadly Friend.

    Announced for publication in 1933; never published.

Edward Noyes Westcott

1847–1898

DAVID HARUM. *New York*, 1898.
  An illustrated edition later published, *New York* [1900], of which there were also 750 large paper copies bound in full vellum.

THE TELLER. *New York*, 1901.
  Also includes the letters of Edward Noyes Westcott. Margaret Westcott Muzzey, editor; and "an account of his life" by Forbes Heermans. The first state does not carry a publisher's list on the verso of the half title.

The Christmas Story From David Harum. *New York*, 1890.
  Reprinted from "David Harum." Illustrated with photographs from the play.

Edith (Newbold Jones) Wharton
1862–1937

VERSES. *Newport, R. I.,* 1878.
Wrappers. *By Edith Newbold Jones.*

THE DECORATION OF HOUSES. *New York,* 1897.
Boards, paper label. With Ogden Codman, Jr.

THE GREATER INCLINATION. *New York,* 1899.
Cloth or boards, no known priority. The first printing has the *Merrymount Press* slug on [p. 257], later on [p. 255]. The first binding has *Wharton* on the spine, later *Edith Wharton.*

THE TOUCHSTONE. *New York,* 1900.
Boards. Issued in London as "A Gift From the Grave."

CRUCIAL INSTANCES. *New York,* 1901.
Cloth or boards.

THE VALLEY OF DECISION. *New York,* 1902.
2 vols. First printed by *Merrymount Press;* later with *Manhattan Press* imprint on copyright page. *Published February, 1902* on copyright page.

SANCTUARY. *New York,* 1903.
Published, October, 1903 on copyright page.

ITALIAN VILLAS AND THEIR GARDENS. *New York,* 1904.

THE DESCENT OF MAN AND OTHER STORIES. *New York,* 1904.

ITALIAN BACKGROUNDS. *New York,* 1905.

THE HOUSE OF MIRTH. *New York,* 1905.
First state printed on laid paper with the *Scribner Press* slug on copyright page. Later, on wove paper with the *Caxton Press* slug on copyright page. Some copies issued in limp leather. Reissued with a new introduction, *London* [1936].

MADAME DE TREYMES. *New York,* 1907.
Published February, 1907 on copyright page.

THE FRUIT OF THE TREE. *New York,* 1907.

A MOTOR-FLIGHT THROUGH FRANCE. *New York,* 1908.

THE HERMIT AND THE WILD WOMAN, AND OTHER STORIES. *New York,* 1908.
Published September, 1908 on copyright page.

WHARTON

ARTEMIS TO ACTÆON AND OTHER VERSE. *New York,* 1909.
Published April, 1909 on copyright page.

TALES OF MEN AND GHOSTS. *New York,* 1910.
Published October, 1910 on copyright page.

ETHAN FROME. *New York,* 1911.
Publisher's records state that the first 2,500 copies bound had top edges gilt, balance (3,500 copies) ungilded. Earliest printed copies have perfect type, last line, p. 135. Reissued, 1922, 2,000 copies only, with new introduction. Dramatization by Owen Davis and Donald Davis, *New York,* 1936, first state has code letter *A* on copyright page.

THE REEF. *New York,* 1912.
First printing has symbol (1) below last line of text.

THE CUSTOM OF THE COUNTRY. *New York,* 1913.
Published October, 1913 on copyright page.

FIGHTING FRANCE: FROM DUNKERQUE TO BELFORT. *New York,* 1915.
Front cover stamped in gold: *Fighting France.*

XINGU AND OTHER STORIES. *New York,* 1916.
Published October 1916 on copyright page.

SUMMER. *New York,* 1917.

THE MARNE. *New York,* 1918.
Boards.

FRENCH WAYS AND THEIR MEANING. *New York,* 1919.

THE AGE OF INNOCENCE. *New York,* 1920.
P. 186, in the early printings, has quotation from the burial, instead of the wedding, service. Boards. The first printing has symbol (1) below last line of text. Dramatized by Margaret Ayer Barnes.

IN MOROCCO. *New York,* 1920.

THE GLIMPSES OF THE MOON. *New York,* 1922.
First printing has symbol (1) below last line of text.

A SON AT THE FRONT. *New York,* 1923.
P. 244, line 6, *lips* for *lids. Published September, 1923* on copyright page.

OLD NEW YORK. *New York,* 1924.
4 vols. "False Dawn—The 'Forties"; "The Old Maid—The 'Fifties"; "The Spark—The 'Sixties"; "New Year's Day—The 'Seventies." First printings have (1) at last page of text. "The Old Maid" dramatized by Zoë Akins, *New York,* 1935.

THE MOTHER'S RECOMPENSE. *New York,* 1925.
First printing has symbol (1) below last line of text.

THE WRITING OF FICTION. *New York*, 1925.
Boards, cloth back, paper label.

HERE AND BEYOND. *New York*, 1926.
Has (1) at last page of text.

TWELVE POEMS. [*London*, 1926].
130 signed copies only. Boards.

TWILIGHT SLEEP. *New York*, 1927.
First printing has symbol (1) below last line of text.

THE CHILDREN. *New York*, 1928.
First printing has symbol (1) below last line of text. Moving picture edition published as "Marriage Playground."

HUDSON RIVER BRACKETED. *New York*, 1929.
First printing has symbol (1) below last line of text.

CERTAIN PEOPLE. *New York*, 1930.
First printing has symbol (1) below last line of text.

THE GODS ARRIVE. *New York and London*, 1932.
First printing has symbol (1) below last line of text.

HUMAN NATURE. *New York*, 1933.
First printing has symbol (1) below last line of text.

A BACKWARD GLANCE. *New York*, 1934.

THE WORLD OVER. *New York*, 1936.

GHOSTS. *New York*, 1937.
First printing has symbol (1) below last line of text.

THE BUCCANEERS. *New York*, 1938.
First printing has symbol (1) below last line of text.

American Sonnets. *Boston*, 1890.
Edwin Markham, editor. Contains Mrs. Wharton's "Euralus."
Stories of New York. *New York*, 1893.
Cloth or wrappers. Contains "Mrs. Manstey's View."
Stories by Foreign Authors. *New York*, 1898.
Contains translations by Mrs. Wharton.
The Joy of Living, by Herman Sudermann. *New York*, 1902.
Translated.
The Book of the Homeless. *Paris*, 1915.
Edited and with a contribution. Also 175 large paper copies and 50 with portfolio of plates. American edition, *New York*, 1916. Contains also several translations.

The Three Best Short Stories of a Year. *New York* [1915].
   Wrappers. Issued as an advertisement by *Scribner's Magazine*. Contains "The Triumph of Night" by Mrs. Wharton.

Theodore Roosevelt, by Herman Hagedorn. *Columbia University*, 1919.
   Boards, vellum back or printed wrappers. Contains "With the Tide" by Mrs. Wharton. Privately printed.

American and British Poetry from *The Yale Review*. *New Haven*, 1920.
   Contributions by Mrs. Wharton.

Futility, by William Gerhardi. *New York*, 1922.
   Introduction.

Edith Wharton, by Robert Morss Lovett. *New York*, 1925.

A Bibliography of the Collected Writings of Edith Wharton, by Lawson McClung Melish. *New York*, 1927.
   500 copies only.

W. C. Brownell. *New York*, 1929.
   Privately printed. Contains a chapter by Mrs. Wharton.

A Bibliography of the Writings of Edith Wharton, by Lavinia Davis. *Portland, Maine*, 1933.
   325 copies only.

Designed For Reading. *New York*, 1934.
   Contribution by Wharton.

Speak to the Earth, by Vivienne de Watteville. *New York*, 1935.
   Preface.

Breaking into Print. *New York*, 1937.
   Elmer Adler, editor. Contribution.

Eternal Passion in English Poetry. *New York*, 1939.
   Co-editor.

James Abbott McNeill Whistler
1834–1903

WHISTLER *v*. RUSKIN. *London* [1878].
Wrappers. Sq. 12mo. Second edition is sm. 4to.

THE PIKER PAPERS. *London*, 1881.
Privately printed.

THE PADDON PAPERS. *Chelsea*, 1882.
Stitched without wrappers.

MR. WHISTLER'S "TEN O'CLOCK." *London*, 1885.
Privately printed, 25 copies only. Published edition, *London* or *New York*, 1888.
Reissued with "The Reply to Swinburne," *Chicago*, 1904, 15 copies on vellum,
55 on French paper, 105 on Italian paper.

PROPOSITIONS. *London*, 1886.

THE GENTLE ART OF MAKING ENEMIES. *Paris* [or *New York*] 1890.
Printed grey wrappers. Sheridan Ford, editor. Printed in Belgium and issued with
American imprint of *Stokes*, Paris imprint of *Delabrosse*. Simultaneously issued.
Unauthorized by Whistler who ordered publication of: (*see item following*).

THE GENTLE ART OF MAKING ENEMIES. *London*, 1890.
Boards, cloth back. *Heinemann*, imprint. Also New York imprint of *Lovell*. Also
150 large paper copies, London imprint; 100 with New York imprint. Reissued,
London, 1892, enlarged by addition of "Nocturne" catalog, three letters by
Whistler. Third authorized edition, *New York*, 1904, *Putnam* imprint, is reprint
of second authorized edition.

EDEN VERSUS WHISTLER. THE BARONET & THE BUTTERFLY. A VALENTINE
WITH A VERDICT. *Paris* [1899].
Boards, cloth back. Also copies on large paper. New York edition. *Russell* imprint,
printed at the Paris office together with sheets there published. American edition
has several variants as to preliminary leaves caused by binder's error in placing;
no priority for misbound copies.

ART DICTA AND OTHER ESSAYS. *Boston and London*, 1904.
Boards, cloth back, paper label. Limited issue.

WILDE *v*. WHISTLER. *London*, 1906.
400 copies on small paper; 100 copies on large paper. Wrappers. Privately printed.

THE ETCHED WORK OF WHISTLER. *New York*, 1910.
Edward G. Kennedy, editor. 1 volume of text; 422 plates. 402 copies only for
members of The Grolier Club.

As an exhibiting artist, Whistler issued or had issued, numerous catalogs. The following list includes only a representative few of these.

A Catalogue of Blue and White Nanking Porcelain ... *London*, 1878.
Notes on the Peacock Room. *London*, 1877.
    Privately printed broadside. Reissued with additions in a privately printed 4to. in wrappers, illustrated [*London*, 1904].
Venice Pastels. [*London*, 1881].
    Catalog.
Etchings and Dry Points: Venice, Second Series. [*London*, 1883].
    Catalog.
"Notes"—"Harmonies"—"Nocturnes." *Chelsea*, 1884.
    First edition does not have *May, 1884.*
The Pageant. *London*, 1896.
    C. Hazelwood Shannon and J. W. Gleeson White, editors. 150 copies only, numbered. Contains two plates by Whistler.
Mr. Whistler's Lithographs. *London*, 1896.
    Thomas R. Way, editor. 140 copies only. Reissued in an edition of 400 copies, *New York*, 1914.
Nocturnes, Marines, Chevalet Pieces. [*London, n.d.*].
    Portfolio.
The Art of James McNeill Whistler, by T. R. Way and G. R. Dennis. *London*, 1903.
Recollections and Impressions of James Abbott McNeill Whistler, by Arthur Jerome Eddy. *Philadelphia*, 1903.
Whistler as I Knew Him, by Mortimer Menpes. *London*, 1904.
The Gentle Art of Resenting Injuries: Being Some Unpublished Correspondence Addressed to the Author of "The Gentle Art of Making Enemies," by Frederick Keppel. *New York*, 1904.
    Wrappers.
In Memoriam: J. McNeill Whistler. Speech ... by Walter Raleigh. *London*, 1905.
With Whistler in Venice, by Otto H. Bacher. *New York*, 1908.
    Boards.
The Life of James McNeill Whistler. *London*, 1908.
    By Elizabeth Robins and Joseph Pennell. 2 vols. Also 150 copies on Japan vellum signed by the publisher. The authorized biography.
Writings By and About James Abbott McNeill Whistler, by Don C. Seitz. *Edinburgh*, 1910.
    Bibliography.
The Whistler Book, by Sadakichi Hartmann. *Boston*, 1910.
The Works of James McNeill Whistler ... by Elizabeth Luther Cary. *New York and London*, 1913.
    With a tentative list of the artist's works.
Whistler, by James Laver. *New York*, 1930.
Whistler, The Friend, by Elizabeth Robins Pennell. *Philadelphia*, 1930.

Stewart Edward White
1873–

THE CLAIM JUMPERS. *New York*, 1901.
Cloth, printed wrappers or marbled board sides with leather back.

THE WESTERNERS. *New York*, 1901.

THE BLAZED TRAIL. *New York*, 1902.

CONJUROR'S HOUSE. *New York*, 1903.
Published, March, 1903, R on copyright page. Reissued, 1914, as "The Call of the North."

THE FOREST. *New York*, 1903.
Also 80 large paper copies, numbered and signed.

THE MAGIC FOREST. *New York*, 1903.

THE SILENT PLACES. *New York*, 1904.

THE MOUNTAINS. *New York*, 1904.

BLAZED TRAIL STORIES. *New York*, 1904.

THE PASS. *New York*, 1906.

THE MYSTERY. *New York*, 1907.
With SAMUEL HOPKINS ADAMS.

ARIZONA NIGHTS. *New York*, 1907.

CAMP AND TRAIL. *New York*, 1907.

THE RIVERMAN. *New York*, 1908.

THE RULES OF THE GAME. *New York*, 1910.

THE ADVENTURES OF BOBBY ORDE. *New York*, 1910.

THE CABIN. *New York*, 1911.

THE SIGN AT SIX. *Indianapolis* [1912].

THE LAND OF FOOTPRINTS. *Garden City*, 1912.

AFRICAN CAMP FIRES. *Garden City*, 1913.

GOLD. *Garden City*, 1913.
Yellow cloth binding preferred. Life of White at end of book must be without illustrations save for the ornamental border enclosing the text.

S. E. WHITE

THE REDISCOVERED COUNTRY. *Garden City*, 1915.

THE GRAY DAWN. *Garden City* [1915].

THE LEOPARD WOMAN. *Garden City*, 1916.

SIMBA. *Garden City*, 1918.

THE FORTY-NINERS. *New Haven*, 1918.

THE KILLER. *Garden City*, 1920.
A few copies in wrappers in advance of trade issue, 1919. The pre-issue has 134 pp.; the published edition, 346 pp.

THE ROSE DAWN. *Garden City*, 1920.

DANIEL BOONE: WILDERNESS SCOUT. *Garden City*, 1922.
First printing indicated on copyright page. Illustrated edition, 1926.

ON TIPTOE. *New York* [1922].
First printing has publisher's monogram on copyright page.

THE GLORY HOLE. *Garden City*, 1924.
First edition so stated on copyright page.

CREDO. *Garden City*, 1925.
First printing indicated on copyright page.

SKOOKUM CHUCK. *Garden City*, 1925.
First printing indicated on copyright page.

SECRET HARBOUR. *Garden City*, 1926.
First printing indicated on copyright page.

LIONS IN THE PATH. *Garden City*, 1926.
First printing indicated on copyright page.

BACK OF BEYOND. *Garden City*, 1927.
First printing indicated on copyright page.

WHY BE A MUD TURTLE? *Garden City*, 1928.
First printing indicated on copyright page.

DOG DAYS. *Garden City*, 1930.
First edition so stated on copyright page.

THE SHEPPER-NEWFOUNDER. *Garden City*, 1931.
First printing indicated on copyright page.

WILD ANIMALS. *Burlingame, California* [1932].
350 copies only of which 50 were signed by author and illustrator.

THE LONG RIFLE. *Garden City*, 1932.
First printing indicated on copyright page.

RANCHERO. *Garden City*, 1933.
First edition so stated on copyright page.

FOLDED HILLS. *Garden City*, 1934.
First edition so stated on copyright page.

POLE STAR. *Garden City*, 1935.
With HARRY DEVIGHNE. First printing indicated on copyright page.

THE BETTY BOOK. *New York*, 1937.
First printing indicated on copyright page.

OLD CALIFORNIA IN PICTURE AND STORY. *Garden City*, 1937.
First printing indicated on copyright page.

ACROSS THE UNKNOWN. *New York*, 1939.

WILD GEESE CALLING. *New York*, 1940.
First printing indicated on copyright page.

THE UNOBSTRUCTED UNIVERSE. *New York*, 1940.

The Birds of Mackinac Island. [*n.p.*] 1893.
Wrappers.
Stories From McClure's: Comedy. *New York*, 1901.
Contains "The Saving Grace."
Golden Stories. *New York*, 1909.
Contains "The Foreman: A Story of the Woods."
The Camper's Own Book. *New York*, 1912.
Contribution.
Little Verses With Big Names. *New York*, 1915.
Contains "The Rime of the Young Lady a-Camping."
Camp Fire Verse. *New York*, 1917.
Edited by Haynes and Hanson. Introduction by White.
The Stag Cook Book. *New York* [1922].
C. MacSheridan, editor. Contribution by White.
The Story of California. *Garden City*, 1923.
Reprint of "Gold," "The Rose Dawn" and "The Gray Dawn."
Hudson's Bay Company, by Robert E. Pinkerton. *New York* [1931].
Introduction.
American Writers on American Literature. *New York* [1931].
John Macy, editor. Contains "Fiction of the Eighties and Nineties" by White.
Post Stories of 1935. *Boston*, 1936.
Contains "The Grampus and the Weasel" by White.
Fernand Lungren: A Biography, by John A. Boerger. *Santa Barbara*, 1936.
Foreword.

William Allen White

1868–

RHYMES BY TWO FRIENDS. *Fort Scott* [1893].
With ALBERT BIGELOW PAINE. 500 copies.

THE REAL ISSUE. *Chicago*, 1896.

THE COURT OF BOYVILLE. *New York*, 1899.
Fore and bottom edges noted both trimmed and untrimmed.

STRATAGEMS AND SPOILS. *New York*, 1901.

IN OUR TOWN. *New York*, 1906.

EMPORIA AND NEW YORK. *Emporia*, 1908.

A CERTAIN RICH MAN. *New York*, 1909.

THE OLD ORDER CHANGETH. *New York*, 1910.

A THEORY OF SPIRITUAL PROGRESS. *Emporia*, 1910.
600 signed copies only.

GOD'S PUPPETS. *New York*, 1916.

IN THE HEART OF A FOOL. *New York*, 1918.

THE MARTIAL ADVENTURES OF HENRY AND ME. *New York*, 1918.

THE EDITOR AND HIS PEOPLE. *New York*, 1924.
Editorials selected from the *Emporia Gazette*, by Helen Ogden Mahin. Introduction and footnotes by White.

POLITICS: THE CITIZEN'S BUSINESS. *New York*, 1924.

WOODROW WILSON: THE MAN, HIS TIMES AND HIS TASK. *Boston*, 1924.

CALVIN COOLIDGE: THE MAN WHO IS PRESIDENT. *New York*, 1925.

SOME CYCLES OF CATHAY. *Chapel Hill*, 1925.

BOYS—THEN AND NOW. *New York*, 1926.

MASKS IN A PAGEANT. *New York*, 1928.

WHAT IT'S ALL ABOUT. *New York*, 1936.
First printing indicated on copyright page.

FORTY YEARS ON MAIN STREET. *New York* [1937].

A PURITAN IN BABYLON: THE STORY OF CALVIN COOLIDGE. *New York*, 1938.
First printing indicated on copyright page.

THE CHANGING WEST. *New York*, 1939.
First printing indicated on copyright page.

"What's the Matter With Kansas?" *Emporia*, 1896.
Pamphlet.

Tales From McClure's: The West. *New York*, 1897.
Contains "The Homecoming of Colonel Hucks."

Tales From McClure's: Humor. *New York*, 1897.
Contains "The King of Boyville."

What Happened at Emporia. [*Topeka*, 1908?].

The Grand Canyon of Arizona. Published by the Passenger Department of the
Santa Fe. [*n.p.*] 1909.
Contains: "On the Bright Angel Trail."

A Theory of Spiritual Progress. *Emporia* [1910].
600 copies only, numbered and signed.

Uncle Walt. *Chicago*, 1910.
The probable first state has the top edges gilded, other edges untrimmed.

The Morris Book Shop. *Chicago*, 1912.
Wrappers. Contribution.

The Sturdy Oak. *New York*, 1917.
One chapter by White.

Cheerful by Request, by Edna Ferber. *Garden City*, 1918.
"Lambskin Edition." Preface by White.

The Stag Cook Book. *New York* [1922].
C. MacSheridan, editor. Contribution.

These United States. *New York* [1923].
"Kansas" by White.

Huckleberry Finn, by Mark Twain. *New York*, 1923.
"Definitive Edition," vol. 13. Contains an introduction by White.

Conflicts in American Public Opinion. *Chicago*, 1925.
In "Reading With a Purpose" series.

Harper's Essays. *New York*, 1927.
Contains "The Country Newspaper" by White.

Rome and the World Today, by Herbert S. Hadley. *New York* [1934].
Introduction.

William Rockhill Nelson and the *Kansas City Star*, by Icie F. Johnson. *Kansas City*
[1935].
Introduction by White.

Alfred M. Landon, or, Deeds Not Deficits, by Richard B. Fowler. *Boston* [1936].
Foreword by White.

Defense for America. *New York*, 1940.
Edited and with an introduction by White.

Freedom of the Press. *New York* [1941].
Contribution.

Walt[er] Whitman
1819–1892

FRANKLIN EVANS; or, THE INEBRIATE. [*New York*, 1842].
Supplement to *The New World*, November, 1842. 32 pp. Brownish red wrappers which may or may not be printed. Author's name as *Walter Whitman*.

LEAVES OF GRASS. *Brooklyn*, 1855.
First state has marbled end papers, cover gold stamped, no advertisements or reviews; second state, plain end papers, no gold on covers, no advertisements or reviews; third state same as second but has 16 pp. advertisements bound in.

For convenience the reissued "Leaves of Grass" are here listed chronologically. Whitman rewrote and added to these editions so that each becomes virtually a new work. The author was in close touch with the printers which may account for the freak and paper bound copies, the exact status of which may never be determined.

———— *Brooklyn*, 1856.
20 additional poems.

———— *Boston*, 1860-61.
Printed by Geo. C. Rand and Avery on verso title page. First state of frontispiece in dispute, but tinted state preferred. Probable first state of binding has gold stamped butterfly on spine. Spurious reprints, without change of date, were made from the same plates, *New York*, 1879, and on.

———— *New York*, 1867.
Five variations with various material. *See:* Wells-Goldsmith Bibliography.

———— *Washington*, 1871.
First state, 384 pp. Edition of 1872 adds "A Passage to India."

———— *Camden*, 1876.
For variants see Wells-Goldsmith Bibliography.

———— *Boston*, 1881-82.
A few copies have *third edition* on title page.

———— *Camden*, 1882.
From same plates as preceding.

———— *Philadelphia*, 1882.
From same plates as preceding.

———— *Philadelphia*, 1888.
With new material including "Sands At Seventy," 404 pp. Freak copies with 1884 title page exist.

———— *Philadelphia*, 1889.
300 signed copies only.

———— *Philadelphia*, 1891.
Some in brown paper wrappers.

WALT WHITMAN'S DRUM TAPS. *New York*, 1865.
Second issue contains added "Sequel." It is claimed that the sequel was also separately issued.

AFTER ALL NOT TO CREATE ONLY. *Washington*, 1871.
Broadside. Published edition, *Boston*, 1871.

DEMOCRATIC VISTAS. *Washington*, 1871.
Wrappers.

PASSAGE TO INDIA. *Washington*, 1871.
Wrappers.

AS A STRONG BIRD ON PINIONS FREE. *Washington*, 1872.

MEMORANDA DURING THE WAR. *Camden*, 1875-76.
Should contain two portraits. First printed page states *Remembrance Copy* with space below for signature.

TWO RIVULETS. *Camden*, 1876.
Half calf binding. First state undetermined.

SPECIMEN DAYS & COLLECT. *Philadelphia*, 1882-83.
Rees Welch & Co. imprint.

NOVEMBER BOUGHS. *Philadelphia*, 1888.
Also large paper state, green cover, untrimmed.

COMPLETE POEMS AND PROSE. 1855-1888. [*Philadelphia*, 1888-89].
Also 600 signed copies, three-quarter buckram and boards, paper label on spine; or, half leather.

GOOD-BYE MY FANCY, 2D ANNEX TO LEAVES OF GRASS. *Philadelphia*, 1891.
Also large paper edition, untrimmed.

COMPLETE PROSE WORKS. *Philadelphia*, 1892.

AUTOBIOGRAPHIA. *New York*, 1892.
Charles L. Webster imprint.

CALAMUS. *Boston*, 1897.
Letters to Peter Doyle. Signed by the editor, R. M. Bucke. Also 35 numbered copies on large paper.

THE WOUND DRESSER. *Boston,* 1898.
> With or without tipped-in title page; no known priority. First printing has **1897** copyright notice; later, 1898. Also 60 copies, numbered and signed by the editor, Richard Maurice Bucke.

NOTES AND FRAGMENTS. ₁*Privately Printed*₁ 1899.
> 225 numbered copies only. Signed by the editor, R. M. Bucke.

LETTERS WRITTEN BY WALT WHITMAN TO HIS MOTHER. *New York,* 1902.
> 5 copies only.

WALT WHITMAN'S DIARY IN CANADA. *Boston,* 1904.
> W. S. Kennedy, editor. 500 copies only. First binding, vellum; later, blue cloth.

AN AMERICAN PRIMER. *Boston,* 1904.
> 500 copies only. First binding in white vellum; second binding, blue cloth. A possible intermediate binding is grey boards, vellum back.

LAFAYETTE IN BROOKLYN. *New York,* 1905.
> 250 numbered copies only; of which 15 on Japan vellum, numbered and signed.

CRITICISM: AN ESSAY. *Newark,* 1913.
> 100 numbered copies only. Privately printed.

THE GATHERING OF THE FORCES. *New York,* 1920.
> 2 vols. Limited letter-press edition. Material gathered from the *Brooklyn Daily Eagle,* 1846-47.

THE UNCOLLECTED POETRY AND PROSE OF WALT WHITMAN. *Garden City,* 1921.
> 2 vols. Emory Holloway, editor.

PICTURES: AN UNPUBLISHED POEM. *New York,* 1927.
> 700 copies only.

THE HALF-BREED AND OTHER STORIES. *New York,* 1927.
> Novel and four sketches reprinted from old periodicals. Thomas Ollive Mabbott, editor. Also 155 copies on handmade paper of which 30 with illustrations signed in the proof by the artist, Allen Lewis.

WALT WHITMAN'S WORKSHOP. *Cambridge,* 1928.
> Clifton Joseph Furness, editor. Hitherto unpublished material.

A LEAF OF GRASS FROM SHADY HILL. ₁*Cambridge,* 1928₁.
> With a review of "Leaves of Grass" by Charles Eliot Norton.

RIVULETS OF PROSE. *New York,* 1928.
> Carolyn Wells and Alfred F. Goldsmith, editors. 499 copies only.

I SIT AND LOOK OUT. *New York,* 1932.
> Editorials from the *Brooklyn Daily Eagle,* selected and edited by Emory Holloway and Vernolian Schwarz.

NEW YORK DISSECTED: A SHEAF OF RECENTLY DISCOVERED NEWSPAPER
ARTICLES. *New York*, 1936.
Emory Holloway and Ralph Adimari, editors. 750 numbered copies only.

Voices From the Press. A Collection of Sketches, Essays and Poems. *New York*, 1850.
James J. Brenton, editor. Contribution.
Abbie Nott and Other Knots, by "Katinka." "It's A' a Muddle." *Philadelphia*, 1856.
John T. Winterich in *The Publishers' Weekly*, March 17, 1928, surmises that
this is by Whitman, attributing the discovery to Alfred F. Goldsmith. Three line
quotation from "Leaves" faces the title.
Leaves of Grass: Preface to the Original 1855 Edition. *London*, 1881.
500 copies only.
The Poets' Tribute to Garfield. *Cambridge*, 1882.
Contribution.
Essays From *The Critic*. *Boston*, 1882.
Contains two essays by Whitman.
Walt Whitman, by Richard Maurice Bucke. *Philadelphia*, 1883.
In Response to an Invitation to Attend the Tertio-Millennial Anniversary at Santa
Fé, N. M. [*n.p.*, 1883].
Broadside.
Leaves of Grass With Sands at Seventy and A Backward Glance O'er Travel'd
Roads, May 31, 1889. [*Philadelphia*] 1889.
300 copies only signed by Whitman on the title page. Printed for Whitman's
birthday.
Camden's Compliment to Walt Whitman. *Philadelphia*, 1889.
Edited by Horace Traubel.
In Re: Walt Whitman. *Philadelphia*, 1893.
Edited by Horace Traubel, R. M. Bucke, Thomas Harned. 1,000 numbered copies
only.
Walt Whitman: A Study by John Addington Symonds. *London*, 1893.
Conversations With Walt Whitman, by Sadakichi Hartmann. *New York*, 1895.
Reminiscences of Walt Whitman, by William Sloane Kennedy. *Boston*, 1896.
The Complete Writings of Walt Whitman. *New York*, 1902.
10 vols. "Autograph Edition" with inserted *ms.*, 32 sets only. "Paumanok Edi-
tion," colored plates, 300 sets. "Booklover's-Camden Edition," 500 sets.
With Walt Whitman in Camden, by Horace Traubel. *Boston*, 1906.
Walt Whitman: His Life and Work, by Bliss Perry. *Boston*, 1906.
Also 250 copies with paper label.
Walt Whitman: A Critical Study, by Basil de Selincourt. *London*, 1914.
Bibliography of Walt Whitman, by Frank Shay. *New York*, 1920.
500 copies only.
A Concise Bibliography of the Works of Walt Whitman, With a Supplement of 50
books About Walt Whitman, by Carolyn Wells and Alfred F. Goldsmith. *Boston*,
1922.
550 numbered copies only. Revised edition, 1930.

WHITMAN

Et Cetera: A Collector's Scrap-Book. *Chicago, 1924.*
  Vincent Starrett, editor. Boards, cloth back, paper label. 625 numbered copies only. Contribution.
The Magnificent Idler, by Cameron Rogers. *New York, 1926.*
  Also 250 signed copies. Narrative biography.
Walt Whitman: A Brief Biography With Reminiscences, by H. S. Morris. *Cambridge, 1929.*
Whitman and Burroughs, Comrades, by Clara Barrus. *New York, 1931.*
Walt Whitman and the Civil War: A Collection of Original Articles and Manuscripts. *Philadelphia, 1933.*
  Charles I. Glicksberg, editor.
Whitman, by Edgar Lee Masters. *New York, 1937.*
  First printing has code letter *A* on copyright page.
Leaves of Music by Walt Whitman, by Bella C. Landauer. *New York, 1937.*
  60 copies only.

See under *Burroughs,* "Notes on Walt Whitman ..." 1867.

John Greenleaf Whittier
1807–1892

LEGENDS OF NEW-ENGLAND. *Hartford,* 1831.
Boards, paper label. First state, p. iv, reads *v* or *vi;* next to last line, p. 98, reads *the go.*

MOLL PITCHER. *Boston,* 1832.
Printed wrappers. So-called facsimile edition differs greatly in appearance.

JUSTICE AND EXPEDIENCY. *Haverhill,* 1833.
Stitched, without wrappers. Not over 10 copies known although 500 were printed. Republished same year with New York imprint, earliest state ending with a poem.

MOGG MEGGONE. *Boston,* 1836.

POEMS WRITTEN ... BETWEEN ... 1830 and 1838, etc. *Boston,* 1837.
First has 96 pp. Later 103 pp.

NARRATIVE OF JAMES WILLIAMS. *New York,* 1838.
Cloth or boards and has comma after *Williams* on title page; no printer's imprint on verso title page, and reads *barbarrity,* p. xv, line 1. Second state and later 4to edition (New York), also a Boston edition in same year.

POEMS. *Philadelphia,* 1838.
Cloth or leather.

MOLL PITCHER, AND THE MINSTREL GIRL. *Philadelphia,* 1840.
Printed wrappers. First and only authorized edition of the second title in book form.

LAYS OF MY HOME. *Boston,* 1843.
Gray or yellow boards, paper label. 3 leaves advts.

THE SONG OF THE VERMONTERS. *Windsor, Vermont* [ca. 1843].
Formerly believed to be 1833 production but issued between March 16, 1842 and December 25, 1843. First state is a folio broadside, only five copies known. Second, about 20 years later, without *Windsor* imprint.

BALLADS AND OTHER POEMS. *London,* 1844.
Authorized. Cloth, paper label on spine; leather; or illuminated wrappers.

THE STRANGER IN LOWELL. *Boston,* 1845.
Wrappers. Anon.

VOICES OF FREEDOM. *Philadelphia,* 1846.
Cloth and rarely in illuminated wrappers. All copies read *Fourth, Fifth, Sixth or*

WHITTIER

Seventh Edition, with no apparent differences. This probably signifies that this is the first collected edition of the preceding 1837, 1838 and 1843 volumes of poetry.

THE SUPERNATURALISM OF NEW ENGLAND. *New York,* 1847.
Wrappers. Whittier's name on wrappers, not title page.

POEMS. *Boston,* 1849.
First state does not have *Star of Bethlehem* plate. Reissued, 1850, with five added poems.

LEAVES FROM MARGARET SMITH'S JOURNAL. *Boston,* 1849.
Anonymous. Cloth or wrappers. A few copies have been noted with illustrations. With or without inserted advertisements.

OLD PORTRAITS AND MODERN SKETCHES. *Boston,* 1850.
Advertisements dated 1849.

SONGS OF LABOR AND OTHER POEMS. *Boston,* 1850.
Cloth or boards with paper label. Advertisements dated *May 1850.*

THE CHAPEL OF THE HERMITS. *Boston,* 1853.
12 pp. advts.

LITERARY RECREATIONS AND MISCELLANIES. *Boston,* 1854.
8 pp. advts. dated *September 1854.* Copies have been noted with the advertisements dated *April 1854.*

THE PANORAMA. *Boston,* 1856.
10 pp. advts. dated *April 1856* seem to be first set. Copies often occur without advertisements.

POETICAL WORKS. *Boston,* 1857.
2 vols. "Blue and Gold" series.

THE SYCAMORES. *Nantucket,* 1857.
Wrappers. Not over 12 copies printed.

HOME BALLADS. *Boston,* 1860.
16 pp. advts. dated *July 1860.*

IN WAR TIME. *Boston,* 1864.
22 pp. advts. dated *November 1863,* with this title listed as *just ready.*

NATIONAL LYRICS. *Boston,* 1865.
Wrappers or cloth.

SNOW-BOUND. *Boston,* 1866.
Bound in various colors of cloth, including white. First state has last page of text numbered, with numerals below the line of printer's slug. Forged copies exist which must be examined for this feature. Large paper copies are later. Later editions contain numerous textual changes.

534

THE TENT ON THE BEACH. *Boston,* 1867.
Four states noted. The first reads, p. 46, first line of second stanza, *With quick heart-glow, as one might meet.* Perfect *N* last page of text, first letter, line 2. Two copies known with *Ticknor & Co.* instead of the *T & F* monogram at the foot of spine.

AMONG THE HILLS. *Boston,* 1869.
No publisher's monogram on spine.

MIRIAM. *Boston,* 1871.
Fields Osgood monogram on spine.

THE PENNSYLVANIA PILGRIM. *Boston,* 1872.
Earliest copies are folded in 12; later in 8.

HAZEL-BLOSSOMS. *Boston,* 1875.
Noted on both thick and thin paper with no known priority. First state has *JRO* monogram on spine. Contains nine poems by Elizabeth H. Whittier.

MABEL MARTIN. *Boston,* 1876.
Two editions: (1st) 8vo, copyright 1874, with 56 illustrations; (2nd) 12mo, copyright 1875, with 21 illustrations. James A. Canny states that the 1867 date called for in the Wakeman catalog "was a transposition of the numerals in the printing of the ... catalog and escaped the proof-reader. My catalog was corrected at the time ..."

THE VISION OF ECHARD. *Boston,* 1878.

THE KING'S MISSIVE. *Boston,* 1881.

THE BAY OF SEVEN ISLANDS. *Boston,* 1883.
Monogram on spine. Noted with printed presentation slip inserted.

SAINT GREGORY'S GUEST. *Boston,* 1886.
Wrappers.

THE WRITINGS OF JOHN GREENLEAF WHITTIER. *Boston,* 1888.
7 vols. "Riverside Edition." Also 400 large paper sets, which were earlier in publication. Many early poems, selected by Whittier, are here first collected.

AT SUNDOWN. *Cambridge,* 1890.
250 copies only, with facsimile autograph on slip inserted. Reissued with additions, *Boston,* 1892, of which there were also 250 large paper copies.

A LEGEND OF THE LAKE. *Dover, N. H.,* 1893.
Printed again by Carl P. Rollins in Newburyport in 1895.

THE DEMON LADY. *Haverhill,* 1894.
Wrappers. It is stated on the cover, but it is certainly untrue, that only 25 copies were printed.

WHITTIER

Only the most important are here listed. The early broadsides, "Pericles," "Psalm 137" and "Sicilian Vespers" are probably forgeries, printed at Haverhill some time after 1900. Beginning about 1882 a number of so-called broadsides occur which may be nothing more than proofs pulled for Whittier's use and supplied by the printer. These are marked thus: *

Hymn ... For The 4th July, 1834 ... at Chatham St. Chapel. *New York,* 1834.

Our Countrymen in Chains. *New York* [1834].

Address Read at the Opening of Pennsylvania Hall. *Philadelphia,* 1838.
> 8 pp. stitched. Thick and ordinary paper.

The Branded Hand. [*Philadelphia,* 1845].

A Tract For The Times: A Sabbath Scene. 1850.
> Reprinted as a book, green glazed wrappers, 1853.

Little Eva, Uncle Tom's Guardian Angel. *Boston,* 1852.
> Music.

Maud Muller. [*Newburyport?* 1854].
> Issued separately, *Boston,* 1867, cloth or leather, with illustrations by W. J. Hennessy.

The Kansas Emigrants. *New York* [1854].

Song [A Lay of Olden Time]. [1856].

We're Free, We're Free. *Boston* [1856].
> Sheet music. Not elsewhere printed.

Charity. February 20, 1858.

Naples. 1860.
> 4 pp. 2 forms noted.

Tribute to Deacon Carruthers. [*Haverhill*] March 7, 1860.
> 2 states noted with no known priority.

The Quakers Are Out. [*Newburyport?*] October 11, 1860.

My Psalm. [1860].

In War Time. *Amesbury,* 1863.
> 4 pp.

Barbara Frietchie. *New York* [1863].
> Follows the magazine printing in the *Atlantic* but precedes the book printing in "In War Time."

Hymn for the Dedication of the Unitarian Church in San Francisco. [1864].
> 4 pp.

The Eternal Goodness. [*Boston,* 1865].

G. L. S. [i.e., George L. Stearns]. *Boston,* 1867.

Letter to *The Friends' Review, Manchester, Eng.,* 1870.
> 4 pp.

To Edward and Elizabeth Gove. [*Lynn*] 1872.
> 4 pp.

Sumner. [*Boston,* 1874].
> 16 pp. uncut and unopened, with a new stanza pasted over the 4th stanza, p. 6.

Later, 8 pp. tied with white silk, with the stanza reprinted in the"paste-on" form. These two issues have 47 stanzas; when reprinted in "A Memorial of Charles Sumner," *Boston*, 1874, 7 stanzas were added.

Centennial Hymn. 1876.
4 forms.

Fitz-Greene Halleck. *New York*, 1877.
4 pp.

The Lost Occasion. ₍Boston?, 1880₎.

In Memory. ₍1881₎.

In Memoriam: Rebecca Chase Grinnell. ₍1882₎.
Card.

Copy of a Letter. *Amesbury*, May 1882.

* A Summer Pilgrimage. ₍ca. 1882₎.

* How The Women Went From Dover. ₍ca. 1883₎.

* Banished From Massachusetts. ₍ca. 1884₎.

* The Two Elizabeths. ₍ca. 1885₎.

The Reunion. 1885.

* Revelation. *Amesbury* ₍1886₎.
2 forms.

* On The Big Horn. 1886.

To a Cape Ann Schooner. 1886.
Exists both as a proof and as a separate printing.

Acknowledgement Leaflet. *Oak Knoll*, December 19, 1887.
Printed in script face type.

R. S. S. at Deer Island on the Merrimack. ₍1888₎.

One of the Signers. ₍Newburyport₎ 1888.
6 forms.

* Burning Driftwood. 1889.

The Captain's Well. *New York*, 1890.
Supplement to *The New York Ledger*, January 11, 1890.
Illustrated by Howard Pyle. Issued in two forms: one apparently printed from the magazine plates; the other in 8vo. No known priority. Both bound in alligator grained imitation leather.

* The Last Eve of Summer. August 31, 1890.

Haverhill, 1640-1890. ₍Haverhill, 1890₎.
3 forms.

* Between the Gates. 1891.

* The Wind of March. ₍Newburyport, 1892₎.

A Letter From John G. Whittier. ₍ca. 1892₎.

The Emerald Isle. ₍Printed by Pickard₎.

A New Year's Address to the Patrons of the *Essex Gazette*, 1828. *Boston*, 1903.
60 copies only.

Whittier's Earliest Poems, 1825-6. *Amesbury*, 1906.
4 pp. leaflet. First printing of two poems.

537

CONTRIBUTIONS TO BOOKS

Over 250 books with Whittier contributions have been noted. Only the most important are listed below.

Incidental Poems, by Robert Dinsmoor. *Haverhill,* 1828.
> Contains "J. G. Whittier to the Rustic Bard," Whittier's first appearance in any book. The prose article, "The Light in the Binnacle," in "The Memorial," [1826] is not by Whittier.

Specimens of American Poetry. *Boston,* 1829.
> 3 vols.

Biography of Henry Clay, by George D. Prentice. *Hartford,* 1831.
> Whittier completed the editing and wrote a part of the book. Second edition contains further re-editing by Whittier.

Literary Remains of John G. C. Brainard. *Hartford* [1832].
> Cloth, or boards with paper label. Edited and with a biography of Brainard by Whittier.

History of Haverhill, by B. L. Mirick. *Haverhill,* 1832.
> Material in large part prepared by Whittier. Manuscript completed and published by Mirick. Boards, paper label.

The Abolition Cause Eventually Triumphant. *Andover,* 1836.
> Wrappers. A sermon by David Root. Edited and with a long note by Whittier.

Views of Slavery and Emancipation, from "Society in America," by Harriet Martineau. *Boston,* 1837.

Letters From John Quincy Adams to His Constituents. *Boston,* 1837.
> Edited and with two poems by Whittier. Stitched, without wrappers.

History of Pennsylvania Hall. *Philadelphia,* 1838.
> Cloth or wrappers. Contains an address by Whittier and a poem. With or without errata slip. Rarely contains portrait plate of Whittier.

The North Star. *Philadelphia,* 1840.
> Edited anonymously by Whittier and with two poems by him. Cloth, leather, or yellow boards.

The Poets and Poetry of America, by Rufus W. Griswold. *Philadelphia,* 1842.
> Contains three poems by Whittier here first collected.

A Wreath for St. Crispin, by J. Prince. *Boston,* 1848.
> First printing of four Whittier poems and a life.

Boston Burns Club, Centennial Festival. *Boston,* 1859.
> Contains a Whittier poem.

The Patience of Hope [by Dora Greenwell]. *Boston,* 1862.
> 32 pp. introduction by Whittier.

Only Once. [*New York,* 1862].
> Printed wrappers. Issued with and without four engraved plates at 50 cents and 25 cents respectively.

In Memoriam: Thomas Starr King. [*n.p., ca.* 1864].
> Wrappers. Contains "Thomas Starr King" by Whittier.

Ballads of New England. *Boston,* 1870.
> **Reprint.**

Winter Poems. *Boston*, 1871.
The Journal of John Woolman. *Boston*, 1871.
  Introduction by Whittier.
Child Life: A Collection of Poems. *Boston*, 1872.
  Edited and with an introduction.
The Prayer of Agassiz. *Cambridge*, 1874.
Child Life in Prose. *Boston*, 1874.
  Edited by and with a biographical introduction and one tale by Whittier.
Order of Exercises, Lexington Anniversary, April 19, 1875. *Cambridge*, 1875.
  This leaflet preceded the wrappered volume entitled "Souvenir of 1775—Lexington—1875."
Songs of Three Centuries. *Boston*, 1876.
  Edited and with a preface by Whittier.
Indian Civilization. *Philadelphia*, 1877.
  Introduction.
The River Path. *Boston*, 1878.
William Lloyd Garrison and His Times. *Boston*, 1879.
  Introduction by Whittier.
The Autograph Birthday Book. *Boston* [1881].
  Contribution.
Letters of Lydia Maria Child. *Boston*, 1883.
  Edited and with a biographical introduction by Whittier.
Jack in the Pulpit. [*New York*] 1884.
  4to pictorial boards. A separate reissue with revisions and a facsimile letter.
American Literature. *Boston*, 1887.
  E. P. Whipple, editor. Introduction by Whittier.

BIBLIOGRAPHY

A Bibliography of John Greenleaf Whittier, by Thomas Franklin Currier. *Cambridge*, 1937.
  A definitive work; one of the finest single-author American bibliographies yet published.

The following sales catalogs contain bibliographical information.

Whittier Library. *New York*, February, 1903.
J. D. Whitney. *Boston*, 1911.
Stephen H. Wakeman. *New York*, April 28-29, 1924.
  Later reissued in facsimile edition.

BIOGRAPHY

John Greenleaf Whittier: His Life, Genius and Writings, by W. Sloane Kennedy. *Boston*, 1882.
John Greenleaf Whittier. A Biography, by Francis H. Underwood. *Boston*, 1884.
  In part authorized.

WHITTIER

Life and Letters, by Samuel T. Pickard. *Boston,* 1894.

2 vols. Also 400 copies on large paper; no priority.

Whittier-Land, by Samuel T. Pickard. *Boston,* 1894.

First printing for many boyhood and humorous poems. Contains information of a more informal character than set forth in the preceding.

Whittier as a Politician. *Boston,* 1900.

150 copies printed by Bruce Rogers. Edited by Samuel T. Pickard.

Whittier's Life at Oak Knoll, by Mrs. Abby J. Woodman. *Salem,* 1908.

200 copies printed. Contains bibliographical checklist.

Whittier's Correspondence From The Oak Knoll Collections. *Salem,* 1911.

John Albree, editor. 189 copies only printed by The Riverside Press for The Essex Book Club.

Whittier's Unknown Romance. *Boston,* 1922.

Letters to Elizabeth Lloyd, etc. 385 copies only.

A Study of Whittier's Apprenticeship as a Poet ... Between 1825 and 1835, by Frances Mary Pray. *Bristol, N. H.,* 1930.

First collection of about 100 of Whittier's youthful poems culled from local newspapers and similar publications. Must be checked with Currier's later findings.

Quaker Militant: John Greenleaf Whittier, by Albert Mordell. *Boston,* 1933.

Elizabeth Lloyd and the Whittiers, by Thomas Franklin Currier. *Cambridge,* 1939.

Whittier: Bard of Freedom, by Whitman Bennett.

Announced for October 1941 publication by the University of North Carolina Press.

Thornton (Niven) Wilder
1897–

THE CABALA. *New York, 1926.*
Tan figured cloth, buckram back, top edges stained blue. Also a few copies in blue figured cloth. The following typographical errors have been noted in the first printing: p. 186, line 16, *doctors.* for *doctors,;* p. 196, line 13, *conversation* for *conversion;* p. 202, line 12, *explaininn* for *explaining.*

THE BRIDGE OF SAN LUIS REY. *New York, 1927.*
There was a preliminary issue of 21 (*10?*) copies printed on paper appreciably heavier than that of the first edition. This preliminary printing has the title page wholly in black, all cover stamping in black, with the front cover either stamped or unstamped. The regularly issued edition has the title page printed in green and black, the cover is stamped in green and black and has an ornament on the front cover. English trade edition issued a few days before American trade edition. Illustrated edition, *New York,* 1929, 1,100 copies only, signed by author and illustrator, Rockwell Kent.

THE ANGEL THAT TROUBLED THE WATERS. *New York, 1928.*
Also 775 copies on handmade paper signed by the author. 2,000 copies of trade edition signed by publishers.

THE WOMAN OF ANDROS. *New York, 1930.*
Also 21 sets of page proofs bound in unprinted wrappers, ñot for sale. Top edges stained brick red.

HEAVEN'S MY DESTINATION. *New York, 1935.*
First edition so stated on copyright page. Code letters *M-I* on copyright page.

THE LONG CHRISTMAS DINNER AND OTHER PLAYS. *New York-New Haven,* 1931.
Also 525 signed copies.

OUR TOWN. *New York* [1938].
Acting version published *New York* [1939]. Synopsis of the moving picture version published *New York* [1940].

THE MERCHANT OF YONKERS. *New York, 1939.*
First printing indicated on copyright page.

The Trumpet Shall Sound: A Play. *New Haven,* 1919-1920.
In: *Yale Literary Magazine,* October-December, 1919 and January, 1920. Uncollected.
A Diary: First and Last Entry. [*Northampton, Mass.*] 1924.
In: *S4N,* February, 1924. Uncollected.

The Third Route, by Philip Sassoon. *Garden City*, 1929.
  Introduction.
Tributes to Henry B. [*Privately Printed*, 1929].
  Anna Morgan, editor. Contribution.
Days From A Year in School, by Elsie Abbott. *New York* [1930].
  Foreword.
Love and How to Cure It. *New York* [1932].
  Reprinted from "The Long Christmas Dinner." Printed wrappers.
The Long Christmas Dinner. *New York*, 1933.
  First separate reprinting. Printed wrappers.
Lucrece: A Play, by André Obey. *Boston*, 1933.
  Translated.
The Happy Journey. *New York*, 1934.
  Reprinted in revised form from "The Long Christmas Dinner." Printed wrappers.
  First Edition June, 1934 on copyright page.
Narration: Four Lectures by Gertrude Stein. *Chicago* [1935].
  Also 120 de luxe copies signed by author and Wilder. Introduction by Wilder.
The Yale Literary Magazine. *New Haven*, 1936.
  Centennial number. Boards or wrappers. Contribution.
The Geographical History of America, by Gertrude Stein. [*New York*, 1936].
  Introduction.
The Intent of the Artist. *Princeton*, 1941.
  Augusto Centeno, editor. Contribution by Wilder.
A Bibliography of Thornton Wilder, by George F. Kelley.
  In preparation.

Harry Leon Wilson

1867–1939

ZIG ZAG TALES. *New York*, 1894.
  Cloth or wrappers.

THE SPENDERS. *Boston* [1902].
  Published May, 1902 on copyright page.

THE LIONS OF THE LORD. *Boston* [1903].
  Published June, 1903 on copyright page.

THE SEEKER. *New York*, 1904.
  Gilt lettered cover.

THE BOSS OF LITTLE ARCADY. *Boston* [1905].
  Published, August, 1905 on copyright page. First printing has imprint of *Lothrop Publishing Company;* later, *Lothrop, Lee and Shepard Company.*

EWING'S LADY. *New York*, 1907.
  Published, November, 1907 on copyright page. First printing has the symbol (1) below last line of text.

THE GUARDIAN. *New York*, 1907.
  Play. With BOOTH TARKINGTON. Reissued, *New York,* 1908, as "The Man From Home." Later novelized by Wilson.

THE MAN FROM HOME. *New York*, 1908.
  See preceding title.

BUNKER BEAN. *Garden City*, 1913.
  Dramatized, *New York,* 1922, as "His Majesty, Bunker Bean."

RUGGLES OF RED GAP. *Garden City*, 1915.

SOMEWHERE IN RED GAP. *Garden City*, 1916.

THE GIBSON UPRIGHT. *Garden City*, 1919.
  Play. With BOOTH TARKINGTON. Issued previously in wrappers as an advertisement for the Eastman Kodak Company.

LIFE. *San Francisco*, 1919.
  17th Grove Play of the Bohemian Club.

MA PETTENGILL. *Garden City*, 1919.

THE WRONG TWIN. *Garden City*, 1921.

H. L. WILSON

MERTON OF THE MOVIES. *Garden City*, 1922.
First edition so stated on copyright page. Cloth or publisher's leather.

OH, DOCTOR! *New York*, 1923.

SO THIS IS GOLF! *New York*, 1923.

PROFESSOR, HOW COULD YOU! *New York*, 1924.

TWEEDLES. *New York*, 1924.
Play. With BOOTH TARKINGTON. Printed wrappers.

COUSIN JANE. *New York*, 1925.

LONE TREE. *New York*, 1929.
First edition so stated on copyright page.

HOW'S YOUR HEALTH? *New York*, 1930.
Play. With BOOTH TARKINGTON. Printed wrappers.

TWO BLACK SHEEP. *New York*, 1931.
First printing indicated on copyright page.

WHEN IN THE COURSE ... *New York*, 1940.

Mavericks. *New York*, 1892.
Boards. Contains "True Love's Triumph."
The Sturdy Oak: A Composite Novel. *New York*, 1917.
Chapter 2 by Wilson.

(Thomas) Woodrow Wilson

1856–1924

CONGRESSIONAL GOVERNMENT. *Boston*, 1885.
Publisher's monogram on spine. Advertisements after text for "American Statesmen" have three titles *In Preparation*.

THE STATE: ELEMENTS OF HISTORICAL AND PRACTICAL POLITICS. *Boston*, 1889.
First binding has slanted lettering on front cover and no advertisements at end of text. It is believed that the large paper edition of this title is a later issue.

DIVISION AND REUNION, 1829-1889. *New York*, 1893.
Sheets of the tall copies measure 7". It is possible that these were for the English trade only. Shorter copies have *Epochs of American History* on cover. Reissues of later dates with new introductions.

AN OLD MASTER AND OTHER POLITICAL ESSAYS. *New York*, 1893.

MERE LITERATURE AND OTHER ESSAYS. *New York*, 1896.

GEORGE WASHINGTON. *New York*, 1897.

A HISTORY OF THE AMERICAN PEOPLE. *New York*, 1902.
5 vols. "Alumni Edition," 350 signed copies; "Subscription Edition" and trade edition. Wilson contributed no new material to the "Documentary Edition," 10 vols. It is claimed that the "Alumni Edition" was issued in August, regular edition in October, the first copies of the regular edition carrying the *October* line on copyright page.

CONSTITUTIONAL GOVERNMENT OF THE UNITED STATES. *New York*, 1908.

THE NEW FREEDOM. *New York*, 1913.
Also advance issue in printed wrappers.

WHEN A MAN COMES TO HIMSELF. *New York*, 1915.
B-P at foot of copyright page.

ON BEING HUMAN. *New York*, 1916.
C-Q on copyright page.

WOODROW WILSON AND WORLD SETTLEMENT. *Garden City*, 1922.
3 vols. Ray Stannard Baker, editor. "Written from his [Woodrow Wilson's] unpublished and personal material ..."

THE ROAD AWAY FROM REVOLUTION. *Boston* [1923].

ROBERT E. LEE. *Chapel Hill*, 1924.

WOODROW WILSON

WOODROW WILSON'S LETTER TO ALMONT BARNES. [*New York*, 1924].

THE PUBLIC PAPERS OF WOODROW WILSON. *New York*, 1925-1927.
2 vols. Ray Stannard Baker, editor.

WOODROW WILSON: LIFE AND LETTERS. *Garden City*, 1927-1935.
5 vols. Ray Stannard Baker, editor. First editions so stated on copyright page.

The above list includes only the so-called principal Wilson productions. No attempt has been made to list the hundreds of pamphlets and books with contributions that Wilson produced during his long career as educator and statesman.

Princeton University has issued a series of pamphlet bibliographies by Harry Clemons, George Dobbin Brown and Howard Savoy Leach.

Of the hundreds of speeches and addresses and state papers the following are only a few that have been issued in cloth or boards: "The Free Life," 1908; "The Minister and the Community," 1911; "Why We Are At War," 1917; "In Our First Year of War," and "Guarantees of Peace," 1919; "International Ideals," 1919; "The Hope of the World," 1920; "War Addresses," 1918; "President Wilson's State Papers and Addresses," 1917.

Owen Wister

1860–1938

THE NEW SWISS FAMILY ROBINSON. *Cambridge,* 1882.

THE DRAGON OF WANTLEY. *Philadelphia,* 1892.

RED MEN AND WHITE. *New York,* 1896.

LIN MC LEAN. *New York,* 1898.
>Reissued with new preface, *New York,* 1908. "A Journey in Search of Christmas," *New York,* 1904, reprinted from this.

THE JIMMYJOHN BOSS. *New York,* 1900.
>"Padre Ignacio," *New York,* 1911, reprinted from this. Reissued in "Collected Works," 1928, as "Hank's Woman."

ULYSSES S. GRANT. *Boston,* 1900.

THE VIRGINIAN. *New York,* 1902.
>A few copies were bound in blue cloth for the author's use, having a printed presentation notice on the end paper. "Theatrical Edition," with added material, 1904. With new preface, *New York,* 1911, of which there were also 100 signed copies in boards. Revised edition, *New York,* 1930.

PHILOSOPHY 4. *New York,* 1903.
>Appeared previously in "Stories of the Colleges," *Philadelphia,* 1901.

LADY BALTIMORE. *New York,* 1906.
>Also 200 signed copies on Japan vellum.

HOW DOTH THE SIMPLE SPELLING BEE. *New York,* 1907.
>What may possibly be a remainder state has been noted in blue and white sunburst paper board binding.

MOTHER. *New York,* 1907.
>*Published, October, 1907* on the copyright page. Appeared previously in "The House Party," *Boston,* 1901.

THE SEVEN AGES OF WASHINGTON. *New York,* 1907.

MEMBERS OF THE FAMILY. *New York,* 1911.
>Copies of the second printing have been noted in printed boards.

THE PENTECOST OF CALAMITY. *New York,* 1915.
>Boards, paper labels.

A STRAIGHT DEAL; or, THE ANCIENT GRUDGE. *New York,* 1920.
>Paper labels.

INDISPENSABLE INFORMATION FOR INFANTS. *New York,* 1921.

NEIGHBORS HENCEFORTH. *New York*, 1922.

WATCH YOUR THIRST. *New York*, 1923.
1,000 signed copies only.

WHEN WEST WAS WEST. *New York*, 1928.

ROOSEVELT: THE STORY OF A FRIENDSHIP, 1880-1919. *New York*, 1930.
First state has *Karow* for *Carow* at head of prolog. P. 100 begins: *I went to my desk* etc.

THE WRITINGS OF OWEN WISTER. *New York*, 1928.
11 vols. New prefaces and first book appearance for some material.

The Demon Lover: A Scotch Ballad. *Philadelphia*, 1878.
Sheet music, composed by Wister.
Ten Notable Stories From *Lippincott's*. *New York*, 1894.
Contribution.
The Year Book of Pegasus: No. 1. *Philadelphia*, 1895.
Two contributions.
A House Party. *Boston*, 1901.
Contains "Mother" by Wister.
Done in the Open. *New York*, 1902.
Introduction and verses by Wister; pictures by Frederic Remington. First state has *R. H. Russell* imprint. Also 250 copies in full leather.
Musk-Ox, Bison, Sheep and Goat. *New York*, 1904.
With Caspar W. Whitney and George Bird Grinnell. The Wister chapters are on the mountain sheep and the white goat. Also 100 large paper copies.
S. Weir Mitchell. *Philadelphia*, 1914.
Contains a memorial address by Wister.
Through the Grand Canyon From Wyoming to Mexico, by Ellsworth L. Kolb. *New York*, 1914.
Preface.
Lives of the Presidents. *New York*, 1914.
4 vols. Contains "Roosevelt" by Wister.
Their True Faith and Allegiance, by Gustavus Ohlinger. *New York*, 1916.
Animal Heroes of the Great War, by Ernest Harold Baynes. [*New York*] 1925.
Contains an account of the author by Wister.
The Pinto Horse, by C. E. Perkins. *Santa Barbara*, 1927.
Foreword by Wister.
The Literary Treasures of 1926. [*New York*, 1927].
Contains "The Right Honorable the Strawberries"; later in "When West Was West."
Mount Vernon: Its Owner and Its Story, by Harrison Howell Dodge. *Philadelphia*, 1932.
Introduction.
Notes on a Cellar Book, by George Saintsbury. *New York*, 1933.
Preface.

Thomas (Clayton) Wolfe

1900–1938

LOOK HOMEWARD, ANGEL. *New York*, 1929.
Scribner Press seal on copyright page. Also 100 copies in plain wrappers in advance of publication.

OF TIME AND THE RIVER. *New York*, 1935.
Has code letter *A* on the copyright page.

FROM DEATH TO MORNING. *New York*, 1935.
Has code letter *A* on the copyright page.

THE STORY OF A NOVEL. *New York*, 1936.
Has code letter *A* on copyright page. An account of the writing of "Look Homeward, Angel."

THE WEB AND THE ROCK. *New York*, 1939.
First printing indicated on the copyright page. Portions of the book were circulated in galley form in advance of publication.

A NOTE ON EXPERTS: DEXTER VESPASIAN JOYNER. *New York*, 1939.
300 numbered copies only.

YOU CAN'T GO HOME AGAIN. *New York* [1940].
First edition indicated on the copyright page.

THE HILLS BEYOND.
Announced.

The Crisis in Industry. *Chapel Hill*, 1919.
Printed wrappers. 200 copies only.
Carolina Folk Plays. *New York*, 1924.
Second Series. Contains a one-act play by Wolfe, "The Return of Buck Gavin, the Tragedy of a Mountain Outlaw."
The Book Buyer. *New York*, 1935.
Wrappers. Contains "What a Writer Reads."
Portraits and Self-Portraits, by Georges Schreiber. *Boston*, 1936.
Contribution.
Press Time: A Book of Post Classics. *New York* [1936].
Contains "An Interview With Thomas Wolfe." Except for the first paragraph entirely by Wolfe.
A Southern Harvest. *Boston*, 1937.
Robert Penn Warren, editor. Contribution.

WOLFE

The Carolina Play-Book. *Chapel Hill*, 1938.
   September, 1938. Contains "The Third Night." Printed wrappers.
The Face of a Nation. *New York*, 1939.
   Reprint.

Elinor (Hoyt) Wylie
1885–1928

INCIDENTAL NUMBERS. *London*, 1912.
Anonymous. Boards. Privately printed in an edition of 65 copies only.

NETS TO CATCH THE WIND. *New York*, 1921.
First printing is on unwatermarked paper; second printing on paper watermarked *Regal Antique*. The binding is ribbed brown cloth with a smooth cloth shelfback of a slightly different shade. All examined copies have *be* for *he*, p. 43, line 11.

BLACK ARMOUR. *New York* [1923].
First printing has publisher's monogram on the copyright page. In both first and later printings the running head on p. 53 is missing and on p. 59 the initial letter of the running head is lacking.

JENNIFER LORN. *New York*, 1923.
Boards, cloth back. As originally printed the title page displays two misprints: *tegmine* for *tegmina*, and *Poyngard* for *Poynyard*. Upon discovery of the errors the copies already distributed were recalled and a new title page was printed. These corrected copies constitute the regular first edition and have the title page tipped in. But one copy with the uncorrected title page is known.

THE VENETIAN GLASS NEPHEW. *New York*, 1925.
The publisher's monogram does *not* appear on the copyright page. Also 250 signed copies.

THE ORPHAN ANGEL. *New York*, 1926.
In the first printing there is a comma after the word *copyright* on the verso of the title page and the colophon at [p. 339] contains thirteen lines. In later printings the comma does not appear on the copyright page and the colophon is in ten lines. The publishers state that the first edition was published October 29, 1926, the Book of the Month Club edition published the same day. However, the latter printing shows all the features of the later printings. Also 190 signed copies, 30 on vellum. Issued in London as "Mortal Image."

MR. HODGE & MR. HAZARD. *New York*, 1928.
An unknown number of the first edition was issued with the preliminary advertisement leaf removed and a substitute leaf, signed by the author, replacing it. It reads in part: "... on the occasion of a little gathering to celebrate the publication of this very exquisite book, March 1, 1928."
In view of the fact that all examined copies of the first printing display a title page pasted in, it may be assumed that, as in the case of "Jennifer Lorn," an earlier title page, having a misprint, was cancelled. Jane Wise states: "No such copy [with an error] has come to light to my knowledge, but I do know a collector

who says he saw a salesman's copy and that the quotation on the title page was incorrect."

Although the certificate of issue states that but 145 de luxe signed copies were printed, the publisher recently stated that 150 copies were actually printed.

TRIVIAL BREATH. *New York*, 1928.

In for *An*, p. 13, line 9. Boards, paper labels. Also 100 signed copies.

ANGELS AND EARTHLY CREATURES. *Henley-on-Thames*, 1928.

Privately printed. 51 copies only. Wrappers. The colophon states that each copy is numbered and signed but because of the poet's death more than half the copies were never signed.

ANGELS AND EARTHLY CREATURES. *New York*, 1929.

Trade edition. Also 200 numbered copies on Oland handmade paper.

BIRTHDAY SONNET. *New York*, 1929.

475 copies only in "The Random House Poetry Quartos."

COLLECTED POEMS OF ELINOR WYLIE. *New York*, 1932.

First printing indicated on the copyright page. William Rose Benét, editor. Also 210 numbered copies, signed by the editor. Reissued with additional material, *New York*, 1933.

COLLECTED PROSE OF ELINOR WYLIE. *New York*, 1933.

First printing indicated on copyright page.

The Year Book of the Poetry Society of South Carolina. *Charleston, S. C.*, 1922.
Contains the first and only printing of "Phases of the Moon."
The Bookman Anthology 1922. *New York* [1922].
John Farrar, editor. Contains "Pretty Words."
A Little Anthology. *Cedar Rapids, Iowa* [n.d., 1922?].
Rolfe Humphries, editor. Contains "Sea Blue Eyes" and "Venetian Interior."
Anthology of Magazine Verse for 1922. *Boston* [1923].
William Stanley Braithwaite, editor. Contains eight poems by Wylie.
This Singing World. *New York*, 1923.
Louis Untermeyer, editor. Contains "The Puritan's Ballad."
The Bowling Green. *Garden City*, 1924.
Christopher Morley, editor. Contains six poems by Wylie.
Anthology of Magazine Verse for 1924. *Boston*, 1924.
William Stanley Braithwaite, editor. Contains "The Innocents."
The Best Poems of 1923. *London* [1924].
Thomas Moult, editor. Contains "Shepherd's Holiday."
The Best Poems of 1924. *Boston*, 1924.
L. A. G. Strong, editor. Contains "King's Ransom" and "Unwilling Admission."
The Way of the Makers, by Marguerite Wilkinson. *New York*, 1925.
Contains "Jewelled Bindings."
A Miscellany of American Poetry, 1925. *New York* [1925].
Contains four poems by Wylie.

The Borzoi 1925. *New York* [1925].
For fuller description see under *Cather*. Contains "Carl Van Vechter "
Best Short Stories of 1925. *Boston* [1926].
E. J. O'Brien, editor. Contains "Gideon's Revenge."
The Best Poems of 1926. *New York*, 1926.
L. A. G. Strong, editor. Contains "A Courtesy."
Elinor Wylie. *New York*, 1926.
Laurence Jordan, editor. Pamphlet. All reprinted material.
Samples. *New York* [1927].
Lillie Ryttenberg and Beatrice Lang, editors. Contains "The Applewood Chair."
Curtain Calls of 1926. *New York* [1927].
Contains "My Silver Dress."
The Second Conning Tower Book. *New York*, 1927.
Edited by F. P. A. [Franklin P. Adams]. Contains "Vale Atque Ave."
A Miscellany of American Poetry, 1927. *New York* [1927].
Contains four poems by Wylie.
The Best Poems of 1929. *London*, 1929.
Thomas Moult, editor. Contains "Portrait."
Prize Poems 1913-1929. *New York*, 1930.
Charles Wagner, editor. Contains two poems by Wylie.
Modern American Poetry. *New York* [1930].
Fourth edition. Louis Untermeyer, editor. Contains "The Pebble."
The Smart Set Anthology. *New York* [1934].
Burton Rascoe and Groff Conklin, editors. *Roscoe* for *Rascoe* on the spine. Contains "Ophelia."
The Prose and Poetry of Elinor Wylie, by William Rose Benét. *Norton, Mass.*, 1934.
Contains no first appearance of Wylie material.
Amy Lowell, by S. Foster Damon. *Boston*, 1935.
Contains a letter by Wylie.
Elinor Wylie: The Portrait of an Unknown Lady, by Nancy Hoyt. *Indianapolis* [1935].
Contains previously unpublished material.
Three Worlds, by Carl Van Doren. *New York*, 1936.
Contains letters.
The Ballad of a Bookshop. *Washington, D. C.* [1936?].
A poem of four stanzas in facsimile of Wylie's handwriting, black ink on blue paper. The poem is dated 1920.
Rondeau. *New York* [1936?].
Pamphlet. 100 copies only printed for Harvey Taylor.
Nadir. *Williamsport, Penna.*, 1937.
Pamphlet. 100 copies only, privately printed for Mahlon Leonard Fisher.
From Another World, by Louis Untermeyer. *New York* [1939].
Contains two letters by Wylie.
A Bibliography of the Writings in Verse and Prose of Elinor Wylie, by Jane Wise.
Completed but unpublished. The present list is based on Miss Wise's bibliography.